Second Edition

D1298761

Understanding
ICD-9-CM Coding
A Worktext

Second Edition

Understanding
ICD-9-CM Coding
A Worktext

Mary Jo Bowie

Regina M. Schaffer

DELMAR
CENGAGE Learning™

Australia • Brazil • Japan • Korea • Mexico • Singapore • Spain • United Kingdom • United States

Understanding ICD-9-CM Coding:
A Worktext
Mary Jo Bowie and Regina M. Schaffer

Vice President, Career and Professional
Editorial: Dave Garza

Director of Learning Solutions: Matthew Kane

Senior Acquisitions Editor: Rhonda Dearborn

Managing Editor: Marah Bellegarde

Product Manager: Jadin Babin-Kavanaugh

Editorial Assistant: Chiara Astriab

Vice President, Career and Professional
Marketing: Jennifer McAvey

Marketing Director: Wendy Mapstone

Senior Marketing Manager: Nancy Bradshaw

Marketing Coordinator: Erica Ropitzky

Production Director: Carolyn Miller

Production Manager: Andrew Crouth

Content Project Manager: Anne Sherman

Senior Art Director: Jack Pendleton

For product information and technology assistance, contact us at
Cengage Learning Customer & Sales Support, 1-800-354-9706
For permission to use material from this text or product,
submit all requests online at **www.cengage.com/permissions.**
Further permissions questions can be e-mailed to
permissionrequest@cengage.com

Library of Congress Control Number: 2008938716

ISBN-13: 978-1-4354-5337-1

ISBN-10: 1-4354-5337-9

Delmar
5 Maxwell Drive
Clifton Park, NY 12065-2919
USA

Cengage Learning is a leading provider of customized learning solutions with office locations around the globe, including Singapore, the United Kingdom, Australia, Mexico, Brazil, and Japan. Locate your local office at: **international .cengage.com/region**

Cengage Learning products are represented in Canada by Nelson Education, Ltd.

To learn more about Delmar, visit **www.cengage.com/delmar**

Purchase any of our products at your local college store or at our preferred online store **www.ichapters.com**

Notice to the Reader

Printed in the United States of America
3 4 5 6 7 XXX 12 11 10

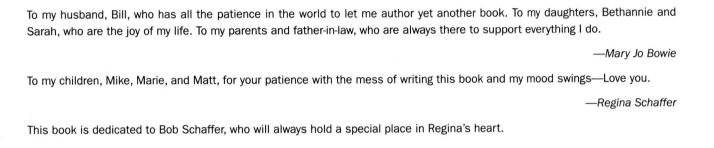

To my husband, Bill, who has all the patience in the world to let me author yet another book. To my daughters, Bethannie and Sarah, who are the joy of my life. To my parents and father-in-law, who are always there to support everything I do.

—*Mary Jo Bowie*

To my children, Mike, Marie, and Matt, for your patience with the mess of writing this book and my mood swings—Love you.

—*Regina Schaffer*

This book is dedicated to Bob Schaffer, who will always hold a special place in Regina's heart.

Contents

SECTION III: ICD-9-CM PROCEDURAL CODING   355

Preface

Understanding ICD-9-CM Coding: A Worktext represents a comprehensive approach to learning and mastering ICD-9-CM coding. This book can be used in the academic setting or as a reference in the work environment.

The approach is fresh and innovative. The book focuses on the fundamentals of ICD-9-CM coding and of the ICD-9-CM Official Coding Guidelines for Coding and Reporting. Many clinical examples are used throughout the text to provide the student with real-life examples. The book provides a standard coding background for all the medical specialties. The second edition also contains expanded coding exercises and case studies.

Organization of the Text

Understanding ICD-9-CM Coding: A Worktext is divided into three sections:

Section 1: Introduction to ICD-9-CM Coding

Section 2: ICD-9-CM Diagnostic Coding

Section 3: ICD-9-CM Procedural Coding

Throughout the textbook, students are given space to take notes. Most chapters contain Internet links, and all have summaries and chapter reviews to facilitate learning. Each diagnostic and procedural chapter contains case studies to enrich the learning process.

Special features of the Text

Several features are incorporated into the chapters to facilitate learning:

* Key terms and learning objectives appear at the beginning of the chapter to familiarize the student with the chapter content. Students should use these features as learning aids and to check their comprehension of the chapter material. Key terms are bold-faced throughout the chapter and in the glossary.

* Exercises throughout the chapters provide students with the opportunity to self-test while learning the material.

* Illustrations of human anatomy and procedures appear throughout the book. The illustrative format is based on the concept that learning is enhanced through visual tools. Throughout the text, anatomical illustrations are used to represent human anatomy and to help the student visualize operative procedures. Current ICD-9-CM books do not provide such visual aids, which can be used by the first-time learner or as a reference by more advanced coders.

* Coding assignment exercises and case studies are provided for all chapters that represent chapters of ICD-9-CM. This hands-on worktext offers learning exercises with room to write in notes.

New to This Edition

* The number of coding assignments and case studies has been expanded.

* Updates have been added for compatibility with the 2008 ICD-9-CM Official Guidelines for Coding and Reporting.

- Disease Highlights have been added to the diseases chapters to discuss the signs and symptoms, clinical tests, and treatments for common diseases.

- EncoderPro, Ingenix's powerful coding software, is available for a 30-day free trial.

- The supplement package for instructors has been expanded.

Supplements

The following supplements are available with the textbook to enhance the classroom experience:

Instructor's Manual

The *Instructor's Manual to Accompany Understanding ICD-9-CM Coding* provides answers to the exercises, chapter reviews, coding assignments, and case studies, as well as sample syllabi and course preparation information (ISBN: 1435470125).

Instructor Resources CD-ROM

The *Instructor Resources to Accompany Understanding ICD-9-CM Coding* on CD-ROM contains a computerized test bank, PowerPoint® studies, and an electronic version of the *Instructor's Manual*. The computerized test bank provides test creation, delivery, and reporting capability. Instructors have the option of adding questions to further individualize tests. Organized by chapter, the test bank contains more than 1,500 questions. A PowerPoint® presentation covers key topics. Organized by chapter, the slides provide organization for the material presented in the text (ISBN: 1435470133).

WebTutor™ Advantage on Blackboard and WebCT

WebTutor™ Advantage is an Internet-based course management and delivery system designed to accompany this text. Its content is available for use in either Blackboard or WebCT. The enhanced WebTutor contains:

- Online quizzes for each chapter

- Discussion topics and learning links

- Additional coding exercises

- Online glossary with flash cards

- PowerPoint® slides

- Computerized test bank

- Communication tools, including a course calendar, chat, email, and threaded discussions

To learn more, visit www.webtutor.cengage.com.

About the Authors

Mary Jo Bowie, MS, RHIA

Consultant and owner, Health Information Professional Services, Binghamton, New York, and instructor, health information technology program, Broome Community College, Binghamton, New York. Active member, American Health Information Management Association, and state and local affiliates. New York State Health Information Management Association: education director and board of directors, 1989–1991; Ambulatory Care Coding Guidelines (ACGC) Committee, 1995–2001; chairperson, ACGC Committee, 1993–1995. American Health Information Management Association: nominee for New York State for National Award for Literary Contribution to Profession, 1993 and 1994.

Regina M. Schaffer, BS, RHIT, CPC

Bachelor's degree in health care administration and an associate's degree in health information technology. Member in good standing of AHIMA as a registered health information technician (RHIT), as well as a member in the American Academy of Professional Coders with her CPC certification. Served two years as the secretary for her local chapter of the AAPC and still an active member. Currently a coding and reimbursement educator specialist. Works closely with providers and their staff in educating them on the proper use of ICD-9-CM coding as well as CPT coding.

Acknowledgments

A special thank-you is extended to the reviewers who have provided recommendations to enhance the content of this work.

Reviewers

Mary M. Cantwell, RHIT, CPC-I, CPC-H, RMC
Instructor, Metro Community College
Health Information Management Department
Omaha, Nebraska

Marie T. Conde, MPA, RHIA, RHIT
Health Information Technology Program Director and instructor
City College of San Francisco
San Francisco, California

Pat King, MA, RHIA
Adjunct faculty
Baker College of Cass City, Michigan

Barbara Marchelletta, BS, CMA (AAMA), CPC (AAPC)
Allied Health Program Director
Beal College
Bangor, Maine

June M. Petillo, MBA, RMC
Instructor—Medical Assisting Program
Manchester Community College & Capital Community College (Hartford)
Senior Implementation Specialist–EMR
Women's Health USA
Avon, Connecticut

SECTION I

Introduction to Coding

Introduction to Coding and Coding Professions

Chapter Outline

Introduction

Professional Coding

History of ICD-9-CM Coding

Health Insurance Portability and
   Accountability Act of 1996

Professional Coding Associations

Employment Opportunities for Coders

Internet Links

Summary

Chapter Review

Objectives

At the conclusion of this chapter, the student will be able to:

1. Describe the purpose of ICD-9-CM coding.
2. Explain the development of the ICD classification system.
3. Identify professional coding certifications and organizations.
4. Discuss the standards mandated by the Health Insurance Portability and
   Accountability Act.

Key Terms

Accrediting Bureau of
   Health Education
   Schools (ABHES)

Administration
   Simplification

American Academy of
   Professional Coders
   (AAPC)

American Association
   of Medical Assistants
   (AAMA)

American Health
   Information
   Management
   Association (AHIMA)

American Medical
   Technologists (AMT)

Centers for Medicare
   and Medicaid
   Services (CMS)

Certified Coding
   Associate (CCA)

Certified Coding
   Specialist (CCS)

Certified Coding
   Specialist, Physician-
   Based (CCS-P)

Certified Healthcare
   Privacy and Security
   (CHPS)

Certified in Healthcare
   Privacy (CHP)

Certified in Healthcare
   Security (CHS)

Certified Medical
   Assistant (CMA)

Certified Professional
   Coder (CPC)

Certified Professional
   Coder, Hospital-Based
   (CPC-H)

Centers for Medicare
   and Medicaid
   Services (CMS)

Coding

Commission on
   Accreditation of Allied
   Health Education
   Programs (CAAHEP)

Health Insurance
   Portability and
   Accountability Act of
   1996 (HIPAA)

ICD-8

International
   Classification of
   Diseases, Ninth
   Revision (ICD-9-CM)

International Classification of Diseases, Ninth Revision, Clinical Modification

Morbidity

Mortality

National Center for Health Statistics (NCHS)

Public Law 104-191

Registered Health Information Administrator (RHIA)

Registered Health Information Technician (RHIT)

Registered Medical Assistant (RMA)

World Health Organization (WHO)

Introduction

Medical coding is the assignment of numerical or alpha-numerical digits and characters to specific diagnostic and procedural phrases. This coding, like any other language, needs to be translated to be understood, and each combination of numbers or of numbers and letters represents a diagnostic or procedural phrase.

> **EXAMPLE:** The diagnostic phrase "appendicitis" is translated into diagnostic code 540.9. The procedural phrase "appendectomy" is translated into procedure code 47.09.

By using ICD-9-CM codes, healthcare professionals can collect, process, and analyze diagnostic and procedural information more effectively.

Professional Coding

Coding is the language used by insurance companies and healthcare providers to tell a story about what brought a person to a facility for treatment and what services were performed. The ability to communicate and translate these codes to another party is vital to the care and treatment rendered to the patient. These codes are also communicated to the insurance company, which is required to make payment on the patient's visit. It is critical that the coding language is fully understood and "spoken" fluently by all the necessary parties so that the essence of the patient's visit and treatment can be conveyed.

In the chapters that follow, the student will gain a greater knowledge of the language of coding, specifically ICD-9-CM. By the completion of this book, the student will have the knowledge base needed to begin "speaking" the language of ICD-9-CM coding, which has increasingly become a tool used in the healthcare industry.

History of ICD-9-CM Coding

ICD-9-CM, an abbreviation for the International Classification of Diseases, Ninth Revision, Clinical Modification, is an arrangement of classes or groups of diagnoses and procedures by systematic division. ICD-9-CM is based on the official version of the International Classification of Diseases, Ninth Revision (ICD-9), which was developed by the World Health Organization (WHO) in Geneva, Switzerland. The WHO assumed responsibility in 1948 for preparing and publishing the revisions to ICD every 10 years. Thus, with every 10-year revision, the name of the current ICD changes. For example, ICD-8 was revised to ICD-9.

The ICD classification system was designed to compile and present statistical data on morbidity, the rate or frequency of disease, and mortality, the rate or frequency of deaths. This form of classification was first used by hospitals to track, store, and retrieve statistical information. However, a more efficient basis for storage and retrieval of diagnostic data was needed. In 1950, the Veterans Administration and the U.S. Public Health Service began independent studies of using the ICD for hospital indexing purposes. By 1956, the American Hospital Association and the American Association of Medical Record Librarians, now the American Health Information Management Association, felt that the ICD form of classification provided an efficient and useful venue for indexing hospital records.

Chapter 1   Introduction to Coding and Coding Professions   **5**

With hospital indexing in mind, the WHO international conference made its eighth revision to the ICD in 1966. Some countries found that ICD-8 lacked the detail needed for diagnostic indexing. In the United States, consultants were asked to study ICD-8 for its applicability to various users. The Advisory Committee to the Central Office on ICD published the International Classification of Diseases, Eighth Revision, adapted for use in the United States in 1968. It became known as ICDA-8 and was used for coding diagnostic data for both morbidity and mortality statistics in the United States.

In 1979, ICD-9-CM replaced earlier, less specific versions of the classification system. The ICD-9-CM streamlined the other versions of the ICD classification system into a single classification system and was intended for use primarily in hospitals in the United States. The ICD-9-CM provides a more complete classification system for morbidity data to be used for indexing and reviewing patient records and medical care.

Within the United States, two agencies are responsible for the annual updates to the ICD-9-CM codes. The National Center for Health Statistics (NCHS) is responsible for maintaining the diagnostic codes that are maintained in volumes 1 and 2 of ICD-9-CM. The Centers for Medicare and Medicaid Services (CMS) is responsible for maintaining the procedure codes of ICD-9-CM, which are found in volume 3.

Since the clinical modifications have been developed, IDC-9-CM has been used to code patient encounters throughout the U.S. healthcare system. The Medicare Catastrophic Coverage Act of 1988 mandated the reporting of ICD-9-CM diagnostic codes on all claims submitted to the Medicare program. In subsequent years private insurance companies required ICD-9-CM codes to be submitted. ICD-9-CM provides a coding system that reflects the signs, symptoms, disorders, diseases, examinations, or other reasons for the services billed by a provider for payment, giving the payer a clear picture of the reason for the patient visit.

ICD-9-CM coding is the key storyteller to the insurance companies, explaining what brought the patient into the office or facility (by use of a diagnostic code), as well as what services were facility provided (by use of a procedural code). Because coding plays such a critical role in reimbursement for service rendered, correct coding practices are essential.

Health Insurance Portability and Accountability Act of 1996

The Health Insurance Portability and Accountability Act of 1996 (HIPAA), Public Law 104-191, was passed by Congress to improve the portability and continuity of healthcare coverage. The Administration Simplification aspect of this legislation developed standards for the electronic exchange of healthcare data by administrative and financial transactions. The final rule on transactions and code sets mandated the use of standardized code sets for the electronic submission of healthcare data. ICD-9-CM diagnostic codes are reported for diagnoses for all levels of care, including all hospital services, clinic services, long-term care, and physician offices. ICD-9-CM procedural codes are reported for inpatient hospital services.

Healthcare providers must now use ICD-9-CM codes to accurately report diagnoses and services provided on submitted insurance claims. The codes are used to determine not only payment but also the medical necessity of care, which is defined by Medicare as "the determination that a service or procedure rendered is reasonable and necessary for the diagnosis or treatment of an illness or injury." Thus, coders perform a vital role in the healthcare system.

Professional Coding Associations

In an effort to assist and promote correct coding and reimbursement, several organizations help educate, train, and credential coders. Credentialing helps to ensure the proper training and education of coders.

American Health Information Management Association (AHIMA)

The American Health Information Management Association (AHIMA) represents health information professionals who manage, organize, process, and manipulate patient data. Health information professionals have knowledge of electronic and paper medical record systems as well as of coding, reimbursement, and research methodologies. The health information managed by these professionals directly impacts patient care and financial decisions made in the healthcare industry. Members of AHIMA feel that the quality of patient care is directly related to the effectiveness of the information available. Healthcare providers, insurance companies, and institutional administrators depend on the accuracy and quality of the health information available. For this reason, AHIMA members are trained to be able to provide a level of service that maintains the quality and accuracy of the medical information they come in contact with.

AHIMA offers certifications and credentialing to ensure that its members meet the level of proficiency that is needed to provide educated professionals to manage healthcare information. The members receive these various certifications or credentials through a combination of education, experience, and performance on national certification exams.

The various certifications and credentials are listed below.

CCA	**Certified Coding Associate**
CCS	**Certified Coding Specialist**
CCS-P	**Certified Coding Specialist, Physician-Based**
CHP	**Certified in Healthcare Privacy**
CHPS	**Certified Healthcare Privacy and Security**
CHS	**Certified in Healthcare Security**
RHIA	**Registered Health Information Administrator**
RHIT	**Registered Health Information Technician**

Continuing education credits are required to maintain the certifications once they have been received. These continuing education credits can be obtained through various conferences, seminars, classes, or other avenues of career development that AHIMA publishes and makes available to its members.

American Academy of Professional Coders (AAPC)

The American Academy of Professional Coders (AAPC) was founded in an effort to elevate the standards of medical coding. The AAPC provides networking opportunities through local chapter memberships and conferences. It also provides ongoing educational opportunities for members. Similar to AHIMA, AAPC offers certifications for professional proficiency. The Certified Professional Coder (CPC) certification is available for coders in physician offices and clinics, and the Certified Professional Coder, Hospital-Based (CPC-H) is available for coders in the hospital setting. There are also two additional certifications for individuals who have not yet met the work experience requirements of the CPC and CPC-H certifications: the Certified Professional Coder Apprentice (CPC-A) and the Certified Professional Coder, Hospital Apprentice (CPC-H-A). Continuing education credits are also required on a biannual basis for the AAPC certification. Whereas AHIMA deals with all aspects of health information, AAPC focuses on coding and reimbursement.

American Association of Medical Assistants (AAMA)

The American Association of Medical Assistants (AAMA) represents individuals trained in performing routine administrative and clinical jobs, including coding, that keep medical offices and clinics running efficiently and smoothly. Credentialing is voluntary in most states. A medical assistant is not required to be certified or registered. However, the AAMA offers the national credential of Certified Medical Assistant (CMA) certification for the medical assisting profession. The Commission on Accreditation of Allied Health Education Programs (CAAHEP) collaborates with the Curriculum Review Board of the AAMA Endowment to accredit medical assisting programs in both public and private postsecondary institutions throughout the United States. This prepares candidates for entry in the medical assisting field. Students who have graduated from a medical assisting program accredited by the CAAHEP or the Accrediting Bureau of Health Education Schools (ABHES) are eligible to take the CMA examination, which tests candidates on tasks that are performed in the workplace. Recertification is required every five years, either by continuing education or by examination.

American Medical Technologists (AMT)

The American Medical Technologists (AMT) offers professional credentials such as Registered Medical Assistant (RMA). These professionals perform the same tasks as those of a CMA but are credentialed by AMT. Students who have completed a college-level program approved by the U.S. Department of Education may voluntarily take the examination that would credential them as an RMA.

Employment Opportunities for Coders

Regardless of the credentialing path that an individual takes, career opportunities are numerous. Coders work in all aspects of health care, including hospitals, physician offices, clinics, long-term care facilities, insurance companies, and billing agencies. With the evolution of the electronic health record, more coders will be needed to review the information that is generated for its accuracy and compliance. The Bureau of Labor Statistics calculates that the growth of coding jobs in the United States will grow faster than will the average of all occupations through 2010. As the population of the United States ages, more individuals will use healthcare services at a greater rate, thus increasing the need for additional services and for coded healthcare data.

Internet Links

To obtain ICD-9-CM updates through a free download, visit *http://www.cdc.gov/nchs/icd9.htm*.

To order a CD-ROM that contains the complete version of ICD-9-CM, see *http://bookstore.gpo.gov*. (This CD-ROM can also be ordered from Superintendent of Documents, U.S. Government Printing Office: 888-293-6498 or 866-512-1800; fax, 202-512-2250. Commercial publishing companies also sell ICD-9-CM books.)

To obtain information on the AAMA, visit *www.aama-ntl.org*.

To obtain information on the AAPC, visit *www.aapc.com*.

To obtain information on the AHIMA, visit *www.ahima.org*.

To obtain information on AMT, visit *www.amt1.com*.

To obtain information on career statistics and opportunities, visit the Bureau of Labor Statistics at *www.bls.gov*.

Summary

- Coding is the assignment of numerical or alpha-numeric digits and characters to diagnostic and procedural phrases.
- ICD-9-CM coding is used in the United States to code diagnoses and procedures.
- The National Center for Health Statistics coordinates the modifications of the disease classification.
- The Centers for Medicare and Medicaid Services coordinates the procedural classification updates.
- The American Health Information Management Association offers the following credentials: Certified Coding Associate; Certified Coding Specialist; Certified Coding Specialist, Physician-Based; Certified in Healthcare Privacy; Certified in Healthcare Security; Certified in Healthcare Privacy and Security; Registered Health Information Administrator; and Registered Health Information Technician.
- The American Academy of Professional Coders offers the following credentials: Certified Professional Coder; Certified Professional Coder, Hospital-Based; Certified Professional Coder Apprentice; and Certified Professional Coder, Hospital Apprentice.
- The American Association of Medical Assistants offers the Certified Medical Assistant credential.
- The American Medical Technologists offers professional credentials such as a Registered Medical Assistant.
- The Administration Simplification aspect of Health Insurance Portability and Accountability Act of 1996 developed standards for the electronic exchange of healthcare data for administrative and financial transactions.

Chapter Review

True/False: Indicate whether each statement is true (T) or false (F).

1. _____ The CPC credential is offered by the American Health Information Management Association.
2. _____ AHIMA requires credentialed professionals to obtain continuing education credits to maintain their credentials.
3. _____ CMAs must be licensed to practice in the United States.
4. _____ The final rule on transactions and code sets mandated the use of ICD-9-CM for the electronic submission of healthcare data.
5. _____ The Centers for Medicare and Medicaid Services coordinates the procedural classification updates.

Fill-in-the-Blank: Enter the appropriate term(s) to complete each statement.

6. The rate or frequency of diseases is known as _____.
7. ICD-9 was developed by the _____.
8. ICD-9-CM is an abbreviation for the International Classification of Diseases, Ninth Revision, _____.
9. Modifications of the ICD-9-CM disease classification is coordinated by _____.
10. Public Law 104-191, known as _____, was passed by Congress to improve the portability and continuity of health care coverage.

Short Answer: Define each abbreviation and acronym listed.

11. AHIMA

12. RHIA

13. CPC-H

14. AMT

15. CPC

16. AAMA

17. RMA

18. CMA

19. CCS

20. CCS-P

An Overview of ICD-9-CM

Chapter Outline

Objectives

At the conclusion of this chapter, the student will be able to:

1. Explain the format ICD-9-CM Coding Book.
2. Identify the chapters of volume I, Tabular List of Diseases and Injuries.
3. List the appendices of volume 1.
4. Discuss the purpose of V codes and E codes.
5. Explain the organization of volume 2, Alphabetic Index.
6. Describe the format of volume 3, Tabular List and Alphabetic Index of Procedures.

Key Terms

Alphabetic Index

Alphabetic Index to External Causes of Injury and Poisoning

Alphabetic Index to Poisoning and External Causes of Adverse Effects of

Drugs and Other Chemical Substances

Anatomical Site

Appendices
Appendix A—Morphology of Neoplasms

Appendix C—Classification of Drugs by American Hospital Formulary Service List Number and Their ICD-9-CM Equivalents
Appendix D—Classification of Industrial Accidents According to Agency

Appendix E—List of Three-Digit Categories

Classification of Diseases and Injuries

Congenital Anomaly

E Code

Reminder

As you work through this chapter, you will need to have a copy of the ICD-9-CM coding book to reference.

Etiology

Index to Diseases and Injuries

Perinatal Period

Supplementary Classification of

External Causes of Injury and Poisoning

Supplementary Classification of Factors Influencing Health Status and

Contact with Health Services

Supplementary Classifications

Table of Drugs and Chemicals

Tabular List and Alphabetic Index of Procedures

Tabular List of Diseases and Injuries

V Code

Introduction

The ICD-9-CM coding system allows healthcare providers and healthcare facilities to answer the question "what brought the patient to my office/facility?" This information is needed for statistical purposes, reimbursement, and continuity of patient care. To accurately convey this information, the coder must become familiar with all aspects of the ICD-9-CM coding book. Within this chapter an overview of ICD-9-CM will be presented.

ICD-9-CM Coding Book Format

The ICD-9-CM coding book consists of three volumes. Volume 1 is the Tabular List of Diseases and Injuries, a numerical listing of diseases and injuries found in ICD-9-CM. Each chapter of this volume is subdivided into sections, categories, and subcategories. The specific organization of volume 1 will be discussed in Chapter 3 of this textbook. (The Tabular List of Diseases and Injuries is most commonly referred to as the "Tabular").

Volume 2 of the ICD-9-CM, known as the Alphabetic Index, is an alphabetic listing of the codes found in volume 1 and is essential for accurate coding. (The Alphabetic Index is most commonly referred to as the "Index"). The three sections of the index include:

- Index to Diseases and Injuries
- Alphabetic Index to Poisoning and External Cause of Adverse Effects of Drugs and Other Chemical Substances
- Alphabetic Index to External Causes of Injury and Poisoning (E codes)

Volume 3 is the Tabular List and Alphabetic Index of Procedures and is used in a facility setting, not routinely in an office or outpatient setting. This particular volume contains both a tabular listing and an alphabetic listing of procedures and surgeries. The format for volume 3 is the same as in volumes 1 and 2 except that procedure codes consist of two digits followed by a decimal point and then one or two additional digits.

EXAMPLE:

Diagnostic Code Description	Diagnostic Code	Procedural Code Description	Procedural Code
Acute appendicitis without mention of peritonitis	540.9	Laparoscopic appendectomy	47.01
Cholelithiais with obstruction	574.21	Cholecystectomy	51.22

Volume 1—Tabular List of Diseases and Injuries.

Volume 1, known as the Tabular List of Diseases and Injuries, is a tabular listing of disease and injuries that has three major subdivisions:

- Classification of Diseases and Injuries
- Supplementary Classifications (V codes and E codes)
- Appendices

The first subdivision consists of the Classification of Diseases and Injuries, a numerical listing of diseases and injuries found in ICD-9-CM and consists of 17 chapters. These diagnostic chapters are organized according to etiology, the cause of disease, or anatomical site, the body system involved.

EXAMPLE: Refer to the information in the following list. Chapter 2, "Neoplasms," is an example of a chapter organized according to etiology, and Chapter 12, "Diseases of the Skin and Subcutaneous Tissue," is a chapter organized by anatomical site.

Chapter Titles of the Classification of Diseases and Injuries

1. Infectious and Parasitic Diseases
2. Neoplasms
3. Endocrine, Nutritional, and Metabolic Diseases and Immunity Disorders
4. Diseases of the Blood and Blood-Forming Organs
5. Mental Disorders
6. Diseases of the Nervous System and Sense Organs
7. Diseases of the Circulatory System
8. Diseases of the Respiratory System
9. Diseases of the Digestive System
10. Diseases of the Genitourinary System
11. Complications of Pregnancy, Childbirth, and the Puerperium
12. Diseases of the Skin and Subcutaneous Tissue
13. Diseases of the Musculoskeletal System and Connective Tissue
14. Congenital Anomalies
15. Certain Conditions Originating in the Perinatal Period
16. Symptoms, Signs, and Ill-Defined Conditions
17. Injury and Poisoning

Exercise 2–1   Identifying Chapters

For each chapter title, indicate whether the chapter is organized by etiology or by anatomical site.

Chapter Title   **Organization**

1. Congenital Anomalies   _____

2. Diseases of the Circulatory System   _____

3. Diseases of the Digestive System   _____

4. Endocrine, Nutritional, and Metabolic
   Diseases and Immunity Disorders   _____

5. Infectious and Parasitic Diseases   _____

6. Diseases of Skin and Subcutaneous
   Tissue   _____

7. Diseases of Mental Disorders   _____

8. Diseases of Nervous System   _____

9. Diseases of Genitourinary System   _____

10. Diseases of Respiratory System   _____

Volume 1—Chapters of the Classification of Diseases and Injuries

The Classification of Diseases and Injuries of volume 1 contains the following 17 chapters.

Chapter 1—Infectious and Parasitic Disease (Code Range 001–139)

This chapter includes diseases generally recognized as communicable or transmissible, as well as a few diseases of unknown but possibly infectious origin.

> **EXAMPLE:** Using volume 1 of your ICD-9-CM book, locate the start of chapter 1. Here you will find the code listing for infectious and parasitic diseases. Reference the following codes to familiarize yourself with this chapter.

Diagnostic Code	Diagnostic Description
050.9	Smallpox, unspecified
008.41	Staphylococcus
036.0	Meningococcal meningitis
102.3	Hyperkeratosis
112.82	Candidal otitis externa

Chapter 2—Neoplasms (Code Range 140–239)

This chapter contains code assignments for malignant, benign, carcinoma in situ, and neoplasms of uncertain and unspecified behavior.

> **EXAMPLE:** Using volume 1 of your ICD-9-CM book, locate the start of chapter 2. Here you will find the code listing for neoplasms. Reference the following codes to familiarize yourself with this chapter.

Diagnostic Code	Diagnostic Description
140.4	Malignant neoplasm of the lower lip, inner aspect
145.4	Malignant neoplasm of the uvula
210.0	Benign neoplasm of the lip
230.2	Carcinoma in situ of stomach
233.0	Carcinoma in situ of breast

Note that this chapter is divided into the following sections:

- Malignant neoplasms (140–208)
- Benign neoplasms (210–229)
- Carcinoma in situ (230–234)
- Uncertain behavior (235–238)
- Unspecified behavior (239)

Chapter 3—Endocrine, Nutritional, and Metabolic Diseases and Immunity Disorders (Code Range 240–279)

Disorders and diseases of the thyroid and other endocrine glands, nutritional deficiencies, metabolic disorders, and disorders of the immune mechanism and immunity deficiencies are contained within this chapter.

EXAMPLE: Using volume 1 of your ICD-9-CM book, locate the start of chapter 3. Here you will find the code listing for diseases of the endocrine system, nutritional and metabolic diseases, and immunity disorders. Reference the following codes to familiarize yourself with this chapter.

Diagnostic Code	Diagnostic Description
240.9	Goiter
244.2	Iodine hypothyroidism
251.2	Hypoglycemia, unspecified
257.0	Testicular hyperfunction
278.01	Morbid obesity

Chapter 4—Diseases of the Blood and Blood-Forming Organs (Code Range 280–289)

Contained within this chapter are types of anemias, coagulation defects, hemorrhagic conditions, and diseases of the white blood cells and other components of the blood. Also contained within this chapter are some diseases of the spleen and lymphatic system.

EXAMPLE: Using volume 1 of your ICD-9-CM book, locate the start of chapter 4. Here you will find the code listing for diseases of the blood and blood-forming organs. Reference the following codes to familiarize yourself with this chapter.

Diagnostic Code	Diagnostic Description
280.9	Iron-deficiency anemia, unspecified
281.1	Other vitamin B_{12} deficiency anemia
282.60	Sickle-cell disease, unspecified
288.3	Eosinophilia
289.1	Chronic lymphadenitis

Chapter 5—Mental Disorders (Code Range 290–319)

This chapter contains mental disorders, including psychotic, personality, neurotic, and nonpsychotic disorders. Chemical dependencies, such as alcoholism and drug dependence, are contained in this chapter, as well as mental retardation and developmental disorders. This chapter also contains psychopathic symptoms that are not part of an organic illness.

EXAMPLE: Using volume 1 of your ICD-9-CM book, locate the start of chapter 5. Here you will find the code listing for mental disorders. Reference the following codes to familiarize yourself with this chapter.

Diagnostic Code	Diagnostic Description
290.11	Presenile dementia with delirium
291.0	Alcohol withdrawal delirium
298.3	Acute paranoid reaction
301.3	Explosive personality disorder
317	Mild mental retardation

Chapter 6—Diseases of the Nervous System and Sense Organs (Code Range 320–389)

This chapter contains diseases of the central and peripheral nervous systems that include the brain, spinal cord, meninges, and nerves. Disorders of the eye, adnexa, ear, and mastoid process are also coded from this chapter.

> **EXAMPLE:** Using volume 1 of your ICD-9CM book, locate the start of chapter 6. Here you will find the code listing for diseases of the nervous system and sense organs. Reference the following codes to familiarize yourself with this chapter.

Diagnostic Code	Diagnostic Description
320.2	Streptococcal meningitis
344.5	Monoplegia
361.32	Horseshoe tear of retina without detachment
370.55	Corneal abscess
382.9	Otitis media, unspecified

Chapter 7—Diseases of the Circulatory System (Code Range 390–459)

The circulatory system includes the heart, arteries, veins, and lymphatic system; therefore, cardiac disorders and arterial, venous, and some lymphatic diseases are contained in this chapter.

> **EXAMPLE:** Using volume 1 of your ICD-9-CM book, locate the start of chapter 7. Here you will find the code listing for diseases of the heart, arteries, arterioles, capillaries, vein, and lymphatic system. Reference the following codes to familiarize yourself with this chapter.

Diagnostic Code	Diagnostic Description
391.0	Acute rheumatic pericarditis
401.0	Malignant hypertension
429.82	Hyperkinetic heart disease
457.2	Lymphangitis
459.0	Hemorrhage

Chapter 8—Diseases of the Respiratory System (Code Range 460–519)

Diseases of the pharynx, larynx, trachea, bronchus, vocal cords, sinuses, nose, tonsils and adenoids, and parts of the lung are coded from this chapter.

> **EXAMPLE:** Using volume 1 of your ICD-9-CM book, locate the start of chapter 8. Here you will find the code listing for diseases of the respiratory system. Reference the following codes to familiarize yourself with this chapter.

Diagnostic Code	Diagnostic Description
461.0	Acute maxillary sinusitis
462	Acute pharyngitis
473.2	Ethmoidal sinusitis
491.0	Simple chronic bronchitis
519.4	Disorders of diaphragm

Chapter 9—Diseases of the Digestive System (Code Range 520–579)

Diseases of the oral cavity, salivary glands, jaws, esophagus, stomach, duodenum, appendix, abdominal cavity, small and large intestine, peritoneum, anus, liver, gallbladder, biliary tract, and pancreas are contained within this chapter.

> **EXAMPLE:** Using volume 1 of your ICD-9-CM book, locate the start of chapter 9. Here you will find the code listing for diseases of the digestive system. Reference the following codes to familiarize yourself with this chapter.

Diagnostic Code	Diagnostic Description
520.3	Mottled teeth
526.1	Fissural cysts of jaw
530.12	Acute esophagitis
537.1	Gastric diverticulum
553.21	Incisional ventral hernia

Chapter 10—Diseases of the Genitourinary System (Code Range 580–629)

Coded from this chapter are diseases of the kidney, ureter, urinary bladder, urethra, male genital organs, male and female breast, and female genital organs (not involving pregnancy, childbirth, and the postpartum period).

> **EXAMPLE:** Using volume 1 of your ICD-9-CM book, locate the start of chapter 10. Here you will find the code listing for diseases of the genitourinary system. Reference the following codes to familiarize yourself with this chapter.

Diagnostic Code	Diagnostic Description
584.6	Acute renal failure with lesion of renal cortical necrosis
592.1	Calculus of ureter
602.2	Atrophy of prostate
614.0	Acute salpingitis and oophoritis
629.1	Hydrocele, canal of neck

Chapter 11—Complications of Pregnancy, Childbirth, and the Puerperium (Code Range 630–677)

This chapter includes ectopic and molar pregnancies, spontaneous abortions, legally and illegally induced abortions, and complications of pregnancy, abortions, labor and delivery, and the postpartum period.

> **EXAMPLE:** Using volume 1 of your ICD-9-CM book, locate the start of chapter 11. Here you will find the code listing for complications of pregnancy, childbirth, and the puerperium. Reference the following codes to familiarize yourself with this chapter.

Diagnostic Code	Diagnostic Description
630	Hydatidiform mole
632	Missed abortion
650	Normal delivery
675.04	Postpartum infection of nipple, 4 weeks after delivery
676.14	Failure of lactation, postpartum, 2 weeks after delivery

Chapter 12—Diseases of the Skin and Subcutaneous Tissue (Code Range 680–709)

This chapter includes inflammatory and infectious conditions of the skin and subcutaneous tissue, as well as diseases of the nail, hair and hair follicles, sweat, and sebaceous glands.

EXAMPLE: Using volume 1 of your ICD-9-CM book, locate the start of chapter 12. Here you will find the code listing for diseases of the subcutaneous tissue and skin. Reference the following codes to familiarize yourself with this chapter.

Diagnostic Code	Diagnostic Description
681.10	Cellulitis and abscess of the toe, unspecified
685.0	Pilonidal cyst with abscess
703.0	Ingrowing nail
708.3	Dermatographic urticaria
709.2	Cicatrix

Chapter 13—Diseases of the Musculoskeletal System and Connective Tissue (Code Range 710–739)

This chapter includes diseases of the bones, joints, bursa, muscles, ligaments, tendons, and soft tissues.

EXAMPLE: Using volume 1 of your ICD-9-CM book, locate the start of chapter 13. Here you will find the code listing for diseases of the musculoskeletal system and connective tissue. Reference the following codes to familiarize yourself with this chapter.

Diagnostic Code	Diagnostic Description
710.1	Systemic sclerosis
714.0	Rheumatoid arthritis
724.5	Backache, unspecified
734	Flat foot
738.4	Acquired spondylolisthesis

Chapter 14—Congenital Anomalies (Code Range 740–759)

This chapter contains any congenital anomaly regardless of the body system involved. A congenital anomaly is an anomaly present at or existing from the time of birth.

EXAMPLE: Using volume 1 of your ICD-9-CM book, locate the start of chapter 14. Here you will find the code listing for congenital anomalies. Reference the following codes to familiarize yourself with this chapter.

Diagnostic Code	Diagnostic Description
740.0	Anencephalus
742.3	Congenital hydrocephalus
747.82	Spinal vessel anomaly
751.62	Congenital cystic disease of the liver
758.0	Down's syndrome

Chapter 15—Certain Conditions Originating in the Perinatal Period (Code Range 760–779)

This chapter includes conditions that have their origin in the perinatal period, a period of time before birth through the first 28 days after birth.

> **EXAMPLE:** Using volume 1 of your ICD-9-CM book, locate the start of chapter 15. Here you will find the code listing for conditions originating in the perinatal period. Reference the following codes to familiarize yourself with this chapter.

Diagnostic Code	Diagnostic Description
760.4	Maternal nutritional disorders
766.22	Prolonged gestation of infant
770.3	Pulmonary hemorrhage of fetus and newborn
776.6	Anemia of prematurity
779.3	Feeding problems in newborn

Chapter 16—Symptoms, Signs, and Ill-Defined Conditions (Code Range 780–799)

This chapter includes symptoms, signs, abnormal results of laboratory tests and investigative procedures, and ill-defined conditions.

> **EXAMPLE:** Using volume 1 of your ICD-9-CM book, locate the start of chapter 16. Here you will find the code listing for symptoms, signs, and ill-defined conditions. Reference the following codes to familiarize yourself with this chapter.

Diagnostic Code	Diagnostic Description
780.01	Coma
780.53	Hypersomnia with sleep apnea, unspecified
781.2	Abnormality of gait
786.2	Cough
796.1	Abnormal reflex

Chapter 17—Injury and Poisoning (Code Range 800–999)

This chapter includes fractures, dislocations, sprains and strains of joints and muscles, intracranial injuries, and internal injuries to chest, abdomen, and pelvis. Open wounds, superficial injuries, contusions, burns, and poisonings by drugs and medicinal and biological substances are also coded from this chapter. Late effects of previous conditions are contained in this chapter as well.

EXAMPLE: Using volume 1 of your ICD-9-CM book, locate the start of chapter 17. Here you will find the code listing for injuries and poisonings. Reference the following codes to familiarize yourself with this chapter.

Diagnostic Code	Diagnostic Description
808.1	Fracture of the acetabulum, open
830.0	Closed dislocation of jaw
845.00	Sprained ankle, unspecified
922.1	Contusion, chest wall
991.2	Frostbite of foot

Exercise 2–2   Identifying Diseases and Chapter Titles

Using the Tabular List of Diseases and Injuries, complete the following table. List the name or description of the disease found in the Tabular and the chapter title. The first one is completed.

Code Number	Description	Chapter Title
078.2	Sweating fever	Infectious and Parasitic Disease
155.0		
003.1		
210.7		
371.40		
729.5		
464.00		
787.02		
537.1		

Volume 1—Supplementary Classifications

The second subdivision of volume 1 consists of Supplementary Classifications, also known as V codes and E codes. These two supplementary classifications are used in combination with codes from the preceding chapters or, in the case of V codes, are used alone to code conditions and/or situations for which there is no code in one of the other chapters. E codes are never used without a code from the 17 chapters.

V Codes—Supplementary Classification of Factors Influencing Health Status and Contact with Health Services (Code Range V01–V86)

The Supplementary Classification of Factors Influencing Health Status and Contact with Health Services section is used to code those conditions or circumstances that are recorded as the reason for the patient encounter when the patient is not currently ill, or when a factor is present that affects the patient's health status and/or medical management of the patient's case. Specific instructions for assigning V codes are found in the chapter entitled "V Codes."

EXAMPLE: Using volume 1 of your ICD-9-CM book, locate the start of "V Codes," which is after chapter 17, "Signs, Symptoms, and Ill-Defined Conditions." Here you will find the Supplementary Classification of Factors Influencing Health Status and Contact with Health Services, or V codes. Reference the following codes to familiarize yourself with this chapter.

V Code	V Code Description
V01.3	Contact with or exposure to smallpox
V12.1	Personal history of nutritional deficiency
V52.2	Fitting and adjustment of artificial eye
V72.0	Examination of eyes and vision
V82.6	Multiphasic screening

E Codes—Supplementary Classification of External Causes of Injury and Poisoning (Code Range E800–E999)

The **Supplementary Classification of External Causes of Injury and Poisoning** section is used to provide a classification for external causes of injuries and poisonings. E codes identify the environmental event, circumstance, or condition that is the cause for the injury or poisoning. These codes are used in addition to a code from one of the main chapters. Specific instructions for assigning these codes are found in the chapter entitled "E Codes."

EXAMPLE: Using volume 1 of your ICD-9-CM book, locate the start of the "E Codes." This follows the chapter on V codes. Here you will find the Supplementary Classification of External Causes of Injury and Poisoning, or E codes. Reference the following codes to familiarize yourself with this chapter.

E Code	E Code Description
E847	Accidents involving cable cars not running on rails
E869.0	Accidental poisoning by nitrogen oxides
E884.2	Fall from chair
E963	Assault by hanging and strangulation
E978	Legal Execution

Exercise 2–3   V Codes and E Codes

True/False: Referencing the chapters for V codes and E codes, answer true (T) or false (F).

1. _____ Code E907 is the code for accidents due to lightning.

2. _____ A family history of a malignant neoplasm of the gastrointestinal tract is coded to V10.00.

3. _____ The E code range E800–E807 codes railway accidents.

4. _____ The V code range V16–V19 codes family histories of conditions.

5. _____ Code E979.4 is the code for terrorism involving firearms.

Volume 1—Appendices

The third subdivision of volume 1 of ICD-9-CM is the Appendices, which contain reference information. There are five appendices in this volume.

Appendix A—Morphology of Neoplasms (Code Range M8000/0–M9970/1)

Appendix A, "Morphology of Neoplasms," contains a nomenclature of the morphology of neoplasms adapted from the International Classification of Diseases (ICD) of Oncology and is used with codes from chapter 2, depending on the setting of the encounter.

Appendix B—Glossary of Mental Disorders

This appendix was officially deleted October 1, 2004.

Appendix C—Classification of Drugs by American Hospital Formulary Service List Number and Their ICD-9-CM Equivalents

Appendix C, "Classification of Drugs by American Hospital Formulary Service List Number and Their ICD-9-CM Equivalents," lists the ICD-9-CM diagnosis code for the coding of poisonings by drugs and medicinal and biological substances in relation to the listing of drugs by the American Hospital Formulary Service.

Appendix D—Classification of Industrial Accidents According to Agency

Appendix D, "Classification of Industrial Accidents According to Agency," lists industrial accidents as defined by the Tenth International Conference of Labor Statisticians.

Appendix E—List of Three-Digit Categories

Appendix E, "List of Three-Digit Categories," is a listing of all the three-digit categories that are found in ICD-9-CM.

Volume 2—Alphabetic Index

Volume 2 of ICD-9-CM has three major subdivisions. The first subdivision is the Index to Diseases and Injuries. This section functions as the key to the coding system. It contains an alphabetical listing of the diseases and injuries classified in ICD-9-CM. This section will be discussed in more detail in a later chapter.

The second subdivision is the Alphabetic Index to Poisoning and External Causes of Adverse Effects of Drugs and Other Chemical Substances, commonly referred to as the Table of Drugs and Chemicals. This table is used to classify poisonings by a drug or chemical, as well as to classify external causes of an adverse effect of a drug or chemical.

The third subdivision is the Alphabetic Index to External Causes of Injury and Poisoning. This is the index for E codes, which classify environmental events, circumstances, and other conditions as the cause of an injury and adverse effects.

The Alphabetic Indices follow alphabetization rules that are unique to ICD-9-CM. These rules will be discussed in Chapter 3.

Volume 3—Tabular List and Alphabetic Index of Procedures

The third volume of ICD-9-CM, known as the Tabular List and Alphabetic Index of Procedures, contains both the alphabetic and tabular list for procedures and surgeries. The Tabular List is organized according to the location of the procedure or is grouped into the chapter for miscellaneous diagnostic and therapeutic procedures. The content of the various chapters will be discussed in detail in later chapters.

> **EXAMPLE:** Refer to the following list. You will see that the chapters are organized by the location of the procedure; for example, chapter 1 is "Operations on the Nervous System" and chapter 4 is "Operations on the Ear."

Chapter Titles and Category Codes of Tabular List of Procedures

00.	Procedures and Interventions, Not Elsewhere Classified (00)
1.	Operations on the Nervous System (01–05)
2.	Operations on the Endocrine System (06–07)
3.	Operations on the Eye (08–16)
4.	Operations on the Ear (18–20)
5.	Operations on the Nose, Mouth, and Pharynx (21–29)
6.	Operations on the Respiratory System (30–34)
7.	Operations on the Cardiovascular System (35–39)
8.	Operations on the Hemic and Lymphatic Systems (40–41)
9.	Operations on the Digestive System (42–54)
10.	Operations on the Urinary System (55–59)
11.	Operations on the Male Genital Organs (60–64)
12.	Operations on the Female Genital Organs (65–71)
13.	Obstetrical Procedures (72–75)
14.	Operations on the Musculoskeletal System (76–84)
15.	Operations on the Integumentary System (85–86)
16.	Miscellaneous Diagnostic and Therapeutic Procedures (87–99)

Exercise 2–4   Tabular List of Procedures

To become familiar with volume 3, complete the following table using the Tabular List of Procedures. The first one is completed.

Procedural Code	Procedural Description	Procedure Chapter Title
22.71	Closure of nasal sinus fistula	Operations on the Nose, Mouth, and Pharynx
07.72	_____	_____
18.31	_____	_____
43.99	_____	_____
35.42	_____	_____
31.45	_____	_____
66.4	_____	_____
55.04	_____	_____
96.41	_____	_____

Procedural Code	Procedural Description	Procedure Chapter Title
08.41		
84.21		
75.7		
00.03		
01.32		
41.06		
85.25		
60.61		
83.31		

Internet Links

The National Center for Health Statistics (NCHS) maintains information about ICD-9-CM. For a wealth of information, explore *http://www.cdc.gov/nchs/icd9.htm*.

Summary

- ICD-9-CM consists of three volumes.

- Volume 1 is the Tabular List of Diseases and Injuries.

- Volume 2 is the Alphabetic Index.

- Volume 3 is the Tabular List and Alphabetic Index of Procedures.

- The Tabular List of Diseases and Injuries has three major subdivisions: the Classification of Diseases and Injuries, Supplementary Classifications, and Appendices.

- The Classification of Diseases and Injuries is a numerical list of diseases and injuries found in ICD-9-CM.

- The Supplementary Classifications of ICD-9-CM are known as V codes and E codes.

- V codes are used to code the conditions or circumstances that are recorded as the reason for the patient encounter, as well as factors that affect the patient's health and/or medical management.

- E codes provide a classification for external causes of injuries and poisonings.

- The appendices in volume 1 serve as reference material for the coder.

- The Alphabetic Index in volume 2 has three major subdivisions: the Index to Diseases and Injuries, the Alphabetic Index to Poisoning and External Causes of Adverse Effects of Drugs and Other Chemical Substances, and the Table of Drugs and Chemicals.

- Volume 3, the Tabular List and Alphabetic Index of Procedures, contains both the tabular and alphabetic list of procedures and surgeries.

Chapter Review

True/False: Indicate whether each statement is true (T) or false (F).

1. _____ Volume 2 is the Tabular List of Diseases and Injuries.

2. _____ V codes and E codes must be used with an additional code from the main chapters of ICD-9-CM.

3. _____ Volume 3 is the Tabular List and Alphabetic Index of Procedures and is used in the facility setting.

4. _____ E codes are used to code conditions or circumstances that are recorded as the reason for the patient encounter when the patient is not currently ill.

5. _____ Family and personal histories of diseases are coded to different V codes.

Fill-in-the-Blank: Enter the appropriate term(s) to complete each statement below.

6. The diagnostic chapters of ICD-9-CM are organized according to _____, the cause of disease, or _____, the body system involved.

7. The _____ contains an alphabetical listing of the diseases and injuries found in ICD-9-CM and serves as a key to the coding system.

8. The codes that provide a classification for external causes of injuries and poisonings are known as _____.

9. Chapter _____, entitled _____, includes fractures, dislocations, sprains and strains of joints and muscles, intracranial injuries, and internal injuries to chest, abdomen, and pelvis.

10. Disorders and diseases of the thyroid and other endocrine glands, nutritional deficiencies, metabolic disorders, and disorders of the immune mechanism and immunity deficiencies are contained in chapter _____, entitled _____.

Short Answer: Briefly respond to each question.

11. Discuss the content of the three volumes of ICD-9-CM.

12. Explain the difference between a diagnostic code and a procedural code. Give an example of each.

13. Summarize the content of chapter 16, "Signs, Symptoms, and Ill-Defined Conditions."

14. Identify the appendices that are found in volume 1 of ICD-9-CM.

15. Explain the purpose of E codes.

ICD-9-CM Volume Organization

Chapter Outline

Objectives

At the conclusion of this chapter, the student will be able to:

1. Discuss the organization of the three volumes of ICD-9-CM.
2. Explain the procedure for referencing main terms in the index of ICD-9-CM.
3. Outline the alphabetizing rules used in the index.
4. Locate main terms in the disease and procedure indices.
5. Identify valid and truncated codes.

Key Terms

Accident

Adverse Effect

Assault

Category

Main Terms

Poisoning

Sections

Subcategory

Subclassification

Suicide Attempt

Therapeutic Use

Truncated Codes

Undetermined

Reminder

As you work through this chapter, you will need to have a copy of the ICD-9-CM coding book to reference.

Introduction

As discussed previously, ICD-9-CM is organized into chapters, appendices, and indices. This chapter will discuss the organization and arrangement of the divisions of the volumes of ICD-9-CM.

Volume 1—Tabular List of Diseases and Injuries

The 17 chapters of the ICD-9-CM, including V codes and E codes, are arranged at the chapter level according to body systems, etiology, or situations affecting the onset of the conditions. A range of codes is assigned to each chapter. For example, chapter 1, "Infectious and Parasitic Diseases," contains codes in the range 001–139. Figure 3-1 illustrates the beginning of chapter 1 and is an example of the code ranges.

---

1. INFECTIOUS AND PARASITIC DISEASES (001–139)

Note: Categories for "late effects" of infectious and parasitic diseases are to be found at 137–139.

Includes: Diseases generally recognized as communicable or transmissible as well as a few diseases of unknown but possibly infectious origin

Excludes: Acute respiratory infections (460–466)
             Carrier or suspected carrier of infectious organism (V02.0–V02.9)
             Certain localized infections
             Influenza (487.0–487.8, 488)

INTESTINAL INFECTIOUS DISEASES (001–009)

Excludes: Helminthiases (120.0–129)

001   Cholera

001.0   Due to Vibrio cholerae
001.1   Due to Vibrio cholerae el tor
001.9   Cholera, unspecified

002   Typhoid and paratyphoid fevers

002.0   Typhoid fever
             Typhoid (fever) (infection) [any site]
002.1   Paratyphoid fever A
002.2   Paratyphoid fever B
002.3   Paratyphoid fever C
002.9   Paratyphoid fever, unspecified

003   Other salmonella infections

Includes: · Infection or food poisoning by Salmonella [any serotype]

003.0   Salmonella gastroenteritis
             Salmonellosis
003.1   Salmonella septicemia
003.2   Localized salmonella infections
             003.20   Localized salmonella infection, unspecified
             003.21   Salmonella meningitis
             003.22   Salmonella pneumonia
             003.23   Salmonella arthritis
             003.24   Salmonella osteomyelitis
             003.29   Other
003.8   Other specified salmonella infections
003.9   Salmonella infection, unspecified

Figure 3-1   ICD-9-CM chapter 1, "Infectious and Parasitic Diseases"

Chapters within ICD-9-CM are divided into sections, which contain a series of three-digit category codes that group conditions or related conditions. Figure 3-1 also illustrates the first section, "Intestinal Infectious Diseases" (001–009), of chapter 1. Reference an ICD-9-CM code book, and note that chapter 1 is divided into the following sections:

Section	Code Range
Intestinal Infectious Diseases	001–009
Tuberculosis	010–018
Zoonotic Bacterial Diseases	020–027
Other Bacterial Diseases	030–041
Human Immunodeficiency Virus Infection	042
Poliomyelitis and Other Non-Arthropod-Borne Viral Diseases and Prion Diseases of Central Nervous System	045–049
Viral Diseases Accompanied by Exanthem	050–059
Arthropod-Borne Viral Diseases	060–066
Other Diseases Due to Viruses and Chlamydiae	070–079
Rickettsioses and Other Arthropod-Borne Diseases	080–088
Syphilis and Other Venereal Diseases	090–099
Other Spirochetal Diseases	100–104
Mycoses	110–118
Helminthiases	120–129
Other Infectious and Parasitic Diseases	130–136

Codes are not assigned from chapter or section levels. Code assignment starts at the category level with three-digit codes. Codes are assigned at this level only if the category level is not further divided into a subcategory, with codes containing four digits, or into a subclassification, with codes containing five digits. An example of a valid category code is code number 490, "Bronchitis, not specified as acute or chronic" (Figure 3-2). Because the category is not divided into subcategory four-digit codes or subclassification five-digit codes, the coder can select 490.

If a category is divided into subcategories, the coder must code at the four-digit level. Category code 491, "Chronic bronchitis," is divided into subcategories, so code 491 would not be valid. The coder must use four digits to code the chronic bronchitis. The acceptable four-digit codes are 491.0, 491.1, 491.8, and 491.9.

Note that subcategory code 491.2 is divided into a subclassification five-digit code; as a result, 491.2 is not valid. Code 491.20 or 491.21 needs to be used. Codes that do not contain all the necessary digits are truncated codes. Truncated codes are codes that are not carried out to the most specific classification available for a category. If invalid truncated codes are used, claims will be rejected by Medicare and other third-party payers.

EXAMPLE: Dr. Matthews' office submits code number 491 as the primary diagnosis code for chronic bronchitis on a claim submitted for third-party reimbursement. The claim is rejected by the third-party payer because the diagnosis was not coded to the fourth or fifth digit. Since Dr. Matthews did not specify the type of chronic bronchitis, the coder should have submitted code 491.9, "unspecified chronic bronchitis." At the time of the initial office visit, a specific diagnosis may not be known. In this situation, either the unspecified diagnosis code or the code(s) for any associated symptoms that required medical attention should be submitted.

Subcategory codes, those containing four digits, can be used only if no subclassification codes are available. Subclassification codes, those codes containing five digits, are the most specific codes available in the coding system. Whenever five-digit codes are present in ICD-9-CM, they must be used.

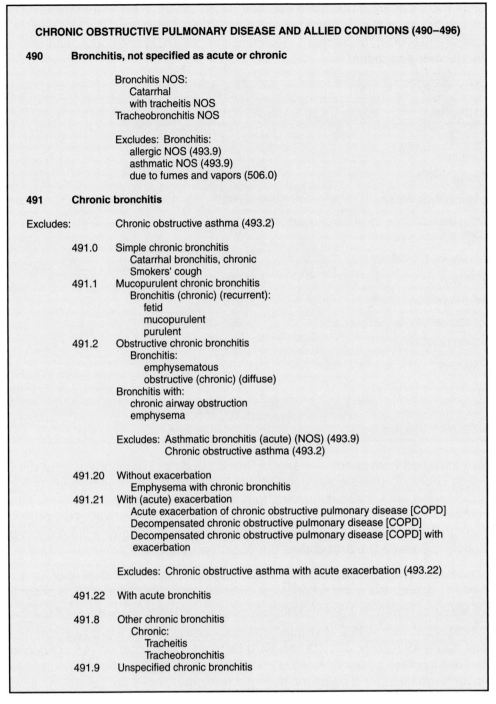

CHRONIC OBSTRUCTIVE PULMONARY DISEASE AND ALLIED CONDITIONS (490–496)

490   Bronchitis, not specified as acute or chronic

Bronchitis NOS:
Catarrhal
with tracheitis NOS
Tracheobronchitis NOS

Excludes: Bronchitis:
allergic NOS (493.9)
asthmatic NOS (493.9)
due to fumes and vapors (506.0)

491   Chronic bronchitis

Excludes: Chronic obstructive asthma (493.2)

491.0   Simple chronic bronchitis
Catarrhal bronchitis, chronic
Smokers' cough
491.1   Mucopurulent chronic bronchitis
Bronchitis (chronic) (recurrent):
fetid
mucopurulent
purulent
491.2   Obstructive chronic bronchitis
Bronchitis:
emphysematous
obstructive (chronic) (diffuse)
Bronchitis with:
chronic airway obstruction
emphysema

Excludes: Asthmatic bronchitis (acute) (NOS) (493.9)
Chronic obstructive asthma (493.2)

491.20   Without exacerbation
Emphysema with chronic bronchitis
491.21   With (acute) exacerbation
Acute exacerbation of chronic obstructive pulmonary disease [COPD]
Decompensated chronic obstructive pulmonary disease [COPD]
Decompensated chronic obstructive pulmonary disease [COPD] with
exacerbation

Excludes: Chronic obstructive asthma with acute exacerbation (493.22)

491.22   With acute bronchitis

491.8   Other chronic bronchitis
Chronic:
Tracheitis
Tracheobronchitis
491.9   Unspecified chronic bronchitis

Figure 3-2 ICD-9-CM code categories 490–491

The fifth digits are displayed in the text of the code description, as in codes 491.20 and 491.21, or displayed after a category heading, as in code 493 (Figure 3-3).

For subcategory codes 493.0, 493.1, 493.2, 493.8, and 493.9, the coder must select the proper fifth digit of 0, 1, or 2. These subcategory codes are not valid codes without the fifth digit. Note that for code 493.8 the fifth digit is displayed in the text of the code description.

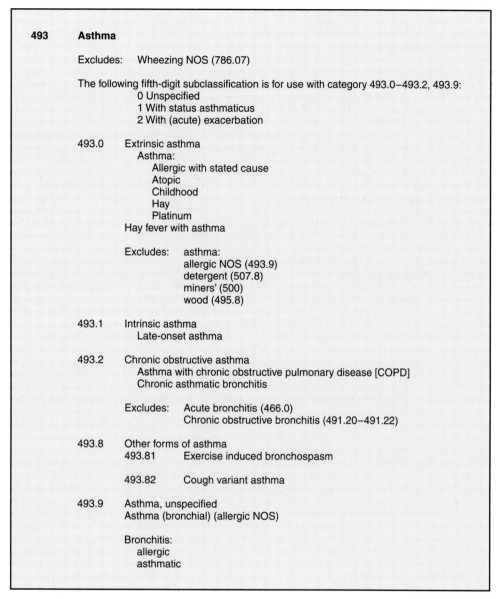

493   Asthma

Excludes: Wheezing NOS (786.07)

The following fifth-digit subclassification is for use with category 493.0–493.2, 493.9:
  0 Unspecified
  1 With status asthmaticus
  2 With (acute) exacerbation

493.0   Extrinsic asthma
        Asthma:
            Allergic with stated cause
            Atopic
            Childhood
            Hay
            Platinum
        Hay fever with asthma

        Excludes: asthma:
                    allergic NOS (493.9)
                    detergent (507.8)
                    miners' (500)
                    wood (495.8)

493.1   Intrinsic asthma
            Late-onset asthma

493.2   Chronic obstructive asthma
            Asthma with chronic obstructive pulmonary disease [COPD]
            Chronic asthmatic bronchitis

        Excludes: Acute bronchitis (466.0)
                    Chronic obstructive bronchitis (491.20–491.22)

493.8   Other forms of asthma
        493.81   Exercise induced bronchospasm

        493.82   Cough variant asthma

493.9   Asthma, unspecified
        Asthma (bronchial) (allergic NOS)

        Bronchitis:
            allergic
            asthmatic

Figure 3-3 ICD-9-CM code category 493

ICD-9-CM Official Coding Guidelines for Coding and Reporting

As you can see, ICD-9-CM diagnosis codes are composed of codes with three, four, or five digits. Diagnosis and procedure codes should be used with the highest number of digits available, with the coder following any subdivisions to obtain the greatest detail. A code is invalid if it has not been coded to the full number of digits required.

EXAMPLE: Acute myocardial infarction, code 410, has fourth digits available to describe the location of the infarction (i.e., 410.2, of inferolateral wall) and fifth digits to identify the episode of care (i.e., 410.21, of inferolateral wall, initial episode of care). It would be incorrect to report a code in category 410 without a fourth and fifth digit.

It should be noted that procedure codes in ICD-9-CM volume 3 should have three or four digits. Two-digit codes are included in ICD-9-CM as headings that may be subdivided into codes with three or four digits, which provide greater detail. This will be discussed later in the chapter.

Volume 2—Alphabetic Index to Diseases and Injuries

The key to locating diagnoses codes is found in volume 2, "Alphabetic Index to Diseases and Injuries." The first section of volume 2, "Index to Diseases and Injuries," is used to locate codes for diseases, injuries, and V codes. V codes are used to code factors that influence health status and contacts with health services. The second section, "Table of Drugs and Chemicals," is used to locate the code for poisonings from drugs and chemicals. The third section of this volume, "The Index to External Causes of Injury," is used to locate E codes. E codes are used to further explain a condition or injury. V codes and E codes will be explained in more detail later in this book.

The alphabetic indices are organized by main terms. These main terms are printed in bold type and follow letter-by-letter alphabetizing. Rules of letter-by-letter alphabetizing are as follows:

1. Ignore single spaces when alphabetizing.
2. Ignore single hyphens when alphabetizing.
3. Numbers or the adjective version of the number (first, second, third, fourth) are placed in numerical order before alphabetical characters.
4. When a diagnostic statement contains the term *with*, the *with* immediately follows the main term, and the second part of the diagnosis follows in alphabetical order.
5. Subterms and modifying terms are indented under the main term. They appear in alphabetical order.

Location of Main Term

Location of the main term in the alphabetic index is the key to correct code selection. **Main terms** identify the disease, sign, symptom, condition, or injury to be coded. Main terms for volume 2 are located in the alphabetic index by referencing the condition or injury that is present, and they start with a capital letter that is printed on the left-hand margin. Figure 3-4 represents a page from volume 2 that shows the main terms *appendage*, *appendicitis*, *appendiclausis*, *appendicolithiasis*, and *appendicopathia oxyurica*.

> **EXAMPLE:** The diagnostic phrase *chronic appendicitis* is located in the index by referencing the term *appendicitis*. Figure 3-4 represents a page from volume 2 for locating the diagnostic phrase *chronic appendicitis*. The coder first references the main term, *appendicitis,* and then locates the subterm *chronic*. The code 542 appears next to the term *chronic (recurrent)*. Note that when in parentheses, the term does or does not need to be included in the diagnostic statement. This coding rule will be discussed in a later chapter.

Locate the following diseases or injuries in volume 2, "Alphabetic Index to Diseases and Injuries," by referencing the main term. Note the codes found in the index.

Disease or Condition	Main Term in Index	Code Found in Index
Chronic appendicitis	Appendicitis	542
Dancing disease	Disease	297.8
Hemorrhagic encephalitis	Encephalitis	323.9
Fracture of arm	Fracture	818.0
Open wound of shin with tendon involvement	Wound	891.2

Appendage
        fallopian tube (cyst of Morgagni) 752.11
        intestine (epiploic) 751.5
        preauricular 744.1
        testicular (organ of Morgagni) 752.89

Appendicitis 541
        with
                perforation, peritonitis (generalized), or rupture 540.0
                      with peritoneal abscess 540.1
                peritoneal abscess 540.1
        acute (catarrhal) (fulminating) (gangrenous) (inflammatory) (obstructive) (retrocecal)
        (suppurative) 540.9
            with
                perforation, peritonitis, or rupture 540.0
                      with peritoneal abscess 540.1
                peritoneal abscess 540.1
        amebic 006.8
        chronic (recurrent) 542
        exacerbation - see Appendicitis, acute
        fulminating - see Appendicitis, acute
        gangrenous - see Appendicitis, acute
        healed (obliterative) 542
        interval 542
        neurogenic 542
        obstructive 542
        pneumococcal 541
        recurrent 542
        relapsing 542
        retrocecal 541
        subacute (adhesive) 542
        subsiding 542
        suppurative—see Appendicitis, acute
        tuberculous (see also Tuberculosis) 014.8

Appendiclausis 543.9

Appendicolithiasis 543.9

Appendicopathia oxyurica 127.4

Figure 3-4 Example of some main terms in the Alphabetic Index to Diseases and Injuries.

Exercise 3–1   Identifying Main Terms

For each diagnostic phrase listed, identify the main term that would be located in the index.

Disease or Condition	Main Term in Index
1. Amnion hematoma	_____
2. Degenerative arthritis	_____
3. Raynaud's gangrene	_____
4. Nonfamilial hemophilia	_____
5. Hepatic infarct	_____
6. Spinal cord injury	_____

Disease or Condition	Main Term in Index
7. Ankle sprain	
8. Patellar tendonitis	
9. Acquired deformity of ankle	
10. Amebic lung abscess	
11. Chronic bronchitis	
12. Senile dementia	
13. Fracture of left 4th rib	
14. Renal hypertension	
15. Allergic enteritis	

Tables of Drugs and Chemicals

The second section of volume 2, "Table of Drugs and Chemicals," is used to locate codes for poisonings and the external cause of the poisoning. Drugs and chemical substances are listed alphabetically. The second column, poisoning, represents the code for the classification of the poisoning, according to the type of drug or chemical that the patient was exposed to. The remaining five columns, listed under external causes, represent the causes of the poisoning or adverse reactions. Figure 3-5 represents an excerpt from a page of the Table of Drugs and Chemicals.

Conditions are classified as a **poisoning** when a drug, chemical, or biological substance has been taken by a patient when it was not given under the direction of a physician. Examples include overdose; intoxication; wrong substance given or taken in error; medications taken with alcohol, prescription, and over-the-counter drugs combined; and wrong dosage taken. These conditions are coded as follows:

1. Reference Table of Drugs and Chemicals, poisoning column, under the main term of the drug or chemical the patient was exposed to. Select poisoning code.

Substance	Poisoning	EXTERNAL CAUSES (E Code)				
		Accident	Therapeutic Use	Suicide Attempt	Assault	Undetermined
Acetone (oils) (vapor)	982.8	E862.4	-----	E950.9	E962.1	E980.9
Acetophenazine (maleate)	969.1	E853.0	E939.1	E950.3	E962.0	E980.3
Acetophenetidin	965.4	E850.4	E935.4	E950.0	E962.0	E980.0
Acetophenone	982.0	E862.4	-----	E950.9	E962.1	E980.9
Acetorphine	965.09	E850.2	E935.2	E950.0	E962.0	E980.0
Acetosulfone (sodium)	961.8	E857	E931.8	E950.4	E962.0	E980.4

Figure 3-5 Excerpt from Table of Drugs and Chemicals

2. Code any manifestation that is present from the Alphabetical Index to Diseases and Injuries (e.g., gastritis, coma, shock).

3. Select the external cause of the poisoning from one of the following columns:

   Accident (E850–E869)—This includes accidental overdose of a drug, wrong substance given or taken in error, drug taken inadvertently, and wrong dosage.

   Suicide attempt (E950–E952)—These are self-inflicted attempts by means of drugs and chemicals.

   Assault (E961–E962)—An injury or poisoning inflicted by another person with the intent to injure or kill.

   Undetermined (E980–E982)—These codes are used when the intent of the poisoning cannot be determined.

The column Therapeutic Use is not to be used with a poisoning code and is used when there is an adverse effect. An adverse effect is defined as a reaction to the correct administration of a drug or a reaction between two or more drugs that were prescribed by a physician. The following steps should be used when coding an adverse effect:

1. Locate the reaction or condition present in the Alphabetic Index to Diseases and Injuries (e.g., rash, vomiting, swelling).

2. Locate the E code for the adverse effect on the Table of Drugs and Chemicals, in the Therapeutic Use column.

   EXAMPLE: A physician prescribes erythromycin, and the patient develops an allergic rash. Because this is an adverse effect to a drug properly taken, the coder codes the allergic rash as 693.0 and then references the Table of Drugs and Chemicals to code the erythromycin as the cause of the rash; this is code E930.3.

Additional E codes are located by using the third section of volume 2, "The Alphabetic Index to External Causes of Injury and Poisoning (E Codes)." E codes have become of interest to third-party payers as well as to governmental agencies and health departments. The presence of the E code shows the cause of an injury or accident and therefore can be helpful in determining the most appropriate financial coverage for the injury, such as workmen's compensation, homeowner's insurance, and so on.

The main terms for this section are organized by the term that describes the accident, the circumstances, or the specific agent that was the cause of the injury or adverse effect. It is important for the coder to use the following rules when selecting E codes:

1. E codes are supplemental codes and are never reported without a code from the main classification (code range 001–999).

2. The letter *E* must always be reported in addition to the numerical characters.

3. The diagnosis being coded is reported first and is followed by the E code.

   E codes are located by one of the following:

   1. Referencing the Table of Drugs and Chemicals for codes for poisonings and adverse effects.

   2. Referencing The Index to External Causes for codes for the cause of an injury or poisoning.

Locate the following external causes for the examples listed in The Index to External Causes of Injury. Note the codes found in the index.

Cause of Injury or Adverse Effect	Main Term in Index	Code Found in Index
Fracture due to fall from tree	Fall	E884.9
Internal injuries from stabbing	Stabbing	E966
Patient struck by lightning	Lightning	E907
Accidental poisoning by carbon monoxide fumes from car in motion, not on public highway	Poisoning	E825.9

Exercise 3–2   Identifying Main Terms for External Causes of Injuries

For each injury listed, identify the main term that would be located in the Alphabetical Index to External Cause of Injury.

Injury	**Main Term in the Index to External Cause of Injury**
1. Burn from contact with dry ice	
2. Choking on an apple	
3. Fall from a stepladder	
4. Third-degree burns from house fire	
5. Puncture wound from BB gun	
6. Multiple lacerations from rape	
7. Fracture of wrist from being trapped by door of elevator	
8. Fainting due to sunstroke	
9. Multiple fractures due to motor vehicle accident	
10. Six-year-old child with multiple bruises from abuse by stepfather	

Volume 3—Tabular List and Alphabetic Index of Procedures

Both the Tabular List of Procedures and Alphabetic Index of Procedures are found in volume 3 of ICD-9-CM. The format of volume 3 is similar to that of volumes 1 and 2 except that procedure codes contain a maximum of four digits; diagnostic codes can contain a maximum of five digits. Figure 3-6 represents the start of the first chapter of the Tabular List of Procedures, entitled "Procedures and Interventions, Not Elsewhere Classified (00)." Note that the codes contain no more than four digits.

Reference an ICD-9-CM code book and locate the second chapter of the Tabular List of Procedures, entitled "Operations on the Nervous System." Note the following category codes found in this chapter.

Category Description	Category Code
Incision and excision of skull, brain, and cerebral meninges	01
Other operations on skull, brain, and cerebral meninges	02
Operations on spinal cord and spinal canal structures	03
Operations on cranial and peripheral nerves	04
Operations on sympathetic nerves or ganglia	05

PROCEDURES AND INTERVENTIONS, NOT ELSEWHERE CLASSIFIED (00)

00   Procedures and interventions, Not Elsewhere Classified

00.0   Therapeutic ultrasound

    00.01   Therapeutic ultrasound of vessels of head and neck
        Anti-restenotic ultrasound
        Intravascular non-ablative ultrasound

        Excludes: Diagnostic ultrasound of:
            eye (95.13)
            head and neck (88.71)
        That of inner ear (20.79)
        Ultrasonic:
            Angioplasty of non-coronary vessel (39.50)
            Embolectomy (38.01, 38.02)
            Endarterectomy (38.11, 38.12)
            Thrombectomy (38.01, 38.02)

    00.02   Therapeutic ultrasound of heart
        Anti-restenotic ultrasound
        Intravascular non-ablative ultrasound

        Excludes: Diagnostic ultrasound of heart (88.72)
            Ultrasonic ablation of heart lesion (37.34)
            Ultrasonic angioplasty of coronary vessels (00.66, 36.09)

    00.03   Therapeutic ultrasound of peripheral vascular vessels
        Anti-restenotic ultrasound
        Intravascular non-ablative ultrasound

        Excludes: Diagnostic ultrasound of peripheral vascular system (88.77)
            Ultrasonic angioplasty of:
            Non-coronary vessel (39.50)

    00.09   Other therapeutic ultrasound

        Excludes: Ultrasonic:
            Fragmentation of urinary stones (59.95)
            Percutaneous nephrostomy with fragmentation (55.04)
            Physical therapy (93.35)
            Transurethral guided laser induced prostatectomy (TULIP) (60.21)

00.1   Pharamaceuticals

    00.10   Implantation of chemotherapeutic agent
        Brain wafer chemotherapy
        Interstitial/intracavitary

        Excludes: Injection or infusion of cancer chemotherapeutic substance (99.25)

        00.11   Infusion of drotrecogin alfa (activated)
            Infusion of recombinant protein

        00.12   Administration of inhaled nitric oxide
            Nitric oxide therapy

        00.13   Injection or infusion of nesiritide
            Human B-type natriuretic peptide (hBNP)

        00.14   Injection or infusion of oxazolidinone class of antibiotics
            Linezolid injection

        00.15   High-dose infusion interleukin-2 [IL-2]
            Infusion (IV bolus, CIV) interleukin
            Injection of aldesleukin

            Excludes: Low-dose infusion interleukin-2 (99.28)

Figure 3-6 Procedures and Interventions, Not Elsewhere Classified (00)

Exercise 3–3   Category Codes for Operations on the Nose, Mouth, and Pharynx

Identify the description for each category code for operations on the nose, mouth, and pharynx in the following list. The first one is done.

Category Code	Description of Category Code
1. 21	Operations on nose
2. 22	_____
3. 23	_____
4. 24	_____
5. 25	_____
6. 26	_____
7. 27	_____
8. 28	_____
9. 29	_____

Alphabetical Index to Procedures

The procedure index follows the same alphabetization rules as in volume 2. Main terms represent procedures and operations. However, there are two exceptions regarding subterms. Subterms that start with *as, by,* and *for* sometimes immediately follow the main term or subterm. The words *with* and *without* will then follow the subterms. Figure 3.7 represents a page from the Alphabetical Index to Procedures. Note that the entry for thoracotomy is followed by the subterm *as operative approach,* and the entry for thrombectomy is followed by the subterm *with endarterectomy.*

> **EXAMPLE:** The term *exploratory thoracotomy* is located in the procedure index by referencing the term *thoracotomy* and then locating the subterm *exploratory.* The code is 34.02, as shown in Figure 3-7.

Exercise 3–4   Using the Alphabetical Index to Procedures

For each procedure or operation listed, identify the main term used to find the procedure in the Alphabetical Index to Procedures.

Procedure or Operation	Main Term in Alphabetical Index to Procedures
1. Incision and drainage of abscess	_____
2. Total hip replacement	_____
3. Coronary artery bypass graft	_____
4. Open reduction of fracture of ankle	_____
5. Fiberglass cast application	_____
6. Exploratory thoractomy	_____

Procedure or Operation   **Main Term in Alphabetical Index to Procedures**

  7. Cryotherapy of warts   _____

  8. Third toe amputation   _____

  9. Bone sequestrectomy   _____

10. Abdominal thrombectomy   _____

Thoracectomy 34.09
        for lung collapse 33.34

Thoracentesis 34.91

Thoracocentesis 34.91

Thoracolysis (for collapse of lung) 33.39

Thoracoplasty (anterior) (extrapleural) (paravertebral) (posterolateral) (complete) (partial) 33.34

Thoracoscopy, transpleural (for exploration) 34.21

Thoracostomy 34.09
        for lung collapse 33.32

Thoracotomy (with drainage) 34.09
        as operative approach—omit code
        exploratory 34.02

Three-snip operation, punctum 09.51

Thrombectomy 38.00
        with endarterectomy—see Endarterectomy
        abdominal
                artery 38.06
                vein 38.07
        aorta (arch) (ascending) (descending) 38.04
        arteriovenous shunt or cannula 39.49
        bovine graft 39.49
        coronary artery 36.09
        head and neck vessel NEC 38.02
        intracranial vessel NEC 38.01
        lower limb
                artery 38.08
                vein 38.09
        mechanical
                endovascular
                      head and neck 39.74
        pulmonary vessel 38.05
        thoracic vessel NEC 38.05
        upper limb (artery) (vein) 38.03

Thromboendarterectomy 38.10
        abdominal 38.16
        aorta (arch) (ascending) (descending) 38.14
        coronary artery 36.09
                open chest approach 36.03
        head and neck NEC 38.12
        intracranial NEC 38.11
        lower limb 38.18
        thoracic NEC 38.15
        upper limb 38.13

Figure 3-7 Alphabetical Index to Procedures

Summary

- The tabular volumes of ICD-9-CM are arranged by chapters.
- Chapters are divided into sections that contain three-digit category codes.
- The assignment of codes start at the category level if the category is not further divided into a subcategory or subclassification.
- Truncated codes are not valid for reporting.
- Diagnosis and procedure codes must be used at their highest number of digits available.
- Volume 2 is used to locate codes for diseases, injuries, V codes, and E codes.
- Main terms identify the term to be referenced in the index.
- The Table of Drugs and Chemicals is used to locate codes for poisonings and the external cause of the poisoning.
- Volume 3 contains both the Tabular List of Procedures and Alphabetic Index of Procedures.

Chapter Review

True/False: Indicate whether each statement is true (T) or false (F).

1. _____ Categories contain a series of three digits that group conditions or related conditions.

2. _____ A subclassification contains codes with five digits.

3. _____ If a category is divided, the coder must code at the subcategory or subclassification level.

4. _____ The tabular sections of ICD-9-CM are organized by main terms.

5. _____ The main term referenced for the diagnostic statement "recurrent infectious bronchitis" would be bronchitis.

Fill-in-the-Blank: Enter the appropriate term(s) to complete each statement.

6. Patient Smith has taken a drug overdose. This is known as a(n) _____.

7. Any injury or poisoning inflicted by another person with the intent to injure or kill is a(n) _____.

8. The cause of an injury or accident is coded by using a(n) _____.

9. Procedure codes contain a maximum of _____ digits.

10. Codes that do not contain all necessary digits are called _____ codes.

Short Answer: Complete each exercise by referencing an ICD-9-CM code book.

11. Use volume 1, "Tabular List of Diseases and Injuries," to complete the following list.

Chapter Title	First Section in Chapter	Code Range of Section
Diseases of Circulatory System	_____	_____
Diseases of Genitourinary System	_____	_____
Neoplasms	_____	_____
Mental Disorders	_____	_____
Congenital Anomalies	_____	_____
Symptoms, Signs, and Ill-Defined Conditions	_____	_____
Diseases of Respiratory System	_____	_____
Diseases of Blood and Blood-Forming Organs	_____	_____
Diseases of Musculoskeletal and Connective Tissue	_____	_____

12. Use the Alphabetical Index to Procedures to identify the main terms for the following procedures or operations.

Procedure or Operation	Main Term
Nasal packing due to severe epistaxis	_____
Biopsy of cervical lymph nodes	_____
Repair of umbilical hernia	_____
Colonoscopy with polypectomy	_____
Left cardiac catheterization	_____
Laparoscopic cholecystectomy	_____
Partial hysterectomy	_____
Colon resection	_____
Manipulation of fracture of femur	_____
Open reduction of left tibia with insertion of screws	_____

ICD-9-CM Coding Conventions and Steps in Coding

Chapter Outline

Introduction
Convention Types
Instructional Notations
Punctuation Marks
Abbreviations

Symbols
Steps in Coding
Summary
Chapter Review

Objectives

At the conclusion of this chapter, the student will be able to:

1. Describe the conventions used in ICD-9-CM.
2. Differentiate among the abbreviations, symbols, and instructional notations used in ICD-9-CM.
3. Identify and select main terms that are referenced in the Alphabetic Indices.
4. Summarize the steps in coding.

Key Terms

Braces
Code First Underlying
  Disease, Cause, or
  Condition
Colon
Conventions
Excludes:

Exclusion Note
Includes:
Inclusion Note
Instructional Notations
Italicized Brackets

Not Elsewhere
  Classifiable (NEC)
Not Otherwise Specified
  (NOS)
Parentheses
See:

See Also:
See Category:
Slanted Brackets
Square Brackets
Use Additional Code

Reminder

As you work through this chapter, you will need to have a copy of the ICD-9-CM coding book to reference.

Introduction

This chapter contains coding rules that highlight concepts that must be followed for accurate coding to occur. Appendix A (Section 1, A) of your textbook also lists the ICD-9-CM Official Guidelines for Coding and Reporting that are relevant to this chapter.

Stop!!! When you see a stop sign, you must stop and then proceed with caution.

ICD-9-CM uses the equivalent of traffic signs to guide coders throughout the coding book. These traffic signs must be followed to ensure accurate coding. The text of ICD-9-CM uses conventions, a group of instructional notations, punctuation marks, abbreviations, and symbols. To code accurately, a coder must have an understanding of the definitions for each of these conventions.

Convention Types

There are four types of conventions used in ICD-9-CM to provide guidance to the coder, including instructional notations, punctuation marks, abbreviations, and symbols.

Instructional Notations

Instructional notations are phrases or notes that appear in all three volumes of the code book and provide information related to code selection.

> **Coding Rule:**
>
> *The placement of the notation determines the code range that is governed by the notation. Coders must refer to the start of chapters, sections, categories, and the fourth- and fifth-digit levels to determine whether an instructional notation is present.*

Includes: Instructional Notation

The notation Includes:, also known as an inclusion note, is used to define and give examples of the content of the chapter, section, category, or subcategory code. (However, Includes: is not actually used at the subcategory level; instead, the code book simply lists the included terms.) Placement of the Includes: notation is important in determining the range of codes that the notation applies to.

Placement of Inclusion Note at Chapter Level

At the beginning of chapter 1, "Infectious and Parasitic Diseases," in the Tabular List of Diseases and Injuries of ICD-9-CM, the following inclusion note appears.

```
Includes:  diseases generally recognized as communicable
           or transmissible as well as a few diseases of unknown
           but possibly infectious origin.
```

Because the notation is placed at the beginning of the chapter, this note applies to the entire "Infectious and Parasitic Diseases" chapter.

Placement of Inclusion Note at Section Level

Placement of the inclusion note at the section level signifies that the note governs an entire section of codes. In chapter 1, "Infectious and Parasitic Diseases," of the Tabular List of Diseases and Injuries of ICD-9-CM, an inclusion note appears after the start of the section entitled "Tuberculosis" (010–018). The inclusion note reads as follows:

```
Includes:  infection by Mycobacterium tuberculosis
           (human) (bovine)
```

The placement of this inclusion notation signifies that only the code range of 010–018 is governed by this note, not the rest of the chapter.

Placement of the Inclusion Note at the Category Code Level

Inclusion notes are also placed at the category code level. In chapter 1, "Infectious and Parasitic Diseases," of the Tabular List of Diseases and Injuries, category code 003 is found. The following inclusion note appears for category code 003:

```
Includes:  infection or food poisoning by Salmonella
           (any serotype)
```

The placement of this inclusion notation indicates that it applies only to category code range 003.0–003.9 because it is placed after the category code 003.

Placement of Inclusion Note at the Fourth- and Fifth-Digit Level

At the fourth- and fifth-digit levels, the notation Includes: does not appear. However, within fourth- and fifth-digit levels, a listing of diagnoses contained within these levels appears. For example, in the listing of code 003.0, found in the Tabular List of Diseases and Injuries, the term *Salmonellosis* appears, indicating that this diseases is classified to this code. The code 003.0 appears as follows:

```
003.0 Salmonella gastroenteritis
      Salmonellosis
```

Salmonellosis represents a diagnosis that is contained or included only in this fourth-digit level.

As seen in the example at the fourth-digit level, the Includes: notation would also hold true at the fifth-digit level. The following is an example of an Includes: notation at the fifth-digit level.

```
008.41 Staphylococcus
       Staphylococcal enterocolitis
```

Exercise 4–1   Identifying Inclusion Notes

For each of the following items, list the diagnosis that is included, as described by the inclusion notation. The first one is completed for you.

1. Category code 070   Viral Hepatitis (Acute) (Chronic)

2. Code 065.8 _____

3. Category code 244 _____

4. Category code 458 _____

5. Code 491.0 _____

6. Section "Hernia of Abdominal Cavity" (550–553) _____

7. Code 372.73 _____

8. Category code 800 _____

9. Category code 710 _____

10. Code 519.9 _____

11. Section "Organic Psychotic Conditions" (290–294) _____

12. Code 600.11 _____

Excludes: Instructional Notation

The **Excludes:** notation, also known as the **exclusion note,** is used to signify that the conditions listed are not assigned to the chapter, section, category, or fourth- or fifth-digit code listed.

Placement at the Chapter Level

In the Tabular List of Diseases and Injuries at the start of chapter 1, "Infectious and Parasitic Diseases," an exclusion notation appears. The Excludes: note reads as follows:

```
Excludes: acute respiratory infections (460-466)
          carrier or suspected carrier of infectious organism (V02.0-V02.9)
          certain localized infections
          influenza (487.0-487.8, 488)
```

If the diagnosis is acute respiratory infection, the Excludes: notation tells the coder that this diagnosis is not included in chapter 1 but that it is included in code range 460–466. Within the exclusion note, following the diagnosis excluded, a code or code range appears in parentheses. The coder should then reference the code or code range in the parentheses. The code in the parentheses is more representative of the diagnosis being coded. This is the code number to be used.

Coding Rule:

The placement of the exclusion notation determines the code range that the note governs. Therefore, the coder must reference the start of the chapter, section, category, and fourth- or fifth-digit codes to determine whether exclusion notations are present.

See: Instructional Notation

The notation of **See:** is used in the Alphabetic Index of ICD-9-CM and instructs the coder to cross-reference the term or diagnosis that follows the notation. For example, in the Alphabetic Index the following appears for the entry of toxicemia.

```
Toxicemia—see Toxemia
```

This notation instructs the coder to cross-reference the term *toxemia* in the Alphabetic Index to obtain the correct code.

See Category: Instructional Notation

The **See category:** notation is also used as a cross-reference in the Alphabetic Index of ICD-9-CM. This notation signals the coder to reference a specific category in the Tabular List.

EXAMPLE: In the Alphabetic Index for the term *late effect(s), of phlebitis or thrombophlebitis of intracranial venous sinuses,* the following appears:

```
Late
 Effect(s) (of)—see also condition
   phlebitis or thrombophlebitis of intracranial venous sinuses
     (conditions classifiable to 325)—see category 326
```

The notation refers the coder to category 326 for the correct code assignment.

See Also: Instructional Notation

This is the third of the cross-reference notations that uses the word *see* in the instructional notation. The See also: notation refers the coder to another location in the Alphabetic Index when the initial listing does not contain all the necessary information to select a code accurately. When coding a diagnosis of palsy of both arms, the coder references the following in the Alphabetic Index:

```
Palsy (see also Paralysis) 344.9
```

Within the listing for palsy, there is no subterm for both arms; therefore, the coder must reference paralysis. When the term *paralysis* is cross-referenced, a subterm for both arms appears. The entry under paralysis appears as follows:

```
Paralysis, paralytic
 arm 344.40
  affecting
   dominant side 344.41
   nondominant side 344.42
  both 344.2
```

The coder uses the 344.2 code because it is the most specific code for the diagnosis.

Coding Rule:

The coder must use the cross-reference to obtain the correct code if a subterm of the diagnosis is not listed. However, if a subterm is listed, the cross-reference does not have to be followed.

EXAMPLE: When coding Bell's palsy, the coder does not have to reference paralysis because Bell's appears as a subterm of palsy. The entry appears as follows:

```
Palsy (see also Paralysis) 344.9
 atrophic diffuse 335.20
 Bell's 351.0
  newborn 767.5
```

Code First Underlying Disease, Cause, or Condition: Instructional Notation

The Code first underlying disease, cause, or condition notation appears in the Tabular List of ICD-9-CM and must always be followed because it instructs the coder to use an additional code to identify an underlying disease, cause, or condition that is present. Therefore, two codes are needed to fully code the diagnostic statement. The two codes must appear in the order stated.

EXAMPLE: In coding the diagnostic statement of "retinal dystrophy" in cerebroretinal lipidosis, the coder First references the main term *dystrophy*. The following appears in the Alphabetic Index.

```
Dystrophy
 Retina, retinal (hereditary)
  in
   cerebroretinal lipidosis 330.1 [362.71]
```

When this code is verified in the Tabular List, code 330.1 is used to code the cerebral lipidosis. Because the code 362.71 appears in the Alphabetic Index, this code, which is the code for retinal dystrophy, must also be used. When the code is verified in the Tabular List, the entry appears as follows:

```
362.71 Retinal dystrophy in systemic or cerebroretinal lipidoses
       Code first underlying disease, as:
          cerebroretinal lipidoses (330.1)
          systemic lipidoses (272.7)
```

The presence of this notation instructs the coder to use both codes to fully identify the diagnosis being coded; code 330.1 should be sequenced first when the codes 330.1 and 362.71 are reported.

Use Additional Code: Instructional Notation

The instructional notation **Use additional code** signals the coder to add a second code to fully code the diagnosis. The coder should assign the additional code if it further describes the diagnosis being coded. The second code should always be assigned to help further define the diagnosis or condition being coded.

> **EXAMPLE:** In the Tabular List, category code 292 has a notation that instructs the coder to use an additional code. The entry appears as follows:
>
> ```
> Includes: organic brain syndrome associated with consumption of drugs
> Use additional code for any associated drug dependence (304.0-304.9)
> Use additional E code to identify drug
> ```

This notation tells the coder that if a patient has a drug-induced mental disorder and any associated drug dependence, an additional code to identify the dependence should be assigned with a code for the drug-induced mental disorder. If the diagnosis to be coded is a paranoid state due to unspecified drug dependence, the codes assigned are 292.11 and 304.90.

Exercise 4–2   Identifying Notations

For each item listed, indicate the type of instructional notation found. The first one is done.

1. Start of chapter 1, "Infectious and Parasitic Diseases"   Includes and Excludes

2. Code 292.2   _____

3. Section entitled "Other Psychoses" (295–299)   _____

4. Code 420.0   _____

5. Chondromatosis, as listed in the Alphabetic Index   _____

6. Boil, as listed in the Alphabetic Index   _____

7. Hematomyelitis, late effect, as it appears in the Alphabetic Index   _____

8. Section "Dorsopathies" (720–724)   _____

9. Code 996.7   _____

10. Category V74   _____

11. Endopericarditis, as it appears in the Alphabetic Index   _____

12. Os, uterus, as it appears in the Alphabetic Index   _____

Punctuation Marks

It is important to understand the meaning of the punctuation marks used in the code book as ICD-9-CM defines them in a manner unique to this coding system.

Parentheses ( )

Parentheses are used in both the Tabular List and Alphabetical Index. Parentheses are used around terms that provide additional information about the main diagnostic term. The presence of the additional information contained within the parentheses does not affect the code assignment for the diagnostic statement being coded, but they help to explain further the diagnosis given by the physician or practitioner. The words contained in the parentheses are sometimes referred to as "nonessential modifiers."

> **EXAMPLE:** In the Alphabetical Index, the term *dermatitis* is found as follows:
>
> ```
> Dermatitis (allergic) (contact) (occupational)
>   (venenata) 692.9
> ```

The parentheses are used around explanatory terms of the main term of dermatitis. If a coder is coding the following diagnoses, the code 692.9 is assigned.

Dermatitis

Allergic dermatitis

Contact dermatitis

Occupational dermatitis

Venenata dermatitis

> **EXAMPLE:** In the Tabular List, the code 692.3 appears as follows:
>
> ```
> 692.3   Due to drugs and medicines in contact with skin
>         Dermatitis (allergic) (contact) due to:
>          arnica
>          fungicides
>          iodine
>          . . .
> ```

The use of the parentheses here is the same as in the Alphabetical Index. The presence or absence of the terms *allergic* or *contact* does not affect code assignment to this subcategory. Examples of some of the diagnoses coded to this subcategory are:

Contact dermatitis due to iodine

Allergic dermatitis due to iodine

Dermatitis due to iodine

Dermatitis due to fungicides

Square Brackets [ ]

Square brackets are used only in the Tabular List. They enclose synonyms, alternative wording, abbreviations, or explanatory phrases. The presence or absence of the phrase in the bracket does not affect code assignment.

> **EXAMPLE:** Code 968.5 appears in the Tabular List as follows:
>
> ```
> 968.5 Surface [topical] and infiltration anesthetics
>       Cocaine                    Procaine
>       Lidocaine [lignocaine]     Tetracaine
> ```

The term *topical* is enclosed in brackets to provide an alternative word for surface; and *lignocaine* is also enclosed in brackets because it is an alternative word for "lidocaine." Therefore, this subcategory is used to code the diagnoses of poisoning by topical application of lidocaine or poisoning by lidocaine. The term *topical* does not have to be present to code to this subcategory.

Square brackets are also used in some editions of ICD-9-CM to enclose fifth digits that are considered valid digits for a code. This use varies from publisher to publisher. To determine whether your code book has this feature, reference code 640.0. The digits 0, 1, and 3 should appear in square brackets if your book has this feature.

Italicized Brackets [ ]

Italicized or slanted brackets are used in the Alphabetic Index to enclose a second code that must be assigned when coding. This is used to record the etiology and/or the manifestation of a disease. These codes should be reported to third-party payers in the order that the codes appear in the Alphabetic Index.

EXAMPLE: In the Alphabetical Index, the term *diabetic gangrene* appears as follows:

```
Diabetes, diabetic
  gangrene 250.7x [785.4]
```

To correctly code this diagnosis, the coder lists 250.7x first, to identify the unspecified type of diabetes, and code 785.4 second, to identify the gangrene. When verifying the codes in the Tabular List, the coder is instructed to use a second code by the presence of an instructional notation: "use additional code for any associated condition" or "use additional code to identify manifestation." Therefore, the Alphabetic Index and Tabular List signal the coder to use two codes to record the diagnoses being coded.

Braces }

Braces are used to connect a series of terms appearing on the left of the brace to a common term on the right of the brace. The terms on the left of the brace must be followed by the term on the right of the brace to be included in the code number being considered.

EXAMPLE: Code 515 in the Tabular List appears as follows:

```
515    Postinflammatory pulmonary fibrosis
          Cirrhosis of lung
          Fibrosis of lung (atrophic)      chronic or
            (confluent) (massive)        } unspecified
            (perialveolar) (peribronchial)
          Induration of lung
```

The terms on the left must be followed by *chronic* or *unspecified* to be included in this category.

Colon :

The colon is used in the Tabular List after a term that is modified by one or more of the terms following the colon. The term on the left of the colon must be modified by a term on the right to be included in the code being considered.

EXAMPLE: Code 291.5 appears in the Tabular List as follows:

```
291.5   Alcohol-induced psychotic disorder with delusions
          Alcoholic:
          paranoia
          psychosis, paranoid type
```

For a psychosis to be coded to this subcategory, it must be of an alcoholic nature and be paranoia or psychosis, paranoid type. If the diagnosis does not specify the terms to the right of the colon, it would not be included in this subcategory.

Abbreviations

Two abbreviations are consistently used in ICD-9-CM: NEC and NOS.

NEC (Not Elsewhere Classifiable)

NEC means **not elsewhere classifiable.** There are two purposes for the abbreviation of NEC. First, it is used with poorly defined terms to warn the coder that specified forms of the diagnosis being coded are classified to different code numbers. The NEC code should only be used if more precise information is not available about the diagnosis. Second, the NEC code should be used when the Tabular List does not provide a separate code for the diagnosis being coded even though the diagnosis is very specific

> **EXAMPLE:** In coding the diagnosis of cervical syndrome of the spine, the coder first references the Alphabetical Index under the main term of *syndrome*. The following appears:

```
Syndrome
  cervical (root) (spine) NEC 723.8
    disc 722.71
    posterior, sympathetic 723.2
    rib 353.0
    sympathetic paralysis 337.0
    traumatic (acute) NEC 847.0
```

After reading through the subterms listed, the coder selects code 723.8 because the diagnosis does not give more specific information. This diagnosis is not elsewhere classified in ICD-9-CM to a specific code. To further complete the coding, the coder would reference code 723.8 in the Tabular List. Here again the abbreviation of NEC appears to signal the coder that a specific code for cervical syndrome is not present in the coding book. The entry in the Tabular List appears as follows:

```
723.8     Other syndromes affecting cervical region
            Cervical syndromes NEC
            Klippel's disease
            Occipital neuralgia
```

NOS (Not Otherwise Specified)

NOS is the abbreviation for **not otherwise specified.** It is also interpreted to mean unspecified. This is used only in the Tabular List. NOS codes are not specific and should be used only after the coder has clarified with the physician that a more specific diagnosis is not available. The coder should also reference the medical record to see whether it contains documentation that can further specify the diagnosis.

> **EXAMPLE:** A patient is seen, and the physician makes a diagnosis of sinusitis and orders a series of sinus X-rays. The physician records sinusitis on the coding form. The coder then references "sinusitis" in the Alphabetic Index and records code 473.9. However, at the time of coding the X-rays are completed and indicate that frontal sinusitis is present.
>
> The coder should then select code 473.1, which identifies frontal sinusitis. If there is no further documentation or findings, that is, no X-rays taken, to expand on the original diagnosis of sinusitis, then code 473.9 would be the correct code to assign. The entry in the Tabular List appears as follows:
>
> ```
> 473.9   Unspecified sinusitis (chronic)
>           Sinusitis (chronic) NOS
> ```

The abbreviation of NOS should signal to the coder to try to clarify the diagnosis more specifically before assigning the code.

Symbols

Section Mark Symbol §

This symbol, §, appears before a code number and denotes the presence of a footnote. The coder should reference the footnote, because it contains additional information relevant to code selection. Footnotes are frequently used in chapter 11, "Complications of Pregnancy, Childbirth, and the Puerperium," to instruct the coder that a fifth digit is needed for the code to be complete. The section mark is not used by all the companies that publish coding books.

Steps in Coding

To accurately assign codes, the coder must understand the conventions that ICD-9-CM uses. Another equally important aspect of coding is having specific written diagnoses and procedures to code. If the diagnoses and procedures are not specifically recorded or recorded in one location in the record, it is necessary for the coder to completely review the record to select all diagnoses and procedures to be coded. Even if the diagnoses and procedures are located on one form in the record, coders should still review the record to obtain the most complete information.

Diagnoses and procedures for inpatient records are typically recorded on a face sheet. In an outpatient setting, various forms are used to record the diagnosis and procedures completed. In a physician's office, an encounter form or a problem list is used to record the diagnoses and procedures.

When reviewing the record, the coder should note any procedures or tests that were ordered for which the results are not available at the time of coding. These test results could change the diagnosis, and therefore the coder should wait for the results of a test to determine the most accurate diagnosis to code. However, in some settings, such as a physician's office, coders do not wait for all test results. Organizations establish coding policies to address this issue.

For accurate coding to occur, the coder should follow these steps indicated:

Step 1. Locate the main term in volume 2, "Alphabetic Index."

When coding a diagnosis, the coder first must select the main term of the diagnostic phrase that is being coded. For example, when coding the diagnostic phrase "chronic allergic sinusitis due to dust," the main term to be located in the Alphabetic Index is *sinusitis.* (This example will be used to illustrate the steps in coding.)

Remember that in the Alphabetic Index the primary arrangement of the diagnostic terms is by condition. When coding procedures in ICD-9-CM, the primary arrangement of terms in the Alphabetic Index of Procedures is by the name of the procedure.

Step 2. Scan the main term entry for any instructional notations.

After locating the main term in the Alphabetic Index, a coder should review the main term entry in the Alphabetic Index for any instructional notations that may appear. If a notation is present, follow it. There are no notations appearing with the diagnosis of sinusitis. (For an example of an instructional notation in the Alphabetic Index, turn to the entry "fracture." Here a note appears.)

Step 3. In the diagnostic phrase being coded, identify any terms that modify the main term.

Terms that serve as modifiers in this example are *chronic* and *allergic. Chronic* appears in parentheses following the main term of *sinusitis,* and *allergic* appears as a subterm, indented under the main term.

Step 4. Follow any cross-reference notations.

Cross-references appear by the use of instructional notations such as see also and see. Next to the term *allergic,* the instructional notation of (see also Fever, hay) appears. The coder should follow this instruction. The coder should now reference "fever, hay" in the Alphabetic Index. The entry of "fever, hay" is further divided into subcategories for the cause of the allergy. The entry lists dust as the allergen; therefore the coder should select the code 477.8.

Step 5. Always verify the code in volume 1, "Tabular List of Diseases and Injuries."

After selecting a code from the Alphabetic Index, the coder must always verify the code in the Tabular List. Additional instructional notations can appear in the Tabular List that are not present in the Alphabetic Index.

Step 6. Follow any instructional terms.

After turning to the Tabular List, scan for any instructional terms that may be present. Coders should scan the following areas:

a. *The start of the chapter*—Here instructional notations appear that govern the entire chapter. In the example of sinusitis, the coder scans the start of chapter 8, "Diseases of the Respiratory System."

Here a note appears that instructs the coder to "use additional code to identify infectious organism." In our example, an infectious organism is not present.

b. *The beginning of the section range*—In the example used, the section range is entitled "Other Diseases of the Upper Respiratory Tract" (470–478). Instructional notations that govern the section range appear here. In our example, no instructional notations appear at this level.

c. *At the beginning of the category, subcategory, or subclassification level*—In our example, the following appears:

```
477 Allergic rhinitis
        Includes: allergic rhinitis (nonseasonal) (seasonal)
                  hay fever
                  spasmodic rhinorrhea
        Excludes: allergic rhinitis with asthma (bronchial) 493.0
```

The presence of the note assures the coder that the correct code is being selected.

Step 7. Select the code.

After completing these steps, the coder can now select the code. In addition, the coder should scan the code selected to ensure that the most specific code has been selected. If fourth and fifth digits are present, the coder must select the code to the highest degree of specificity. In our example, the category of 477, "Allergic rhinitis," was divided into fourth-digit, subcategory levels. This is the most specific level that can be coded. However, if fifth-digit levels are present, they must be selected.

The ICD-9-CM Official Guidelines for Coding and Reporting include the following guidelines that address conventions for ICD-9-CM.

Official ICD-9-CM Coding Guidelines:

A. Conventions for the ICD-9-CM

The conventions for the ICD-9-CM are the general rules for use of the classification independent of the guidelines. These conventions are incorporated within the index and tabular of the ICD-9-CM as instructional notes. The conventions are as follows:

1. Format: The ICD-9-CM uses an indented format for ease in reference

2. Abbreviations

   a. Index abbreviations

   NEC "Not elsewhere classifiable"   This abbreviation in the index represents "other specified" when a specific code is not available for a condition the index directs the coder to the "other specified" code in the tabular.

   b. Tabular abbreviations

   NEC "Not elsewhere classifiable"   This abbreviation in the tabular represents "other specified." When a specific code is not available for a condition the tabular includes an NEC entry under a code to identify the code as the "other specified" code. (See Section I.A.5.a, "Other" codes.)

NOS "Not otherwise specified"   This abbreviation is the equivalent of unspecified. (See Section I.A.5.b, "Unspecified" codes.)

3. Punctuation

[ ]   Brackets are used in the tabular list to enclose synonyms, alternative wording or explanatory phrases. Brackets are used in the index to identify manifestation codes. (See Section I.A.6, "Etiology/manifestations.")

( )   Parentheses are used in both the index and tabular to enclose supplementary words that may be present or absent in the statement of a disease or procedure without affecting the code number to which it is assigned. The terms within the parentheses are referred to as nonessential modifiers.

:   Colons are used in the Tabular list after an incomplete term which needs one or more of the modifiers following the colon to make it assignable to a given category.

4. Includes and Excludes Notes and Inclusion Terms

Includes: This note appears immediately under a three-digit code title to further define, or give examples of, the content of the category.

Excludes: An excludes note under a code indicates that the terms excluded from the code are to be coded elsewhere. In some cases the codes for the excluded terms should not be used in conjunction with the code from which it is excluded. An example of this is a congenital condition excluded from an acquired form of the same condition. The congenital and acquired codes should not be used together. In other cases, the excluded terms may be used together with an excluded code. An example of this is when fractures of different bones are coded to different codes. Both codes may be used together if both types of fractures are present.

Inclusion terms: List of terms is included under certain four and five digit codes. These terms are the conditions for which that code number is to be used. The terms may be synonyms of the code title, or, in the case of "other specified" codes, the terms are a list of the various conditions assigned to that code. The inclusion terms are not necessarily exhaustive. Additional terms found only in the index may also be assigned to a code.

5. Other and Unspecified codes

a. "Other" codes

Codes titled "other" or "other specified" (usually a code with a 4th digit 8 or fifth-digit 9 for diagnosis codes) are for use when the information in the medical record provides detail for which a specific code does not exist. Index entries with NEC in the line designate "other" codes in the tabular. These index entries represent specific disease entities for which no specific code exists so the term is included within an "other" code.

b. "Unspecified" codes

Codes (usually a code with a 4th digit 9 or 5th digit 0 for diagnosis codes) titled "unspecified" are for use when the information in the medical record is insufficient to assign a more specific code.

6. Etiology/manifestation convention ("code first," "use additional code," and "in diseases classified elsewhere" notes)

Certain conditions have both an underlying etiology and multiple body system manifestations due to the underlying etiology. For such conditions, the ICD-9-CM has a coding convention that requires the underlying condition be sequenced first followed by the manifestation. Wherever such a combination exists, there is a "use additional code" note at the etiology code, and a "code first" note at the manifestation code. These instructional notes indicate the proper sequencing order of the codes, etiology followed by manifestation.

In most cases the manifestation codes will have in the code title, "in diseases classified elsewhere." Codes with this title are a component of the etiology/manifestation convention. The code title indicates that it is a manifestation code. "In diseases classified elsewhere" codes are never permitted to be used as first listed or principal diagnosis codes. They must be used in conjunction with an underlying condition code and they must be listed following the underlying condition.

There are manifestation codes that do not have "in diseases classified elsewhere" in the title. For such codes a "use additional code" note will still be present and the rules for sequencing apply.

In addition to the notes in the tabular, these conditions also have a specific index entry structure. In the index both conditions are listed together with the etiology code first followed by the manifestation codes in brackets. The code in brackets is always to be sequenced second.

The most commonly used etiology/manifestation combinations are the codes for Diabetes mellitus, category 250. For each code under category 250 there is a use additional code note for the manifestation that is specific for that particular diabetic manifestation. Should a patient have more than one manifestation of diabetes, more than one code from category 250 may be used with as many manifestation codes as are needed to fully describe the patient's complete diabetic condition. The category 250 diabetes codes should be sequenced first, followed by the manifestation codes.

"Code first" and "Use additional code" notes are also used as sequencing rules in the classification for certain codes that are not part of an etiology/ manifestation combination. See Section I.B.9, "Multiple coding for a single condition."

7. "And"

The word "and" should be interpreted to mean either "and" or "or" when it appears in a title.

8. "With"

The word "with" in the alphabetic index is sequenced immediately following the main term, not in alphabetical order.

9. "See" and "See Also"

The "see" instruction following a main term in the index indicates that another term should be referenced. It is necessary to go to the main term referenced with the "see" note to locate the correct code.

A "see also" instruction following a main term in the index instructs that there is another main term that may also be referenced that may provide additional index entries that may be useful. It is not necessary to follow the "see also" note when the original main term provides the necessary code.

B. General Coding Guidelines

1. Use of Both Alphabetic Index and Tabular List

Use both the Alphabetic Index and the Tabular List when locating and assigning a code. Reliance on only the Alphabetic Index or the Tabular List leads to errors in code assignments and less specificity in code selection.

2. Locate each term in the Alphabetic Index

Locate each term in the Alphabetic Index and verify the code selected in the Tabular List. Read and be guided by instructional notations that appear in both the Alphabetic Index and the Tabular List.

Summary

- ICD-9-CM uses a group of instructional notations, abbreviations, punctuation marks, and symbols to guide the coder.

- An Includes: note gives examples of the content of a section of the code book.

- An Excludes: note indicates terms that are excluded from a section of the code book.

- *NEC* means not elsewhere classifiable.

- *NOS* means not otherwise specified.

- Brackets are used to enclose synonyms, alterative wording, or explanatory phrases.

- Parentheses are used to enclose supplementary words.

- Colons are used after an incomplete term to identify one or more modifiers.

- The phrases *code first* and *use additional code notes* are used to identify sequencing of codes.

- The Alphabetic Index and the Tabular List must both be used when assigning codes.

- All instructional notations that appear in the Alphabetic Index and the Tabular List should be read and used as a guide when selecting codes.

Chapter Review

True/False: Indicate whether each statement is true (T) or false (F).

1. _____ *NEC* means not elsewhere coded.

2. _____ Terms that appear in parentheses must appear in the diagnostic statement being coded.

3. _____ NOS means not otherwise specified.

4. _____ The placement of an inclusion note signifies the section of the code book that the note governs.

5. _____ At the fourth- and fifth-digit levels, the notation Includes: does not appear; however, a listing of diagnoses contained within these levels appears.

6. _____ NOS is used with poorly defined terms to warn the coder that specified forms of the diagnosis being coded are classified to different code numbers.

7. _____ The See also: notation refers the coder to another location in the Tabular List.

8. _____ At times, two codes are used to code a diagnostic statement.

9. _____ In the diagnostic phrase "acute frontal sinusitis," the main term to reference in the Alphabetic Index is *frontal*.

10. _____ The first step in coding is to locate the main term in the Tabular List.

Short Answer: For each diagnostic or procedural statement listed, identify the main term that would be used in the Alphabetic Index of ICD-9-CM.

11. Unstable angina _____

12. Congestive heart failure _____

13. Acute punctured eardrum _____

14. Repair of fracture _____

15. Excision of lesion _____

16. Ulcerative chronic tonsillitis _____

17. Chronic left quadrant abdominal pain _____

18. Gastritis due to diet deficiency _____

19. Primary neoplasm of stomach _____

20. Abscess of vas deferens _____

21. Release of carpal tunnel _____

22. Streptococcal peritonitis _____

23. Ileo-jejunal bypass _____

24. Ulcer with gangrene _____

25. Reconstruction of eye socket _____

26. Acute broncholitis _____

27. Tarsal synostosis _____

28. Congenital nipple retraction _____

29. Postsurgical lordosis _____

30. Open Wound _____

Short Answer: Briefly respond to the following.

31. List the steps in coding.

32. Differentiate between the abbreviations *NOS* and *NEC*.

33. Explain why coders must reference both the Alphabetic Index and Tabular List.

34. Explain what a nonessential modifier is.

35. Explain why it is important that all instructional notation are followed.

Coding Guidelines

Chapter Outline

Objectives

At the conclusion of this chapter, the student will be able to:

1. List the Cooperating Parties for ICD-9-CM.
2. Explain the purpose of the ICD-9-CM Official Guidelines for Coding and Reporting.
3. Identify the four sections of the ICD-9-CM Official Guidelines for Coding and Reporting.
4. Differentiate and explain the guidelines for inpatient versus outpatient and physician office visits.
5. Summarize the guidelines for the sequencing of diagnostic codes.
6. Explain the purpose of the Present on Admission Guidelines.

Key Terms

Appendix I—Present on Admission Reporting Guidelines

Combination Code

Cooperating Parties for ICD-9-CM

ICD-9-CM Official Guidelines for Coding and Reporting

Late Effect

POA Indicator

Reminder

As you work through this chapter, you will need to reference the ICD-9-CM Official Guidelines for Coding and Reporting. These guidelines can be found in Appendix A of this book.

Principal Diagnosis

Secondary Diagnosis

Section I—Conventions, General Coding Guidelines, and Chapter-Specific Guidelines

Section II—Selection of Principal Diagnosis

Section III—Reporting Additional Diagnoses

Section IV—Diagnostic Coding and Reporting Guidelines for Outpatient Services

Introduction

To ensure accurate diagnostic and procedural information, ICD-9-CM is used to capture information for third-party reimbursement, continuity of patient care, healthcare statistics, and other reporting functions. In an effort to assist coders in consistently using ICD-9-CM, the ICD-9-CM Official Guidelines for Coding and Reporting were developed by the Cooperating Parties for ICD-9-CM. The Cooperating Parties for ICD-9-CM included the following organizations:

- American Hospital Association

- American Health Information Management Association

- Centers for Medicare and Medicaid Services (CMS)

- National Center for Health Statistics (NCHS)

These parties cooperatively developed and approved the ICD-9-CM Official Guidelines for Coding and Reporting for publication by the Department of Health and Human Services.

The guidelines are organized into four sections with one appendix, as follows:

- Section I—Conventions, General Coding Guidelines, and Chapter-Specific Guidelines. In this section the guidelines address the structure and conventions of ICD-9-CM and provide general guidelines that apply to the entire classification, as well as chapter-specific guidelines.

- Section II—Selection of Principal Diagnosis. This section includes guidelines for the selection of principal diagnosis for nonoutpatient settings. Nonoutpatient settings include acute care, short-term care, long-term care, and psychiatric hospitals; home health agencies; rehab facilities; nursing homes; and the like.

- Section III—Reporting Additional Diagnoses. In this section the guidelines cover the reporting of additional diagnoses that affect patient care in nonoutpatient settings.

- Section IV—Diagnostic Coding and Reporting Guidelines for Outpatient Services. This section outlines the guidelines for outpatient coding and reporting. These coding guidelines for outpatient diagnoses have been approved for use by hospitals and providers in coding and reporting hospital-based outpatient services and provider-based office visits.

- Appendix I—Present on Admission Reporting Guidelines. Effective October 1, 2007, CMS required that for all Medicare inpatient acute care discharges, facilities must report all diagnoses and external cause of injury codes that are present on admission of the patient. This appendix outlines the guidelines for implementation of the present on admission indicators.

Section I—ICD-9-CM Conventions, General Coding Guidelines, and Chapter-Specific Guidelines

Section I provides guidelines for conventions as well as general coding guidelines and chapter-specific guidelines. The guidelines for conventions were previously reviewed in Chapter 4 of this book. The general coding guidelines will be reviewed in this chapter, and the chapter-specific guidelines will be reviewed in the remaining chapters of this book. The chapter-specific guidelines are sequenced in the

Official Guidelines in the same order as they appear in the ICD-9-CM Tabular List. For example, chapter 1 of the ICD-9-CM Tabular List is entitled "Infectious and Parasitic Diseases," and the first subsection in the chapter-specific guidelines is C1, entitled "Chapter 1: Infectious and Parasitic Diseases (001–139)."

Numerous guidelines have been used in the development of this book and appear throughout the book in the highlighted Coding Guideline areas. However, all coders need to read and become familiar with all of the Official Guidelines to enhance coding accuracy. (Author Bowie encourages her new coding students to read the Official Guidelines from front to back numerous times! She thinks of the guidelines as the directions for the ingredients when baking. If you don't follow the directions when baking, your cake will not turn out as it should. If you don't follow the coding guidelines, you will not select the proper codes. Coding is also like baking: the more you bake, the better baker you become. The more you code, the better coder you become!)

Acute and Chronic Conditions

This guideline is used when coding the diagnostic statement "acute and chronic bronchitis." Both codes 466.0, Acute bronchitis, and 491.9, Chronic bronchitis, are assigned, with 466.0 sequenced first. To assign both codes the medical documentation must clearly document both the acute and chronic condition. If both terms do not appear in the patient's record, then only one code should be used as documented in the record, or the physician should be asked for clarification.

> **Official ICD-9-CM Coding Guideline:**
>
> *If the same condition is described as both acute (subacute) and chronic, and separate subentries exist in the Alphabetic Index at the same indentation level, code both and sequence the acute (subacute) code first. (See Appendix A, Section I, B10.)*

Combination Code

> **Official ICD-9-CM Coding Guideline:**
>
> *A **combination code** is a single code used to classify two diagnoses, a diagnosis with an associated secondary process (manifestation), or a diagnosis with an associated complication.*
>
> *Combination codes are identified by referring to subterm entries in the Alphabetic Index and by reading the inclusion and exclusion notes in the Tabular List. Assign only the combination code when that code fully identifies the diagnostic conditions involved or when the Alphabetic Index so directs. Multiple coding should not be used when the classification provides a combination code that clearly identifies all of the elements documented in the diagnosis. When the combination code lacks necessary specificity in describing the manifestation or complication, an additional code should be used as a secondary code. (See Appendix A, Section I, B11.)*

An example of a combination code occurs when the diagnostic phrase "acute appendicitis with generalized peritonitis" is coded. In this example two diagnoses are present: acute appendicitis and generalized peritonitis. When the Alphabetic Index is referenced for appendicitis, the following appears:

```
Appendicitis 541
 with
  perforation, peritonitis (generalized), or rupture 540.0
   with peritoneal abscess 540.1
  peritoneal abscess 540.1
   . . .
```

This signifies that one code is to be used to code both diagnoses.

Codes That Describe Symptoms and Signs

> **Official ICD-9-CM Coding Guideline:**
>
> *Codes that describe symptoms and signs, as opposed to diagnoses, are acceptable for reporting purposes when a related definitive diagnosis has not been established (confirmed) by the provider. Chapter 16 of ICD-9-CM, "Symptoms, Signs, and Ill-Defined Conditions" (codes 780.0–799.9) contain many, but not all codes for symptoms. (See Appendix A, Section I, B6.)*

Codes that describe symptoms and signs, such as pain and fever, are acceptable for coding when a definitive diagnosis has not been established. For example, when a patient presents in a physician's office for abdominal pain and the cause has not been confirmed, the abdominal pain is coded.

Conditions That Are an Integral Part of a Disease Process

> **Official ICD-9-CM Coding Guideline:**
>
> *Signs and symptoms that are associated routinely with a disease process should not be assigned as additional codes, unless otherwise instructed by the classification. (See Appendix A, Section I, B7.)*

When a definitive diagnosis is recorded and signs and symptoms are recorded, the coder should code the definitive diagnosis only if the signs and symptoms are integral to the disease process. Symptoms such as cough and fever are not recorded for a patient who has been diagnosed with a respiratory infection.

Conditions That Are Not an Integral Part of a Disease Process

> **Official ICD-9-CM Coding Guideline:**
>
> *Additional signs and symptoms that may not be associated routinely with a disease process should be coded when present. (See Appendix A, Section I, B8.)*

If signs and symptoms exist that are not routinely associated with a disease process, the signs and symptoms should be coded. If a patient presents for a sprained ankle and is also experiencing vomiting, both the ankle sprain and the symptom of vomiting are recorded.

Multiple Coding for a Single Condition

> **Official ICD-9-CM Coding Guideline:**
>
> *In addition to the etiology/manifestation convention that requires two codes to fully describe a single condition that affects multiple body systems, there are other single conditions that also require more than one code. "Use additional code" notes are found in the tabular at codes that are not part of an etiology/manifestation pair where a secondary code is useful to fully describe a condition. The sequencing rule is the same as for the etiology/manifestation pair; "use additional code" indicates that a secondary code should be added. (See Appendix A, Section I, B, 9.)*

As described in Chapter 4, there are conventions that instruct coders to assign multiple codes to a single condition. These conventions include the instruction notations of Use additional code and Code first underlying condition. Because these conventions are commonly used with codes for infectious diseases, they will be discussed in greater detail in Chapter 6 of this book. Multiple codes are also used for late effects, complication codes, and obstetric codes. These will also be described in their respective chapters.

Impending or Threatened Conditions

Official ICD-9-CM Coding Guideline:

Code any condition described at the time of discharge as "impending" or "threatened" as follows:

If it did occur, code as confirmed diagnosis.

If it did not occur, reference the Alphabetic Index to determine whether the condition has a subentry term for "impending" or "threatened" and also reference main term entries for "Impending" and "Threatened."

If the subterms are listed, assign the given code.

If the subterms are not listed, code the existing underlying condition(s) and not the condition described as impending or threatened. (See Appendix A, Section I, B13.)

To accurately code a diagnosis that is modified by the terms *impending* or *threatened*, the coder must answer the question "did the condition actually occur?"

If the condition occurred, then code the diagnosis as confirmed. For example, if a physician recorded "impending rupture of spleen due to enlarged spleen" and the spleen ruptured, then the diagnostic statement of ruptured spleen is coded by using code 289.59.

If the condition did not occur, the coder needs to reference the Alphabetic Index to determine whether the condition has a subentry term for "impending" or "threatened" and also reference main term entries for "impending" and "threatened." For example, if a physician recorded the diagnostic statement of "impending rupture of spleen due to enlarged spleen" but treatment prevented the rupture, the code for enlarged spleen, 789.2, is recorded, because there is no code for the impending rupture of spleen in the main term entries in the Alphabetic Index.

At times, ICD-9-CM does use the terms *impending* or *threatened* in the Alphabetic Index. When the condition does not occur, but the terms *impending* or *threatened* are used in the diagnostic statement and ICD-9-CM provides a main term entry or subterm entry of *impending* or *threatened*, the code is assigned that appears in the Alphabetic Index.

EXAMPLE: A physician records the diagnostic statement of "threatened miscarriage," but the miscarriage does not occur. Because ICD-9-CM provides an entry in the Alphabetic Index for "threatened miscarriage," code 640.0X is assigned.

Late Effects

Official ICD-9-CM Coding Guideline:

*A **late effect** is the residual effect (condition produced) after the acute phase of an illness or injury has terminated. There is no time limit on when a late effect code can be used. The residual may be apparent early, such as in cerebrovascular accident cases, or it may occur months or years later, such as that due to a previous injury. Coding of late effects generally requires two codes sequenced in the following order: The condition or nature of the late effect is sequenced first; the late effect code is sequenced second.*

An exception to these guidelines are instances where the code for late effect is followed by a manifestation code identified in the Tabular List and title or where the late effect code has been expanded (at the fourth- and fifth-digit levels) to include the manifestation(s). The code for the acute phase of an illness or injury that led to the late effect is never used with a code for the late effect. (See Appendix A, Section I, B 12.)

A physician records the diagnostic phrase "malunion of fracture of left tibia." The malunion is the residual condition that was caused by the fracture, known as the late effect. Common terms that are used to describe residual conditions include:

```
Due to old illness or injury
Due to previous illness or injury
Following previous illness or injury
Late
Malunion
Nonunion
Old
Scarring
Secondary to illness or injury in previous time
Sequela of
```

When these terms are used, the coder can assume that a late effect exists. To code *late* effects, the coder should reference the main term of *late* in the Alphabetic Index. Here a subterm *effects* also appears.

It should be noted that two codes are needed to code late effects: One code is used to code the residual condition, and one code is used to code the cause of the late effect. The code for the residual condition is listed first, followed by the code for the cause. (There are some exceptions to this, and the coder should be guided by instructions found in the Alphabetic Index and Tabular List.)

EXAMPLE: Sally Smith is a patient at Sunny View Nursing Home who has been admitted with the following diagnosis: traumatic arthritis due to old fracture of left ankle. This would be coded to 716.17, coding traumatic arthritis, and 905.4, coding the cause of the arthritis.

The coder first references the Alphabetic Index for the main term of *arthritis* and the subterm *traumatic*. Code 716.1x appears. (The *x* indicates that a fifth digit is needed for the code to be valid.) To code the cause of the arthritis, the coder then references the main term of *Late* in the Alphabetic Index, followed by the subterms of *effects, fractures, extremity, lower.* Code 905.4 appears, which codes late effect of fracture of lower extremities.

Exercise 5–1   Identifying Late Effects

For each of the following diagnostic statements, identify the residual condition and the late effect or cause of the residual.

Diagnostic Statement	Residual Condition	Late Effect or Cause
1. Paralysis due to old cerebrovascular accident	_____	_____
2. Mental retardation due to brain injury	_____	_____
3. Blindness due to chicken pox	_____	_____
4. Scarring due to third-degree burns	_____	_____
5. Kyphosis due to poliomyelitis	_____	_____
6. Past history of polio patient now presents with scoliosis	_____	_____
7. Hemiplegia resulting from spinal cord injury that occurred five years ago	_____	_____

8. Grand mal seizure due to encephalitis three
   years ago   _____ _____

9. Neural deafness caused by childhood
   measles 15 years ago   _____ _____

10. Malunion of spinal fracture   _____ _____

Exceptions for Code Assignment for Late Effects

As previously discussed, most coding of late effects requires two codes, with the residual condition sequenced first, followed by the cause of the late effect. However, the following exceptions exist:

1. A second code is not needed when medical documentation does not identify the residual. If a physician records "late effect of injury to hand," only the code for the late effect is used.

2. Sequencing is reversed if the Alphabetic Index indicates a different sequence. For example, in coding scoliosis due to poliomyelitis, coders are instructed to first list code 138, the late effect code, followed by the code 737.43.

3. Only one code is needed if ICD-9-CM does not provide a code to describe the cause of the late effect.

4. Only one code is needed when the late effect code has been expanded at the fourth- and fifth-digit level to code both the late effect and residual. The only category code that this occurs with is code 438, Late effect of cerebrovascular disease.

Exercise 5–2   Coding Late Effects

For each of the following diagnostic statements, select the appropriate ICD-9-CM code(s).

1. Kyphosis due to polio   _____

2. Ataxia due to cerebrovascular accident   _____

3. Scarring of leg due to multiple lacerations from motor vehicle
   accident   _____

4. Aphasia from previous cerebrovascular disease   _____

5. Late effect of burn on face   _____

6. Mental retardation due to viral encephalitis   _____

7. Contracture of ankle due to previous fracture   _____

8. Paralysis of right arm due to poliomyelitis   _____

9. Scoliosis due to polio at age nine   _____

10. Residuals of poliomyelitis   _____

Chapter-Specific Coding Guidelines

The Official ICD-9-CM Guidelines for Coding and Reporting outline the chapter-specific coding guidelines in Section I, C. These guidelines are for specific diagnoses and complications found in ICD-9-CM. These chapter-specific guidelines will be discussed throughout the remaining chapters of this book.

Section II—Selection of Principal Diagnosis

Section II of the ICD-9-CM Official Guidelines for Coding and Reporting is entitled "Section II—Selection of Principal Diagnosis." This section of the guidelines is used to provide consistency in selecting the principal diagnosis, which is defined in the Uniform Hospital Discharge Data Set (UHDDS) as "that condition established after study to be chiefly responsible for occasioning the admission of the patient to the hospital for care." The UHDDS definitions are used by hospitals to report inpatient data elements in a consistent, standardized manner. To review the definitions and the data elements that the definitions apply to, review the July 31, 1985, *Federal Register* (Vol. 50, No, 147), pp. 31038–40. It should be noted that the guidelines in this section are for all nonoutpatient settings (acute care; short-term care, long-term care, and psychiatric hospitals; home health agencies; rehab facilities; nursing homes; and the like). The guidelines for coding and reporting outpatient services, which include hospital-based outpatient services and physician office visits, are outlined in section IV of the ICD-9-CM Official Guidelines for Coding and Reporting.

Codes for Symptoms, Signs, and Ill-Defined Conditions

Codes from chapter 16 of ICD-9-CM, "Symptoms, Signs, and Ill-Defined Conditions," are not to be used as a principal diagnosis when a related definitive diagnosis has been established.

> **EXAMPLE:** A patient is admitted because of severe abdominal pain. After diagnostic testing, it was determined that the patient has a gastric ulcer. The gastric ulcer is the principal diagnosis.

Two or More Interrelated Conditions That Equally Meet the Definition for Principal Diagnosis

When two or more interrelated conditions equally meet the definition for principal diagnosis, the guidelines state that any one of the diagnoses may be sequenced first.

> **EXAMPLE:** Tom Pick was admitted due to severe vomiting, nausea, and abdominal pain. After study it has determined that he had a gastric ulcer and diverticulitis. Treatment was equally directed at both diagnoses, and the physician documents that both conditions prompted the admission. Either condition could be listed as the principal diagnosis.

Two or More Comparative or Contrasting Conditions

At times physicians record comparative or contrasting diagnoses by using the terms *either* or *versus*. The coding guideline states the following:

> ### Official ICD-9-CM Coding Guideline:
>
> *In those rare instances when two or more comparative or contrasting diagnoses are documented as "either/or" (or similar terminology), they are coded as if the diagnoses were confirmed and the diagnoses are sequenced according to the circumstances of the admission. If no further determination can be made as to which diagnosis should be principal, either diagnosis may be sequenced first. (See Appendix A, Section II, D.)*

> **EXAMPLE:** Two comparative diagnoses, appendicitis versus diverticulitis, were recorded as the final diagnoses. The patient's symptoms were controlled, and he was discharged. In this case either could be assigned as the principal diagnosis.

Symptom(s) Followed by Contrasting or Comparative Diagnoses

At the time of discharge, physicians may not be able to distinguish a definitive diagnosis and may record a symptom, followed by contrasting or comparative diagnoses. The guidelines instruct coders to sequence these cases as follows:

Official ICD-9-CM Coding Guideline:

When a symptom(s) is followed by contrasting/comparative diagnoses, the symptom code is sequenced first. All the contrasting/comparative diagnoses should be coded as additional diagnoses. (See Appendix A, Section II, E.)

Original Treatment Plan Not Carried Out

When treatment is not carried out, the coder must still answer the question "what diagnosis, after study, occasioned the admission to the hospital?" The principal diagnosis remains the same even if the treatment was not carried out.

Official ICD-9-CM Coding Guideline:

Sequence as the principal diagnosis the condition, which after study occasioned the admission to the hospital, even though treatment may not have been carried out due to unforeseen circumstances. (See Appendix A, Section II, F.)

EXAMPLE: Denny Sams is an 80-year-old man with a past history of gastric ulcer. He was admitted because of severe abdominal pain and back pain. After diagnostic study it was determined that he had kidney stones, and lithotripsy was planned. Before the lithotripsy, he was discharged at his request because he felt he needed to go home to care for his wife. The procedure was not performed.

In this example the kidney stones are the reason for the admission and are therefore reported as the principal diagnosis.

Complications of Surgery and Other Medical Care

Complications may result after surgery or from other medical care. In these cases the complication is considered the principal diagnosis.

Official ICD-9-CM Coding Guideline:

When the admission is for treatment of a complication resulting from surgery or other medical care, the complication code is sequenced as the principal diagnosis. If the complication is classified to the 996–999 series and the code lacks the necessary specificity in describing the complication, an additional code for the specific complication may be assigned. (See Appendix A, Section II, G.)

Uncertain Diagnosis

At times a physician does not have sufficient knowledge to make a definitive diagnosis at the time of discharge. In these cases the physician commonly records the diagnosis as questionable or suspected. In these cases the following guideline should be followed.

Official ICD-9-CM Coding Guideline:

If the diagnosis documented at the time of discharge is qualified as "probable," "suspected," "likely," "questionable," "possible," or "still to be ruled out," or other similar terms indicating uncertainty, code the condition as if it existed or was established. The bases for these guidelines are the diagnostic workup, arrangements for further workup or observation, and initial therapeutic approach that correspond most closely with the established diagnosis. (See Appendix A, Section II, H.)

It should be noted that this guideline is relevant only to the selection of a principal diagnosis for inpatient admissions to short-term, acute, or long-term care, and psychiatric hospitals. This guideline is not used for outpatient hospital records or physician office records. This will be discussed further later in this chapter under diagnostic coding and reporting guidelines for outpatient services.

Admission from Observation Unit or Outpatient Surgery

At times patients are admitted as inpatients following medical observation, for postoperative observation following outpatient surgery, or for continuing inpatient care following outpatient surgery. The ICD-9-CM Official Guidelines for Coding and Reporting direct coders to select the principal diagnosis for these cases based on the following guidelines.

Official ICD-9-CM Coding Guideline:

I. Admission from Observation Unit

1. Admission Following Medical Observation

When a patient is admitted to an observation unit for a medical condition, which either worsens or does not improve, and is subsequently admitted as an inpatient of the same hospital for this same medical condition, the principal diagnosis would be the medical condition which led to the hospital admission.

2. Admission Following Post-Operative Observation

When a patient is admitted to an observation unit to monitor a condition (or complication) that develops following outpatient surgery, and then is subsequently admitted as an inpatient of the same hospital, hospitals should apply the Uniform Hospital Discharge Data Set (UHDDS) definition of principal diagnosis as "that condition established after study to be chiefly responsible for occasioning the admission of the patient to the hospital for care."

J. Admission from Outpatient Surgery

When a patient receives surgery in the hospital's outpatient surgery department and is subsequently admitted for continuing inpatient care at the same hospital, the following guidelines should be followed in selecting the principal diagnosis for the inpatient admission:

- *· If the reason for the inpatient admission is a complication, assign the complication as the principal diagnosis.*
- *If no complication, or other condition, is documented as the reason for the inpatient admission, assign the reason for the outpatient surgery as the principal diagnosis.*
- *If the reason for the inpatient admission is another condition unrelated to the surgery, assign the unrelated condition as the principal diagnosis. (See Appendix A, Section II, I-J.)*

EXAMPLE: Tom Smith was placed in observation due to extreme renal colic. He was admitted because it was determined that he had kidney stones that were not going to pass. Surgery was completed to remove the kidney stones. The principal diagnosis for the admission is the kidney stones.

Section III—Reporting Additional Diagnoses

In additional to the principal diagnosis, additional diagnoses are coded and reported. UHDDS defines other diagnoses, commonly called secondary diagnoses, as "all conditions that coexist at the time of admission, that develop subsequently, or that affect the treatment received and/or length of stay. Diagnoses that relate to an earlier episode which have no bearing on the current hospital stay are to be excluded." This definition is used for inpatients in acute care, short-term care, long-term care, and psychiatric hospitals home health agencies, rehab facilities, nursing homes and the like to standardize reporting.

Previous Conditions

Most facilities establish written policies for the coding of previous conditions. The Official Coding Guidelines states the following, which can be used as a basis for facility policy:

Official ICD-9-CM Coding Guideline:

If the physician has included a diagnosis in the final diagnostic statement, such as the discharge summary or the face sheet, it should ordinarily be coded. Some providers include in the diagnostic statement resolved conditions or diagnoses and status-post procedures from previous admission that have no bearing on the current stay. Such conditions are not to be reported and are coded only if required by hospital policy.

However, history codes (V10–V19) may be used as secondary codes if the historical condition or family history has an impact on current care or influences treatment. (See Appendix A, Section III, A.)

EXAMPLE: Polly Jones was admitted because of severe headaches, nausea, weight loss, and dehydration. Four years ago she was treated for cancer of colon, which was resected; she has been in remission. The physician recorded dehydration as the principal diagnosis and history of cancer of the colon at time of discharge. History of cancer of colon is coded as a secondary diagnosis.

Abnormal Findings

Abnormal findings are not coded and reported for inpatients unless the physician documents the significance of the findings.

Official ICD-9-CM Coding Guideline:

Abnormal findings (laboratory, X-ray, pathologic, and other diagnostic results) are not coded and reported unless the provider indicates their clinical significance. If the findings are outside the normal range and the attending provider has ordered other tests to evaluate the condition or prescribed treatment, it is appropriate to ask the provider whether the abnormal finding should be coded. (See Appendix A, Section III, B.)

Uncertain Diagnosis

If at the time of discharge the diagnosis documented is qualified, the condition should be coded as if it existed.

Official ICD-9-CM Coding Guideline:

If the diagnosis documented at the time of discharge is qualified as "probable," "suspected," "likely," "questionable," "possible," or "still to be ruled out," code the condition as if it existed or was established. (See Appendix A, Section III, C.)

EXAMPLE: Tim Mack is admitted to Hill Hospital for abdominal cramping, fever, rectal pressure, and pain that have been present for the past five days. After admission he develops episodes of bloody diarrhea and an urgency to defecate. The physician records suspected ulcerative colitis at the time of discharge. Code 556.9 is assigned for this case.

Section IV—Diagnostic Coding and Reporting Guidelines for Outpatient Services

Section IV of the ICD-9-CM Official Guidelines for Coding and Reporting is approved for use by hospitals and providers for reporting hospital-based outpatient services and provider-based office visits. It is important to note that the guidelines just discussed differ at times from the guidelines for outpatient and provider-based office visits.

In the outpatient or office setting, the definition of principal diagnosis does not apply. In the outpatient setting, the term *first-listed diagnosis* is used.

First-Listed Diagnosis

> ## Official ICD-9-CM Coding Guideline:
>
> *In the outpatient setting, the term* first-listed diagnosis *is used in lieu of principal diagnosis.*
>
> *In determining the first-listed diagnosis, the coding conventions of ICD-9-CM, as well as the general and disease-specific guidelines take precedence over the outpatient guidelines.*
>
> *Diagnoses often are not established at the time of the initial encounter/visit. It may take two or more visits before the diagnosis is confirmed. (See Appendix A, Section IV, A.)*

Because providers are often not able to establish a definitive diagnosis at the time of initial or subsequent visits, outpatient and physician office coders use codes from chapter 16 of ICD-9-CM, "Symptoms, Signs, and Ill-Defined Conditions," as well as other symptom codes from disease chapters. Each code can be used when a definitive diagnosis has not been established.

Accurate Reporting of Diagnosis Codes and Symptoms and Signs

> ## Official ICD-9-CM Coding Guideline:
>
> *For accurate reporting of ICD-9-CM diagnosis, the documentation should describe the patient's condition, using terminology which includes specific diagnoses as well as symptoms, problems, or reasons for the encounter. (See Appendix A, Section IV, C.)*
>
> *Codes that describe symptoms and signs, as opposed to diagnoses, are acceptable for reporting when a diagnosis has not been established (i.e., confirmed) by the provider. (See Appendix A, Section IV, E.)*

EXAMPLE: Mary Banks presents with low back pain. She was working in her garden when she bent down and felt a "pop" in her lower back next to her spine. She is in severe pain, which radiates into her legs. She has had previous back pain, and her physician suspects that she may have a protruding disc. He orders X-rays and magnetic resonance imaging.

At the conclusion of this encounter, the symptom of back pain should be coded because the suspected protruding disc has not been confirmed.

Observation Stay

The following guideline should be followed when selecting a first-listed diagnosis for patients who are admitted for observation for a medical condition.

> ## Official ICD-9-CM Coding Guideline:
>
> *When a patient is admitted for observation for a medical condition, assign a code for the medical condition as the first-listed diagnosis.*
>
> *When a patient presents for outpatient surgery and develops complications requiring admission to observation, code the reason for the surgery as the first-reported diagnosis (reason for the encounter), followed by codes for the complications as secondary diagnoses.*

Encounters for Circumstances Other Than a Disease or Injury

It is common in physicians' offices for patients to seek care, such as preventative medical care, when a disease or injury is not present. For these encounters, ICD-9-CM provides a supplementary classification known as the V codes, which will be further discussed later in this book.

> ### Official ICD-9-CM Coding Guideline:
>
> *ICD-9-CM provides codes to deal with encounters for circumstances other than a disease or injury. The Supplementary Classification of Factors Influencing Health Status and Contact with Health Services (V01.0–V84.8) is provided to deal with occasions when circumstances other than a disease or injury are recorded as diagnoses or problems. See Section I. C. 18 for information on V codes. (See Appendix A, Section IV, F.)*

EXAMPLE: Tim Smith and his wife, Sue, have been trying unsuccessfully to conceive a child. Sue has been seen by a physician, and it has been determined that she should be able to conceive. Tim is now presenting to undergo sperm count testing for fertility. This encounter would be coded by using code V26.21, Fertility testing.

Sequencing and Multiple Codes for Outpatient and Physician Office Visits

For outpatient and physician office visits, the code that is listed first for coding and reporting purposes is the reason for the encounter.

> ### Official ICD-9-CM Coding Guideline:
>
> *List first the ICD-9-CM code for the diagnosis, condition, problem, or other reason for encounter/visit shown in the medical record to be chiefly responsible for the services provided. List additional codes that describe any coexisting conditions. In some cases the first-listed diagnosis may be a symptom when a diagnosis has not been established (confirmed) by the physician. (See Appendix A, Section IV, H.)*

EXAMPLE: Edward Smith presented to his primary care provider because of an upper respiratory infection and a reoccurrence of migraine headaches, which he experienced yesterday. Currently he does not have a headache, but he would like his prescription renewed for his medication for migraines. The upper respiratory infection is listed as the first diagnosis, followed by the migraine headaches.

> ### Official ICD-9-CM Coding Guideline:
>
> *Chronic disease treated on an ongoing basis may be coded and reported as many times as the patient receives treatment and care for the condition(s). (See Appendix A, Section IV, J.)*
>
> *Code all documented conditions that coexist at the time of the encounter/visit and that require or affect patient care, treatment, or management. Do not code conditions that were previously treated and no longer exist. However, history codes (V10–V19) may be used as secondary codes if the historical condition or family history has an impact on current care or influences treatment. (See Appendix A, Section IV, K.)*

EXAMPLE: Pam Lord is diabetic and is being seen for gastritis. Her blood sugar was taken, and she was given Prevacid for the gastritis. Gastritis would be listed first, followed by the code for diabetes mellitus.

Diabetes is a chronic condition that should be coded because the patient received treatment for the condition on this visit as well as for the gastritis.

Encounters for Diagnostic Services

The Official Guidelines provide the following instruction for coding encounters when a diagnostic service is the only service provided during the encounter:

Official ICD-9-CM Coding Guideline:

For patients receiving diagnostic services only during an encounter/visit, sequence first the diagnosis, condition, problem, or other reason for the encounter/visit shown in the medical record to be chiefly responsible for the outpatient services provided during the encounter/visit. Codes for other diagnoses (e.g., chronic conditions) may be sequenced as additional diagnoses.

For outpatient encounters for diagnostic tests that have been interpreted by a physician, and the final report is available at the time of coding, code any confirmed or definitive diagnosis(es) documented in the interpretation. Do not code related signs and symptoms on test results. (See Appendix A, Section IV, L.)

EXAMPLE: Gretchen Rose has noticed a lump in her left breast. She presents to her primary care provider to discuss this. Her mother had breast cancer at the age of 54 and died. The provider orders a mammogram. The mass in the breast would be listed first, code 611.72, as the reason for the visit, followed by a code for family history of malignant neoplasm of breast, V16.3.

EXAMPLE: The mammogram for Gretchen Rose revealed a mass in the breast and she had a biopsy on 9/10/XX. At the time of coding for the biopsy, the physician has recorded a diagnosis of primary carcinoma of the breast, lower-inner quadrant. This would be coded by using code 174.3.

Encounters for Therapeutic Services

The following guideline is provided for coding encounters for therapeutic services:

Official ICD-9-CM Coding Guideline:

For patients receiving therapeutic services only during an encounter/visit, sequence first the diagnosis, condition, problem, or other reason for encounter/visit shown in the medical record to be chiefly responsible for the outpatient services provided during the encounter/visit. Codes for other diagnoses (e.g., chronic conditions) may be sequenced as additional diagnoses.

The only exception to this rule is that when the primary reason for the admission/encounter is chemotherapy, radiation therapy, or rehabilitation, the appropriate V code for the service is listed first, and the diagnosis or problem for which the service is being performed listed second. (See Appendix A, Section IV, M.)

EXAMPLE: Penny Black, a dialysis patient, is seen in the clinic for a therapeutic injection of Aranesp for anemia due to end-stage renal disease. Codes 585, Chronic renal failure, and 285.21, Anemia in end-stage renal disease, are assigned for this case because they are the reasons for the therapeutic service.

Preoperative Evaluations

At times, before surgery, surgeons require patients to obtain preoperative clearance from their primary care provider.

Official ICD-9-CM Coding Guideline:

For patients receiving preoperative evaluations only, sequence first a code from category V72.8, Other specified examinations, to describe the preop consultations. Assign a code for the condition to describe the reason for the surgery as an additional diagnosis. Code also any findings related to the preop evaluation. (See Appendix A, Section IV, N.)

Ambulatory/Outpatient Surgery

The following guidelines give direction to the coder when ambulatory/outpatient surgery episodes of care are coded:

Official ICD-9-CM Coding Guideline:

For ambulatory surgery, code the diagnosis for which the surgery was performed. If the postoperative diagnosis is known to be different from the preoperative diagnosis at the time the diagnosis is confirmed, select the postoperative diagnosis for coding since it is the most definitive. (See Appendix A, Section IV, O.)

When a patient presents for outpatient surgery, code the reason for the surgery as the first-listed diagnosis (reason for the encounter), even if the surgery is not performed due to a contraindication. (See Appendix A, Section IV, A, 1)

EXAMPLE: Bill Best is admitted for ambulatory surgery for an umbilical hernia. On the operative report, the physician records the following: preoperative diagnosis, umbilical hernia; postoperative diagnosis, umbilical hernia with gangrene.

Because the postoperative diagnosis was available at the time of coding, the postoperative diagnosis of umbilical hernia with gangrene would be coded as code 551.1, because it represents the more definitive diagnosis.

Routine Outpatient Prenatal Visits

During pregnancy, many prenatal visits will occur. For routine visits during the pregnancy when no other abnormal condition exists, the following guideline should be used:

Official ICD-9-CM Coding Guideline:

For routine outpatient prenatal visits when no complications are present, codes V22.0, Supervision of normal first pregnancy, or V22.1, Supervision of other normal pregnancy, should be used as the principal diagnoses. These codes should not be used in conjunction with chapter 11 codes. (See Appendix A, Section I, V, P.)

EXAMPLE: Sherrie Gage presents to her obstetrician for her third prenatal visit during her first pregnancy. He completes the exam and finds her pregnancy to be progressing normally. This encounter is coded during code V22.0, Supervision of normal first pregnancy.

Appendix I of the ICD-9-CM Official Guidelines for Coding and Reporting—Present on Admission Reporting Guidelines

Effective October 1, 2007, CMS required that present on admission (POA) indicators be assigned for all diagnoses and external causes of injury codes for inpatient acute care discharges as part of changes to the DRG reimbursement system. The POA indicator is used to report whether the diagnosis and/or external cause of the injury was present at the time of admission. Appendix I of the Official Guidelines states that "present on admission is defined as present at the time the order for inpatient admission occurs—conditions that develop during an outpatient encounter, including emergency department, observation, or outpatient surgery, are considered as present on admission." POA indicators are assigned to principal and secondary diagnoses and the external cause of injury codes, according to this definition.

It should be noted that the POA guidelines provide guidance to coders on how to apply the POA indicators to the codes selected for the discharge. The POA indicator is assigned after coders have selected the principal and secondary diagnosis(es) for the case. When selecting codes, the coder is to be guided by Sections I to III of the ICD-9-CM Official Guidelines for Coding and Reporting. Do not confuse the purpose of Appendix I of the Guidelines. To learn more about how to select POA indicators, read the Present on Admission Reporting Guidelines in Appendix A of this textbook.

Internet Links

The ICD-9-CM Official Guidelines for Coding and Reporting can be found online at *http://www.cdc.gov/nchs/datawh/ftpserv/ftpicd9/icdguide08.pdf*.

Summary

- The ICD-9-CM Official Guidelines for Coding and Reporting were developed by the Cooperating Parties for ICD-9-CM.

- The Cooperating Parties for ICD-9-CM include the American Hospital Association, American Health Information Association, Centers for Medicare and Medicaid Services, and the National Center for Health Statistics.

- There are four sections of the ICD-9-CM Official Guidelines for Coding and Reporting.

- Section I contains the ICD-9-CM Conventions, General Coding Guidelines, and Chapter-Specific Guidelines.

- Section II describes the Selection of Principal Diagnosis(es) for Inpatient, Short-Term, Acute Care, and Long-Term Care Hospital Records.

- Section III describes the Reporting of Additional Diagnoses for Inpatient, Short-Term, Acute Care, and Long-Term Care Hospital Records.

- Section IV describes the Diagnostic Coding and Reporting Guidelines for Outpatient Services.

- Appendix A provides a complete listing of all the ICD-9-CM Official Guidelines for Coding and Reporting.

Chapter Review

True/False: Indicate whether each statement is true (T) or false (F).

1. _____ The ICD-9-CM Official Guidelines for Coding and Reporting were developed by the American Health Information Management Association.

2. _____ For outpatient and physician office visits, the code that is listed first for coding and reporting purposes is the reason for the encounter.

3. _____ Codes that describe symptoms and signs are acceptable for coding when a definitive diagnosis has not been established in a physician's office.

4. _____ If signs and symptoms exist that are not routinely associated with a disease process, the signs and symptoms should not be coded.

5. _____ Late effect codes should be used only within six months after the initial injury or disease.

6. _____ The principal diagnosis is defined as "that condition established after study to be chiefly responsible for occasioning the outpatient visit of the patient to the hospital for care."

7. _____ If the diagnosis documented at the time of discharge is qualified as "probable" or "suspected," do not code the condition.

8. _____ Codes from chapter 16 of ICD-9-CM, "Symptoms, Signs, and Ill-Defined Conditions," are not to be used as a principal diagnosis when a related definitive diagnosis has been established.

9. _____ A patient is admitted because of severe abdominal pain. After diagnostic testing, it was determined that the patient has appendicitis. The abdominal pain is the principal diagnosis.

10. _____ In a physician's office, a chronic disease treated on an ongoing basis may be coded and reported as many times as the patient receives treatment and care for the condition.

Fill-in-the-Blank: Enter the appropriate term(s) to complete each statement.

11. A _____ is the residual effect (condition produced) after the acute phase of an illness or injury has terminated.

12. For ambulatory surgery, if the postoperative diagnosis is known to be different from the preoperative diagnosis at the time the diagnosis is confirmed, select the _____ diagnosis for coding.

13. In the _____ setting, the definition of principal diagnosis does not apply.

14. For outpatient and physician office visits, the code that is listed first for coding and reporting purposes is the _____.

15. Rule out conditions are not coded in the _____ setting.

16. When the final report is available at the time of coding for outpatient diagnostic tests, code the _____ diagnosis(es) documented in the interpretation.

17. Abnormal findings are not coded and reported for _____ unless the physician documents the significance of the findings.

18. In the outpatient setting, the term _____ is used in lieu of principal diagnosis.

19. In most cases when coding late effects, two codes are required, with the _____ sequenced first followed by the cause of the late effect.

20. When coding a late effect, a second code is not needed when medical documentation does not identify the _____.

Short Answer: Briefly answer each of the following.

21. Explain the ICD-9-CM Official Guideline for coding two or more interrelated conditions that equally meet the definition for principal diagnosis.

22. Discuss how to code a diagnosis recorded as "suspected" in both an inpatient and an outpatient record.

23. List the Cooperating Parties that developed the ICD-9-CM Official Coding Guidelines.

24. List the sections of the ICD-9-CM Official Guidelines for Coding and Reporting.

25. Define the term *present on admission* as it applies to POA indicators.

SECTION II

ICD-9-CM Diagnostic Coding

Infectious and Parasitic Diseases

Chapter Outline

Objectives

At the conclusion of this chapter, the student will be able to:

1. Identify infectious and parasitic diseases.
2. Explain single code, combination code, and dual code assignment.
3. Discuss ICD-9-CM coding guidelines for infectious and parasitic diseases.
4. Summarize the coding of symptomatic and asymptomatic cases of HIV.
5. List the types of hepatitis and the codes for each.
6. Accurately code infectious and parasitic diseases.
7. Select and code diagnoses from case studies.

Key Terms

Arthropods

Bacilli

Bacillus

Bacteria

Candial Vulvovaginitis

Candidal Onychia

Candidiasis

Cocci

Coccus

Combination Code
  Assignment

Culture and Sensitivity
  Test (C&S)

Diplo-

Dual Code Assignment

E. Coli

Escherichia Coli

Fungi

Helminths

Host

Infectious Diseases

Molds

Monilial Vulvovaginitis

Moniliasis

Opportunistic Infections

Opportunistic Mycotic
  Infections

Opportunistic Parasites

Parasite

Parasitic Diseases

Pathogen

Protozoa

Reminder

As you work through this chapter, you will need to have a copy of the ICD-9-CM coding book to reference.

Sepsis

Septicemia

Septic Shock

Severe Sepsis

Single Code Assignment

Spirilla

Spirillum

Staphylo-

Strepto-

Systemic Inflammatory Response Syndrome (SIRS)

Thrush

Toxic Shock Syndrome

Viruses

Yeast Infections

Introduction

Infectious and parasitic diseases, category code range 001–139, are classified in chapter 1 of ICD-9-CM. Infectious diseases are diseases that occur when a pathogen, a micro-organism that can cause disease in humans, invades the body and causes disease. Parasitic diseases occur when an organism, known as a parasite, lives on or within another organism, known as the host. In this relationship, the parasite benefits and the host is harmed. An easy way to remember the diseases that fall into this chapter can be found by referencing the start of chapter 1 in the code book. The Includes: note found at the start of the chapter describes this chapter as:

> Diseases generally recognized as communicable or transmissible as well as a few diseases of unknown but possibly infectious origin.

Introduction to Body Systems

This chapter of ICD-9-CM is organized by organisms and body sites. Diseases are organized into the sections of chapter 1 by organism type or by body site. For example, intestinal infectious diseases fall into category codes 001–009, representing a body site, and category 042, human immunodeficiency virus, represents a category code for a specific organism. Figure 6-1 represents the sections of chapter 1 and the category codes.

Section Title	Category Codes
Infestional Infectious Diseases	001–009
Tuberculosis	010–018
Zoonotic Bacterial Diseases	020–027
Other Bacterial Diseases	030–041
Human Immunodeficiency Virus Infection	042
Poliomyelitis and Other Non-Arthropod-Borne Viral Diseases and Prion Diseases of Central Nervous System	045–049
Viral Diseases Accompanied by Exanthem	050–059
Arthropod-Borne Viral Diseases	060–066
Other Diseases Due to Virus and Chlamydiae	070–079
Rickettsioses and Other Arthropod-Borne Diseases	080–088
Syphilis and Other Venereal Diseases	090–099
Other Spirochetal Diseases	100–104
Mycoses	110–118
Helminthiases	120–129
Other Infectious and Parasitic Diseases	130–136
Late Effects of Infectious and Parasitic Diseases	137–139

Figure 6-1 Infectious and Parasitic Diseases sections and category codes

The various sections of chapter one identify the different types of organisms that cause infections. Organisms are classified into the following groups:

- Bacteria
- Fungi
- Parasites
- Viruses

Bacteria

Bacteria are one-celled organisms named according to their shapes and arrangements (Figures 6-2, 6-3, and 6-4). For example, diplococci bacteria are round, spherical, or coffee bean–shaped bacteria that occur in pairs.

Common bacterial infection sites include the bloodstream, skin, gastrointestinal, respiratory, and urinary tracts. Some organisms are commonly found in the human body and do not cause disease in a particular body site but can cause disease in another body site. Because a specific organism can cause disease in different body sites, it is important for a coder to note the type of organism and body site when coding.

EXAMPLE: *Escherichia coli,* also known as *E. coli,* is a rod-shaped bacillus found in the large intestine of humans. When found in the large intestine, it is normally nonpathogenic. However, when *E. coli* is found outside the intestine, it can cause disease in the urinary tract or infections in pressure ulcers.

To accurately diagnose a specific bacterial infection that is affecting a patient, a physician will order a culture and sensitivity test, also known as a C&S. The culture identifies the type of organism causing

Singular Name of Bacterial Shape	Plural Form	Description
Coccus	Cocci	Spherical or round
Bacillus	Bacilli	Straight rod
Spirillum	Spirilla	Spiral, corkscrew, or slightly curved

Figure 6-2 Bacterial shapes

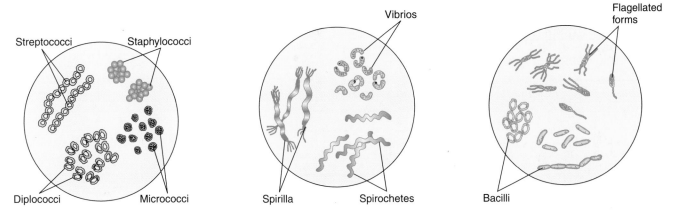

Figure 6-3 Forms of cocci, bacilli, and spirilla (From Bowie MJ, Schaffer RM. *Nursing Assistant: A Nursing Process Approach,* 9th ed. Clifton Park, NY: Delmar, Cengage Learning, 2003.)

Arrangement	Medical Word Part
Single	There is no specific medical term.
Pairs	**diplo-**
Chains	**strepto-**
Clusters	**staphylo-**

Figure 6-4 Arrangements of bacteria

the infection, and the sensitivity identifies the antibiotic that should be used to treat the infection. It is important that a coder reference the culture and sensitivity report to identify the specific bacteria that is causing the infection.

Common bacterial infections include:

Name of Infection	Common Pathogen
Pseudomembraneous colitis	*Clostridium difficile*
Salmonella food poisoning	*Salmonella*
Urinary tract infection	*E. coli*
	Pseudomonas aeruginosa
Tuberculosis	*Mycobacterium tuberculosis*
Impetigo	*Streptococci A*
Strep throat	*Streptococcus*

Fungi

Fungi are microscopic plant life that lack chlorophyll and must have a source of matter for nutrition because they cannot manufacture their own food. The two common forms of fungal infections that affect humans are molds and yeast. **Yeast infections** are caused by an unicellular fungi that reproduce by budding; **molds** are caused by long filament-shaped fungi. Yeasts and molds that infect human tissues are known as **opportunistic parasites**. Opportunistic parasites cause **opportunistic infections** when a patient has a weakened immune system. Opportunistic infections commonly occur in the following types of individuals:

- Patients with chronic conditions, such as AIDS, diabetes, and cancer
- Infants and newborns
- Patients who are postsurgery
- Patients who have taken antibiotics
- Steroid users

Common yeasts and molds that affect humans are:

Name of Infection	Common Pathogen
Athlete's foot	*Tinea pedis*
Thrush	*Candida albicans*
Ringworm	*Tinea capitis*
Chicago disease	*Blastomyces dermatitidis*

Parasites

Parasites are organisms that feed on other organisms to nourish themselves. Specific parasitic organisms are:

- **Protozoa**—one-celled organisms that live on living matter and are classified by the way they move.

- **Helminths**—organisms that include flatworms, roundworms, and flukes.

- **Arthropods**—organisms that include insects, ticks, spiders, and mites.

Parasitic infections are found in the intestinal tract, bloodstream, lymph nodes, central nervous system, and skin. Some parasitic infections multiply in the bloodstream and move into body organ tissue, such as the liver and spleen. Figure 6-5 illustrates malarial parasites in red blood cells. Other parasites, such as a tapeworm, attach to body structures and cause disorders. A tapeworm uses hooks and suckers to attach to the intestinal wall of its host, thus causing weight loss (Figure 6-6). Common parasitic infections include:

Name of Infection	Common Pathogen
African sleeping sickness	*Trypanosoma gambiense*
Chagas' disease	*Trypanosoma cruzi*
Malaria	*Plasmodium falciparum*
	Plasmodium vivax
	Plasmodium malariae
	Plasmodium ovale
Pinworm	*Enterobius vermicularis*
Head lice	*Pediculus*
Scabies	*Sarcoptes*

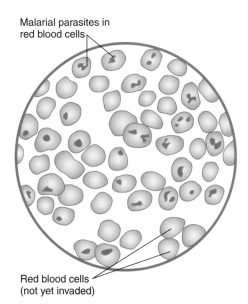

Figure 6-5 Malarial parasites in red blood cells (From Grover-Lakomia LL, Fong E. *Microbiology for Health Careers,* 6th ed. Clifton Park, NY: Delmar, Cengage Learning, 1999, p. 177.)

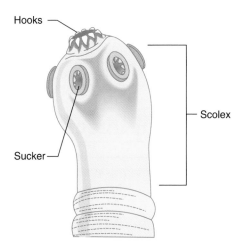

Figure 6-6 Tapeworm (From Grover-Lakomia LL, Fong E. *Microbiology for Health Careers,* 6th ed. Clifton Park, NY: Delmar, Cengage Learning, 1999, p. 181.)

Viruses

Viruses are the smallest of infectious pathogens. They penetrate cells and release their DNA or RNA into the nucleus of a cell, causing damage to the human cell. Viruses are completely dependent on the nutrients inside the cells for reproduction and metabolism and vary in their effects from a common cold to viral hepatitis and AIDS.

Common viral infections include:

Name of Disease	Name of Pathogen
Shingles	*Herpes zoster*
Chickenpox	*Varicella*
AIDS	Human immunodeficiency virus
Genital herpes	*Herpes simplex*
German measles	RNA virus
West Nile fever	*Flavivirus*

Exercise 6–1   Identifying Pathogens

For each of the diseases listed, state whether the pathogen is bacterial (B), fungal (F), parasitic (P), or viral (V).

Disease	**Pathogens**
1. Athlete's foot	_____
2. Chickenpox	_____
3. Impetigo	_____
4. Ringworm	_____
5. Malaria	_____
6. Genital herpes	_____
7. Head lice	_____
8. *Salmonella* food poisoning	_____

Coding of Infectious and Parasitic Diseases

Infectious and parasitic diseases are coded in ICD-9-CM in one of three ways: single code assignment, combination code assignment, or dual code assignment. Therefore, at times only one code is needed to code an infectious or parasitic disease; at other times two codes are needed.

Single Code Assignment

Single code assignment occurs when only one code is needed to code the diagnostic statement.

> **EXAMPLE:** A patient presents with acute scarlet fever. To code this diagnostic statement, the coder references the term *fever* or *scarlet fever* in the Alphabetic Index. For this example, assume

that the coder references the term *scarlet fever*. The entry appears in the Alphabetic Index as shown in Figure 6-7.

Scarlatina 034.1
        anginosa 034.1
        maligna 034.1
        myocarditis, acute 034.1 *[422.0]*
          old (see also Myocarditis) 429.0
        otitis media 034.1 *[382.02]*
        ulcerosa 034.1
Scarlatinella 057.8
Scarlet fever (albuminuria) (angina) (convulsions) (lesions of lid) (rash) 034.1

Figure 6-7 Alphabetic Index listing for scarlet fever

After referencing the index, the coder must now verify the code in the Tabular List. Code 034.1 appears as shown in Figure 6-8. Therefore, code 034.1 is the single code that is needed to accurately code acute scarlet fever.

034   **Streptococcal sore throat and scarlet fever**

      034.0   Streptococcal sore throat
            Septic:
                angina
                sore throat
            Streptococcal:
                angina
                laryngitis
                pharyngitis
                tonsillitis

      034.1   Scarlet fever
            Scarlatina

            Excludes: parascarlatina (057.8)

Figure 6-8 Tabular List entry for scarlet fever

Combination Code Assignment

Combination code assignment occurs when a single code is used to identify the organism and the condition caused by the organism. Here, only one code is needed to code the diagnostic statement.

> **EXAMPLE:** A patient is diagnosed with herpes simplex meningitis. To code this diagnostic statement, the coder references the term *meningitis* in the Alphabetic Index. The entry appears in the Alphabetic Index as shown in Figure 6-9.

```
Meningitis
     gram-negative cocci NEC 036.0
             specified NEC 320.82
     gram-positive cocci NEC 320.9
     herpes (simplex) virus 054.72
             zoster 053.0
     H. influenzae 320.0
     infectious NEC 320.9
     influenzal 320.0
     Klebsiella pneumoniae 320.82
```

Figure 6-9 Alphabetic Index listing for meningitis

After referencing the Alphabetic Index, the coder notes that code 054.72 is listed for herpes simplex meningitis. The coder verifies the code in the Tabular List. Code 054.72 appears as shown in Figure 6-10. Therefore, only one code, 054.72, is needed to code the organism, herpes simplex, and the manifestation, meningitis.

```
054.7    With other specified complications

     054.71   Visceral herpes simplex
     054.72   Herpes simplex meningitis
     054.73   Herpes simplex otitis externa
     054.74   Herpes simplex myelitis
     054.79   Other
```

Figure 6-10 Category code 054.7

Dual Code Assignment

Dual code assignment occurs when two codes are needed to code a diagnostic statement. The infectious and parasitic disease codes are sequenced before the code from another ICD-9-CM chapter when two codes are used to code a diagnostic statement.

> **EXAMPLE:** A patient is diagnosed with anthrax pneumonia. To code this diagnostic statement, the coder references the term *pneumonia* and the subterm *anthrax* in the Alphabetic Index. The entry appears in the Alphabetic Index as shown in Figure 6-11.
>
> Note that in the Alphabetic Index, two codes are listed: code 022.1 and code 484.5. Code 022.1 identifies the organism, anthrax, and code 484.5 identifies the pneumonia. Note that code 484.5 appears in brackets in the Alphabetic Index to signal to the coder that the code in the brackets should be listed as the second code.

Official ICD-9-CM Coding Guideline:

In the index, both conditions are listed together with the etiology code first, followed by the manifestation codes in brackets. The code in brackets is always to be sequenced second. (See Appendix A, Section I, A, 6—Etiology/ manifestation convention.)

In referencing the tabular listing of code 484.5, the coder is instructed to code first the underlying disease (022.1), anthrax. The tabular listing of 484.5 appears as shown in Figure 6-12.

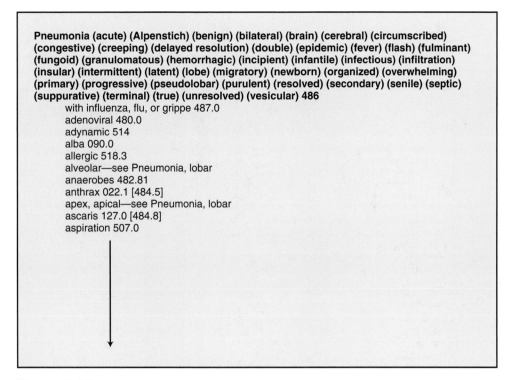

Figure 6-11 Alphabetic Index listing for pneumonia

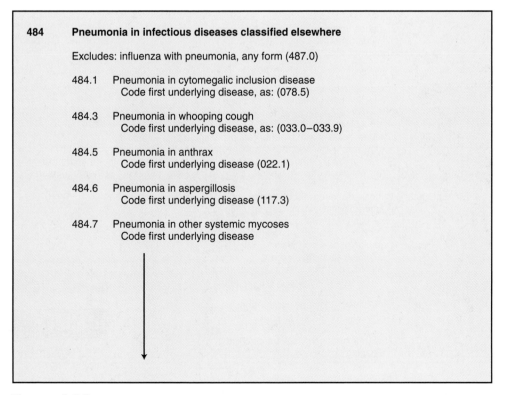

Figure 6-12 Tabular List entry for pneumonia

EXAMPLE: A patient is diagnosed with trypanosomiasis meningitis. The coder references the main term *meningitis* and the subterm *trypanosomiasis* in the Alphabetic Index. The entry appears as shown in Figure 6-13. Note that both codes appear in the Alphabetic Index, with 086.1 listed first and 321.3 listed in the brackets.

Meningitis
    streptococcal (acute) 320.2
    suppurative 320.9
        specified organism NEC 320.89
    syphilitic 094.2
        acute 091.81
        congenital 090.42
        secondary 091.81
    torula 117.5 [321.0]
    traumatic (complication of injury) 958.8
    Treponema (denticola) (macrodenticum) 320.81
    trypanosomiasis 086.1 [321.3]
    tuberculous (see also Tuberculosis, meninges) 013.0
    typhoid 002.0 [320.7]
    Veillonella 320.81
    Vibrio vulnificus 320.82
    viral, virus NEC (see also Meningitis, aseptic) 047.9
    Wallgren's (see also Meningitis, aseptic) 047.9

Figure 6-13 Alphabetic Index listing for meningitis, streptococcal to Wallgren's

In the Tabular List, the entry for code 086.1 is as shown in Figure 6-14.

Note that after the main heading for trypanosomiasis, an instructional notation appears that instructs the coder to use an additional code to identify the manifestation.

086   **Trypanosomiasis**
    Use additional code to identify manifestations, as:
        trypanosomiasis:
            encephalitis (323.2)
            meningitis (321.3)

    086.0   Chagas' disease with heart involvement
          American trypanosomiasis with heart involvement
          Infection by Trypanosoma cruzi with heart involvement
          Any condition classifiable to 086.2 with heart involvement

    086.1   Chagas' disease with other organ involvement
          American trypanosomiasis with involvement of organ other than heart
          Infection by Trypanosoma cruzi with involvement of organ other than heart
          Any condition classifiable to 086.2 with involvement of organ other than heart

    086.2   Chagas' disease without mention of organ involvement
          American trypanosomiasis
          Infection by Trypanosoma cruzi

    086.3   Gambian trypanosomiasis
          Gambian sleeping sickness
          Infection by Trypanosoma gambiense

    086.4   Rhodesian trypanosomiasis
          Infection by Trypanosoma rhodesiense
          Rhodesian sleeping sickness

    086.5   African trypanosomiasis, unspecified
          Sleeping sickness NOS

    086.9   Trypanosomiasis, unspecified

Figure 6-14 Tabular List entry for trypanosomiasis

In the Tabular List, the entry for code 321.3 is as shown in Figure 6.15. Here the coder is again instructed to list the code for trypanosomiasis first.

321.3   Meningitis due to trypanosomiasis
        Code first underlying disease (086.0–086.9)

321.4   Meningitis in sarcoidosis
        Code first underlying disease (135)

321.8   Meningitis due to other nonbacterial organisms classified elsewhere
        Code first underlying disease

        Excludes: leptospiral meningitis (100.81)

Figure 6-15 Tabular List entry for meningitis

Official ICD-9-CM Coding Guideline:

Certain conditions have both an underlying etiology and multiple body system manifestations due to the underlying etiology. For such conditions the ICD-9-CM has a coding convention that requires the underlying condition be sequenced first, followed by the manifestation. Wherever such a combination exists, there is a "use additional code" note at the etiology code, and a "code first" note at the manifestation code. These instructional notes indicate the proper sequencing order of the codes, etiology followed by manifestation. (See Appendix A, Section I, A, 6—Etiology/manifestation convention.)

Intestinal Infectious Diseases (Category Codes 001–009)

This range of codes includes infections that occur in the stomach, intestines, and colon. The codes are organized according to the type of organisms causing the infection and the site of the infection.

Codes found in this section include:

- Cholera (001.0–001.9)
- Typhoid and paratyphoid fevers (002.0–002.9)
- Salmonella infections (003.0–003.9)
- Shigellosis (004.0–004.9)
- Bacterial food poisoning (005.0–005.9)
- Amebiasis (006.0–006.9)
- Protozoal intestinal diseases (007.0–007.9)
- Intestinal infections due to other organisms (008.00–008.8)
- Ill-defined intestinal infections (009.0–009.3)

Patients who are diagnosed with an infectious intestinal disease typically display the same signs and symptoms regardless of the type of infectious intestinal disease.

Disease Highlight—Infectious Intestinal Diseases

Signs and Symptoms:

- Nausea
- Vomiting

- Anorexia

- Abdominal pain

- Fever

- Muscular aches

- Malaise

Clinical Tests:

- Blood and stool cultures to identify the type of infectious organisms

Treatment:

- Patients are given an antiemetric drug to reduce the vomiting.

- Antimotility drugs are used to relieve the abdominal pain.

- To replace lost fluids, patients are encouraged to increase fluid intake.

- In severe cases patients are given IV replacement therapy.

Tuberculosis (Category Codes 010–018)

Tuberculosis is an infection caused by *Mycobacterium tuberculosis* that spreads through the body via lymph and blood vessels and that most commonly localizes in the lungs. At the start of the ICD-9-CM code book, section 010–018, an Includes: notation states that infections by *Mycobacterium tuberculosis* are coded from this section. An additional Excludes: notation notes that congenital tuberculosis (771.2) and late effects of tuberculosis (137.0–137.4) are excluded. Symptoms of the disease include fatigue and weakness, loss of appetite and weight, coughing, hemoptysis, night sweats, and increased temperature later in the day and evening. Clinical tests used to diagnosis tuberculosis include:

- Chest X-rays

- Mantoux skin test

- Sputum culture

```
All codes for tuberculosis have five digits. The fifth digits used are:
0   Unspecified
1   Bacteriological or histological examination not done
2   Bacteriological or histological examination unknown (at present)
3   Tubercle bacilli found (in sputum) by microscopy
4   Tubercle bacilli not found (in sputum) by microscopy but found by bacterial
    culture
5   Tubercle bacilli not found by bacteriological examination, but tuberculosis
    confirmed histologically
6   Tubercle bacilli not found by bacteriological or histological examination, but
    tuberculosis confirmed by other methods [inoculation of animals]
```

The fifth digit 0 is used when the medical documentation at the time of coding does not specify the type of examination used to identify the tuberculosis or when the information is not documented. The fifth digit 1 is used when the medical documentation records that no bacteriological or histological examination was completed. The fifth digit 2 is used when a bacteriological or histological examination was completed but the method is unknown or the results are not available. The fifth digit 3 is used when the organism was found by microscopy. The fifth digit 4 is used when the organism was found not by microscopy but by bacterial culture. The fifth digit 5 is used when the organism was not found by bacteriological examination but confirmed histologically. The fifth digit 6 is used when the organism is not found by bacteriological or histological examination but was confirmed by other methods.

When coding from this section, the coder needs also to identify the site of the infection. It is most common of tuberculosis to localize in the lungs; however, tuberculosis can also infect other organs.

Zoonotic Bacterial Diseases (Category Codes 020–027)

This section includes zoonotic bacterial diseases that are transmitted to humans by contact with infected animals, insects, fleas, ticks, or their discharges or products. Common symptoms of diseases in this range include fever, chills, headache, sweating, body aches, weakness, and fatigue. Blood specimens are used for diagnosis. Common diseases in this section include:

- Anthrax
- Bubonic plague
- Listeriosis meningitis
- Mediterranean fever

Other Bacterial Diseases (Category Codes 030–041)

This range of codes classifies a wide range of bacterial diseases. One of the most common codes in this section is 034.0, Streptococcal sore throat. This is commonly seen in pediatric patients and is diagnosed by a throat culture.

A less commonly seen infection, but a potentially life-threatening condition, that is coded from this range is septicemia. Physicians commonly use the terms *septicemia* and *sepsis* synonymously; however, current medical practice makes a distinction between these terms and other related conditions. The ICD-9-CM Official Guidelines for Coding and Reporting state the following in reference to SIRS, septicemia, and sepsis:

Official ICD-9-CM Coding Guidelines:

SIRS, Septicemia, and Sepsis

(a) The terms septicemia *and* sepsis *are often used interchangeably by providers, however they are not considered synonymous terms. The following descriptions are provided for reference but do not preclude querying the provider for clarification about terms used in the documentation:*

  (i) **Septicemia** *generally refers to a systemic disease associated with the presence of pathological microorganisms or toxins in the blood, which can include bacteria, viruses, fungi, or other organisms.*

  (ii) **Systemic inflammatory response syndrome (SIRS)** *generally refers to the systemic response to infection, trauma/burns, or other insult (such as cancer), with symptoms including fever, tachycardia, tachypnea, and leukocytosis.*

  (iii) **Sepsis** *generally refers to SIRS due to infection.*

  (iv) **Severe sepsis** *generally refers to sepsis with associated acute organ dysfunction. (See Appendix A, Section I, C1b)*

ICD-9-CM classifies septicemia to category 038 and subdivides into fourth digits that identify specific bacteria. Instructional notes appear after the 038 category, as shown in Figure 6-16.

The coder needs to identify the organism that has caused the infection and take note of whether the Excludes: notation applies to the case being coded. It should also be noted that the coder is instructed to use an additional code for SIRS.

```
038        Septicemia

           Use additional code for systemic inflammatory response syndrome (SIRS) (995.91–995.92)

           Excludes:        bacteremia (790.7)
                            during labor (659.3)
                            following ectopic or molar pregnancy (639.0)
                            following infusion, injection, transfusion or vaccination (999.3)
                            postpartum, puerperal (670)
                            septicemia (sepsis) of newborn (771.81)
                            that complicating abortion (634–638 with .0, 639.0)
```

Figure 6-16 Tabular List entry for septicemia

SIRS is classified to subcategory code 995.9, with fifth digits identifying the following:

995.90 SIRS, unspecified

995.91 Sepsis

995.92 Severe sepsis

995.93 SIRS due to noninfectious process without acute organ dysfunction

995.94 SIRS due to noninfectious process with acute organ dysfunction

Patients who have septicemia can also develop septic shock. Septic shock is coded to a number of different codes depending on the circumstances of the case. The excerpt from the ICD-9-CM Alphabetic Index summarizes the codes used; see Figure 6-17.

Septic shock is classified to 785.52 with an instructional notation in the Tabular List as follows:

Code first:

Systemic inflammatory response syndrome

  due to infectious process with organ dysfunction (995.92)

The tabular List entry for code 995.92 also instructs the coder to use an additional code to identify septic shock. In other words, coders needs to make sure that all instructional notations are read!

Please note that the ICD-9-CM Official Coding Guidelines guide the coder as follows:

```
Shock
    septic 785.52
        with
                abortion—see Abortion, by type, with shock
                ectopic pregnancy (see also categories 633.0–633.9) 639.5
                molar pregnancy (see also categories 630–632) 639.5
        due to
                surgical procedure 998.0
                transfusion NEC 999.8X
                        bone marrow 996.85
        following
                abortion 639.5
                ectopic or molar pregnancy 639.5
                surgical procedure 998.0
                transfusion NEC 999.8X
                        bone marrow 996.85
```

Figure 6-17 Alphabetical Index listing for septic shock

Official ICD-9-CM Coding Guidelines:

6) Septic shock

(a) Sequencing of septic shock

Septic shock *generally refers to circulatory failure associated with severe sepsis, and, therefore, it represents a type of acute organ dysfunction.*

For all cases of septic shock, the code for the systemic infection should be sequenced first, followed by codes 995.92 and 785.52. Any additional codes for other acute organ dysfunctions should also be assigned. As noted in the sequencing instructions in the Tabular List, the code for septic shock cannot be assigned as a principal diagnosis.

(b) Septic Shock without documentation of severe sepsis

Septic shock indicates the presence of severe sepsis.

Code 995.92, Severe sepsis, must be assigned with code 785.52, Septic shock, even if the term severe sepsis is not documented in the record. The "use additional code" note and the "code first" note in the tabular support this guideline. (See Appendix A, Section I, C1, b,6 a-b)

Septic shock related to obstetrical and gynecological patients is coded from ICD-9-CM chapter 11, "Complications of Pregnancy, Childbirth, and the Puerperium." Septic shock that is due to or following a surgical procedure or transfusion is classified to chapter 16, "Symptoms, Signs, and Ill-Defined Conditions." Reference Figure 6-17 for specific codes.

The ICD-CM Official Guidelines for Coding and Reporting include the following guidelines for coding septicemia, SIRS, sepsis, severe sepsis, and septic shock.

Official ICD-9-CM Coding Guidelines:

(b) The Coding of SIRS, sepsis, and severe sepsis

The coding of SIRS, sepsis, and severe sepsis requires a minimum of two codes: a code for the underlying cause (such as infection or trauma) and a code from subcategory 995.9, Systemic inflammatory response syndrome (SIRS).

(i) The code for the underlying cause (such as infection or trauma) must be sequenced before the code from subcategory 995.9, Systemic inflammatory response syndrome (SIRS).

(ii) Sepsis and severe sepsis require a code for the systemic infection (038.xx, 112.5, etc.) and either code 995.91, Sepsis, or 995.92, Severe sepsis. If the causal organism is not documented, assign code 038.9, Unspecified septicemia.

(iii) Severe sepsis requires additional code(s) for the associated acute organ dysfunction(s).

(iv) If a patient has sepsis with multiple organ dysfunctions, follow the instructions for coding severe sepsis.

(v) Either the term sepsis or SIRS must be documented to assign a code from subcategory 995.9.

(vi) See Section I.C.17.g, Injury and poisoning, for information regarding systemic inflammatory response syndrome (SIRS) due to trauma/burns and other noninfectious processes.

(c) Due to the complex nature of sepsis and severe sepsis, some cases may require querying the provider prior to assignment of the codes.

2) Sequencing Sepsis and Severe Sepsis

(a) Sepsis and severe sepsis as principal diagnosis

If sepsis or severe sepsis is present on admission and meets the definition of principal diagnosis, the systemic infection code (e.g., 038.xx, 112.5, etc.) should be assigned as the principal diagnosis, followed by code 995.91, Sepsis, or 995.92, Severe sepsis, as required by the sequencing rules in the Tabular List. Codes from subcategory 995.9 can never be assigned as a principal diagnosis. A code should also be assigned for any localized infection, if present.

If the sepsis or severe sepsis is due to a postprocedural infection, see Section I.C.10 for guidelines related to sepsis due to postprocedural infection.

(b) Sepsis and severe sepsis as secondary diagnoses

When sepsis or severe sepsis develops during the encounter (it was not present on admission), the systemic infection code and code 995.91 or 995.92 should be assigned as secondary diagnoses.

(c) Documentation unclear as to whether sepsis or severe sepsis is present on admission

Sepsis or severe sepsis may be present on admission but the diagnosis may not be confirmed until sometime after admission. If the documentation is not clear whether the sepsis or severe sepsis was present on admission, the provider should be queried.

3) Sepsis/SIRS with Localized Infection

If the reason for admission is both sepsis, severe sepsis, or SIRS and a localized infection, such as pneumonia or cellulitis, a code for the systemic infection (038.xx, 112.5, etc) should be assigned first, then code 995.91 or 995.92, followed by the code for the localized infection. If the patient is admitted with a localized infection, such as pneumonia, and sepsis/SIRS doesn't develop until after admission, see guideline I.C.1.b.2.b.

If the localized infection is postprocedural, see Section I.C.10 for guidelines related to sepsis due to postprocedural infection.

Note: The term urosepsis is a nonspecific term. If that is the only term documented, then only code 599.0 should be assigned based on the default for the term in the ICD-9-CM index, in addition to the code for the causal organism if known.

4) Bacterial Sepsis and Septicemia

In most cases, it will be a code from category 038, Septicemia, that will be used in conjunction with a code from subcategory 995.9, such as the following:

(a) Streptococcal sepsis

If the documentation in the record states streptococcal sepsis, codes 038.0, Streptococcal septicemia, and code 995.91 should be used, in that sequence.

(b) Streptococcal septicemia

If the documentation states streptococcal septicemia, only code 038.0 should be assigned; however, the provider should be queried whether the patient has sepsis, an infection with SIRS.

5) Acute Organ Dysfunction That Is Not Clearly Associated with the Sepsis

If a patient has sepsis and an acute organ dysfunction, but the medical record documentation indicates that the acute organ dysfunction is related to a medical condition other than the sepsis, do not assign code 995.92, Severe sepsis. An acute organ dysfunction must be associated with the sepsis in order to assign the severe sepsis code. If the documentation is not clear as to whether an acute organ dysfunction is related to the sepsis or another medical condition, query the provider.

7) Sepsis and septic shock complicating abortion and pregnancy

Sepsis and septic shock complicating abortion, ectopic pregnancy, and molar pregnancy are classified to category codes in Chapter 11 (630–639). See Section I.C.11.

8) Negative or inconclusive blood cultures

Negative or inconclusive blood cultures do not preclude a diagnosis of septicemia or sepsis in patients with clinical evidence of the condition, however, the provider should be queried. (See Section I, C 1-2)

Exercise 6–2   Coding Septicemia, SIRS, Sepsis, Severe Sepsis, and Septic Shock

For each diagnostic phrase, select the appropriate ICD-9-CM diagnostic code(s).

1. Septic shock _____

2. Septic shock following surgery _____

3. Streptococcal sepsis _____

4. Streptococcal septicemia, no sepsis _____

5. SIRS _____

6. Severe sepsis due to infection _____

Toxic Shock Syndrome (Code 040.82)

Toxic shock syndrome is an acute infection, caused by staphylococcus or streptococcus bacteria, with an abrupt onset of symptoms. Symptoms include high fever, rash, diarrhea, vomiting, and myalgia. In severe cases patients experience hypotension, shock, and organ failure. Toxic shock syndrome has most commonly been observed in women using tampons, but cases have also occurred in children and males. When toxic shock syndrome code 040.82 is used, an additional code should be assigned to identify the organism present.

Human Immunodeficiency Virus (HIV) Disease (Code 042)

Code 042 is used to identify patients who are symptomatic and have the diagnoses listed in ICD-9-CM Tabular List that are as shown in Figure 6-18.

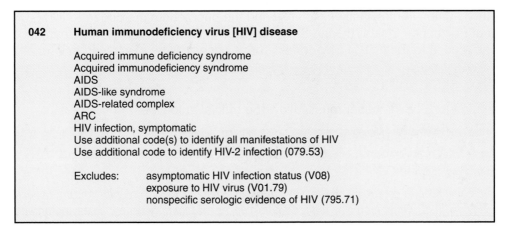

Figure 6-18 Tabular List entry for HIV

This code is not used for patients who are asymptomatic. Asymptomatic cases are coded to V08, Asymptomatic human immunodeficiency virus (HIV) infection. Cases with inconclusive HIV test results are coded to 795.71, Nonspecific serologic evidence of HIV.

The following guidelines should be followed when coding HIV infections.

Official ICD-9-CM Coding Guidelines:

1. *Code only confirmed cases of HIV infection/illness. This is an exception to the hospital inpatient guideline Section II, H.*

   In this context, confirmation does not require documentation of positive serology or culture for HIV; the provider's diagnostic statement that the patient is HIV positive or has an HIV-related illness is sufficient.

2. *Selection and sequencing of HIV cases*

   a. **Patient admitted for HIV-related condition.** *If a patient is admitted for an HIV-related condition, the principal diagnosis should be 042, followed by additional diagnosis codes for all reported HIV-related conditions.*

   b. **Patient with HIV disease admitted for unrelated condition.** *If a patient with HIV disease is admitted for an unrelated condition (such as a traumatic injury), the code for the unrelated condition (e.g., the nature of injury code) should be the principal diagnosis. Other diagnoses would be 042 followed by additional diagnosis codes for all reported HIV-related conditions.*

   c. **Whether the patient is newly diagnosed.** *Whether the patient is newly diagnosed or has had previous admissions/encounters for HIV conditions is irrelevant to the sequencing decision.*

   d. **Asymptomatic human immunodeficiency virus.** *V08, Asymptomatic human immunodeficiency virus [HIV] infection, is to be applied when the patient without any documentation of symptoms is listed as being "HIV positive," "known HIV," "HIV test positive," or similar terminology. Do not use this code if the term AIDS is used or if the patient is treated for any HIV-related illness or is described as having any condition(s) resulting from his/her HIV positive status; use 042 in these cases.*

   e. **Patients with inconclusive HIV serology.** *Patients with inconclusive HIV serology, but no definitive diagnosis or manifestations of the illness, may be assigned code 795.71, Inconclusive serologic test for Human Immunodeficiency Virus [HIV].*

   f. **Previously diagnosed HIV-related illness.** *Patients with any known prior diagnosis of an HIV-related illness should be coded to 042. Once a patient had developed an HIV-related illness, the patient should always be assigned code 042 on every subsequent admission/encounter. Patients previously diagnosed with any HIV illness (042) should never be assigned to 795.71 or V08. (See Appendix A, Section C1, a, 1 to 2a-f.)*

Note that HIV infection in pregnancy, childbirth, and the puerperium are coded to ICD-9-CM chapter 11, "Complications of Pregnancy, Childbirth, and the Puerperium." Exposure to HIV virus and encounters for testing for HIV are coded to the ICD-9-CM V codes. These cases will be discussed in later chapters.

Encounters for Testing HIV

When coding testing for HIV, the coder must follow the official guidelines.

Official ICD-9-CM Coding Guidelines:

(h) *Encounters for testing for HIV*

If a patient is being seen to determine his/her HIV status, use code V73.89, Screening for other specified viral disease. Use code V69.8, Other problems related to lifestyle, as a secondary code if an asymptomatic patient is in a known high-risk group for HIV. Should a patient with signs or symptoms or illness, or a confirmed HIV-related diagnosis be tested for HIV, code the signs and symptoms or the diagnosis. An additional counseling code V65.44 may be used if counseling is provided during the encounter for the test.

When a patient returns to be informed of his/her HIV test results, use code V65.44, HIV counseling, if the results of the test are negative.

If the results are positive but the patient is asymptomatic, use code V08, Asymptomatic HIV infection. If the results are positive and the patient is symptomatic use code 042, HIV infection, with codes for the HIV-related symptoms or diagnosis. The HIV counseling code may also be used if counseling is provided for patients with positive test results. (See Appendix A, Section C1, a, 1h)

Viral Diseases Accompanied by Exanthem (Category Codes 050–059)

Common diseases coded to this range include smallpox, chickenpox, herpes zoster, herpes simplex, congenital herpes, measles, and rubella. In this section it is common to use a combination code to identify the organism and any complications of the disease.

EXAMPLE: Measles without mention of complications is coded to code 055.9. Measles keratitis, an inflammation of the cornea that can occur as a complication of measles, is coded to code 055.71.

When coding in this section, the coder needs to note any complications that occur so that the complication is reflected in the code selected. Figure 6-19 illustrates the use of fifth digits to capture complications from herpes zoster.

Disease	Body System of Complication	ICD-9-CM Code
Postherpetic polyneuropathy	Neurologic	053.13
Herpes zoster iridocyclitis	Ophthalmic	053.22
Otitis externa due to herpes zoster	Auditory	053.71

Figure 6-19 Herpes zoster

Exercise 6–3   Confirming Codes Found in the Tabular List

Using the Tabular List of ICD-9-CM, confirm the following code numbers to verify whether the diagnostic phrase listed is included (I) or excluded (E) for the category code number listed.

1. 004   Bacillary dysentery   _____
2. 005   *Salmonella* infections   _____
3. 007   Diarrhea due to protozoa   _____
4. 012   Tuberculosis respiratory infection   _____
5. 030   Hansen's disease   _____
6. 035   Postpartum erysipelas   _____
7. 047   Meningitis due to leptospira   _____
8. 050   Boston exanthem   _____
9. 053   Shingles   _____
10. 056   German measles   _____

Other Diseases Due to Viruses and Chlamydiae (Category Codes 070–079)

Codes in this section of ICD-9-CM use fourth and fifth digits to identify the organism and manifestations or complications of the disease. This section includes diseases due to viruses and chlamydiae, including the following diseases:

- Viral hepatitis
- Rabies
- Mumps

- Hand, foot, and mouth disease
- Infectious mononucleosis
- Viral warts

Disease Highlight—Infectious Mononucleosis

Signs and Symptoms:

- Enlarged lymph nodes
- Fever
- Sore throat
- Malaise
- Anorexia
- Myalgia
- Splenomegaly

Clinical Testing:

- The patient presents with an elevated WBC and atypical lymphocytes.
- A monopsot test is positive and liver function tests are abnormal.

Treatment:

- Steroid therapy is common.
- Symptomatic treatment includes over-the-counter pain relievers and throat gargles using warm saline.

Viral Hepatitis

Viral hepatitis is found in this section of ICD-9-CM. The various types of hepatitis are:

- Hepatitis A (HAV)
- Hepatitis B (HBV)
- Hepatitis C (HCV)
- Hepatitis D (HDV-delta)
- Hepatitis E (HEV)

    It is imperative that the coder identifies the type of hepatitis present and any complications that occur.

    EXAMPLE: Category codes 070.0 and 070.1 identify HAV, and category codes 070.2 and 070.3 identify HBV. Codes 070.41–070.49 identify "Other specified viral hepatitis with hepatic coma," and codes 070.51–070.59 identify "Other specified viral hepatitis without mention of hepatic coma." It is important for the coder to read the diagnostic phrase thoroughly to identify all components of the ICD-9-CM hepatitis codes.

Disease Highlight—Viral Hepatitis (code category 070)

Signs and Symptoms:

- Nausea
- Vomiting
- Fever

- Anorexia

- Malaise

- Enlarged and tender liver

- Jaundice

Clinical Testing:

- White blood cell count is in the normal to low range.

- Abnormal liver tests show that especially markedly elevated aminotransferases are present early in the course of the disease.

- Biopsy of the liver shows hepatocellular necrosis and mononuclear infiltrates.

- Mild proteinuria and bilirubinuria are present.

Treatment:

Recommended are:

- Antiviral drug therapy

- Bed rest

- A gradual return to normal activity without overexertion

Syphilis and Other Venereal Diseases (Category Codes 090–099)

Diseases in this section include bacterial and unspecified venereal diseases that are transmitted sexually or transplacentally to a fetus from an infected pregnant woman. Syphilis, an infectious chronic disease caused by *Treponema pallidum,* can affect any organ of the body. ICD-9-CM classifies syphilis into categories, as shown in Figure 6-20.

It is important for the coder to identify the type of syphilis (congenital, early, symptomatic, etc.) to accurately assign a code.

Title of Category	Category Code
Congenital Syphilis	090
Early Syphilis, Symptomatic	091
Early Syphilis, Latent	092
Cardiovascular Syphilis	093
Neurosyphilis	094
Other Forms of Late Syphilis, with Symptoms	095
Late Syphilis, Latent	096
Other and Unspecified Syphilis	097

Figure 6-20 Categories of syphilis

Mycoses (Category Codes 110–118)

This section includes fungal infections that affect various body sites. An instructional notation at the start of the section directs coders to use additional codes to identify associated manifestations.

Candidiasis or moniliasis infections, category code 112, are fungal infections caused by the fungus *Candida,* which can affect various sites. ICD-9-CM uses fourth and fifth digits to identify the various sites affected by *Candida.* Common sites and codes are:

• Mouth—Commonly called thrush, code 112.0

• Vulva and vagina—Commonly called candial or monilial vulvovaginitis, code 112.1

• Skin and nails—Commonly called candidal onychia, code 112.3

Opportunistic mycotic infections are coded to code 118, Opportunistic mycoses. These infections include a wide variety of fungal infections that occur in a compromised host, typically a patient who has a chronic disease or weakened immune system. Infectious sites include the skin, subcutaneous tissue, and other organs.

Late Effects of Infectious and Parasitic Diseases (Category Codes 137–139)

Late effect codes are used to code residual conditions due to a previous disease or injury. In chapter 1 of ICD-9-CM, three late effect codes are used:

• Code 137—Late effects of tuberculosis

• Code 138—Late effect of acute poliomyelitis

• Code 139—Late effects of other infectious and parasitic diseases

These codes are used when a patient has previously had an infection and now has a residual condition due to the infection. The code for the residual is listed first, and the late effect code is listed second.

EXAMPLE: A patient presents with constrictive pericarditis and a history of tuberculous pericarditis four years ago. The physician states that the constrictive pericarditis is a late effect of the tuberculosis. At the current time, the patient does not have tuberculosis. A coder would select code 423.2, Constrictive pericarditis, to code the residual effect and code 137.4 to identify that the constrictive pericarditis is a late effect of tuberculosis. A code for the infection is not assigned because the infection no longer exists.

Exercise 6–4   Selecting Codes

For each diagnostic phrase, circle the correct code from the codes listed.

1. Candidiasis infection		112.89	112.9
2. Acute gonococcal vulvovaginitis		098.0	098.2
3. Latent early syphilis		091.2	092.9
4. Meningoencephalitis due to rubella		056.01	056.09
5. Chronic HBV with hepatic coma		070.22	070.23

For each diagnostic phrase, select the appropriate ICD-9-CM code.

6. Herpes simplex iridocyclitis _____

7. Hepatitis E without mention of hepatic coma _____

8. Mixed malaria _____

9. Syphilitic meningitis, congenital _____

10. Tinea cruris _____

Internet Links

A comprehensive infectious disease syllabus can be found at *www.atsu.edu/kcom.*

Categories of acquired immunity can be found at *www.wisc-online.com.*

For information on infectious and parasitic diseases, search the Centers for Disease Control and Prevention Web site at *www.cdc.gov* and the National Institutes of Health Web site at *www.nih.gov.*

For recent research on infectious diseases from the National Foundation on Infectious Diseases, go to *www.nfid.org.*

For more information regarding parasitic diseases, reference the Karolinska Institute Web site at *www.mic.ki.se/Diseases.*

Summary

- ICD-9-CM chapter 1 includes infectious and parasitic diseases.
- Organisms are classified into the following groups: bacteria, fungi, parasites, and viruses.
- Opportunistic infections occur when a patient has a weakened immune system.
- Single code assignment, combination code assignment, and dual code assignment are used in chapter 1.
- An underlying condition/infection code is sequenced first, followed by the manifestation code.
- Septicemia occurs when there is a systematic infection with presence of organisms or their toxins in the blood.
- Code only confirmed cases of HIV infection or illness.
- If a patient is admitted for an HIV-related condition, the principal diagnosis should be code 042, followed by additional diagnosis codes for all reported HIV-related conditions.
- Asymptomatic HIV cases are coded to code V08.
- Patients with inconclusive HIV serology and no definitive diagnosis or manifestations of HIV should be assigned code 795.71.
- Viral hepatitis includes hepatitis A, B, C, D, and E.

Chapter Review

True/False: Indicate whether each statement is true (T) or false (F).

1. _____ Cocci, bacilli, and spirilla describe fungal shapes.

2. _____ To describe clusters of bacteria, the medical word part *staphylo-* is used.

3. _____ A culture and sensitivity test is used to identify parasitic infections.

4. _____ Yeast infections are caused by fungi.

5. _____ Dual code assignment is mandatory for all bacterial infections.

Fill-in-the-Blank: Enter the appropriate term(s) to complete each statement.

6. In dual code assignment, two codes appear in the Alphabetic Index. This is to signal to the coder that the code in the brackets should be listed as the _____ code.

7. Clinical tests used to diagnosis tuberculosis include chest X-rays, _____, and sputum cultures.

8. Candidiases, also known as _____ infections, are fungal infections caused by the fungus *Candida*.

9. Thrush is a common candidiasis infection of the _____.

10. Patients previously diagnosed with any HIV illness (code 042) should never be assigned to codes _____ or _____.

Coding Assignments

Instructions: Using an ICD-9-CM coding book, select the code for each diagnostic statement.

1. Botulism   _____

2. Gonococcal keratitis   _____

3. Scarlet fever   _____

4. Infectious diarrhea   _____

5. Herpes simplex meningitis   _____

6. Sweating fever   _____

7. Warts   _____

8. Congential syphilis   _____

9. Hyperkeratosis of pinta   _____

10. Scabies   _____

11. Behcet's syndrome   _____

12. Syphilitic bursitis   _____

13. Malaria   _____

14. Foot and mouth disease   _____

15. Conjunctivitis, viral   _____

16. Chronic viral hepatitis   _____

17. West Nile virus   _____

18. Rubella   _____

19. Shingles   _____

20. Genital herpes   _____

21. Mumps without mention of complications _____

22. Tuberculosis of bronchus   _____

23. Astrovirus   _____

24. Shigella sonnei   _____

25. Oxyurasis   _____

Case Studies

Instructions: Review each case study and select the correct ICD-9-CM diagnostic code.

CASE 1

S: Fifty-yr-old male presents today with severe abdominal pain, nausea, and vomiting, persistent over the last 24 hours. Diarrhea has developed, and abdominal cramping is also present. Pt states he cannot keep anything down. Upon questioning, he states he attended a neighborhood clambake and ate at least a dozen raw clams. No OTC medications were tried because pt cannot keep anything down.

O: Pleasant, alert gentleman who appears in mild discomfort. **Vital signs:** Temp—99, pulse—70, resp—22, BP—120/00. **Skin:** Warm and clammy. **HEENT:** Unremarkable except for dryness around conjunctiva and the mouth. Patient appears slightly dehydrated. Neck: No JVD; no thyromegaly or bruits. **Lungs:** Clear to auscultation and percussion. **Heart:** No murmurs. **Extremities:** No edema.

A: Food poisoning due to salmonella

P: Will order a suppository to help with the nausea. Stressed the importance of forcing fluids once the suppository has had time to work. Patient will call in the morning if not better. If he is improving, he will follow up as needed.

ICD-9-CM Code Assignment: _____

CASE 2

S: Nineteen-year-old woman presents today with slight fever, cough, and fatigue x 4 days. OTC medications were tried with little relief. No other family members are symptomatic. No nausea or vomiting, no shortness of breath.

O: **Vital Signs:** Temp—98.7, BP—100/72; **Skin:** warm and dry; **HEENT:** TM's normal; throat is slightly red; **Neck:** normal; **Lungs:** clear; **Heart:** RRR.

A: Viral Infection

P: I explained to patient that I feel this is a viral infection and could have come on in a variety of different ways. I suggested Advil for comfort and plenty of fluids. Patient requested an antibiotic. I explained that since this was viral in nature, an antibiotic would not be effective. She said she would try the Advil and notify us if she is not improved in 7–10 days.

ICD-9-CM Code Assignment: _____

CASE 3

S: This is a 29-year-old female who presents today with fever and nausea for 3 days. Patient has tried over-the-counter cold and flu medicine with no results. No other family members are ill at this time. Temp has been running anywhere from 99 to 102. When asked about any other symptoms, patient states that she "feels like my heart is racing sometimes." Patient has not voided in 2 days.

O: Respirations: 31; Pulse: 100; BP: 150/00. She is alert, oriented, and in no acute distress. Lungs: Clear, no rhonci or wheezing. HEENT: WNL. Skin: Clammy to touch. Heart: RRR with no murmurs. Abdomen: Soft and nontender. Extremities: Ankle edema +12.

A: Staphylococcus septicemia

P: Patient is admitted to hospital and will follow staphylococcus septicemia protocol.

ICD-9-CM Code Assignment: _____

CASE 4

Dr. Malik had just returned from a trip to overseas. He was providing free medical care to the people of a small village in a very desolate region of central Africa. Upon his return, he suddenly developed a severe headache, pain in his joints and back, and an extremely high fever. After extensive testing, combined with the fact that he had just returned from overseas, it was determined that Dr. Malik had contracted African tick typhus.

ICD-9-CM Code Assignment: _____

CASE 5

Kaley presented today with an unsightly sore on the lower lip and onto the skin. The patient said this is extremely painful and occurs usually around the time of her period. After a brief examination, Dr. Snyder diagnoses Kaley with herpes simplex, at which time he prescribes medication that will help relieve her symptoms.

ICD-9-Cm Code Assignment: _____

Neoplasms

Chapter Outline

Objectives

At the conclusion of this chapter, the student will be able to:

1. Define the types of neoplasm.
2. Identify common benign and malignant neoplasms.
3. Select codes from the neoplasm table.
4. Select and code diagnoses from case studies.

Key Terms

Anemia	Contiguous	Malignant Secondary	Nonmalignant Tumors
Benign Neoplasm	Dehydration	Melanoma	Paracentesis
Biopsy	Encapsulated	Metastasize	Sarcoma
Ca In Situ	Leukemia	Morphology	Thoracentesis
Cancer	Lipoma	Neoplasm	Tumor
Cancerous Growths	Lymphoma	Neoplasms of Uncertain	
Carcinoma	Malignant Neoplasm	Behavior	
Carcinoma In Situ (CIS)	Malignant Primary	Neoplasms of	
		Unspecified Nature	

Reminder

As you work through this chapter, you will need to have a copy of the ICD-9-CM coding book to reference.

Introduction

Chapter 2 of ICD-9-CM, "Neoplasms," is used to code malignant and benign neoplasms. Neoplasms, or tumors, are defined as an uncontrolled abnormal growth of cells and are characterized as malignant or benign. Malignant neoplasms, called cancerous growths, are life threatening, whereas benign or nonmalignant tumors are usually not life threatening.

Introduction to the Body System

ICD-9-CM codes neoplasms according to the form and structure of the cell, also known as morphology, and anatomical site. Neoplastic conditions are located in the Alphabetic Index by referring to the morphological term or referencing the neoplasm table. Coders must be familiar with the medical terms used to characterize neoplasms before attempting to locate the terms in ICD-9-CM.

Malignant Versus Benign Neoplasms

Malignant neoplasms, also called cancer, grow relatively rapidly and may metastasize, or spread, to other body parts. The malignant cells multiply excessively and can invade or infiltrate normal tissue, making the condition life threatening if untreated. The cancerous cells interfere with normal cell growth (Figure 7-1) and draw nutrients away from body tissue. Compared with normal tissue, cancerous cells appear disorderly and do not look like the tissue of origin. Patients with malignant conditions may experience:

- Anorexia

- Abnormal bleeding or bruising

- Difficulty swallowing

- Indigestion

- Malaise

- Fever

- Sores that will not heal or that change to the appearance of a wart or mole

- Bladder and bowel habit changes

- Mass in breast or other body site

- Persistent cough

- Weight loss

    To determine whether a patient has a tumor present, various laboratory tests and procedures [such as endoscopies, magnetic resonance imaging (MRI), computed tomography (CT) scans, X-rays, and ultrasound] are used. A biopsy, or removal of tissues for pathological examination, is completed to differentiate between malignant and benign tumors.

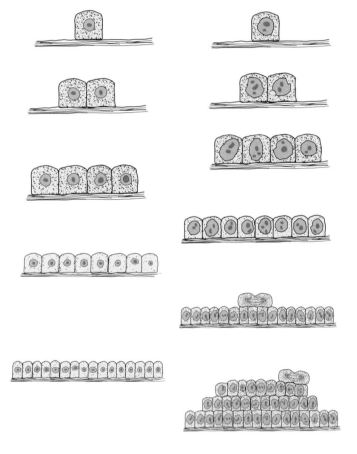

Figure 7-1 Cellular growth patterns: (A) Normal cells, (B) cancer cells

Benign neoplasms usually grow slowly, typically are encapsulated (surrounded by a capsule), and do not metastasize. Under a microscope, benign neoplastic cells appear similar to the tissue of origin. Benign tumors do not cause death unless they are located in vital organs. For example, if a patient has a benign tumor located in the spinal cord or brain, removal may be complicated because of the location of the tumor.

Both benign and malignant neoplasms are named and classified by the tissue of origin. Neoplasms are typically named by adding the suffix *oma* to the name of the body part, such as in lipoma, a benign neoplasm of adipose tissue. Malignant tumors include:

- Carcinoma—Cancer of the epithelial cells of connective tissue
- Lymphoma—Cancer of the lymph nodes and immune system
- Leukemia—Cancer of the blood-forming organs
- Melanoma—Cancer of melanin-producing cells
- Sarcoma—Cancer of supportive tissue such as blood vessels, bones, cartilage, and muscles

Disease Highlight—Basal Cell Carcinoma of Skin

Basal cell carcinoma of the skin is the most common form of skin cancer. The cancer forms at the epidermal layer of the skin. The types of basal cell carcinoma are sclerosing, noduloulcerative, and superficial. The most common cause of basal cell carcinoma is prolonged sun exposure, but it can also be a result of radiation exposure, immunosuppression, or even arsenic ingestion.

Signs and Symptoms:

- In the noduloulcerative type of basal cell carcinoma, small, smooth, pinkish, or translucent lesions form in the early stages; ulcerations and tumors spread and become infected in later stages.
- Sclerosing basal cell carcinoma looks waxy and has yellowish plaques without any distinct border.
- Superficial types of basal cell carcinoma are most often found on the chest and back, and they are irregularly shaped lesions. The lesion may appear to have a scaly look with atrophic areas in the center of it.

Clinical Tests:

- For basal cell carcinoma, biopsy and examination.

Treatment:

- Excision
- Chemotherapy
- Radiotherapy
- Cryotherapy

Common benign and malignant neoplasms are listed in Table 7-1.

Note:
Rather than being classified by organ system, this chapter codes malignancies according to adjacent or adjoining anatomic sites.

Table 7-1 Benign and Malignant Neoplasms

Tissue of Origin	Benign Neoplasms	Malignant Neoplasms
Adipose	Lipoma	Liposacroma
Blood vessel	Hemangioma	Hemangiosacroma
Bone	Osteoma	Osteogenic sarcoma Osteosarcoma
Bone marrow		Ewing sarcoma Multiple myeloma Leukemia
Breast		Carcinoma of breast
Cartilage	Chondroma	Chondrosarcoma
Cervix		Epidermoid carcinoma of the cervix
Colon		Carcinoma of colon
Esophagus		Esophageal adenocarcinoma
Fibrous	Fibroma	Fibrosarcoma
Ganglion cells	Ganglioneuroma	Neuroblastoma
Kidney		Hypernephroma Wilm's tumor
Lung		Adenocarcinoma of the lung Oat cell carcinoma
Meninges	Meningioma	Malignant meningioma
Muscle tissue, smooth	Leiomyoma	Leiomyosarcoma
Muscle tissue, striated	Rhabdomyoma	Rhabdomyosacroma
Nerve tissue	Neuroma Neurinoma Neurofibroma	Neurogenic sarcoma
Ovaries		Cystadenocarcinoma of the ovaries
Penis		Carcinoma of penis
Skin		Basal cell carcinoma
Stomach		Gastric adenocarcinoma Melanoma Squamous cell carcinoma
Testes		Seminona
Uterus	Fibroid	Adenocarcinoma of the uterus

Exercise 7–1   Identifying Neoplasms

For each of the terms listed, determine whether the neoplasm is benign (B) or malignant (M).

   1. Choriocarcinoma   _____

   2. Reticulosarcoma   _____

   3. Uterine leiomyoma

   4. Adenomatous polyp   _____

   5. Giant-cell sarcoma   _____

   6. Juxtacortical chondroma   _____

   7. Fibromyxosarcoma of connective tissue _____

   8. Osteofibroma   _____

   9. Psammocarcinoma   _____

   10. Angiomyolipoma   _____

Coding of Neoplasms

ICD-9-CM groups neoplasms into the following behavior groups:

- Malignant (primary and secondary)—Code range 140–208

- Benign—Code range 210–229

- Cancer in situ—Code range 230–234

- Uncertain behavior—Code range 235–238

- Unspecified—Code range 239

To select a code, the coder must reference the patient's record to determine the type of neoplasm present. A biopsy or pathology report gives the most definitive information. Chapter 2, "Neoplasms," of ICD-9-CM contains all of the codes for malignant conditions and most of the codes for benign conditions. Adenocarcinoma of the breast is a malignant neoplasm that is coded to category 174 with fourth and fifth digits used to identify the location of the neoplasm. It is the most common malignancy affecting females.

Disease Highlight—Adenocarcinoma of the Breast

Adenocarcinoma of the breast, commonly called breast cancer, is a malignant neoplastic condition.

Signs and Symptoms:

- A lump or mass in the breast or in the area of the armpit that is firm to hard when palpated

- Unusual drainage or discharge from nipple

- A change in the breast or nipple size or shape

- Change in the skin with redness or pitting of the skin

- Edema of the arm

Clinical Tests:

- To confirm adenocarcinoma of the breast, a biopsy is completed.

- Several types of biopsies can be completed: incisional biopsy, fine-needle aspiration biopsy, and needle biopsy.

Treatment:

Treatment depends on the extent of the cancer. Options are:

- Surgical intervention
- Chemotherapy
- Radiation therapy
- Tamoxifen and other hormonal therapies are all treatment options

    Some codes for benign conditions are found in specific body system chapters.

    EXAMPLE: The following benign neoplasms are coded to specific body systems.

Neoplasm	Code	Specific Body System
Polyp of nasal cavity	471.0	Respiratory
Cyst of oral soft tissue	528.4	Digestive
Ovarian cyst	620.2	Genitourinary
Prostatic adenoma	600.20–600.21	Genitourinary
Cyst of bone	733.20–733.29	Musculoskeletal

Chapter 2 of ICD-9-CM also contains codes for carcinoma in situ, neoplasms of uncertain behavior, and neoplasms of unspecified nature.

Carcinoma in situ, also referred to as **ca in situ** or **CIS,** is defined as neoplastic cells undergoing malignant changes that are confined to the original epithelium site without invading surrounding tissues. Common sites of ca in situ include the bladder, breast, cervix, and vulva. Ca in situ is also referred to as transitional cell, noninfiltrating, noninvasive, and preinvasive carcinoma.

Neoplasms of uncertain behavior include cases in which the neoplasm exhibits characteristics of both benign and malignant behavior after pathological investigation. Codes in ICD-9-CM range 235–238 should be assigned only when the pathological documentation concludes that the behavior of the neoplasm cannot be confirmed and further study is needed to arrive at a definitive diagnosis. To specify the purpose of this code range, the following notes appears in the Tabular List after the section heading (Figure 7-2).

NEOPLASMS OF UNCERTAIN BEHAVIOR (235–238)

Note: Categories 235–238 classify by site certain histomorphologically well-defined neoplasms, the subsequent behavior of which cannot be predicted from the present appearance.

Figure 7-2   Note for neoplasms of uncertain behavior

Category 239 is used for **neoplasms of unspecified nature.** This includes cases in which the behavior or **morphology** of the neoplasm is not specified in the patient's medical record. Cases in which this category is used include the following situations:

- A patient is transferred from one facility to another without accompanying medical information, or complete diagnostic studies were not completed at the first facility.
- Complete pathological workup is not completed.
- Patient is an outpatient and pathological study is pending.
- A patient is transferred to a facility to determine the definitive nature of the neoplasm.

NEOPLASMS OF UNSPECIFIED NATURE (239)

239   Neoplasms of unspecified nature

Note: Category 239 classifies by site neoplasms of unspecified morphology and behavior. The term "mass," unless otherwise stated, is not to be regarded as a neoplastic growth.

Includes: "growth" NOS
                 neoplasm NOS
                 new growth NOS
                 tumor NOS

Figure 7-3 Neoplasms of unspecified nature

To specify the purpose of this category, a note is included in the Tabular List after the category heading Neoplasms of unspecified nature (239) (Figure 7-3).

Neoplasm Table

In the Alphabetic Index, codes for neoplasms are located by referencing the name of the neoplasm and using the neoplasm table. The neoplasm table is organized alphabetically by anatomical structure. Once the anatomical site is located, the table lists codes for malignant, benign, uncertain, and unspecified behaviors.

Malignant neoplasms are organized in three columns in the table: primary, secondary, and ca in situ. Ca in situ is used when the pathological report or diagnostic statement records "ca in situ." The column for malignant primary is used when the neoplasm originated from the site being coded. The column for malignant secondary is used when the neoplasm metastasized or spread to the site being coded.

EXAMPLE: To code the term *basal cell carcinoma of the chin*, the coder first references the term *carcinoma* in the Alphabetic Index. The entry appears as shown in Figure 7-4.

Note that the Alphabetic Index instructs the coder to reference "Neoplasm, skin, malignant."

This refers the coder to the neoplasm table. The coder must follow the instruction given to locate the proper type of neoplasm. In this case the neoplasm is malignant. The table groups neoplasms as shown in Figure 7-5.

The table lists anatomical sites and then subterms for some sites. To code basal cell carcinoma of the chin, the coder searches the table for the anatomical site of "skin" and then the subterm *chin*. Columns to the right of the terms list the codes for each type of neoplasm. The appropriate code is then selected from the columns.

To ensure accurate coding, the coder has to carefully read the diagnostic statement to determine whether the site is primary or secondary. The following guidelines should be followed:

1. When a diagnostic phrase reads "metastatic from," the site mentioned is the primary site. A diagnosis of "metastatic carcinoma from the kidneys" means that the carcinoma originated in the kidneys.

2. When a diagnostic phrase reads "metastatic to," the site mentioned is the secondary site. A diagnosis of "metastatic carcinoma to the pancreas" means that the secondary site is the pancreas.

3. When only one site is given without any further information defining the site as primary or secondary, the coder's first reference should always be the medical record. If this is not available or if the information contained in the record is not of help, the following steps should be taken. Suppose the diagnostic phrase to be coded is "metastatic basosquamous carcinoma of the leg."

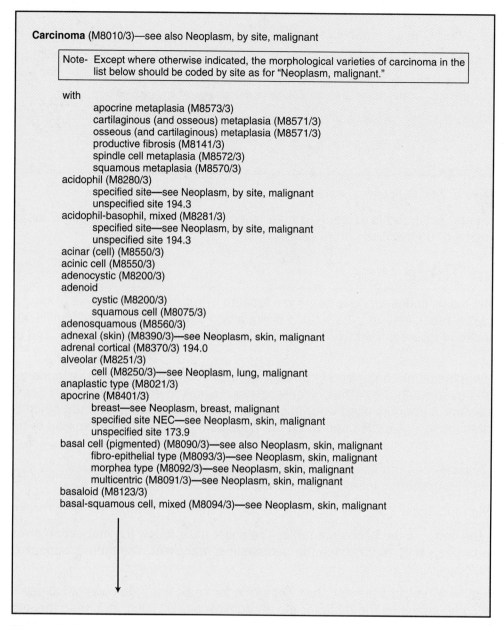

Carcinoma (M8010/3)—see also Neoplasm, by site, malignant

> Note- Except where otherwise indicated, the morphological varieties of carcinoma in the list below should be coded by site as for "Neoplasm, malignant."

with
    apocrine metaplasia (M8573/3)
    cartilaginous (and osseous) metaplasia (M8571/3)
    osseous (and cartilaginous) metaplasia (M8571/3)
    productive fibrosis (M8141/3)
    spindle cell metaplasia (M8572/3)
    squamous metaplasia (M8570/3)
acidophil (M8280/3)
    specified site—see Neoplasm, by site, malignant
    unspecified site 194.3
acidophil-basophil, mixed (M8281/3)
    specified site—see Neoplasm, by site, malignant
    unspecified site 194.3
acinar (cell) (M8550/3)
acinic cell (M8550/3)
adenocystic (M8200/3)
adenoid
    cystic (M8200/3)
    squamous cell (M8075/3)
adenosquamous (M8560/3)
adnexal (skin) (M8390/3)—see Neoplasm, skin, malignant
adrenal cortical (M8370/3) 194.0
alveolar (M8251/3)
    cell (M8250/3)—see Neoplasm, lung, malignant
anaplastic type (M8021/3)
apocrine (M8401/3)
    breast—see Neoplasm, breast, malignant
    specified site NEC—see Neoplasm, skin, malignant
    unspecified site 173.9
basal cell (pigmented) (M8090/3)—see also Neoplasm, skin, malignant
    fibro-epithelial type (M8093/3)—see Neoplasm, skin, malignant
    morphea type (M8092/3)—see Neoplasm, skin, malignant
    multicentric (M8091/3)—see Neoplasm, skin, malignant
basaloid (M8123/3)
basal-squamous cell, mixed (M8094/3)—see Neoplasm, skin, malignant

Figure 7-4 Alphabetical Listing for carcinoma

a. As with any other diagnosis code that needs to be located, the coder first goes to the Alphabetic Index and locates the morphology type of neoplasm. In this case, under "carcinoma" in the Alphabetic Index, "basosquamous" is found. The Alphabetic Index then refers the coder to see "Neoplasm, skin, malignant."

b. The coder now checks the diagnostic statement for subterms that lead to a more specific code assignment. In our example, leg is the site we are looking for.

c. We know this is a metastasis, but we do not know the primary site. Because we do not have a primary site, the code assigned is 198.2 as the primary diagnosis.

d. Because we do not have a primary site assigned, the coder uses the "unknown site or unspecified" on the neoplasm table. The code 199.1, Malignant, primary, is the secondary code reflecting the metastasis.

| | MALIGNANT | | | | Uncertain Behavior | Unspecified |
	Primary	Secondary	Ca in Situ	Benign		
Skin NEC	173.9	198.2	232.9	216.9	238.2	239.2
abdominal wall	173.5	198.2	232.5	216.5	238.2	239.2
ala nasi	173.3	198.2	232.3	216.3	238.2	239.2
ankle	173.7	198.2	232.7	216.7	238.2	239.2
antecubital space	173.6	198.2	232.6	216.6	238.2	239.2
anus	173.5	198.2	232.5	216.5	238.2	239.2
arm	173.6	198.2	232.6	216.6	238.2	239.2
auditory canal (external)	173.2	198.2	232.2	216.2	238.2	239.2
auricle (ear)	173.2	198.2	232.2	216.2	238.2	239.2
auricular canal (external)	173.2	198.2	232.2	216.2	238.2	239.2
axilla, axillary fold	173.5	198.2	232.5	216.5	238.2	239.2
back	173.5	198.2	232.5	216.5	238.2	239.2
breast	173.5	198.2	232.5	216.5	238.2	239.2
brow	173.3	198.2	232.3	216.3	238.2	239.2
buttock	173.5	198.2	232.5	216.5	238.2	239.2
calf	173.7	198.2	232.7	216.7	238.2	239.2
canthus (eye) (inner) (outer)	173.1	198.2	232.1	216.1	238.2	239.2
cervical region	173.4	198.2	232.4	216.4	238.2	239.2
cheek (external)	173.3	198.2	232.3	216.3	238.2	239.2
chest (wall)	173.5	198.2	232.5	216.5	238.2	239.2
chin	173.3	198.2	232.3	216.3	238.2	239.2
clavicular area	173.5	198.2	232.5	216.5	238.2	239.2
clitoris	184.3	198.82	233.3	221.2	236.2	239.5
columnella	173.3	198.2	232.3	216.3	238.2	239.2
concha	173.2	198.2	232.2	216.2	238.2	239.2

Figure 7-5 Alphabetical listing for neoplasms, skin

When the only code that can be used is 199.1 or if the morphology type is not given in the diagnostic explanation, the coder uses 199.1 as primary diagnosis unless the site is one of the following:

- Bone
- Brain
- Diaphragm
- Heart
- Liver
- Lymph nodes
- Mediastinum
- Meninges
- Peritoneum
- Pleura
- Retroperitoneum
- Spinal cord
- Sites classifiable to code 195

When not otherwise specified in the diagnostic description or the medical record, malignant neoplasms of these sites are coded by using the Malignant/Secondary column. The exception to this is the liver. When there is a malignant neoplasm of the liver that is not specified as primary or secondary, a special code designation is given, code 155.2, Liver, not specified as primary or secondary.

When the coder is not given a specific site but does have the morphology type, the morphology type in the Alphabetic Index is referenced to assign the code.

Exercise 7–2   Coding for Neoplasms

For each diagnostic statement listed, select the appropriate code.

1. Subependymal glioma   _____

2. Breast mass   _____

3. Ca of lung   _____

4. Ceruminous adenocarcinoma   _____

5. Metastatic carcinoma to lung   _____

6. Liposarcoma of the shoulder   _____

7. Pheochromocytoma (benign) of
   the adrenal gland   _____

8. Metastatic tumor to the
   common bile duct   _____

9. Amelolbastic odontoma   _____

10. Fibromyoma of the uterus   _____

Sequencing of Codes

When coding for treatment of neoplasms, the coder must read the patient's record to determine the reason for the visit or admission. The record governs the sequencing of the codes used.

Malignancy as Principal Diagnosis

If a patient is seen and the focus of the visit is to treat the neoplasm, then the neoplasm is sequenced as the principal diagnosis, unless the treatment is solely for the purpose of radiotherapy or chemotherapy. (The specific guidelines for coding encounters or admissions involving radiotherapy or chemotherapy will be discussed later in this chapter.) If a patient with cancer is seen for an acute or chronic condition and the treatment is focused on the acute or chronic condition, then the acute or chronic condition becomes the principal diagnosis.

> **Official ICD-9-CM Coding Guidelines:**
>
> *If the treatment is directed at the malignancy, designate the malignancy as the principal diagnosis. (See Appendix A, Section I, C2, A.)*

EXAMPLE: On May 1, Sally Jones was admitted to Hill Top Hospital with a blood sugar level of 375. The following diagnoses were on the face sheet at admission: carcinoma of the breast, uncontrolled insulin-dependent diabetes, and hypertension. She was admitted to control the diabetes. Therefore, for this admission, the diabetes is the principal diagnosis.

The same patient was admitted on September 1 for a mastectomy due to carcinoma of the breast. Although her medical condition also includes insulin-dependent diabetes and hypertension, on this admission the principal diagnosis is the carcinoma of the breast.

Eradication of Malignancy and Follow-Up Examinations

Cancer patients are monitored on a regular basis to monitor recurrence or metastasis. Code selection is based on the status of the patient at the time of the encounter.

Treatment Followed by Recurrence

When a patient is treated for a malignancy, whether it is with chemotherapy, radiation, or surgery, and there is evidence that the cancer has recurred, the code for the primary malignancy is coded as the principal diagnosis.

Follow-Up Visit with No Recurrence

Code category V67 is used when a patient is seen for follow-up after undergoing surgery, chemotherapy, or radiation and no evidence of a recurrence or metastasis exists. An appropriate code from the following should be used:

- V67.09—Follow-up exam following other surgery
- V67.1—Follow-up exam following radiotherapy
- V67.2—Follow-up exam following chemotherapy
- V67.6—Follow-up exam following combined treatment

Excised Malignancy Followed by Recurrence

When a previously excised malignancy recurs, the code for the malignancy is used as the principal diagnosis.

Two Primary Sites

In some malignant cancer cases, two primary sites are present. The coder must determine whether the treatment is directed at one site or both sites. When the treatment is directed at one site, that site should be designated as the principal diagnosis. When the treatment is directed at both sites, either site can be designated as the principal diagnosis.

> **EXAMPLE:** Tom Top has a diagnosis of primary carcinoma of the esophagus and primary carcinoma of the stomach. On February 1, he was admitted for partial removal of carcinogenic esophageal tissue. There was no treatment for the carcinoma of the stomach. In this case the principal diagnosis is the primary carcinoma of esophagus, code 150.9.
>
> On May 1, he was admitted for removal of tissue of the esophagus and stomach due to carcinoma. Because the treatment was directed at two primary sites, either site can be used as the principal diagnosis.

Primary and Secondary Malignancies

When a patient has both primary and secondary malignancies, the coder must determine the focus of treatment to ensure correct code sequencing. Patients with primary and secondary malignancies can be admitted or seen for the following reasons:

- To address the primary malignancy only
- To address the secondary malignancy only
- To address both the primary and secondary malignancies
- To address the secondary site when a primary site has been excised or eradicated

Primary Malignancy Only

When the primary malignancy is the only condition treated, designate the primary malignancy as the principal diagnosis.

Secondary Malignancy Only

When treatment is directed at the secondary or metastatic malignancy only, the secondary site is designated as the principal diagnosis, unless the admission is for radiotherapy or chemotherapy. An additional code is also assigned for the primary site.

> **EXAMPLE:** Bob Pint is admitted for removal of a metastatic tumor of the spinal cord from the lung. The secondary malignant tumor of the spinal cord is the principal diagnosis, and the primary malignant cancer of the lung is used as an additional code.

Official ICD-9-CM Coding Guideline:

When a patient is admitted because of a primary neoplasm with metastasis and treatment is directed toward the secondary site only, the secondary neoplasm is designated as the principal diagnosis even though the primary malignancy is still present. (See Appendix A, Section I, C2, b.)

Primary and Secondary Malignancy

In cases in which treatment is equally directed at both a primary and a secondary malignancy, the primary malignancy is sequenced as the principal diagnosis and the secondary malignancy is sequenced as an additional code.

> **EXAMPLE:** Nate Newman was admitted to the hospital for surgery on a malignant tumor of the pancreas and a malignant tumor of the spleen, which had been discovered with the latest CT scan done before admission. The tumor of the spleen is believed to have metastasized from the pancreas, but this will be confirmed when the pathology report comes back after surgery.
>
> In this case, the pancreatic tumor had already been diagnosed, which made it the primary malignancy. The tumor in the spleen was a new tumor that was going to be removed during the same surgery and is coded as a secondary diagnosis.

Secondary Sites with Excision or Eradication of Primary Site

A patient may undergo treatment for a primary site that could include excision, chemotherapy, and radiation therapy. After such treatment, the site may show no evidence of any existing primary malignancy, and therefore further treatment would not be directed to the primary site. Treatment may then be directed at the secondary site. The secondary site is then used as the principal diagnosis, and the former primary site is assigned a code from category V10, Personal history of a malignant neoplasm.

> **EXAMPLE:** Steve Smith was treated for carcinoma of the gallbladder with metastasis to the lungs. In January he underwent removal of the gallbladder, and currently there is no evidence of the carcinoma in the biliary area. He is now being admitted for removal of his left lung due to cancer. The secondary site of cancer of the lungs is coded and sequenced first, and the previous primary site is coded to V10.09, Personal history of malignant neoplasm.

Official ICD-9-CM Coding Guideline:

When a primary malignancy has been previously excised or eradicated from its site and there is no further treatment directed to that site, and there is no evidence of any existing primary malignancy, a code from category V10, Personal history of malignant neoplasm, should be used to indicate the former site of the malignancy. Any mention of extension, invasion, or metastasis to another site is coded as a secondary malignant neoplasm to that site. The secondary site may be the principal or first-listed with the V10 code used as a secondary code. (See Appendix A, Section I, C2, d.)

Coders should be cautious when looking up "personal history of a malignant neoplasm" in the Alphabetic Index. Be sure to pay particular attention to the indentations because there is also a category for family history of malignant neoplasms.

EXAMPLE: Adriana Romano was diagnosed with breast cancer, code 174.9, in 2002 and underwent treatment with no evidence of malignancy in 2008. Today (December 30, 2008), she presents with fatigue. Today's visit is coded 780.79 to code the fatigue, and code V10.3 is added to report the personal history of breast cancer.

Contiguous Sites

In some cases, a physician cannot determine the origin of the neoplasm because the site or origin appears to be contiguous, meaning that it is of two adjacent sites. In these cases a fourth digit of 8 is used to signify that there are overlapping sites.

EXAMPLE: Jim Brooks has been diagnosed with cancer of the gallbladder and hepatic ducts. The primary site cannot be determined. Code 156.8 is used to code a malignant neoplasm of the gallbladder and hepatic bile ducts. When the Tabular List for code 156.8 is referenced, the entry appears as shown in Figure 7-6.

156	**Malignant neoplasm of gallbladder and extrahepatic bile ducts**
156.0	Gallbladder
156.1	Extrahepatic bile ducts
	Biliary duct or passage NOS
	Common bile duct
	Cystic duct
	Hepatic duct
	Sphincter of Oddi
156.2	Ampulla of Vater
156.8	Other specified sites of gallbladder and extrahepatic bile ducts
	Malignant neoplasm of contiguous or overlapping sites of gallbladder and extrahepatic bile ducts whose point of origin cannot be determined
156.9	Biliary tract, part unspecified
	Malignant neoplasm involving both intrahepatic and extrahepatic bile ducts

Figure 7-6 Tabular listing for malignant neoplasm of gallbladder and extrahepatic bile ducts

Complications Associated with Neoplasms

There are numerous complications associated with malignant neoplasms and their treatment. Patients commonly seek healthcare that is directed at the treatment of the complications and not at the treatment of the neoplasm.

Anemia

Cancer patients can experience anemia, a deficiency of the red blood cells, caused by the malignancy or chemotherapy. When encounters or admissions occur for the management of the anemia, the following coding guidelines should be followed:

Official ICD-9-CM Coding Guideline:

1. *When the admission/encounter is for management of an anemia associated with the malignancy and the treatment is only for anemia, the appropriate anemia code (such as code 285.22, Anemia in neoplastic disease) is designated as the principal diagnosis and is followed by the appropriate code(s) for the malignancy. Code 285.22 may also be used as a secondary code if the patient suffers from anemia and is being treated for the malignancy.*

2. *When the admission/encounter is for management of an anemia associated with chemotherapy, immunotherapy or radiotherapy and the only treatment is for the anemia, the anemia is sequenced first, followed by code E933.1. The appropriate neoplasm code should be assigned as an additional code. (See Appendix A, Section I, C2, c, 1–2.)*

EXAMPLE: Patty Pink is diagnosed with carcinoma of the breast and is undergoing chemotherapy. She has developed anemia from the chemotherapy and is being admitted for management of the anemia. Because she is being admitted for the treatment of the anemia, the anemia is sequenced first, followed by the code for the carcinoma of the breast.

Dehydration

Dehydration, excess loss of fluids, is also a complication that can occur owing to vomiting and diarrhea caused by the malignancy, chemotherapy, or radiation therapy. When a patient has experienced dehydration, an encounter or admission may be necessary to rehydrate the patient.

EXAMPLE: Sally Smith has been undergoing radiation therapy for leukemia on an outpatient basis. She has experienced diarrhea and vomiting and is now dehydrated. Her physician is admitting her to Sunny Hill Hospital to receive intravenous rehydration. In this case the dehydration is sequenced as the principal diagnosis, followed by a code for the leukemia.

Official ICD-9-CM Coding Guideline:

When the admission/encounter is for management of dehydration due to the malignancy or the therapy or a combination of both, and only the dehydration is being treated (intravenous rehydration), the dehydration is sequenced first, followed by the code(s)for the malignancy. (See Appendix A, Section I, C2, c, 3.)

Surgical Procedure Performed for Treatment of a Malignancy

Sometimes a malignancy requires surgical intervention. If a complication is results from the surgery, the complication is coded as the primary diagnosis when an admission or encounter is needed.

EXAMPLE: Amanda Pan had surgery on a malignant tumor of the small intestine. One month after the surgery, Amanda developed an infection that required treatment with antibiotics. In this example, the infection is coded first, then the tumor.

Official ICD-9-CM Coding Guideline:

When the admission/encounter is for treatment of a complication resulting from a surgical procedure designate the complication as the principal or first-listed diagnosis if treatment is directed at resolving the complication. (See Appendix A, Section I, C2, c, 4.)

Pain

As the malignancy progresses and as treatment occurs, cancer patients sometimes experience pain that can result in depression, anxiety, difficulty sleeping, and loss of appetite. Narcotic medications may be necessary to control the pain. If a patient seeks medical care or is admitted for control of the pain, the malignancy code is designated as the principal diagnosis. Even though ICD-9-CM has codes for pain, which are mostly found in chapter 16, "Symptoms, Signs, and Ill-Defined Conditions," the malignancy code is used.

Official ICD-9-CM Coding Guideline:

Symptoms, signs, and ill-defined conditions listed in chapter 16 characteristic of, or associated with, an existing primary or secondary site malignancy cannot be used to replace the malignancy as principal or first-listed diagnosis, regardless of the number of admissions or encounters for treatment and care of the neoplasm. (See Appendix A, Section I, C2, g.)

Admissions or Encounters Involving Surgery, Chemotherapy, and Radiation Therapy

After a patient has been diagnosed with a malignant condition, treatment options can include surgery, chemotherapy, radiation therapy, or a combination of treatments. A coder must identify the treatment occurring during the current encounter or admission.

Surgery Followed by Chemotherapy or Radiation

In some cases a patient will undergo surgery to remove the cancerous tissue and then undergo chemotherapy or radiation.

>   **EXAMPLE:** Sally Pink, who was diagnosed with carcinoma of the breast, was admitted for a total mastectomy followed by radiation therapy. In this case the carcinoma of the breast is the principal diagnosis.

Official ICD-9-CM Coding Guideline:

When an episode of care involves the surgical removal of a neoplasm, primary or secondary site, followed by adjunct chemotherapy or radiation treatment during the same episode of care, the neoplasm code should be assigned as the principal or first-listed diagnosis, using codes in the 140–198 series or where appropriate in the 200–203 series. (See Appendix A, Section I, C2, e, 1.)

Encounter or Admission Solely for Administration of Chemotherapy or Radiation

ICD-9-CM provides the following two codes for encounters or admissions solely for treatment by chemotherapy or radiation:

V58.0—Encounters for radiation therapy

V58.11—Encounters for antineoplastic chemotherapy

V58.12—Encounters for antineoplastic immunotherapy

>   **EXAMPLE:** Mary Ann Jones was admitted for chemotherapy for plasma cell leukemia. The principal diagnosis or code listed first is V58.11, Encounters for antineoplastic chemotherapy. A code for the plasma cell leukemia, 203.10, is also assigned as an additional code.

>   **EXAMPLE:** Mary Ann Jones's physician has decided not only to have her receive chemotherapy but also to follow the treatment with radiation therapy. Codes V58.0, Encounters for radiation therapy, and V58.11, Encounters for antineoplastic chemotherapy, should be used. Either can be sequenced first.

Official ICD-9-CM Coding Guideline:

If a patient admission/encounter is solely for the administration of chemotherapy, immunotherapy, or radiation therapy, assign code V58.0, Encounter for radiation therapy, or V58.11, Encounter for antineoplastic chemotherapy, or V58.12, Encounter for antineoplastic immunotherapy, as the first-listed or principal diagnosis. If a patient receives more than one of these therapies during the same admission more than one of these codes may be assigned, in any sequence. (See Appendix A, Section I, C2, e, 2.)

Chemotherapy or Radiation Therapy Followed by Complications

It is common for patients to experience nausea, vomiting, and dehydration after chemotherapy or radiation therapy. When a patient is admitted for the purpose of chemotherapy or radiation and subsequently develops a complication, the principal diagnosis code is the code for the chemotherapy or radiation therapy, followed by the code for the malignancy and the complication.

> **EXAMPLE:** Sally Jones was admitted for radiation therapy for giant-cell leukemia, and immediately after the treatment, she developed nausea and excessive vomiting. She was treated for the nausea and vomiting. Code V58.0, Encounter for radiation therapy, is sequenced first, followed by code 207.20, Giant-cell leukemia, and code 787.01, Nausea and vomiting.

Official ICD-9-CM Coding Guidelines:

When a patient is admitted for the purpose of radiotherapy, immunotherapy, or chemotherapy and develops complications such as uncontrolled nausea and vomiting or dehydration, the principal or first-listed diagnosis is V58.0, Encounter for radiotherapy, or V58.11, Encounter for antineoplastic chemotherapy, or V58.12, Encounter for antineoplastic immunotherapy, followed by any codes for the complications. (See Appendix A, Section I, C2, e, 3.)

Admission or Encounter to Determine Extent of Malignancy or to Perform a Procedure

At times patients are seen for a paracentesis, which is a surgical puncture of the abdominal cavity for aspiration of fluid, or a thoracentesis, which is a surgical procedure for aspiration of fluid in the chest wall or to determine the extent of a malignancy. In these cases the primary malignancy or metastatic site is the primary diagnosis, even if radiation or chemotherapy is administered.

When an admission or encounter occurs to determine the extent of malignancy or to perform a procedure, the following guideline should be followed:

Official ICD-9-CM Coding Guideline:

When the reason for the admission/encounter is to determine the extent of the malignancy, or for a procedure such as paracentesis or thoracentesis, the primary malignancy or appropriate metastatic site is designated as the principal or first-listed diagnosis, even though chemotherapy or radiotherapy is administered. (See Appendix A, Section I, C2, f.)

Internet Links

For a complete list of approved cancer drugs, go to *www.fda.gov/cder/cancer*.

For information on cancer, visit the American Cancer Society Web site at *www.cancer.org*.

For information on cancer research, visit *www.cancer.gov/cancerinfo/literature*.

For guidelines for the sequencing of neoplasms visit *www.fortherecordmag.com/archives*. Reference the July 9, 2007, issue.

Summary

- Neoplasms are classified as malignant, benign, cancer in situ, of uncertain behavior, and unspecified.

- A biopsy is completed to determine whether a neoplasm is malignant or benign.

- Carcinoma in situ is defined as neoplastic cells undergoing malignant changes that are confined to the original epithelium site without invading surrounding tissues.

- Neoplasms of uncertain behavior include cases in which the neoplasm exhibits characteristics of both benign and malignant behavior.

- Neoplasms of unspecified nature include cases in which the behavior or morphology of the neoplasm is not specified in the patient's medical record.

- In the Alphabetic Index, codes for neoplasms are located by referencing the name of the neoplasm and by using the neoplasm table.

- Sequencing of codes for neoplasms depends on the reason for the encounter or admission.

Chapter Review

True/False: Indicate whether each statement is true (T) or false (F).

1. _____ There is no differentiation between malignant and benign neoplasm in ICD-9-CM.

2. _____ Lipoma and chondroma are malignant neoplasms.

3. _____ Carcinoma of the breast is malignant.

4. _____ The neoplasm table is organized by anatomical site.

5. _____ In the neoplasm table, benign neoplasms are divided into primary and secondary sites.

6. _____ When a patient is seen for chemotherapy, the neoplasm is sequenced as the principal diagnosis.

7. _____ If treatment is directed at a malignancy and the patient is also treated for an acute condition, the malignancy is designated as the principal diagnosis.

8. _____ When cancer treatment is equally directed at both a primary and a secondary site, the principal diagnosis is the primary site.

9. _____ Narcotic medications are used to control the pain of cancer patients.

10. _____ When a patient is admitted with a primary neoplasm with metastasis and treatment is directed toward the secondary site, the secondary neoplasm is designated as the principal diagnosis.

Fill-in-the-Blank: Enter the appropriate term(s) to complete each statement.

11. Carcinoma in situ is also referred to as _____.

12. If a cancer patient is seen for an acute condition and the treatment is focused on the acute condition, then the _____ is the principal diagnosis.

13. Cancer patients are seen on a regular basis to monitor recurrence or _____.

14. Benign neoplasm usually grow _____ and do not _____.

15. A benign neoplasm of adipose tissue is known as a(n) _____.

16. A biopsy or _____ report will provide definitive information about the type of neoplasm present.

17. When a diagnostic phrase reads "metastatic from," the site mentioned is the _____ site.

18. When a previously excised malignancy recurs, the code for the _____ is used as the principal diagnosis.

19. Carcinoma of two adjacent sites is known as _____.

20. When an admission occurs for the management of anemia associated with a malignancy and the treatment is for the anemia, the _____ is designated as the principal diagnosis.

Coding Assignments

Instructions: Using an ICD-9-CM coding book, select the code for each diagnostic statement.

Diagnosis	Code
1. Carcinoma of mouth	_____
2. Adenocarcinoma of adrenal cortical	_____
3. Left kidney lipoma	_____
4. Leiomyoma of uterus	_____
5. Neoplasm of anterior wall of urinary bladder, malignant	_____
6. Plasma cell leukemia	_____
7. Lymphosarcoma	_____
8. Acute promyelocytic leukemia	_____
9. Secondary malignant neoplasm of skin	_____
10. Carcinoma of uterine cervix	_____
11. Carcinoma of bone	_____
12. Carcinoma in situ of bladder	_____
13. Primary neoplasm of ovary	_____
14. Secondary cancer of islet cells of pancreas	_____
15. Cancer of prostate gland	_____
16. Neoplasm of uncertain behavior of renal pelvis	_____
17. Basal cell carcinoma of skin on scalp	_____

18. Sampson's tumor _____

19. Wilm's nephroblastoma _____

20. Benign neoplasm of abdomen _____

21. Benign neoplasm of the bursa of the shoulder _____

22. CIS of the rectosigmoid junction _____

23. Malignant neoplasm of the adrenal gland with metastasis to the kidney _____

24. Metastatic cancer from the bladder to the ureter _____

25. Cancer of the stomach _____

Case Studies

Instructions: Review each case study, and select the correct ICD-9-CM diagnostic code.

CASE 1

Physician's Office Note

4/25/XX   Weight: 154 pounds, decrease from 2 weeks ago; weight then was 160.

CHIEF COMPLAINT: loss of weight, here for follow-up from breast biopsy.

Sally was seen 2 weeks ago, and I palpated a mass in her left breast. She was sent for a biopsy. She is here today for follow-up.

BREAST: Mass present in left breast; right breast has no masses present.

ABDOMEN: Normal, no masses or tenderness.

Patient is anxious about results of biopsy.

Pathology report reviewed with patient that confirmed cancer of breast. Patient was referred to Dr. Smith at West Oncology.

ICD-9-CM Code Assignment: _____

CASE 2

Inpatient Discharge Summary

HISTORY OF PRESENT ILLNESS:

The patient is a 76-year-old with a known history of cancer of the lung with metastasis to the brain. Cancer of lung was resected 6 months ago. The patient was admitted because his daughter noticed him getting weaker and because he was not eating or drinking well for the last 2 days. He has undergone chemotherapy and radiation in the past 5 months, and he has asked for the treatment to be stopped. Upon examination at the time of admission, he was dehydrated and weak due to lack of eating.

HOSPITAL COURSE:

Patient requested that he receive care only for his dehydration. He was given IV hydration and refused all other treatment.

MEDICATIONS AT DISCHARGE: Patient was discharged on Vicodin for pain management, 1 every 4 hours as needed for pain.

DISCHARGE DIAGNOSES: Dehydration, metastatic cancer to lung

ICD-9-CM Code Assignment: _____

CASE 3

Oncology Clinic Note

Patient is seen today to establish a schedule for his chemotherapy regime for his diagnosis of acute lymphoid leukemia.

EXAM:

VITALS: Temperature 98.9, B/P 125/80. Pulse: regular.

LUNGS: Normal

ABDOMEN: Soft, no masses noted.

HEENT: Normal

HEART: Normal rate and rhythm

Chemotherapy schedule was reviewed, and side effects of treatment were discussed. Chemotherapy to start on 4/23/XX.

ICD-9-CM Code Assignment: _____

CASE 4

Ellen is a 65-year-old female who presents today with severe headaches and blurred vision. She said these symptoms have been going on for approximately 2 weeks. She says that the pain is 10 out of 10 and that nothing seems to help relieve it. She has a history of breast cancer, which has been in remission for one year. A CT scan of the head and neck reveals a tumor in the temporal lobe of the brain. A biopsy was performed and confirmed this to be a metastasis from the breast tumor.

ICD-9-CM Code Assignment: _____

CASE 5

A 52-year-old female presented with a 1-year history of epiphora. During this year, the tears were not bloodstained but very much a nuisance to the patient. CT revealed a small tumor connected to the lacrimal sac and duct. Incisional biopsy revealed a benign tumor of the lacrimal sac. The patient was treated by removing the tumor.

ICD-9-CM Code Assignment: _____

Endocrine, Nutritional, and Metabolic Diseases and Immunity Disorders

CHAPTER 8

Chapter Outline

Introduction

Introduction to the Body System

Coding of Endocrine, Nutritional, and Metabolic Diseases and Immunity Disorders

Internet Links

Summary

Chapter Review

Coding Assignments

Case Studies

Objectives

At the conclusion of this chapter, the student will be able to:

1. Understand how hormones influence functions within the body.
2. Distinguish between the different types of diabetes and select ICD-9-CM codes for the various types of diabetes.
3. Apply the ICD-9-CM coding guidelines to endocrine and metabolic disorders.
4. Describe diseases that are classified to this chapter.
5. Accurately code endocrine, nutritional, metabolic, and immune diseases.
6. Select and code diagnoses and procedures from case studies.

Key Terms

Adult Onset Diabetes

Diabetes Mellitus

Endocrine System

Glucose

Goiter

Gout

Hormones

Hyperthyroidism

Hypothyroidism

Insulin

Insulin-Dependent Diabetes Mellitus (IDDM)

Juvenile Diabetes

Metabolism

Non-Insulin-Dependent Diabetes Mellitus (NIDDM)

Pancreas

Thyroid Gland

Thyroiditis

Thyrotoxic Crisis

Thyrotoxic Storm

Type I Diabetes Mellitus

Type II Diabetes Mellitus

> **Reminder**
>
> *As you work through this chapter, you will need to have a copy of the ICD-9-CM coding book to reference.*

Introduction

Chapter 3 of the ICD-9-CM, "Endocrine, Nutritional, and Metabolic Diseases and Immunity Disorders," classifies conditions that affect the endocrine system, nutritional deficiencies unrelated to diseases of blood, metabolic diseases, and immunity disorders. The most commonly used codes in this chapter relate to diabetes mellitus, which is a chronic disorder resulting from a problem with the pancreas. The pancreas is anatomically located under the stomach in the upper abdomen and performs various physiological functions. One of these functions is secreting digestive hormones into the gastrointestinal tract to aid in digestion. The other function is to regulate insulin in the body. Insulin is used in the body to process glucose. If the pancreas does not regulate the insulin properly or does not produce insulin at all, glucose levels are thrown out of control. Glucose is needed for the cells to properly supply energy for the body's metabolic functions.

Nutritional and metabolic disorders, with the exception of anemias caused by nutritional deficiencies, are also classified to this chapter. Anemias caused by nutritional deficiencies are classified to chapter 4 of ICD-9-CM, "Diseases of the Blood and Blood-Forming Organs." The nutritional and metabolic disorders classified to chapter 3 of ICD-9-CM are caused by deficiencies of vitamins, minerals, and proteins, as well as other conditions such as obesity, gout, and carbohydrate and lipid imbalances.

It should be noted that some endocrine and metabolic disturbances—such as conditions that affect pregnancy and neonates and certain types of anemia resulting from nutritional deficiencies—are coded to other chapters in ICD-9-CM. Coders should read the Exclude: notes throughout chapter 3 to become familiar with the conditions that are excluded from this chapter.

Introduction to the Body System

The endocrine system (endo means "within, -crin means "to secrete") consists of several different internal groups of glands and structures that produce or secrete hormones. Figure 8-1 illustrates the structures of the endocrine system. Hormones are chemical substances produced by the body to keep organs and tissues functioning properly. Each hormone has a specific function, as summarized in Figure 8-2.

When chemical changes occur within the body, hormone release may be either increased or decreased, provided that the organ producing the hormone is functioning properly. When endocrine body structures do not function properly, hormones are not released.

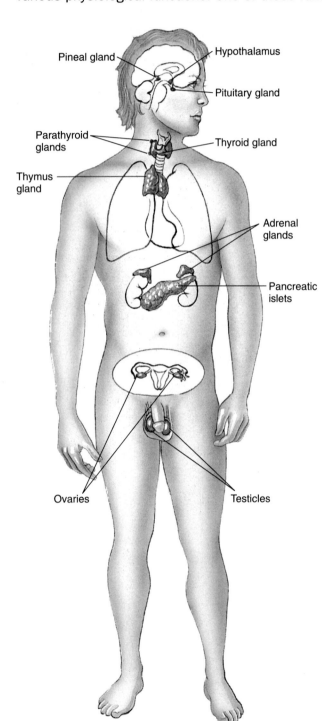

Pineal gland
Hypothalamus
Pituitary gland
Parathyroid glands
Thyroid gland
Thymus gland
Adrenal glands
Pancreatic islets
Ovaries
Testicles

Figure 8-1   Structures of the endocrine system

Hormone	Functions
Aldosterone	Aids in regulating the levels of salt and water in the body.
Androgens	Influence sex-related characteristics.
Adrenocorticotropic hormone (ACTH)	Stimulates the growth and secretions of the adrenal cortex.
Antidiuretic hormone (ADH)	Helps control blood pressure by reducing the amount of water that is excreted.
Calcitonin	Works with the parathyroid hormone to regulate calcium levels in the blood and tissues.
Cortisol	Regulates the metabolism of carbohydrates, fats, and proteins in the body. Also has an anti-inflammatory action.
Epinephrine	Stimulates the sympathetic nervous system.
Estrogen	Develops and maintains the female secondary sex characteristics and regulates the menstrual cycle.
Follicle-stimulating hormone (FSH)	In the female, stimulates the secretion of estrogen and the growth of ova (eggs). In the male, stimulates the production of sperm.
Glucagon	Increases the level of glucose in the bloodstream.
Growth hormone (GH)	Regulates the growth of bone, muscle, and other body tissues.
Human chorionic gonadotropin (HCG)	Stimulates the secretion of the hormones required to maintain the pregnancy.
Insulin (In)	Regulates the transport of glucose to body cells and stimulates the conversion of excess glucose to glycogen for storage.
Lactogenic hormone (LTH)	Stimulates and maintains the secretion of breast milk.
Luteinizing hormone (LH)	In the female, stimulates ovulation. In the male, stimulates testosterone secretion.
Melatonin	Influences the sleep-wakefulness cycles.
Norepinephrine	Stimulates the sympathetic nervous system.
Oxytocin (OXT)	Stimulates uterine contractions during childbirth. Causes milk to flow from the mammary glands after birth.
Parathyroid hormone (PTH)	Works with calcitonin to regulate calcium levels in the blood and tissues.
Progesterone	Completes preparation of the uterus for possible pregnancy.
Testosterone	Stimulates the development of male secondary sex characteristics.
Thymosin	Plays an important role in the immune system.
Thyroid hormones (T_4 and T_3)	Regulates the rate of metabolism.
Thyroid-stimulating hormone (TSH)	Stimulates the secretion of hormones by the thyroid gland.

Figure 8-2 Hormones and functions

EXAMPLE: The thyroid gland secretes hormones that regulate growth and metabolism. A condition known as hypothyroidism occurs when the thyroid is not as active as it should be, thus creating a deficiency of thyroid hormone secretion. An underactive thyroid, left undiagnosed, can cause conditions such as depression, sensitivity to cold, and fatigue. Medications can be prescribed to stimulate or replace the needed hormones to get the thyroid hormones back in balance.

Coding of Endocrine, Nutritional, and Metabolic Diseases and Immunity Disorders

Chapter 3 of ICD-9-CM is organized into the following sections:

- Disorders of the thyroid gland—Category codes 240–246

- Diseases of other endocrine glands—Category codes 249–259

- Nutritional deficiencies—Category codes 260–269

- Other metabolic and immunity disorders—Category codes 270–279

Disorders of the Thyroid Gland (Category Codes 240–246)

ICD-9-CM classifies disorders of the thyroid gland to category codes 240–246. The primary function of the thyroid gland is to regulate the body's metabolism, which is the rate at which energy is used by the body and at which body functions occur.

Common conditions that are classified to this code range are different types of goiters. When hormone secretions fall within normal limits but the thyroid itself becomes enlarged, this condition is known as a goiter. Lack of iodine in the system may be the cause of an enlarged thyroid.

Other conditions affecting the thyroid include hypothyroidism, which is an underactive thyroid, and hyperthyroidism, which occurs when the thyroid oversecretes hormones, causing excessive amounts of thyroid hormones in the blood. Hyperthyroidism can cause weight loss, nervousness, tachycardia, and goiters. In some extreme cases of hyperthyroidism, known as thyrotoxic crisis or thyrotoxic storm, the symptoms of hyperthyroidism are so severe that it puts the patient in a life-threatening situation or crisis.

Codes 242.0–242.9, which classify various types of hyperthyroidsm, require a fifth digit to identify whether the record documents the presence of a thyrotoxic crisis or storm. The following fifth digits are used:

```
0—without mention of thyrotoxic crisis or storm
1—with mention of thyrotoxic crisis or storm
```

Another common condition, thyroiditis (an inflammation of the thyroid gland) is classified to category code 245. It should be noted that fourth digits are used to identify whether the condition is acute, subacute, chronic, or unspecified. Documentation needs to be reviewed to justify the fourth-digit selection.

Disease Highlight—Hypothyroidism

Hypothyroidism occurs when there is a decrease in the production of the thyroid hormone secondary to the dysfunction of the thyroid gland. The causes of the decreased function may relate to surgery, inflammatory conditions, irradiation therapy, and chronic autoimmune thyroid diseases.

Signs and Symptoms:

In the early stages of hypothyroidism the patient presents with:

- Fatigue

- Weakness

- Muscle cramps
- Constipation
- Arthralgias
- Headache
- Thinning of nails and hair

In the later stages the patient may have:

- Slow speech
- Thickening of the tongue
- Puffiness of the face and eyelids
- Decreased sense of smell and taste
- Dyspnea
- Pitting edema
- Hypoventilation
- Hypoxia
- Hypothermia
- Hyponatremia
- Hypotension

Clinical Testing:

The following results of lab testing indicate hypothyroidism:

- An increase in serum cholesterol and prolactin
- Elevated liver enzymes and creatine
- An increase in TSH
- Low to normal serum T4 levels

Treatment:

Patients are treated with medication, the most common of which is Levothyroxine.

Exercise 8–1   Coding of Category Codes 240–246

Select the appropriate ICD-9-CM code for each diagnostic statement listed.

1. Multinodular goiter _____

2. Congenital hypothyroidism _____

3. Atrophy of thyroid _____

4. Congenital thyroid insufficiency _____

5. Cyst of thyroid _____

6. Pyogenic thyroiditis _____

7. Hashimoto's disease   _____

8. Thyroiditis   _____

9. Iatrogenic hypothyroidism   _____

10. Thyrotoxicosis from ingestion of excessive thyroid material with mention of thyrotoxic crisis   _____

Diseases of Other Endocrine Glands (Category Codes 249–259)

One of the most used sections of chapter 3 are codes 249–259, Diseases of other endocrine glands. This section includes codes for diabetes mellitus, a complex metabolic disease characterized by hyperglycemia caused by defects in insulin secretion, insulin action, or both. There are various types of diabetes that are identified by the severity of the disorder within the pancreas and the onset of the disease. It should be noted that category code 249 codes secondary diabetes mellitus. Secondary diabetes mellitus develops as a result of or secondary to another disease of condition. Coders need to be familiar with the includes and excludes notes that appear under the heading for category code 249.

When the pancreas does not secrete insulin at all or when an insufficient amount of insulin is secreted, the patients are diagnosed as having type I diabetes mellitus. The onset for type I diabetes is generally between puberty and adulthood, but it can also occur at birth; thus the term juvenile diabetes is used to describe this type of diabetes. Type I diabetes is also referred to as juvenile type, juvenile-onset, or ketosis-prone diabetes. Symptoms of the disease are increased hunger, frequent urination, and thirst. The person with type I diabetes takes injections of insulin to replace the insulin not being produced by the pancreas. These insulin injections are necessary to keep the person alive. Blood sugars need to be monitored very carefully to prevent serious or life-threatening conditions.

The other type of diabetes is type II diabetes mellitus, or adult-onset diabetes. Type II diabetes results from the body's inability to produce sufficient amounts of insulin or its inability to process the insulin it does produce. This type of diabetes is usually the type that develops later on in life; type II diabetes is far more common than type I diabetes. The symptoms of type II diabetes are the same as that of type I. Whereas patients with type I diabetes require injections of insulin to maintain control of their diabetes, type II diabetes is controlled by diet, exercise, and oral medications. If the oral medications are not successful in bringing insulin levels under control, then insulin injections may be necessary.

> **Official ICD-9-CM Coding Guideline:**
>
> *If the type of diabetes mellitus is not documented in the medical record, the default is type II. (See Appendix A, Section I, C3, a2.)*

Providers rarely write out the insulin dependency of a patient; the abbreviations IDDM or NIDDM are used instead. These two abbreviations stand for insulin-dependent diabetes mellitus and non-insulin-dependent diabetes mellitus, respectively. The coder may see type II NIDDM or type II IDDM on the note to distinguish the use of insulin or not. Type II diabetics can be either insulin-dependent or non-insulin-dependent, and clarification needs to be made before the encounter is coded. Type I diabetes is always insulin-dependent. The other factor in determining proper code selection depends on whether the diabetic is controlled. The determination as to whether the patient is under control is a clinical determination that needs to be clarified for the coder by the provider if this information is not documented in the patient's medical record.

Official ICD-9-CM Coding Guideline:

If the documentation in a medical record does not indicate the type of diabetes but does indicate that the patient uses insulin, the appropriate fifth-digit for type II must be used. For type II patients who routinely use insulin, code V58.67, Long-term (current) use of insulin, should be assigned to indicate that the patient uses insulin. Code V58.67 should not be assigned if insulin is given temporarily to bring a type II patient's blood sugar under control during an encounter. (See Appendix A, Section I, C3, a3.)

Because diabetes can cause such a wide range of complications involving the eyes, circulation, kidneys, skin, and heart, the coder must carefully read the record to determine the relationship of the diabetes to the conditions that a patient has. Sometimes a note will state "with diabetes," but clarification needs to be made as to whether a condition is "caused by" or "secondary to" before diabetic complications are assigned codes. The diabetes section is one of the few categories in ICD-9-CM that is used as a primary code when classifying the disease (diabetes) and its major manifestations (e.g., neuropathy, hyperosmolarity, peripheral circulatory disorders).

Official ICD-9-CM Coding Guideline:

When assigning codes for diabetes and its associated conditions, the code(s) from category 250 must be sequenced before the codes for the associated conditions. The diabetes codes and the secondary codes that correspond to them are paired codes that follow the etiology/manifestation convention of the classification. (See Section I.A.6., Etiology/manifestation convention.) Assign as many codes from category 250 as needed to identify all of the associated conditions that the patient has. The corresponding secondary codes are listed under each of the diabetes codes. (See Appendix A, Section I, C3, A4.)

EXAMPLE: A provider's note reads as follows: Patient presents with type II, uncontrolled IDDM and an ulceration of the calf of the leg, due to his type II IDDM. The codes assigned are 250.82 Diabetes with other manifestations, 707.12 for the ulceration of the lower leg, and V58.67 for the insulin use.

The 250 series of codes used to code diabetes requires a fourth- and fifth-digit assignment. The fourth digit is used to indicate the presence of a complication that is a direct result of the diabetes. The fifth digit distinguishes whether the condition was controlled or uncontrolled, and until October 2004, the fifth-digit assignment also indicated whether there was insulin dependence or not. In October 2004 the Centers for Medicare and Medicaid Services (CMS) announced that it was deleting the insulin/non-insulin designations from the descriptions listed in the box for fifth-digit assignment. The fifth digits currently read as follows:

Fifth Digit	Description
0	Type II or unspecified type, not stated as uncontrolled
1	Type I (juvenile type), not stated as uncontrolled
2	Type II or unspecified type, uncontrolled
3	Type I (juvenile type), uncontrolled

This change occurred because providers have been assigning a type I descriptor to patients who really have type II diabetes. Fifth digits are still needed, and providers will assign the fifth digit according to the actual type of diabetes the patient has. The hope is that with the deletion of the insulin descriptors, coding confusion will be avoided. The provider's documentation is key and still needs to be as accurate as possible. It should clearly state which type of diabetes the patient has.

EXAMPLE: An elderly patient presents for follow-up of his diabetic neuropathy. He brought the log of his blood sugar readings for the past month. This log was reviewed with him and showed him to be in good control. He has been insulin dependent now for 6 years.

This visit was due to the man's diabetic neuropathy. To code this visit, the coder starts with the Alphabetic Index, locating the term *diabetes* and then the subterm *neuropathy*. The codes listed are 250.6X and 357.2. Note that an instructional note appears after the main term *diabetes* instructing the coder that fifth digits are needed for category code 250. Verification of the code in the Tabular Listing indicates the correct code assignment. The 250 indicates the diabetes, and the fourth digit of 6 indicates that the patient has a neuropathy.

The fifth digit still has to be determined. The patient has been "insulin dependent for 6 years" and is elderly, indicating type II diabetes. The note also states that this gentleman is "in good control." Because of these two factors, the fifth digit assigned here is 0. Our code assignment for this visit is 250.60. Keep in mind that diabetes is never coded as "out of control" unless the provider clearly documents this.

The code of 357.2 is assigned to identify the neurological manifestations and code V58.67 to identify the insulin dependence.

As diabetes progresses, complications of the disease occur. Figure 8-3 describes complications and manifestations of the disease and the subcategory codes for the various complications.

Exercise 8–2   Endocrine and Metabolic Disorders

Fill-in-the-Blank: Enter the appropriate term(s) to complete each statement.

1. A condition that occurs when the thyroid is not as active as it should be is referred to as _____.

2. A chronic disorder that results from a problem with the pancreas not secreting insulin properly is called _____.

3. The thyroid gland secretes hormones that regulate _____.

4. Diabetes mellitus falls into the _____ series of codes.

5. The fourth digit in the assignment of codes for diabetes indicates the presence of a _____.

6. The fifth digit in this assignment of codes for diabetes distinguishes whether the condition is _____ or _____.

7. _____ diabetes is a type of diabetes that occurs in pregnant women.

8. When you see code 250.4X, you are able to tell that this patient has _____, which involves complications due to diabetes.

9. The type of diabetes that is always insulin dependent is type _____.

10. Because of the complications and manifestations that can occur with diabetic patients, provider _____ is key to correct code assignment.

Complications/ Manifestations	Description	Code Range	Notes
Ketoacidosis	Large quantities of ketones cause elevated acid levels in blood and urine.	250.1X	Most commonly found in type I diabetes; reference to provider note is key.
Hyperosmolarity	Causes dehydration due to the cells not functioning properly.	250.2X	Coma may or may not be present and most often occurs in type II diabetes; reference to provider note is key.
Diabetes with other coma	Some diabetics can go into a coma if there is an imbalance in their eating and exercise patterns; coma can also be caused by insulin when adjustments are being made in dosage.	250.3X	Coding will be different if patient is not a diabetic; this code set is only for diabetic patients; some of the conditions that would cause a coma in a diabetic patient can be present without the person being in a coma; in this case the coder refers to the 250.8X section.
Renal complications	Causes chronic renal failure, nephrosis, nephritis.	250.4X	Because of a cause-and-effect relationship between diabetes and renal conditions, the diabetes is coded first with the renal disease second; if documentation is not clear on this, then the codes are reversed with the renal disease first and the diabetes second; reference to provider note is key.
Eye disease	Includes diseases of the retina known as diabetic retinopathy where the diabetes has caused damage to the retina; complications involving the eyes are common in diabetics.	250.5X	A direct connection must be made by the physician with regard to diabetes and eye conditions.
Peripheral vascular disease	This common complication in diabetic can lead to gangrene or ischemia of the lower limbs.	250.7X	Unless a causal relationship is documented, cerebrovascular disease, coronary artery disease, and cardiomyopathy are not included in this subsection and are coded separately.
Gestational diabetes	Occurs in pregnant women only during their pregnancy; abnormal glucose tolerance is present and may require insulin for duration of the pregnancy.	648.0X 250.0X	Because this is not a permanent diabetic condition, the 648 category is coded first, with the type of diabetes coded second; discussed further in the chapter on obstetrics.

Figure 8-3 Complications and manifestations of diabetes and code ranges

Nutritional and Metabolic Immunity (Category Codes 260–269)

Nutritional deficiencies are classified to category codes 260–269. Nutritional and vitamin deficiencies are commonly seen as a result of poverty or substance abuse. The diagnosis of obesity and the complications that accompany it are on the rise as a direct result of fast foods, food fad, or diets that cause extreme weight loss and then are abruptly stopped. The so-called diet craze also contributes to the diagnoses of malnutrition as well because the body may not be getting enough nutrients to function efficiently.

It is common to have vitamin deficiencies in patients who are malnourished, but these deficiencies can also be found in patients who exhibit problems such as malabsorption of nutrients. Although malabsorption most commonly is found in infants, children, and the elderly, these conditions can be found in anyone.

Category codes in this section of the code book classify the nutritional deficiencies according to the type of deficiency. Examples of conditions that are classified to this section are:

Vitamin A deficiency—Category code 264

Thiamine and niacin deficiency—Category code 265

Vitamin D deficiency—Category code 268

Other Metabolic and Immunity Disorders (Category Codes 270–279)

Conditions covered in this section include disorders of lipid metabolism, gout, and mineral metabolism. It should be noted that the entire range of category codes 270–279 is governed by the following instructional notation that appears after the section heading:

```
Use additional code to identify any associated mental retardation.
```

Disease Highlight—Gout

Gout is a form of arthritis that can become disabling when an acute attack occurs. Gout most commonly affects the peripheral joints. Acute attacks are caused by too much uric acid in the blood, which in some patients forms hard crystals in the joint area. Gout can be brought on by too much alcohol, being overweight, and/or eating meat or fish in excess. There are indications that patients who have a family history of gout may be more prone to getting it.

Signs and Symptoms:

It is common for sudden onsets of gout to occur at night. Symptoms include:

- Fever
- Swollen, tender joints that are red and warm to touch

Any joint can be affected, but the most common joint affected is the tatarsophalangeal joint of the great toe. Other joints of the feet, ankles, and knees are common sites of gout.

Clinical Testing:

Laboratory testing will show an increase in:

- Serum uric acid
- White blood cell count
- Sedimentation rate

Treatment:

- Patients are advised to increase liquid intake and to avoid fatty foods or alcoholic beverages.
- Medications given include NSAIDs or corticosteroids for patients who cannot tolerate NSAIDs.

Internet Links

An interactive Web site that explains diabetes can be found at *www.heartcenteronline.com.*

Education information about the endocrine system can be found at *www.ndei.org* and *www.endocrineweb.com.*

Additional information about the endocrine system can be found at *www.nrdc.org/health/effects/qendoc.asp.*

The National Institute of Diabetes and Digestive and Kidney Diseases has a Web site that contains a wealth of information at *www.endocrine.niddk.nih.gov.*

Summary

- The endocrine system is made up of structures that produce or secrete hormones.

- Hormones keep organs and tissues functioning properly.

- The thyroid gland secretes hormones that regulate growth and metabolism.

- Diabetes is a chronic condition that can affect the proper functioning of organs and systems in the body.

- There are two types of diabetes. The types are determined by the functioning of the pancreas.

- Documentation is key to coding diabetes and any associated conditions correctly.

- Nutritional deficiencies and other metabolic and immunity disorders are also coded from this section.

Chapter Review

True/False: Indicate whether the statement is true (T) or false (F).

1. _____ When the pancreas does not secrete insulin, these patients typically have type II diabetes.

2. _____ Hypothyroidism is a thyroid that is not as active as it should be.

3. _____ Type II diabetes is also known as adult-onset diabetes.

4. _____ Ketoacidosis is most commonly found in type II diabetics.

5. _____ Gestational diabetes develops during childhood.

Fill-in-the-Blanks: Enter the appropriate term(s) to complete the phrase.

6. The types of diabetes are determined by the functioning of the _____.

7. Ketoacidosis is when large quantities of ketones cause elevated acid levels in _____ and _____.

8. An inflammation of the thyroid gland is called _____.

9. The condition in which hormone secretions fall within normal limits but the thyroid itself is enlarged is called _____.

10. Type I diabetes is also referred to as juvenile type, juvenile-onset, or _____ diabetes.

Coding Assignments

Instructions: Using an ICD-9-CM coding book, select the code for each diagnostic statement.

Diagnosis	Code
1. Hyperthyroidism	_____
2. Fructose intolerance	_____
3. Hyperlipidemia NOS	_____
4. Morbid obesity	_____

5. Wilson's disease _____

6. Hypoglycemia _____

7. Vitamin D–resistant rickets _____

8. Type I diabetes _____

9. Type II diabetes with hyperosmolarity _____

10. Bronzed diabetes _____

11. Simple goiter _____

12. Cystathioninemia _____

13. Mild-degree of malnutrition _____

14. Type I diabetic, under good control, with gangrene of the right great toe _____

15. Type I diabetic, uncontrolled with hyperosmolarity _____

16. Nondiabetic insulin coma _____

17. Vitamin B_{12} deficiency _____

18. Galactosemia _____

19. Vitamin A deficiencies with night blindness _____

20. Hypophosphatasia _____

21. Secondary thyroid hyperplasia _____

22. Sporadic goiter _____

23. Iodine hypothyroidism _____

24. Nutritional dwarfism _____

25. Hypopotassemia _____

Case Studies

Instructions: Review each case study and select the correct ICD-9-CM diagnostic code.

CASE 1

An 8-year-old female presents with frequent urination. According to mom, patient complains frequently of muscle cramping and "being tired all the time." When patient is questioned directly, she nods in positive response to the above. It should also be noted that the patient appears smaller than a typical 8-year-old.

Vital signs are normal and noted in the nurse's note for this date. Heart sounds are normal. Lungs are clear. Abdomen is soft and nontender.

Stat labs are positive for elevated levels of plasma renin and plasma aldosterone; they also show hypokalemia and metabolic acidosis.

ASSESSMENT: Bartter's syndrome

ICD-9-CM Code Assignment: _____

CASE 2

Patient presents today with symptoms of excessive thirst and frequent urination, which has been going on for approximately 1 month. Patient states that these symptoms are affecting her sleep, and she is concerned that there might be something wrong. Patient denies any shortness of breath, nausea, or stomach cramping. Patient does state that mother had type II diabetes, and she is fearful since the symptoms are similar. Patient states that she was borderline diabetic during her pregnancy.

WEIGHT: 198 lbs   Temp: 98.7   BP: 110/70

HEART: No murmurs, RRR

LUNGS: Normal

SKIN: Warm and dry

EXTREMITIES: No edema

We did a finger stick, which indicated an elevated blood sugar level of 201. A HgA1C was ordered, which came back at a level 9. With these results and the symptoms involved, diabetes is the diagnosis here. We will try and control her diabetes with diet, exercise, and Glucophage. She will be set up for diabetic education as soon as possible.

ICD-9-CM Code Assignment: _____

CASE 3

S: This patient is a 68-year-old female presenting with severe muscle cramps most evenings. Sometimes the cramping wakes her out of a sound sleep. This has been going on for several months and doesn't seem to be getting better.

O: Pleasant older female, well nourished and in no acute distress. Weight is 175 lbs; blood pressure is 176/72; temperature, 98.4; pulse, 72; and respirations, 18. Skin: Normal and dry to touch; no rashes. Heart: No murmurs. Lungs: Clear. Extremities: No edema, clubbing, or cyanosis.

LAB RESULTS: Hemoglobin, 11.6; hematocrit, 35.3; potassium is 5.6, which is slightly elevated.

A & P: Hyperkalemia. I gave the patient a form that lists foods high in potassium content. I asked her to limit her intake of these foods as much as possible. If this approach works and the cramping lessens, we can avoid medication. She is willing to try this for 2 weeks. If she has not improved over that time, we will explore other options.

ICD-9-CM Code Assignment: _____

CASE 4

This patient presents today with a history of thyroidectomy 6 years prior to today's visit. Today she is complaining of some tingling in the hands and feet, some lethargy, and some anxiety. We ran some lab tests, which showed low serum and urinary calcium, as well as low urinary phosphate with increase in the serum phosphate. Parathyroid hormone levels were almost absent. It was determined that the patient has hypoparathyroidism.

ICD-9-CM Code Assignment: _____

CASE 5

A 2-month-old male presents with chronic, severe diarrhea and fatigue. His growth is stunted. His family is concerned because he has been treated for several different disorders, none of which have been the problem. After extensive lab testing over the last week, we found very low-density lipoprotein levels. We now have a definite diagnosis of Anderson's disease and will begin vitamin E therapy.

ICD-9-CM Code Assignment: _____

Diseases of the Blood and Blood-Forming Organs

Chapter Outline

Objectives

At the conclusion of this chapter, the student will be able to:

1. Identify diseases of the blood and blood-forming organs.
2. List the three types of blood cells.
3. Explain the various types of anemia and the codes for each.
4. Define various coagulation defects.
5. Explain diseases of white blood cells.
6. Accurately code diseases of the blood and blood-forming organs.
7. Select and code diagnoses from case studies.

Key Terms

Agranulocytes
Anemia
Angiohemophilia
Anticoagulants
Aplastic Anemia
Coagulation
Coagulation Defects

Diff
Differential Leukocyte
   Count
Differential White Blood
   Cell Count
Erythrocyte Count

Erythrocyte
   Sedimentation Rate
   (ESR)
Erythrocytes
Granulocytes
Hematocrit (Hct)
Hemoglobin (Hgb)

Hemolytic Anemia
Iron Deficiency Anemia
Leukocyte Count
Leukocytes
Mean Corpuscular
   Hemoglobin (MCH)

Reminder

As you work through this chapter, you will need to have a copy of the ICD-9-CM coding book to reference.

Mean Corpuscular Hemoglobin Concentration (MCHC)

Mean Corpuscular Volume (MCV)

Neutropenia

Packed Cell Volume (PCV)

Pernicious Anemia

Plasma

Platelets

Prothrombin Time

Protime

Purpura

Red Blood Cell Count

Red Blood Cells (RBC)

Sed Rate

Sickle-Cell Anemia

Sickle-Cell Trait

Thrombocytes

Thrombocytopenia

Von Willebrand's Disease

White Blood Cell Count

White Blood Cells (WBC)

Introduction

Chapter four of ICD-9-CM contains codes for diseases of the blood and blood-forming organs, except for diseases of the blood and blood-forming organs that are complicating pregnancy or the puerperium and neoplastic blood diseases. Conditions that complicate pregnancy or the puerperium are coded with chapter 11 of ICD-9-CM, "Complications of Pregnancy, Childbirth, and the Puerperium," with an additional code assigned from ICD-9-CM chapter 4 to identify the type of blood disease. Neoplastic diseases of the blood are coded with chapter 2 of ICD-9-CM, "Neoplasms."

Introduction to the Body Systems

Blood transports various nutrients and substances—such as oxygen, fats, waste products, and so on—from one part of the body to another. The various functions of the blood include the following:

Defensive—Transporting antibodies throughout the body to fight infection and disease

Excretory—Transporting waste products, such as creatinine and urea, from the cells to the excretory organs

Nutritive—Transporting nutrients to body tissue

Regulatory—Transporting hormones, controlling body temperature, and maintaining water balance and a steady environment for tissue cells

Respiratory—Transporting oxygen to and carbon dioxide from the tissues of the body

Blood Composition

Blood is composed of plasma, which is the liquid portion of the blood without its cellular elements. Blood is also composed of cellular or formed elements such as erythrocytes, leukocytes, and thrombocytes.

Erythrocytes, also known as red blood cells (RBC), are disc-shaped red blood cells that contain hemoglobin. Hemoglobin absorbs oxygen and transports it to the tissues of the body.

Leukocytes, also known as white blood cells (WBC), are pale-colored cells with an irregular ball-like shape; they provide the body's natural defense against injury and disease. Leukocytes are classified into two major groups: granulocytes (cells with a granular appearance) and agranulocytes (cells that are not granular). The various types of granulocytes and agranulocytes are as follows. See Figure 9-1 for an illustration of the formed elements of the blood.

Type of Leukocyte	Specific Type of Granulocyte or Agranulocyte
Granulocyte	Neutrophils
	Eosinophils
	Basophils
Agranulocytes/Nongranular	Lymphocytes
	Monocytes

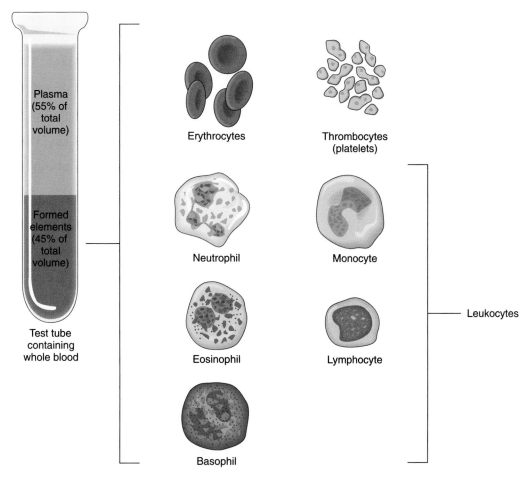

Figure 9-1 Formed elements of the blood (From Rizzo, Donald. *Fundamentals of Anatomy and Physiology*. 2nd ed. Albany, NY: Delmar, Cengage Learning, p. 298.)

Thrombocytes, also known as platelets, are ovoid-shaped structures that initiate blood clotting, or coagulation. When a blood vessel is damaged, from a cut or other injury, a "platelet plug" is formed to stop the bleeding. If coagulation does not occur, bleeding will continue and a person could bleed to death.

Coders should understand the blood components so that they can review blood test reports to substantiate the diagnoses. These reports provide the medical documentation to justify the codes selected. Figure 9-2 provides a listing of normal ranges for blood tests.

Coding of Diseases of the Blood and Blood-Forming Organs

ICD-9-CM chapter 4, "Diseases of the Blood and Blood-Forming Organs," classifies diseases into the following category codes:

280—Iron deficiency anemias

281—Other deficiency anemias

282—Hereditary hemolytic anemias

283—Acquired hemolytic anemias

284—Aplastic anemias and other bone marrow failure syndromes

Blood Test	Definition of Test	Normal Range		Examples of Diseases Indicated by Abnormal Value
White blood cell count, also known as **leukocyte count** or **WBC**	Identifies the number of white blood cells found in a cubic millimeter of blood (mm^3).	Adults and children	5000–10,000/mm^3	Leukocytosis Leukopenia
		Children 2 years or younger	6200–17,000/mm^3	
		Newborns	9000–30,000/mm^3	
Differential white blood cell count, also known as **Differential leukocyte count,** or **(diff)**	Identifies the percentage of each type of white cell relative to the total number of leukocytes.	Neutrophils Monocytes Lymphocytes Basophils Eosinophils	55–70% 2–8% 20–40% 0.5–1% 1–4%	Neutrophilia Neutropenia Measles Mumps Hepatitis Lymphocytosis Monocytosis Asthma Allergies
Red blood cell count, also known as **erythrocyte count** or **RBC**	Identifies the number of red blood cells found in a cubic millimeter of blood (mm^3).	Men Women Infants and children Newborns	4.7–6.1 million/mm^3 4.2–5.4 million/mm^3 3.8–5.5 million/mm^3 4.8–7.1 million/mm^3	Anemia Erythrocytosis Rheumatic fever
Hematocrit (Hct) also known as **packed cell volume (PCV)**	Determines the percentage of red blood cells in whole blood.	Men Women Children Newborns	42–52% 37–47% (in pregnancy: >33%) 30–42% 44–64%	Anemia
Hemoglobin (Hgb)	Evaluates the oxygen-carrying capacity of the red blood cells by determining the grams of hemoglobin per deciliter of blood.	Men Women Children Newborns	14–18 g/dl 12–16 g/dl (in pregnancy: >11 g/dl) 11–16 g/dl 14–24 g/dl	Anemias Hyperthyroidism Lymphoma
Mean corpuscular volume (MCV)	Describes the average size of an individual red blood cell in cubic microns.	Adults and children Newborns	80–95 um^3 96–108 um^3	Iron deficiency Anemia Thalassemia Pernicious anemia
Mean corpuscular hemoglobin (MCH)	Identifies the average weight of hemoglobin in an average red blood cell reported in picograms (pg).	Adults and children Newborns	27–31pg 32–38 pg	Macrocytic and Microcytic anemia
Mean corpuscular hemoglobin concentration (MCHC)	Measures the average concentration or percentage of hemoglobin within each red blood cell.	Adults and children Newborns	32–36% 32–33%	Hypochromic Anemia Spherocytosis
Erythrocyte sedimentation rate (ESR, sed rate)	Measures the rate at which red blood cells settle out of unclotted blood in an hour. Expressed as millimeters per hour (mm/hr).	Men <50 yrs Men >50 yrs Women <50 yrs Women >50 yrs Children	0–10 mm/hr 0–13 mm/hr 0–13 mm/hr 0–20 mm/hr 0–10 mm/hr	Polycythemia vera Sickle cell anemia
Platelet count	Measures the number of platelets per cubic millimeter of blood (mm^3).	Adults and children	150,000– 400,00/mm^3	Thrombocytosis Thrombopenia
Mean platelet volume (MPV)	Measures the relative size of platelets expressed in micrometers.	Adults and children	2–4 um diameter	Systematic lupus Erythematosus Anemia

Figure 9-2 Blood test values

285—Other and unspecified anemias

286—Coagulation defects

287—Purpura and other hemorrhagic conditions

288—Diseases of white blood cells

289—Other diseases of blood and blood-forming organs

Exercise 9–1   Blood Test Values

Using Figure 9-2, answer the following questions:

1. The normal range of a WBC for a child 2 years or younger is:
   a. 5,000–10,000/mm³
   b. 6,200–17,000/mm³
   c. 9,000–30,000/mm³

2. A normal MCH in an adult is 27–31 pg. The *pg* stands for:
   a. picograms
   b. pecometer
   c. pacogram

3. When looking at an Hgb level, a provider is looking at:
   a. the number of platelets per cubic millimeter of blood
   b. the oxygen-carrying capacity of the red blood cells
   c. the rate at which red blood cells settle out of unclotted blood in an hour

4. If the mean corpuscular volume does not fall within normal limits, it might be an indication of:
   a. hyperthyroidism
   b. thrombocytopenia
   c. thalassemia

5. The test that gives an indication of the percentage of red blood cells in whole blood is:
   a. MCV
   b. Hct
   c. Differential leukocyte count

Anemia

Anemia is a condition marked by a decrease in red blood cells, hemoglobin, hematocrit, or a combination thereof. There are numerous causes and types of anemia. When anemia is coded, it is important that the type of anemia is identified. If the diagnostic statement does not identify the type of anemia, the coder should review the medical record or query the physician before assigning a code.

Iron Deficiency Anemia (Category Code 280)

Iron deficiency anemia occurs when there is an insufficient supply of iron in the blood, which can be caused by blood loss or inadequate dietary iron intake. Category code 280, Iron deficiency anemias, requires the assignment of a fourth digit to identify the specific type of iron deficiency anemia. The fourth-digit subcategories are as follows:

```
0    Secondary to blood loss (chronic)
1    Secondary to inadequate dietary iron intake
8    Other specified iron deficiency anemias
9    Iron deficiency anemia, unspecified
```

Other Deficiency Anemias (Category Code 281)

Category code 281, Other deficiency anemias, is used to classify other types of deficiency anemias and requires the use of a fourth digit to indicate the specific type of deficiency. The fourth-digit subcategories are as follows:

```
0    Pernicious anemia
1    Other vitamin B₁₂ deficiency anemia
2    Folate-deficiency anemia
3    Other specified megaloblastic anemias, not elsewhere classified
4    Protein-deficiency anemia
5    Anemia associated with other specified nutritional deficiency
9    Unspecified deficiency anemia
```

Coders should review the medical record to determine the specific deficiency anemia that is supported by the physician documentation or laboratory reports.

Disease Highlight—Pernicious Anemia

Pernicious anemia is an autoimmune disorder in which the stomach is unable to produce intrinsic factor, which is needed to absorb vitamin B_{12}. This type of anemia can be caused by gastritis, gastric surgery, or endocrine or metabolic disorders.

Signs and Symptoms:

Patients with pernicious anemia have:

- Anorexia
- Gastrointestinal symptoms that include diarrhea or intermittent constipation
- Nonlocalized abdominal pain
- Atrophic gastritis
- Fatigue
- Shortness of breath
- Pallor
- Positive Babinski's reflex

Clinical Testing:

Pernicious anemia is confirmed by a positive Schilling test. Additional laboratory testing shows an:

- Increased MCV
- Increased serum LDH
- Increased bilirubin
- Decreased WBC and platelet count

- A decrease in vitamin B_{12} serum

- Abnormal bone marrow

Treatment:

Because the patient's body is not producing intrinsic factor, it inadequately absorbs vitamin B_{12}. Therefore a patient with pernicious anemia will receive monthly injections of vitamin B_{12} for his or her lifetime.

Hemolytic Anemias (Category Codes 282–283)

Hemolytic anemia occurs when red blood cells are broken down at a faster rate than bone marrow can produce them; as a result, an abnormal reduction of red blood cells occurs. This disease can be acquired or hereditary. Hereditary hemolytic anemias are classified to category 282, whereas acquired forms of hemolytic anemias are classified to category 283. Acquired hemolytic anemias are caused by outside elements, such as infectious organisms or another physical element.

Sickle-cell anemia and sickle-cell trait are inherited conditions that are classified to category 282. **Sickle-cell trait** is an asymptomatic condition in which the patient received the genetic trait from only one parent. **Sickle-cell anemia** occurs when a patient receives the genetic trait from both parents, thus developing an abnormal type of hemoglobin in the red blood cell that causes decreased oxygenation in the tissues. Sickle-cell trait is classified to code 282.5, and sickle-cell anemia is classified to 282.6X with fifth digits identifying various types. It should be noted that when a patient is in crisis, that is, the patient is experiencing painful symptoms, an additional code for the type of crisis should be identified. Patients with sickle-cell anemia can develop complications that include problems with their eyes, congestive heart failure, heart murmurs, jaundice, enlarged liver, hematuria, gallstones, urine concentration reduction, osteomyelitis, and ulcerations of the lower extremities. The following instructional notation appears at the fifth-digit level for the codes that identify patients in crisis.

```
Use additional code for type of crisis, such as:

 Acute chest syndrome (517.3)

 Splenic sequestration (289.52)
```

EXAMPLE: Frank Jones is admitted to Valley View Hospital. His discharge summary records splenic sequestration and sickle-cell anemia. This admission is coded with codes 282.64 and 289.52.

Aplastic Anemia (Category Code 284)

Aplastic anemia is caused by the failure of bone marrow to produce blood components. Constitutional and congenital aplastic anemia is classified to code 284.01 and 284.09. Acquired forms may be due to a chronic systemic disease, infection, exposure to drugs, radiation, or other chemicals and are classified to codes 284.81 and 284.89. Acquired forms often result from treatment for cancer malignancies, such as radiation therapy.

It should also be noted that subcategory code 284.89 instructs the coder to use an additional E code to identify the cause of the aplastic anemia. The coder should determine the type and cause of the anemia by reviewing the patient record or querying the physician if the documentation is not specific.

Other and Unspecified Anemia (Category Code 285)

Anemia due to acute blood loss, caused by an abrupt significant blood loss from trauma or injury, is classified to code 285.1. Acute blood loss can occur because of external and internal injuries, or it can occur during or after surgery.

EXAMPLE 1: Sally Jones was in a motor vehicle accident and transported via ambulance to the emergency department. The physician determined that she has acute blood loss anemia, coded as 285.1, due to a ruptured spleen, coded as 865.04, but notes no external injuries.

EXAMPLE 2: Tim Smith was cutting his hedges with electric hedge clippers, which slipped and severely cut his wrist. He was taken to the emergency department, and the physician determined that he had acute blood loss anemia, code 285.1, due to an open wound of the wrist with tendon involvement, code 881.22.

EXAMPLE 3: Beth Briggs had a hysterectomy and lost a significant amount of blood during the procedure. At her discharge from the hospital, the physician recorded acute blood-loss anemia as a diagnosis on the discharge summary. This diagnosis is coded as 285.1.

It is important that coders closely review the patient record to determine whether the blood-loss anemia is acute or chronic. Acute blood-loss anemia is classified as code 285.1, whereas unspecified or chronic blood-loss anemia is classified as code 280.0.

Anemia in Chronic Illness

Anemia that occurs when a patient has a chronic illness is classified to category code 285.2, with a fifth digit assigned to identify the type of chronic illness as follows:

285.21	Anemia in chronic kidney disease
285.22	Anemia in neoplastic disease
285.29	Anemia of other chronic disease

Patients with chronic illness are commonly admitted for treatment of the anemia that develops as a result of the chronic illness. When a patient is admitted to treat the anemia, for example, to receive a transfusion, the code for the anemia is used as the principal diagnosis. However, when the patient is admitted for treatment of the chronic illness and anemia is also treated, the anemia code is used as a secondary diagnosis.

EXAMPLE 1: Sally Jones has breast cancer and has received chemotherapy. She is admitted to Sunny Valley Hospital because her doctor determined that she needs a transfusion because she is anemic. This would be coded to 285.22.

EXAMPLE 2: Tom Hart has end-stage renal disease and is admitted for treatment of the disease. During the hospitalization, his doctor determined that he is anemic. Code 285.21 is used as a secondary diagnosis.

The following Official ICD-9-CM Coding Guidelines give direction to coders for the assignment of codes 285.21, 285.22, and 285.29.

Official ICD-9-CM Coding Guideline:

Subcategory 285.2, Anemia in chronic illness, has codes for anemia in chronic kidney disease, code 285.21; anemia in neoplastic disease, code 285.22; and anemia in other chronic illness, code 285.29. These codes can be used as the principal/first-listed code if the reason for the encounter is to treat the anemia. They may also be used as secondary codes if treatment of the anemia is a component of an encounter, but not the primary reason for the encounter. When using a code from subcategory 285, it is also necessary to use the code for the chronic condition causing the anemia.

(1) Anemia in chronic kidney disease

   When assigning code 285.21, Anemia in chronic kidney disease, it is also necessary to assign a code from category 585, Chronic kidney disease, to indicate the stage of chronic kidney disease. [See I.C.10.a, Chronic kidney disease (CKD).]

(2) Anemia in neoplastic disease

   When assigning code 285.22, Anemia in neoplastic disease, it is also necessary to assign the neoplasm code that is responsible for the anemia. Code 285.22 is for use for anemia that is due to the malignancy, not for anemia due to antineoplastic chemotherapy drugs, which is an adverse effect. (See I.C.2.c.1, Anemia associated with malignancy. See I.C.2.c.2, Anemia associated with chemotherapy, immunotherapy, and radiation therapy. See I.C.17. e.1, Adverse effects.) (See Appendix A, Section I, C4, a, 1–2.)

Exercise 9–2   Types of Anemia

Match the diagnostic statement in the first column with the correct ICD-9-CM diagnostic code from the right-hand column.

Diagnostic Statement		ICD-9-CM Diagnostic Codes
1. Aplastic anemia	_____	280.0
2. Anemia due to blood loss	_____	280.9
3. Hemolytic anemia	_____	281.0
4. Acute hemorrhagic anemia	_____	281.8
5. Profound anemia	_____	281.9
6. Chlorotic anemia	_____	283.9
7. Congenital pernicious anemia	_____	284.01
8. Blackfan-Diamond anemia	_____	284.9
9. Macrocytic anemia	_____	285.1
10. Diphasic anemia	_____	285.9

Coagulation Defects (Category Code 286)

Coagulation defects occur when there is a deficiency in one or more of the blood-clotting factors, resulting in prolonged clotting time and possibly serious bleeding. The normal stages of blood clotting are summarized in Figure 9-3. A coagulation defect occurs when there is a disruption in this process because of heredity or acquired conditions. Coagulation defects are classified with category code 286, with fourth digits identifying whether the defect is congenital or acquired. Hereditary coagulation defects, such as hemophilia, Christmas disease, and Von Willebrand's disease, are classified to codes 286.0–286.4.

Disease Highlight—Von Willebrand's Disease

Von Willebrand's disease, also known as angiohemophilia, is the most common of the inherited bleeding disorders. This disease is caused by a deficiency in clotting factor and platelet function and is categorized as a hereditary autosomal dominant disorder.

Signs and Symptoms:

Patients with Von Willebrand's disease have an increase in mucosal bleeding that will include:

- Epistaxis
- Gingival bleeding
- Monorrhagia
- Gastrointestinal bleeding

These patients also have an increased amount of bleeding following surgery, injury, and dental procedures.

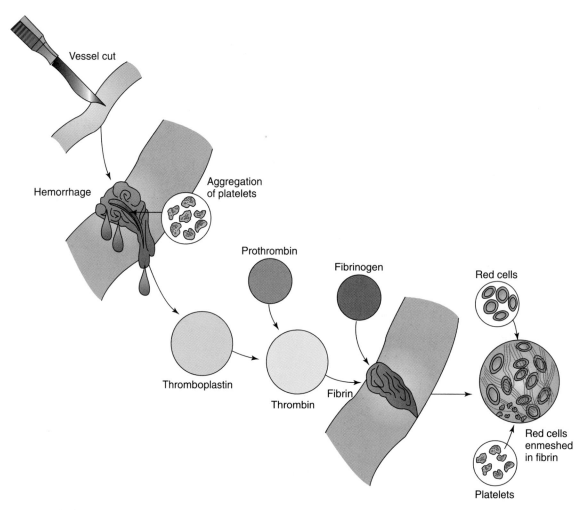

Figure 9-3 Normal stages of blood clotting (From Rizzo, Donald. *Fundamentals of Anatomy and Physiology*. 2nd ed. Albany, NY: Delmar, Cengage Learning, p. 306.)

Clinical Testing:

Laboratory tests show:

- Prolonged bleeding time
- A decrease in the vW factor level in plasma

Treatment:

- Patients diagnosed with Von Willebrand's disease are to avoid using aspirin because this exacerbates bleeding.
- Patients who have lost a significant amount of blood should have a transfusion of plasma cryoprecipitate.
- Antifibrinolytic agents are administered to patients during surgery and dental procedures to decrease bleeding.
- Desmopressin acetate is also given to patients to control the disease.

Hemorrhagic disorders due to intrinsic circulating anticoagulants, an acquired disorder of circulating antibodies, inhibit the normal blood-clotting process. These disorders are classified with code 286.5.

Delayed Blood Clotting Due to Coagulation Defects Versus Anticoagulant Therapy

It should be noted that patients who are being treated with anticoagulants, medications that prevent the formation of blood clots such as heparin or warfarin (Coumadin), may develop bleeding and/or organ hemorrhage. When a patient who is receiving anticoagulant therapy develops a complication, code 286.5 is not assigned because this disorder is not due to a circulating anticoagulant. When bleeding or hemorrhage occurs because of anticoagulant therapy, a code for the condition and code E934.2 are assigned.

> **EXAMPLE:** Tim Mack has been taking Coumadin and is now experiencing gastric discomfort. Dr. Tops examines him and orders diagnostic testing that determines that Tim has acute gastritis with hemorrhage secondary to Coumadin. This diagnosis is coded as 535.01 and E934.2. (It should be noted that when billing for physician charges, some third-party payers will not accept an E code. This needs to be clarified with the payer before a claim is submitted.)

Patients who receive Coumadin therapy may have a prolonged bleeding time. Prolonged bleeding time is evaluated by a blood test, known as prothrombin time (protime), which measures the time it takes for blood to clot. When a patient is receiving Coumadin, a prolonged prothrombin time is expected and providing a code for the prolonged prothrombin time is not needed. However, ICD-9-CM classifies patients who are not receiving Coumadin but have an abnormal prothrombin time or other abnormal coagulation profile to code 790.92, Abnormal coagulation profile. Therefore, before assigning code 790.92, the coder must determine whether the patient is receiving Coumadin.

Purpura and Other Hemorrhagic Conditions (Category Code 287)

The following diseases are classified to this category:

- **Purpura**—An accumulation of blood under the skin that forms multiple pinpoint hemorrhages

- **Thrombocytopenia**—An abnormal decrease in platelet count that causes purpural hemorrhages

It should be noted that code 287.4 instructs coders to use an additional E code to identify the cause of secondary thrombocytopenia.

Diseases of White Blood Cells (Category Code 288)

Category 288 classifies diseases of white blood cells except for leukemia, which is classified to category codes 204.0–208.9. Neutropenia, an abnormal decrease of granular leukocytes in the blood, is classified with 288.0. This condition occurs in patients who receive chemotherapy and have a decrease in the number of white blood cells. Patients with neutropenia can also have fever and chills, sores in the stomach, throat, or on the skin.

Internet Links

To learn about the various types of anemia, visit *www.anemiainstitute.org*.

For a comprehensive review of blood coagulation, visit *http://tollefsen.wustl.edu*.

To learn about neutropenia, visit *www.neutropenia.ca*.

Diseases of the blood are explained at the following two sites: *www.nhlbi.nih.gov/health/public/blood/index.htm* and *www.umm.edu/blood/index.htm*.

Summary

- ICD-9-CM chapter 4 includes diseases of the blood and blood-forming organs.

- Diseases of the blood and blood-forming organs complicating pregnancy or the puerperium are classified to chapter 11 of ICD-9-CM, "Complications of Pregnancy, Childbirth, and the Puerperium."

- Neoplastic diseases of the blood are classified to chapter 2 of ICD-9-CM, "Neoplasms."

- Erythrocytes are red blood cells; leukocytes are white blood cells.

- Leukocytes are divided into two groups: granuloyctes and agranulocytes.
- Thrombocytes function in the initiation of blood clotting.
- Anemia occurs when there is decrease in red blood cells, hemoglobin, and/or hematocrit.
- Sickle-cell trait and sickle-cell anemia are separately identifiable conditions that are classified to different codes in ICD-9-CM.
- Aplastic anemia can be congenital or acquired.
- Coagulation defects cause prolonged clotting time and can result in serious bleeding, which can lead to death.
- Diseases of the white blood cells, except leukemia, are classified to chapter 4 of ICD-9-CM.

Chapter Review

True/False: Indicate whether each statement is true (T) or false (F).

1. _____ Sally Smith is pregnant and anemic. Her anemia is coded to ICD-9-CM chapter 4, "Diseases of the Blood and Blood-Forming Organs."

2. _____ Leukemia is classified to ICD-9-CM chapter 4, "Diseases of the Blood and Blood-Forming Organs."

3. _____ Acute anemia and chronic anemia are classified to separate codes in ICD-9-CM.

4. _____ Coagulation defects are always congenital.

5. _____ Sickle-cell trait and sickle-cell anemia are classified to the same code in ICD-9-CM.

Fill-in-the-Blank: Enter the appropriate term(s) to complete each statement.

6. Platelets, also known as _____, function in the initiation of clotting.

7. Coumadin and heparin are used in _____ therapy.

8. Coumadin can cause a(n) _____ bleeding time.

9. Anemia that results after an excessive loss of blood during surgery is known as _____.

10. The failure of bone marrow to produce blood components is known as _____.

Short Answer: Briefly respond to each question.

11. Explain the difference between sickle-cell trait and sickle-cell anemia.

12. Define hemolytic anemia.

13. Discuss the cause of aplastic anemia.

14. List and define the subcategories of category code 280, Iron deficiency anemias.

15. Summarize the causes of acute blood loss anemia.

Coding Assignments

Instructions: Using an ICD-9-CM coding book, select the code for each diagnostic statement.

Diagnosis	Code
1. Cytogenic anemia	
2. Atypical anemia	
3. B_{12} deficiency anemia	
4. Macrocytic anemia	

5. Pernicious anemia _____

6. Anemia due to hemorrhage _____

7. Protein deficiency anemia _____

8. Congenital aplastic anemia _____

9. Acute blood loss resulting in anemia _____

10. Simple chronic anemia _____

11. Congenital aregenerative anemia _____

12. Anemia due to glutathione metabolism disorder _____

13. Anemia due to folate acid deficiency _____

14. Acute hemolytic anemia _____

15. Splenic anemia _____

16. Anemia due to blood loss from a chronic ulcer of the stomach _____

17. Addison's anemia _____

18. Plummer-Vinson syndrome _____

19. Nutritional megaloblastic anemia _____

20. Aplastic anemia due to radiation _____

21. Chronic lymphadenitis _____

22. Neutropenia _____

23. Secondary benign polycythemia _____

24. Secondary eosinophilia _____

25. May-Hegglin syndrome _____

Case Studies

Instructions: Review each case study, and select the correct ICD-9-CM diagnostic code.

CASE 1

Discharge Summary

PATIENT NAME: Polly Patch

AGE: 72 years old

Polly was admitted from home because she passed out from dizziness. Her daughter called my office, and I admitted her to the medical unit because this is the third time in 2 weeks that she has passed out.

On initial examination she was conscious and alert and appeared pale. Physical findings can be found on the history and physical dated 2/13/XX.

CBC, chest X-ray, and EKG were ordered.

CBC revealed a low platelet count of 53,000, supporting a diagnosis of thrombocytopenia. Chest X-ray and EKG were normal.

The rest of her 2-day admission was uneventful, and she was discharged home. She was instructed to follow up in my office in 2 weeks or to call my office if her symptoms increase.

ICD-9-CM Code Assignment: _____

CASE 2

Hospital Note for 3/4/XX

Bob was admitted on Monday with a diagnosis of anemia associated with a primary malignancy of the prostate. Today I ordered a blood transfusion due to his low blood count. CBC is to be repeated after the transfusion. I instructed the charge nurse to call me with the results.

ICD-9-CM Code Assignment: _____

CASE 3

Postsurgical Note

Mary is now 1-day postop for a right breast mass excision. During the surgery she lost a significant amount of blood due to uncontrolled bleeding. A CBC was ordered that showed an abnormally low hematocrit and hemogloblin, confirming anemia due to blood loss. She was given a transfusion and has tolerated the transfusion well.

ICD-9-CM Code Assignment: _____

CASE 4

Office Note

Terry was extremely tired and began suffering from some abdominal pain. She really couldn't give a specific site of the pain, but she was in pain. When the diarrhea began, she called to schedule an appointment. She presented to me and explained her symptoms. Tests confirmed a diagnosis of pernicious anemia. Terry was started on Vitamin B_{12} injections and began to feel much better.

ICD-9-CM Code Assignment: _____

CASE 5

Kala was feeling very weak and lethargic over the past month. She began to suffer from pain in her major joints even when she had not been exercising or participating in sports. Her mother decided it was time to go to the doctor to find out what was causing her symptoms. Kala's doctor found her to be slightly dehydrated and decided that she needed some testing done given her other symptoms. When the tests came back, Kala was told she had sickle-cell anemia and would need to be hospitalized for IV therapy.

ICD-9-CM Code Assignment: _____

10 Mental Disorders

Chapter Outline

Introduction to the Body System

Coding of Mental Disorders

Internet Links

Summary

Chapter Review

Coding Assignments

Case Studies

Objectives

At the conclusion of this chapter, the student will be able to:

1. Define mental health disorders and conditions.
2. Discuss the sequencing of codes for drug and alcohol abuse and dependence.
3. Summarize how the coding for this specialty is different from the other specialties and why the coding is challenging.
4. Select and code diagnoses from case studies.

Key Terms

Alcohol Abuse

Alcohol Dependence

Alcoholism

Bipolar Disorders

Delirium

Delusional Disorders

Delusions

Dementia

Depressive Features

Diagnostic and Statistical Manual of Mental Disorders, Fourth Revision (DSM-IV)

Drug Abuse

Drug Dependence

Manic-Depressive Episodes

Mental Retardation

Mild Mental Retardation

Moderate Mental Retardation

Neurotic Disorders

Personality Disorders

Profound Mental Retardation

Psychoses

Schizophrenic Disorders

Severe Mental Retardation

Unspecified Mental Retardation

Reminder

As you work through this chapter, you will need to have a copy of the ICD-9-CM coding book to reference.

Introduction to the Body System

Mental disorders are disorders that affect the ability of a person to function in a healthy, socially acceptable way and are classified to chapter 5 of ICD-9-CM, "Mental Disorders." It should be noted that persons with the same mental disorder are not always affected the same way. The severity may be different, or a person's reaction to treatment may differ from that of other patients.

Effective with the October 1, 2004, update of ICD-9-CM, the Glossary of Mental Disorders, also known as Appendix B, was removed from the official ICD-9-CM manual. The Glossary of Mental Disorders contained the definitions of psychiatric conditions found in ICD-9-CM and provided a quick reference for the coder when assigning codes. Because psychiatric terminology changes frequently, the glossary was removed. For the most current definitions of psychiatric conditions, coders should reference http://allpsych.com.

Psychiatric disorders diagnosed by psychiatrists most commonly are recorded by using a nomenclature established by the American Psychiatric Association that is known as the Diagnostic and Statistical Manual of Mental Disorders, Fourth Revision (DSM-IV). The codes found in the nomenclature and ICD-9-CM are the same, but the terminology occasionally differs between the two systems. Although most psychiatrists use the terminology from DSM-IV, the ICD-9-CM codes are used to report mental disorders to third-party payers. To learn more about the *Diagnostic and Statistical Manual of Mental Disorders,* visit http//allpsych.com/disorders/dsm.html. At the time of writing, DSM-V has been tentatively slated for release in 2011.

Exercise 10–1   Defining Psychiatric Terms

Define the following psychiatric terms by using the Web site listed above or by using a medical dictionary.

1. Anxiety

_____

_____

_____

2. Depression

_____

_____

_____

3. Panic attack

_____

_____

4. Hallucination

_____

_____

5. Personality disorder

_____

_____

Coding of Mental Disorders

Chapter 5, "Mental Disorders," in the ICD-9-CM coding book is divided into three sections of codes containing the following category codes:

- Psychoses—Category codes 290–299

- Neurotic disorders, personality disorders, and other nonpsychotic mental disorders—Category codes 300–316

- Mental retardation—Category codes 317–319

Psychoses (Category Codes 290–299)

The first section of chapter 5 of ICD-9-CM, "Psychoses," classifies conditions that interfere with a person's ability to perform the activities of daily living. Persons with these types of disorders tend to have a distorted view of reality and are not able to comprehend the inappropriateness of their behavior.

The codes in this section represent psychotic behaviors and conditions such as different types of dementia, alcoholic psychoses, organic psychotic conditions, schizophrenic disorders, and other specified psychoses. Provider documentation is critical to correctly coding the conditions in this section.

Dementias (Category Code 290)

Various forms of dementia, a slowly progressive decrease in mental abilities that includes lack of judgment, decreased memory, and a decreased ability to pay attention, are classified to category code 290. Fourth-digit sub-categories are used to identify the following:

- Senile dementia, uncomplicated—290.0

- Presenile dementia—290.1

- Senile dementia with delusional or depressive features—290.2

- Senile dementia with delirium—290.3

- Vascular dementia—290.4

Fifth-digit sub-classifications are used with subcategory codes 290.1X, 290.2X and 290.4X to identify dementia associated with related conditions such as

Delirium—A confused, disoriented state with the inability to think clearly

Delusions—A false perception that is maintained by a person despite proof that it is contrary to reality

Depressive features—Loss of interest or pleasure in activities or a depressed mood state

Provider documentation should specify the associated conditions by stating "with acute confusional state," "with delirium," "depressed type," and so on. Coders need to review the medical documentation to select the correct fifth digit.

EXAMPLE: Mary Ellen is a patient in Valley Nursing Home. The staff has noticed a marked change in her behavior lately. She is exhibiting signs of paranoia, especially with regard to food. Mary Ellen won't eat food at meal time unless a staff member tastes it in front of her; then she eats. Staff continually assure her that she is being given the same food as everyone else, but she insists someone taste her food before she will eat it. Her physician diagnoses her with presenile dementia with delusional features. Code assignment in this case is 290.12, Presenile dementia with delusional features.

An instructional notation appears at the category code level 290.4 that instructs the coder to "use additional code to identify cerebral atherosclerosis." This instructional notation does not appear in the Alphabetic Index and would be missed if the Tabular List is not referenced.

EXAMPLE: Connie Coder is coding the diagnostic statement "cerebral arteriosclerotic dementia with delusional features, paranoid type." She references the term *dementia,* followed by the subterms *arteriosclerosis* and *delusions* in the Alphabetic Index. If Connie does not reference the Tabular List, the code 437.0 would be omitted. The proper code assignment should be 290.42 and 437.0 for this diagnosis.

When coding dementia, it is imperative that the medical documentation is completely reviewed and that both the Alphabetic Index and Tabular List of ICD-9-CM are referenced.

Alcohol-Induced Mental Disorders (Category Code 291) and Drug-Induced Mental Disorders (Category Code 292)

Mental disorders related to excessive alcohol use are coded to category code 291. A history of alcohol abuse does not support a diagnosis of alcohol-induced mental disorders unless the provider's documentation supports this relationship in the current episode of care or if this history has a direct relationship to the treatment. This same rule holds true for a history of drug abuse.

Drug-induced mental disorders are coded to category 292 only with documentation that the mental disorder is associated with the consumption of drugs. Note that an instructional notation appears at the category code level 292 to instruct coders to use an additional code for any associated drug dependence and to use an additional E code to identify the specific drug used.

In the coding of drug-induced mental disorders, the psychosis code from category code 292 should be listed first, followed by the code for any associated drug dependence, codes 304.0–304.9. However, if there is no indication of psychosis or symptoms of withdrawal, then the code for substance dependence is listed alone.

EXAMPLE: Tom Thomas is admitted for drug-induced delirium due to opiate dependence. This is coded as 292.81 and 304.00.

Exercise 10–2   Coding Category Codes 290–294

Select the correct ICD-9-CM code for the diagnoses. Do not select E codes.

1. Paranoid state induced by drugs   _____

2. Alcohol amnestic syndrome   _____

3. Senile dementia with delirium   _____

4. Alcoholic paranoia   _____

5. Senile psychosis   _____

6. Presenile dementia with depressive features   _____

7. Alcoholic hallucinations   _____

8. Multi-infarct dementia   _____

9. Drug-induced anxiety disorder   _____

10. Korsaloff's psychosis   _____

11. Vascular dementia with delirium   _____

12. Chronic alcoholic brain syndrome   _____

13. Posttraumatic organic psychosis _____

14. Insomnia due to drugs _____

15. Alcoholic mania _____

Other Psychoses (Category Codes 295–299)

Category codes 295–299 classify various forms of psychoses that include:

Schizophrenic disorders—A psychotic disorder characterized by disruptive behavior, hallucinations, delusions, and disorganized speech

Bipolar disorders—Also known as manic-depressive episodes, includes the occurrence of an elevated mood alternating with depressive episodes

Delusional disorders—Include the feeling of paranoia in which the patient has a constant distrust and suspicion of others

In the 295–299 code series, many fifth digits are used. Coders must become familiar with the fifth digits and the Include: and Exclude: notes that are found in this section. The assignment of fifth digits is to be based on physician documentation, and the physician should be queried if diagnostic statements need to be specified. If diagnostic statements cannot be clarified, codes for unspecified conditions should be used.

EXAMPLE: Dr. Jones records paraphrenic schizophrenia on a patient's record. The coder is unable to get a more specific diagnostic statement. Code 295.30 assigned.

Neurotic Disorders, Personality Disorders, and Other Nonpsychotic Mental Disorders (Category Codes 300–316)

This category of codes classifies neurotic, personality, and other nonpsychotic disorders in which the person's ability to distinguish reality from fantasy is not impaired; they live within socially acceptable limits but experience anxiety, phobias, and other nonpsychotic disorders. This section of codes, 300–316, includes such conditions as anxiety, phobias, personality disorders, sexual and gender identity disorders, alcohol and drug dependence, acute reactions to stress, anxiety, and nonpsychotic mental disorders owing to brain damage.

Neurotic Disorders

Neurotic disorders are defined as disturbances or symptoms that cause a person to feel distressed. The person feels that the disturbance is not acceptable or desirable. Their behavior is socially acceptable, and their perception of reality is intact. The disorders that fall under neurotic behavior include phobias, obsessive/compulsive symptoms, and excessive anxiety.

Personality Disorders

Personality disorders are defined as a pattern of maladaptive and inflexible traits that last throughout an individual's lifetime. They include such conditions as paranoid personality disorder, histrionic personality disorder, and antisocial personality disorder.

Opiates
  Buprenex (buprenorphine)
  Darvon, Darvocet (propoxyphene)
  Demerol (meperidine)
  Dilaudid (hydromorphone)
  Fentanyl
  Heroin
  Immodium (loperamide)
  Lomotil (diphenoxylate)
  Lorcet (hydrocodone)
  MS Contin/morphine
  Methadone (Dolophine, Dolobid),
        LAAM (levomethadyl)
  Nubain (nalbuphine)
  Nyquil, cough syrups (dextromethorphan)
  OxyContin (oxycodone)
  Percocet, Percodan
  Stadol (butorphanol)
  Talwin (pentazocine)
  Ultram (trammodol)
  Vicodin (hydrocodone)

Benzodiazipines
  Ambien (zoldipem)
  Ativan (lorazepam)
  Dalmane (flurazepam)
  Halcion (triazolam)
  Klonopin (clonazepam)
  Librium (chlordiazepoxide)
  Restoril (temazepam)
  Serax (oxazepam)
  Tranzene (chlorazepate)
  Valium (diazepam)
  Versed (midlazolam)
  Xanax (alprazolam)

Barbituates
  Amytal (amobarbital)
  Fiorinal (butalbital)
  Nembutal (pentobarbital)
  Phenobarbital
  Seconal (secobarbital)

Hallucinogens
  Ecstasy (methylenedioxymethamphetamine
        or MDMA)
  Ketamine
  LSD (lysergic acid diethylamide)
  Marijuana
  Mescaline
  MDA (methylenedioxyamphetamine)
  Mushrooms
  PCP (phtencyclidine)
  Peyote
  XTC

Stimulants
  Amphetamine diet pills
  Cocaine
  Dexadrine
  Ephedrine
  Methamphetamine
  Pseudoephedrine
  Ritalin (methylphenidate)

Inhalants
  Anesthetic gases
  Diprivan (propofol)
  Gasoline/paint thinner
  Poppers, snappers (nitrous oxide)
  Propellant

Others
  Benadryl (diphenhydramine)
  Chloral hydrate
  Flexeril (cyclobenzaprine)
  Miltown (meprobamate)
  Placidyl (ethchlorvynol)
  Skelaxin (methaxalone)
  Soma (carisoprodol)

Figure 10-1 Common addictive drugs

Substance Abuse and Dependency

Alcohol and drug abuse and dependence are classified to this section of the code book. Alcohol abuse is defined as drinking alcohol to excess but not having a physical dependence on the alcohol. Alcohol dependence, also known as alcoholism, occurs when a person has become dependent on alcohol and is unable to stop drinking even though the alcoholism has negative effects on the person's health, social relationships, and normal daily activities such as work. Drug abuse is defined as taking drugs to excess but not having a dependence on them. Drug dependence occurs when there is a chronic use of drugs that creates a compulsion to take the drug in order to experience the effects from the drug. Figure 10-1 lists common addictive drugs. The following fifth digits are used with category codes 303, Alcohol dependence; 304, Drug dependence; and 305, Nondependent abuse of drugs:

0   Unspecified

1   Continuous

2   Episodic

3   In remission

Medical documentation needs to be reviewed to accurately select the fifth digits. If documentation does not justify fifth digits 1, 2, or 3, then the fifth digit of 0 must be selected to indicate that the abuse or dependence is unspecified.

Patients who are dependent on drugs and alcohol may experience withdrawal when they are not using the substances. Codes 291.0, 291.3, and 291.81 code alcohol withdrawal. Drug withdrawal is coded to 292.0.

The sequencing of codes for drug and alcohol abuse and dependence depends on the circumstances of the care and on the type of facility to which the patient is admitted.

When a patient is admitted for treatment of the substance abuse or dependence, the code for the abuse or dependence is sequenced first.

When the patient is admitted for a condition unrelated to their substance abuse but is a substance abuser or has a dependency, the code for the unrelated condition should be listed first.

When patients are admitted to substance abuse facilities, the code for the abuse or dependency should be sequenced first.

Depressive Disorder (Category Code 311)

Category code 311, Depressive disorder, not elsewhere classified is also in this section of codes. This code is used frequently by primary care providers in an office setting. Use of this code as a primary diagnosis by providers other than psychiatrists or psychologists is not widely accepted by insurance companies because it falls outside their scope of practice. Before this code can be assigned, conclusive documentation must support the diagnosis. The Exclude: note found in category 311 helps to further explain the use of code 311 or other more appropriate codes.

EXAMPLE: Tom Tic has experienced a brief depressed state because he lost his job. Code 309.0 is assigned.

Mary Mat is seen because she is experiencing depression because of marital stress. The physician records depression in her record. Code 311 is assigned.

Exercise 10–3   Coding of Category Codes 295–316

Select the correct ICD-9-CM code for the diagnoses listed.

1. Childhood schizophrenia _____

2. Acute hysterical psychosis _____

3. Depression with anxiety _____

4. Continual methadone dependence _____

5. Stuttering _____

6. Psychogenic dyspepsia _____

7. Hypomanic personality disorder _____

8. Chronic paranoid psychosis _____

9. Borderline schizophrenia _____

10. Claustrophobia _____

11. Heller's syndrome, active   _____

12. Reactive depressive psychosis   _____

13. Paraphrenia   _____

14. Tobacco dependence   _____

15. Atypical psychosis   _____

Mental Retardation (Category Codes 317–319)

Mental retardation is a condition in which the mind of the patient never fully develops. The coding in this section is based on the person's current level of functioning. When mental retardation is a result of injury or disease, an additional diagnosis should be coded to reflect the associated conditions.

Mental retardation is defined in ICD-9-CM as follows:

- **Mild mental retardation**—Code 317, an IQ of 50 to 70

- **Moderate mental retardation**—Code 318.0, an IQ of 35 to 49

- **Severe mental retardation**—Code 318.1, an IQ of 20 to 34

- **Profound mental retardation**—Code 318.2, an IQ under 20

- **Unspecified mental retardation**—Code 319, used when the medical documentation states that the patient is mentally retarded but the level of functioning is not recorded

Disease Highlight—Mental Retardation

Mental retardation is a genetic or acquired condition in which there is decreased intelligence. The genetic causes of mental retardation are:

- Down's syndrome

- Hypothyroidism

- Phenylketonuria

Acquired causes include:

- Birth injuries

- Anoxia

- Head trauma

- Poor nutrition

- Premature birth

- Prenatal maternal rubella or syphilis

- Blood type incompatibility

Signs and Symptoms:

Children with mental retardation show signs of decreased mental functioning compared to other children of the same age.

Clinical Testing:

IQ testing and observation of a child's functional levels confirm the diagnosis.

Treatment:

Treatment of patients with mental retardation varies depending on their functioning level. Severely retarded persons are institutionalized because they are unable to care for themselves without assistance. Mildly retarded persons are able to live fairly normal lives and to find employment with little psychological and social assistance.

Internet Links

To learn about addictions, Alzheimer's, depression, stress, personality disorders, and other psychiatric conditions, go to *www.apa.org*, the homepage of the American Psychological Association.

To learn more about the diagnosis and treatment of mental and emotional illness and substance use disorders, go the *www.psych.org*, the homepage of the American Psychiatric Association.

For information on current treatment, research, and prevention of drug abuse, go to *www.drugabuse.gov*, the homepage of the National Institute on Drug Abuse.

The American Academy of Addiction Psychiatry provides information about the treatment of addiction and research on the etiology, prevention, and identification of addictions at *www.aaap.org.*

The Alcohol Medical Scholars Program provides information on the identification and care of individuals with alcohol use disorders and other substance-related problems at *www.alcoholmedicalscholars.org.*

To learn more about the treatment of mental disorders, visit *www.mentalhealth.org* and *http://psychcentral.com/disorders.*

Summary

- Chapter 5 of ICD-9-CM classifies mental disorders.

- Provider documentation must be reviewed, and it must be used to justify codes selected for the coding of mental disorders.

- ICD-9-CM and DSM-IV are both used to classify mental disorders.

- Dementia is a form of psychosis and is classified in ICD-9-CM by etiology.

- Fourth and fifth digits are frequently used with chapter 5 of ICD-9-CM; therefore, coders need to thoroughly review provider documentation before selecting codes.

- Delusional and depressive features associated with dementia are identified at the fourth-digit level of ICD-9-CM.

- Alcohol abuse and alcohol dependence are classified separately in ICD-9-CM.

- Drug abuse and drug dependence are classified separately in ICD-9-CM.

- Abuse occurs when there is excess use of a substance; dependence occurs when person has become dependent on a substance and is unable to stop using the substance.

- A diagnosis of depression must be clearly supported by provider documentation for code selection.

- Mental retardation is classified in ICD-9-CM by a person's functional level and is described as mild, moderate, severe, profound, or unspecified.

Chapter Review

True/False: Indicate whether each question is true (T) or false (F).

1. _____ DSM-IV is the preferred nomenclature of mental disorders for third-party reimbursement.

2. _____ Alcohol abuse and dependence are classified to different codes in ICD-9-CM.

3. _____ Mild retardation is diagnosed when a person has an IQ of 30.

4. _____ Mental disorders are always congenital.

5. _____ Ginger Gin is admitted to New Days Drug and Alcohol Treatment Facility with the following diagnoses: gastritis due to alcoholism, continuous alcohol dependence. The code for the alcohol dependence should be sequenced first when payment for services is billed.

Fill-in-the-Blank: Enter the appropriate term(s) to complete each statement.

6. A slowly progressive decrease in mental abilities that includes lack of judgment, decreased memory, and a decrease in the ability to pay attention is known as _____.

7. A chronic use of drugs that creates a compulsion to take the drug in order to experience the effects from the drug is known as _____.

8. Psychiatric disorders diagnosed most commonly by psychiatrists are recorded by using _____ _____.

9. Manic-depressive episodes, also known as _____, occur when a person has elevated moods alternating with depressive episodes.

10. A person with an IQ of 40 would be diagnosed as having _____ mental retardation.

Coding Assignments

Instructions: Using an ICD-9-CM coding book, select the code for each diagnostic statement.

Diagnosis   **Code**

1. Presenile dementia with depressive features   _____

2. Obsessive-compulsive disorder   _____

3. Anxiety   _____

4. Borderline personality disorder   _____

5. Social phobia   _____

6. Narcissistic personality disorder   _____

7. Mental retardation, IQ 29   _____

8. Premature ejaculation   _____

9. Heroin dependence   _____

10. Passive personality disorder _____

11. Stress reaction due to family crisis _____

12. Anorexia nervosa _____

13. Psychogenic dysuria _____

14. Neurotic depression _____

15. Marijuana abuse, current _____

16. Alcoholic paranoia _____

17. Alcohol withdrawal syndrome _____

18. Senile dementia _____

19. Alcoholic dementia _____

20. Chronic paranoid schizophrenia _____

21. Senile dementia with depressive features _____

22. Vascular dementia with delusions _____

23. Transient organic psychosis _____

24. Subacute delirium _____

25. Excitative type psychosis _____

Case Studies

Instructions: Review each case study, and select the correct ICD-9-CM diagnostic code.

CASE 1

PATIENT: Tom Smith   DATE OF SERVICE: 9/10/XX

BLOOD PRESSURE: 140/90   WEIGHT: 164   PULSE: Rapid   TEMPERATURE: 100

Tom was seen today at the request of his wife for what she suspects is a recurrence of his cocaine dependence.

On physical examination, the following was noted:

EARS, EYES, NOSE, AND THROAT: Pupils are dilated.

HEART: Heart rate is increased; blood pressure is 140/90.

ABDOMEN: Soft, nontender, no abnormal masses

PSYCHIATRIC: Oriented to time and place. Patient is very talkative and admits to not eating for the last 36 hours with no sleep for the last 48 hours. Patient admits to using cocaine over the last month.

Referral made for inpatient treatment.

ICD-9-CM Code Assignment: _____

CASE 2

Nursing Facility Note of 2/7/XX

Sally Smith was admitted on 2/5/XX because of her medical conditions and her inability to care for herself at home. She was mildly cooperative throughout the exam; however, her dementia makes her obviously confused and at times she has delusions resulting from her senile dementia. Her psychoactive medications were reviewed and adjusted today. Her full medical history and physical was completed 2/5/XX by Dr. Jones. I am examining her today because she is experiencing a cough and fever.

HEENT: Normal

LUNGS: Congested, bronchitis present

ABDOMEN: Soft, nontender; active bowel sound; no masses noted

HEART: Regular rhythm without murmurs, pulses normal.

TEMPERATURE: 101.3   BLOOD PRESSURE: 125/85   PULSE: Regular

Medication orders written.

ICD-9-CM Code Assignment: _____

CASE 3

Psychiatric Office Note

Terry was seen today experiencing symptoms of mania, speech disturbances, and lack of sleep for 3 days due to his bipolar disorder. Patient states that he has not been taking his medications. I discussed with the patient the importance of taking his medications and instructed him to regularly take them. Current issues that present stress for the patient were discussed, including marital distress and financial issues. Patient was instructed to follow up at 1 month.

ICD-9-CM Code Assignment: _____

CASE 4

Emergency Department Note

PATIENT: Mary Hill   DATE OF SERVICE: 12/31/XX

AGE: 23

Mary was brought in by ambulance. She was at a New Year's Eve's Party and she has been drinking alcohol for 4 hours and passed out. According to her friend who accompanied her to the ER, Mary does not have an alcohol addiction and has no known medical conditions.

Physical Exam

Pupils are dilated.

HEART: Heart rate is decreased.

ABDOMEN: No abnormal findings

Patient has limited response to questions. While she was in the emergency room, she started to vomit. She was observed for 7 hours and then sent home. She was advised to seek counseling for possible alcohol addiction.

ICD-9-CM Code Assignment: _____

CASE 5

Physician's Office Note

NAME: John Nown   DATE OF SERVICE: 3/1/XX

BLOOD PRESSURE: 130/83   WEIGHT: 168   TEMPERATURE: 98.6

John is being seen today at his request because he has felt tired and has lost his appetite for the last 3 weeks since his wife died. He has no other complaints at this time.

He said he wants to make sure that he has no physical problems. Reviewing his record, I noted that all of his immunizations are current and that he is not due for any additional preventative medicine testing at this time.

Physical Exam:

HEENT: Within normal limits

HEART: Normal R&R, no murmurs

ABDOMEN: Soft and nontender, no masses; active bowel sounds

EXTREMITIES: Within normal limits

Patient is oriented to time, person, and surroundings with no confusion. Patient expressed that he is sad because of the loss of his wife. I told the patient that his tiredness is most likely due to the loss of his wife and that there are no abnormal physical findings at this time.

DIAGNOSIS: Adjustment disorder with depressed mood.

PLAN: Patient refused antidepressive medications and said he would seek counseling if he felt he needed it. He was instructed to call the office if he experienced any other symptoms and said he wanted to follow up with me in 3 weeks.

ICD-9-CM Code Assignment: _____

Diseases of the Nervous System and Sense Organs

Chapter Outline

Introduction

Introduction to the Body System

Coding of the Diseases of the Central
   Nervous System

Internet Links

Summary

Chapter Review

Coding Assignments

Case Studies

Objectives

At the conclusion of this chapter, the student will be able to:

1. Identify the major structures of the nervous system.
2. Explain conditions that involve the nervous system.
3. Explain conditions that involve the sensory organs.
4. Summarize the coding guidelines for this chapter.
5. Become familiar with the terminology used when coding conditions from this section.
6. Select and code diagnoses and procedures from case studies.

Key Terms

Adnexa

Alzheimer's Disease

Autonomic Nervous
   System

Bell's Palsy

Cataract

Central Nervous System
   (CNS)

Cerebrovascular
   Accident (CVA)

Conductive Hearing
   Loss

Conjunctivitis

Dementia

Encephalitis

Encephalomyelitis

Epilepsy

Glaucoma

Gram-Negative Bacteria

Gram-Positive Bacteria

Grand Mal

Hemiparesis

Hemiplegia

Infantile Cerebral Palsy

Meningitis

Multiple Sclerosis

Myelitis

Nervous System

Otosclerosis

Reminder

As you work through this chapter, you will need to have a copy of the ICD-9-CM coding book to reference.

Parasympathetic Nervous System	Peripheral Nervous System (PNS)	Retina	Sympathetic Nervous System
Parkinson's Disease	Petit Mal	Stapes	

Introduction

This chapter will discuss coding for conditions of the nervous system and sensory organs. The coding for the nervous system is very detailed and requires the coder to pay close attention to the provider documentation in order to assign the correct code.

Introduction to the Body System

The **nervous system** is the system that controls all bodily activities. The nervous system is divided into two main parts. The **central nervous system (CNS)** is the part of the nervous system that is made up of the brain and spinal cord. Codes 320–349 in the ICD-9-CM coding book classify diseases of the central nervous system. The **peripheral nervous system (PNS)** is the part of the nervous system that directly branches off the central nervous system. The 12 pairs of cranial nerves and 31 pairs of spinal nerves make up this system. Included in the peripheral nervous system is what is known as the **autonomic nervous system**. The autonomic nervous system encompasses the regulation of the activities of the cardiac muscle, smooth muscle, and glands. Codes 350–359 classify the remaining diagnoses of the nervous system. Ultimately, the brain controls all activities of the body's functions. If the brain dies, the body also dies. Figure 11-1 illustrates the organization of the central nervous system and the peripheral nervous system.

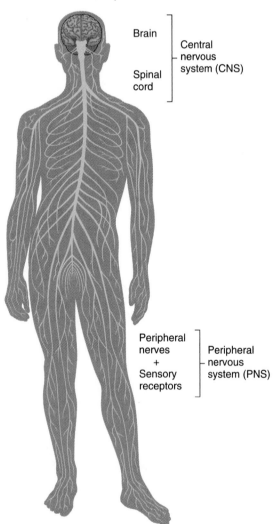

Figure 11-1 Central and peripheral nervous systems (From Ehrlich A, Schroeder CL. *Medical Terminology for Health Professions,* 4th ed. Clifton Park, NY: Delmar, Cengage Learning, 2001.)

Coding of the Diseases of the Central Nervous System

Chapter 6 of ICD-9-CM, "Diseases of the Nervous System and Sense Organs," is divided into the following sections:

Category Codes	Section Title
320–326	Inflammatory Diseases of the Central Nervous System
327	Organic Sleep Disorder
330–337	Hereditary and Degenerative Diseases of the Central Nervous System
338	Pain
339	Other Headache Syndromes
340–349	Other Disorders of the Central Nervous System
350–359	Disorders of the Peripheral Nervous System
360–379	Disorders of the Eye and Adnexa
380–389	Diseases of the Ear and Mastoid Process

Inflammatory Diseases of the Central Nervous System (Category Codes 320–326)

The first section of this chapter classifies diseases of the central nervous system. This is one of the more difficult sections of the coding book because of the notes associated with each code. It is vital to read all notes in the Alphabetic Index as well as in the Tabular List before assigning a code. This subsection requires the assignment of two codes in many cases to accurately code a condition.

> **EXAMPLE:** Patient is diagnosed with meningitis due to Lyme disease. In the Alphabetic Index under meningitis, due to Lyme disease, code 088.81 is listed first for the Lyme disease and then code 320.7 for the meningitis. The note in the Tabular List under code 320.7 reads "code first underlying disease," which is the Lyme disease.

The coder may encounter the terms *Gram-negative* and *Gram-positive* when reading documentation for bacterial meningitis. The terms refer to the differential staining test for bacterial identification. Gram-positive bacteria retain the dye color of violet, and Gram-negative bacteria change the dye color from violet to colorless. It is essential that the coder reference the patient's record to determine whether Gram-negative or Gram-positive bacteria have been identified during diagnostic laboratory studies.

Meningitis

Meningitis is an inflammation of the membranes, or the meninges, of the spinal cord or brain. Meningitis can be bacterial, nonbacterial, viral, or aseptic. ICD-9-CM classifies meningitis according to the type of organism or cause. It is important to note that if the documentation states nonbacterial, viral, or aseptic meningitis without further clarification, then the meningitis is coded to the 047 category, "Meningitis due to enterovirus." Diseases in these categories may result from bacterial infection spreading from another nearby infection such as a middle ear infection. When meningitis is a manifestation of another disease, code the underlying disease first.

Other conditions that code to these categories of the nervous system include encephalitis, an inflammation of the brain; myelitis, an inflammation of the spinal cord; and encephalomyelitis, an inflammation of both the brain and the spinal cord. Abscesses within the brain, spinal cord, or both, along with phlebitis and thrombophlebitis of intracranial venous sinuses, are all coded in these categories.

Hereditary and Degenerative Diseases of the Central Nervous System (Category Codes 330–337)

The conditions encountered in this section include Alzheimer's disease, a disease in which brain structure changes lead to memory loss, personality changes, and ultimately impaired ability to function. Another condition is dementia, which is a slow decline in mental function that impairs judgment and the ability to think. When a provider documents "dementia with Alzheimer's disease," both codes are needed. Clarification should also be made regarding the type of dementia.

Parkinson's disease, a progressive disease characterized by a masklike facial expression, weakened muscles, tremors, and involuntary movement, is classified by this section of ICD-9-CM. When Parkinson's disease is coded, it is important for the coder to identify any other associated conditions that may exist because these can affect code assignment. For example, the following codes are used to classify Parkinson's disease associated with other conditions:

Parkinson's disease	332.0
Secondary Parkinsonism	332.1
Parkinsonism in Huntington's disease	333.4
Dementia with Parkinsonism	331.82

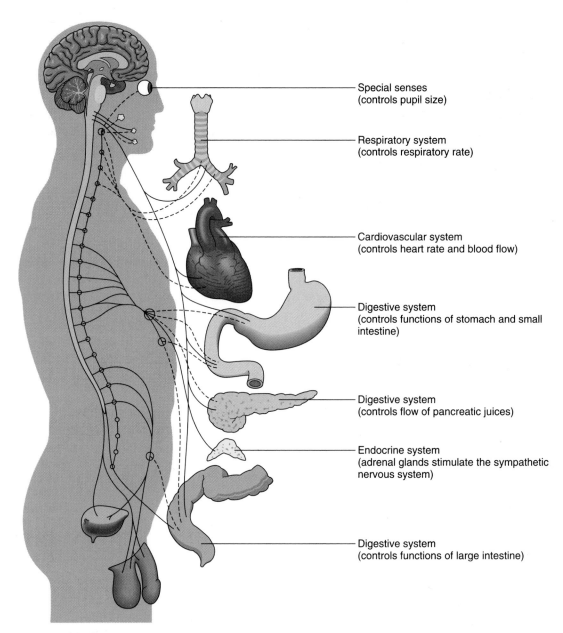

Figure 11-2 Autonomic nervous system and the major body systems involved (From Ehrlich A, Schroeder CL. *Medical Terminology for Health Professions,* 4th ed. Clifton Park, NY: Delmar, Cengage Learning, 2001.)

Disorders of the spinal cord and the autonomic nervous system are also coded to these categories of codes. These categories contain many notes, and the coder needs to be extremely diligent in reading all the information before assigning codes from this section.

Disorders of the autonomic nervous system conclude this section of codes. The autonomic processes are subdivided into parasympathetic and sympathetic. The parasympathetic nervous system controls digestion, constriction of the pupil of the eye, and smooth muscle contraction. When the body is not undergoing stressful events the parasympathetic system works to keep the body functions normal. The sympathetic nervous system controls reaction to stress, sometimes called the "fight-flight" reaction. The sympathetic nervous system will tell the brain that heart rate and blood flow need to increase. Figure 11-2 shows examples of major body systems affected by the autonomic nervous system.

Pain (Category Code 338)

Codes that fall in the 338 category were designed to be used along with codes from other chapters or categories to lend a more accurate reflection about acute or chronic pain and pain associated with neoplasms.

If a patient is assigned a diagnosis of "generalized pain," "pain attributed exclusively to psychological factors," or pain that is localized to a specific area, codes are not selected from this category. This is highlighted in the code book as an Exclude: note under the heading in the Tabular List for category 338. However, post-thoracotomy pain, as well as other postoperative pain, may be coded from this category. The Coding Guidelines give very detailed and specific instructions as to when code selection is allowed from this category.

Official ICD-9-CM Coding Guidelines:

Pain—Category 338

(1) General coding information

Codes in category 338 may be used in conjunction with codes from other categories and chapters to provide more detail about acute or chronic pain and neoplasm-related pain, unless otherwise indicated below.

If the pain is not specified as acute or chronic, do not assign codes from category 338, except for post-thoracotomy pain, postoperative pain, neoplasm-related pain, or central pain syndrome.

A code from subcategories 338.1 and 338.2 should not be assigned if the underlying (definitive) diagnosis is known, unless the reason for the encounter is pain control/management and not management of the underlying condition.

(a) Category 338 Codes as Principal or First-Listed Diagnosis

Category 338 codes are acceptable as the principal diagnosis or the first-listed code:

- *When pain control or pain management is the reason for the admission/encounter (e.g., a patient with displaced intervertebral disc, nerve impingement, and severe back pain presents for injection of steroid into the spinal canal). The underlying cause of the pain should be reported as an additional diagnosis, if known.*

- *When an admission or encounter is for a procedure aimed at treating the underlying condition (e.g., spinal fusion, kyphoplasty), a code for the underlying condition (e.g., vertebral fracture, spinal stenosis) should be assigned as the principal diagnosis. No code from category 338 should be assigned.*

- *When a patient is admitted for the insertion of a neurostimulator for pain control, assign the appropriate pain code as the principal or first-listed diagnosis. When an admission or encounter is for a procedure aimed at treating the underlying condition and a neurostimulator is inserted for pain control during the same admission/ encounter, a code for the underlying condition should be assigned as the principal diagnosis, and the appropriate pain code should be assigned as a secondary diagnosis.*

(b) Use of Category 338 Codes in Conjunction with Site-Specific Pain Codes

(i) Assigning Category 338 Codes and Site-Specific Pain Codes

Codes from category 338 may be used in conjunction with codes that identify the site of pain (including codes from chapter 16) if the category 338 code provides additional information. For example, if the code describes the site of the pain but does not fully describe whether the pain is acute or chronic, then both codes should be assigned.

(ii) Sequencing of Category 338 Codes with Site-Specific Pain Codes

The sequencing of category 338 codes with site-specific pain codes (including chapter 16 codes), is dependent on the circumstances of the encounter/admission as follows:

- *If the encounter is for pain control or pain management, assign the code from category 338, followed by the code identifying the specific site of pain (e.g., encounter for pain management for acute neck pain from trauma is assigned code 338.11, Acute pain due to trauma, followed by code 723.1, Cervicalgia, to identify the site of pain).*

- *If the encounter is for any other reason except pain control or pain management, and a related definitive diagnosis has not been established (confirmed) by the provider, assign the code for the specific site of pain first, followed by the appropriate code from category 338.*

(2) Pain due to devices, implants, and grafts

Pain associated with devices, implants, or grafts left in a surgical site (for example, painful hip prosthesis) is assigned to the appropriate code(s) found in chapter 17, "Injury and Poisoning." Use additional code(s) from category 338 to identify acute or chronic pain due to presence of the device, implant, or graft (338.18, 338.19, or 338.28–338.29).

(3) Postoperative pain

Post-thoracotomy pain and other postoperative pain are classified to subcategories 338.1 and 338.2, depending on whether the pain is acute or chronic. The default for post-thoracotomy and other postoperative pain not specified as acute or chronic is the code for the acute form.

Routine or expected postoperative pain immediately after surgery should not be coded.

(a) Postoperative pain not associated with specific postoperative complication

Postoperative pain not associated with a specific postoperative complication is assigned to the appropriate postoperative pain code in category 338.

(b) Postoperative pain associated with specific postoperative complication

Postoperative pain associated with a specific postoperative complication (such as painful wire sutures) is assigned to the appropriate code(s) found in chapter 17, "Injury and Poisoning." If appropriate, use additional code(s) from category 338 to identify acute or chronic pain (338.18 or 338.28). If pain control/management is the reason for the encounter, a code from category 338 should be assigned as the principal or first-listed diagnosis, in accordance with Section I.C.6.a.1.a above.

(c) Postoperative pain as principal or first-listed diagnosis

Postoperative pain may be reported as the principal or first-listed diagnosis when the stated reason for the admission/encounter is documented as postoperative pain control/management.

(d) Postoperative pain as secondary diagnosis

Postoperative pain may be reported as a secondary diagnosis code when a patient presents for outpatient surgery and develops an unusual or inordinate amount of postoperative pain.

The provider's documentation should be used to guide the coding of postoperative pain, as well as Section III, "Reporting Additional Diagnoses," and Section IV, "Diagnostic Coding and Reporting in the Outpatient Setting."

See Section II.I.2 for information on the sequencing of diagnoses for patients admitted to hospital inpatient care following postoperative observation.

See Section II.J for information on the sequencing of diagnoses for patients admitted to hospital inpatient care from outpatient surgery.

See Section IV.A.2 for information on the sequencing of diagnoses for patients admitted for observation.

(4) Chronic pain

Chronic pain is classified to subcategory 338.2. There is no time frame defining when pain becomes chronic pain. The provider's documentation should be used to guide the use of these codes.

(5) Neoplasm-Related Pain

Code 338.3 is assigned to pain documented as being related, associated or due to cancer, primary or secondary malignancy, or tumor. This code is assigned regardless of whether the pain is acute or chronic.

This code may be assigned as the principal or first-listed code when the stated reason for the admission/ encounter is documented as pain control/pain management. The underlying neoplasm should be reported as an additional diagnosis.

When the reason for the admission/encounter is management of the neoplasm and the pain associated with the neoplasm is also documented, code 338.3 may be assigned as an additional diagnosis.

See Section I.C.2 for instructions on the sequencing of neoplasms for all other stated reasons for the admission/encounter (except for pain control/pain management).

(6) *Chronic pain syndrome*

This condition is different than the term chronic pain, and therefore this code should only be used when the provider has specifically documented this condition. (See Appendix A, Section I, C6, a, 1–6.)

Other Disorders of the Central Nervous System (Category Codes 340–349)

Categories of codes 340–349 classify the remaining diseases of the central nervous system. Multiple sclerosis, an inflammatory disease of the central nervous system in which T cells and macrophages break down myelin fibers, is coded to this section.

Disease Highlight—Multiple Sclerosis

Multiple sclerosis (MS) is a chronic, disease that attacks the central nervous system. The patient's own body attacks the myelin fibers, causing scarring or sclerosis. This sclerosis interrupts the nerve impulses traveling to and from the brain and spinal cord. There is no clear conclusive clinical evidence of any type of pathogenesis that would cause MS.

Signs and Symptoms:

The symptoms of MS vary from person to person and include:

- Numbness in the limbs

- Visual disturbances

- Muscle weakness

- Emotional problems, such as mood swings and depression

- Urinary problems may also occur, such as incontinence, urgency, or frequency.

Clinical Testing:

MS is difficult to diagnose. Testing may include:

- Electrophoresis

- CT and MRI scans

- Lumbar puncture

- EEG

Treatment:

Patients with MS receive symptomatic treatment, such as physical therapy and steroid treatment, to relieve the symptoms.

Hemiplegia and hemiparesis are also classified to this category of codes, category 342. Hemiplegia is a condition in which one side of the body is paralyzed due to brain hemorrhage, cerebral thrombosis, embolis, or a tumor of the cerebrum. Hemiparesis is a synonym for hemiplegia. This section of codes requires a fifth digit to indicate which side of the body is affected. The sides are not listed as right or left, but as dominant, nondominant, or unspecified. It is the responsibility of the coder to bring this to the attention of the provider to note which of these modifying terms is appropriate. These codes are assigned only if they occur during the current episode of care, usually a hospital admission with relation to a cerebrovascular accident (CVA), or what is commonly known as a stroke. If further encounters take place outside the hospital, then the hemiplegia is coded as a late effect of the CVA using code 438.2X.

Infantile cerebral palsy, a disorder that is present at birth, is chronic and nonprogressive and is coded in this section. Motor function of the brain is impaired when a patient is diagnosed with infantile cerebral palsy.

Epilepsy is a transient disturbance of cerebral function that is recurrent and characterized by episodes of seizures. The most severe seizure is the grand mal. Less severe seizures are identified as petit mal. There may be convulsions, abnormal behavior, and loss of consciousness when a seizure occurs. Because seizures can occur in other diseases or conditions, the coder should not assume that epilepsy is present unless the provider specifically documents the seizure as being caused by the patient's epilepsy. A diagnosis of epilepsy carries serious legal consequences, such as loss of a driver's license or the inability to obtain insurance, so extreme care needs to be taken when assigning this diagnosis.

Disorders of the Peripheral Nervous System (Category Codes 350–359)

There are 12 pairs of cranial nerves. They originate in the brain from the brain stem. The pairs are identified by Roman numerals in the order in which they arise from the anterior to posterior portion of the brain. Figure 11-3 illustrates the nerves, their origins, and their names.

Disorders or injury to any of the cranial nerves can cause severe loss of function, such as Bell's palsy, code 351.0, which is a disorder of the facial nerves caused by a lesion on a facial nerve, producing facial distortion and unilateral paralysis of the face. See Figure 11-4 for an illustration of a person with Bell's palsy. Documentation is essential for coding in this section because specific nerve identification is sometimes necessary to assign the correct code.

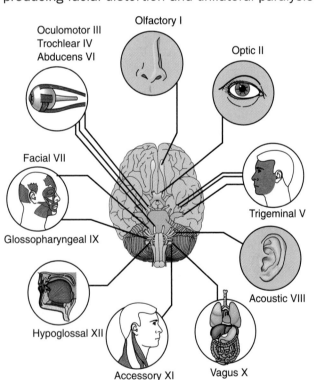

Figure 11-3 Cranial nerves are identified with Roman numerals and are named for the areas or functions they serve (From Ehrlich A, Schroeder CL. *Medical Terminology for Health Professions,* 4th ed. Clifton Park, NY: Delmar, Cengage Learning, 2001.)

Disorders of the Eye and Adnexa (Category Codes 360–379)

Coding disorders of the eye can be difficult because it is very detailed. It is important that the coder understand the anatomy of the eye or have detailed diagrams and well documented provider notes to assist with the coding. Figures 11-5 and 11-6 illustrate the complexity of the eye anatomy.

The adnexa means the accessory or appendage of an organ. Figure 11-7 diagrams the adnexa of the eyes.

Codes beginning with category 361 classify disorders of the retina. The retina is the innermost layer of the eye. The retina is where the rods and cones are located, which distinguish color receptors from black-and-white receptors. If the coder encounters a diagnosis of hypertensive retinopathy, the code for 362.11 should also be accompanied by the specific code for the type of hypertension the patient has.

EXAMPLE: The patient presents today with some visual disturbances such as blurry vision and headaches. The patient is also being treated for uncontrolled benign hypertension, which is now causing a problem with his eyes. After preliminary testing, it has been determined that patient is suffering from hypertensive retinopathy.

In our example, there is a direct correlation being made between the hypertension and the retinopathy. The hypertension is stated as benign. So our code assignment is 362.11 with 401.1.

Also classified in this section of the chapter are conjunctivitis, cataracts, and glaucoma. These are all commonly encountered diagnoses. Conjunctivitis is an inflammation of the conjunctiva. Cataracts are opacities of the lens of the eye. If a patient has developed cataracts due to the use of high-risk medications over a long period of time, the diagnosis of V58.69, Long-term (current) use of other medications, needs to be added to the cataracts.

Glaucoma is an increase in intraocular pressure, which can damage the optic nerve. There are different types of glaucoma, so provider documentation is important to assign the correct codes from the series of codes on glaucoma. Modifying terms associated with a diagnoses of glaucoma include *borderline, open-angle, primary angle-closure, corticosteriod-induced,* and so on. Reference category code 365 to become familiar with the classifications of glaucoma.

Figure 11-4 Bell's palsy (From Neighbors M, Tannehill-Jones R. *Human Diseases,* 2nd ed. Clifton Park, NY: Delmar, Cengage Learning, p. 273.)

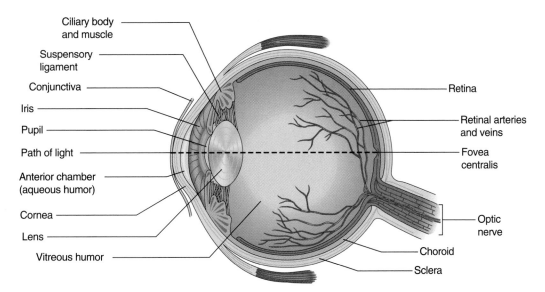

Figure 11-5 Cross-section of the structures of the eyeball (From Ehrlich A, Schroeder CL. *Medical Terminology for Health professions*, 4th ed. Clifton Park, NY: Delmar, Cengage Learning, 2001.)

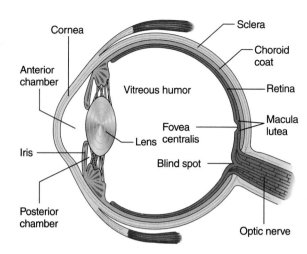

Figure 11-6 Structures of the eye (From Ehrlich A, Schroeder CL. *Medical Terminology for Health Professions,* 4th ed. Clifton Park, NY: Delmar, Cengage Learning, 2001.)

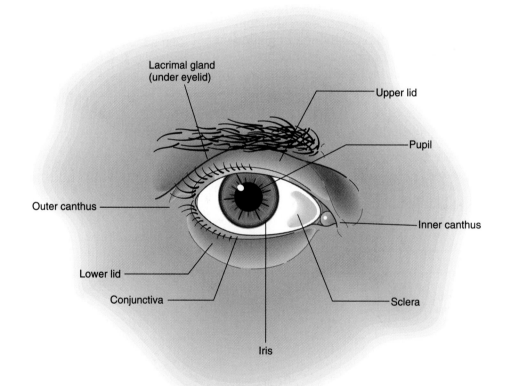

Figure 11-7 Major structures and adnexa of the right eye (From Ehrlich A, Schroeder CL. *Medical Terminology for Health Professions*, 4th ed. Clifton Park, NY: Delmar, Cengage Learning, 2001.)

Exercise 11–1   Assigning Diagnostic Codes

For each diagnostic statement, assign an ICD-9-CM code:

1. Acute follicular conjunctivitis _____
2. Angular blepharoconjunctivitis _____
3. Macular keratitis _____
4. Blindness in one eye and low vision in the other—impairment level not specified _____
5. Transient visual loss _____
6. After-cataract, obscuring vision _____
7. Binocular vision disorder _____
8. Paracecal scotoma _____
9. Total internal ophthalmoplegia _____
10. Atrophy of sphincter of iris _____

Diseases of the Ear and Mastoid Process (Category Codes 380–389)

This section includes codes that involve the external, middle, and inner ear. The external ear includes the external auditory canal, auricle, and helix. The middle ear is where the eustachian tubes and the auditory tubes are found. The inner ear houses the cochlea, acoustic nerves, and the organ of Corti. Figure 11-8 shows a cross-section of the ear and the various structures found there.

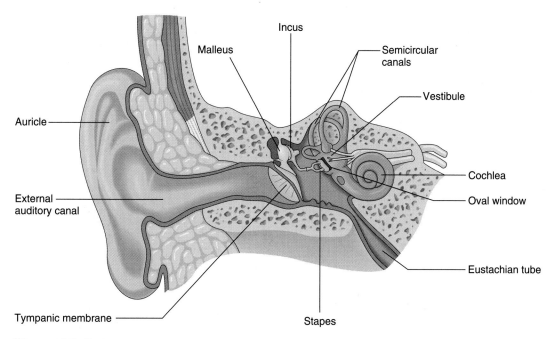

Figure 11-8 Cross-section of the structures of the ear (From Ehrlich A, Schroeder CL. *Medical Terminology for Health Professions,* 4th ed. Clifton Park, NY: Delmar, Cengage Learning, 2001.)

When coding hearing loss, the coder needs to distinguish between conductive hearing loss and sensory hearing loss. **Conductive hearing loss** usually involves the external or middle ear. Otitis media is a common condition of conductive hearing loss in children. In adults, a more common condition involves the stapes. The **stapes** is the third bone in the middle ear. If this bone becomes fixed and does not move any more, a condition called **otosclerosis** occurs and causes hearing loss.

Internet Links

To learn more about diseases of the nervous system and sense organs, visit the following sites for more information:

Parkinson's disease: *www.apdaparkinson.com* and *www.pdf.org*.

Disorders of the eye: *www.artifical-eye.com* and *www.stlukeseye.com/Conditions*.

Epilepsy: *www.epilepsyfoundation.org*.

Neurological disorders: *www.biausa.org* and *www.neuroexam.com*.

Nervous system and sense organs: *http://stdavids.com/ebsco.aspx*

Summary

- The nervous system controls all bodily activity.

- The nervous system is divided into the central nervous system, the brain and spinal cord, and the peripheral nervous system, which branches off the central nervous system.

- Reading all the notes in the Alphabetic Index and Tabular List is essential to correct code assignment because numerous notes appear for the coding of the nervous system and sense organs.

- Provider documentation is critical to correct code assignment.

- Coding for the eye is very detailed. Care should be given to understanding the provider's note with regard to these conditions.

- Coding conditions of the ear entails understanding whether you are selecting codes for conditions that impact with the external, middle, or inner ear.

Chapter Review

True/False: Indicate whether each statement is true (T) or false (F).

1. _____ The nervous system is divided into three main parts.

2. _____ The autonomic nervous system regulates the activity of the smooth muscle.

3. _____ Gram-positive bacteria turn dye color to blue.

4. _____ Diseases of the CNS are coded to the categories 320–326.

5. _____ Dementia is a relatively quick decline in mental function.

6. _____ Infantile cerebral palsy is present at birth.

7. _____ V58.69 is the correct code to use if the patient is on high-risk medications over a long period of time.

8. _____ The retina is the innermost layer of the eye.

9. _____ The most severe form of seizure is grand mal.

10. _____ Conductive hearing loss involves the inner ear.

Fill-in-the-Blank: Enter the appropriate term(s) to complete each statement.

11. _____ is an inflammation of the membranes of the spinal cord or brain.

12. For a patient with the diagnosis of Alzheimer's dementia, _____ code(s) are needed to properly code this diagnosis.

13. The _____ controls all bodily activities.

14. The _____ division of the autonomic nervous system is what controls digestion.

15. PNS stands for _____.

16. Alzheimer's disease falls into the _____ category of codes.

17. The _____ is the third bone in the middle ear.

18. A synonym for hemiplegia is _____.

19. _____ is an increase in intraocular pressure, which can damage the optic nerve.

20. The inflammatory disease of the CNS in which T cells and macrophages break down myelin fibers is called _____.

Coding Assignments

Instructions: Using an ICD-9-CM coding book, select the code for each diagnostic statement.

Diagnosis	Code
1. Conductive hearing loss of the external ear	_____
2. Retinal detachment, partial with multiple defects	_____
3. Gram-negative anaerobic meningitis	_____
4. Mycotic meningitis	_____
5. Exophoria	_____
6. Eustachian tube dysfunction	_____
7. Hyperacusis	_____
8. Reflex sympathetic dystrophy of the arm	_____
9. Staphylococcal meningitis	_____
10. Anterior scleritis	_____
11. Duane's syndrome	_____
12. Iridoschisis	_____

13. Phantom limb syndrome _____

14. Narcolepsy without cataplexy _____

15. Postviral encephalitis _____

16. Hemiplegia, right side _____

17. Migraine headache _____

18. Clonic epilepsy _____

19. Foreign body in lens of eye (retained) _____

20. Diabetic cataract _____

21. Retained intraocular foreign body _____

22. Leucocoria _____

23. Vestibular neuronitis _____

24. Cholesterin granuloma _____

25. Fistula of the mastoid _____

Case Studies

Instructions: Review each case study, and select the correct ICD-9-CM diagnostic code.

CASE 1

Physician's Office Note

9/1/XX

Patient presents for reevaluation of eyes.

Patient states that both eyes are "very itchy and dry, and are driving me crazy."

In the morning her eyes are dry and have matter all around them.

EXAM:

    EYES: Appear crusty

    OD 20/30 + 2

    OS 20/20 – 1

    PUPILS: Within normal limits

    EOM: Within normal limits

    TONO: 17/13

    SLIT LAMP: Marginal blepharitis in both eyes

  PLAN: Tobradex QID both eyes. Follow up in 7 days or if symptoms worsen.

ICD-9-CM Code Assignment: _____

CASE 2

Patient presents as a follow-up to her decreased ability to see when reading at night. Patient states that her activities of daily living have been decreased due to her sight.

EYE EXAM: Reveals decreased visual acuity to the 20/200 level in her left eye. The decreased acuity is caused by a 2+ nuclear sclerotic and cortical spoking and 2+ posterior subcapsular cataract.

Treatment options were discussed with the patient. She has requested surgery to correct the left senile cataract. She will be scheduled for a cataract extraction with posterior chamber intraocular lens implant.

ICD-9-CM Code Assignment: _____

CASE 3

Patient presents as follow-up to review symptoms that include weakness and involuntary muscular contractions of the hands and arms. Patient has experienced these symptoms for the last 8 months. Patient is also here to discuss findings from EMG and muscle biopsy.

EXAM:

HEENT: Within normal limits

EXTREMITIES: Involuntary muscle contractions observed, weakness noted in forearms.

HEART: Normal

ABDOMEN: Soft, nontender; no masses

PSYCH: Oriented to time and place

Findings from EMG and muscle biopsy confirm amyotrophic lateral sclerosis. This was discussed with patient. It was suggested to the patient that he should be seen at the ALS Clinic by Dr. Smith. Patient was agreeable.

ICD-9-CM Code Assignment: _____

CASE 4

Darcy was brought to the doctor's office by her parents. She is a 5-year-old female who is running a fever of 103°, has been vomiting for the past 12 hours, appears to be dehydrated, and has a bit of a rash on the trunk. Blood, nasal, and urine cultures were run. as well as a CT scan of the brain. The cultures came back with a positive diagnosis of pneumococcal meningitis. Darcy was started on IV therapy and admitted to the hospital until she stabilized.

ICD-9-CM Code Assignment: _____

CASE 5

Emergency Department Note

This 4-year-old female was brought into the emergency room. Her left eye appeared inflamed. Her mother said that there was a sudden onset of inflammation in her left eye.

Examination of the left eye revealed inflammation of the conjunctiva.

Her ears, nose, and throat were normal.

She was given an ophthalmic ointment to apply to both eyes for 10 days.

ICD-9-CM Code Assignment: _____

Chapter Outline

Introduction

Introduction to the Body Systems

Coding of Diseases of the Circulatory
  System

Internet Links

Summary

Chapter Review

Coding Assignment

Case Studies

Objectives

At the conclusion of this chapter, the student will be able to:

1. Identify diseases of the circulatory system.
2. Discuss ICD-9-CM coding guidelines for diseases of the circulatory system.
3. Summarize the coding guidelines for coding mitral and aortic valve disorders.
4. List the types of hypertension and the codes for each.
5. Accurately code diseases of the circulatory system.
6. Select and code diagnoses from case studies.

Key Terms

Angina Pectoris

Arteries

Arteriosclerotic Heart
  Disease

Benign Hypertension

Cardiac Dysrhythmias

Cardiomyopathy

Cerebral Hemorrhage

Cerebral Infarction

Cerebrovascular
  Accident (CVA)

Cerebrovascular
  Disease

Chorea

Chronic Ischemic Heart
  Disease

Diastolic Blood
  Pressure

Endocarditis

Healed Myocardial
  Infarction

Heart

Heart Attack

Heart Failure

Hemorrhoids

Hypertension

Hypertension Table

Reminder

As you work through this chapter, you will need to have a copy of the ICD-9-CM coding book to reference.

Hypertensive Heart Disease

Hypertensive Chronic Kidney Disease

Hypotension

Ischemic Heart Disease

Malignant Hypertension

Myocardial Infarction (MI)

Myocarditis

Obstetrical Period

Occlusion

Old Myocardial Infarction

Pericarditis

Pericardium

Phlebitis

Portal Vein Thrombosis

Pulmonary Artery

Pulmonary Vein

Secondary Hypertension

Stenosis

Stroke

Systolic Blood Pressure

Thrombolytic Therapy

Thrombophlebitis

Transient Cerebral Ischemia

Transient Hypertension

Unspecified Hypertension

Unstable Angina

Varicose Veins

Veins

Introduction

Chapter 7 of ICD-9-CM contains codes for diseases of the circulatory system, except circulatory conditions that occur during an obstetrical period, the time from pregnancy until 6 weeks after delivery, or that are determined to be a congenital anomaly. Circulatory disorders that occur during the obstetrical period are coded to chapter 11 of ICD-9-CM, "Complications of Pregnancy, Childbirth, and the Puerperium," and circulatory congenital anomalies are coded to chapter 14 of ICD-9-CM, "Congenital Anomalies."

> **EXAMPLE:** Hypertensive diseases code to 401–405 excluding hypertensive diseases that complicate pregnancy, childbirth, or the puerperium, which code to 642.0X–642.9X. The diagnosis of malignant hypertension codes to 401.0, whereas a diagnosis of malignant hypertension complicating pregnancy codes to 642.2X, as found in chapter 11 of ICD-9-CM, "Complications of Pregnancy, Childbirth, and the Puerperium."

The body structures found in this chapter of ICD-9-CM are also referred to as the cardiovascular system. As discussed earlier in Chapter 9 of this text, the cardiovascular system includes the heart and the blood vessels.

Introduction to the Body System

The circulatory system consists of the following organs and body structures:

- Arteries—Carry oxygen-rich blood from the heart to the body (with the exception of the pulmonary artery, which carries deoxygenated blood from the heart to the lungs)

- Veins—Carry deoxygenated blood from the body back to the heart (with the exception of the pulmonary vein, which carries oxygenated blood back to the heart)

- Heart—A muscular organ, located between the lungs and to the left of the midline of the body, that pumps blood throughout the body

The blood vessels of the body are considered the longest system of the body. The heart is considered one of the strongest organs of the body, pumping an average of 4,000 gallons of blood a day for an adult. It is important for coders to be able to identify the various arteries, veins, and specific parts and structures of the heart.

> **EXAMPLE:** A patient has been diagnosed with left posterior tibial artery occlusion. To accurately code this diagnosis, the coder must be able to identify that this artery is found in the lower extremities. To select a code, the term *occlusion* is located in the Alphabetic Index, which is further divided into anatomical structures. Figure 12-1 illustrates the index entry.

Arterial circulation (Figure 12-2), venous circulation (Figure 12-3), and heart pulmonary circulation (Figure 12-4) must be understood for correct code selection.

Occlusion
    anus 569.49
        congenital 751.2
        infantile 751.2
    aortoiliac (chronic) 444.0
    aqueduct of Sylvius 331.4
        congenital 742.3
            with spina bifida (see also Spina bifida) 741.0
    arteries of extremities, lower 444.22
        without thrombus or embolus (see also Arteriosclerosis, extremities) 440.20
        due to stricture or stenosis 447.1
        upper 444.21
            without thrombus or embolus (see also Arteriosclerosis, extremities) 440.20
            due to stricture or stenosis 447.1
    artery NEC (see also Embolism, artery) 444.9
        auditory, internal 433.8
        basilar 433.0
            with other precerebral artery 433.3
            bilateral 433.3
        brain or cerebral (see also Infarct, brain) 434.9
        carotid 433.1
            with other precerebral artery 433.3
            bilateral 433.3
        cerebellar (anterior inferior) (posterior inferior) (superior) 433.8
        cerebral (see also Infarct, brain) 434.9
        choroidal (anterior) 433.8
        chronic total
            coronary 414.2
            extremity(ies) 440.4
        communicating posterior 433.8
        complete
            coronary 414.2
            extremity(ies) 440.4
        coronary (thrombotic) (see also Infarct, myocardium) 410.9
            acute 410.9
                without myocardial infarction 411.81
            chronic total 414.2
            complete 414.2
            healed or old 412
            total 414.2
        extremity(ies)
            chronic total 440.4
            complete 440.4
            total 440.4
        hypophyseal 433.8
        iliac 444.81
        mesenteric (embolic) (thrombotic) (with gangrene) 557.0
        pontine 433.8
        precerebral NEC 433.9
            late effect—see Late effect(s) (of) cerebrovascular disease
            multiple or bilateral 433.3
            puerperal, postpartum, childbirth 674.0
            specified NEC 433.8
        renal 593.81
        retinal—see Occlusion, retina, artery
        spinal 433.8
        vertebral 433.2
            with other precerebral artery 433.3
            bilateral 433.3

Figure 12-1 Alphabetic Index listing of occlusion

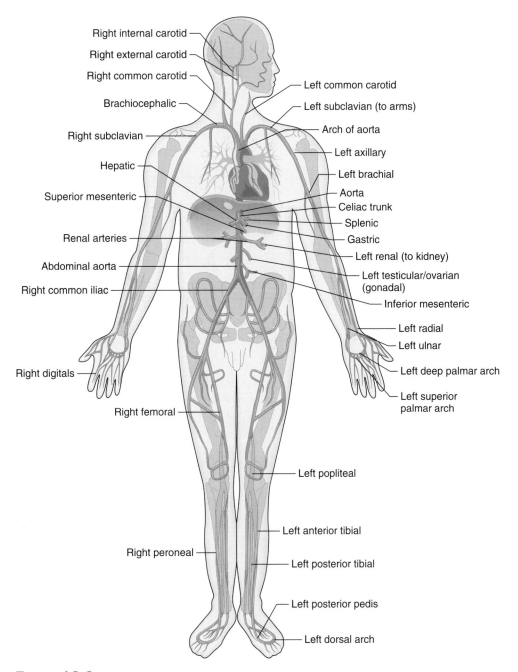

Figure 12-2 Arterial circulation

Exercise 12–1   Identifying Arteries and Veins

For each of the arteries and veins listed, state where the structure is located: abdominal cavity (A), lower extremities (L), thoracic (T), and upper extremities (U). (Reference Figures 12-2, 12-3, and 12-4.)

1. Right femoral artery   _____

2. Left renal vein   _____

3. Left great saphenous vein _____

4. Right ulnar artery   _____

5. Arch of aorta   _____

6. Left ovarian vein   _____

7. Pulmonary artery   _____

8. Superior palmar arch   _____

9. Peroneal artery   _____

10. Hepatic artery   _____

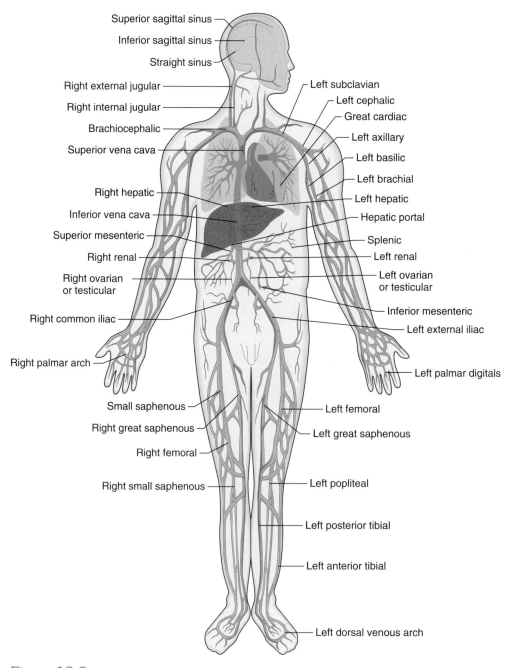

Figure 12-3 Venous circulation

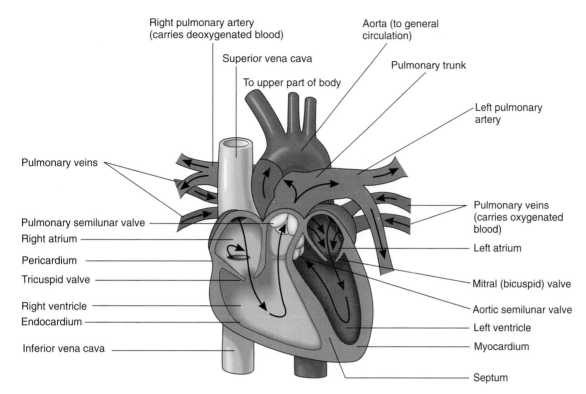

Figure 12-4 Heart pulmonary circulation

Coding of Diseases of the Circulatory System

Many circulatory system disorders are interrelated. When a patient has a cardiovascular disease, it can affect many vessels throughout the entire cardiovascular system and damage various organs. Circulatory system disorders can be caused by infections as well as by physiological factors.

Acute Rheumatic Fever and Rheumatic Heart Disease (Category Codes 390–398)

Acute rheumatic fever develops, usually in children ages 5 to 15 years, following a group A hemolytic *Streptococci* infection of the pharynx. ICD-9-CM classifies acute cases of the disease to codes 390–392 and chronic rheumatic heart disease to codes 393–398. Symptoms of acute rheumatic fever include abdominal pain, fever, joint pain, skin changes, chorea (involuntary movements of the face, tongue, and upper extremities), and lesions of the heart, blood vessels, and connective tissue. Chronic rheumatic heart disease results from an attack or attacks of rheumatic fever that cause damage to the heart, particularly the aortic and mitral valves.

ICD-9-CM assumes that certain valve disorders have a rheumatic etiology. The Alphabetic Index provides guidance to coders for determining whether a valvular disorder has a rheumatic etiology. ICD-9-CM assumes the following:

- A disorder involving both the mitral and aortic valve is rheumatic in origin; for example, mitral valve stenosis with aortic obstruction codes to 396.0.

- Some mitral valve disorders of unspecified origin are presumed to be rheumatic in origin unless specified in the diagnostic statement; for example, mitral stenosis (394.0) versus congenital mitral stenosis (746.5).

- Aortic disorders are assumed to be nonrheumatic unless the diagnostic statement specifies that the aortic disorder is rheumatic in origin. For example, aortic stenosis codes to 424.1, whereas rheumatic aortic stenosis codes to 395.0.

Let the Alphabetic Index be your guide to code disorders of the heart valves. Completing the following exercise illustrates how ICD-9-CM assumes that certain valve disorders are rheumatic in etiology.

Exercise 12–2   Coding Mitral and Aortic Valve Disorders

Select the appropriate ICD-9-CM code for the following diagnoses, noting whether the disorder is considered of rheumatic (R) etiology or of nonrheumatic (N) etiology. The first two examples are completed for you.

Etiology	Code	
1. Rheumatic aortic stenosis	395.0	R
2. Aortic stenosis	424.1	N
3. Aortic and mitral valve insufficiency		
4. Mitral valve stenosis		
5. Stenosis of mitral and aortic valve		
6. Mitral valve insufficiency and stenosis		
7. Mitral valve insufficiency		
8. Aortic valve insufficiency		
9. Aortic valve insufficiency and stenosis		
10. Rheumatic aortic insufficiency		

Hypertensive Disease (Category Codes 401–405)

Codes for hypertenison, hypertensive heart disease, and hypertensive chronic kidney disease are coded to category codes 401–405. Because of the interrelationship of hypertension and other hypertensive conditions, coders must pay close attention to the instructional notations found in both the Alphabetic Index and the Tabular List.

Hypertension

Hypertension is an increase in systolic blood pressure (the pressure on the arterial walls during the heart muscle contraction), in diastolic blood pressure (the pressure on the arterial walls during relaxation of the heart muscle), or in both.

ICD-9-CM uses a table in the Alphabetic Index, commonly known as the hypertension table, to index the various forms of hypertension. The hypertension table can be difficult to read because of the various levels of indentations. Remember to pull out a ruler or straight edge to identify the identations! The first subterm of the table lists conditions that are associated with hypertension, such as heart involvement, renal involvement, and renal sclerosis or failure. The table alphabetically lists subterms such as accelerated, antepartum, cardiorenal, and so on. It should also be noted that the table contains an entry for the subterm due to. This entry identifies hypertension that is caused by the various conditions listed, such as hypertension due to a brain tumor. Figure 12-5 illustrates the hypertension table.

Hypertension Table	Malignant	Benign	Unspecified
Hypertension, hypertensive (arterial) (arteriolar) (crisis) (degeneration) (disease) (essential) (fluctuating) (idiopathic) (intermittent) (labile) (low renin) (orthostatic) (paroxysmal) (primary) (systemic) (uncontrolled) (vascular)	401.0	401.1	401.9
with			
chronic kidney disease			
stage I through stage IV, or unspecified	403.00	403.10	403.90
stage V or end stage renal disease	403.01	403.11	403.91
heart involvement (conditions classifiable to 429.0–429.3, 429.8, 429.9 due to hypertension) (see also Hypertension, heart)	402.00	402.10	402.90
with kidney involvement—see Hypertension, cardiorenal			
renal involvement (only conditions classifiable to 585, 586, 587) (excludes conditions classifiable to 584) (see also Hypertension, kidney)	403.00	403.10	403.90
with heart involvement—see Hypertension, cardiorenal failure (and sclerosis) (see also Hypertension, kidney)	403.01	403.11	403.91
sclerosis without failure (see also Hypertension, kidney)	403.00	403.10	403.90
accelerated (see also Hypertension, by type, malignant)	401.0	-	-
antepartum—see Hypertension, complicating pregnancy, childbirth, or the puerperium			
cardiorenal (disease)	404.00	404.10	404.90
with			
chronic kidney disease			
stage I through stage IV, or unspecified	404.00	404.10	404.90
and heart failure	404.01	404.11	404.91
stage V or end stage renal disease	404.02	404.12	404.92
and heart failure	404.03	404.13	404.93
heart failure	404.01	404.11	404.91
and chronic kidney disease	404.01	404.11	404.91
stage I through stage IV or unspecified	404.01	404.11	404.91
stage V or end stage renal disease	404.03	404.13	404.93
cardiovascular disease (arteriosclerotic) (sclerotic)	402.00	402.10	402.90
with			
heart failure	402.01	402.11	402.91
renal involvement (conditions classifiable to 403) (see also Hypertension, cardiorenal)	404.00	404.10	404.90

Figure 12-5 Hypertension table

The hypertension table is also divided into three columns that identify the various subcategories of hypertension:

- Malignant hypertension—A severe form of hypertension, with common blood pressure readings of 200/140 mm Hg or higher, that frequently has an abrupt onset and a duration of a few months [Immediate treatment is crucial. Malignant hypertension, even with treatment, can lead to cerebral hemorrhages, encephalopathy, nephropathy (such as renal failure), retinopathy, heart failure, or myocardial ischemia.]

- Benign hypertension—Mildly elevated blood pressure that remains relatively stable over many years

- Unspecified hypertension—Hypertension that is not specified as malignant or benign in the diagnostic statement

If the patient's record does not specify that the hypertension is malignant or benign, the unspecified code should be assigned.

Official ICD-9-CM Coding Guideline:

The Hypertension Table, found under the main term, Hypertension, in the Alphabetic Index, contains a complete listing of all conditions due to or associated with hypertension and classifies them according to malignant, benign, and unspecified. (See Appendix A, Section I, C7, a.)

Hypertension, Essential, or NOS—Assign hypertension (arterial) (essential) (primary) (systemic) (NOS) to category code 401 with the appropriate fourth digit to indicate malignant (.0), benign (.1), or unspecified (.9). Do not use either .0 malignant or .1 benign unless medical record documentation supports such a designation. (See Appendix A, Section I, C7, a, 1.)

At times physicians may describe hypertension as controlled or uncontrolled. There is no way to differentiate between controlled and uncontrolled states of hypertension within the ICD-9-CM coding system. Therefore, the following guidelines should be followed.

Official ICD-9-CM Coding Guideline:

Hypertension, Controlled

Assign appropriate code from categories 401–405. This diagnostic statement usually refers to an existing state of hypertension under control by therapy. (See Appendix A, Section I, C7, a, 9.)

Hypertension, Uncontrolled

Uncontrolled hypertension may refer to untreated hypertension or hypertension not responding to current therapeutic regimen. In either case, assign the appropriate code from categories 401–405 to designate the stage and type of hypertension. Code to the type of hypertension. (See Appendix A, Section I, C7, a, 10.)

EXAMPLE: Tim Long was seen by Dr. Hardy for uncontrolled hypertension, and his medications were adjusted. The appropriate code to assign is 401.9.

Before assigning a code for hypertension, medical documentation must be available clearly stating that the patient has hypertension rather than an elevated blood pressure reading. ICD-9-CM code 796.2 is used when a patient has elevated blood pressure but the physician has not made a diagnosis of hypertension. Some physicians refer to elevated blood pressure as transient hypertension.

Official ICD-9-CM Coding Guideline:

Hypertension, Transient

Assign code 796.2, Elevated blood pressure reading without diagnosis of hypertension, unless the patient has an established diagnosis of hypertension. Assign code 642.3X for transient hypertension of pregnancy. (See Appendix A, Section I, C7, a, 8.)

Elevated Blood Pressure

For a statement of elevated blood pressure without further specificity, assign code 796.2, Elevated blood pressure reading without diagnosis of hypertension, rather than a code from category 401. (See Appendix A, Section I, C7, a, 11.)

Secondary Hypertension

Secondary hypertension is defined as high arterial blood pressure due to another disease such as central nervous system disorders, renal disorders, and endocrine and vascular diseases. Secondary hypertension is coded to category code 405, which is divided into malignant, benign, and unspecified secondary hypertension. An underlying condition of renovascular origin or of another origin is defined by use of a fifth digit. The 405 codes code only the secondary hypertension, and a second code is necessary to code the disease causing the hypertension.

Official ICD-9-CM Coding Guideline:

Hypertension, Secondary

Two codes are required: one to identify the underlying etiology and one from category 405 to identify the hypertension. Sequencing of codes is determined by the reason for admission/encounter. (See Appendix A, Section I, C7, a, 7.)

EXAMPLE: Gale Smith is admitted to Sunny Valley Hospital to address her secondary malignant hypertension that is caused by polycystic kidney disease. Because she was admitted to treat the secondary malignant hypertension, that would be sequenced first. The appropriate codes to assign are 405.09 and 753.12.

Harry Health is seen by Dr. Jones, a urologist, for follow-up because he is being treated for chronic pyelonephritis and secondary hypertension. The appropriate codes to assign are 590.00 and 405.99.

Exercise 12–3   Coding of Hypertension

Select the appropriate ICD-9-CM diagnostic code(s) for the diagnoses listed.

1. Essential hypertension _____

2. Hypertension due to malignant neoplasm of brain _____

3. Uncontrolled malignant hypertension _____

4. Vascular hypertension, benign _____

5. Hypertension due to Cushing's disease _____

6. Malignant hypertensive disease _____

7. Elevated blood pressure _____

8. Periarteritis nodosa causing hypertension _____

9. Accelerated hypertension _____

10. Labile hypertension _____

Hypertensive Heart Disease

Hypertensive heart disease includes heart diseases due to hypertension, such as hypertensive cardiomegaly, hypertensive cardiopathy, hypertensive heart failure, and so on. The Includes: note in the Tabular List is shown in Figure 12-6 and can be used as a guide for hypertensive heart diseases.

```
402      Hypertensive heart disease

         Includes:        Hypertensive:
                                  Cardiomegaly
                                  Cardiopathy
                                  Cardiovascular disease
                                  Heart (disease) (failure)
                          Any condition classifiable to 429.0–429.3,
                                  429.8, 429.9 due to hypertension

         Use additional code to specify type of heart failure (428.0–429.43),
         if known
```

Figure 12-6 Tabular List entry for hypertensive heart disease

When heart conditions are caused by hypertension, a code from category 402 is assigned with an additional code from category 428.

Official ICD-9-CM Coding Guideline:

Hypertension with Heart Disease

Heart conditions (425.8, 429.0–429.3, 429.8, 429.9) are assigned to a code from category 402 when a causal relationship is stated (due to hypertension) or implied (hypertensive). Use an additional code from category 428 to identify the type of heart failure in patients with heart failure. More than one code from category 428 may be assigned if the patient has systolic or diastolic failure and congestive heart failure.

The same heart conditions (425.8, 429.0–429.3, 429.8, 429.9) with hypertension, but without a stated causal relationship, are coded separately. Sequence according to the circumstances of the admission/encounter. (See Appendix A, Section I, C7, a, 2.)

When assigning codes, the coder must pay attention to the wording found in the diagnostic statement. When a causal relationship is stated in the diagnostic statement, a code from 402 and a code from category 428 should be assigned. If a causal relationship is not stated, then separate codes are assigned.

> **EXAMPLE:** Maggie Baggie was being closely followed by her doctor because she was diagnosed with myocarditis due to benign hypertension. The codes assigned to her visit are 429.0 and 402.10.
>
> Sally Smith has a diagnosis of congestive heart failure due to hypertension. The appropriate codes to assign are 402.91 and 428.0.
>
> Tom Thomas has a diagnosis of congestive heart failure and hypertension. (In this statement no relationship exists.) The appropriate codes to assign are 428.0 and 401.9.

Hypertensive Chronic Kidney Disease

Hypertensive chronic kidney disease includes renal diseases that are caused by hypertension and include arteriolar nephritis, hypertensive renal failure, renal sclerosis with hypertension, and so on. Figure 12-7 illustrates the conditions that are included and excluded from category 403 as they appear in the Tabular List. (Note that acute renal failure is not included in category 403.) ICD-9-CM most commonly assumes a cause-and-effect relationship between hypertension and renal disease, using a fifth digit to indicate whether renal failure is present.

Official ICD-9-CM Coding Guideline:

Hypertensive Chronic Kidney Disease

Assign codes from category 403, Hypertensive chronic kidney disease, when conditions classified to categories 585 are present. Unlike hypertension with heart disease, ICD-9-CM presumes a cause-and-effect relationship and classifies chronic kidney disease (CKD) with hypertension as hypertensive chronic kidney disease.

Fifth digits for category 403 should be assigned as follows:

- *0 with CKD stage I through stage IV, or unspecified*
- *1 with CKD stage V or end stage renal disease*

The appropriate code from category 585, Chronic kidney disease, should be used as a secondary code with a code from category 403 to identify the stage of chronic kidney disease. (See Section I.C.10a for information on the coding of chronic kidney disease.) (See Appendix A Section I, C7, a, 3.)

403	**Hypertensive chronic kidney disease**
Includes:	Arteriolar nephritis
	Arteriosclerosis of:
	Kidney
	Renal arterioles
	Arteriosclerotic nephritis (chronic) (interstitial)
	Hypertensive:
	Nephropathy
	Renal failure
	Uremia (chronic)
	Nephrosclerosis
	Renal sclerosis with hypertension
	Any condition classifiable to 585, 586, or 587 with any condition
	classifiable to 401
Excludes:	Acute renal failure (584.5–584.9)
	Renal disease stated as not due to hypertension
	Renovascular hypertension (405.0–405.9 with fifth-digit 1)

The following fifth-digit subclassification is for use with category 403:
> 0 With chronic kidney disease stage I through stage IV, or unspecified
> Use additional code to identify the stage of chronic kidney disease
> (585.1–585.4, 585.9).
> 1 With chronic kidney disease stage V or end-stage renal disease
> Use additional code to identify the stage of chronic kidney disease
> (585.5, 585.6).

403.0	Malignant
403.1	Benign
403.9	Unspecified

Figure 12-7 Tabular List entry for hypertensive chronic kidney disease

EXAMPLE: Tim Time is diagnosed with chronic hypertensive uremia. The appropriate code is 403.90.

Sue Short is diagnosed with acute renal failure and hypertension. The appropriate codes are 584.9 and 401.9.

Hypertensive Heart and Chronic Kidney Disease

Category code 404 represents a combination code for diagnoses when a heart condition, from category 402, and hypertensive chronic kidney disease, from category 403, both exist. Figure 12-8 illustrates category code 404. Note that a fifth digit is used to identify heart failure and the stage of the chronic kidney disease.

Official ICD-9-CM Coding Guideline:

Hypertensive Heart and Chronic Kidney Disease

Assign codes from combination category 404, Hypertensive heart and chronic kidney disease, when both hypertensive renal disease and hypertensive heart disease are stated in the diagnosis. Assume a relationship between the hypertension and the chronic kidney disease, whether or not the condition is so designated. Assign an additional code from category 428, to identify the type of heart failure. More than one code from category 428 may be assigned if the patient has systolic or diastolic failure and congestive heart failure. (See Appendix A, Section I, C7, A, 4.)

EXAMPLE: Joan Smith is diagnosed with hypertensive cardiovascular chronic kidney disease, stage III. The appropriate codes to assign are 404.90 and 585.3.

404 **Hypertensive heart and renal disease**

Includes: Disease:
Cardiorenal
Cardiovascular renal
Any condition classifiable to 402 with any condition classifiable to 403

Use additional code to specify type of heart failure (428.0, 428.20–428.23, 428.30–428.33, 428.40–428.43)

The following fifth-digit subclassification is for use with category 404:
0 Without heart failure and with chronic kidney disease stage I through stage IV, or unspecified
Use additional code to identify the stage of chronic kidney disease (585.1–585.4, 585.9).
1 With heart failure and with chronic kidney disease stage I through stage IV, or unspecified
Use additional code to identify the stage of chronic kidney disease (585.1–585.4, 585.9).
2 Without heart failure and with chronic kidney disease stage V or end-stage renal disease
Use additional code to identify the stage of chronic kidney disease (585.5–585.6).
3 With heart failure and with chronic kidney disease stage V or end-stage renal disease
Use additional code to identify the stage of chronic kidney disease (585.5–585.6).

404.0 Malignant
404.1 Benign
404.9 Unspecified

Figure 12-8 Tabular List entry for hypertensive heart and chronic kidney disease

Ischemic Heart Disease (Category Codes 410–414)

Ischemic heart disease occurs when there is an inadequate supply of blood to the heart, which is caused by a blockage, also called an occlusion, or constriction of an arterial blood vessel. The vessels commonly become blocked or constricted because of the presence of fatty deposits on the walls of the arteries. Ischemic heart disease is also referred to as the following:

- Arteriosclerotic coronary artery disease (ACAD)
- Arteriosclerotic heart disease (ASHD)
- Atherosclerosis
- Coronary artery disease (CAD)
- Coronary arteriosclerosis
- Coronary heart disease
- Coronary ischemia

Myocardial Infarction

An acute myocardial infarction (MI), commonly called a heart attack, occurs when there is inadequate blood supply to a section or sections of the heart.

Disease Highlight—Myocardial Infarction

A myocardial infarction (MI) occurs when there is a decrease in the blood flow through one of the coronary arteries, causing a decrease in the amount of oxygen that is supplied to the heart tissue. The decreased blood flow causes myocardial ischemia and necrosis.

Sign and Symptoms:

The classic symptoms of an MI include:

- Severe chest pain that typically radiates down the left arm and up to the neck and jaw
- Sweating
- Nausea
- Vomiting
- Shortness of breath
- Weakness
- Dysrhythmias

Clinical Testing:

The following clinical tests are completed to confirm a diagnosis of myocardial infarction:

- Electrocardiography—An ST segment elevation or depression, symmetric inversion of T waves, and evolving Q waves
- Blood tests—Elevation of cardiac enzymes in the blood
- Cardiac imaging studies—Appearance of segmental wall motion abnormality
- Chest X-ray—Possible signs of congestive heart failure, which may develop behind other clinical findings

Treatment:

If the patient is currently having an MI:

- Place the patient in a lying position. If cardiac arrest occurs, cardiopulmonary resuscitation should be administered.
- Medical treatment is directed at pain management and the administration of oxygen.
- If the patient is experiencing arrhythmias, medications are administered.
- **Thrombolytic therapy**, the intravenous administration of thrombolytic agents, is often completed to open the coronary artery occlusion and to restore blood flow to the cardiac tissue.

Following the management of the acute MI:

- Patients may undergo cardiac catheterization to evaluate the heart.
- Angioplasty and/or coronary artery bypass surgery may be indicated depending on the clinical findings.
- Cardiac rehabilitation and patient education are also part of the treatment regimen.

Acute myocardial infarctions are coded to category 410 with fourth-digit subcategories and fifth-digit subclassifications. The fourth-digit subcategories identify the specific site of the infarction such as anterolateral wall, inferolateral wall, inferoposterior wall, and so on. The fifth-digit subclassification identifies the episode of care. The fifth digits for category 410 are defined as follows:

0—Episode of Care Unspecified—Use when the source document does not contain sufficient information for the assignment of fifth digit 1 or 2.

1—Initial Episode of Care—Use to designate the first episode of care for a newly diagnosed myocardial infarction. The fifth digit of 1 is assigned regardless of the number of times a patient may be transferred during the initial episode of care.

For example, if a patient is diagnosed as having an MI in Sunny Valley Hospital and then transferred to Hill Top Hospital for additional cardiac workup, the fifth digit of 1 would be used by both facilities.

2—Subsequent Episode of Care—Use the fifth digit of 2 to designate an episode of care after the initial episode when the patient is admitted for further observation, evaluation, or treatment for a myocardial infarction that has received initial treatment but is still less than 8 weeks old.

For example, Tom Jones had an MI on January 1 and was an inpatient for 2 days and sent home. On February 1 his doctor readmitted him for further observation due to the MI. The fifth digit of 2 would be used for the second admission but the initial episode of care was less then 8 weeks old.

To select the proper fourth digit, the coder must identify the affected wall of the heart.

This information is not commonly recorded in the diagnostic statement; therefore, it is necessary for the coder to reference other documents found in the patient's record, such as an EKG report. If the coder is unable to determine the site of the MI, then code 410.9, Myocardial infarction, unspecified, should be used, but only after the coder has reviewed all information present in the patient's record.

Old Myocardial Infarction

Category code 412, Old myocardial infarction, sometimes referred to as a healed myocardial infarction, is used when a patient has had an MI in the past but currently is not experiencing any symptoms. This code is not assigned when current symptoms or ischemic heart disease is present; it actually records a history of an MI. This code is most commonly used when a past MI has been diagnosed after a diagnostic study or EKG has been completed. It is important that the coder determine from the medical documentation that no symptoms are present before this code is assigned.

> **EXAMPLE:** Don Duckster presented to the physician's office for a follow-up visit six months after an EKG showed a slight MI. The patient complained of no symptoms. Code 412 is appropriately assigned for this visit.

Angina Pectoris and Unstable Angina

Angina pectoris, which is assigned to ICD-9-CM category code 413, is defined as severe chest pains caused by an insufficient amount of blood reaching the heart. It is relieved rapidly by rest or nitrates. Factors that usually bring on an angina attack include exertion, heavy eating, and stress.

Unstable angina, which is assigned to ICD-9-CM code 411.1, is an accelerating, or crescendo, pattern of chest pain that occurs at rest or during mild exertion, typically lasting longer than does angina pectoris and is not responsive to medications. Unstable angina can progress to infarction or may heal and return to a stable condition. This code is assigned only when there is no documentation of infarction. Diseases that code to 411.1 include accelerating angina, impending infarction, preinfarction syndrome, and preinfarction angina. Figure 12-9 illustrates the most common patterns of angina. Patients typically complain of tightness in the chest that radiates to the left arm, neck, and jaw.

Chronic Ischemic Heart Disease

Chronic ischemic heart disease, also referred to as arteriosclerotic heart disease, is a condition of arteries narrowing over a long period of time. This narrowing causes myocardial atrophy and areas of interstitial scarring. These patients may ultimately suffer from an acute MI or unstable angina. This form of heart disease is classified to the 414 category, which is further subdivided into fourth- and fifth-digit subcategories. The fourth digit identifies the specific types of ischemic heart disease. The fifth digit identifies the specific vessels where atherosclerosis is found, such as a native artery, a bypass graft, or an artery or vein of a transplanted heart.

> **EXAMPLE:** Code 414.03 is the code assignment for a patient with atherosclerosis of nonautologous biological bypass graft. The atherosclerosis is identified with the fourth digit of 0. The nonautologous bypass graft is identified by use of the 3.

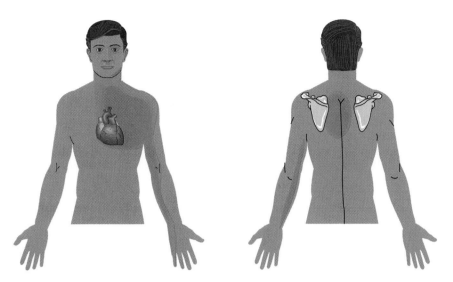

Figure 12-9 Most common patterns of angina (From Marianne Neighbors & Ruth Tannehill-Jones, ISBN: 1-4180-7088-0, page 141. Delmar, Cengage Learning.)

Other Forms of Heart Disease (Category Codes 420–429)

This range of codes classifies other forms of heart disease including:

- Pericarditis, category code 420—Inflammation of the outer layers of the heart, known as the pericardium

- Endocarditis, category code 421—Inflammation of the inner layer of the heart

- Myocarditis, category code 422—Inflammation of the heart muscle

- Cardiomyopathy, category code 425—Diseases of the heart muscle

- Cardiac dysrhythmias, category code 427—Abnormal cardiac rhythm

- Heart failure, category code 428—A decreased ability of the heart to pump a sufficient amount of blood to the body's tissue. Code 428.0 is used report congestive heart failure, unspecified. Figure 12-10 illustrates signs of congestive heart failure.

When selecting codes in this section of the code book, the coder must be able to identify modifying terms that are associated with the main diagnostic term.

Myocarditis has numerous causes, including tuberculous, bacterial infections, and toxic reaction due to drugs or other toxins. The coder must identify the cause to select the correct code because different fourth- and fifth-digit codes are used when coding myocarditis.

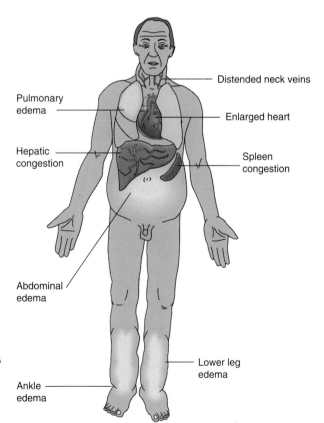

Figure 12-10 Signs of congestive heart failure (From Marianne Neighbors & Ruth Tannehill-Jones, ISBN: 1-4180-7088-0, page 143. Delmar, Cengage Learning.)

Cerebrovascular Disease (Category Codes 430–438)

ICD-9-CM category codes 430–438 are used to code cerebrovascular disease. Cerebrovascular disease includes abnormal nontraumatic conditions that affect the cerebral arteries and include the following:

- Cerebral hemorrhage—Bleeding within the brain or layers of brain lining

- Cerebrovascular accident (CVA)—The disruption in the normal blood supply to the brain, commonly called a stroke

- Occlusion of cerebral and precerebral arteries—The blocking of the artery

- Stenosis of the cerebral arteries—The narrowing of the cerebral arteries that supply blood to the brain

- Transient cerebral ischemia—The temporary restriction of blood flow to cerebral arteries

Official ICD-9-CM Coding Guideline:

The terms stroke *and* CVA *are often used interchangeably to refer to a cerebral infarction. The terms* stroke, CVA, *and* cerebral infarction NOS *are all indexed to the default code 434.91, Cerebral artery occlusion, unspecified, with infarction. Code 436, Acute, but ill-defined, cerebrovascular disease, should not be used when the documentation states "stroke" or "CVA." (See Appendix A, Section I, C7, b.)*

EXAMPLE: Dr. Mike admitted a patient through the Emergency Department last week with a diagnosis of stroke. Documentation was referenced with no other diagnosis available except for "stroke." The coder assigns code 434.91.

In the Tabular List, at the start of categories 430–438, a notation appears that instructs coders to use an additional code to identify the presence of hypertension when it occurs with a cerebrovascular disease. Therefore, two codes are needed to code hypertensive cerebrovascular disease.

EXAMPLE: Mary Mad is diagnosed with a cerebral hemorrhage and hypertension. The appropriate codes to use are 431 and 401.9.

Official ICD-9-CM Coding Guideline:

Hypertensive Cerebrovascular Disease

First assign codes from 430–438, Cerebrovascular disease, then the appropriate hypertension code from categories 401–405. (See Appendix A, Section I, C7, a5.)

It should also be noted that when codes 437 and 438 are used, fifth digits are necessary to indicate whether cerebral infarction, death of cerebral tissue due to inadequate blood supply, has occurred. A fifth digit of 0 is used when there is no mention of cerebral infarction in the medical documentation. A fifth digit of 1 is used when there is mention of cerebral infarction during this episode of treatment. The coder must carefully read the medical documentation before assigning the fifth digits for categories 437 and 438.

EXAMPLE: Tom Tiny is diagnosed with cerebral thrombosis. The appropriate code to assign is 434.00.

Tina Little is diagnosed with a cerebral embolism that caused cerebral infarction. The appropriate code to assign is 434.11.

Diseases of Arteries, Arterioles, and Capillaries (Category Codes 440–449)

It is most helpful for coders to reference a diagram of the body's arteries when coding in this section. Many of the codes identify the specific artery that is diseased. It is also important for coders to identify whether the disease is affecting the patient's own arteries or grafted or transplanted arteries.

EXAMPLE: Atherosclerosis, category code 440, is divided at the fourth- and fifth-digit levels to identify atherosclerosis of the native arteries of the extremities, codes 440.20–440.24, and atherosclerosis of bypass grafts, codes 440.30–440.32.

Diseases of Veins and Lymphatics and Other Diseases of Circulatory System (Category Codes 451–459)

Code range 451–459 includes numerous conditions that are commonly treated. The category codes found in this section of the code book include:

- Category code 451—Phlebitis—Inflammation of a vein, and thrombophlebitis—Inflammation of a vein with the formation of a thrombus

- Category code 452—Portal vein thrombosis—The formation of a blood clot in the main vein of the liver

- Category code 453—Other venous embolism and thrombosis—Venous embolism and thrombosis, with fourth digits to identify specific syndromes and the sites of the embolism and thrombosis

- Category code 454—Varicose veins of the lower extremities—Dilated superficial veins of the legs

- Category code 455—Hemorrhoids—Enlarged veins in or near the anus

- Category code 456—Varicose veins of other sites—Varicose veins of the esophagus, nasal septum, sublingual, scrotal, pelvic, and vulval areas

- Category code 457—Noninfectious disorders of lymphatic channels—Disorders of the lymphatic channels that include lymphangitis, lymphangiectasis, lymphedema, and elephantiasis

- Category code 458—Hypotension—Low blood pressure

- Category code 459—Other disorders of circulatory system—Hemorrhage, postphlebitic syndrome, compression of vein, chronic venous hypertension, chronic venous insufficiency, and other circulatory system disorders

Coders must also determine whether any modifying factors impact the disease because codes in this range identify whether ulceration, inflammation, bleeding, or other conditions accompany the disease.

EXAMPLE: Category code 454 is divided at the fourth-digit level to identify varicose veins of the lower extremities as follows:

454.0 Varicose veins of the lower extremities with ulcer

454.1 Varicose veins of the lower extremities with inflammation

454.2 Varicose veins of the lower extremities with ulcer and inflammation

454.8 Varicose veins of the lower extremities with other complications

454.9 Asymptomatic varicose veins

Internet Links

For general cardiology information, visit *http://cardio-info.com*.

To learn more about peripheral vascular disease, visit *http://www.footcare4u.com*.

To better understand the various forms of heart disease, visit *www.medicinenet.com/vascular_disease/ article.htm, www.naturalhealthschool.com/8_1.html* and *www.americanheart.org*.

Summary

- ICD-9-CM chapter 7 includes diseases of the circulatory system.

- The primary structures of the circulatory system include arteries, veins, and the heart.

- Cardiovascular disease can affect many vessels throughout the entire body.
- ICD-9-CM uses a table in the Alphabetic Index to index the various forms of hypertension.
- Hypertension is described as malignant, benign, and unspecified.
- Secondary hypertension is high arterial blood pressure owing to another disease.
- Hypertensive heart disease includes heart diseases that are caused by hypertension.
- Hypertensive renal disease includes renal diseases that are caused by hypertension.
- Cerebrovascular disease includes abnormal nontraumatic conditions that affect the cerebral arteries.
- Category 410, Acute myocardial infarctions, has fourth and fifth digits. The fourth-digit subcategories identify the specific site of the infarction, and the fifth-digit subclassification identifies the episode of care.
- Chronic ischemic heart disease is also referred to as arteriosclerotic heart disease.
- Cerebrovascular disease includes abnormal nontraumatic conditions that affect the cerebral arteries.

Chapter Review

True/False: Indicate whether each statement is true (T) or false (F).

1. _____ Angina pectoris and unstable angina are classified to the same code.

2. _____ Veins carry deoxygenated blood from the body back to the heart with one exception, the pulmonary vein.

3. _____ Aortic disorders are assumed to be nonrheumatic unless the diagnostic statement specifies that the aortic disorder is rheumatic in origin.

4. _____ Diastolic blood pressure is the pressure on the arterial walls during heart muscle contraction.

5. _____ Benign hypertension is mildly elevated blood pressure that remains stable over many years.

Fill-in-the-Blank: Enter the appropriate term(s) to complete each statement.

6. Uncontrolled hypertension may refer to _____ hypertension or hypertension not responding to current _____.

7. Hypertensive cardiomegaly and hypertensive heart failure are types of _____ disease.

8. Stenosis of the cerebral arteries is caused by a _____ of the cerebral arteries that supply blood to the brain.

9. Circulatory system disorders can be caused by infections as well as _____ factors.

10. A severe form of hypertension, known as _____, occurs when there is an abrupt onset of a pressure reading of 200/140 or higher.

Coding Assignment

Instructions: Using an ICD-9-CM coding book, select the code for each diagnostic statement.

1. Benign essential hypertension   _____

2. Moderate arterial hypertension _____

3. Raynaud's syndrome with gangrene _____

4. Family history of ischemic heart disease _____

5. Rheumatic aortic regurgitation _____

6. Unstable angina _____

7. Angina pectoris with essential hypertension _____

8. Labile hypertension _____

9. Congestive heart failure _____

10. Peripheral venous insufficiency _____

11. Alcoholic cardiomyopathy _____

12. Cardiac arrest _____

13. Dressler's syndrome _____

14. Congenital atrial septal defect _____

15. Acute pericarditis _____

16. Atrial flutter _____

17. Cardiomegaly _____

18. Aortic aneurysm _____

19. Chronic ischemic heart disease _____

20. Acute myocardial infarction _____

21. Obstructive cardiomyopathy _____

22. Extrasystolic arrhythmia _____

23. Aneurysm of renal artery _____

24. Arterial stricture _____

25. Bleeding external hemorroids _____

26. Chronic venous hypertension with ulcer _____

27. Subacute lymphangitis _____

28. Atheroembolism of lower extremity _____

29. Endomyocardial fibrosis _____

30. Idiopathic pulmonary arteriosclerosis _____

Case Studies

Instructions: Review each case study and select the correct ICD-9-CM diagnostic code.

CASE 1

Physician's Office Note

VITAL SIGNS: Temperature 100.2;   Blood pressure 130/80;   Weight 175 pounds

Sally presents today with a chief compliant of pain in her left leg that has been present on and off for the last week. She has previously experienced phlebitis in her left leg.

EXAM:

HEENT: Normal

CHEST: Clear

EXTREMITIES: There is edema in her left leg. An area on her calf is tender to palpation. She states that the pain is also unbearable when I touch it.

Because of her previous phlebitis, I sent her to the X-ray department for a STAT venogram that revealed a thrombus in her left calf, confirming thrombophlebitis.

Patient was given heparin, and a prescription was written for antibiotics. The left leg was immobilized, and she was instructed to return to me in 3 days.

ICD-9-CM Code Assignment: _____

CASE 2

DISCHARGE SUMMARY:

Admitted 2/03/XX

Discharged 2/7/XX

Admitting Diagnosis:

Unstable angina

Atrial fibrillation

HISTORY:

This 69-year-old man was admitted through the ER with chest pain that began while he eating his lunch. After lunch he went to do his grocery shopping, and he began to develop discomfort in his chest as well as in his jaw. He drove himself to the ER. The ER physician admitted the patient due to unstable angina.

Vital signs at time of admission: BP 140/60, heart rate 110 to 120

HEART: There was a systolic murmur in the pericardium. Patient complains of chest pain.

All other physical findings were within normal limits.

HOSPITAL COURSE:

Cardiac enzymes—CPK of 105, Troponin—4.7 with a relative index of 5.4

Digoxin level was 1.8.

All other lab values were normal.

EKG showed arterial fibrillation with rapid ventricular response and was positive for a new anterior wall infarction.

The patient was maintained on Imdur 30 mg daily and metrprolol 50 mg in the morning and evening.

The patient stabilized and was instructed to see me in 7 days.

Discharge Diagnosis:

Acute MI, anterior wall

Chronic atrial fibrillation

Hypertension

ICD-9-CM Coding Assignment: _____

CASE 3

Skilled Nursing Facility Physician Monthly Progress Note

4/22/XX

This patient was admitted in January of 2003 with a primary diagnosis of ischemic heart disease, history of bladder cancer, and uncontrolled malignant hypertension. Patient continues to be stable. On exam he appears comfortable and still has some coughing spells during my physical examination.

Vital signs include a weight of 223.8 lb, compared to last 3 months, it varies from 222 to 225. No weight gain or weight loss.

BLOOD PRESSURE: 160/90, which is not under control; pulse—70 per minute; regular, respirations—24.

LUNGS: Still occasional rhonchi but no wheeze

HEART: Regular rhythm with no change in systolic murmur

Abdomen is soft. Bowel sounds are active.

EXTREMITIES: No pedal edema; no clubbing or cyanosis

Medications, including Advil, Cytotec, Ascriptin, Tylenol, Tenormin, Pulmoaid therapy, Senna laxative, Artificial Tears, Analgesic balm, Casadex, Mycolog, to be continued, along with the standing orders.

I will see the patient in 30 days or at the request of the charge nurse.

ICD-9-CM Code Assignment: _____

CASE 4

Physician's Office Note

Mr. Cafferty presents today with some ascites and complaint of exertional dyspnea. When queried about any other symptoms, he stated that at night he sometimes wakes up coughing, which in his words is described as "real dry." He has a history of congestive heart failure and microvascular spasms.

On physical examination, mild ascites, tachycardia, and peripheral edema are noted. Previous diagnostic testing was reviewed, which confirmed cardiomyopathy.

ICD-9-CM Code Assignment: _____

CASE 5

Physician's Office Note

VITAL SIGNS: Temperature 98.8;   blood pressure 120/70;   weight 185 pounds

This 42-year-old male presents today with shortness of breath, fatigue, ankle edema, and anxiety. He states that these symptoms have begun to increase in severity, and he is concerned.

Chest X-ray and EKG confirmed congestive heart failure.

ICD-9-CM Code Assignment: _____

13 Diseases of the Respiratory System

Chapter Outline

Introduction
Introduction to the Body System
Coding for the Respiratory System
Internet Links

Summary
Chapter Review
Coding Assignments
Case Studies

Objectives

At the conclusion of this chapter, the student will be able to:

1. Identify some of the major structures of the respiratory system.
2. Explain some of the conditions that are encountered in the respiratory system.
3. Understand some of the terminology associated with the respiratory system.
4. Summarize coding guidelines for this chapter.
5. Assign the proper diagnostic codes for diseases of the respiratory system.

Key Terms

Acute Bronchitis
Asbestosis
Aspiration Pneumonia
Asthma
Bronchi
Bronchitis
Chronic Bronchitis

Chronic Obstructive
 Pulmonary (Lung)
 Disease (COPD)
Chronic Sinusitis
Emphysema
Empyema
Larynx
Legionnaire's Disease

Lobar Pneumonia
Lungs
Obstructive Lung
 Disease
Pharyngitis
Pharynx
Pleurisy

Pneumonia
Respiratory Failure
Respiratory System
Status Asthmaticus
Tonsils
Trachea
Vocal Cords

Reminder

As you work through this chapter, you will need to have a copy of the ICD-9-CM coding book to reference.

Introduction

Chapter 8 of ICD-9-CM, Diseases of the Respiratory System, (category codes 460–519) classifies conditions such acute respiratory infections, diseases of the upper respiratory tract, pneumonia, influenza, and chronic obstructive pulmonary disease.

Introduction to the Body System

The respiratory system begins its function when air enters the body through the nose or mouth. The respiratory system is comprised of structures that exchange oxygen and carbon dioxide in the body. The main organs of the respiratory system are the lungs, where this gas exchange occurs. The lungs also work as a purification or filtering system for the air the body takes in. There are two lobes, one on the right and one on the left, which hold the bronchi. The bronchi are formed when the trachea, or windpipe, branches off in the chest. Figure 13-1 illustrates the structures of the respiratory system.

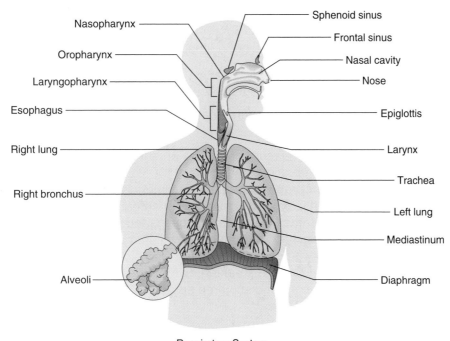

Respiratory System

Figure 13-1 Structures of the respiratory system (From Ehrlich A, Schroeder CL. *Medical Terminology for Health Professions,* 4th ed. Clifton Park, NY: Delmar, Cengage Learning, 2001.)

The larynx and pharynx are also part of the respiratory system. The larynx is the made up of cartilage and ligaments that compose the vocal cords, or the voice box. When air passes through the vocal cords, sound or speech is produced. The pharynx is also known as the throat. This structure connects the mouth and nose to the larynx. Once air has passed from the nose or mouth through the pharynx, the air then moves into the trachea.

Coding for the Respiratory System

Categories 460–519 are the classifications for any disease of the respiratory system except for neoplastic disease and some major infectious diseases. Provider documentation is key in the diagnosis coding for respiratory disease. Laboratory results, on their own, are not enough to assign a diagnosis code in this chapter.

Acute Respiratory Infections (Category Codes 460–466)

This subcategory of codes contains some of the more common diagnosis codes used by a primary care office. The common cold, code 460, along with acute sinusitis and acute bronchitis, is coded to this section. Pharyngitis, or what is commonly called a sore throat, is coded to code 462. There can be many causes of pharyngitis, such as a virus, bacteria, and tobacco abuse. The code 462 is for acute pharyngitis and should not be used if the condition is chronic, which would code to 472.1. If the pharyngitis is due to an infection, codes from the "Infectious and Parasitic Diseases" chapter should be reported to identify the cause of the infection. Infections such as Coxsackievirus, flu, or streptococcus that cause pharyngitis are coded using one code instead of two separate codes because the pharyngitis is considered an integral part of the infection. If the pharyngitis is not caused by infection, then 462 is coded along with other conditions.

> **EXAMPLE:** An 8-year-old girl presents today with a runny nose, cough, and sore throat. A rapid strep test is done, which comes back negative.
>
> DX: Cold and sore throat   Code assignment: 460 and 462
>
> Different Patient
>
> An 8-year-old girl presents today with a runny nose, cough, and sore throat. A rapid strep test is done, which comes back positive.
>
> DX: Strep throat   Code assignment: 034.0

When coding in this section, be sure your documentation supports an acute condition. If there is any question, consult the provider for clarification.

Also coded to this category of codes are acute bronchitis and bronchiolitis. Bronchitis, an inflammation of the bronchus, can be diagnosed as both acute and chronic. ICD-9-CM provides separate codes for the acute and chronic manifestations of bronchitis. Acute bronchitis is a inflammation of the bronchus that lasts for a short period of time and is typically caused by a spreading of an inflammation from the nasopharynx. Symptoms of acute bronchitis include fever, cough, and substernal pain. Acute bronchitis is classified to code 466.0. Chronic bronchitis is a prolonged inflammation of the bronchus, lasting for more than 3 months and occurring for two consecutive years. Chronic bronchitis can occur because of exposure to bronchial irritants such as cigarette smoking. Symptoms of chronic bronchitis include a severe, persistent cough and large amounts of discolored sputum. Chronic bronchitis is classified to category codes 491.

If a patient is diagnosed with an acute bronchitis with emphysema, a progressive loss of lung function, two codes are needed.

> **EXAMPLE:** A 72-year-old man presents today with history of emphysema. He now presents with low-grade fever, cough, and some back pain. After examination and chest X-ray, diagnosis at this time is acute bronchitis with emphysema.
>
> Code assignment: 466.0 and 492.8

Exercise 13–1   Coding from Category Codes 460–466

Instructions: Select the appropriate code for each diagnosis listed.

1. Acute laryngitis   _____

2. Acute maxillary sinusitis _____

3. Multiple URI   _____

4. Croup _____

5. Acute bronchiolitis due to RSV _____

6. Viral epiglottitis without obstruction _____

7. Viral pharyngitis _____

8. Supraglottitis, with obstruction _____

9. Subacute viral bronchitis _____

10. Acute URI _____

Other Diseases of the Upper Respiratory Tract (Category Codes 470–478)

This section of the chapter contains many of the codes needed to code the chronic inflammatory diseases of the upper respiratory tract. Figure 13-2 illustrates the structures of the upper respiratory tract.

This section also classifies conditions that affect the accessory structures of the respiratory system such as the sinus cavities and middle ear. These accessory structures are coded from this category

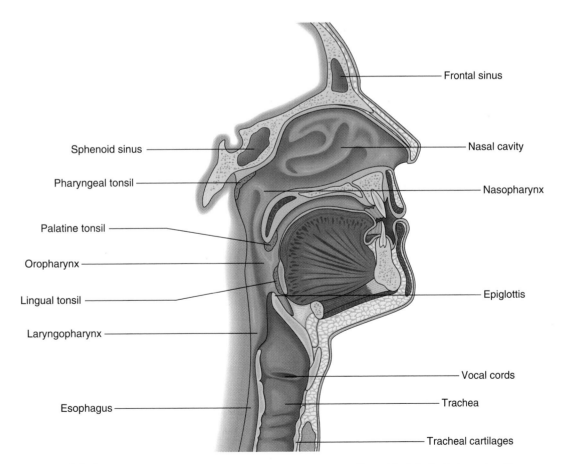

Figure 13-2 Structures of the upper respiratory system (From Ehrlich A, Schroeder CL. *Medical Terminology for Health Professions,* 4th ed. Clifton Park, NY: Delmar, Cengage Learning, 2001.)

because they are lined with mucous membrane that is connected to the nasal cavity. One of the more common conditions coded to this section is chronic sinusitis, code 473.9, which is a prolonged inflammation of one or more of the sinus cavities. Chronic sinusitis can be a result of exposure to something the patient may be allergic to or an infective agent. Acute sinusitis is coded to the 461 category.

Chronic diseases of the tonsils are coded to this section. The tonsils protect the entrance to the respiratory system from invading organisms. Abscess of the tonsils is coded to 475, Peritonsillar abscess. Acute tonsillitis is coded to 463. Other chronic conditions found here are chronic laryngitis and allergic rhinitis.

Pneumonia and Influenza (Category Codes 480–488)

Pneumonia is a condition in which liquid, known as exudate, and pus infiltrate the lung and cause an inflammation. Bacteria, viruses, inhaled irritants, or fungi can cause pneumonia. There are many types of pneumonia, so it is very important to verify the type of pneumonia documented in the medical record. ICD-9-CM classifies pneumonia by the organism or irritant causing the pneumonia. The following category codes for pneumonia are used in ICD-9-CM:

480   Viral pneumonia

481   Pneumococcal pneumonia

482   Other bacterial pneumonia

483   Pneumonia due to other specified organism

484   Pneumonia in infectious diseases classified elsewhere

485   Bronchopneumonia, organism unspecified

486   Pneumonia, organism unspecified

507   Pneumonitis, due to solids and liquids

At times a provider documents the term *lobar pneumonia*. When there is mention of pneumonia in a lobe of the lung, it is only lobar pneumonia if documented by the provider as such. Lobar pneumonia, code 481, is usually caused by *Streptococcus pneumoniae.*

Another type of pneumonia that may be encountered by a coder is Legionnaire's disease, which occurs when a contaminated water source becomes airborne via humidifiers, water faucets, and air conditioning. The code for Legionnaire's disease is 482.84.

Disease Highlight—Legionnaire's Disease

Legionnaire's disease is a severe and often fatal disease caused by a bacterial infection that is spread by water vapor containing *Legionella pneumophila*. The water vapor is transmitted via the air through systems that contain water vapors such as shower heads, water faucets, humidifiers, spas, and air conditioners. The *Legionella pneumophila* infection causes pneumonia and ranks among the three or four most common causes of community acquired pneumonia.

Signs and Symptoms:

Patients with Legionnaire's disease present with the following signs and symptoms:

- High fever and chills
- Toxic appearance
- Pleurisy
- Headache

- Gastrointestinal pain
- Muscle aches
- Fatigue
- Cough
- Diagnosis of pneumonia

Legionnaire's disease is more common in smokers, patients with chronic lung disease, and immunocompromised patients.

It should be noted that a milder form of Legionnaire's disease, known as Pontiac fever, can occur in patients. These patients present with all of the same symptoms except pneumonia.

Clinical Testing:

For a definitive diagnosis of Legionnaire's disease, the following tests are typically performed:

- Chest X-rays to confirm the pneumonia
- Blood tests
- Sputum cultures
- Urinalysis

Treatment:

Treatments regimens include:

- Antibiotic therapy—Rifampin and erythromycin are commonly given in combination. Other antibiotics that are effective are azithromycin and clarithromycin.
- Respiratory therapy—Patients with severe cases of pneumonia are given respiratory care and therapy.
- Rest

Aspiration pneumonia occurs when a solid or liquid is inhaled into the lung. Aspiration pneumonia is classified to category code 507, Pneumonitis due to solids and liquids. Fourth digits describe the cause of the aspiration pneumonia as follows:

0   Due to inhalation of food or vomitus

1   Due to inhalation of oils and essences

8   Due to other solids and liquids

At times a patient can develop both bacterial pneumonia and aspiration pneumonia. When this occurs, both types of pneumonia are coded.

Exercise 13–2   Coding Pneumonia

Instructions: Select the appropriate ICD-9-CM code for the diagnosis listed.

1. Group A streptococcus pneumonia   _____

2. Mycoplasma pneumoniae   _____

3. *E. coli* pneumonia   _____

4. Adenovirus pneumonia _____

5. Viral pneumonia _____

6. Gram-negative pneumonia _____

7. Parainfluenza viral pneumonia _____

8. Chlamydia _____

9. Pneumonia due to *Staphylococcus aureus* _____

10. Bacterial pneumonia _____

Chronic Obstructive Pulmonary Disease and Allied Conditions (Category Codes 490–496)

Category codes 490–496 include:

- Category 490—Bronchitis, not specified as acute or chronic

- Category 491—Chronic bronchitis

- Category 492—Emphysema

- Category 493—Asthma

- Category 494—Bronchiectasis

- Category 495—Extrinsic allergic alveolitis

- Category 496—Chronic airway obstruction, not elsewhere classified

It is essential that coders read the medical documentation to be able to accurately select codes from this section of the code book. Coders must determine whether the condition being coding is acute or chronic or whether there is an acute exacerbation of a condition. Fourth and fifth digits are used to denote when conditions are with or without exacerbations.

Bronchitis, an inflammation of one or more of the bronchi, can be acute or chronic. As mentioned earlier in this textbook, code 466.0 is used to report acute bronchitis. Code 490 is used to code bronchitis not specified as acute or chronic, and category code 491 is used to code chronic bronchitis.

As discussed earlier in this chapter, unlike acute bronchitis, chronic bronchitis is a condition that lasts more than 3 months. Documentation must specifically state that the condition is chronic. It is not unusual for chronic bronchitis to be combined with obstructive lung disease. Obstructive lung disease is a decrease in airflow within the lungs. When this condition is chronic, it is known as chronic obstructive pulmonary (lung) disease (COPD).

Official ICD-9-CM Coding Guideline:

Conditions that constitute COPD are obstructive chronic bronchitis, subcategory 491.2, and emphysema, category 492. All asthma codes are under category 493, Asthma. Code 496, Chronic airway obstruction, not elsewhere classified, is a nonspecific code that should only be used when the documentation in a medical record does not specify the type of COPD being treated. (See Appendix A, Section I, C8, a, 1.)

Emphysema, a loss of lung function due to progressive decrease in the number of alveoli in the bronchus of the lung, is coded to category code 492. Asthma is a stricture of the airway that causes difficulty breathing. Asthma is usually an allergic disorder in which wheezing and coughing are common indicators. The 493 category, Asthma, requires a fifth-digit subclassification to indicate whether there is an acute exacerbation or status asthmaticus is present. Status asthmaticus is a severe asthmatic attack that does not respond to treatment. The attack is prolonged and usually includes severe respiratory distress. The provider must clearly document the status asthmaticus to be coded with a fifth digit of 1 "with status asthmaticus," or the fifth-digit must be 0 (unspecified) or 2 (with acute exacerbation).

Official ICD-9-CM Coding Guideline:

An acute exacerbation of asthma is an increased severity of the asthma symptoms, such as wheezing and shortness of breath. Status asthmaticus refers to a patient's failure to respond to therapy administered during an asthmatic episode and is a life-threatening complication that requires emergency care. If status asthmaticus is documented by the provider with any type of COPD or with acute bronchitis, the status asthmaticus should be sequenced first. It supersedes any type of COPD including that with acute exacerbation or acute bronchitis. It is inappropriate to assign an asthma code with fifth digit 2, with acute exacerbation, together with an asthma code with fifth digit 1, with status asthmaticus. Only the fifth digit 1 should be assigned. (See Appendix A, Section I, C8, a, 4.)

The ICD-9-CM Official Guidelines for Coding and Reporting give coders further directions for coding an acute exacerbation of chronic obstructive bronchitis and asthma.

Official ICD-9-CM Coding Guideline:

The code for chronic obstructive bronchitis and asthma distinguishes between uncomplicated cases and those in acute exacerbation. An acute exacerbation is a worsening or a decompensation of a chronic condition. An acute exacerbation is not equivalent to an infection superimposed on a chronic condition, though an exacerbation may be triggered by an infection. (See Appendix A, Section I, C8, a, 2.)

For example, code 491.21 is used to code chronic obstructive bronchitis with acute exacerbation.

Many of the conditions coded to categories 490–496 are overlapping in their nature. The Official Coding Guidelines for Coding and Reporting give further instructions for these cases.

Official ICD-9-CM Coding Guideline:

Due to the overlapping nature of the conditions that make up COPD and asthma, there are many variations in the way these conditions are documented. Code selection must be based on the terms as documented. When selecting the correct code for the documented type of COPD and asthma, it is essential to first review the index, and then verify the code in the tabular list. There are many instructional notes under the different COPD subcategories and codes. It is important that all such notes be reviewed to assure correct code assignment. (See Appendix A, Section I, C8, a, 3.)

The coding guidelines also address cases in which acute bronchitis is documented with COPD.

Official ICD-9-CM Coding Guideline:

Acute bronchitis, code 466.0, is due to an infectious organism. When acute bronchitis is documented with COPD, code 491.22, Obstructive chronic bronchitis with acute bronchitis, should be assigned. It is not necessary to also assign code 466.0. If a medical record documents acute bronchitis with COPD with acute exacerbation, only code 491.22 should be assigned. The acute bronchitis included in code 491.22 supersedes the acute exacerbation. If a medical record documents COPD with acute exacerbation without mention of acute bronchitis, only code 491.21 should be assigned. (See Appendix A, Section I, C8, b, 1.)

Other Lung Diseases

The remainder of the chapter on the respiratory system contains codes for conditions that are caused by external agents. Such conditions include asbestosis, which is a result of exposure to asbestos. Another respiratory disease, empyema, is an infection in the pleural cavity and is coded to category 510. The fourth digit depends on whether a fistula is present.

Inflammation of the thoracic cavity is known as pleurisy. This condition is sometimes associated with pneumonia, but in most cases it is caused by an infection. Pleurisy is a symptom of other disorders, and for this reason the underlying disorder needs to be identified and treated.

Respiratory failure is a severe condition that interrupts the flow of oxygen or carbon dioxide unless the patient is in danger. ICD-9-CM classifies respiratory failure as follows:

518.81   Acute respiratory failure

518.83   Chronic respiratory failure

518.84   Acute and chronic respiratory failure

The medical record must be reviewed by the coder before a code for respiratory failure is assigned. The documentation must clearly support the use of these codes. One item that needs to be included in the documentation is an arterial blood gas pH of less than 7.35. If respiratory failure is due to trauma, drug overdose, or nonrespiratory conditions, these condition should be identified in the provider documentation as well.

The sequencing of code 518.81, Acute respiratory failure, for inpatient admissions is governed by the following ICD-9-CM Official Guidelines for Coding and Reporting.

Official ICD-9-CM Coding Guideline:

(1) Acute respiratory failure as principal diagnosis

Code 518.81, Acute respiratory failure, may be assigned as a principal diagnosis when it is the condition established after study to be chiefly responsible for occasioning the admission to the hospital and the selection is supported by the Alphabetic Index and Tabular List. However, chapter-specific coding guidelines (such as obstetrics, poisoning, HIV, newborn) that provide sequencing direction take precedence.

(2) Acute respiratory failure as secondary diagnosis

Respiratory failure may be listed as a secondary diagnosis if it occurs after admission or if it is present on admission but does not meet the definition of principal diagnosis.

(3) Sequencing of acute respiratory failure and another acute condition

When a patient is admitted with respiratory failure and another acute condition (e.g., myocardial infarction, cerebrovascular accident), the principal diagnosis will not be the same in every situation. This applies whether the other acute condition is a respiratory or nonrespiratory condition. Selection of the principal diagnosis will be dependent on the circumstances of admission. If both the respiratory failure and the other acute condition are equally responsible for occasioning the admission to the hospital and there are no chapter-specific sequencing rules, the guideline regarding two or more diagnoses that equally meet the definition for principal diagnosis (Section II, C) may be applied in these situations.

If the documentation is not clear as to whether acute respiratory failure and another condition are equally responsible for occasioning the admission, query the provider for clarification. (See Appendix A, Section I, C8, c1–3)

Internet Links

To learn more about diseases of the respiratory system, visit *www.lungusa.org* and *www.emphysema.net.*

The Pulmonary Education and Research Foundation also provides current information at *www.perf2ndwind.org.*

For additional illustrations of the respiratory system and additional information about diseases of the respiratory system, visit *http://users.rcn.com/jkimball.ma.ultranet/BiologyPages/P/Pulmonary.html.*

Summary

- The respiratory system works as a purifying system, filtering air and carrying oxygen to the blood cells and carrying carbon dioxide out of the body.
- The lungs are the main organ of the respiratory system.
- The larynx is where the vocal cords are located.
- The trachea branches off into each lung; the branches are called bronchi.
- Respiratory conditions are commonly identified as acute, chronic, or both acute and chronic.
- ICD-9-CM classifies pneumonia by the organism or irritant causing the pneumonia.
- ICD-9-CM provides separate codes for the acute and chronic manifestations of bronchitis.
- Acute and chronic sinusitis is classified to different category codes within ICD-9-CM.
- The ICD-9-CM Official Guidelines for Coding and Reporting give instructions for coding chronic obstructive pulmonary disease and asthma, chronic obstructive pulmonary disease and bronchitis, and respiratory failure.

Chapter Review

True/False: Indicate whether each statement is true (T) or false (F).

1. _____ Lungs are where the bronchi are located.

2. _____ The respiratory system begins its function when air enters the body.

3. _____ Oxygen is carried into the blood cells, and carbon dioxide is carried out.

4. _____ Code 462 is used for acute pharyngitis.

5. _____ The code for Legionnaire's disease is 482.84.

Fill-in-the-Blank: Enter the appropriate term(s) to complete each statement below.

6. Sinus conditions are coded to this chapter because they are lined with the same _____ that is connected to the nasal cavity.

7. An infection of the pleural cavity is called _____.

8. The _____ is where the vocal cords are located.

9. Chronic bronchitis is a bronchial infection that lasts longer than _____.

10. Another name for windpipe is _____.

Coding Assignments

Instructions: Using and ICD-9-CM coding book, select the code for each diagnositic statement.

Diagnosis	Code
1. Acute tonsillitis	_____
2. Edema of pharynx	_____
3. Chronic ethmoidal sinusitis	_____
4. Acute tracheitis without obstruction	_____
5. Farmer's lung	_____
6. Acute and chronic respiratory failure	_____
7. Diaphragmitis	_____
8. Chronic laryngitis	_____
9. Allergic rhinitis due to dog hair	_____
10. Chronic tonsillitis and adenoiditis	_____
11. COPD	_____
12. Parapharyngeal abscess	_____
13. Acute bronchitis with emphysema	_____
14. Hypertrophy of nasal turbinates	_____
15. Acute epiglottitis with obstruction	_____
16. Acute and chronic obstructive bronchitis	_____
17. Hay fever with asthma	_____
18. Necrotic pneumonia	_____
19. Mediastinal fistula	_____
20. Acute pleurisy	_____
21. Loffler's syndrome	_____
22. Hypostatic bronchopneumonia	_____
23. Acute pulmonary manifestations due to radiation	_____
24. Malt workers' lung	_____
25. Smokers' cough	_____

Case Studies

Instructions: Review each case study and select the correct ICD-9-CM diagnostic code.

CASE 1

CHIEF COMPLAINT: This 71-old-year male, whom I have treated for a number of years, returns today with a persistent cough.

HISTORY OF THE PRESENT ILLNESS: The patient has a 4-month history of a cough. He also experienced this last year.

PAST MEDICAL HISTORY: Acute bronchitis and pneumonia

SOCIAL HISTORY: Patient is a 2-pack-a-day smoker. Denies alcohol.

ALLERGIES; NKA

EXAM: BP 125/80, pulse 72, respirations 22

HEENT: No findings.

LUNGS: Bilateral wheezing and scattered rales. Sputum is discolored. Abdomen: no findings.

Chest X-ray ordered. Sputum C&S.

I feel that the patient has progressed to a chronic state of bronchitis. Patient to follow up in 2 weeks. Medications ordered as per med sheet.

ICD-9-CM Code Assignment: _____

CASE 2

CHIEF COMPLAINT: A 36-year-old male patient presents with headache and pressure in his head.

VITAL SIGNS: Temperature 100.3, BP 130/70

HEENT: Pain over the eyes in the frontal area of the forehead. Palpation increases pain. Throat appears red. There is a discolored discharge from his nose.

LUNGS: Clear

ABDOMEN: Normal findings

Patient has responded to Z-pac in the past for acute sinusitis; therefore, this was ordered.

ICD-9-CM Code Assignment: _____

CASE 3

Katy presented to the ED at 5:00 am very flushed with difficulty breathing, chest tightness, and tachycardia. She was examined by the ED physician, who ordered a pulmonary function test, arterial blood gases, chest X-ray, and ECG. Katy was diagnosed with an acute exacerbation of asthma. She was given two nebulizer treatments, which helped. After 12 hours observation, she was sent home.

ICD-9-CM Code Assignment: _____

CASE 4

This 72-year-old male presents today with productive cough, fever, chills, dyspnea, and chest pain. He was given a complete examination, which included a chest X-ray, EKG, and blood and sputum cultures. The cultures came back with a positive for pneumonia infection due to streptococcus, group A. We have begun antibiotic therapy and will have him set up with 1 liter of O_2 at night if he needs it.

ICD-9-CM Code Assignment: _____

CASE 5

Mary, age 14, presented to our office today with complaints of tearing, sneezing, headache, and problems "catching her breath." When asked whether she noted any changes in her routine, body lotions, or laundry soap, she said no. She did say that she is spending more time outside. Her mother said she noticed this same thing happening last spring as well. We did a blood chemistry as well as some allergy sensitivity testing. Mary was diagnosed with allergic rhinitis. She was started on antihistamine therapy.

ICD-9-CM Code Assignment: _____

Diseases of the Digestive System

Chapter Outline

Objectives

At the conclusion of this chapter, the student will be able to:

1. Identify the various anatomical structures of the digestive system.
2. Explain different conditions that are related to the digestive system.
3. Discuss the specific coding related to the different conditions encountered in the digestive system.
4. Select and code diagnoses from case studies.

Key Terms

Accessory Organs	Colitis	Enteritis	Gastrointestinal (GI) Tract
Alimentary Canal	Crohn's Disease	Esophagitis	Gastrojejunal Ulcer
Appendicitis	Direct Inguinal Hernia	Esophagus	Geographic Tongue
Appendix	Diverticula	Gallbladder	Hepatic
Bile	Diverticulitis	Gastric Ulcer	Hernia
Cecum	Diverticulosis	Gastroesophageal	Hiatal Hernia
Cholecystitis	Duodenal Ulcer	Reflux Disease (GERD)	Ileum
Cholelithiasis	Duodenum		

Reminder

As you work through this chapter, you will need to have a copy of the ICD-9-CM coding book to reference.

Indirect Inguinal Hernia	Liver	Periapical Abscess	Regional Enteritis
Inguinal Canal	Malocclusion	Peritonitis	Stomach
Inguinal Hernia	Pancreas	Pulp	Ulcerative Colitis
Jejunum	Peptic Ulcer	Pulpitis	

Introduction

Chapter 9 of ICD-9-CM, "Diseases of the Digestive System," classifies conditions of the digestive system, which is also known as the gastrointestinal (GI) tract. The category codes found in this chapter of the code book include the following:

520–529   Diseases of oral cavity, salivary glands, and jaws

530–538   Diseases of esophagus, stomach, and duodenum

540–543   Appendicitis

550–553   Hernia of abdominal cavity

555–558   Noninfectious enteritis and colitis

560–569   Other diseases of intestine and peritoneum

570–579   Other diseases of digestive system

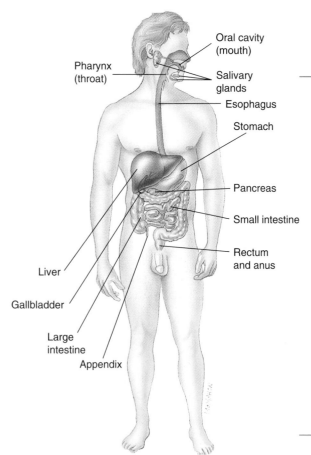

Figure 14-1 Major and accessory structures of the digestive system (From Ehrlich A, Schroeder CL. *Medical Terminology for Health Professions,* 4th ed. Clifton Park, NY: Delmar, Cengage Learning, 2001, p. 166.)

Introduction to the Body System

The digestive system is also referred to as the alimentary canal (*aliment* means "nourishment" and *ary* means "pertaining to"; thus *alimentary* means "pertaining to nourishment"). The oral cavity (mouth), the pharynx (throat), esophagus, stomach, small intestine, large intestine, rectum, and the anus are the major organs of the digestive system. Figure 14-1 illustrates the major organs and anatomical structures of this system.

The digestive process begins when food is taken into the mouth for nourishment and is broken down for digestion, absorption, or nutrients. The process ends with the elimination of waste. The breakdown of food begins with chewing and continues as chemicals within the body further break food down and assist in the absorption and elimination process.

Coding for the Digestive System

This chapter of ICD-9-CM is organized according to the anatomical order of the digestive tract, starting with the mouth through the intestines to the rectum and anus. This helps the coder determine the correct areas of the chapter for code assignments. Disorders of the liver, gallbladder, and pancreas also code to this section because they are considered accessory organs, or secondary organs, of the digestive system.

Diseases of Oral Cavity, Salivary Glands, and Jaws (Category Codes 520–529)

These categories of codes classify disorders of the oral cavity, such as tooth development anomalies, disturbances of tooth formation, and other periodontal diseases. These categories of codes include congenital anomalies, and hereditary problems of the oral cavity are therefore not found in chapter 14 of ICD-9-CM, "Congenital Anomalies" (740–759).

When coding disorders of the oral cavity, it is helpful for the coder to refer to a diagram of the mouth and teeth. Figures 14-2 and 14-3 illustrate the structures of the oral cavity.

Diseases of the enamel, hard tissue of the teeth, and center of the teeth, known as pulp, are classified to this section of the book. Pulpitis, code 522.0, is an abscess of the pulp, usually of bacterial origin. Another condition that is encountered in this category of codes is periapical abscess, which is an infection of the pulp and surrounding tissue.

Category 524 includes malocclusion, a condition in which the bite alignment is abnormal. This type of condition usually requires orthodontic correction. Other conditions coded to this section of the chapter are gingivitis, diseases of the jaw and salivary glands, and diseases and conditions of the tongue, such as geographic tongue. Geographic tongue is a condition in which irregularly shaped patches show on the tongue and resemble landforms on a map. The cause is unknown, but the condition usually goes away on its own or, in some cases, with a topical steroid.

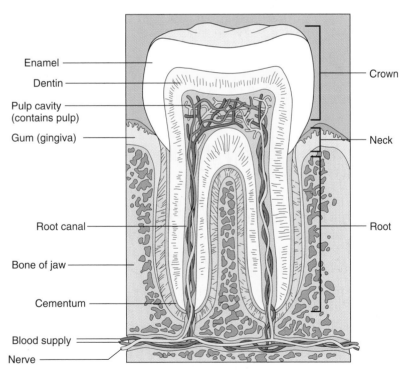

Figure 14-2 Structures and tissues of the tooth (From Ehrlich A, Schroeder CL. *Medical Terminology for Health Professions,* 4th ed. Clifton Park, NY: Delmar, Cengage Learning, 2001, p. 168.)

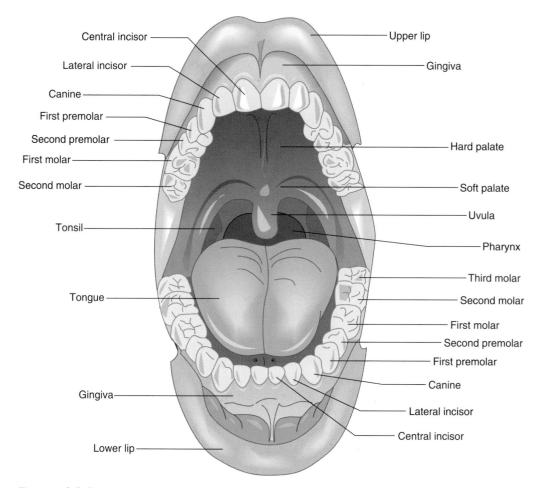

Figure 14-3 Structures of the oral cavity (From Ehrlich A, Schroeder CL. *Medical Terminology for Health Professions,* 4th ed. Clifton Park, NY: Delmar, Cengage Learning, 2001, p. 167.)

Diseases of Esophagus, Stomach, and Duodenum (Category Codes 530–538)

The esophagus connects the throat to the stomach. When food and water pass through the oral cavity, they travel down the esophagus to the stomach. When a person has an upset stomach and vomiting is involved, the reverse occurs. Esophagitis is an inflammation of the esophagus due to reflux of acid and pepsin from the stomach into the esophagus. Gastroesophageal reflux disease (GERD), is a common condition that primary care providers treat.

The esophagus connects to the stomach, a pouchlike structure. The stomach connects to the duodenum. The duodenum is where the small intestine begins. Figure 14-4 illustrates the stomach and its structures as well as its relation to the esophagus and the duodenum.

The duodenum extends to the jejunum, which is the middle portion of the small intestine. The jejunum connects the duodenum to the ileum, which is the last part of the small intestine. The ileum connects to the cecum, which is the beginning of the large intestine. It is important for a coder to know where certain structures stop and start so that the correct codes can be assigned.

Coding of Gastrointestinal Ulcers

Ulcerations of the gastrointestinal (GI) tract occur when there is erosion of the mucous membrane.

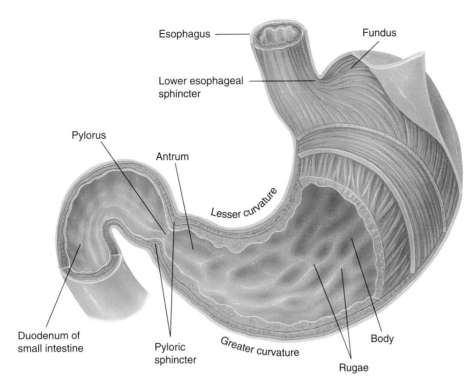

Figure 14-4 Structures of the stomach (From Ehrlich A, Schroeder CL. *Medical Terminology for Health Professions,* 4th ed. Clifton Park, NY: Delmar, Cengage Learning, 2001, p. 169.)

Disease Highlight—Gastrointestinal Ulcers

Gastrointestinal ulcers occur throughout the gastrointestinal tract and include gastric, duodenal, peptic, and gastrojejunal ulcers. All ulcers involve the destruction of tissue occurring in areas that are exposed to acid and/or pepsin. The mucous membrane penetrates through the muscularis mucosa and becomes inflamed. The etiology of ulcers is unclear, but contributing factors include reflux of bile or hyperacidity in the stomach, the extended use of anti-inflammatory drugs such as aspirin, the heavy intake of steroids and alcohol, smoking, and the presence of *Helicobacter pylori* bacteria.

Signs and Symptoms:

Patients with gastrointestinal ulcers complain of burning pain in the stomach or epigastric region, which may or may not subside with food intake or use of antacids. Patients also experience:

- Weight loss
- Nausea
- Vomiting
- Anemia

Clinical Testing:

Ulcers are diagnosed by:

- Upper GI and barium studies (endoscopy), which shows the ulceration
- Lab tests that review the patient's hemoglobin, hematocrit, and serum gastric and amylase levels. Hemoglobin and hematocrit are decreased in patients with bleeding from the ulcer. Serum gastrin and serum amylase levels are increased.
- Stool sample, which can be positive for occult blood

Treatment:

Treatment for patients with ulcers is directed at decreasing the acidity of the ulcer site, which promotes healing of the mucosa.

- Elimination of contributing factors is essential.
- Antacids and dietary restrictions neutralize the gastric acids.
- If *Helicobacter* bacteria is present, patients are given antibiotics.
- Patients are encouraged to eat nutritious regular meals.
- Anticholinergic drugs are prescribed to reduce the secretion of acid.
- Surgical intervention is necessary in severe cases when a patient has a hemorrhage, perforation, obstruction, or severe pain from the ulcer site.

    ICD-9-CM classifies the ulcers according to the site of the ulcer by using the following category codes:

- Gastric ulcer, category code 531—Ulcers that occur in the stomach
- Duodenal ulcer category code 532—Ulcers that occur in the upper part of the small intestine
- Peptic ulcer (site unspecified), category code 533—Ulcers that occur in an unspecified site of the GI tract
- Gastrojejunal ulcer, category code 534—Ulcers that occur in the stomach and jejunum

    EXAMPLE: An 82-year-old man presents today for persistent pain in the stomach. The patient states that he suffers from indigestion, nausea, and darker-than-normal stools. Lab results indicate that the patient is anemic and that the guaiac is positive. When the stomach area is palpated, pain is noted around the lower stomach area. After endoscopic examination, the patient is confirmed to have an acute gastrojejunal ulcer, which has not yet begun to hemorrhage. No obstructions are noted, and as we have not encountered hemorrhaging, medication is prescribed at this time for treatment.

    Because the confirmed diagnosis of acute gastrojejunal ulcer is given, the code assigned is 534.30, Acute gastrojejunal ulcer without mention of hemorrhage or perforation. A fifth digit of 0, without mention of obstruction, is needed to complete the code assignment. Many of the codes in this section require a fifth-digit code assignment of either 0, without mention of obstruction, or 1, with mention of obstruction.

Exercise 14–1   Identifying Fourth and Fifth Digits for Codes 531–534

For each code listed, identify the meaning of the fourth and fifth digit used in the code. The first one is completed.

Diagnostic Code	Fourth Digit	Fifth Digit
1. 533.00—Peptic ulcer	acute with hemorrhage	without mention of obstruction
2. 534.11—Gastrojejunal ulcer		
3. 531.40—Gastric ulcer		
4. 532.90—Duodenal ulcer		
5. 533.21—Peptic ulcer		

   6. 531.71—Gastric ulcer _____ _____

   7. 532.31—Duodenal ulcer _____ _____

   8. 534.40—Gastrojejunal ulcer _____ _____

   9. 532.60—Duodenal ulcer _____ _____

   10. 534.10—Gastrojejunal ulcer _____ _____

Appendicitis (Category Codes 540–543)

The **appendix** is a wormlike structure that is found, in most people, at the blind end of the cecum. When the appendix becomes inflamed or infected, known as **appendicitis,** the patient may experience pain and the white blood cell count becomes elevated. The appendix does not serve any known purpose in the digestive system, but it is the most common nonobstetrical problem encountered during pregnancy. Figure 14-5 illustrates the location of the appendix.

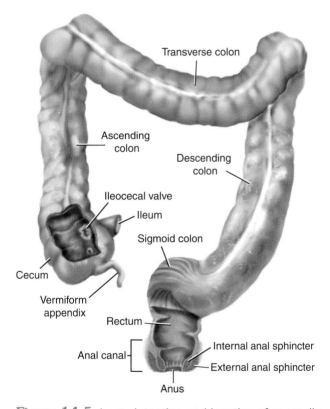

Figure 14-5 Large intestine and location of appendix

When coding appendicitis, the coder must determine whether any other complications are associated with the appendicitis, such as generalized peritonitis or peritoneal abscess. The coder should also note whether the term is modified by "acute," "chronic," or "subacute." These complications and terms all affect code assignment.

   EXAMPLE: The diagnostic statement of appendicitis codes to 541, acute appendicitis codes to 540.9, and chronic appendicitis and subacute appendicitis code to 542.

It should also be noted that the following fourth digits are used with category 540 to identify the presence or absence of complications.

540.0   Acute appendicitis with generalized peritonitis

540.1   Acute appendicitis with peritoneal abscess

540.9   Acute appendicitis without mention of peritonitis

Hernia of Abdominal Cavity (Category Codes 550–553)

A hernia, quite simply, is a protrusion or bulge through the tissue that normally contains the structure. There are several different types of hernias.

The tubular structure that passes through the lower layers of the abdominal wall is called the inguinal canal. An inguinal hernia occurs when a part of the intestine passes through a weak point or tear in the wall that holds the abdominal organs. Sometimes the doctor's note refers to a "direct inguinal hernia," which is a protrusion in the groin area. An indirect inguinal hernia is a protrusion that has moved to the scrotum. These types of hernias code to the 550 category and require a fifth digit to indicate whether the hernia is unilateral or bilateral and whether it is recurrent.

> **EXAMPLE:** A 23-year-old man presents with a bulging in the scrotal area on the right side. The patient experiences sharp pain on the right when urinating. Over the last week, patient has noticed pain in the area at the end of his workday. The patient has not experienced this before and is quite concerned. Upon examination, it was determined that the patient is suffering from an indirect inguinal hernia. We will refer him to a surgeon for further evaluation.

Code assignment in our example is 550.90. The 550.90, Inguinal hernia, without mention of obstruction or gangrene, with a fifth digit of 0, unilateral or unspecified (not specified as recurrent), is chosen based on the information given in the note. There is no mention of obstruction or gangrene, which may change with the surgeon's evaluation. With the information given, it appears the hernia is only on the right side and is not recurrent.

Other types of hernias that are encountered by a coder are a femoral hernia, an umbilical hernia, ventral hernia, incisional hernia, and hiatal hernia. Hiatal hernias are common. A hiatal hernia is the sliding of part of the stomach into the chest cavity. Figure 14-6 illustrates a hiatal hernia. The coder needs to indicate whether the hernia is recurrent and whether it is unilateral or bilateral by the selection of proper fourth and fifth digits. Many hernia repairs are now being done laparoscopically instead of through an incision. The codes in this area should be reviewed carefully because code changes occur almost annually.

Exercise 14–2   Coding Hernias

Code the following hernias using an appropriate ICD-9CM code.

Diagnosis	**Code**
1. Femoral hernia, bilateral with gangrene	_____
2. Incisional hernia with obstruction	_____
3. Inguinal hernia with gangrene	_____
4. Bilateral femoral hernia with obstruction	_____
5. Umbilical hernia with gangrene	_____

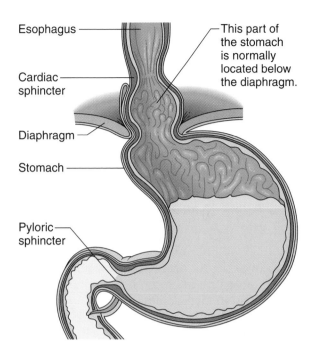

Esophagus

This part of
the stomach
is normally
located below
the diaphragm.

Cardiac
sphincter

Diaphragm

Stomach

Pyloric
sphincter

Figure 14-6 Hiatal hernia (From Neighbors M,
Tannehill-Jones R. *Human Diseases,* 2nd ed. Clifton
Park, NY: Delmar, Cengage Learning, p. 191.)

Noninfectious Enteritis and Colitis (Category Codes 555–558)

Noninfectious enteritis and colitis are classified to category codes 555–558, whereas infectious enteritis and colitis are classified in chapter 1 of ICD-9-CM, "Infectious and Parasitic Diseases." Enteritis is an inflammation of the intestines, and colitis is an inflammation of the colon. Conditions that are classified to this section include Crohn's disease and ulcerative colitis. Crohn's disease (codes 555.0–555.9), also known as regional enteritis, is a form of inflammatory bowel disease that can cause thickening and scarring of the abdominal wall, most commonly found in the large intestine, it can attack anywhere in the GI tract. Fourth digits are used to identify the specific site affected.

> **EXAMPLE:** Michelle presented with diarrhea, which has been going on for the last week along with abdominal pain, fever, and noticeable weight loss. The physician ordered a barium enema and small bowel X-ray. The results of these tests confirmed a diagnosis of Crohn's disease of the small intestine.

Crohn's disease of the small intestine is classified to code 555.0, and Crohn's disease of the large intestine is classified to code 555.1.

Ulcerative colitis affects the colon by causing frequent diarrhea. The colon becomes inflamed, and ulcers develop in the lining of the intestine. Ulcerative colitis is classified to category code 556, with fifth digits used to identify the site affected.

The coder needs to identify the site by reviewing the patient's medical record to accurately code Crohn's disease and ulcerative colitis. If the site cannot be determined from review of the medical documentation, then the following codes should be used:

Crohn's disease, 555.9

Ulcerative colitis, 556.9

Other Diseases of Intestines and Peritoneum (Category Codes 560–569)

Common conditions that are classified to this section of the code book include diverticulosis and diverticulitis. Diverticula are pouches or sacs in the lining of the intestine that cause a condition known as diverticulosis. If these sacs become inflamed, the patient is diagnosed with diverticulitis. A note at the beginning of the 562 category instructs the coder to "use additional code to identify any associated peritonitis (567.0–567.9)." Peritonitis is an inflammation of the lining of the abdominal cavity.

When coding diverticulosis or diverticulitis, coders must determine the site of the condition, either the small intestine (fourth-digit code 562.0) or colon (fourth-digit code 562.1). Coders must also determine whether the condition occurs with or without hemorrhage, which is identified by the selection of a fifth digit. It should be noted that an instructional notation appears after the category heading for category 562, Diverticula of intestine, that instructs the coder to "Use additional code to identify any associated peritonitis (567.0–567.9)."

> **EXAMPLE:** Mary presents to the ER with severe abdominal pain. She is running a fever of 101. She has been suffering for several days but states that with bowel movement the pain subsides a little. Stool guaiac shows trace amounts of blood. A GI consult resulted in an endoscopic exam, which confirmed the diagnosis of diverticulitis with minimal hemorrhaging of the lower portion of the small intestine. Peritonitis was confirmed by the endoscopy. Lab results were inconclusive, but white cell count was elevated. We will monitor for 24 hours and run further labs at that time. Patient was started on antibiotics for peritonitis.

Mary was diagnosed with diverticulitis of the small intestine. The guaiac showed traces of blood but a GI consult confirmed the hemorrhaging, so the code assigned is 562.02. An additional code is necessary for the peritonitis. Because the type was not confirmed, code assignment in this case is 567.9, Unspecified peritonitis.

Other Diseases of Digestive System (Category Codes 570–579)

This subsection of the chapter includes codes for the accessory organs of the digestive system, which include the liver, gallbladder, and pancreas. Figure 14-7 illustrates the accessory organs of the digestive system. The liver filters red blood cells, produces glycogen, and secretes bile, which breaks down fat. A coder may encounter the term hepatic, which means pertaining to the liver.

The gallbladder is found under the liver and is connected to the liver via the cystic duct. The purpose of the gallbladder is to store bile secreted by the liver until the bile is needed in digestion.

The pancreas is located behind the stomach and is connected to the gallbladder and the liver by way of the common bile duct. This organ has a function in both the digestive system and the endocrine system. The pancreas secretes juices necessary for digestion but also regulates blood sugar levels through the release of the hormone insulin.

Cholecystitis and Cholelithiasis

Cholecystitis, a sudden and severe onset of inflammation of the gallbladder, and cholelithiasis, the formation or presence of gallstones, are classified to this section of the code book. Cholecystitis and cholelithiasis can occur with or without the other condition. The coder must therefore review the medical documentation carefully to identify the clinical picture of the patient.

Cholelithiasis is classified to category code 574, with fourth digits used to identify the location of the gallstones and whether cholecystitis is present or not present. The following fifth digits are used with the 574 category codes:

0   Without mention of obstruction

1   With obstruction

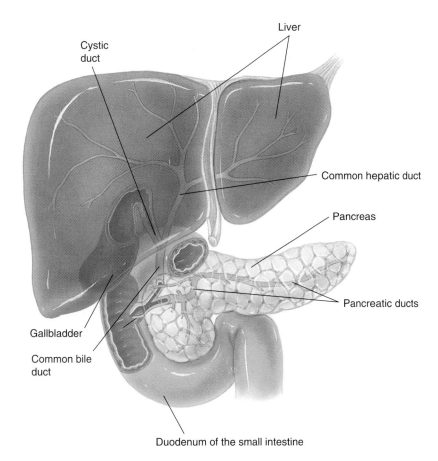

Liver

Cystic
duct

Common hepatic duct

Pancreas

Pancreatic ducts

Gallbladder

Common bile
duct

Duodenum of the small intestine

Figure 14-7 Accessory digestive organs (From Ehrlich A, Schroeder CL. *Medical Terminology for Health Professions,* 4th ed. Clifton Park, NY: Delmar, Cengage Learning, 2001, p. 170.)

Cholecystitis without the mention of cholelithiasis is classified to category code 575 with the following fourth digits used:

0   Acute cholecystitis

1   Other cholecystitis

2   Obstruction of gallbladder

3   Hydrops of gallbaldder

4   Perforation of gallbladder

5   Fistula of gallbaldder

6   Cholesterolosis of gallbladder

8   Other specified disorders of gallbladder

9   Unspecified disorders of gallbladder

It should be noted that subcategory 575.1 is further divided to the fifth-digit level. This subcategory is used to code other types of cholecystitis. Cholecystitis, unspecified is coded to 575.10, and chronic cholecystitis is coded to code 575.11. Code 575.12 is used to report cholecystitis that is described as acute and chronic cholecystitis. It is essential that the provider's documentation be reviewed prior to code selection for accurate coding.

Gastrointestinal Hemorrhage (Category Code 578)

Category 578, Gastrointestinal hemorrhage, has a detailed exclusion note that the coder should read carefully before assigning a code. The exclusion note appears as follows:

```
EXCLUDES: that with mention of:
        angiodysplasia of stomach and duodenum (537.83)
        angiodysplasia of intestine (569.85)
        diverticulitis, intestine:
         large (562.13)
         small (562.03)
        diverticulosis, intestine:
         large (562.12)
         small (562.02)
        gastritis and duodenitis (535.0-535.6)
        ulcer:
         duodenal, gastric, gastrojejunal, or peptic (531.00-534.91)
```

Several conditions that might include GI bleeding are coded not to this category of codes but to other categories of ICD-9-CM.

EXAMPLE: Mary Barry presents to the ER with stomach pain and blood in stool. Upon questioning, Mary states she has diverticulosis. She admits to not watching her diet over the last 2 days, and she may be having a flare-up. After GI consult, it is determined that Mary does indeed have diverticulitis in the small intestine. She is on a round of antibiotics along with Flagyl.

The diagnosis in this example is 562.03, Diverticulitis of small intestine with hemorrhage. The coder does not include code 578.1, Blood in stool.

A second patient presented to the ER with stomach pain and blood in stool, but no history of diverticulosis and no GI consult was completed, the coding assignment would be 536.8, Dyspepsia and other specified disorders of stomach function, along with 578.1, Blood in stool.

Therefore, coders must remember to carefully read the medical documentation and notations that are present in the code book to ensure accurate coding.

Internet Links

To learn more about diseases and conditions of the digestive system, visit the following sites: *http://www.gastro.org*, *http://www.jr2.ox.ac.uk*, and *http://www.saem.org*.

The Cleveland Clinic has a Web site that can be found at: *http://my.clevelandclinic.org/disorders/ Gastrointestinal_Tract_disorders/hic_Gastrointestinal_Disorders.aspx*. This site has adundant information on gastrointestinal disorders.

Additional information can also be found at *www.iffgd.org*. This site is maintained by the International Foundation for Functional Gastrointestinal Disorders.

Summary

- The digestive process begins when food is taken into the mouth for nourishment and finishes its work with the elimination of waste.

- The *alimentary canal* and the *gastrointestinal tract* are terms used to describe the digestive system.

- Diseases of the oral cavity, including the teeth, are included in chapter 9 of ICD-9-CM.
- Accessory organs such as the appendix, liver, gallbladder, and pancreas are also classified to chapter 9 of ICD-9-CM.
- Appendicitis can be accompanied with peritonitis or peritoneal abscess.
- Hernias are classified in ICD-9-CM according to the site of the hernia.
- Noninfectious enteritis and colitis are classified to chapter 9 of ICD-9-CM, whereas infectious enteritis and colitis are classified to chapter 1 of ICD-9-CM.
- Diverticula are abnormal sacs in the lining of the intestine.
- Diverticulitis occurs when there is an inflammation of the diverticula.

Chapter Review

True/False: Indicate whether the statement is true (T) or false (F).

1. _____ Food is broken down for nourishment by the digestive tract.

2. _____ Cholelithiasis means kidney stones.

3. _____ The pancreas is not an accessory organ.

4. _____ Irregularly shaped patches that appear on the tongue are known as mapped tongue.

5. _____ The stomach is a pouchlike structure that connects to the esophagus on one end and to the ileum on the other.

Fill-in-the-Blank: Enter the appropriate term(s) to complete each statement.

6. An infection of the pulp and the surrounding tissue in the mouth is called _____.

7. An inflammation of the esophagus due to acid reflux is known as _____.

8. The _____ secretes bile, which breaks down fat.

9. The _____ has functions in both the digestive and endocrine system.

10. Hernias are classified in ICD-9-CM according to _____.

Coding Assignments

Instructions: Using an ICD-9-CM coding book, select the code for each diagnostic statement.

Diagnosis	Code
1. Chronic pulpitis	_____
2. Reflux esophagitis	_____
3. Anterior soft tissue impingement	_____
4. Recurrent femoral hernia	_____
5. Hematemesis	_____
6. Mandibular hyperplasia	_____

7. Phlebitis of portal vein _____

8. Stenosis of cystic duct _____

9. Sliding hiatal hernia _____

10. GERD _____

11. Gastric diverticulum _____

12. Umbilical hernia _____

13. Dental pulp degeneration _____

14. Granulomatous colitis _____

15. Odontogenesis imperfecta _____

16. Temporomandibular joint arthralgia _____

17. Abnormal jaw closure _____

18. Barrett's esophagus _____

19. Hypertophic gastritis with hemorrhage _____

20. Biliary cirrhosis _____

21. Adynamic ileus _____

22. Calculus of gallbladder and bile duct with acute cholecystitis with obstruction _____

23. Hepatic infarction _____

24. Fistula of bile duct _____

25. Pancreatic steatorrhea _____

Case Studies

Instructions: Review each case study, and select the correct ICD-9-CM diagnostic code.

CASE 1

CHIEF COMPLAINT: Abdominal pain

HISTORY: This is a 70-year-old man who had a diagnostic sigmoidoscopy done 3 days ago for rectal bleeding. He is having some abdominal pain. He has noted some nausea and pain when he eats solid food. He said he feels better if he has only liquids, and once he has a bowel movement he feels better. When asked if he knew the results of his sigmoidoscopy, he replied that the doctor had told him he had some diverticula. He denies any diarrhea but said there is some constipation. He also denies chest pain or shortness of breath. He has had some coughing, but no other symptoms are noted. All other reviews of systems are noted as normal.

PAST MEDICAL HISTORY: Positive for diverticulosis. No known allergies, no diabetes. Patient had thyroidectomy 25 years ago.

EXAM:

HEENT: Normal

MOUTH: Partially edentulous; gums look healthy.

HEART: Regular sinus rate and rhythm; heart sounds are good.

LUNGS: Clear to auscultation and percussion.

ABDOMEN: Soft; slight tenderness on palpation in lower left quadrant; no organomegaly; no masses palpable; bowel sounds good.

GENITALIA: Normal male.

RECTAL: Good sphincter tone; guaiac testing shows occult blood; blood is noted upon visual exam.

EXTREMITIES: No edema, ulceration, or discoloration; pedal pulses are normal.

NEUROLOGICAL: Normal

IMPRESSION: Diverticulitis with hemorrhage

PLAN: We will begin antibiotic therapy with Flagyl.

ICD-9-CM Code Assignment: _____

CASE 2

This is a 25-year-old female with a history of ulcerative colitis who presents today with diarrhea and bleeding. She was hospitalized last June with a similar problem and had been on IV steroids and then oral steroids prior to discharge. She has been off the steroids now for approximately 2 months and had been doing fairly well. She now is having abdominal cramping and loose stools, which have become bloody. She noted that over the last 48 hours, her bowel movements have increased dramatically, which is why she has presented to the ER. She has been drinking and eating very bland foods, as well as avoiding dairy products. Nothing seems to help.

PHYSICAL EXAM: This is a 25-year-old female who appears slightly dehydrated and in mild distress. Temp: 98.1; respiratory rate: 20; pulse: 110 and regular; BP: 100/70.

HEENT: Normal; oral cavity is moist without lesions.

NECK: Supple, no thyromegaly or lymphadenopathy

CHEST: Clear to auscultation and percussion

HEART: No murmurs, rubs, or gallops

ABDOMEN: Nondistended. Normal bowel sounds. Some epigastric tenderness with deep palpation, without radiation. Has some right lower quadrant discomfort without rebound or guarding associated.

RECTAL: Some internal hemorrhoids noted. Stool is light brown and not bloody at this time.

IMPRESSION and PLAN: Exacerbation of ulcerative colitis. Admit patient at this time. Would like to start IV rehydration and also intravenous steroids. Will observe stool count, consistency, and whether there is blood in the stool. Amylase, creatinine, BUN, WBC, Hgb, and MCV ordered.

ICD-9-CM Code Assignment: _____

CASE 3

Skilled Nursing Facility Monthly Progress Note:

This resident was admitted in May of this year with the primary diagnoses of diabetes mellitus and chronic gastritis. The patient has been complaining of heartburn and is occasionally irritated by banana and other cereals. She denies any nausea or vomiting, but she thinks that every time she eats there is fullness in the stomach.

PHYSICAL EXAMINATION:

She is alert, conscious, not in any acute pain or distress. Fasting blood sugar is 86; BP, 120/74; P, 80 per minute and regular; R, 20; and temp, 95.7. Her weight is 110.

Abdomen is soft. Bowel sounds are positive; it is not distended, and there is tenderness.

Heart, regular rhythm with no change in the systolic murmur.

Lung is clear to auscultation.

Medications include: See medication list for her current medications. Start Maalox 15cc 3 times a day for gastritis. I will reevaluate her if she needs additional medication for her gastritis.

ICD-9-CM Code Assignment: _____

CASE 4

ED Summary Note:

Sylvia presented to the ED with abdominal distention and pain, along with nausea, and reported an earlier bout of vomiting. Upon examination, no bowel sounds were noted, but an increase in white cell count was noted. Barium studies showed a twisting of the intestine. A surgical consult was requested for Sylvia.

ICD-9-CM Code Assignment: _____

CASE 5

ED Summary Note:

Kyle presented to the ED with abdominal distention and tenderness, a fever of 102°, and a complaint of nausea. Kyle has a history of perforated peptic ulcer. Physical exam was performed, along with arterial blood gases (which showed lowered potassium and carbon dioxide), urinalysis, and lab tests, all of which confirm the diagnosis of generalized acute peritonitis.

ICD-9-CM Code Assignment: _____

Diseases of the Genitourinary System

Chapter Outline

Objectives

At the conclusion of this chapter, the student will be able to:

1. Identify the anatomical structures of the urinary system.
2. Identify the anatomical structures of the male and female genital tracts.
3. Explain the conditions that are related to the genitourinary system.
4. Discuss specific coding guidelines related to the conditions encountered in the genitourinary system.
5. Select and code diagnoses from case studies.

Key Terms

Acute Renal Failure

Benign Prostatic Hypertrophy (BPH)

Chronic Renal Failure

Complete Prolapse

Cyst of Breast

Cystitis

Dysplasia of Cervix

Endometriosis

End-Stage Renal Disease (ESRD)

Female Genitalia

Fibrocystic Disease of the Breast

Genital Prolapse

Glomerulonephritis

Hematuria

Incomplete Prolapse

Kidney

Male Genitalia

Menopause

Micturate

Nephritis

Nephrons

Nephropathy

Nephrosis

Ovarian Cyst

Penis

Perimenopausal

Postmenopausal

Premenopausal

Prostate Gland

Reminder

As you work through this chapter, you will need to have a copy of the ICD-9-CM coding book to reference.

Sebaceous Cyst of
the Breast

Urethra

Urinary System

Urine

Ureters

Urinary Bladder

Urinary Tract Infections
(UTI)

Voiding

Introduction

Chapter 10 of ICD-9-CM, "Diseases of the Genitourinary System," classifies conditions of the urinary system and the male and female genital tracts except for certain genitourinary transmissible infections, neoplasms, and conditions associated with pregnancy, childbirth, and the puerperium. Symptoms that are just emerging, such as frequent urination, or conditions that are familial linked, such as family history of malignant neoplasm of the kidney (V16.51), are not found in this chapter.

It should also be noted that hypertensive renal disease is classified to conditions of the circulatory system, category 403, not in this chapter.

Introduction to the Body System

The urinary system is comprised of the kidneys, ureter, bladder, and urethra. The main function of the urinary system is to maintain a balance of the contents of the fluids within the body. Urea is removed from the bloodstream and then, along with other excess fluids and waste products, is converted to urine, which is expelled from the body by way of the bladder. Figure 15-1 illustrates the structures of the urinary system.

The kidneys are the primary organs of the urinary system. There are usually two kidneys, which are located against the dorsal wall of the abdominal cavity and lie on either side of the vertebral column.

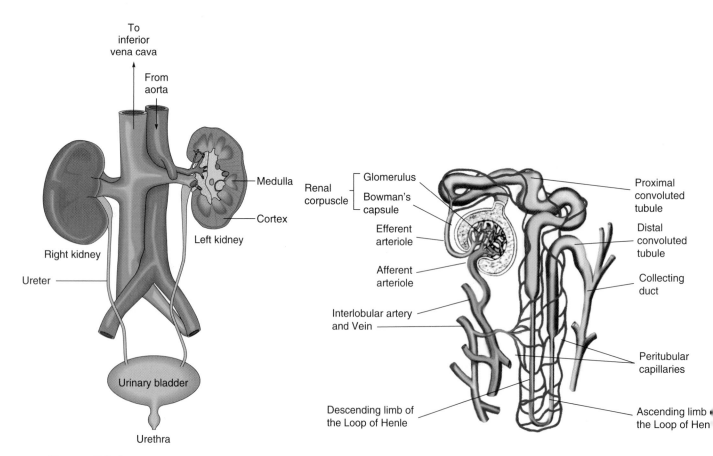

Figure 15-1 Structures and blood flow of the kidneys (From Ehrlich A, Schroeder CL. *Medical Terminology for Health Professions,* 4th ed. Clifton Park, NY: Delmar, Cengage Learning, 2001, p. 189.)

The kidney filters blood constantly to remove waste. The kidneys contain nephrons, which work to filter, reabsorb, and secrete urine. The nephrons are the structures that actually form urine.

Urine is moved from the kidney to the bladder by way of the ureters. The ureters are very narrow tubes, which can easily be damaged in certain types of surgery. It is important that they function properly for the urinary system to do its job.

The ureters connect to the urinary bladder, which holds urine until it moves to the urethra. The urethra is a small tube extending from the bladder to outside the body. When the bladder fills, pressure is exerted on the urethra, causing the urge to urinate. The coder may note the terms *micturate* or *voiding,* which are synonymous terms for urination. Coders must be very careful to identify the proper body part and the spelling of urethra and ureter. The spelling of these structures is very close, so attention to spelling when locating a code is critical.

The male genitalia are made up of the scrotum, testicles, and the penis. The function of these organs is primarily for reproduction, but they also function as part of the urinary system, which is why they are included in this chapter.

In the male, the urethra passes through the penis to outside the body. The penis functions in both the urinary and reproductive systems. The ureters move urine from the kidneys to the bladder. Urine is moved via the urethra from the urinary bladder to outside the body. In the reproductive function, semen moves through the vas deferens to the urethra from the ejaculatory duct.

The prostate gland is also part of the male genitalia. The prostate gland is located under the bladder and on the upper end of the urethra. The prostate gland secretes a fluid that is part of the semen and also aids in the motility of the sperm. Figure 15-2 illustrates a cross-section of the male genitalia and its relation to the urethra and the urinary bladder.

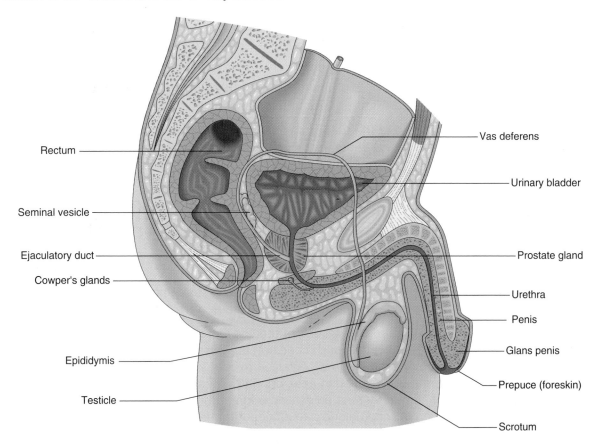

Figure 15-2 Cross-section of the male reproductive organs (From Ehrlich A, Schroeder CL. *Medical Terminology for Health Professions,* 4th ed. Clifton Park, NY: Delmar, Cengage Learning, 2001, p. 296.)

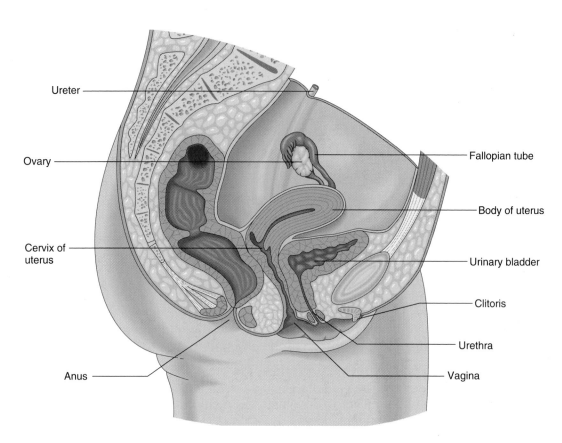

Figure 15-3 Cross-section of the female reproductive organs (From Ehrlich A, Schroeder CL. *Medical Terminology for Health Professions,* 4th ed. Clifton Park, NY: Delmar, Cengage Learning, 2001, p. 301.)

The function of the female genitalia is the same as that of the male genitalia. Reproduction is the primary function, but because of its proximity to the urinary system, it is included in this chapter.

The female genitalia are made up of the uterus, vagina, ovaries, fallopian tubes, cervix, perineum, clitoris, labia, and mammary glands, or breasts. Figure 15-3 illustrates a cross-section of the female genitalia and its relation to the urinary system.

Coding for the Genitourinary System

Nephritis, Nephrotic Syndrome, and Nephrosis (Category Codes 580–589)

Nephritis is an inflammation of the kidneys. Nephrosis refers to a disease or disorder of the kidney. The coder may encounter the term *nephropathy,* which is a synonymous term for nephrosis.

Some conditions that are classified to this section of the code book have separate codes for the acute and chronic manifestation of the disease. One such condition is glomerulonephritis, an inflammation of the glomeruli of the kidney. Acute glomerulonephritis is classified to category 580, Acute glomerulonephritis, whereas chronic glomerulonephritis is classified to category 582. These two codes are not usually billed together in the same episode of care. If there is an exacerbation of the chronic glomerulonephritis, the condition causing the exacerbation is coded along with a code from the 582 section.

EXAMPLE: Polly Patient came in for a follow-up of her chronic glomerulonephritis. Polly also has type II, insulin-dependent uncontrolled diabetes. She has been feeling a little tired, and her blood sugars have been running high. We will run labs to see what is going on.

To code this example, code the diabetes first, using code 250.42, Diabetes, type II uncontrolled with renal involvement, as the primary diagnosis. Code 582.81 codes the chronic glomerulonephritis. The key here is to pay attention to the brackets in the Alphabetic Index and then to verify your code selection in the Tabular List.

Two of the most serious conditions encountered in this section of the chapter are acute and chronic renal failure. For acute renal failure, use codes in the 584 category when the renal function is interrupted suddenly. The cause can be any number of reasons, and the renal function usually returns with treatment. Causes of acute renal failure include blockage of urine flow caused by stones, tumors, or an enlarged prostate; embolism; congestive heart failure; surgical shock; hemorrhagic shock; and dehydration. In the event that renal function does not return, the condition may progress to chronic renal insufficiency or failure and ultimately death.

Chronic renal failure, also known as chronic kidney disease, is a progressive disease in which renal function deteriorates, causing multisystem problems. As the disease progresses, other organs are affected until the patient advances to the late states of chronic renal failure, which is then considered end-stage renal disease (ESRD). Patients with chronic renal failure may be on dialysis or awaiting a kidney transplant. Chronic kidney disease (CKD) code determination is based on the stage of the disease. The diagnosis code category for chronic kidney disease is 585, and fourth digits are used to indicate the stage. Stage 1 involves some kidney damage with a glomerular filtration rate (GFR) slightly greater than 90, which is considered a normal GFR. Stage 2 has a GFR of 60–89 with mild or minor kidney damage. Stage 3 involves more damage to the kidney with a GFR of 30–59. Stage 4 has a GFR of 15–29 with severe kidney damage. Stage 5 involves severe kidney damage with a GFR less than 15. At stage 5, the patient is on dialysis or awaiting a transplant. Category 585 contains instructional notations that appear in the Tabular List as follows:

```
585    Chronic kidney disease (CKD)
       Chronic uremia
       Code first hypertensive chronic kidney disease, if applicable,
       (403.00-403.91, 404.00-404.93)
       Use additional code to identify kidney transplant status, if applicable
       (V42.0)
       Use additional code to identify manifestation as:
          uremic:
                neuropathy (357.4)
                pericarditis (420.0)
```

Documentation is key when coding for chronic renal failure/chronic kidney disease. The coder may encounter such phrases as "chronic renal insufficiency, chronic renal failure, chronic renal disease, which are all coded to 585.9 because the terms are unspecified as to the stage of the disease," which is coded to 585.9. Laboratory tests are generally an indication of chronic renal failure. Elevated serum creatinine or blood urea nitrogen (BUN) values may indicate this condition. Clinical manifestations such as anemia, hypocalcemia, and renal osteodystrophy may be documented. Unless the provider has documented specifically that the patient has ESRD, renal failure, chronic renal failure, or renal insufficiency, clarification must be made before a code is assigned. It is vital that a coder assign only a diagnosis that can be supported by medical documentation, so it is essential that there be communication with the provider for clarification of the diagnosis before a code is assigned.

If the patient has renal involvement with diabetes, documentation needs to be clear as to the cause and effect relationship. If renal failure is due to diabetes, the code for diabetes is coded first, followed by the type of renal failure. Patients with hypertension due to renal failure are coded to the 403 category. The documentation must be clear that the two conditions are related. If this relationship is not documented as a causal condition, code each condition separately.

The ICD-9-CM Official Guidelines for Coding and Reporting instructs coders to follow the following guidelines for the coding of chronic kidney disease.

Official ICD-9-CM Coding Guideline:

a. Chronic kidney disease

(1) Stages of chronic kidney disease (CKD)

The ICD-9-CM classifies CKD based on severity. The severity of CKD is designated by stages I–V. Stage II, code 585.2, equates to mild CKD; stage III, code 585.3, equates to moderate CKD; and stage IV, code 585.4, equates to severe CKD. Code 585.6, End-stage renal disease (ESRD), is assigned when the provider has documented end-stage renal disease (ESRD). If both a stage of CKD and ESRD are documented, assign code 585.6 only.

(2) Chronic kidney disease and kidney transplant status

Patients who have undergone kidney transplant may still have some form of CKD because the kidney transplant may not fully restore kidney function. Therefore, the presence of CKD alone does not constitute a transplant complication. Assign the appropriate 585 code for the patient's stage of CKD and code V42.0. If a transplant complication such as failure or rejection is documented, see Section I.C.17.f.1.b for information on coding complications of a kidney transplant. If the documentation is unclear as to whether the patient has a complication of the transplant, query the provider.

(3) Chronic kidney disease with other conditions

Patients with CKD may also suffer from other serious conditions, most commonly diabetes mellitus and hypertension. The sequencing of the CKD code in relationship to codes for other contributing conditions is based on the conventions in the tabular list.

(See I.C.3.a.4 for sequencing instructions for diabetes. See I.C.4.a.1 for anemia in CKD. See I.C.7.a.3 for hypertensive chronic kidney disease. See I.C.17.f.1.b, Kidney transplant complications, for instructions on coding of documented rejection or failure.) (See Appendix A, Section I, C10, a1–2)

Other Diseases of Urinary System (Category Codes 590–599)

The coder needs to be cautious in this section because there are many notes for coding underlying disease or additional codes to identify organisms. Therefore, it is imperative that coders thoroughly read the coding notations in the Tabular List of ICD-9-CM for this chapter.

EXAMPLE: Katy Kidney has presented to the ER with severe abdominal pain as well as painful urination. She has had lab work ordered and a sterile urine catch done. At this time it appears that she is suffering from acute cystitis with *E. coli* present.

In our example the diagnosis for cystitis, which is an inflammation of the bladder, needs to include the code for the *E. coli* organism. Our code assignment should be 595.0, Acute cystitis, and 041.4, *E. coli,* because our note for the 595 code assignment states "use additional code to identify organism."

Other disorders of the bladder, urethra, and urinary tract are included in this subsection of the chapter. Hematuria, a condition in which blood appears in the urine, is classified to this section. Hematuria is commonly a symptom of a more definitive condition. When hematuria is present as a symptom of a more definitive condition and considered an inherent part of that condition, hematuria is not coded; only the more definitive condition is coded.

EXAMPLE: Bill Best presents with back pain and difficulty urinating. He has had previous bouts with kidney stones, so his physician orders the following STAT diagnostic tests. A urinalysis reveals hematuria, and a scan reveals two kidney stones. For this encounter, only the renal calculus is coded, using 592.0, because the physician records the following as a diagnosis: "hematuria due to renal calculus."

Another commonly seen condition that is classified to this chapter of ICD-9-CM is urinary tract infections (UTI), which is an abnormal presence of micro-organisms in the urine. UTIs are classified to code 599.0, Urinary tract infection, site not specified. The following two notations appear in the Tabular List for subcategory code 599.0, which must be used by coders when coding UTIs.

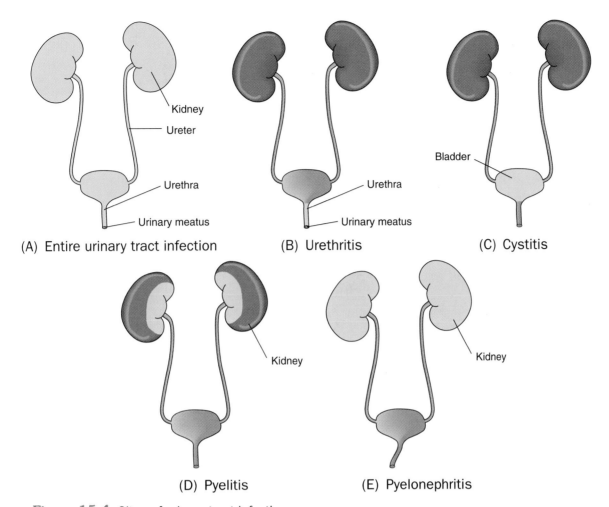

(A) Entire urinary tract infection   (B) Urethritis   (C) Cystitis

(D) Pyelitis   (E) Pyelonephritis

Figure 15-4 Sites of urinary tract infections

```
Use additional code to identify organism, such as Escherichia coli [E. coli]
(041.4)
EXCLUDES: candidiasis of urinary tract (112.2)
          urinary tract infection of newborn (771.82)
```

It should be noted that subcategory code 599.7 is differentiated by the use of fifth digits to identify unspecified hematuria (code 599.70), gross hematuria (code 599.71), and microscopic hematuria (code 599.72).

Urinary tract infections can occur in various sites throughout the urinary tract. Figure 15-4 identifies various UTI sites. When a specific site of the infection is identified, ICD-9-CM assigns the following codes:

- 597.8   Urethritis
- 595.9   Cystitis, unspecified
- 595.0   Acute cystitis
- 595.2   Chronic cystitis
- 590.80   Pyelitis or pyelonephritis
- 590.10   Acute pyelitis or acute pyelonephritis
- 590.00   Chronic pyelitis or chronic pyelonephritis

It should be noted that many of these codes have instructional notations at the category and subcategory levels. Be sure to reference the Tabular List when selecting these codes to identify the instructional notations.

Exercise 15–1 Identifying Notations for Category Codes 590–599

Instructions: For each category or code listed, identify the applicable notation(s).

Category or Code	Notation
1. 590.81	_____
2. Category 590	_____
3. 599.8	_____
4. 598.01	_____
5. 599.6	_____

Diseases of the Male Genital Organs (Category Codes 600–608)

Category codes 600–608 classify conditions of the male genital organs, which include the prostate gland and penis. The prostate gland is located in front of the rectum and under the urinary bladder. This gland also surrounds the opening of the bladder leading into the urethra.

The prostate gland can become enlarged and affect a person's ability to urinate. It is important for physicians to determine the reason why a male is unable to urinate. Inability to urinate can be caused by hyperplasia, an enlargement of the prostate, and by prostatic cancer. Both conditions can cause urinary obstruction and are typically the reasons why patients will seek care. The physician, through diagnostic testing, determines whether the patient has a neoplastic condition or hyperplasia. Neoplastic conditions are classified in ICD-9-CM to chapter 2, "Neoplasms." Hyperplasia and inflammatory diseases of the prostate are classified to category codes 600 and 601.

Benign prostatic hypertrophy (BPH) is an abnormal enlargement of the prostate, a common condition that affects men over 60 years of age. BPH is classified in ICD-9-CM to category code 600. Fourth digits are used in this category to identify the nature of the hypertrophy. Fifth digits are used to identify the presence or absence of urinary obstruction. Category 601 is used to code inflammatory disease of the prostate. Fourth digits are used to indicate acute or chronic prostatitis, abscess of prostate, prostatocystitis, or prostatitis in diseases classified elsewhere and other specified inflammatory diseases of prostate. The following notation also appears in the Tabular List for category 601:

```
Use additional code to identify the organism, such as Staphylococcus (041.1) or
Streptococcus (041.8)
```

Therefore, it is important for the coder to identify whether a specific organism has been identified as the cause of the prostatitis. It should also be noted that an additional instructional notation appears for subcategory 601.4 that instructs coders to code first underlying diseases. Reference the code book to make note of these instructional notations.

The remaining codes found in this section of the code book classify disorders of the testes, penis, and seminal vesicles. Male infertility, category code 606, uses fourth digits to identify the cause of the infertility.

Exercise 15–2   Coding from Category Codes 600–608

Instructions: Select the appropriate ICD-9-CM code for each diagnostic statement.

Diagnosis	Code
1. Leukoplakia of penis	_____
2. BPH with urinary obstruction	_____
3. Chronic prostatitis	_____
4. Dysplasia of prostate	_____
5. Staphylococcus infection causing orchitis with abscess	_____
6. Nodular prostate	_____
7. Abscess of vas deferens	_____
8. Stricture of spermatic cord	_____
9. Cyst of prostate	_____
10. Abscess of prostate	_____

Disorders of the Breast (Category Codes 610–612)

Disorders of the breast are coded to different chapters within ICD-9-CM. Neoplastic conditions are classified to chapter 2, "Neoplasms," and other disorders of the breast that occur during pregnancy or during the postpartum period are classified to chapter 11, "Complications of Pregnancy, Childbirth, and the Puerperium." The remaining disorders of the breast are classified to category code 610, Benign mammary dysplasias, and to category code 611, Other disorders of the breast.

Review of the medical record is essential when you are coding disorders of the breast. If there are any questions as to the cause of the disorders, the provider should be queried. When a provider documents terms such as "breast lump," "cyst," or "growth," clarification is needed to determine whether the condition is of neoplastic origin. Biopsies of breast tissue are completed to determine whether the growth is neoplastic, and coders need to reference pathology reports before assigning codes for neoplastic conditions. When a provider records "mass in breast," "lump," "cyst," or "growth," the coder should use code 611.72, Lump or mass in breast, until further diagnostic testing reveals the cause of the mass.

Other common non-neoplastic disorders of the breast that are classified to these codes include:

- Cyst of breast, code 610.0—A single encapsulated fluid-filled sac of the breast

- Fibrocystic disease of the breast, code 610.1—The presence of a single cyst or multiple cysts of the breast

- Sebaceous cyst of the breast, code 610.8—An encapsulated cyst of a sebaceous gland of the breast that contains yellowish, fatty material

Inflammatory Diseases of Female Pelvic Organs (Category Codes 614–616)

At the start of category codes 614–616, the following instructional notations appear:

```
Use additional code to identify organism such as Staphylococcus (041.1) or
Streptococcus (041.0).
```

`EXCLUDES: that associated with pregnancy, abortion, childbirth, or the puerperium (630-676.9)`

The first note instructs the coder to use two codes: one for the condition and one to identify the type of infection present.

The Excludes: note signals to the coder that if any of the conditions being coded are associated with pregnancy, abortion, childbirth, or the puerperium, the condition is classified to chapter 16 of ICD-9-CM.

EXAMPLE: A female patient presents with lower abdominal discomfort, low back pain, and leukorrhea. A vaginal exam and culture reveal cervicitis of streptococcal origin. This is coded by using codes 616.0, Cervicitis, and 041.0, Streptococcal infection.

Six months later the same patient is pregnant and has a repeat streptococcal infection during her pregnancy. This is coded by using codes 646.6x, Infections of genitourinary tract in pregnancy, and code 041.0, Streptococcal infection.

Other Disorders of the Female Genital Tract (Category Codes 617–629)

The following disorders of the female genital tract are classified in this chapter of ICD-9-CM:

- **Endometriosis,** code 617—An abnormal growth of the endometrium outside the uterus.

- **Genital prolapse,** code 618—The downward displacement of the genital organs (Fourth digits are used to identify whether the condition involves the vaginal wall, the uterus, or both. Coders must also identify whether the prolapse is diagnosed as a complete prolapse, when the entire uterus descends and protrudes beyond the introitus and the vagina becomes inverted, or as an incomplete prolapse, when the uterus descends into the introitus.)

- **Ovarian cyst,** codes 620.0–620.2—The encapsulated sac of the ovary that is filled with a semisolid or liquid material

- **Dysplasia of cervix,** subcategory code 622.1—The abnormal development or growth of cells of the cervix [Fifth digits are used to identify cervical intraepithelial neoplasia I (CIN I) and intraepithelial neoplasia II (CIN II).]

Another section of codes frequently used in this chapter classify menopausal disorders. Menopause refers to the time of a woman's life when her menstrual cycle ceases. A woman may experience problems that are premenopausal (the time period right before menopause), perimenopausal (when symptoms of menopause begin, such as hot flashes), menopausal (which is marked by a woman not having a period for one year), and postmenopausal (when a woman has not had a period for at least one year until the time she celebrates her 100th birthday). It should be noted that premature menopause is coded not to this section of codes but to 256.31. Menopausal and postmenopausal disorders are classified to category code 627.

Exercise 15–3   Coding for Category Codes 617–629

For each diagnostic statement listed, select the appropriate ICD-9-CM diagnostic codes.

Diagnosis	Codes
1. Uterovesical fistula (female)	_____
2. Hypertrophy of uterus	_____
3. Dysmenorrhea	_____
4. Leukoplakia of vagina	_____

  5. Female stress incontinence   _____

  6. Eversion of cervix   _____

  7. Endometriosis of rectum   _____

  8. Midline cystocele   _____

  9. Rectovaginal fistula   _____

  10. Pelvic muscle wasting of female   _____

Internet Links

To learn more about the urinary system, visit the *Digital Urology Journal* at *http://www.duj.com* and the following sites from various medical universities: *http://urology.jhu.edu*, *http://www.med.stanford.edu*, and *http://www.urology.medsch.ucla.edu*.

To learn more about male and female reproductive systems, visit *http://www.malehealthcenter.com* and *http://healthywomen.org*.

Summary

- The urinary system and the genital system are so closely connected that in some cases the function of one depends on the ability of the other to work properly.

- Certain genitourinary transmissible infections, neoplasms, and conditions associated with pregnancy, childbirth, and the puerperium are not classified in chapter 10 of ICD-9-CM, "Diseases of the Genitourinary System."

- The late state of chronic renal failure is considered end-stage renal disease.

- The coder needs to be cautious in this chapter because there are many notes for coding underlying disease or additional codes to identify organisms.

Chapter Review

True/False: Indicate whether the statement is true (T) or false (F).

  1. _____ The urethra is a narrow tube connecting the kidney to the bladder.

  2. _____ The mammary glands are located in the breasts.

  3. _____ The prostate gland is part of the male urinary system.

  4. _____ Nephrosis refers to a disease or disorder of the kidney.

  5. _____ If renal failure is confirmed as being a direct result of a diabetic condition, the diabetes code is listed first, followed by the code identifying the type of renal failure.

Fill-in–the-Blank: Enter the appropriate term(s) to complete each statement.

  6. The _____ holds urine until it is expelled from the body.

  7. _____ is a progressive disease in which renal function deteriorates.

8. _____ is a synonymous term for nephropathy.

9. _____ marks the end of a woman's menstrual cycle.

10. The _____ filters blood to remove waste, and the _____ actually form urine.

Coding Assignments

Instructions: Using and ICD-9-CM coding book, select the appropriate code for each diagnostic statement.

Diagnosis	Code
1. Atrophy of kidney	_____
2. Galactorrhea not associated with childbirth	_____
3. Bilateral small kidneys	_____
4. Paralysis of the bladder	_____
5. Chronic renal failure	_____
6. Postmenopausal bleeding	_____
7. Dysplasia of the cervix	_____
8. Acute renal failure with lesion of renal cortical	_____
9. Hyperplasia of prostate with urinary obstruction	_____
10. Prolapsed urethral mucosa	_____
11. Lobar glomerulonephritis	_____
12. Benign prostatic hypertrophy	_____
13. UTI	_____
14. Weakening of pubocervical tissue	_____
15. Ureterolithiasis	_____
16. Renal cortical necrosis NOS	_____
17. Chronic interstitial cystitis	_____
18. Peyronie's disease	_____
19. Acute salpingo-oophoritis	_____
20. Overactive bladder	_____
21. Fibrosclerosis of breast	_____

22. Atrophy of the spermatic cord   _____

23. Azoospermia   _____

24. Abscess of the epididymis   _____

25. Acute nephritis with lesion of necrotizing glomerulitis   _____

Case Studies

Instructions: Review each case study, and select the correct ICD-9-CM diagnostic code.

CASE 1

Physician's Office Note

This 50-year-old patient was seen today in follow-up for renal insufficiency.

HISTORY OF THE PRESENT ILLNESS: The patient had a renal biopsy that showed focal and segmental glomerular sclerosis. He was placed on Vasotec but developed hyperkalemia, and then the Vasotec was stopped.

PAST MEDICAL HISTORY: Hypertension in 1990, coronary artery disease in 1992

ALLERGIES: NKA

PHYSICAL EXAM:

BP 170/90   Pulse 88   Respirations 19

HEENT: Fundi are unremarkable. PERRLA

NECK: No JVD, adenopathy, or goiter

LUNGS: Clear

CARDIAC: Regular rate and rhythm without murmurs, rubs, or gallops

ABDOMEN: Soft, nontender, no masses

LABORATORY DATA: His most recent data completed on August 1, 200X, showed his sedimentation rate at 50, potassium at 5.3, BUN 75, creatinine 3.8, potassium down to 5.1, and calcium 9.6 with an albumin of 3.2. WBC is 16.4, hemoglobin 9.1, and platelets 530.

DIAGNOSTIC IMPRESSION: Focal and segmental glomerulosclerosis

MEDICATIONS ORDERED: Diovan 80 mg daily

Instructed him to follow a low-potassium diet and follow up with me in 1 month.

ICD-9-CM Code Assignment: _____

CASE 2

Discharge Summary

PERTINENT HISTORY: The patient is a 31-year-old white female admitted from my office because of increasing abdominal pain. The patient is gravida II, para II. The pain has been present for the last 6 months, occurring more severely the day before the onset of menses. The pain radiated down her back, vagina, and her lower abdomen.

HOSPITAL COURSE:

Pelvis exam revealed generalized tenderness. A laparoscopy revealed endometriosis of pelvic peritoneum. The patient was counseled as to available treatment options, which include hormonal therapy, surgical resection, or electrocautery. After pain management, she was discharged in 1 day. She wishes to discuss the treatment options with her husband.

DISCHARGE INSTRUCTIONS TO PATIENT: Patient was instructed to see me in my office in 3 days.

ICD-9-CM Code Assignment: _____

CASE 3

Skilled Nursing Facility Progress Note

VITAL SIGNS: B/P 1250/80   Weight 165 pounds   Temperature 100.1

This 84-year-old man was seen today at the request of the charge nurse. The patient is experiencing urinary retention. No other complaints were noted by patient.

EXAM:

HEENT: Normal

CHEST: Lungs are clear.

HEART: Normal sinus rhythm, no murmurs noted.

ABDOMEN: Soft, nontender. No masses noted.

RECTAL: Smooth enlarged prostate, no other findings noted.

Because of the enlarged prostate I ordered a PSA to rule out prostate cancer since the patient has not had a previous PSA completed. The following tests were also ordered: urinalysis and urine culture. Patient will be seen again when results are received.

ICD-9-CM Code Assignment: _____

CASE 4

ED Summary Note

Eric presented to the ED with severe flank pain, hematuria, and a palpable flank mass. He said the pain was 10 on the pain scale. He had a dull pain for most of the day but pain escalated over the last hour. Dr. Smith ordered a renal scan and ultrasound. Eric was diagnosed with hydronephrosis. He was sent home on pain medications and antibiotic therapy.

ICD-9-CM Code Assignment: _____

CASE 5

Physician's Office Visit

Mrs. Vinton presents with complaint of painful urination. She states she has pain and burning when urinating. She also notes that she feels urgency and has recently started with low back pain over the last 24 hours. A urinalysis was positive for pyuria, the culture showing 150,000 organisms/mL. She was diagnosed with cystitis. She was started on antibiotics.

ICD-9-CM Code Assignment: _____

Complications of Pregnancy, Childbirth, and Puerperium

Chapter Outline

Introduction

Introduction to the Body System

Coding of Complications of Pregnancy, Childbirth, and the Puerperium

Internet Links

Summary

Chapter Review

Coding Assignments

Case Studies

Objectives

At the conclusion of this chapter, the student will be able to:

1. Identify the stages of pregnancy.
2. Explain different complications encountered during pregnancy and how they affect code assignment.
3. Discuss specific coding guidelines related to different stages of pregnancy.
4. Summarize the use of fifth digits in the chapter.
5. List the different types of abortions and explain how the code assignments are affected.
6. Select and code diagnoses from case studies.

Key Terms

Abruptio Placentae

Antepartum

Antepartum Complication

Cesarean Delivery

Childbirth

Complete Placenta Previa

Ectopic Pregnancy

Embryo

Fetus

Gestational Diabetes

Gravida

Incomplete Abortion

Labor

Labor and Delivery

Legally Induced Abortion

Missed Abortion

Molar Pregnancy

Multiple Gestation

Reminder

As you work through this chapter, you will need to have a copy of the ICD-9-CM coding book to reference.

Obstetrical Care	Partial Placenta Previa	Postpartum Complication	Spontaneous Abortion
Occult Prolapse	Placenta Previa		Uterus
Overt Prolapse	Postpartum	Puerperium	Vasa Previa
Para			

Introduction

Chapter 11 of ICD-9-CM, "Complications of Pregnancy, Childbirth, and the Puerperium," classifies conditions that occur during pregnancy, childbirth, and six weeks after delivery. This chapter also codes normal deliveries. Obstetrical care, medical care that occurs during pregnancy and delivery, is divided into the antepartum period, labor and delivery, and the postpartum period.

Introduction to the Body System

It is important to understand the terminology associated with the different stages of maternity and delivery care in order to code from this section correctly. Through the eighth week of pregnancy, the developing child is known as an embryo. From the ninth week until birth, the developing child is referred to as a fetus. When a fetus has reached the point at which it is capable of living outside the uterus, childbirth occurs. Figure 16-1 illustrates the position of a fetus at term. The uterus sits above the cervix and is the part of the female anatomy that houses the fetus until birth. Pregnancy, in most cases, takes 40 weeks. In some instances, conditions or problems alter the length of time a woman is pregnant.

Antepartum encompasses the time before childbirth. Childbirth refers to the delivery of one or more infants and is referred to as labor and delivery. The three stages of labor will be further discussed later in this chapter.

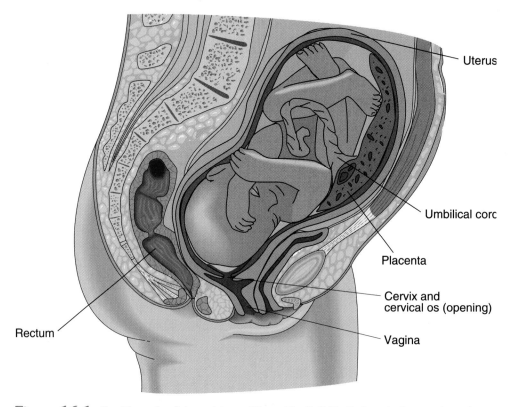

Figure 16-1 Position of a fetus at term (From Lindh WQ. *Delmar's Comprehensive Medical Assisting: Administrative and Clinical Competencies*, 2nd ed. Clifton Park, NY: Delmar, Cengage Learning, 2002, p. 461.)

The term *puerperium* relates to the postpartum period, which begins immediately after delivery and lasts for six weeks. Postpartum means after childbirth.

The ICD-9-CM Official Guidelines for Coding and Reporting define the postpartum and peripartum periods in the guidelines.

Official ICD-9-CM Coding Guideline:

Postpartum and Peripartum Periods

The postpartum period begins immediately after delivery and continues for six weeks following delivery. The peripartum period is defined as the last month of pregnancy to five months postpartum. (See Appendix A, Section I, C11, i, 1.)

Coding of Complications of Pregnancy, Childbirth, and the Puerperium

The coding of diagnoses in this chapter can be confusing and complex. For this reason, specific coding guidelines have been established in the ICD-9-CM Official Guidelines for Coding and Reporting. These guidelines must be followed.

Official ICD-9-CM Coding Guideline:

Chapter 11 codes are to be used only on the maternal record, never on the record of the newborn. (See Appendix A, Section I, C11, a, 2.)

The codes from this chapter are to be used *only* on the mother's record. These codes are *never* used in the medical record of the newborn. The codes related to the newborn will be discussed in another chapter.

The Official Coding Guidelines for Coding and Reporting also specify the following with regard to codes from chapter 11 and sequencing priority.

Official ICD-9-CM Coding Guideline:

Obstetric cases require codes from chapter 11, codes in the range 630–679, Complications of pregnancy, childbirth, and the puerperium. Chapter 11 codes have sequencing priority over codes from other chapters. Additional codes from other chapters may be used in conjunction with chapter 11 codes to further specify conditions. Should the provider document that the pregnancy is incidental to the encounter, then code V22.2 should be used in place of any chapter 11 codes. It is the provider's responsibility to state that the condition being treated is not affecting the pregnancy. (See Appendix A, Section I, C 11, a, 1.)

Any conditions encountered during a pregnancy or postpartum period are coded to this chapter as a complication unless the provider documents that such a condition is incidental to the pregnancy. The documentation must clearly state that the visit was not directly related to the pregnancy. In this case, a V22.2, Pregnant state, incidental, should be used instead of codes from this chapter.

EXAMPLE: Female presents for sinus pressure and pain, for the past 3 days; no OTC medications were tried because she is pregnant for approximately 24 weeks. Diagnosis is sinusitis. Although the decision for medication is affected by the pregnancy, the visit is for a condition not directly related to it. The code assignment is 461.9 as the primary diagnosis for the sinusitis, along with the V22.2 as the second code.

Fifth digits are frequently used in this chapter to indicate whether the encounter is antepartum or postpartum and whether a delivery has also occurred. An antepartum complication occurs while the patient is pregnant and ends when the patient delivers. A postpartum complication is any complication occurring within the six-week period after delivery.

> ## Official ICD-9-CM Coding Guideline:
>
> *Categories 640–648, 651–676 have required fifth digits, which indicate whether the encounter is antepartum or postpartum and whether a delivery has occurred. (See Appendix A, Section I, C11, a, 3.).*
>
> *The fifth digits, which are appropriate for each code number, are listed in brackets under each code. The fifth digits on each code should all be consistent with each other. That is, should a delivery occur, all of the fifth digits should indicate the delivery. (See Appendix A, Section I, C11, a, 4.).*

Should the provider document that a condition or complication that might occur outside the six-week time period is related to the pregnancy, codes from this chapter can be used. A postpartum complication that occurs during the same admission as the delivery is identified with a fifth digit of 2. Subsequent encounters for postpartum complications should be identified with a fifth digit of 4. Fifth digits identify the current episode of care (i.e., antepartum or postpartum, or whether delivery has occurred) and are discussed in more detail throughout this chapter.

Ectopic and Molar Pregnancy (Category Codes 630–633)

The first category range in this chapter classifies ectopic and molar pregnancy. This section includes ectopic pregnancy, or a pregnancy that occurs outside the uterus. Abdominal, tubal, and ovarian pregnancies are all included in this section. If a blighted ovum in the uterus develops into a mole or benign tumor, this is considered a molar pregnancy. The products of conception have not yet developed into a fetus in these cases. When the current episode of care is for an ectopic or molar pregnancy, a code from this series is the primary diagnosis. A code from the 639 category can be used as a secondary code to describe the complication. Figure 16-2 illustrates an ectopic pregnancy.

Also included in this category is code 632 for a missed abortion. A missed abortion is a term that refers to a fetus that has died before the completion of 22 weeks' gestation with the retention of the dead fetus or products of conception up to four weeks after demise. This period of completion varies legally from state to state and in some states may be as few as 19 weeks. The coder needs to be aware

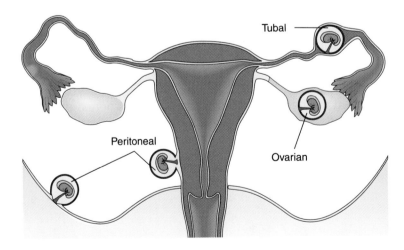

Figure 16-2 An ectopic pregnancy (From Lindh WQ. *Delmar's Comprehensive Medical Assisting: Administrative and Clinical Competencies*, 2nd ed. Clifton Park, NY: Delmar, Cengage Learning, 2002, p. 463.)

of state and local laws regarding this so that the correct code assignment can be made. Abnormal products of conception, which would include carneous mole, hydatidiform mole, and blighted ovum, are reported by using codes 630 or 631.

Other Pregnancy with Abortive Outcome (Category Codes 634–639)

For abortion categories 634–637, fifth digits are required. Fifth-digit 1, incomplete, indicates that all of the products of conception have not been expelled from the uterus. This is known as an incomplete abortion. Fifth-digit 2, complete, indicates that all products of conception have been expelled from the uterus before the episode of care.

A code from categories 640–649 and 651–657 may be used as additional codes with an abortion code to indicate the complication leading to the abortion. Fifth-digit 0 is assigned with codes from these categories when used with an abortion code because the other fifth digits do not apply. Codes from the 660–669 series are not to be used for complications of abortion.

Spontaneous abortion, code 634, is also coded in this section. A spontaneous abortion is the complete or incomplete expulsion of products of conception before a pregnancy goes beyond 22 weeks' gestation.

An abortion that is induced by medical personnel working within the law is considered a legally induced abortion. The legally induced abortion can be elective or for therapeutic reasons such as the mother's health being in danger. Fifth-digit assignment is used to identify the state of abortion. If a patient is admitted to the hospital with a complication resulting from an illegally induced abortion, codes from the 636 series are used. When an attempted termination of pregnancy results in a liveborn fetus, code 644.21, Early onset of delivery, is assigned with the appropriate V27 code, Outcome of delivery. The procedure code for the attempted termination of pregnancy should be assigned.

If there is a subsequent encounter for retained products of conception after a spontaneous or legally induced abortion, codes from the 634 series are used. Spontaneous abortion, or legally induced abortion, with a fifth digit of 1 (incomplete) is also used. This is appropriate even when the patient was discharged previously with a discharge diagnosis of complete abortion.

> **EXAMPLE:** Patient presents 2 days after elective abortion with excessive hemorrhaging. She was taken to the OR, and a D&C was performed to remove additional products of conception. The code assignment is 635.11.

Please note that The ICD-9-CM Official Guidelines for Coding and Reporting summarize the guidelines that relate to abortion as follows:

Official ICD-9-CM Coding Guideline:

(1) *Fifth digits required for abortion categories*

Fifth digits are required for abortion categories 634-637. Fifth digit 1, incomplete, indicates that all of the products of conception have not been expelled from the uterus. Fifth digit 2, complete, indicates that all products of conception have been expelled from the uterus prior to the episode of care.

(2) *Code from categories 640-648 and 651-659*

A code from categories 640-648 and 651-659 may be used as additional codes with an abortion code to indicate the complication leading to the abortion.

Fifth digit 3 is assigned with codes from these categories when used with an abortion code because the other fifth digits will not apply. Codes from the 660-669 series are not to be used for complications of abortion.

(3) *Code 639 for complications*

Code 639 is to be used for all complications following abortion. Code 639 cannot be assigned with codes from categories 634-638.

(4) Abortion with liveborn fetus

When an attempted termination of pregnancy results in a liveborn fetus, assign code 644.21, Early onset of delivery, with an appropriate code from category V27, Outcome of delivery. The procedure code for the attempted termination of pregnancy should also be assigned.

(5) Retained products of conception following an abortion

Subsequent admissions for retained products of conception following a spontaneous or legally induced abortion are assigned the appropriate code from category 634, Spontaneous abortion, or 635, Legally induced abortion, with a fifth digit of 1 (incomplete). This advice is appropriate even when the patient was discharged previously with a discharge diagnosis of complete abortion. (See Appendix A, Section I, C11, k, 1–5.)

Complications Mainly Related to Pregnancy (Category Codes 640–649)

The complications listed in this section include conditions even if they arose or were present during labor, delivery, or the puerperium. This section requires fifth-digit assignments, which indicate whether the encounter is antepartum or postpartum and also whether a delivery has occurred.

A box appears at the beginning of this section in most coding books that explains each of the fifth digits available in this section. As stated in the box found in most coding books, and with a subscript sign next to each code, valid fifth digits are in brackets under each code. In cases in which no delivery occurs, the principal diagnosis should correspond to the principal complication of the pregnancy that necessitated the encounter. If more than one complication exists, all the complications that were treated or monitored should be coded and may be sequenced in any order.

The fifth digits that would be appropriate for use with a particular code are listed in brackets under the code. If more than one code in this chapter is used, the fifth-digit code assignment should be consistent. The coder needs to be aware that certain fifth digits cannot be used together for the same episode of care. The 0, unspecified as to episode of care or not applicable, is used only if absolutely no other information is available. This fifth digit should not be used for a hospital admission because there is almost always more information available. The 1, delivered, with or without mention of antepartum condition, and the 2, delivered with mention of postpartum complication, can be used together but not with any other fifth digit for the same episode of care. The fifth digits of 3, antepartum condition or complication, and 4, postpartum condition or complication, are used alone and cannot be assigned with any other fifth digit.

EXAMPLE: Polly Patient presents with slight hemorrhaging, which is diagnosed as marginal placenta previa. No delivery occurred at this encounter. Code 641.13 is the code assignment.

Sally Second presents with marginal placenta previa and is also experiencing gestational hypertension. The code assignment is 641.13 along with 642.33. The fifth digit in each case is a 3, antepartum condition or complication.

Note that the fifth-digit assignments on the second case are consist with each other.

Should a condition arise that affects the management of the pregnancy, childbirth, or the puerperium, additional secondary codes from other chapters might be needed to identify the conditions. A complication that should be noted here is gestational diabetes. The ICD-9-CM Official Guidelines for Coding and Reporting instructs coders to be guided by the following guidelines:

Official ICD-9-CM Coding Guideline:

Diabetes mellitus is a significant complicating factor in pregnancy. Pregnant women who are diabetic should be assigned code 648.0X, Diabetes mellitus complicating pregnancy, and a secondary code from category 250, Diabetes mellitus, to identify the type of diabetes. (See Appendix A, Section I, C11, f.)

Official ICD-9-CM Coding Guideline:

Gestational diabetes can occur during the second and third trimester of pregnancy in women who were not diabetic prior to pregnancy. Gestational diabetes can cause complications in the pregnancy similar to those of preexisting diabetes mellitus. It also puts the woman at greater risk of developing diabetes after the pregnancy. Gestational diabetes is coded to 648.8X, abnormal glucose tolerance. Codes 648.0 and 648.8X should never be used together on the same record. Code V58.67, Long-term (current) use of insulin, should also be assigned if the gestational diabetes is being treated with insulin. (See Appendix A, Section 1, C11, g.)

Two other conditions that can complicate pregnancies are abruptio placentae and placenta previa. Both are conditions affect the placenta.

Disease Highlight—Abruptio Placentae

When there is a premature sudden separation of the placenta from the uterus prior to or during labor, the patient is said to have abruptio placentae. The abrupt separation can be caused by trauma, chronic hypertension, convulsions, and multiple births. See Figure 16-3.

Signs and Symptoms:

The presenting signs and symptoms are determined by the amount of separation of the placenta. When a partial separation occurs, the patient may be asymptomatic. When a complete separation occurs:

- The patient needs to seek medical care quickly because a complete separation can lead to maternal and fetal death.
- The mother may experience severe abdominal pain with vaginal bleeding.
- Shock can also occur.
- There is a decrease in fetal heart tones and in fetal activity due to the lack of oxygen and nutrition being supplied to the fetus.

Clinical Testing:

Because of the urgency of the condition, diagnosis is made based on clinical history and observation. At times a uterine ultrasound is completed.

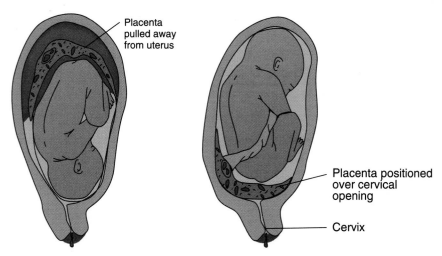

Placenta pulled away from uterus

Placenta positioned over cervical opening

Cervix

Figure 16-3 Abruptio placentae (From Marianne Neighbors & Ruth Tannehill-Jones, *Human Diseases,* Second Edition, Delmar, Cengage Learning, ISBN: 1-4018-7088-0, page 323.

Treatment:

If the placenta separation is partial, the patient is placed on bed rest and may be hospitalized to monitor the mother and fetus.

If the placenta separation is complete:

- The patient is prepared for delivery.

- Continuous fetal monitoring is started to determine fetal distress.

- Often a cesarean section is performed.

- If the mother has lost a significant amount of blood, she is given units of blood.

    Placenta previa is another complication that occurs during pregnancy.

Disease Highlight—Placenta previa

Placenta previa is the abnormal positioning of the placenta in the lower uterus that partially or completely covers the cervical os.

- A complete placenta previa occurs when the placenta entirely covers the cervical os.

- A partial placenta previa occurs when the placenta covers part of the cervical os.

Risk factors include:

- Maternal age greater than 35

- Large or abnormal placenta formation

- Multiparity

- Previous uterine surgery

- Smoking

Signs and Symptoms:

The patient has spotting during the first and second trimester. During the third trimester, the patient may have bright red vaginal bleeding and uterine cramping. If the bleeding is severe, the patient may experience shock, which can be life threatening.

Clinical Testing:

Pelvic ultrasound is completed to visualize the placenta.

Treatment:

The treatment course of action is determined by the extent of the placenta previa.

- Medications may be administered to prevent premature labor and stop contractions.

- If there is minimal bleeding, the patient is placed on bed rest and observed.

- If the bleeding is severe or if the fetus is in distress, an emergency cesarean section is performed. Blood transfusions may also be necessary.

HIV-Related Illness During Pregnancy, Childbirth, or the Puerperium

The following ICD-9-CM Official Guidelines are for coding HIV-related illness during pregnancy, childbirth, and the puerperium.

Official ICD-9-CM Coding Guideline:

During pregnancy, childbirth, or the puerperium, a patient admitted because of an HIV-related illness should receive a principal diagnosis of 647.6X, Other specified infectious and parasitic diseases in the mother classifiable elsewhere, but complicating the pregnancy, childbirth, or the puerperium, followed by 042 and the code(s) for the HIV-related illness(es).

Patients with asymptomatic HIV infection status admitted during pregnancy, childbirth, or the puerperium should receive codes of 647.6X and V08. (See Appendix A, Section I, C11, d.)

Exercise 16–1   Identifying Fifth Digits

Instructions: Match the following description with the correct fifth digit used with category codes 640–648.

Description	Fifth Digit
1. Postpartum condition or complication	_____
2. Delivered, with mention of postpartum complication	_____
3. Unspecified as to episode of care or not applicable	_____
4. Antepartum condition or complication	_____
5. Delivered, with or without mention of antepartum condition	_____

Normal Delivery and Other Indications for Care in Pregnancy, Labor, and Delivery (Category Codes 650–659)

This section of codes is used to classify normal deliveries, malposition and malpresentation of fetus, and other maternal or fetal abnormalities that affect the management of the mother.

Normal Delivery (Code 650)

Code 650, Normal delivery, is assigned when the delivery requires no assistance, there is no fetal manipulation, there may or may not be an episiotomy, a vaginal delivery occurs, and a full-term, live-born infant is born. Code 650 is not to be used with any other code in the 630–676 code range. There are no fourth or fifth digits assigned with the 650 code.

An additional code for the outcome of delivery, code V27.0, may be assigned with the 650 code. The outcome of delivery code identifies the number of children born and whether the children were liveborn or stillborn. The only outcome of delivery code used with the 650 code is V27.0, Single liveborn. The V27 series of codes are used only for coding the mother's encounter and should not be used on the medical record for the baby. The baby's record contains codes from the V30 series. Figure 16-4 illustrates the presentation of a fetus during normal delivery.

Figure 16-4 Presentation of a fetus during normal delivery (From Ehrlich A, Schroeder CL. *Medical Terminology for Health Professions*, 4th ed. Clifton Park, NY: Delmar, Cengage Learning, 2001, p. 311.)

EXAMPLE: A 24-year-old woman was admitted for a normal vaginal delivery. A single, live, full-term male was delivered with no forceps or manipulation necessary. Episiotomy was not necessary for this delivery. No complications were noted during the pregnancy and postpartum; patient is doing well. Code assignment is 650.

Because our example meets all the criteria outlined for use of the 650 code, this is the code assigned and submitted to insurance along with a V27.0 as a secondary code for the outcome of the delivery.

Official ICD-9-CM Coding Guideline:

(1) Normal Delivery

Code 650 is for use in cases when a woman is admitted for a full-term normal delivery and delivers a single, healthy infant without any complications antepartum, during the delivery, or postpartum during the delivery episode. Code 650 is always a principal diagnosis. It is not to be used if any other code from chapter 11 is needed to describe a current complication of the antenatal, delivery, or perinatal period. Additional codes from other chapters may be used with code 650 if they are not related to or are in any way complicating the pregnancy.

(2) Normal delivery with resolved antepartum complication

Code 650 may be used if the patient had a complication at some point during her pregnancy, but the complication is not present at the time of the admission for delivery.

(3) V27.0, Single liveborn, outcome of delivery

V27.0, Single liveborn, is the only outcome of delivery code appropriate for use with 650 (See Appendix A, C11, h, 1-3.)

EXAMPLE: A woman, who suffered from excessive vomiting for the last 3 months of her pregnancy, delivered a single, live, full-term male. The vomiting had subsided 2 weeks before delivery. The delivery was an uneventful, normal vaginal delivery.

This example is coded in the same way as the prior example, with codes 650 and V27.0. The vomiting is not coded because it had stopped before delivery.

Category Codes 651–659

Category codes 651–659 require the use of the following fifth digits:

    0   Unspecified as to episode of care or not applicable
    1   Delivered, with or without mention of antepartum condition
    2   Delivered, with mention of postpartum complication
    3   Antepartum condition or complication
    4   Postpartum condition or complication

Category 651 is for a multiple gestation, which indicates twins, triplets, quadruplets, or other specified multiple fetus. The 651 category also has codes for multiple gestation with the loss of one or more fetus, as in vanishing twin syndrome (651.33).

Categories 652 and 653 describe fetal position, problems with presentation, and abnormalities of organs and soft tissue of the pelvis such as scarring from a previous cesarean, cervical incompetence, and tumor of cervix or vagina. Figure 16-5 illustrates normal and abnormal fetal delivery positions.

Category 655 and category 656 contain codes from known or suspected fetal abnormalities affecting the medical management of the mother.

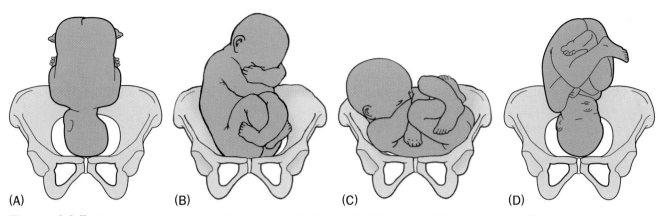

Figure 16-5 Delivery positions: (A) Occiput anterior (normal); (B) breech; (C) transverse; (D) occiput posterior (From Sormunen C. *Terminology for Allied Health Professions*, 5th ed. Clifton Park, NY: Delmar, Cengage Learning, 2003, p. 420.)

Official ICD-9-CM Coding Guideline:

Codes from category 655

Known or suspected fetal abnormality affecting the management of the mother, and category 656, other fetal and placental problems affecting the management of the mother, are assigned only when the fetal condition is actually responsible for modifying the management of the mother, i.e., by requiring diagnostic studies, additional observation, special care, or termination of pregnancy. The fact that the fetal condition exists does not justify assigning a code from this series to the mother's record. (See Appendix A, Section I, C11, c, 1.)

There has to be a direct effect on the mother caused by the fetus for these code assignments. The provider documentation should clearly make this connection. The only fifth digits that apply in these categories are 0, 1, and 3.

EXAMPLE: A 34-year-old pregnant woman presents to the ER for a broken ankle and decreased fetal movement after a fall down a flight of stairs at her home. Patient is at 30 weeks' gestation. We are admitting her to set the ankle as well as for ordering an ultrasound and monitoring the fetus for 24 hours. The codes assigned are 824.8 for the fracture and 655.73 for decreased fetal movement.

In some cases surgery needs to be completed on the fetus while it is still in utero. The following guideline should be followed when coding this type of case.

Official ICD-9-CM Coding Guideline:

In utero surgery

In cases when surgery is performed on the fetus, a diagnosis code from category 655, known or suspected fetal abnormalities affecting management of the mother, should be assigned identifying the fetal condition. Procedure code 75.36, Correction of fetal defect, should be assigned on the hospital inpatient record.

No code from chapter 15, the perinatal codes, should be used on the mother's record to identify fetal conditions. Surgery performed in utero on a fetus is still to be coded as an obstetric encounter. (See Appendix A, Section I, C11, c, 2.)

Exercise 16–2   Identifying Normal Deliveries

For each description listed, state whether the case is a normal delivery (N) or complicated delivery (C).

1. Vaginal full-term birth with fetal malposition   _____

2. Full-term birth, hyperemesis during pregnancy, vaginal delivery   _____

3. Delivery with use of forceps   _____

4. Delivery of full-term liveborn twins   _____

5. Full-term liveborn infant, cesarean section   _____

Complications Occurring Mainly in the Course of Labor and Delivery (Category Codes 660–669)

Labor is the process by which the fetus moves from the uterus to birth. As discussed earlier, labor occurs in three stages. Stage one starts when the contractions become regular until the cervix is fully dilated. Stage two is the time from complete dilation of the cervix through the birth of the fetus. Stage three begins after the fetal birth until the time of complete expulsion of the placenta and membranes.

Category 660, Obstructed labor codes, encompasses the codes that describe breech presentation, presentation other than normal head down, or anatomical abnormalities. This type of labor is the most common cause of maternal and fetal death. The only fifth digits that apply to this category are 0, 1, or 3.

Complications involving the umbilical cord fall under category 663. To code in this section, knowledge of certain terminology is necessary. Occult prolapse is when the umbilical cord is trapped in front of a shoulder or is expelled before the presenting part. Overt prolapse occurs with ruptured membranes when the cord is in front of the presenting part. Vasa previa is a dangerous condition in which the umbilical cord is the presenting part; the vessels can become pinched off or rupture because they are compressed between the fetus and the walls of the birth canal. The only fifth digits used in this category are 0, 1, or 3.

Also included in this subsection is obstetrical trauma, which includes injury to pelvic organs or rupture of the uterus during labor. Postpartum hemorrhage and retained placenta or membranes are coded from this subsection. Other complications of labor and delivery, such as shock during or after labor and delivery and also renal failure after labor and delivery, are also in this subsection.

Complications of the Puerperium (Category Codes 670–677)

Major infection after childbirth is coded to code 670.0X with 0, 2, or 4 as a fifth digit. To be coded to this section, the infection is usually bacterial and serious. Infections after abortion, minor genital tract infections, and urinary tract infections are not coded to this code.

Code 677, Late effect of complication of pregnancy, childbirth, and the puerperium, is for use in cases when an initial complication of a pregnancy develops sequelae requiring care or treatment at a future date. This code may be used at any time after the initial postpartum period. This code, like all late effect codes, is to be sequenced following the code describing the sequelae of the complication. No fifth digits are needed for this code.

The ICD-9-CM Official Guidelines for Coding and Reporting give specific guidelines for reporting code 677, Late effect of complication of pregnancy.

Official ICD-9-CM Coding Guideline:

(1) Code 677

Code 677, Late effect of complication of pregnancy, childbirth, and the puerperium, is for use in cases when an initial complication of a pregnancy develops a sequelae requiring care or treatment at a future date.

(2) After the initial postpartum period

This code may be used at any time after the initial postpartum period.

(3) Sequencing of Code 677

This code, like all late effect codes, is to be sequenced following the code describing the sequelae of the complication. (See Appendix A, Section I, C11, j 1–3.)

Other Situations Regarding Pregnancy and Childbirth

For prenatal outpatient visits for patients with high-risk pregnancies, a code from category V23, Supervision of high-risk pregnancy, should be used as the principal or first-listed diagnosis. Secondary codes from this chapter may be used in conjunction with these codes if appropriate. A thorough review of any pertinent Excludes: note is necessary to be certain that these V codes are being used properly.

For routine outpatient prenatal visits when no complications are present, codes V22.0, Supervision of normal first pregnancy, and V22.1, Supervision of other normal pregnancy, should be used as the first-listed diagnoses and should not be used in conjunction with other codes from this chapter.

In cases of cesarean delivery, the selection of the principal diagnosis should correspond to the reason the cesarean delivery was performed unless the reason for the admission or encounter was unrelated to the condition resulting in the cesarean delivery. A cesarean delivery, sometimes referred to as a cesarean section, is delivery of the fetus by way of an incision through the abdominal wall into the uterus and removal the fetus.

When the mother delivers outside the hospital before admission and is admitted for routine postpartum care with no complication noted, code V24.0, Postpartum care and examination immediately after delivery, should be assigned as the principal diagnosis. A delivery diagnosis should not be used for a woman who has delivered before admission to the hospital. Any postpartum procedures should be coded.

Please note that in office and hospital notes the providers give a pregnant woman's past history regarding pregnancy using the following terms: gravida, which means pregnant woman, and para, which means that a woman has produced a viable infant weighing more than 500 grams or reaching the age of more than 20 weeks' gestation. The infant may or may not have been alive at birth. When a woman has twins, it is still considered para 1, or a single birth experience. A woman who has had three pregnancies and three live births would have a note that reads gravida 3 (meaning she was pregnant three times) and para 3 (meaning she delivered three children). A woman who has had three pregnancies but who lost a fetus at 12 weeks would have a note that reads gravida 3 (meaning three pregnancies) and para 2 (meaning she gave birth to two viable infants).

Coders should also be guided by the following guidelines when selecting obstetric principal or first-listed diagnosis:

Official ICD-9-CM Coding Guideline:

Selection of OB Principal or First-Listed Diagnosis

(1) Routine outpatient prenatal visits

For routine outpatient prenatal visits when no complications are present, codes V22.0, Supervision of normal first pregnancy, and V22.1, Supervision of other normal pregnancy, should be used as the first-listed diagnoses. These codes should not be used in conjunction with chapter 11 codes.

(2) Prenatal outpatient visits for high-risk patients

For prenatal outpatient visits for patients with high-risk pregnancies, a code from category V23, Supervision of high-risk pregnancy, should be used as the first-listed diagnosis. Secondary chapter 11 codes may be used in conjunction with these codes if appropriate.

(3) Episodes when no delivery occurs

In episodes when no delivery occurs, the principal diagnosis should correspond to the principal complication of the pregnancy, which necessitated the encounter. Should more than one complication exist, all of which are treated or monitored, any of the complications codes may be sequenced first.

(4) When a delivery occurs

When a delivery occurs, the principal diagnosis should correspond to the main circumstances or complication of the delivery. In cases of cesarean delivery, the selection of the principal diagnosis should correspond to the reason the cesarean delivery was performed unless the reason for the admission/encounter was unrelated to the condition resulting in the cesarean delivery.

(5) Outcome of delivery

An outcome of delivery code, V27.0–V27.9, should be included on every maternal record when a delivery has occurred. These codes are not to be used on subsequent records or on the newborn record. (See Appendix A, Section I, C11, b 1–5.)

Internet Links

To learn more about pregnancy, childbirth, and the puerperium, visit Dr. Donnica's Woman's Health site at *http://www.drdonnica.com* and the National Women's Health Resource Center at *www.healthywomen.org.*

For information on labor and delivery, visit *http://babies.sutterhealth.org* and *http://www.nlm.nih.gov/medlineplus/childbirth.html.*

Summary

- Understanding terminology is extremely important to be able to assign the correct codes.

- The codes in chapter 11 of ICD-9-CM apply to the medical record or encounter of the mother.

- Any conditions encountered during a pregnancy or postpartum period are coded to this chapter as a complication unless the provider documents that such a condition is incidental to the pregnancy.

- Different types of abortions need to be identified as ICD-9-CM provides different codes for each type of abortion.

- Complications of childbirth, including problems that could be encountered with the umbilical cord, require complete documentation to code correctly.

- Fifth-digit code assignment is critical, as well as understanding the notes that appear in the Tabular List of the ICD-9-CM coding book.

Chapter Review

True/False: Indicate whether each statement is true (T) or false (F).

1. _____ Through the 10th week of pregnancy, the developing child is known as an embryo.

2. _____ The second stage of labor is the time from the complete dilation of the cervix through the birth of the fetus.

3. _____ Unspecified episode of care is used only if there is absolutely no other information available.

4. _____ A spontaneous abortion is coded to category code 644.

5. _____ Codes from this chapter should appear only on the mother's encounter.

Fill-in-the-Blanks: Enter the appropriate term(s) to complete each statement.

6. A blighted ovum that has developed into a benign tumor is called a _____.

7. A pregnancy that occurs outside the uterus is called an _____.

8. A developing child from nine weeks until birth is known as a _____.

9. When the umbilical cord is trapped in front of a shoulder or is expelled before the presenting part, this is known as _____.

10. The time before childbirth is called _____.

11. Through eight weeks of pregnancy, the developing child is known as an _____.

12. The puerperium, or postpartum period, lasts up to _____ weeks after delivery.

13. A dangerous condition in which the umbilical cord is the presenting part during delivery is known as _____.

14. The only outcome of delivery code assigned with code 650 is _____.

15. During pregnancy, childbirth, or the puerperium, a patient admitted because of an HIV-related illness should be coded with a principal diagnosis of _____.

Coding Assignments

Instructions: Using an ICD-9-CM coding book, select the appropriate code for each diagnostic statement.

Diagnosis	Code
1. Hyperfibrinolysis (30 weeks, no delivery)	_____
2. Severe pre-eclampsia 2 days after delivery	_____
3. Accident causing hemorrhage at 15 weeks (no delivery)	_____
4. Vomiting complicating pregnancy	_____
5. Low-lying placenta (during pregnancy, no hemorrhage)	_____
6. Intrauterine tubal pregnancy	_____

7. Termination of pregnancy complicated by renal failure   _____

8. Miscarriage at 10 weeks' gestation   _____

9. Tubal pregnancy with intrauterine pregnancy   _____

10. Uterine fibroid found during last ultrasound before delivery   _____

11. Twins, both delivered without complication   _____

12. Cervical incompetence, Shirodkar suture needed to hold pregnancy   _____

13. Premature rupture of membranes   _____

14. Threatened abortion at 15 weeks' gestation, no delivery   _____

15. Obstruction of delivery during labor caused by prolapsed arm of fetus   _____

16. Term pregnancy, delivery of premature stillborn twins   _____

17. Delivery with retained placenta with manual removal of retained placenta   _____

18. Normal prenatal care   _____

19. Postpartum hemorrhage   _____

20. Pregnancy complicated by bacteriuria, asymptomatic   _____

21. Hydatidform mole   _____

22. Pelvic peritonitis following an ectopic pregnancy   _____

23. Syphilis during pregnancy   _____

24. Threatened premature labor   _____

25. Antepartum anemia complicating pregnancy   _____

Case Studies

Instructions: Review each case study and select the correct ICD-9-CM diagnostic code.

CASE 1

Physician's Office Note of 2/04/XX

WEIGHT: 150 pounds. This is a weight gain of 7 pounds since her last visit 3 weeks ago. Blood pressure: 140/80. Lab: Urinalysis reveals protein present.

Patient is complaining of increased headaches and dizziness.

VAGINAL EXAM: Normal

HEENT: Face appears swollen.

EXTREMITIES: Edema of hands and feet

Patient symptoms indicate pre-eclampsia. Patient advised to decrease salt intake and to follow up in 2 weeks.

ICD-9-CM Code Assignment: _____

CASE 2

Discharge Summary

ADMISSION DATE: 5/6/XX Discharge date: 5/8/XX

HISTORY:

This patient is gravida 2, para 1 and was seen in my office for all of her prenatal visits. Her prenatal course was uneventful. She was admitted with a history of contractions every 3 to 5 minutes. Cervix was 100% effaced and 9 cm dilated.

HOSPITAL COURSE:

At the time of admission, patient received IV and was placed on a fetal monitor. Her water broke at 2 am. After 3 hours the patient delivered a baby boy with apgar scores of 8 at 1 minute and 10 at 5 minutes. Postpartum care was uneventful. The patient was discharged 2 days later.

INSTRUCTIONS TO PATIENT: Diet as tolerated. Tylenol every 4 hours for pain. She is to follow up in my office in 2 weeks.

ICD-9-CM Code Assignment: _____

CASE 3

Physician's Office Note

This patient presents today in the eighth month of her pregnancy. She complains of increase fatigue over the last month, edema of both legs, shortness of breath, and difficulty breathing when lying down. Because she has pre-eclampsia, I have monitored her closely for the last 2 months. Last week I sent her for an EKG, chest X-ray, and coronary angiography. Today I am reviewing the results with her.

EXAM: Reveals an obese, gravida 1, para 0, 29-year-old woman.

HEENT: Normocephalic, palpebrale conjunctiva, pinkish, PERRLA

NECK: Supple. No mass noted.

HEART: Tachycardia present. Slight murmur.

LUNGS: There is congestion in both lungs.

ABDOMEN: Protuberant, soft, and nontender. Liver and spleen not palpable. Uterus enlarged to gestational size. Fetal heart tones are noted to be normal.

PELVIC: External genitalia—normal. Vagina—clear. Membranes are intact.

EXTREMITIES: There is edema in both legs.

Review of diagnostic testing: EKG, chest X-ray, and coronary angiography results support a diagnosis of peripartum cardiomyopathy.

I discussed with the patient the need for medications to improve her heart function, decrease edema, and prevent the formation of blood clots that can occur with the diagnosis of peripartum cardiomyopathy.

Medications were orders as per medication record.

INSTRUCTIONS TO PATIENT: I explained to the patient the need to take her medications as prescribed. She is to follow up with me in 5 days.

ICD-9-CM Code Assignment: _____

CASE 4

Discharge Note

Linda presented to the hospital in active labor. She was admitted, and a fetal monitor was used, which showed that there was a very unstable fetal heart rate of 100–125. After physical examination, it was determined that she was fully dilated but the baby was in breech position. Linda was instructed to begin pushing, at which time the fetal heart rate dropped. It was decided that an attempt would be made to turn the baby, but this attempt was unsuccessful. At this point, an emergency cesarean delivery was successfully performed.

ICD-9-CM Code Assignment: _____

CASE 5

Physician's Office Visit

This 27-year-old female, who is 12 weeks pregnant, is experiencing increased thirst, increased urination, increased fatigue, and bouts of nausea. An in-office blood sugar reading was 245, so a glucose tolerance test was ordered. The results confirmed gestational diabetes. Insulin is not necessary at this time.

ICD-9-CM Code Assignment: _____

Diseases of the Skin and Subcutaneous Tissue

Chapter Outline

Introduction
Introduction to the Body System
Coding of Diseases of the Skin and
    Subcutaneous Tissue
Internet Links

Summary
Chapter Review
Coding Assignments
Case Studies

Objectives

At the conclusion of this chapter, the student will be able to:

1. Identify and name the layers of the skin.
2. Explain the conditions classified in this chapter.
3. Identify the three sections of ICD-9-CM chapter 12, "Diseases of the Skin and Subcutaneous Tissue."
4. Select and code diagnoses and procedures from case studies.

Key Terms

Abscess
Acne
Alopecia
Bedsores
Boils
Carbuncle
Cellulitis

Decubitus Ulcer
Dermatitis
Dermis
Epidermis
Erythematosquamous
    Dermatosis
Furuncle

Hair
Hirsutism
Hives
Integumentary
Melanocytes
Melanoma
Nails

Pressure Ulcers
Sebaceous Glands
Subcutaneous
Ulcers
Urticaria

Reminder

As you work through this chapter, you will need to have a copy of the ICD-9-CM coding book to reference.

Introduction

Diseases of the skin and subcutaneous tissue, category code range 680–709, are classified in chapter 12 of ICD-9-CM, "Diseases of the Skin and Subcutaneous Tissue." There are only three sections found in this chapter of ICD-9-CM:

- Infections of Skin and Subcutaneous Tissue—Category codes 680–686

- Other Inflammatory Conditions of Skin and Subcutaneous Tissue—Category codes 690–698

- Other Diseases of Skin and Subcutaneous Tissue—Category codes 700–709

Introduction to the Body System

The coding in this chapter classifies disorders and diseases of the integumentary system, or the skin. *Integumentary* means "covering" or "outer layer." The integumentary system acts as a shield for the body and is considered the largest body system. The functions of the integumentary system include the protection of deeper tissue by retaining fluid in the body and the regulation of body temperature by controlling the amount of heat loss. This natural shield also works as a factor in the immune system by blocking bacteria and other foreign bodies from entering the body. Receptors for touch are located on the skin. Because the skin is porous, it protects the body from ultraviolet radiation from the sun while letting the ultraviolet light in so that vitamin D can be produced by the body. The skin also temporarily stores fat, glucose, water, and salts that are absorbed by the blood and used by various organs of the body.

The skin is specialized tissue made up of three layers. The epidermis is the outermost layer of the skin. Epithelial tissues make up the epidermis. There are no blood vessels or connective tissue within the epidermis, so this layer of skin depends on the lower layers for nourishment.

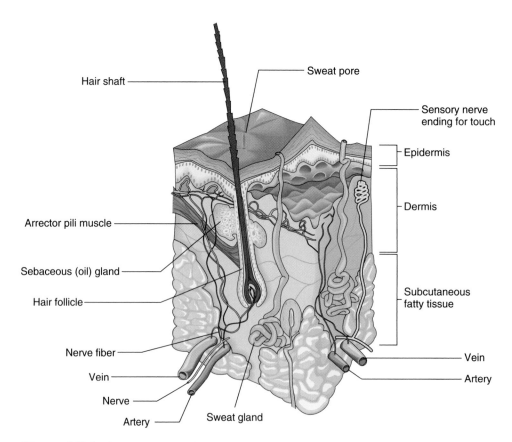

Figure 17-1 Cross-section of the skin (From Scott AS, Fong E. *Body Structures and Functions,* 9th ed. Clifton Park, NY: Delmar, Cengage Learning, 1998, p. 58.)

The color of the skin is determined by the amount of melanin pigment contained in melanocytes, or cells that produce dark pigment. When these cells exhibit abnormal behavior, a person might be diagnosed with melanoma. Melanoma is a fast-growing cancer of the skin, usually identified as a mole that has changed in some way.

The dermis is the thick layer of tissue located directly below the epidermis. This is the layer of skin that enables a person to recognize touch, pain, pressure, and temperature changes. This layer of skin contains blood and lymph vessels, so it is more sensitive and self-sufficient than the epidermis.

The layer of skin that connects to the muscle surface is called the subcutaneous layer. *Cutane* means "skin," so *subcutaneous* means "below the skin." Fat cells are found in this layer of skin. Figure 17-1 illustrates the three layers of skin and some of the structures contained in them.

Coding of Diseases of the Skin and Subcutaneous Tissue

In the ICD-9-CM Official Guidelines for Coding and Reporting, no guidelines are present for chapter 12 of ICD-9-CM. Coding for this chapter includes diseases and disorders not only of the skin but also of the nails, sweat glands, hair, and hair follicles. Figure 17-2 illustrates various diseases of the skin.

Infections of Skin and Subcutaneous Tissue (Category Codes 680–686)

The first section of this chapter classifies disorders such as cellulitis, carbuncles, and furuncles, which may be caused by bacterial organisms. It is important for the coder to note, however, that the following Exclude: notation appears after the section heading:

```
Infections of Skin and Subcutaneous Tissue (680–686)

Excludes: certain infections of skin classified under "Infectious and Parasitic
Diseases," such as:

          erysipelas (035)

          erysipeloid of Rosenbach (027.1)

          herpes:

           simplex (054.0–054.9)

           zoster (053.0–053.9)

        molluscum contagiosum (078.0)

        viral warts (078.1)
```

Category code 680 classifies furuncles, or boils, as a staphylococcal infection around hair follicles. Carbuncles occur when furuncles cluster and form a pus-filled sac. The fourth-digit assignment for category code 680 indicates the anatomic location of the boil. The only body areas that are not covered in this section are the eye and the genital system. Carbuncles of the eye are coded to ICD-9-CM chapter six, "Diseases of the Nervous System and Sense Organs," and carbuncles of the genital area are coded to ICD-9-CM chapter 10, "Diseases of the Genitourinary System."

EXAMPLE:

S: Patient presents with a "bump on my neck" that is beginning to hurt. Patient cannot recall any injury to the area. Patient has started with a low-grade fever of 99.3 and has noticed an increase in the pain over the last day or two.

O: Upon examination, a large red lump is located at the base of the posterior side of the neck. The lump is fluctuating and causes pain upon touch.

A & P: Carbuncle of the neck. At this time we will start antibiotics and warm compresses. If this does not relieve some of the pain and some improvement is not noticed in the next 5 days, he will return and we will look at other options.

NONPALPABLE

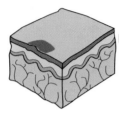

Macule:
Localized changes in skin color of less than 1 cm in diameter
Example: Freckle

Patch:
Localized changes in skin color of greater than 1 cm in diameter
Examples: Vitiligo, stage 1 of pressure ulcer

PALPABLE

Papule:
Solid, elevated lesion less than 0.5 cm in diameter
Examples: Warts, elevated nevus

Plaque:
Solid, elevated lesion greater than 0.5 cm in diameter
Example: Psoriasis

Nodules:
Solid and elevated, but extending deeper than papules into the dermis or subcutaneous tissues, 0.5–2.0 cm
Examples: Lipoma, erythema nodosum, cyst

Wheal:
Localized edema in the epidermis causing irregular elevation that may be red or pale
Examples: Insect bite, hives

FLUID-FILLED CAVITIES WITHIN THE SKIN

Vesicle:
Accumulation of fluid between the upper layers of the skin; elevated mass containing serous fluid; less than 0.5 cm
Examples: Herpes simplex, herpes zoster, chickenpox

Bulla:
Same as a vesicle only greater than 0.5 cm
Examples: Contact dermatitis, large second degree burns, bulbous impetigo, pemphigus

Pustule:
Vesicles or bullae that become filled with pus, usually described as less than 0.5 cm in diameter
Examples: Acne, impetigo, furuncles, carbuncles, folliculitis

Figure 17-2 Disorders of the skin (From Sormunen C. *Terminology for Allied Health Professions*, 5th ed. Clifton Park, NY: Delmar, Cengage Learning, 2003, p. 103.)

The code for this example is 680.1, Carbuncle and furuncle of neck.

Categories 681 and 682 classify cellulitis and abscess. Cellulitis is another type of infection within the layers of the skin that can be a result of an ulcer, laceration, or wound. In some cases, two codes are necessary when coding a patient encounter for cellulitis. Reference to provider documentation is necessary for determining the need for two codes and also their sequencing. If cellulitis is noticed when a patient is being treated for an open wound or a burn, the open wound or burn is coded first with an additional code for the cellulitis. If the cellulitis is what brought the patient in after treatment has already been rendered for the other condition such as a burn or open wound, the cellulitis is coded first with the burn or open wound second. The open wound is coded as complicated in either case because complication indicates infection. It also should be noted that if cellulitis is associated with an open wound that has been repaired, the documentation should reflect whether the cellulitis is a postoperative infection. These issues will be discussed further in Chapter 22 of this textbook when injuries are discussed.

This section of the chapter also classifies abscesses. An abscess is a localized collection of pus and indicates tissue destruction. As with cellulitis, if an organism is identified as the cause of the abscess, this fact should be coded in addition to the code for the abscess.

Documentation is critical for these categories of the chapter. The coder needs to reference the provider note to accurately code the condition, the sequencing, and the site of the cellulitis or abscess.

Exercise 17–1   Coding Category Codes 680–686

Instructions: For each diagnostic statement, select the appropriate ICD-9-CM code(s).

Diagnosis	Code(s)
1. Staphylococcus cellulitis and abscess of finger	_____
2. Boil on right shoulder	_____
3. Acute lymphangitis of neck	_____
4. Pyoderma gangrenosum	_____
5. Fistula of skin	_____
6. Acute lymphadenitis	_____
7. Cellulitis of toes	_____
8. Pilonidal fistula without abscess	_____
9. Cellulitis of scalp	_____
10. Furuncle of the temple region	_____

Other Inflammatory Conditions of Skin and Subcutaneous Tissue (Category Codes 690–698)

This section of the chapter contains codes for common conditions such as cradle cap, dermatitis, eczema, and erythematosquamous dermatosis. Erythematosquamous dermatosis, which is classified to category code 690, is a condition that affects the scalp and face. It is a condition that presents as a scaly inflammation. Conditions coded to this category include itchy, dry skin and dandruff.

Dermatitis is an inflammation of the upper layer of the skin and is also classified to this section of the chapter. Various types of dermatitis exist; therefore, if a provider documents a specific type of dermatitis, a coder must select a code to identify the type of dermatitis such as category code 692, contact dermatitis, versus category code 691, atopic dermatitis.

Another type of dermatitis coded to this section of the chapter is dermatitis due to medication. A distinction is made here between drugs ingested and drugs or plants that come in contact with the skin topically. Category 693, Dermatitis due to substances taken internally, is used if the coder sees the diagnosis of drug eruption, dermatitis medicamentosa, or medication properly administered with an allergic reaction or adverse side effect. It should also be noted that a reaction to medication ingested is when the proper medication prescribed by a medical professional has been ingested at the proper dosage. Use of the E code is used in addition to the 693 code to identify the drug. This will be further discussed in the chapter on E codes, but E codes are *never* listed as the primary diagnosis.

EXAMPLE

S: A 21-month-old male presents today with low-grade fever, hives, and slight swelling in the joints of the lower extremities. Mother notes that child was started on Amoxicillin, 500 mg, for an ear infection. Child started medication 1 day ago. Review was made with mom on the dosage. Child was given proper dosage but now appears to have had an allergic reaction.

O: Upon examination, child is alert and in no acute distress. He is a bit lethargic but is not crying or fussy. He allows examination of ears: TMs red, some fluid. Rest of HEENT is unremarkable. Skin is warm to touch, and it should be noted that child has low-grade temp of 99.8. He is showing mild rash on the trunk, and it is now moving to the extremities. Joints of the upper extremities are fine, but the lower extremities are showing signs of slight swelling. As for rest of exam, heart and lungs are normal. No other problems noted in either of these areas.

A: Allergic reaction to Amoxicillin

P: Will start child on Benydryl and change the antibiotic to Ceclor for the ear infection. If he is not exhibiting signs of reduced hives and disappearence of joint swelling in 24 hours or if temperature spikes and reation starts to become worse, mom will bring child back here, if during regular office hours, or to the Emergency Room, if after hours.

This example clearly describes an allergic reaction to Amoxicillin. Documentation supports that the medication was given properly. The coding for this example is 693.0 as well as E930.0.

Sunburn is also coded to the 692 category. ICD-9-CM does not require coding for a first-, second-, or third-degree sunburn with regard to total area of the body that suffered the burn, as it does with other burns. Burns that occur because of a tanning bed or tanning booth are coded to 692.82 instead of 692.71, which is noted in the Excludes: note under 692.7. Dermatitis due to radiation from gamma rays, X-rays, or ultraviolet lights are coded to the 692.8 section of this chapter.

Other Diseases of Skin and Subcutaneous Tissue (Category Codes 700–709)

Some of the common diagnosis codes found in this section of the chapter are coding for corns and calluses. Podiatrists frequently reference these codes because corns and calluses are most commonly found on the feet and hands. The cause is usually constant rubbing or friction from shoes or, in the case of hands, continuous rubbing of something across the hand such as a handle of a tool. Generally, no treatment is rendered unless these become painful or irritated.

Also found within these categories are codes for diseases of nails, hair, and hair follicles; skin ulcers; and diseases of the sebaceous glands. Disorders of **nails** are coded to this section because nails are hardened cells of the epidermis. Some of the conditions a coder sees are ingrown nail, code 703.0, and onycholysis, code 703.8.

Conditions involving the hair are coded to this section because hair follicles extend out of the dermis. **Hair** is a form of protection used by the body to keep foreign material from entering through the skin. Some of the conditions a coder might have to code from this section are **hirsutism,** excessive hair growth, coded to 704.1, and **alopecia,** loss of hair, coded to 704.00.

The sebaceous glands are located in the skin and produce an oily secretion that conditions the skin. Oversecretion of the sebaceous glands can cause acne. Acne is coded to the 706 category of codes, with fourth digits used to identify the type of acne.

The 707 category of the chapter also contains codes for decubitus ulcers. Ulcers are erosions of the skin in which the tissue becomes inflamed and then is lost. Ulcers not only appear on the skin but can be found within the body. A decubitus ulcer is a result of continuous pressure in an area that eventually limits or stops circulation and oxygen flow to an area. Decubitus ulcers are also called pressure ulcers or bedsores. They are staged as one through six depending on ulcer severity. This staging does not affect the coding assignment, but knowledge of the staging may be necessary when reviewing documentation. Patients who are confined to bed or in a wheelchair are at risk for developing decubitius ulcers. Figures 17-3 and 17-4 illustrate common sites of decubitus ulcers for patients confined to bed or a wheelchair.

When ulcers, other than decubitus, are caused by another condition, such as venous hypertension or diabetes, the causal condition should be coded first.

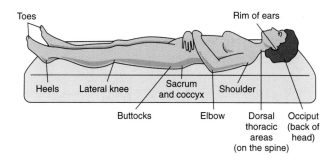

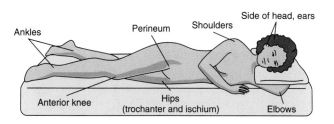

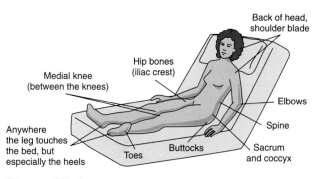

Figure 17-3 Decubitus ulcer sites of bed-bound patient (From Hegner BR, Acello B, Caldwell E. *Nursing Assistant: A Nursing Process Approach*, 9th ed. Clifton Park, NY: Delmar, Cengage Learning, 2004, p. 591.)

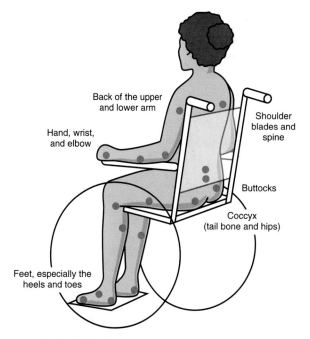

Figure 17-4 Decubitus ulcer sites of wheelchairbound patient (From Hegner BR, Acello B, Caldwell, E. *Nursing Assistant: A Nursing Process Approach*, 9th ed. Clifton Park, NY: Delmar, Cengage Learning, 2004, p. 591.)

EXAMPLE: Debbie Diabetic presents with a heel ulcer. Review of her blood sugars shows that they are slightly out of control. She has been good about her insulin but admits that she has not been following her diet very closely. The ulcer is still small, and we should be able to treat it fairly easily; however, it was explained to the patient that if she doesn't watch her diet more closely, healing will be difficult and she may develop more sores. She understands and she will be careful. She will return in approximately 1 week.

The codes for our example are 250.82 for the diabetic condition and 707.14 for the heel ulcer.

As with all coding, the medical documentation must be used to guide a coder in the selection of the codes and in the sequencing of the codes.

The 708 category is used to report urticaria, commonly known as hives. Fourth digits are needed to specify the type of urticaria: allergic, idiopathic, dermatographic, thermal, vibratory, cholinergic, and other forms.

Disease Highlight—Urticaria

Urticaria is a skin disorder in which there are raised edematous areas of skin accompanied by intense itching. Urticaria may be an indication of an allergic reaction to foods, inhaled allergens, drugs, or an insect bite. Nonallergic reactions can be caused by an infection or some type of external physical stimuli.

Signs and Symptoms:

The patient presents with lesions that have very distinct dermal wheals accompanied by erythematous areas surrounding the lesions. In the areas of the wheals there is severe itching.

Clinical Testing:

The following tests may be performed:

- Allergy testing
- Urinalysis
- Sedimentation rate
- CBC

These tests are completed to confirm or rule out an inflammatory process.

Treatment:

Patients are given antihistamines and instructed to avoid the allergen if the urticaria is caused by an allergic reaction. Topical ointments may also be given.

Internet Links

To learn more about disorders of the skin and subcutaneous system, visit *http://www.sirinet.net* and *www.emedicine.com.*

To learn more about decubitus ulcers, visit *www.ldhpmed.com.*

Summary

- Because some of the conditions in this chapter are similar to those coded in other areas of the coding book, it is very important to review the documentation and ask for clarification if necessary.
- This chapter codes diseases of the skin, hair, nails, and sebaceous glands.
- The skin is also known as the integumentary system and is made up of three layers: the epidermis, the dermis, and the subcutaneous layer.

- Conditions of the integumentary system include melanoma, furuncles, carbuncles, cellulitis, abscesses, and dermatitis.
- Conditions of the nails are coded to this chapter.
- Codes for skin ulcers are found in this chapter.

Chapter Review

True/False: Indicate whether each statement is true (T) or false (F).

1. _____ Vitamin D is produced by the body with the help of ultraviolet rays from the sun passing through the skin.

2. _____ Patient presents with an open wound of the leg area. During the examination, it is noted that the patient has cellulitis. The wound is coded first, then the cellulitis.

3. _____ The dermis layer is located below the subcutaneous layer of skin.

4. _____ An E code is used as the primary diagnosis when coding the adverse effect of a drug properly administered.

5. _____ An inflammation of the upper layer of the skin is called alopecia.

Fill-in- the-Blank: Enter the appropriate term(s) to complete each statement.

6. Another name for bedsore or pressure ulcer is _____.

7. The outermost layer of the skin is called the _____.

8. Dermatitis due to radiation from gamma rays or X-rays is coded to _____.

9. The subcutaneous layer connects the bottom layer of the skin to the top surface of _____.

10. Another name for skin is _____.

Coding Assigments

Instructions: Using an ICD-9-CM coding book, select the code for each diagnostic statement.

Diagnosis	Code
1. Seborrheic infantile dermatitis	_____
2. Cellulitis of cheek	_____
3. Decubitus ulcer, buttock	_____
4. Hidradenitis	_____
5. Paronychia of toe	_____
6. Pyogenic granuloma	_____
7. Impetigo	_____
8. Vitiligo	_____

9. Acne varioliformis _____

10. Intrinsic infantile dermatitis _____

11. Ingrown toenail _____

12. Carbuncle of leg _____

13. Ulcer of ankle _____

14. Pilonidal cyst with abscess _____

15. Cheloid _____

16. Sunburn _____

17. Acne vulgaris _____

18. Subcutaneous calcification _____

19. Urticaria due to cold and heat _____

20. Bed sore _____

21. Xerosis cutis _____

22. Cicatrix _____

23. Lichen nitidus _____

24. Skin tag _____

25. Benign pemphigus _____

Case Studies

Instructions: Review each case study, and select the correct ICD-9-CM diagnostic code.

CASE 1

S: A 15-year-old male presents with acne. Patient says that he has had continual breakouts over the last 6 months, which appear, to the patient, to be getting worse. He tries not to touch his face and washes it three and four times a day.

O: Examination reveals a well nourished, well developed 15-year-old male with acne lesions on the face. There are also a few lesions on the chest and back. The rest of the skin exam is unremarkable.

A: Acne

P: I explained to patient that washing the face too much is just as harmful as not washing enough. Patient will wash once in the morning and then again before bed with a mild soap, followed by Differin q.h.s., and will start doxycycline once a day, 100 mg p.o. q.d. He will return in 1 month for follow-up.

ICD-9-CM Code Assignment: _____

CASE 2

Skilled Nursing Facility Note

VITAL SIGNS: See nurse's vital signs sheet.

This patient was admitted in March because of dementia, and she is wheelchair bound.

EXAM:

HEENT: Within normal limits

ABDOMEN: Soft, no masses

HEART: Normal

SKIN: There is skin breakdown in the sacrum area, which shows some necrotic tissue in the ulcerative area. It shows some granulation, and there is drainage at this time. Stage 4 decubitus present.

PLAN: I have instructed the nurses to treat with Sorbsan, packing twice a day and using a dry sterile dressing.

ICD-9-CM Code Assignment: _____

CASE 3

Physician's Office Note

Patient presents with a complaint of pain in left hand and has been running a low-grade fever.

EXAM:

EXTREMITIES: Right arm and hand within normal limits. Left hand and thumb are sore to touch. The nail around the thumb is swollen, and the cuticle is edematous and red. The cuticle lifts away from the base, and there is pus present. Paronychia of thumb present.

Antibiotics ordered as per med sheet. Patient encouraged to wash hands frequently.

Patient instructed to follow up in 10 days or if symptoms worsen.

ICD-9-CM Code Assignment: _____

CASE 4

Physician's Office Note

Tim is a 5-year-old male who presents today with a dark spot on the interior portion of the upper lip. Mom noticed this spot about 3 weeks ago and said that it has gotten darker than when it first appeared. The child is having no problems eating or drinking. Upon examination, it is noted that there is a 2.5-mm dark spot noted on the midline of the upper lip. This spot is not tender, is nonthickened, and appears to be the only one present. No other spots, lesions, or abnormalities are noted. The diagnosis for this child is purpura annularis telangiectodes.

ICD-9-CM Code Assignment: _____

CASE 5

Physician's Office Note

Tess presented today with a complaint of burning and itching around her abdominal scar. The scar is a result of an automobile accident she was in approximately 3 years ago. Upon examination, the scar is approximately 15 cm in length and appears to be elevated and slightly irregular in shape. I believe this to be a keloid and will administer a steroid injection at the site to relieve the symptoms. Tess will return to the office in 2 weeks for follow-up or sooner if necessary.

ICD-9-CM Code Assignment: _____

18

Diseases of the Musculoskeletal System and Connective Tissue

Chapter Outline

Objectives

At the conclusion of this chapter, the student will be able to:

1. Identify the anatomical structures of the musculoskeletal system.
2. Explain the conditions and disorders that affect the musculoskeletal system.
3. Discuss specific coding guidelines related to the conditions encountered in the musculoskeletal system.
4. Explain the coding guidelines for coding acute fractures versus aftercare.
5. Select and code diagnoses from case studies.

Key Terms

Acquired Deformity	Chondropathy	Fascia	Osteoarthritis (OA)
Ankylosis	Colles' Fracture	Herniated Disc	Osteomyelitis
Ankylosing Spondylitis	Compression Fractures of the Spine	Joints	Osteopathy
Arthritis		Ligaments	Osteoporosis
Arthropathies	Degenerative Joint Disease	Malunion Fracture	Pathologic Fracture
Bones	Dorsopathy	Muscles	Primary Osteoarthritis
Bursa	Dowager's Hump	Myelopathy	Rheumatism
Cartilage		Nonunion Fracture	

Reminder

As you work through this chapter, you will need to have a copy of the ICD-9-CM coding book to reference.

Rheumatoid Arthritis
(RA)

Secondary
Osteoarthritis

Spondylosis

Stress Fracture

Synovia

Tendons

Introduction

Chapter 13 of ICD-9-CM, "Diseases of the Musculoskeletal System and Connective Tissue," category codes 710–739, classifies diseases into the following categories and sections:

Category Codes	Section Title	Definition
710–719	Arthropathies and Related Disorders	**Arthropathy**—disorder of the joint
720–724	Dorsopathies	**Dorsopathy**—disorder of the back
725–729	Rheumatism, Excluding the Back	**Rheumatism**—disorder of the joints, muscles, and tendons and their attachments.
730–739	Osteopathies, Chondropathies, and Acquired Musculoskeletal Deformities	**Osteopathy**—disorder of the bone **Chondropathy**—disorder of the cartilage

This chapter of ICD-9-CM classifies musculoskeletal disorders and conditions that occur as a disease process. Injuries that affect the musculoskeletal system, such as a fracture, are classified to chapter 17 of ICD-9-CM, "Injury and Poisoning," with the exception of stress fractures, pathologic fractures, and malunion of a fracture; these are classified to this chapter of ICD-9-CM.

Introduction to the Body System

Some main terms will be discussed here to help basic understanding, but it is essential that the coder have good reference materials, a good understanding of anatomy and physiology, and documentation from the provider that is specific enough to guide the coder to the correct code assignment.

This chapter of the coding book classifies diseases of the musculoskeletal system. *Musculoskeletal* refers to the muscles, which hold the body erect and allow movement, and the bones, which are connective tissue that protect the internal organs and form the framework of the body. For correct code assignments to be made from this chapter, the coder must understand the terms that are associated with the musculoskeletal system.

Cartilage is smooth, nonvascular connective tissue that comprises the more flexible parts of the skeleton such as the outer ear. Joints allow for bending and rotating movements. Ligaments are bands of connective tissue that connect the joints, and tendons connect muscle to bone. Synovia is the

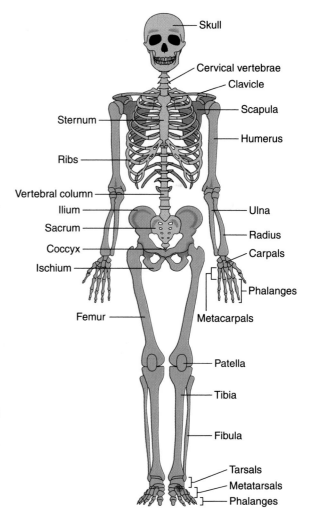

Figure 18-1 Anterior view of the human skeleton (From Ehrlich A, Schroeder CL. *Medical Terminology for Health Professions,* 4th ed. Clifton Park, NY: Delmar, Cengage Learning, 2001, p. 49.)

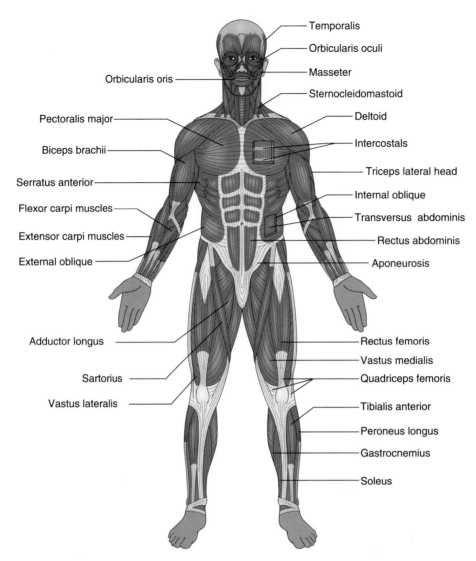

Figure 18-2 Anterior view of the major muscles of the body (From Ehrlich A, Schroeder CL. *Medical Terminology for Health Professions,* 4th ed. Clifton Park, NY: Delmar, Cengage Learning, 2001, p. 78.)

fluid that acts as a lubricant for the joints, tendon sheath, or bursa. The bursa is the synovial-filled sac that works as a cushion to assist in movement. Fascia is the connective tissue that not only covers but supports and separates muscles. Figures 18-1, 18-2, and 18-3 illustrate the anatomical features of the musculoskeletal system.

Coding of Diseases of the Musculoskeletal System and Connective Tissue

At the beginning of ICD-9-CM chapter 13, a note appears that lists fifth-digit subclassifications for categories 711–712, 715–716, 718–719, and 730. The fifth-digit subclassification identifies the site along with specific joints and bones included. It is imperative that coders reference this notation to assign codes.

EXAMPLE:

The following appears for the fifth digit of 1

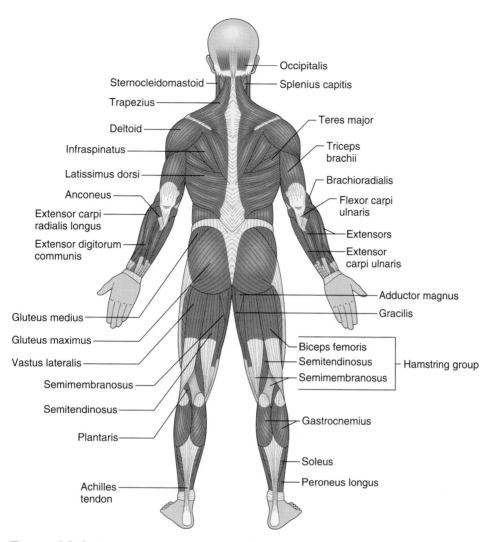

Figure 18-3 Posterior view of the major muscles of the body (From Ehrlich A, Schroeder CL. *Medical Terminology for Health Professions,* 4th ed. Clifton Park, NY: Delmar, Cengage Learning, 2001, p. 78.)

1   shoulder region

Acromioclavicular joint(s)

Clavicle

Gleohumeral joint(s)

Scapula

Sternoclavicular joint(s)

When the diagnostic statement "crystal-induced arthritis, sternoclavicular joint" is coded, a fifth digit of 1 is used to identify the region affected. Code assignment is 712.91.

Fifth digits appear in the Tabular List under the code numbers and indicate the fifth-digit assignments that can be assigned with a particular code. As in our example, in the Tabular List under 712.9, the brackets appear with [0–9], which indicates that the fifth-digit assignment indicating the site of the condition can be any fifth digit from 0 through 9.

Arthropathies and Related Disorders (Category Codes 710–719)

Arthropathies are disorders of the joints. **Arthritis,** an inflammation of a joint, is a common condition coded to this section of the musculoskeletal chapter. Dual coding guidelines apply if arthritis is a manifestation of other conditions. Notations appear throughout this section that instruct coders to assign additional codes.

> **EXAMPLE:** When coding the diagnostic statement "arthritis due to ulcerative colitis," two codes are used. This condition codes to 556.9 for the ulcerative colitis as the primary diagnosis, with 713.1, arthropathy associated with gastrointestinal conditions other than infections, listed as a secondary diagnosis. The note under this 713 category instructs the coder to code first any underlying disease.

Rheumatism is a general term for the deterioration and inflammation of connective tissues, including muscles, tendons, synovium, and bursa. One of the most painful types of arthritis is **rheumatoid arthritis (RA)**, which is a disease of the autoimmune system in which the synovial membranes are inflamed and thickened. Rheumatoid arthritis can affect children or adults and can affect one site or many sites throughout the body. Rheumatoid arthritis may also be referenced as "progressive arthritis" and "proliferative arthritis." Medical documentation needs to specify the site or sites affected so that the appropriate code can be assigned. Because joint swelling and pain are considered an integral part of the condition, they should not be coded separately when a definitive diagnosis of rheumatoid arthritis is given.

The most common form of arthritis is known as **osteoarthritis (OA)**. Osteoarthritis is also referred to as degenerative arthritis because it causes degeneration of the articular cartilage. Osteoarthritis also causes enlargement of the bone. It occurs almost always in older patients. The term *degenerative joint disease* is frequently used to describe this type of osteoarthritis. Osteoarthritis is classified to 715.0X, Osteoarthrosis, generalized. Care needs to be taken when assigning a fifth digit because only 0, 4, and 9 are valid for this code. When more specific osteoarthritis codes are used, such as 715.1X–715.9X, additional fifth digits can be assigned.

Fourth-digit assignments reflect whether the code assignment is for a condition that is localized or generalized and whether it is primary or secondary. For this reason, it is difficult to assign codes for osteoarthritis from the Alphabetic Index only. Reference to the Tabular List is necessary to correctly code these conditions.

Primary osteoarthritis is a form of localized osteoarthritis that most often affects joints of the spine, knee, and hip, as well as the small joints of the hands and feet. This is sometimes referred to as idiopathic or polyarticular degenerative arthritis.

Secondary osteoarthritis is the other category of localized osteoarthritis and is most often due to illness or injury. It affects the joint of one area and can be caused by diseases, injuries, or trauma that change the normal function and structure of the cartilage.

> **EXAMPLE:** A 76-year-old man presents today for follow-up of his degenerative joint disease. He has not noticed any increased pain in his knees but now has noticed pain in the fingers. Upon examination, joints of the first and second phalanges on the right hand are slightly swollen. Knees don't appear any more swollen than at last visit; pulses in all extremities are good. The right hand is a new problem. We will be ordering lab work today to be reviewed at the next visit in 3 months.
>
> Dx: Localized degenerative joint disease in fingers and knees. Plan: Continue on current medication.

The diagnosis in the example is "Localized degenerative joint disease." By referencing the term *disease* in the Alphabetic Index, the coder then has to locate "joint," then follow the indentations to "degenerative," where "degenerative (see also Osteoarthrosis) 715.9X" is found. Reference needs to be made to the Tabular List for the fifth digit. When the coder references the Tabular List, attention should be drawn to the fact that the 715.9X, Osteoarthrosis, unspecified whether generalized or localized, is not the correct code. The diagnosis clearly states "localized." The code assignment is now 715.89, Osteoarthrosis, involving, or with mention of more than one site, but not specified as generalized.

Exercise 18-1   Coding for Categories 710–719

Instructions: For each diagnostic statement listed, select the appropriate ICD-9-CM code.

Diagnosis	Code
1. Libman-Sacks disease with nephrotic syndrome	_____
2. Polymyositis	_____
3. Polyarthritis of ankle and foot due to pneumococcus	_____
4. Rheumatoid carditis	_____
5. Localized secondary degenerative joint disease of hand	_____

Dorsopathies (Category Codes 720–724)

Dorsopathies are disorders of the back. One of the conditions encountered in this section is ankylosing spondylitis, a form of rheumatoid arthritis. It is a chronic inflammation of the spine and sacroiliac joints, which leads to stiffening of the spine. Ankylosis is the complete fusion of the vertebrae. Spondylitis is an inflammation of the vertebrae. Ankylosing spondylitis is also referred to as Marie-Strumpell or Bekhterev's disease. The cause is unknown, but it is progressive and affects mainly the small joints of the spine. This condition is classified to code 720.0.

Category code 721, Spondylosis and allied disorders, requires a fourth digit to indicate with or without myelopathy. The term *myelopathy* refers to any disorder of the spinal cord. Back disorders that involve herniation of the intervertebral disc or spondylitis need the distinction of with myelopathy or without myelopathy. Paralysis is not included in the codes for herniated disc, but paresthesia is.

A herniated disc is a result of the rupture of the nucleus pulposus, or the material in the center of the disc. The rupture causes the nucleus pulposus to move outward, placing pressure on the spinal cord. Because back pain is an integral part of a herniated disc, it is not coded separately. Sciatica is another symptom and is not coded separately. Provider documentation should include whether myelopathy is present. Codes 722.0–722.2X are used to classify a herniated disc, which is also referred to as a displacement of the disc.

Osteopathies, Chondropathies, and Acquired Musculoskeletal Deformities (Category Codes 730–739)

This subsection of the chapter contains some of the most commonly coded disorders of the musculoskeletal system. Osteomyelitis is an inflammation of bone tissue and marrow caused by a bacterial organism. Osteoporosis (codes 733.00–733.09) is a reduction in bone mass that is responsible for different conditions that can affect a person's health. The more severe condition that affect patients with osteoporosis is fractures.

Disease Highlight—Osteoporosis

Osteoporosis is a bone disorder related to metabolism where there is a loss of bone mass due to decreased bone formation and increased bone resorption. The disease causes aporosity, or a Swiss cheese appearance, of the bones, creating a decrease in bone mass. The numerous causes of osteoporosis include:

- Malnutrition
- Decreased calcium absorption

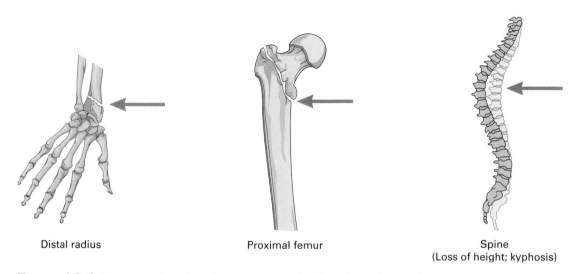

Distal radius   Proximal femur   Spine
                                                                    (Loss of height; kyphosis)

Figure 18-4 Fracture site related to osteoporosis (From Neighbors, Marianne and Tannehill-Jones. *Human Disease*, 2nd edition. Clifton Park, NY: Delmar, Cengage Learning, p 91.)

- Inadequate calcium intake
- Estrogen deficiency
- As a side effect of some chronic diseases

Signs and Symptoms:

Osteoporosis is a slow developing disease that may take decades before symptoms present. Compression fractures of the spine and pathologic wrist fractures commonly present as an early sign of osteoporosis. As the disease progresses, the patient may have:

- A loss of height
- Kyphosis (see Figure 18-4)
- Pain in the back and trunk area
- A decrease in the size of the chest and abdominal cavity
- The appearance of Dowager's hump, an abnormal curvature in the upper thoracic spine (Figure 18-5 illustrates the loss in height and the appearance of Dowager's hump in a patient with osteoporosis.)

As the disease advances, the patient's risk of fracturing a bone increases. Common fracture sites include the distal radius and proximal femur. Figure 18-4 illustrates these fracture sites.

Clinical Testing:

Osteoporosis is diagnosed by:

- Taking bone mass measurements, bone biopsy, and X-rays
- Completing blood testing to determine the serum calcium, phosphorus, and alkaline phosphatase levels

Treatment:

Since osteoporosis is irreversible, there is no treatment to reverse the bone mass loss.

- Patients are encouraged to take calcium and vitamin D and to complete a daily exercise routine.
- Reducing risk factors, such as decreasing caffeine and alcohol consumption and not smoking, is a treatment option that is also encouraged.

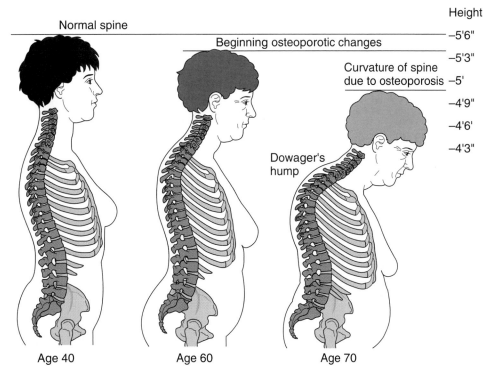

Figure 18-5 Osteoporosis: loss in height and the Dowager's hump (From Neighbors, Marianne and Tannehill-Jones. *Human Disease*, 2nd edition. Clifton Park, NY: Delmar, Cengage Learning, p 91.)

- Physical therapy, estrogen therapy, and the surgical correction of pathological fractures are also treatment options for some patients.

- The drug alendronate, Fosamax, is often prescribed in an effort to increase bone mass.

Three types of fractures are commonly associated with osteoporosis. Pathologic or compression fractures of the spine occur when the vertebrae in the spine become weak and collapse under low stress. Colles' fracture is a wrist fracture that typically occurs when a person tries to break a fall by extending the arm. The last type, and the most dangerous, is a hip fracture. The hip fracture can be caused by a fall or, in some cases, can occur spontaneously. Loss of mobility or even death can be the result of this type of fracture. Coders must determine whether the fracture occurred because of a weakened diseased bone or as a result of an injury. It should be noted that fractures that occur because of a traumatic injury, such as a child who falls and breaks his arm while playing, are classified to chapter 17 of ICD-9-CM, "Injury and Poisoning." For correct code assignment, coders must read the medical record to identify whether the fracture is pathologic or due to a traumatic injury.

The following types of fractures are coded to this section of chapter 13 of the ICD-9-CM code book:

- Pathologic fractures, 733.1X—A pathologic fracture is a break of a diseased bone that occurs from a minor stress or injury that would not normally occur in healthy bone. Pathologic fractures can also occur spontaneously. A fifth digit is used to identify the site of the fracture.

- Malunion fractures, 733.81, and nonunion fractures, 733.82—A malunion occurs when the fracture site is misaligned. A nonunion occurs when the fracture fragments fail to unite.

- Stress fractures, 733.93–733.95—Stress fractures occur when there is repetitive force applied to a bone over a period of time. Another term used for stress fractures is *stress reaction*. Individuals who run or exercise frequently may develop stress fractures. Stress fractures are not always visualized by X-ray initially when they are suspected.

The ICD-9-CM Official Guidelines for Coding and Reporting gives coders directions for the coding of pathologic fractures. It should be noted that this guideline also refers coders to Section I.C.17.b of the ICD-9-CM Official Guidelines for Coding and Reporting for information on the coding of traumatic fractures, because traumatic fractures are coded in chapter 17 of ICD-9-CM, "Injury and Poisonings."

Official ICD-9-CM Coding Guideline:

Coding of Pathologic Fractures

Acute Fractures vs. Aftercare

Pathologic fractures are reported using subcategory 733.1, when the fracture is newly diagnosed. Subcategory 733.1 may be used while the patient is receiving active treatment for the fracture. Examples of active treatment are surgical treatment, emergency department encounter, and evaluation and treatment by a new physician.

Fractures are coded using the aftercare codes (subcategory V54.0, V54.2, V54.8, or V54.9) for encounters after the patient has completed active treatment of the fracture and is receiving routine care for the fracture during the healing or recovery phase. Examples of fracture aftercare are cast change or removal, removal of external or internal fixation device, medication adjustment, and follow-up visits following fracture treatment.

Care for complications of surgical treatment for fracture repairs during the healing or recovery phase should be coded with the appropriate complication codes.

Care of complications of fractures, such as malunion and nonunion, should be reported with the appropriate codes. (See Section I. C. 17.b for information on the coding of traumatic fractures.) (See Appendix A, Section I, C13, a, 1.)

Acquired deformities are coded at the end of this chapter. An acquired deformity is a malformation of an anatomical structure that is caused by infections, injury to soft tissue, or a late effect of a fracture. It should be noted that the conditions coded to this chapter are acquired and are not congenital. Congenital musculoskeletal deformities are classified to chapter 14 of ICD-9-CM, "Congenital Anomalies."

Internet Links

To learn more about the musculoskeletal system and disorders, visit *www.eicd.com*, *www.aihw.gov.au*, *www.aaos.org*, and *www.gwc.maricopa.edu/class/bio201/muscle/mustut.htm*.

For information on treatment and prevention of osteoporosis, visit *www.umassmemorial.org*.

Summary

- Chapter 13 of ICD-9-CM classifies diseases of the musculoskeletal system and connective tissue.

- Congenital disorders of the musculoskeletal system are classified to chapter 14 of ICD-9-CM, "Congenital Anomalies."

- Fifth-digit subclassifications are frequently used in chapter 13 of ICD-9-CM.

- Arthritis is classified by its type or cause.

- Degenerative joint disease is commonly seen in elderly patients.

- Back pain and sciatica are common symptoms of a herniated disc and are not coded separately.

- Stress fractures, pathological fractures, and malunion or nonunion fractures are classified to chapter 13 of ICD-9-CM.

- Fractures that have occurred due to a traumatic injury are coded to chapter 17 of ICD-9-CM, "Injury and Poisoning."

Chapter Review

True/False: Indicate whether each statement is true (T) or false (F).

1. _____ All fractures are coded to chapter 13 of ICD-9-CM, "Diseases of the Musculoskeletal System."

2. _____ A compression fracture can occur when a person tries to break a fall by extending an arm.

3. _____ All congenital disorders of the back are classified to chapter 13 of ICD-9-CM.

4. _____ Fourth and fifth digits are frequently used in chapter 13 of ICD-9-CM.

5. _____ A fifth digit of 2 is valid with code 715.0.

Fill-in- the-Blank: Enter the appropriate term(s) to complete each statement.

6. Tendons connect _____ to _____.

7. _____ is an inflammation of a joint.

8. _____ separates and covers the muscles.

9. Code 715.3 can have _____ as a fifth-digit code assignment, as indicated in the Tabular List.

10. _____ acts as a lubricant for joints.

Coding Assignments

Instructions: Using an ICD-9-CM coding book, select the code for each diagnostic statement.

Diagnosis	Code
1. Cauliflower ear	_____
2. Coccygodynia	_____
3. Kyphosis due to radiation	_____
4. Pelvic obliquity	_____
5. Senile osteoporosis	_____
6. Pathological fracture of humerus	_____
7. Pain in limb	_____
8. Polymyositis	_____
9. Spinal stenosis	_____
10. Joint mice, knee	_____
11. Arthropathy with hyperparathyroidism	_____
12. Rheumatoid arthritis	_____
13. Acute osteomyelitis of shoulder	_____

14. Low back pain   _____

15. Baker's cyst   _____

16. Zygomatic hyperplasia   _____

17. Effusion of elbow   _____

18. Cervical spondylosis with myelopathy   _____

19. Osteoporosis   _____

20. Contracture of fingers   _____

21. Pelvic obliquity   _____

22. Cavus deformity of foot   _____

23. Cubitus varus (acquired)   _____

24. Displacement of cervical intervertebral disc without myelopathy   _____

25. Bunion   _____

Case Studies

Instructions: Review each case study, and select the correct ICD-9-CM diagnostic code.

CASE 1

Physician's Office Visit

VITAL SIGNS: B/P 125/80   Temperature 98.9   Weight 164 pounds

Sally is here today to follow up on her blood sugar levels.

HEENT: Normal, no pathological changes due to diabetes

ABDOMEN: Soft, tender. No masses, spleen normal.

CHEST/HEART: Within normal limits

EXTREMITIES: Feet were examined and revealed joint inflammation due to Charcot's arthritis. The arthritis is a result of the advancing diabetes. Patient was instructed to avoid wearing tight footwear and to file calluses that are present on feet with an emery board. Patient was advised to schedule an appointment with Dr. Town, a podiatrist, for ongoing care.

Diabetes is controlled at this time. Follow up in 1 month.

ICD-9-CM Code Assignment: _____

CASE 2

Emergency Room Visit

This 16-year-old female was running at track practice today and started to experience foot pain. This has occurred in the past when she runs, but today the pain is at an increased level.

VITAL SIGNS: Temperature 98.6   B/P 120/75   Weight 124 pounds

EXAM:

HEENT: Within normal limits

HEART: Normal

ABDOMEN: Normal, with no complaints

EXTREMITIES: Left foot pain present, and pain increases to touch in the metatarsal area.

X-ray ordered.

X-RAY RESULTS: Negative

Clinical diagnosis of stress reaction of metatarsals.

Referred to orthopedics.

ICD-9-CM Code Assignment: _____

CASE 3

Skilled Nursing Facility Note

Mary was admitted in June of 200X with a diagnosis of dementia and osteoporosis. She is seen today at the request of the charge nurse because she is complaining of pain in her right midthigh area. She has not fallen or injured herself.

EXAM:

EXTREMITIES: When the patient's right leg is moved, she complains of pain in her thigh. She does not complain of pain in her left leg.

Onsite X-ray was ordered, which showed a fracture of the shaft of the femur.

Patient was sent to hospital for treatment.

CLINICAL IMPRESSION: Fracture due to postmenopausal osteoporosis.

ICD-9-CM Code Assignment: _____

CASE 4

Physician's Office Visit

Mark presents today for follow-up of a torn meniscus. The injury occurred while skiing 2 years ago. He was going downhill, fell, and twisted his knee during this fall. He was in a wheelchair for 2 weeks and then moved to crutches and physical therapy. He is now walking and performing activities of daily living without assistance. The diagnosis given for today's visit is old bucket handle tear of medial meniscus of the knee.

ICD-9-CM Coding Assignment: _____

CASE 5

Physician's Office Visit

Mrs. Kennedy presents today with "terrible pain in my knees." It has been 6 months since I have seen her. We discussed the medications she is taking, which are limited to Advil or Tylenol. Examination reveals decreased range of motion and a slight change in gait. It was decided to run a few lab tests and also take some X-rays, which confirmed the diagnosis of osteoarthritis of the knee, bilaterally. We decided that glucosamine plus chondroitin sulfate, which are OTC medications, could be tried at this time prior to anything stronger. If she experiences no relief in the next 3 to 4 weeks, we will explore other options.

ICD-9-CM Coding Assignment: _____

Chapter Outline

Objectives

At the conclusion of this chapter, the student will be able to:

1. Define the terms *congenital anomaly* and *deformity*.
2. Explain the conditions classified to chapter 14 of ICD-9-CM.
3. Discuss the organization of chapter 14 of ICD-9-CM.
4. Differentiate between congenital and acquired conditions.
5. Discuss the coding guidelines that relate to congenital anomalies.
6. Select and code diagnoses from case studies.

Key Terms

Acquired Condition	Cleft Lip	Harelip	Talipes
Anencephalus	Cleft Palate	Hydrocephalus	Teratogens
Anisorcoria	Clubfoot	Polycystic Kidney	Volkmann's Deformity
Anomaly	Congenital Anomaly	Disease	
Birth Defect	Deformity	Spina Bifida	

Reminder

As you work through this chapter, you will need to have a copy of the ICD-9-CM coding book to reference.

Introduction

Congenital anomalies, category codes 740–759, are classified in Chapter 14 of ICD-9-CM. This chapter is organized according to anatomical site and, at times, groups anomalies of the same site to the same code when ICD-9-CM does not provide a specified code for an anomaly. For example, code 742.8, Other specified anomalies of nervous system, is used to code a diagnosis that is specified as a certain type but is not specifically listed in ICD-9-CM. When a specific code is not present in ICD-9-CM, the coder should assign the nonspecific code and an additional code for the manifestation of the anomaly.

> **EXAMPLE:** Kelly was born with a congenital malposition of the gastrointestinal tract that has caused a gastrointestional obstruction. This malposition is coded using code 751.8, Other specified anomalies of digestive system. Code 560.9 is used to code the manifestation—a gastrointestional obstruction.

To locate congenital anomalies in the Alphabetic Index, the coder should first reference the specific anomaly. However, at times ICD-9-CM does not provide a specific entry for the congenital anomaly; then the coder should reference the entries of "anomaly" or "deformity" to locate the term.

Introduction to the Body System

To understand the conditions that are classified to this chapter of ICD-9-CM, it is important to understand its terminology. A congenital anomaly is a disorder that exists at the time of birth and may be a result of genetic factors, agents causing defects in the embryo, or both. Agents that cause defects in an embryo are called teratogens. ICD-9-CM makes a definite distinction between an anomaly and a deformity. A deformity is a problem in the structure or form, which may or may not be disfiguring. An example of this is Volkmann's deformity, which is a congential dislocation of the tibiotarsal. An anomaly, or birth defect, is a deviation from what is normal in the development of a structure or organ. An example of an anomaly is spina bifida cystica. Spina bifida is a congenital condition in which the spinal canal fails to close around the spinal cord.

When selecting codes for congenital anomalies and defects, coders must closely review the Alphabetic Index. Many conditions are identified in ICD-9-CM as both congenital and acquired. Acquired conditions are conditions that occur during a person's life. ICD-9-CM makes a distinction in the Alphabetic Index between congenital and acquired conditions, with the terms *acquired* or *congenital* in parentheses for some conditions. The terms in parentheses act as modifiers for the condition being coded because they further describe the condition.

> **EXAMPLE:** Holly presented to the Emergency Room with extreme pain in the right little finger. Holly is 10 years old. Upon examination, it was noted that the joint was somewhat deformed in that it indented in the middle of the joint. Patient cannot flex the finger. She noted that the finger has been like this since birth, but until she has finished growing, surgery is not an option. Will treat with ibuprofen and ice until patient can be seen by primary care.

When coding the diagnostic statement "deformity of the joint," the coder finds the following in the Alphabetic Index:

```
Deformity
 joint (acquired) NEC 738.8
  congenital 755.9
  contraction (abduction) (adduction) (extension)
   (flexion)—see Contraction, joint
```

In the Alphabetic Index, both acquired and congenital are listed, with the term *congenital* appearing in parentheses and the term *acquired* appearing as an indentation. It is imperative that the coder be able to read the documentation when confronted with this type of situation in order to assign the correct code. If this is not possible, then the coder needs to communicate with the provider for clarification.

It should also be noted that the codes in this chapter are not assigned by age. Some congenital conditions do not manifest themselves until later in life even though they may have been present at birth.

Another clarification needs to be made regarding conditions that occur during the birthing process. If a condition occurs during the birthing process, the condition is considered a perinatal condition; conditions that are due to birth injury are coded to chapter 15, "Conditions in the Perinatal Period," with category 767, Birth trauma.

EXAMPLE: Billy Baby was delivered at 6:15 am, weighing in at 7 pound 9 unces. The physician noticed an anomaly of the clavicle area, and an X-ray confirmed a fractured clavicle. It was determined that the fracture occurred as the infant was proceeding down the birth canal.

Even though the injury occurred during birth, the diagnosis of clavicle fracture due to birth trauma is coded as 767.2, Fracture of clavicle due to birth trauma. Codes regarding perinatal conditions are discussed in more detail in Chapter 20 of this textbook.

Coding of Congenital Anomalies

The ICD-9-CM Official Guidelines for Coding and Reporting state the following for codes in categories 740-559, congenital anomalies:

Official ICD-9-CM Coding Guideline:

Codes in categories 740–759, Congenital Anomalies

Assign an appropriate code(s) from categories 740–759, Congenital Anomalies, when an anomaly is documented. A congenital anomaly may be the principal/first-listed diagnosis on a record or a secondary diagnosis.

When a congenital anomaly does not have a unique code assignment, assign additional code(s) for any manifestations that may be present.

When the code assignment specifically identifies the congenital anomaly, manifestations that are an inherent component of the anomaly should not be coded separately. Additional codes should be assigned for manifestations that are not an inherent component.

Codes from chapter 14 may be used throughout the life of the patient. If a congenital anomaly has been corrected, a personal history code should be used to identify the history of the anomaly. Although present at birth, a congenital anomaly may not be identified until later in life. Whenever the condition is diagnosed by the physician, it is appropriate to assign a code from codes 740–759.

For the birth admission, the appropriate code from category V30, Liveborn infants, according to type of birth, should be sequenced as the principal diagnosis, followed by any congenital anomaly codes, 740–759. (See Appendix A, Section I, C14, a.)

To assign codes according to this guideline, it is imperative that the coder determine whether the condition being coded is congenital and whether all of the manifestations of the congenital condition are captured via code assignment.

Congenital Anomalies of the Nervous System, Eye, Ear, Face and Neck (Category Codes 740–744)

The first part of this chapter of ICD-9-CM classifies congenital anomalies of the nervous system, that affect the brain, spinal cord, and other nervous system tissues, and the eyes, ears, face and neck. Anencephalus, which is classified to category 740, is a birth defect in newborns in which the neural groove closes early in the first trimester. The brain maybe abnormally shaped, or there may be no cranial vault. The coder needs to look for clues in the medical record to code this condition. The coder may see "partial or total absence of the skull, brain, or spinal cord." The coder may identify anencephalus in

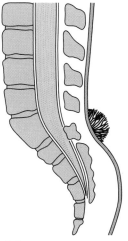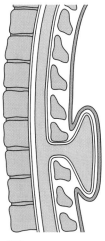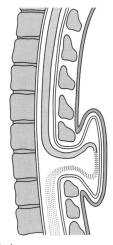

(A) Spina bifida occulta   (B) Meningocele   (C) Myelomeningocele

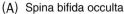

Figure 19-1 Types of spina bifida (From Neighbors, Marianne and Tannehill-Jones. *Human Disease*, 2nd edition. Clifton Park, NY: Delmar, Cengage Learning, p 374.)

the medical record by "absence of half of the brain" or "missing one of the hemispheres of the brain." Clarification of the diagnosis needs to be discussed with the physician.

Spina bifida, a congenital defect of the closure of the spinal column, is classified to category code 741, except for spina bifida occulta, which is classified to code 756.17. Figure 19-1 illustrates the different types of spina bifida. Fourth digits are used for category code 741 to identify the presence or absence of hydrocephalus, an accumulation of fluid within the cranial meninges. The following fifth-digit subclassification is used to identify the site of the spina bifida:

    0   Unspecified region
    1   Cervical region
    2   Dorsal (thoracic) region
    3   Lumbar region

Therefore, to code the term *spina bifida*, the coder should identify the region of the vertebral column that the condition affects and whether hypocephalus is present.

The 743 category of this chapter is devoted to congenital anomalies of the eye. The anomalies are classified according to the specific site and type of defect encountered. One of the common conditions that may be encountered is congenital anisorcoria. Anisorcoria is also known as unequal pupils, and congenital anisorcoria is classified to code 743.46.

Exercise 19–1   Coding Category Codes 740–744

Instructions: For each diagnostic statement, select the appropriate ICD-9-CM code.

Diagnosis	**Code**
1. Congenital entropion	_____
2. Congenital absence of auditory canal	_____
3. Cerebral cyst, congenital	_____
4. Hydrocephalus due to lumbar region spina bifida	_____
5. Riley-Day syndrome	_____

Congenital Anomalies of the Cardiovascular System (Category Codes 745–747)

Congenital anomalies of the cardiovascular system involve the heart and other structures of the circulatory system. The category codes are organized according to the anatomical structures affected by the anomaly. For example, congenital anomalies of the heart are classified to category codes 745 and 746, and other congenital anomalies of the circulatory system are classified to category codes 747. The most challenging aspect of coding in this part of the code book is the terminology used. Because of the complexity of some of the conditions encountered in this part of the chapter, it is very important that any questions a coder has regarding terminology, site, or abbreviations used are researched by the coder for proper code assignment. Once a coder is familiar with the provider's documentation with regard to these types of anomalies, code assignment becomes easier.

Coders also need to identify that the cardiac condition being coded is congenital. For example, stenosis of the mitral valve can be congenital or acquired. Congenital stenosis of the mitral valve is coded to 746.5, and mitral valve stenosis is coded to 394.0.

Exercise 19–2 Coding Congenital Anomalies of the Cardiovascular System

Instructions: For each of the diagnostic statements, select the appropriate ICD-9-CM code.

Diagnosis	Code
1. Coarctation of the aorta	_____
2. Tetralogy of Fallot	_____
3. Absence of pulmonary valve, present at birth	_____
4. Ostium primum defect	_____
5. Defect of the ventricular septum	_____

Congenital Anomalies of Respiratory System (Category Code 748)

Congenital anomalies of the respiratory system affect the lungs, trachea, nose, larynx, trachea, bronchus, and other respiratory system structures. Category code 748 is the only category for congenital anomalies of the respiratory system.

Congenital Anomalies of the Digestive System (Category Codes 749–750)

Digestive system congenital anomalies include conditions that are present at birth and that affect the gastrointestinal tract and conditions or defects of the mouth and lips. Common defects that are classified to category code 749 are the cleft palate and cleft lip. A cleft palate is a congenital groove or opening of the palate that involves the hard palate, soft palate, or both, as well as the upper lip. A cleft lip, also referred to as harelip, is a congenital defect that results in a deep groove or opening of the lip running upward to the nose. Fourth digits are used in category code 749 as follows:

749.0   Cleft palate

749.1   Cleft lip

749.2   Cleft palate with cleft lip

Fifth-digit subclassifications are used with these fourth digits. Coders must review the record to identify whether both cleft lip and cleft palate exist together or separately and whether the condition is bilateral or unilateral and complete or incomplete. Fifth digits identify bilateral or unilateral, as well as complete or incomplete (partial). If the record does not clearly identify all these necessary elements, the coder needs to clarify the documentation with the provider.

When the medical documentation is reviewed, determine whether the digestive system condition is congenital in nature, rather than an acquired condition, because separate codes exist for acquired versus congenital digestive system conditions.

Exercise 19–3   Congenital versus Acquired Digestive System Conditions

Instructions: For each diagnostic statement list the code for both the congenital and acquired digestive system condition. The first one is completed.

Diagnostic Statement	Code for Congenital Condition	Code for Acquired Condition
1. Diverticulum of colon	751.5	562.10
2. Displacement of stomach		
3. Esophageal displacement		
4. Spasm of the pylorus		
5. Hypertorphy of the tongue		
6. Atresia of the salivary duct		
7. Stenosis of small intestine		
8. Disorder of the intestines		
9. Deformity of the ileum		
10. Esophageal stenosis		

Congenital Anomalies of the Genitourinary System (Category Codes 752–753)

Category code 752, Congenital anomalies of the genital organs, classifies both female and male anomalies. Fourth and fifth digits are used to identify the specific anomaly. Category code 753, Congenital anomalies of the urinary system, classifies anomalies that affect the kidneys, urether, urinary bladder, urethra, and other renal pelvis conditions. Subcategory 753.1 classifies polycystic kidney disease, a slowly progressive disorder in which the normal tissue of the kidneys is replaced with multiple grapelike cysts. Fifth-digit subclassifications are used to identify the various types of cystic kidney disease. If the medical record does not document the specific type of the disease, then code 753.12, Polycystic kidney, unspecified type, should be assigned. Complications of the disease, such as renal failure, can also occur. When other complications are present, additional codes should be assigned to identify the complication.

Disease Highlight—Polycystic Kidney Disease

Polycystic kidney disease is an inherited disorder in which the kidneys gradually lose the ability to function due to the grapelike clusters of cysts that form. The fluid-filled cysts cause a gradual inability of the kidneys to function as the renal tissue becomes compressed and eventually stops working. Figure 19-2 illustrates a polycystic kidney.

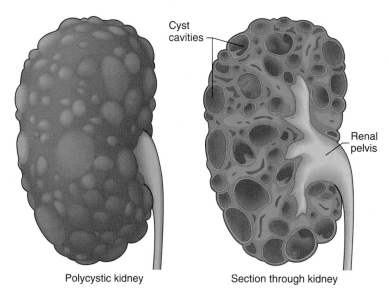

Cyst cavities

Renal pelvis

Polycystic kidney   Section through kidney

Figure 19-2 Polycystic kidney (From Neighbors, Marianne, and RuthTannehill-Jones. *Human Disease*, 2nd edition. Clifton Park, NY: Delmar, Cengage Learning, p 230.)

Signs and Symptoms:

As the disease progresses, renal tissue is destroyed and hypertension typically develops. Lumbar pain, blood in the urine, and frequent urinary tract infections occur. In some cases renal failure occurs.

Clinical Testing:

- Family history of polycystic kidney disease determines whether a patient is at risk.

- An intravenous pyelogram confirms the diagnosis.

- Urine tests, ultrasound, CT scans, lab tests, used to check creatinine levels, also confirm the diagnosis.

Treatment:

- There is no cure for the disease, but treatment of symptoms and surgical intervention may be necessary.

- If the kidney fails, dialysis is necessary.

- A kidney transplant is needed for end-stage management of the disease.

- Treatment is also directed by managing the hypertension and urinary tract infections.

Congenital Anomalies of the Musculoskeletal System (Category Codes 754–756)

These category codes include deformities of the musculoskeletal system as well as nonteratogenic deformities that are considered to be due to intrauterine malposition and pressure. These congenital conditions can affect a child's functional ability, which can vary greatly in severity. Most of these conditions are corrected through surgical interventions. A common congenital anomaly that occurs involves the feet, clubfoot or talipes, code 754.70. ICD-9-CM also provides the following category codes that identify the type of talipes:

754.5   Varus deformities of feet—the congenital turning inward of the feet

754.6   Valgus deformities of feet—the congenital outward turning of the feet

The fifth-digit subclassification further identifies the section of the foot that the disorder affects. Figure 19-3 illustrates a talipes varus deformity of the feet.

Congenital Anomalies of the Integument (Category Code 757)

This category classifies anomalies of the skin, subcutaneous tissue, hair, nails, and breast. Common anomalies classified to this category include the following:

757.32   Birthmarks, port-wine stain, strawberry nevus

757.4   Congenital alopecia

757.6   Anomalies of the breast, such as hypoplasia of breast, formation of an additional breast or nipple

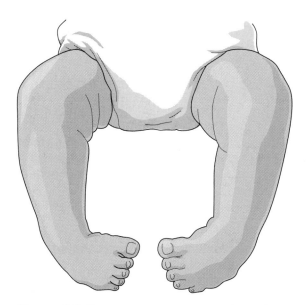

Figure 19-3 Varus deformity of the foot (From Ehrlich A, Schroeder CL. *Medical Terminology for Health Professions,* 4th ed. Clifton Park, NY: Delmar, Cengage Learning, 2001, p. 58.)

Chromosomal Anomalies (Category Code 758)

This category classifies anomalies, and syndromes associated with an anomaly, in the number and form of chromosomes. An Include: notation directs the coder to use an additional code for conditions associated with the chromosomal anomalies. Fourth digits are used in this category to identify specific syndromes, including:

758.0   Down's syndrome

758.1   Patau's syndrome

758.2   Edwards' syndrome

758.7   Klinefelter's syndrome

Internet Links

To learn more about congenital anomalies, visit the National Institutes of Health at *http://health.nih.gov* and the National Library of Medicine at *http://www.nlm.nih.gov.*

Summary

- Congenital anomalies may be a result of genetic factors, teratogens, or both.

- The anomalies can be present at birth and obvious, or they may not be identified until later in life.

- Some anomalies are more serious than others. Anencephalus is a severe defect and usually results in death.

- Documentation is critical, and it is essential that the coder have clarification of the diagnoses to be certain of the code assignment.

- ICD-9-CM classifies anomalies to congenital and acquired states; therefore, for accurate coding to occur, medical documentation must clearly identify whether the anomaly is congenital.

Chapter Review

True/False: Indicate whether each statement is true (T) or false (F).

1. _____ The agents causing defects in an embryo are called teratogens.

2. _____ The codes in this chapter are assigned by age.

3. _____ The first part of the chapter deals with anomalies of the nervous system.

4. _____ Anomalies of the eye are coded to the specific site of the defect.

5. _____ Spina bifida is a congenital condition in which the spinal canal fails to close around the spinal cord.

Fill-in-the-Blank: Enter the appropriate term(s) to complete each statement.

6. A _____ is a disorder that exists at the time of birth.

7. The code for the congenital deformity of a joint is _____.

8. A birth defect is also known as a _____.

9. A birth defect in newborns in which the neural groove fails to close in the first trimester is known as _____.

10. A _____ is a problem in the structure or form that may or may not be disfiguring.

Coding Assignments

Instructions: Using an ICD-9-CM coding book, select the appropriate code for each diagnostic statement.

Diagnosis	Code
1. Congenital hydrocephalus	_____
2. Macrocheilia	_____
3. Unspecified anomaly of ear with impairment of hearing	_____
4. Congenital deformity of auricle of the heart	_____
5. Arnold-Chiari syndrome	_____
6. Congenital brachial cleft cyst	_____
7. Klipple-Feil syndrome	_____
8. Corrected transposition of great vessels	_____
9. Congenital upper-limb vessel anomaly	_____
10. Hydromyelia	_____
11. Congenital renal dysplasia	_____

12. Exstrophy of urinary bladder   _____

13. Microcephalus   _____

14. Congenital longitudinal deficiency, ulnar, complete   _____

15. Congenital deformity of lip   _____

16. Multiple epiphyseal dysplasia   _____

17. Tuberous sclerosis   _____

18. Macrotia   _____

19. Meckel's diverticulum   _____

20. Congenital coronary artery anomaly   _____

21. Fragile X syndrome   _____

22. Velo-cardio-facial syndrome   _____

23. Scrotal transposition   _____

24. Nuclear cataract   _____

25. Hemicephaly   _____

Case Studies

Instructions: Review each case study, and select the correct ICD-9-CM diagnostic code.

CASE 1

Inpatient Orthopedic Consultation

Mary is a 3-year-old female child I am seeing at the request of Dr. Sharp. She is presently admitted to remove a cystic hygroma on her neck. I was asked to see her because she has severe congenital spastic quadriplegia with more involvement on the left than on the right. She was born 4 weeks premature and spent 5 weeks in the NICU and was diagnosed with congenital adduction contracture of the left hip. Her development has been extremely delayed due to cerebral palsy.

EXAM:

Generalized spastic quadriplegia. Increased tone on her left side than her right. There is a significant adduction contracture of her left hip, with abduction to 10 degrees.

IMPRESSION:

Congenital adduction contracture of left hip.

RECOMMENDATIONS: The spasticity in her hip adductors may cause her hip to dislocate, and an X-ray was ordered. She was scheduled for an adductor tenotomy to prevent her hip from dislocating.

ICD-9-CM Code Assignment: _____

CASE 2

Office Visit

Samantha returns today for follow-up of her elbow and knee flexion contractures.

EXAM:

UPPER EXTREMITIES: Rigid bilateral 37 degree elbow flexion contractures.

PELVIC JOINTS: She has no contractures of her hips.

LOWER EXTREMITIES: Rigid bilateral 40-degree knee flexion contractures

ANKLES: There are no contractures of her ankles.

X-RAYS REVIEWED: AP pelvis, AP and lateral knee, and AP and lateral elbow X-rays show no significant findings. The findings are consistent with mulitpex, congenital arthrogryposis involving the elbows and knees.

RECOMMENDATIONS:

Measurements have been taken to have elbow and knee night splints made. She was scheduled for fitting and a 1-month follow-up visit.

ICD-9-CM Code Assignment: _____

CASE 3

Ambulatory Surgery Discharge Note

This is a 7-year-old female who presented with a problem swallowing. The mother states that she took the child to her pediatrician for evaluation when she started having problems eating and holding food down. The pediatric office sent over results of CT scans of the neck, chest, and trunk as well as lab test results. Upon review of the CT scans, it is noted that a slight mass is present on the esophagus that has probably been present since birth. Today a surgical removal of the mass and path examination was completed. The postoperative diagnosis of esophageal cyst (congenital) was made.

ICD-9-CM Coding Assignment: _____

CASE 4

Physician's Office Note

This is a 5-year-old male who presents today with a complaint of abdominal pain. His mother has noted a history of complaints of abdominal pain in the past. He is now experiencing vomiting since last night around 1 am and is quite lethargic and in mild distress. Examination reveals the abdomen is distended and tender. An abdominopelvic CT scan reveals a stricture in the small bowel. This appears to have been present since birth but due to the child's growth it has now become a problem. He will be admitted to the hospital for surgical correction.

ICD-9-CM Coding Assignment: _____

CASE 5

Pediatric Office Note

Theresa Louise presents today for a 2-week checkup after normal vaginal delivery. Mom says baby is eating well and is alert, responds appropriately when she hears noise, and is overall healthy. Upon examination there is a slight murmur when listening to the heart. We performed an EKG and chest X-ray. There appears to be a small ventricular septal defect which would have been present at birth. We will not do anything further at this time but monitor this condition to see if it corrects itself over this coming year.

ICD-9-CM Coding Assignment: _____

Certain Conditions Originating in the Perinatal Period

Chapter Outline

Introduction

Coding Guidelines for Certain Conditions
  Originating in the Perinatal Period

Internet Links

Summary

Chapter Review

Coding Assignments

Case Studies

Objectives

At the conclusion of this chapter, the student will be able to:

1. Understand how perinatal conditions of the mother affect the fetus or newborn.
2. Describe conditions that may affect the fetus or newborn.
3. Define various perinatal conditions.
4. Discuss the specific coding guidelines that relate to conditions originating in the perinatal period.
5. Select and code diagnoses from case studies.

Key Terms

ABO Isoimmunization	Birth Trauma	Hypoxia	Meconium
Anoxia	Fetal Immaturity	Isoimmunization	Noxious Influence
Asphyxia	Heavy-for-Dates	Jaundice	Perinatal Period
Bilirubin	Hemolysis	Light-for-Dates	Preterm Infant

Reminder

As you work through this chapter, you will need to have a copy of the ICD-9-CM coding book to reference.

Introduction

The time surrounding the birth of a child up to 28 days after birth is considered the perinatal period. The codes in chapter 15 of ICD-9-CM, "Certain Conditions Originating in the Perinatal Period," are for the medical record of the fetus or newborn *only* and are *never* found in the medical record of the mother.

Some of the conditions that are classified to this chapter are conditions that can affect persons throughout their lives; other conditions are temporary and disappear after several days, months, or even years.

> **EXAMPLE:** Billy Baby is a preterm newborn, 16 hours old, who is now developing jaundice. Jaundice in a newborn is usually taken care of after 24 hours under a sun lamp. Code 774.2, Neonatal jaundice associated with preterm delivery, is the code assignment for this temporary form of jaundice.

Coding Guidelines for Certain Conditions Originating in the Perinatal Period

General coding guidelines are followed to find the correct code assignments from this chapter. Physician documentation plays a key role in determining when to assign codes. The ICD-9-CM Official Guidelines for Coding and Reporting give the following guidance for coding conditions originating in the perinatal period:

Official ICD-9-CM Coding Guideline:

1. *Assigning codes for conditions that require treatment.*

   Assign codes for conditions that require treatment or further investigation, prolong the length of stay, or require resource utilization.

2. *Codes for conditions specified as having implications for future health care needs.*

   Assign codes for conditions that have been specified by the provider as having implications for future health care needs. Note: This guideline should not be used for adult patients.

3. *Codes for newborn conditions originating in the perinatal period.*

   Assign a code for newborn conditions originating in the perinatal period (categories 760–779), as well as complications arising during the current episode of care classified in other chapters, only if the diagnoses have been documented by the responsible provider at the time of transfer or discharge as having affected the fetus or newborn. (See Appendix A, Section I, C15, h 1–3.)

> **EXAMPLE:** A physician notices a problem with the clavicle of a newborn infant immediately after birth. X-rays revealed a fractured clavicle. The physician determines the fracture is a result of birth trauma. Code assignment is 767.2.

In the example given, a fractured clavicle due to birth trauma can be located under "fracture" or "birth." Either term takes the coder to code 767.2. Please note when locating codes that are classified to this chapter of ICD-9-CM, a term that can be referenced in the Alphabetic Index is the main term *birth*. This entry in the Alphabetic Index provides a listing of various conditions that code to this chapter. The entry in the Alphabetic Index appears as follows:

```
Birth
  abnormal fetus or newborn 763.9
  accident, fetus or newborn—see Birth, injury
  complications in mother—see Delivery, complicated
  compression during NEC 767.9
  defect—see Anomaly
  delayed, fetus 763.9
  difficult NEC, affecting fetus or newborn 763.9
```

```
dry, affecting fetus or newborn 761.1
forced, NEC, affecting fetus or newborn 763.89
forceps, affecting fetus or newborn 763.2
hematoma of sternomastoid 767.8
immature 765.1
  extremely 765.0
inattention, after or at 995.52
induced, affecting fetus or newborn 763.89
infant—see Newborn
injury NEC 767.9
 adrenal gland 767.8
 basal ganglia 767.0
 brachial plexus (paralysis) 767.6
 brain (compression) (pressure) 767.0
 cerebellum 767.0
 cerebral hemorrhage 767.0
 conjunctiva 767.8
 eye 767.8
 fracture
  bone, any except clavicle or spine 767.3
  clavicle 767.2
  femur 767.3
  humerus 767.3
```

Systemic, infectious, or metabolic diseases of the mother that affect the fetus should be coded from this chapter of ICD-9-CM. Perinatal conditions that are not detected until later in life should also be coded from this section. Age is not a factor when coding from this chapter. These codes can still be used if a problem or condition should appear later in life or if the condition is not diagnosed until later in life.

EXAMPLE: Tom Thomas is a 7-year-old who is diagnosed with Erb's palsy who is being seen in the Cerebral Palsy Clinic for a physical. There are no other abnormal findings. This encounter is coded using code 767.6.

When coding a condition that is identified at birth, codes from the V30–V39 categories are also assigned with codes from chapter 15 of ICD-9-CM. The V codes indicate that a birth occurred during the current episode of care. Remember that the codes from these categories are assigned only to the medical record of the newborn.

Official ICD-9-CM Coding Guideline:

When coding the birth of an infant, assign a code from categories V30–V39, according to the type of birth. A code from this series is assigned as a principal diagnosis, and assigned only once to a newborn at the time of birth. (See Appendix A, Section I, C15, b.)

EXAMPLE: Tammy Tiny was born premature at 27 weeks of gestation with a birth weight of 980 grams. At the time of discharge, the codes assigned are:

- V30.00, Single liveborn infant born in hospital without mention of cesarean delivery

- 765.03, Extreme immaturity

- 765.24, Weeks of gestation, 27 to 28 completed weeks of gestation

Note that the V code is sequenced first.

The V codes are used only if the perinatal condition is found during the episode of care in which the birth took place. If the newborn is discharged home and returns hours later with a problem that occurred during birth, the codes from the V30 series are *not* used. If the newborn is transferred to a facility other than the one in which the infant was born, the V codes are also not assigned.

EXAMPLE: Tammy Tiny, the infant from the previous example, was transferred from Hospital A to Hospital B because of the need to be in a neonatal intensive care nursery. At the time of discharge from Hospital B, the V code is not assigned. Codes assigned for this discharge are:

- 765.03, Extreme immaturity

- 765.24, Weeks of gestation, 27 to 28 completed weeks of gestation

If an infant is born outside a hospital and then later admitted because of a complication, the complication code is assigned as the principal diagnosis, and no code from the V30 to V39 series is assigned.

The ICD-9-CM Official Guidelines for Coding and Reporting also give coders instructions for the sequencing of perinatal codes, birth process or community acquired conditions, and the coding of clinically significant conditions.

Official ICD-9-CM Coding Guideline:

(2) *Sequencing of perinatal codes*

Generally, codes from chapter 15 should be sequenced as the principal/first-listed diagnosis on the newborn record, with the exception of the appropriate V30 code for the birth episode, followed by codes from any other chapter that provide additional detail. The "use additional code" note at the beginning of the chapter supports this guideline. If the index does not provide a specific code for a perinatal condition, assign code 779.89, Other specified conditions originating in the perinatal period, followed by the code from another chapter that specifies the condition. Codes for signs and symptoms may be assigned when a definitive diagnosis has not been established.

(3) *Birth process or community acquired conditions*

If a newborn has a condition that may be either due to the birth process or community acquired and the documentation does not indicate which, the default is due to the birth process and the code from chapter 15 should be used. If the condition is community acquired, a code from chapter 15 should not be assigned.

(4) *Code all clinically significant conditions*

All clinically significant conditions noted on routine newborn examination should be coded. A condition is clinically significant if it requires:

- *Clinical evaluation or*
- *Therapeutic treatment or*
- *Diagnostic procedures or*
- *Extended length of hospital stay or*
- *Increased nursing care and/or monitoring or*
- *Has implications for future health care needs*

Note: These perinatal guidelines are the same as the general coding guidelines for "additional diagnoses," except for the final point regarding implications for future health care needs. Codes should be assigned for conditions that have been specified by the provider as having implications for future health care needs. Codes from the perinatal chapter should not be assigned unless the provider has established a definitive diagnosis. (See Appendix A, Section I, C15, 2–4.)

Maternal Causes of Perinatal Morbidity and Mortality (Category Codes 760–763)

Codes from these categories are assigned only when the maternal condition has actually affected the fetus or newborn. The fact that the mother has an associated medical condition or experiences some complication of pregnancy, labor, or delivery does not justify the routine assignment of codes from these categories to the newborn record.

Such conditions as hypertension, renal disease, or respiratory infections, along with circulatory or urinary diseases, can affect the health or life of a newborn infant or a fetus. The conditions might have an immediate effect, or the effect may not be apparent until later in life.

Other conditions that are coded to these subsections of the chapter are noxious influences that affect the fetus or newborn. Noxious influences, or substances that are harmful to one's health, include such things as drug use and alcohol abuse. Drug or alcohol use during pregnancy can cause many birth defects and can cause the newborn to be born with a dependency. Once the umbilical cord is cut and the newborn goes without the alcohol or drugs that the baby has become dependent on, symptoms of withdrawal can occur. It should be noted here that just because the mother has a condition that *could* affect the fetus or newborn does not mean that the code is assigned. A code from these categories is assigned only if the mother's condition causes the morbidity or mortality in the fetus or newborn. Fetal alcohol syndrome occurs when a fetus has been exposed to alcohol prior to birth.

Disease Highlight—Fetal Alcohol Syndrome

Fetal alcohol syndrome (FAS) is a result of a woman's use or abuse of alcohol during pregnancy. Children may be developmentally delayed or in some cases mentally retarded, and they may have problems with their central nervous system.

Fetal alcohol syndrome is caused by the mother's intake of alcohol, which travels through her bloodsteam, across the placenta, and on to the fetus. The alcohol remains in the system of the fetus much longer than in the mother's due to the fact that there is a higher concentration of blood in the fetus and a slower metabolism.

Signs and Symptoms:

When the child is born, there may be:

- Facial malformations

- A delay in the development of gross and fine motor skills

- Slowed growth

- Mental retardation

- Deformities of joints, limbs, and fingers

Clinical Testing:

There is no formal way to diagnose FAS, but obtaining a complete clinical history of the pregnancy helps to confirm the diagnosis.

Treatment:

There is no cure for FAS; therefore, treatment consists of treating and managing the patient's existing symptoms and defects.

Official ICD-9-CM Coding Guideline:

Codes from categories 760–763, Maternal causes of perinatal morbidity and mortality, are assigned only when the maternal condition has actually affected the fetus or newborn. The fact that the mother has an associated medical condition or experiences some complication of pregnancy, labor, or delivery does not justify the routine assignment of codes from these categories to the newborn record. (See Appendix A, Section I, C15, f.)

EXAMPLE: Harry Heart was born on 12/20/XX, and during delivery the cord was around the infant's neck, causing anoxia. The codes to assign for this discharge are:

- V30.00, Single liveborn infant
- 762.5, Other compression of umbilical cord
- 768.9, Unspecified birth asphyxia in liveborn

Other Conditions Originating in the Perinatal Period (Category Code 764–779)

Categories 764–779 are used to classify other conditions that originate in the perinatal period.

Birth Weight and Newborn Maturity

Some of the conditions coded to these categories relate to size of a fetus. For categories 764 and 765, a fifth-digit classification is necessary to denote birth weight. The coder may see "light-for-dates" or "small for dates" in the diagnosis or in documentation review. These terms refer to underweight infants that show signs of fetal malnutrition.

A light-for-dates notation should not be confused with immature or premature birth. **Fetal immaturity** refers to a birth weight of less than 1,000 grams. A **preterm infant** is a newborn born before the completion of 40 weeks with a birth weight of 1,000 to 2,499 grams.

> ## Official ICD-9-CM Coding Guideline:
>
> *Providers utilize different criteria in determining prematurity. A code for prematurity should not be assigned unless it is documented. The fifth-digit assignment for codes from category 764 and subcategories 765.0 and 765.1 should be based on the recorded birth weight and estimated gestational age.*
>
> *A code from subcategory 765.2, Weeks of gestation, should be assigned as an additional code with category 764 and codes from 765.0 and 765.1 to specify weeks of gestation as documented by the provider in the record. (See Appendix A, Section I, C15, i.)*

Category 766 is used when the infant is exceptionally large or post-term or when prolonged gestation occurs. An exceptionally large baby or a baby who is **heavy-for-dates** has a birth weight of 4,500 grams or more regardless of gestation period. The post-term period is from 40 weeks through 42 completed weeks. Over 42 completed weeks is coded to prolonged gestation of infant, code 766.22.

Birth Trauma, Lack of Oxygen, and Insufficient Lung Development

Birth trauma, such as a fractured clavicle or injury to the spine, is coded to the 767 category. **Birth trauma** is said to occur when there is injury to the fetus during the delivery process. The cause of this trauma can be a result of breech presentation or even forceps delivery.

Category 768 contains codes for hypoxia and asphyxia. **Hypoxia** is a condition in which there are below-normal levels of oxygen in the cells. **Asphyxia** is a condition in which there is a lack of oxygen in the air that is inhaled, usually due to pathological changes. **Anoxia** is a complete lack of oxygen and is the most serious of these conditions. It is sometimes confused with hypoxia in the fetus or newborn. Careful attention to details in the documentation is necessary to note the difference for correct coding assignment. Any of these conditions can cause permanent damage to vital organs should the fetus or newborn survive them.

Because of insufficient lung development, the fetus or newborn can suffer from a variety of respiratory problems. Respiratory conditions tend to occur in premature infants because the lungs are the last vital organ to fully form before birth. Before 37 weeks' gestation, there is an increased danger of respiratory problems. Respiratory conditions of the fetus and newborn are coded to category 770.

Isoimmunization, Jaundice, and Meconium Obstruction

Blood typing the mother at the onset of pregnancy is done for several reasons; one of the most important is isoimmunization. Isoimmunization is the immunization or incompatability of the blood of an Rh-negative mother mixing with the Rh-positive blood of the fetus. If both the mother and fetus are Rh-positive, there is not an issue. An Rh-negative mother may have to go through a series of shots to avoid the possibility of complications such as pleural effusion, heart failure, and anemia in the fetus or newborn. ABO isoimmunization is another condition in which the mother with type O blood carries a fetus with blood type A or B. Hemolysis, or the destruction of red blood cells, of the fetal blood can occur when the antibodies from the mother cross the placenta into the fetus.

Jaundice, also known as hyperbilirubinemia or icterus, is a common condition in newborns. Bilirubin is the pigment in bile, which is produced from the destruction of hemoglobin and released by the liver. When excess bilirubin is released into the blood stream, jaundice occurs.

Coding issues that may be encountered with jaundice revolve around documentation. Laboratory results may indicate an elevated bilirubin; however, if there is no indication of treatment, then the elevated bilirubin should not be coded unless the provider confirms the diagnosis of jaundice and the treatment initiated. Code 773.1, Hemolytic disease due to ABO isoimmunization, should be reported when the documentation supports that the newborn has jaundice due to blood group incompatibility. Additional codes for jaundice are not necessary because jaundice is already included in the 773.1 code.

The remaining categories in this chapter deal with a variety of conditions found in the fetus or newborn. One such condition is meconium obstruction, which is classified to code 777.1, Meconium obstruction. Meconium is a tarlike material that collects in the intestine of the fetus and is usually the first stools of the newborn. When the newborn has no stools for the first 24 hours, abnormal distention meconium obstruction may be the cause. Documentation clarification is needed for a definitive diagnosis.

Internet Links

To learn more about conditions that arise in the perinatal period, go to the following Web sites: U.S. Department of Health and Human Services at *www.hhs.gov,* Combined Health Information Database at *http://chid.nih.gov/subfile/subfile.html,* Neonatal Resuscitation Program at *www.aap.org,* and U.S. Department of Health and Human Services at *www.hhs.gov.*

Summary

- The codes from chapter 15 of ICD-9-CM classify conditions that affect the fetus or newborn.

- These codes are used on the chart of the newborn *only* and *never* appear in the mother's medical record.

- To locate conditions for coding from this section, the coder references the condition or the main term *birth*.

- Congenital conditions that are not detected until later in life should be coded from this section.

- Codes from the V30–V39 categories are usually assigned first when a condition from this chapter is coded for a newborn.

- Conditions such as light-for-dates and heavy-for-dates are classified to chapter 15 of ICD-9-CM.

Chapter Review

True/False: Indicate whether each statement is true (T) or false (F).

1. _____ A child is born at 11:55 pm and discharged for home at 5 pm the next day. The child returns to the ER at 10 pm that evening with jaundice. Both the jaundice and the V30 code are coded to the child's chart.

2. _____ Codes from this chapter can be found in the record of either the mother or the newborn.

3. _____ Low birthweight may be referred to as fetal immaturity.

4. _____ Hemolysis occurs when the antibodies from the mother cross the placenta into the fetus.

5. _____ Jaundice is also known as isoimmunization.

Fill-in-the-Blank: Enter the appropriate term(s) to complete each statement.

6. The perinatal period extends from birth up to _____.

7. When a newborn has a condition coded from this chapter, a code from the _____ series is added to indicate that a birth has occurred.

8. Underweight infants who show signs of fetal malnutrition are sometimes referred to as
_____.

9. Anoxia is a complete lack of _____ to the fetus.

10. Injury to the fetus that occurs during the delivery process is known as _____.

Coding Assignments

Instructions: Using an ICD-9-CM coding book, select the code for each diagnostic statement.

Diagnosis	Code
1. Maternal hypertension affecting the fetus	_____
2. Fetal alcohol syndrome	_____
3. Acute hydramnios	_____
4. Post-term infant, 41 weeks	_____
5. Cocaine addiction in newborn	_____
6. Premature baby, birth weight of 1,900 grams	_____
7. Fetal malnutrition, 6 days old, 1,300 grams	_____
8. Meconium peritonitis	_____
9. Bilirubin encephalopathy	_____
10. Cold injury syndrome of newborn	_____
11. Light-for-dates newborn, 1,550 grams	_____
12. Neonatal thyrotoxicosis	_____

13. CNS dysfunction in newborn _____

14. Polycythemia neonatorum _____

15. Neonatal tachycardia _____

16. Stillbirth _____

17. Mild birth asphyxia _____

18. Pulmonary hemorrhage _____

19. Bronchopulmonary dysplasia _____

20. Neonatal moniliasis _____

21. Polyhydramnios _____

22. Placenta previa affecting the fetus _____

23. Abnormality in fetal heart rate before the onset of labor _____

24. Moderate birth asphyxia _____

25. Injury to brachial plexus _____

Case Studies

Instructions: Review each case study, and select the correct ICD-9-CM diagnostic code.

CASE 1

Inpatient Physician's Progress Note

12/20/XX Two-day-old infant examined today to follow up after the results of diagnostic tests.

BLOOD GAS: Study indicates reduced oxygen tension and ineffective gas exchange.

CHEST X-RAY: Presence of infiltrate

Infant continues to exhibit signs of infant respiratory distress syndrome.

ORDERS: Continue titrated oxygen and aerosol infusion of Survanta.

ICD-9-CM Code Assignment: _____

CASE 2

Inpatient Physician's Progress Note

2/3/XX Five-hour-old neonate is jaundiced, and delivering physician has just determined that the child is Rh-positive and mother is Rh-negative. The mother just moved to the area, and it cannot be determined from history whether the mother had screening for Rh incompatibility prior to delivery.

EXAM:

ABDOMEN: Liver and spleen are enlarged.

CHEST: Lungs are clear.

PLAN: Phototherapy and albumin infusion standard protocol as per written orders.

IMPRESSION: Hemolytic disease of the newborn due to Rh isoimmunization.

ICD-9-CM Code Assignment: _____

CASE 3

Discharge Summary

The patient was discharged in stable condition on 1/20/XX. She is to continue on breast milk and can be supplemented with Similac with iron.

This patient is the product of a full-term gestation. The Apgars were 9 and 10. Birth weight was 6 pounds 10 ounces. Physical examination shortly after birth was negative. The infant's temperature was elevated, and urinalysis revealed a urinary tract infection due to *Staphylococcus aureus*. The plan was to observe the patient. Antibiotic therapy was started.

She had no difficulty nursing and ate well while she was in the hospital. She had no problems with her bowel movements. On the day of discharge, the patient's weight was down 3 ounces from birth. She will be seen in my office in 7 days.

ICD-9-CM Code Assignment: _____

CASE 4

Hospital Visit Note

The patient is a female, born 36 hours ago and now experiencing convulsions. Product of normal delivery with birth weight of 7 pounds 2 ounces. Her vital signs are normal at this time. The nursing staff contacted this physician immediately upon noting the convulsions, which they said lasted several seconds. An EEG and ECG have been ordered, along with a complete blood workup. The baby will be monitored closely until all test results are back.

ICD-9-CM Code Assignment: _____

CASE 5

Hospital Visit Note

The patient is a newborn infant male, born 2 hours ago to a mother who was experiencing severe hypertension prior to her pregnancy. The mother was being monitored closely for this condition during her current pregnancy because she had difficulty during her last one. It appears now that this baby boy is experiencing some respiratory distress due to the maternal hypertension. Pulse ox reading was 70, and his respirations were elevated. His vital signs at this time are all within normal limits since we started the oxygen. His pulse ox reading is now at 98. He will be monitored until such time as there is no need for the oxygen and his vital signs remain normal.

ICD-9-CM Code Assignment: _____

Symptoms, Signs, and Ill-Defined Conditions

Chapter Outline

Coding of Symptoms, Signs, and Ill-Defined
  Conditions
Coding Guidelines for Symptoms, Signs,
  and Ill-Defined Conditions

Summary
Chapter Review
Coding Assignments
Case Studies

Objectives

At the conclusion of this chapter, the student will be able to:

1. Identify terms used in locating codes for symptoms, signs, and ill-defined conditions found in chapter 16 of ICD-9-CM.
2. Explain terms found in documentation that would lead a coder to chapter 16 of ICD-9-CM.
3. Describe and understand the conditions classified to chapter 16 of ICD-9-CM.
4. Discuss the specific coding guidelines that relate to signs, symptoms, and ill-defined conditions.
5. Select and code signs, symptoms, and ill-defined conditions from case studies.

Key Terms

Altered States of
  Consciousness

Coma
Morbidity

Mortality
Sign

Symptom

Reminder

As you work through this chapter, you will need to have a copy of the ICD-9-CM coding book to reference.

Introduction

Chapter 16 of ICD-9-CM, "Symptoms, Signs, and Ill-Defined Conditions," classifies the abnormal results of laboratory or other investigative procedures and signs, symptoms, and ill-defined conditions for which no diagnoses are classified elsewhere in the ICD-9-CM. The codes for symptoms that affect only one body system are classified to the relevant chapter of ICD-9-CM, whereas symptoms that affect multiple systems or more than one disease are found in chapter 16.

Coding of Symptoms, Signs, and Ill-Defined Conditions

Chapter 16 of ICD-9-CM contains codes for signs, symptoms, and ill-defined conditions that affect medical care and management of the patient. A symptom is reported by the patient and typically is what brings the patient to seek medical attention. A symptom is considered subjective information because it can be evaluated or measured only by the patient. A sign is observed by the physician and is objective evidence of a disease. It can be measured or evaluated.

EXAMPLE: Marie Merry presents with itching and burning of the right forearm. Upon examination, a patch of small blisters is noticed.

In this example, the itching and burning is considered a symptom because it can be described and evaluated only by the patient. The blisters are a sign because they can be observed and evaluated by the physician.

Ill-defined conditions also code to this chapter but should never be used if a more definitive diagnosis has been made. These codes are used when there is absolutely no diagnosis found in the medical information available. Until a specific diagnosis is assigned, the signs and symptoms are coded. When a definitive diagnosis is made, codes from this chapter do not apply.

EXAMPLE: Mrs. Marble presents today with her 3-week-old infant daughter, who is not eating well and is quite fussy. She cries after she has had her bottle, sometimes to the point that she vomits. She has been like this over the last several days, and now Mrs. Marble would like her to be examined.

Examination revealed nothing out of the ordinary. This is a normal, 3-week-old infant girl. Heart and lungs are clear; bowel sounds are active and normal. Abdomen is soft with no spleenomegaly.

Diagnosis: Fussy infant

Plan: Will contact the pediatric GI office and set up a consult with possible workup.

The diagnosis in this example is 780.91, Fussy infant (baby), because a definitive diagnosis is not made. If a definitive diagnosis is made by the pediatric gastroenterologist (GI), then the diagnosis is *not* 780.91 but changes to the diagnosis given by that doctor.

Before selecting codes from this chapter, coders should be familiar with the notations that appear in the Tabular List after the chapter heading. The notations explain the purpose and use of chapter 16 of ICD-9-CM. The following is an excerpt from the notation that explains the codes found in this chapter of ICD-9-CM:

The conditions and signs or symptoms included in categories 780-796 consist of:

a. Cases for which no more specific diagnosis can be made even after all facts bearing on the case have been investigated.

b. Signs or symptoms existing at the time of initial encounter that proved to be transient and whose causes could not be determined.

c. Provisional diagnoses in a patient who failed to return for further investigation or care.

d. Cases referred elsewhere for investigation or treatment before the diagnosis was made.

e. Cases in which a more precise diagnosis was not available for any other reason.

f. Certain symptoms which represent important problems in medical care and which it might be desired to classify in addition to a known cause.

It is common that codes from chapter 16 are used for coding outpatient encounters, because patients seek care for relief of symptoms and results of diagnostic workups are not always available at the time of the encounter. The codes from chapter 16 are used to describe the reason for the encounter.

Coding Guidelines for Symptoms, Signs, and Ill-Defined Conditions

The ICD-9-CM Official Guidelines for Coding and Reporting provides the coder with guidance as to when to use codes from chapter 16. These guidelines at times are different for inpatient and outpatient encounters; however, some of the guidelines apply to both the inpatient and the outpatient settings. The first guideline that applies to coding symptoms and signs appears in Section I, B6 of the ICD-9-CM Official Guidelines for Coding and Reporting and reads as follows:

Official ICD-9-CM Coding Guideline:

Signs and Symptoms

Codes that describe symptoms and signs, as opposed to diagnoses, are acceptable for reporting purposes when a related definitive diagnosis has not been established (confirmed by the physician). Chapter 16 of ICD-9-CM, Symptoms, Signs, and Ill-Defined Conditions (codes 780.0–799.9) contain many but not all codes for symptoms. (See Appendix A, Section I, B, 6.)

Guideline for Principal Diagnosis

An additional guideline in Section II, A of the ICD-9-CM Official Guidelines for Coding and Reporting states the following, which applies to the selection of a principal diagnosis(es) for inpatient, short-term, acute care, and long-term care records.

Official ICD-9-CM Coding Guideline:

Codes for symptoms, signs, and ill-defined conditions from Chapter 16 are not to be used as a principal diagnosis when a related definitive diagnosis has been established. (See Appendix A, section II, A.)

This guideline instructs the coder to report a definitive diagnosis when it is established and not use a code from chapter 16. If a definitive diagnosis is not established, then a code from chapter 16 can be used. In an inpatient setting, symptom codes are not sequenced as a principal diagnosis when a related condition has been confirmed unless the patient was admitted for the purpose of treating the symptom and no care, treatment, or evaluation of the underlying disease occurred. For example, if a patient was admitted with intractable renal colic known to be caused by kidney stones and only pain management occurred, the code for renal colic, 788.0, is used. Therefore, the symptom can be coded as a principal diagnosis if the patient is being treated for only the symptom and not for the underlying condition. The coder should always go back to the reason for the encounter if there is any question as to sequencing.

Guideline for Symptoms Followed by Contrasting or Comparative Diagnoses

The following guideline applies to the selection of a principal diagnosis for inpatient, short-term, acute care, and long-term care hospitals.

> **Official ICD-9-CM Coding Guideline:**
>
> *When a symptom(s) is followed by contrasting/comparative diagnoses, the symptom code is sequenced first. All the contrasting/comparative diagnoses should be coded as additional diagnoses. (See Appendix A, Section II, E.)*

For example, if a patient is experiencing right lower abdominal pain and the physician records the statement "abdominal pain due to appendicitis versus renal colic," all the contrasting or comparative diagnoses are coded as additional codes, with the symptom code listed first. This guideline applies only to the selection of principal diagnoses and not to the reporting of secondary diagnosis. If the physician listed the same statement as a secondary diagnosis, only the abdominal pain is reported.

Symptoms and Signs as Secondary Codes

The ICD-9-CM Official Guidelines for Coding and Reporting state the following in relation to reporting signs and symptoms as additional diagnosis. This guideline applies to both inpatient and outpatient settings.

> **Official ICD-9-CM Coding Guideline:**
>
> *Conditions that are an integral part of a disease process*
>
> *Signs and symptoms that are associated routinely with a disease process should not be assigned as additional codes unless otherwise instructed by the classification. (See Appendix A, Section I, B, 7.)*

It is important for the coder to have clear medical documentation, as well as reference materials available, in order to properly code patient admissions and encounters in which signs and symptoms are described in addition to disease processes. The coder must be able to identify the signs and symptoms that are implicit in a diagnostic statement, because these signs and symptoms are not coded. For example, if a patient presents with abdominal pain and it is determined that the patient has gastroenteritis, the abdominal pain is not coded because the abdominal pain is an integral part of the disease.

However, when a patient presents with signs and symptoms that are not routinely associated with a disease, the following coding guideline applies:

> **Official ICD-9-CM Coding Guideline:**
>
> *Conditions that are not an integral part of a disease process*
>
> *Additional signs and symptoms that may not be associated routinely with a disease process should be coded when present. (See Appendix A, Section I, B, 8.)*

Difference in Inpatient and Outpatient Coding Guideline

When coding for inpatient hospital visits, suspected, rule-out, and possible diagnoses can be coded. When coding for outpatient or office visits, the suspected, rule-out, and possible diagnoses cannot be coded. Therefore, often in the outpatient settings, codes from chapter 16 of ICD-9-CM are used until a physician can establish a definitive diagnosis. The following guideline applies to outpatient settings and is found in section IV of the ICD-9-CM Official Guidelines for Coding and Reporting.

Official ICD-9-CM Coding Guideline:

Do not code diagnoses documented as "probable," "suspected," "questionable," "rule out," or "working diagnosis" or other similar terms indicating uncertainty. Rather, code the conditions(s) to the highest degree of certainty for that encounter/visit, such as symptoms, signs, abnormal test results, or other reason for the visit. Please note: This differs from the coding practices used by short-term, acute care, long-term care, and psychiatric hospitals. (See Appendix A, Section IV, I.)

EXAMPLE: Patty Patient presents to the ER with acute rebound tenderness in the abdomen and a fever of 99. The ER doctor orders a lab workup to be done to rule out appendicitis.

Diagnosis on lab order: Rebound tenderness, fever, possible appendicitis.

The coding is going to hinge on the fact that this patient is being seen in the emergency room and is therefore still considered an outpatient. The diagnosis of "possible appendicitis" cannot be coded. In the outpatient setting, the symptoms of rebound tenderness, 789.60, and fever, 780.60, are coded because these are the reasons the patient presented to the emergency room in the first place.

Symptoms (Category Codes 780–789)

Category codes 780–789 classify multiple symptoms that include altered states of consciousness and coma, category code 780.0X. A coma is a condition in which the person is in a deep state of unconsciousness. There is usually no spontaneous eye movement or response to painful stimuli. In altered states of consciousness, such as transient alteration of awareness, the patient does not lose consciousness completely but may stare or have an altered loss of awareness.

Also coded to this section of codes is syncope. Syncope is a condition in which there is a brief loss of consciousness due to a lack of oxygen to the brain. This is also known as fainting. When no specific disease process is identified as causing the condition, syncope in any form is coded to 780.2.

Symptoms involving the cardiovascular system, the respiratory system, the digestive system, and the urinary system are coded to this chapter unless there is a definitive diagnosis that encompasses the symptoms involved.

Nonspecific Abnormal Findings (Category Codes 790–796)

Coding for conditions that are classified as abnormal findings without a definitive diagnosis is classified to category codes 790–796, Nonspecific abnormal findings. Such conditions can be located in the Alphabetic Index under terms such as "Findings, abnormal, without diagnosis," "Elevation," and "Abnormal, abnormality, abnormalities." If the documentation infers but does not specifically state a diagnosis, clarification needs to be sought from the provider; then an addendum is added to the documentation if the physician clarifies previous documentation.

A problem that is frequently encountered by a primary care office is a patient who presents with elevated blood pressure but has no history of elevated blood pressure or hypertension. There is nothing in the history or examination to indicate that this is a chronic condition. The code of 796.2, Elevated blood pressure, is assigned in this case. If this same patient presents to the office with elevated blood pressure, has a documented history of benign hypertension, and is on medication to control the blood pressure, it is correct to assign the 401.1, Benign hypertension code.

Before category codes 790–796 are assigned, clarify with the provider that a definitive diagnosis has not been established.

Ill-Defined and Unknown Causes of Morbidity and Mortality (Category Codes 797–799)

Morbidity refers to a diseased state, mortality to death. Conditions such as sudden infant death syndrome (SIDS) and unattended deaths are coded to this section of the chapter. Before assigning these codes, the coder needs to review all medical documentation available to ensure that a more definitive diagnosis has not been determined. If a definitive diagnosis is given, the definitive diagnosis is coded and category codes 797–799 are not used. As always, coders must review all medical documentation that is present at the time of the patient encounter to ensure coding accuracy.

Summary

- Chapter 16 of ICD-9-CM, "Symptoms, Signs and Ill-Defined Conditions," contains codes for symptoms and signs that affect medical care and management of the patient.
- Abnormal findings and ill-defined conditions are also coded to chapter 16 of ICD-9-CM.
- Codes from this chapter should not be used if a more definitive diagnosis is available.
- Until a specific diagnosis is assigned, the signs and symptoms are coded instead.
- Symptoms are not usually sequenced as a principal diagnosis when a related condition has been confirmed.
- Suspected, rule-out, and possible diagnoses cannot be coded in an outpatient setting.

Chapter Review

True/False: Indicate whether the statement is true (T) or false (F).

1. _____ A symptom is objective and a sign is subjective.

2. _____ Diagnosis codes from chapter 16 of ICD-9-CM are not used if a definitive diagnosis is given.

3. _____ In an outpatient setting, rule-out diagnoses can be coded.

4. _____ Symptoms involving the respiratory and digestive systems are coded to the 780–789 categories of codes.

5. _____ When a patient does not completely lose consciousness, it is a form of syncope.

Fill-in-the-Blank: Enter the appropriate term(s) to complete each statement.

6. Until a specific diagnosis is assigned, the _____ and _____ are coded instead.

7. Another term for fainting is _____.

8. A _____ is a condition in which the person is in a deep state of unconsciousness.

9. The term _____ refers to death.

10. An acronym for sudden infant death syndrome is _____.

Coding Assignments

Instructions: Using an ICD-9-CM coding book, select the appropriate code for each diagnostic statement.

Diagnosis	Code
1. Shortness of breath	
2. Hemoptysis	
3. Syncope	
4. Chyluria	
5. Unattended death	
6. Pyrexial seizure	
7. Orthopnea	
8. SIDS	
9. Male stress incontinence	
10. Nervousness	
11. Abnormal glucose tolerance test	
12. Hyperventilation	
13. Tachycardia	
14. Nosebleed	
15. Abnormal thyroid uptake	
16. Palpitations	
17. Symbolic dysfunction	
18. Slow urinary stream	
19. Diarrhea	
20. Dysphagia	
21. Elevated PSA	
22. Abnormal findings in amniotic fluid	
23. Flushing	
24. Parageusia	
25. Aphonia	

Case Studies

Instructions: Review each case study, and select the correct ICD-9-CM diagnostic code.

CASE 1

Physician's Office Visit

CHIEF COMPLIANT: Patient fell walking up her steps last night. She states she twisted her right ankle and applied ice on it in the evening. This morning she noticed increased swelling, and the pain has increased. She states that she is also having a severe headache since the fall.

PHYSICAL EXAMINATION:

HEENT: Normal

CHEST: Normal

On examination, the ankle is tender and swollen and has very limited motion. The patient is not able to bear weight on the ankle.

The patient was instructed to go to the hospital radiology department as I suspect a fracture. Pending results, will be referred to an orthopedic surgeon if necessary.

Tylenol 3 was ordered for her headache. Patient will be contacted following results of X-ray.

ICD-9-CM Code Assignment: _____

CASE 2

Emergency Room Visit—Physician's Note

S: This 75-year-old patient was shoveling snow when he became short of breath. His wife insisted that he come to the emergency room to be evaluated. He states that he has had no other symptoms.

O: HEENT: Normal

CHEST: Normal heart rate, no significant findings; EKG normal

LUNGS: Clear, no congestion

ABDOMEN: Soft, nontender; no organ enlargement

LABS: All returned normal.

A: Shortness of breath, ruled out MI.

P: Instructed patient to see his primary care provider for full physical examination.

ICD-9-CM Code Assignment: _____

CASE 3

Physician's Office Note

The patient is a 72-year-old male who presents today with complaints of abdominal discomfort, some shortness of breath, and pain "in my gut." The patient denied any recent injury or trauma to the abdomen. He says he feels fine otherwise. Social history is positive for alcohol x 6 per day, and cigarette smoking x 1 pack per day.

Examination reveals an obese Caucasian male who has a distended abdomen. No palpable masses in the abdomen.

SKIN: Skin color is normal; no bruises or discoloration

HEENT: No significant findings

HEART: Normal rate and rhythm

Lab results reveal WBC count to be at 400 cells/milliliter.

The diagnosis at this time is generalized ascites. The patient has been counseled on limiting sodium intake and is now taking Aldactone.

ICD-9-CM Code Assignment: _____

CASE 4

Physician's Office Visit

Marcus is an 8-year-old male who presented yesterday to the nurse's office at school with a nosebleed that occurred on the playground after Marcus and another student collided on the swing set. Other than the nosebleed, he was fine and able to go back to class.

Today Marcus presents to this office with another nosebleed after he fell out of his bed while wrestling with his brother. His mother is concerned because of the two incidents happening so close together and because she had a bit of difficulty getting this nosebleed to stop.

On examination, Marcus is a normal, healthy, 8-year-old male in NAD with evidence of a recent nosebleed. At this time, there is a slight trickle of blood coming from the right nare. Internal exam reveals no serious problems. Marcus does not complain of a headache, blurred vision, or any other pain in the head and neck. We packed the nostril and told the mother to return if any further bleeding occurs. Diagnosis for today's visit is nosebleed. We will continue to follow him to rule out possible chronic blood disorders.

ICD-9-CM Code Assignment: _____

CASE 5

Physician's Clinic Note

Mrs. Black presents today with complaints of "feeling tired" all the time. Upon questioning, she notes that for the most part her routine has not changed very much. She is a 56-year-old female who has 2 grown children who do not live with her. Her husband is 57 years old and semiretired. She said that her husband helps her around the house and also that she helps him around the yard. When asked if she is sleeping all right, she said she is getting up once or twice a night but falls right back to sleep. At this time, I advised Mrs. Black that maybe she should try to get a good walk in during the day and also watch her diet. If the malaise and fatigue don't subside or do not improve over the next two months with these changes, we will do further testing. Labs were drawn today to look at levels.

EXAM:

HEENT: Normal

ABDOMEN: Nondistended, no masses

HEART: RRR

EXTREMITIES: Normal

Oriented to time, person, and place

No significant physical findings noted.

ICD-9-CM Code Assignment: _____

22 Injury and Poisoning

Chapter Outline

Introduction

Coding Guidelines

Summary

Chapter Review

Coding Assignments

Case Studies

Objectives

At the conclusion of this chapter, the student will be able to:

1. Identify when to assign combination codes for injuries.

2. Explain the various types of fractures.

3. Differentiate among abrasions, contusions, and superficial and complex injuries.

4. Describe the types of open wounds.

5. Discuss the specific coding guidelines that relate to injuries and poisoning.

6. Select and code diagnoses from case studies.

Key Terms

Adverse Effect

Anterior

Avulsion

Burn

Closed Fracture

Complete Fracture

Complicated Fracture

Compound Fracture

Concussion

Dislocation

Fracture (Fx)

Lateral

Luxation

Medial

Open Fracture

Paralysis

Poisoning

Postconcussion
  Syndrome

Posterior

Reduction

Simple Fracture

Sprain

Strain

Subluxation

Vault of the Skull

Vertebral Column

Reminder

As you work through this chapter, you will need to have a copy of the ICD-9-CM coding book to reference.

Introduction

This chapter is quite different from the chapters encountered to this point. This chapter is not confined to one part of the body or to one body system. It is an eclectic collection of injuries that can occur on almost any area of the body. The injuries range from fractures and crush injuries to burns, spinal cord injuries, and late effects of injuries.

Injuries are coded according to the type of injury first and then the location of the injury. It is imperative to use the Tabular List in conjunction with the Alphabetic Index because the Include: and Exclude: notes are used extensively. Correct code assignments cannot be made if the notes are not followed and if documentation is not clear.

Coding Guidelines

The ICD-9-CM Official Guidelines for Coding and Reporting provides many guidelines for the coding of injuries and poisoning. Because more than one injury can occur at the same time, the official guidelines state the following:

Official ICD-9-CM Coding Guideline:

When coding injuries, assign a separate code for each injury unless a combination code is provided, in which case the combination code is assigned. Multiple injury codes are provided in ICD-9-CM but should not be assigned unless information for a more specific code is not available. These codes are not to be used for normal, healing surgical wounds or to identify complications of surgical wounds.

The code for the most serious injury, as determined by the provider, is sequenced first.

1. Superficial injuries

Superficial injuries such as abrasions or contusions are not coded when associated with more severe injuries of the same site.

2. Primary injury with damage to nerves/blood vessels

When a primary injury results in minor damage to peripheral nerves or blood vessels, the primary injury is sequenced first with additional code(s) from categories 950–957, Injury to nerves and spinal cord, and/or 900–904, Injury to blood vessels. When the primary injury is to the blood vessels or nerves, that injury should be sequenced first. (See Appendix A, Section I, C17, a.)

Fractures (Category Codes 800–829)

Official ICD-9-CM Coding Guideline:

Coding of traumatic fractures

The principles of multiple coding of injuries should be followed in coding fractures. Fractures of specified sites are coded individually by site in accordance with both the provisions within categories 800–829 and the level of detail furnished by medical record content. Combination categories for multiple fractures are provided for use when there is insufficient detail in the medical record (such as trauma cases transferred to another hospital), when the reporting form limits the number of codes that can be used in reporting pertinent clinical data, or when there is insufficient specificity at the fourth-digit level or fifth-digit level. (See Appendix A, Section I, C17, b.)

Terminology is very important when coding fractures. Fractures, sometimes seen in a provider note as Fx, are broken bones resulting from undue force or pathological changes. Malunions (code 733.81) or nonunions (code 733.82) are not found in this chapter. These types of fractures were described in Chapter 18 of this textbook as part of the chapter "Diseases of the Musculoskeletal System and Connective Tissue."

Knowledge of whether the fracture is open or closed is the starting point for coding fractures. An open fracture, also known as a compound fracture, is a fracture that has broken through the skin at the fracture site. The bone may or may not be protuding through the skin, but there is always an open wound associated with this type of fracture. Because the tissues are exposed, there is a high risk for infection in these types of fractures. Surgery is almost always required. Foreign bodies or "missiles" may need to be removed during surgery from the tissues.

A closed fracture is a type of fracture in which the bone is broken but the skin has not been broken. This type of fracture is also known as a complete or simple fracture. The note box at the beginning of the Alphabetic Index identifies terms that may be encountered as either open or closed.

A quick reference has been provided here for closed fractures, but it is not comprehensive. Should the coder encounter a term that is not listed here, clarification from the provider may be necessary. It is important to note that if the fracture is not specified as open or closed and the coder cannot get any further information from the provider, then it is coded as closed.

Type of Closed Fracture	Definition
Comminuted	Bone is crushed, may be splintered.
Compression	Bone is pressed on itself.
Depressed	Relating to skull, bone is broken but pushed inward.
Fissured	Bone has a narrow split that does not go through to the other side.
Greenstick	As with a greenstick of a tree, the bone bends as well as breaks.
Impacted	One end of the broken bone is wedged into the other bone.
Spiral	Severe twisting motion causes bone to twist apart.
Stress	Excessive impact on bone causes small hairline crack in the bone.

Figure 22-1 illustrates types and patterns of fractures.

If an internal organ has been injured as a direct result of the fracture, it is called a complicated fracture. The injury can be a result of the bone itself causing the injury or just a fragment of the bone causing the injury.

The categories in this section of the chapter begin with the skull and work down the body to the bones of the toes. The fourth and fifth digits offer more specific coding and are necessary when coding in these categories. Fourth digits refer to whether the fracture is open or closed, and the fifth digit usually identifies a specific site within the category.

Coders should also be guided by the following guidelines:

Official ICD-9-CM Coding Guideline:

(1) Acute Fractures Versus Aftercare

Traumatic fractures are coded using the acute fracture codes (800–829) while the patient is receiving active treatment for the fracture. Examples of active treatment are surgical treatment, emergency department encounter, and evaluation and treatment by a new physician.

Fractures are coded using the aftercare codes (subcategories V54.0, V54.1, V54.8, or V54.9) for encounters after the patient has completed active treatment of the fracture and is receiving routine care for the fracture during the healing or recovery phase. Examples of fracture aftercare are cast change or removal, removal of external or internal fixation device, medication adjustment, and follow-up visits following fracture treatment.

Care for complications of surgical treatment for fracture repairs during the healing or recovery phase should be coded with the appropriate complication codes.

Care of complications of fractures, such as malunion and nonunion, should be reported with the appropriate codes.

Pathologic fractures are not coded in the 800–829 range but instead are assigned to subcategory 733.1. See Section I.C.13.a for additional information.

(2) *Multiple fractures of same limb*

Multiple fractures of the same limb classifiable to the same three-digit or four-digit category are coded to that category.

(3) *Multiple unilateral or bilateral fractures of same bone*

Multiple unilateral or bilateral fractures of the same bone(s) but classified to different fourth-digit subdivisions (bone part) within the same three-digit category are coded individually by site.

(4) *Multiple fracture categories 819 and 828*

Multiple fracture categories 819 and 828 classify bilateral fractures of both upper limbs (819) and both lower limbs (828), but without any detail at the fourth-digit level other than open and closed type of fractures.

(5) *Multiple fractures sequencing*

Multiple fractures are sequenced in accordance with the severity of the fracture. The provider should be asked to list the fracture diagnoses in the order of severity. (See Appendix A, Section C17, b, 1–5.)

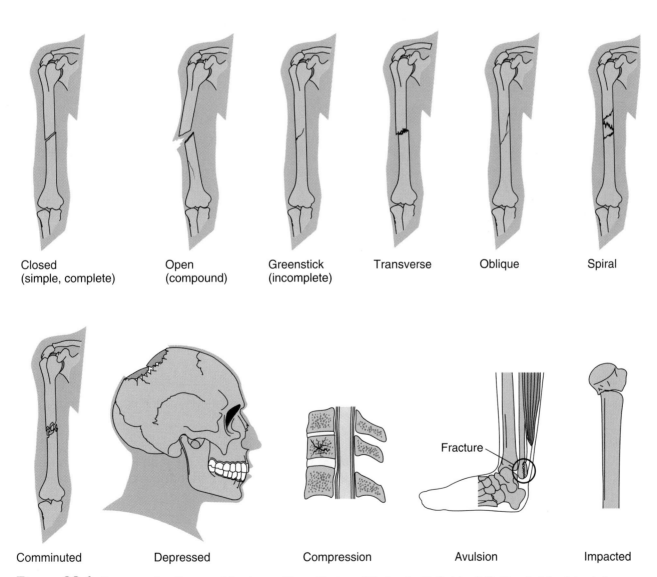

| Closed (simple, complete) | Open (compound) | Greenstick (incomplete) | Transverse | Oblique | Spiral |

| Comminuted | Depressed | Compression | Avulsion | Impacted |

Figure 22-1 Types and patterns of fractures (From Hegner BR, Acello B, Caldwell E. *Nursing Assistant: A Nursing Process Approach,* 9th ed. Clifton Park, NY: Delmar, Cengage Learning, 2004, p. 644.)

Should the coder encounter a diagnosis that indicates both open and closed fractures, the open fracture is coded because this takes priority over the closed fracture.

As stated earlier, the categories in this section of the chapter begin at the top of the head with the 800 category, Fracture of vault of skull. The vault of the skull is made up of three bones: the two parietal bones and the frontal bone. The chapter moves on to different types of fractures of the head and face. The next section deals with fractures of the neck and trunk. Some knowledge of anatomy is necessary to maneuver around these sections when coding. The vertebral column, which shields the spinal column, is made up of cervical, thoracic, and lumbar vertebra. To properly code an injury to the spinal column or a vertebra, location of the injury is necessary. An injury to this area of the body can cause paralysis. Paralysis is the loss of sensation or voluntary motion. This loss may be permanent or temporary, depending on the type and site of the injury.

Fractures of the spinal column move into fractures of the ribs, sternum, larynx, and trachea. Coding for rib fractures should be meticulous and should capture all the ribs affected. It is important to code as specifically as possible because, in this case, reimbursement can be affected if all information is not relayed.

Fracture of the pelvis completes the coding of the trunk. The next categories code fractures of the extremities, beginning with the upper limbs and including the clavicle and the scapula.

Codes 820–829, Fracture of lower limb, conclude the fracture categories of this chapter. As in any coding of fractures, attention to location and type of fracture is important and affects the proper code assignment. Should a fracture be bilateral, it is coded twice to reflect this. This is sometimes seen in motor vehicle accidents.

Dislocation (Category Codes 830–839)

The term *dislocation* means that a body part has moved out of place, in this case a bone. The bone has moved or displaced completely from where it should be. A synonymous term for dislocation is luxation. In cases in which a partial dislocation, or subluxation, has occurred, only part of the joint surface has moved away from where it should be.

Like fractures, dislocations can be open or closed. An open dislocation is prone to infection, and a reduction is the usual procedure needed to put the joint back into place whether the dislocation is open or closed.

Coding of dislocations requires knowledge of whether the dislocation is open or closed, as well as the location of the displaced bone in relation to where its proper placement should be within the joint. The terms to look for in provider documentation are "anterior," "posterior," "lateral," and "medial."

Anterior means in front of or forward of. Posterior is the opposite of anterior and means in back of or behind. Medial is closest or nearest to the midline of a structure. Lateral means away from midline toward the side.

Dislocations can be very serious when major joints are involved, specifically the shoulders, knees, and hips. Vascular complications can occur with these types of dislocations, which can have long-lasting or even permanent adverse affects.

When a dislocation occurs with a fracture, the dislocation is included in the code for the fracture and is not coded separately. This category of codes is used when no fracture is present. As with fractures, dislocations are coded as closed unless the provider has specifically stated that the dislocation was open.

Sprains and Strains of Joints and Adjacent Muscles (Category Codes 840–848)

Sometimes the terms *sprain* and *strain* are used interchangeably. They are not the same, and clarification needs to be made if there is any question as to which condition the patient has.

A sprain is an injury to a joint, specifically the ligament of the joint, which becomes stretched. A strain is not an injury at the joint site but to the muscle or to the tendon attachment. In provider documentation, the coder may note that the severity of sprain or strain has been graded or typed, with type I as the least severe through type III as the most severe. When there are more than one of these types of injuries, the typing of sprains and strains is helpful in determining which site to code first. Commonly RICE therapy (rest, ice, compression, and elevation) is used to treat strains and sprains. These are the measures that a patient commonly takes to treat the strain or sprain.

EXAMPLE: Patient presents after an MVA (motor vehicle accident) in which the car was rear-ended and pushed forward into a telephone pole. Because the patient was not wearing a seatbelt, whiplash has occurred, as well as a type II strain of the wrist from bracing for impact along with a type III sprain of the ankle as the patient was worked free by EMTs. The neck and back were stabilized before transport. According to the EMT at the scene, the patient was in a great deal of pain: at the scene, 10+ on the pain scale. Now in the ER, pain is probably at a 9+ without movement.

Whiplash is coded first because it is the main focus of treatment and probably the more severe injury. The term *whiplash* is looked at in the Alphabetic Index, which sends us to 847.0 in the Tabular List and that gives us 847.0, Neck sprain and strain. We then code the type III ankle sprain, because this is the next severe injury. Look up *sprain* then *ankle;* reference is to 845.00, Unspecified site of ankle sprain and strain, in the Tabular List. The last thing coded is the type II strain of the wrist. In the Alphabetic Index under the main term *strain,* the term *wrist* is not found, but there is a See also note: see also sprain, by site. The coder would then go to the term sprain and find wrist and code 842.00, Sprain and strain of unspecified site of wrist.

Exercise 22–1   Category Codes 800–839

Instructions: Indicate whether each statement is true (T) or false (F).

1. _____ Injuries are coded according to location first, then type of injury.

2. _____ Sprains and strains are not the same type of injury.

3. _____ When coding fractures, attention to the type of fracture and the location is important.

4. _____ To properly code fractures, the coder needs to know whether the fracture is dislocated or not.

5. _____ The vertebral column shields the spinal column and the back.

Fill-in-the-Blank: Enter the appropriate term(s) to complete each statement.

6. "Fx" in a provider note refers to a _____.

7. A _____ is an injury to a ligament, whereas a _____ is an injury to a muscle.

8. Comminuted is a type of _____ fracture.

9. A synonymous term for luxation is _____.

10. A _____ fracture occurs when bones are pressed together.

Instructions: Using an ICD-9-CM coding book, select the code for each diagnostic statement.

Diagnosis	Code
11. Comminuted ankle fracture	_____
12. Extracapsular fracture of the femur	_____
13. Sprain of the sternoclavicular joint	_____
14. Broken leg, lower end, three places	_____
15. Closed dislocation of the seventh cervical vertebra	_____
16. Open fracture, sternum	_____
17. Open posterior dislocation of tibia, proximal end	_____
18. Closed fracture and dislocation of the lateral malleolus	_____
19. Open dislocation of the carpometacarpal joint	_____
20. Closed fracture of femoral condyle	_____

Intracranial Injury, Excluding Those with Skull Fracture (Category Codes 850–854)

These categories classify intracranial injury, such as concussions. A concussion is a violent shaking or jarring of the brain. The main axis for coding concussions hinges on whether the patient lost consciousness and, if so, to what degree. The provider documentation needs to indicate whether there was brief, moderate, or prolonged loss of consciousness, as well as whether the patient regained consciousness. Codes from the 850 category are used if the concussion is still in the current stage, usually within 24 to 48 hours of the injury. If the diagnosis is postconcussion syndrome, code 310.2 is used instead. Postconcussion syndrome describes the symptoms after a concussion, such as headache, fatigue, depression, and anxiety.

Codes from the 851 category are used if a condition is diagnosed as conclusion with cerebral laceration. Two codes are not necessary in this instance; only one code from the 851 category is needed to encompass both problems. Attention needs to be directed to the fifth-digit assignment as to the duration of loss of consciousness, if any.

Internal Injury of Thorax, Abdomen, and Pelvis (Category Codes 860–869)

Internal injuries can occur as a result of a concussion of internal organs, a blast from explosive force, blunt trauma, a puncture, crush injuries, a laceration, and hematoma. Some of the codes in this section contain the phrase "with open wound." The coder should be aware that in these instances the phrase includes those with mention of infection or foreign body. The coder should also be aware that many categories in this section require a fifth-digit assignment.

Open Wound (Category Codes 870–897)

The note at the start of this section includes open wounds caused by animal bites, cuts, lacerations, puncture wounds, and traumatic amputations. Also included here are avulsions. An avulsion is a ripping or tearing away. Avulsions are usually documented in reference to fingernails or toenails or a portion of an organ, but they can also be used in reference to arms or legs as well.

Sometimes the coder encounters the term *complicated*, referring to an open wound, such as "complicated open wound of the back." It would code out to 876.1, Open wound of back, complicated. This is easy to understand because the diagnosis is telling you that it is a complicated open wound. However, if you encountered the diagnosis "open wound of the back with major infection," where would you go? The term complicated indicates delayed healing, delayed treatment, foreign body in wound, and major infection.

Sequencing these codes can sometimes be confusing if the wound itself is not the reason for the encounter. There are occasions when a diabetic patient may have an open wound, in which, several weeks after the wound occurred, cellulitis is now present. The patient's wound itself doesn't require treatment, but the cellulitis does. The cellulitis is coded first, with the open wound as a secondary diagnosis.

Late Effects of Injuries, Poisonings, Toxic Effects, and Other External Causes (Category Codes 905–909)

A late effect is defined by ICD-9-CM as the following:

> **Official ICD-9-CM Coding Guideline:**
>
> *The residual effect (condition produced) after the acute phase of an illness or injury has terminated. (See Appendix A, Section I, B, 12.)*

A late effect is found in the Alphabetic Index under "late." Attention to the indentations, followed by a check of the code in the Tabular List, is essential in assigning the correct code. A late effect may be apparent early, or it may not show up until months or years later. There is no time limit on when a late effect code can be used. Coding late effects generally requires two codes: the cause of the late effect is sequenced first and then the late effect. The coder needs to be sure that the late effect code being assigned is truly a late effect and not a current injury.

The ICD-9-CM Official Guidelines for Coding and Reporting state the following in relation to the coding of late effects:

> **Official ICD-9-CM Coding Guideline:**
>
> *There is no time limit on when a late effect code can be used. The residual may be apparent early, such as in cerebrovascular accident cases, or it may occur months or years later, such as that due to a previous injury. Coding of late effects generally requires two codes sequenced in the following order: The condition or nature of the late effect is sequenced first; the late effect code is sequenced second.*
>
> *An exceptions to the above guidelines are instances where the code for late effect is followed by a manifestation code identified in the Tabular List and title or where the late effect code has been expanded (at the fourth- and fifth-digit levels) to include the manifestation(s). The code for the acute phase of an illness or injury that led to the late effect is never used with a code for the late effect. (See Appendix A, Section I, B, 12.)*

EXAMPLE: Carter is a 76-year-old male who presents today for follow-up to a stroke he had one year ago. Since the stroke, Carter has been going to physical therapy because of the hemiplegia affecting his right side. The hemiplegia is a residual to the stroke. He has learned to use his left hand for writing, though he is hoping to be able to go back to using his right hand, which is his dominant hand.

In our example, code 438.21 is the only code used to report this visit because the hemiplegia is a late effect of the stroke. The stroke itself does not need to be coded because the 438 code also indicates that the condition is due to the stroke.

Burns (Category Codes 940–949)

Coding for burns can be very difficult and confusing if the coding guidelines are not followed. A **burn** is an injury to body tissue as a result of heat, flame, sun, chemicals, radiation, and electricity. Coding a burn is determined by the percentage of body surface affected and the severity, or degree, of the burn. Burns are classified as first, second, and third degree.

First-degree burns do not present a danger to the patient and are limited to the outer layer of the epidermis. An example is a mild sunburn. Second-degree burns are partial-thickness burns, which form blisters. A second-degree burn, not properly treated, can result in an infection at the burn site.

Third-degree burns are full-thickness burns and affect the epidermis, dermis, and subcutaneous layers. This type of burn can lead to necrosis and even loss of the body part. Because a burn is the destruction of the skin, which protects the body from infection, it is important that the patient receive proper treatment. Infection is a very serious problem in burn victims, as is loss of blood supply to the areas of third-degree burns. Without blood supply to the area, necrosis can occur. Figure 22-2 illustrates the types of burns.

In some cases, a patient may present with multiple burns of varying degrees. Guidelines for proper sequencing of burns are as follows:

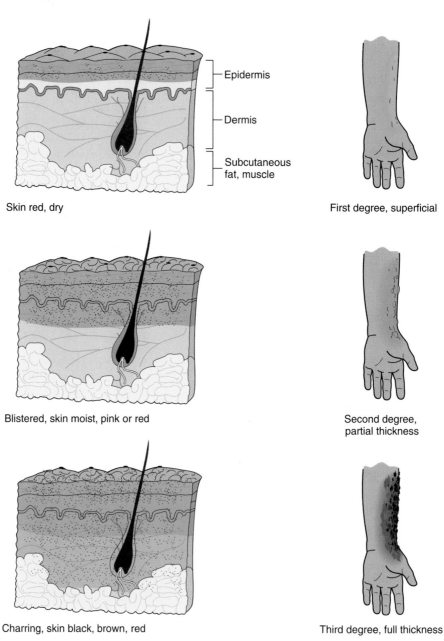

Figure 22-2 First-, second-, and third-degree burns (From Ehrlich A, Schroeder CL. *Medical Terminology for Health Professions*, 4th ed. Clifton Park, NY: Delmar, Cengage Learning, 2001, p. 264.)

Official ICD-9-CM Coding Guideline:

Coding of Burns

Current burns (940–948) are classified by depth, extent, and agent (E code). Burns are classified by depth as first-degree (erythema), second-degree (blistering), and third-degree (full-thickness involvement).

(1) Sequencing of burn and related condition codes

Sequence first the code that reflects the highest degree of burn when more than one burn is present.

a. *When the reason for the admission or encounter is for treatment of external multiple burns, sequence first the code that reflects the burn of the highest degree.*

b. *When a patient has both internal and external burns, the circumstances of admission govern the selection of the principal or first-listed diagnosis.*

c. *When a patient is admitted for burn injuries and other related conditions such as smoke inhalation and/or respiratory failure, the circumstances of admission govern the selection of the principal or first-listed diagnosis.*

(2) Burns of the same local site

Classify burns of the same local site (three-digit category level, 940–947) but of different degrees to the subcategory identifying the highest degree recorded in the diagnosis.

(3) Nonhealing burns

Nonhealing burns are coded as acute burns.

Necrosis of burned skin should be coded as a nonhealed burn.

(4) Code 958.3, Post-traumatic wound infection

Assign code 958.3, Post-traumatic wound infection, not elsewhere classified, as an additional code for any documented infected burn site.

(5) Assign separate codes for each burn site

When coding burns, assign separate codes for each burn site. Category 946, Burns of multiple specified sites, should be used only if the locations of the burns are not documented.

Category 949, Burn, unspecified, is extremely vague and should rarely be used.

(6) Assign codes from category 948, Burns

Burns classified according to extent of body surface involved, when the site of the burn is not specified or when there is a need for additional data. It is advisable to use category 948 as additional coding when needed to provide data for evaluating burn mortality, such as that needed by burn units. It is also advisable to use category 948 as an additional code for reporting purposes when there is mention of a third-degree burn involving 20 percent or more of the body surface.

In assigning a code from category 948:

Fourth-digit codes are used to identify the percentage of total body surface involved in a burn (all degrees).

Fifth-digits are assigned to identify the percentage of body surface involved in third-degree burn.

Fifth-digit zero (0) is assigned when less than 10 percent or when no body surface is involved in a third-degree burn.

Category 948 is based on the classic "rule of nines" in estimating body surface involved: head and neck are assigned nine percent, each arm nine percent, each leg 18 percent, the anterior trunk 18 percent, posterior trunk 18 percent, and genitalia one percent. Providers may change these percentage assignments where necessary to accommodate infants and children who have proportionately larger heads than adults and patients who have large buttocks, thighs, or abdomen that involve burns.

(7) Encounters for treatment of late effects of burns

Encounters for the treatment of the late effects of burns (i.e., scars or joint contractures) should be coded to the residual condition (sequelae) followed by the appropriate late effect code (906.5-906.9). A late effect E code may also be used, if desired.

(8) Sequelae with a late effect code and current burn

When appropriate, both a sequelae with a late effect code, and a current burn code may be assigned on the same record (when both a current burn and sequelae of an old burn exist). (See Appendix A, Section I, C17, c, 1–7.)

With these few guidelines in mind, this example illustrates how they are applied.

EXAMPLE: A fire victim presents to ER with first- and second-degree burns on the right arm. The right leg contains third-degree burns to the hip and thigh area.

To properly code this example, attention is directed to the category necessary. The three-digit categories identify the site. Because the hip and thigh area contain third-degree burns (the most severe of the burns to be dealt with), we locate the 945 category, Burn of lower limb(s). Third-degree burns are specified by the fourth digit, 945.3, Full-thickness skin loss due to burn (third-degree nos) of lower limb(s). A fifth digit is required for use with 945. Because the hip and thigh are involved, the fifth digit of 9, Multiple sites of lower limb(s), is used. The code assignment for our example is 945.39.

The extent of the body surface burned is coded according to the so-called rule of nines. The rule of nines is based on the premise that the adult body can be divided into anatomic regions that have surface area percentages that are multiples of nine. The rule of nines breaks down as follows:

Head and neck—9%

Arms—9% each

Legs—18% each

Anterior trunk—18%

Posterior trunk—18%

Genitalia—1%

As in the degree of burn code assignment, the codes from category 948 for the percentages of total body surface involved require fourth- and fifth-digit code assignments. The ICD-9-CM Official Guidelines for Coding and Reporting detail guidelines in this area (refer to Section I, C17, c, 6 for the complete guideline). Infants and children are coded differently. Coders are not to assign a code from this category unless the provider has indicated the degree of the burn in the documentation. Fifth-digit code assignment is made for the percentage of body surface burned.

Sometimes late effects of burn such as joint contractures or scars are present. Treatment of these late effects should be coded to the residual condition, followed by the late effect code from the 906 category. The E code for late effects may also be used. E codes are discussed in further detail in a later chapter.

Injury to Nerves and Spinal Cord (Category Codes 950–957)

The central nervous system (CNS), as discussed earlier in this book, is made up of the brain and spinal cord. There are 31 pairs of spinal nerves that originate directly from the spinal cord and 12 pairs of cranial nerves that originate from the brain. Peripheral nerves branch off these main pair of nerves. Almost any injury to these main nerves and the peripheral nerves is coded from this section.

Certain Traumatic Complications and Unspecified Injuries (Category Codes 958–959)

This category of codes rounds out the section of this chapter dealing with injuries. Injuries that can be coded more specifically anywhere else within ICD-9-CM should be assigned from codes outside this category.

Poisoning by Drugs, Medicinal and Biological Substances (Category Codes 960–979)

This section classifies substances, whether they are drugs or medicinal or biological substances, that are used incorrectly. This is one of the main causes of accidents in the home involving children. When coding a possible poisoning, the coder needs to determine whether it was actually a poisoning or an adverse effect. When a drug or other substance is used as prescribed or used correctly according to directions, this is an adverse effect. The coder may encounter certain terms that indicate an adverse effect, for example, "allergic reaction," "paradoxical," "synergistic," or "idiosyncratic reaction." "Hypersensitivity to drugs" or "toxicity," "toxic effect," or "intoxication due to prescription drugs" may also be seen in documentation. (Refer to the complete guideline located in Appendix A, Section 1, C17, E1.)

When the substance is not used as prescribed or not used properly, this is poisoning. If the documentation does not state specifically that the situation was a poisoning, then it is coded as an adverse effect. (Refer to the complete guideline located in Appendix A, Section 1, C17, E2.)

If the situation is actually a poisoning, the coder refers to the Table of Drugs and Chemicals. The table is located at the end of the Alphabetic Index.

The first column in the table is labeled Poisoning. When a statement of poisoning, overdose, wrong substance given or taken, or intoxication is used in the diagnosis and identified as such in the medical record, these codes are used.

Also found in the Table of Drugs and Chemicals are columns labeled Accidental Poisoning, Therapeutic Use, Suicide Attempt, Assault, and Undetermined. These columns contain E codes indicating external causes. The E codes are only used as secondary codes and *never* as the primary diagnosis. In situations involving poisonings or adverse effects, more than one E code may be necessary to fully describe what took place at the encounter.

Codes from the category 980–989, Toxic effects of substances chiefly nonmedicinal as to source, complete the poisoning and toxic effects section of codes in this chapter. Alcohol toxicity, lead, metals, and food are contained in these categories of codes. Also in this section are the codes for snake venom. Because 48 states in the United States contain venomous snakes, coders may encounter a situation that would take them to this section of the coding book.

The remainder of this chapter, codes 990–999, contains codes that encompass some of the more unusual circumstances encountered in coding or codes that are not more specifically coded in any other chapters of ICD-9-CM. Codes 990–995 report other and unspecified effects of external causes that are not defined elsewhere in ICD-9-CM. Codes 996–999 report complications of surgical and medical care that are not elsewhere classified. This range includes mechanical complications of various devices, implants, and grafts, as well as other reactions to prosthetics.

Summary

- When coding injuries, assign a separate code for each injury unless a combination code is provided.
- The Official ICD-9-CM Coding Guidelines for coding multiple fractures should be followed when coding multiple fractures.
- When a dislocation occurs with a fracture, the dislocation is included in the code for the fracture.
- A sprain is an injury to a joint, and a strain is an injury to the muscle or the tendon attachment.
- Intracranial injuries that are diagnosed with cerebral lacerations are coded with a combination code.
- Fifth digits are commonly used when coding injuries of the thorax, abdomen, and pelvis.
- A burn is an injury to body tissue as a result of heat, flame, sun, chemicals, radiation, or electricity.
- Burns are classified by the severity: first, second, or third degree.
- The extent of the body surface burned is coded according to the rule of nines.
- An adverse effect occurs when a drug or other substance is used as prescribed or correctly according to directions.

Chapter Review

True/False: Indicate whether the statement is true (T) or false (F).

1. _____ The main axis for coding concussions hinges on whether the patient lost consciousness.

2. _____ Codes in the category of open wounds include fractures.

3. _____ There is a time limit on when a late effect code can be assigned.

4. _____ The rule of nines is used to describe the total body surface burned.

5. _____ If documentation does not state "poisoning," then it is coded as an adverse effect.

Fill-in-the-Blank: Enter the appropriate term(s) to complete each statement.

6. The term _____ indicates delayed healing of a wound.

7. The first column listed in the Table of Drugs and Chemicals is _____.

8. A violent shaking or jarring of the brain is known as a _____.

9. A substance that causes an allergic reaction even though it is used correctly is called a(n) _____.

10. According to the rule of nines, each arm is valued at _____%.

Coding Assignments

Instructions: Using an ICD-9-CM coding book, select the appropriate code for each statement.

Diagnosis	Code
1. A 3-year-old child was brought to ER after swallowing too much Benadryl. Dr. Michaels is listing this as an accidental poisoning.	_____
2. Open wound of large toe	_____
3. Anaphylactic shock due to properly administered substance	_____
4. Open wound of finger with splinter that had to be removed (do not code procedure at this time)	_____
5. Phlebitis after transfusion	_____
6. Complete below-knee amputation (traumatic)	_____
7. Mechanical complication due to cardiac pacemaker electrode	_____
8. Traumatic subdural hemorrhage with loss of consciousness for 2 hours	_____
9. Seasickness	_____
10. Laceration of eyelid, $1/2$ inch	_____
11. Late effect of lower-end leg fracture	_____
12. Toxic effect of gasoline	_____
13. Open wound of forehead	_____
14. Frostbite of hand	_____
15. Infected insect bite of forearm	_____

16. Late effect of radiation   _____

17. Injury to hepatic veins   _____

18. Vitreous touch syndrome   _____

19. Friction burn of finger   _____

20. Urticaria (reaction) due to serum   _____

21. Closed fracture of the frontal bone of the skull, no intracranial injury   _____

22. Fracture of the greater tuberosity of the humerus   _____

23. Open fracture at the base of the neck of the femur   _____

24. Sprain of the medial collateral ligament of the knee   _____

25. Lung contusion   _____

Case Studies

Instructions: Review each case study, and select the correct ICD-9-CM diagnostic code.

CASE 1

Physician's Office Note

S: The patient's wife brought the patient to my office after the patient tried to separate a raccoon and their dog, which were fighting. While trying to separate the animals, the patient was bitten. He is not sure whether the raccoon or the dog bit him.

EXAM:

The patient's left hand has bite marks on it. The wound is bleeding and is deep, and there is tendon involvement.

The nurse cleaned the wound, and a tetanus shot was given. Because the wound is deep and there is tendon involvement, I called Dr. Black for a surgical consult. The wound was dressed to control the bleeding.

ICD-9-CM Code Assignment: _____

CASE 2

ER Note

CHIEF COMPLIANT: This 2-year-old patient presents with a cut on his face.

History of the present illness: Patient fell off a kitchen chair and struck his face on the seat of the chair.

VITAL SIGNS: Pulse 117, Respirations 28, BP 103/43

RESPIRATORY: Airway clear

BREATH SOUNDS: Clear

SKIN: Laceration to the bridge of the nose.

LACERATION REPAIR NOTE: The patient was papoosed with his mother's knowledge and presence. The wound was injected with 2% plain Lidocaine, and the wound edges were approximated with three #6-0 nylon sutures.

The patient was sent for an X-ray to rule out any facial bone fractures.

PLAN: Follow up with family physician in 1 week.

ICD-9-CM Code Assignment: _____

CASE 3

Physician's Office Note

CHIEF COMPLIANT: Pain in right arm.

HISTORY OF PRESENT ILLNESS: This 39-year-old female was carrying groceries into her house when she slipped on ice and fell. She landed on her right side and on her arm.

EXAM:

EXTREMITIES: Her right arm is swollen, and it appears to be broken due to the abnormal appearance.

An in-office X-ray was completed that showed a complete fracture of the shaft of the humerus. Patient was referred to Dr. Break, the orthopedic surgeon on call. Patient was sent to Dr. Break's office.

ICD-9-CM Code Assignment: _____

CASE 4

Clinic Visit Note

This is a 63-year-old type II diabetic male who presents 4 weeks after cutting his leg on piece of plastic while at his summer home. The patient presented to this office at the time of the injury due to concerns he had regarding possible complications stemming from his diabetes. No stitches were necessary; we cleaned the wound and educated the patient on wound care.

The wound is located on the back part of the calf area and is now red and painful. Upon examination, there was no streaking at this time, but some clear drainage is noted. The patient is afebrile, and other vital signs are within normal limits.

The diagnosis at this time is cellulitis secondary to the leg wound. We are starting the patient on antibiotics and have also treated and dressed the wound.

ICD-9-CM Code Assignment: _____

CASE 5

Emergency Department Note

This patient is a 27-year-old male who was brought to the emergency department by ambulance after being bitten by a rattlesnake while hiking in the desert. The bite is located just above the ankle. The patient was wearing sneakers instead of hiking boots. The area of the bite is now red and a bit swollen. The patient says the pain is about 9 out of 10 on the pain scale. The exact type of snake is not known because the patient wasn't sure.

Examination reveals two small puncture marks on the medial side of the lower leg above the ankle. Vital signs are within normal limits. The skin is swollen, red, and warm to touch. Patient was given a shot of antivenom and admitted for 24-hour observation.

ICD-9-CM Code Assignment: _____

V Codes—Supplementary Classification of Factors Influencing Health Status and Contact with Health Services

Chapter Outline

Objectives

At the conclusion of this chapter, the student will be able to:

1. Explain the purpose of V codes.
2. Identify key terms that are used to locate V codes in the Alphabetic Index.
3. Describe and identify encounters for which V codes are used.
4. Explain when to use codes from the V30–V39 series.
5. Identify the V codes used to code status and postsurgical states.
6. Discuss the specific coding guidelines that relate to V codes.
7. Select and code V codes from case studies.

Key Terms

Family History Codes   Isolation   Personal History Codes   Status Code

---

Reminder

As you work through this chapter, you will need to have a copy of the ICD-9-CM coding book to reference.

Introduction

In ICD-9-CM, there are two supplementary chapters. The first supplementary chapter, entitled "V Codes—Supplementary Classification of Factors Influencing Health Status and Contact with Health Services," classifies those encounters for which circumstances other than a disease or injury prompts the encounter. V codes are listed in the Tabular Volume of ICD-9-CM, following chapter 17 of the Disease Tabular List. V codes are used to indicate the reason for the encounter and are used in both the inpatient and outpatient settings but are generally more applicable to the outpatient setting. V codes can be used in any healthcare setting as either primary or secondary codes, depending on the circumstances.

Introduction to V Codes (Category Codes V01–V84)

As defined in the ICD-9-CM Official Guidelines for Coding and Reporting, there are four primary uses of V codes.

Official ICD-9-CM Coding Guideline:

There are four primary circumstances for the use of V Codes:

1. *A person who is not currently sick encounters the health services for some specific reason, such as to act as an organ donor, to receive prophylactic care, such as inoculations or health screenings, or to receive counseling on health-related issues.*

2. *A person with a resolving disease or injury or a chronic, long-term condition requiring continuous care encounters the health care system for specific aftercare of that disease or injury (e.g., dialysis for renal disease, chemotherapy for malignancy, cast change). A diagnosis/symptom code should be used whenever a current, acute diagnosis is being treated or a sign or symptom is being studied.*

3. *Circumstances or problems influence a person's health status but are not in themselves a current illness or injury.*

4. *Newborns, to indicate birth status. (See Appendix A, Section I, C18, a.)*

The following circumstances describe encounters for which V codes would be used.

- To report encounters for specific purposes, even though the patient is not currently ill, such as to receive vaccinations, obtain routine physical examinations, and have well-baby visits

- To report a circumstance or problem that is influencing a patient's health status but is not in itself a current illness or injury, such as a personal history of malignant neoplasm or a family history of heart disease

- To report an encounter for a therapy, such as chemotherapy or dialysis

- To indicate the outcome of delivery for obstetric patients and to indicate the birth status of a newborn

V codes are located in the same manner as diagnostic codes. Main terms are listed in the Alphabetic Index. When V codes are reported, all numerical entries must be preceded by a *V*. Locating a V code in the Alphabetic Index can sometimes be difficult because of the differences in documentation practices by physicians. Terminology used within ICD-9-CM does not always parallel terminology used by providers. To use the V codes most effectively, it is recommended that coders become familiar with this chapter of the code book by understanding the category codes within the chapter.

Persons with Potential Health Hazards Related to Communicable Diseases (Category Codes V01–V06)

Category code V01 is used to designate when a patient has had contact with or exposure to communicable diseases but has not contracted the condition. Reference to the exposure needs to be made in the documentation along with the note that the patient is not symptomatic at this time.

Official ICD-9-CM Coding Guideline:

Contact/exposure

Category V01 indicates contact with or exposure to communicable diseases. These codes are for patients who do not show any sign or symptom of a disease but have been exposed to it by close personal contact with an infected individual or are in an area where a disease is epidemic. These codes may be used as a first-listed code to explain an encounter for testing or, more commonly, as a secondary code to identify a potential risk. (See Appendix A, Section I, C18, d, 1.)

V codes from category V01 are located in the Alphabetic Index by referencing *contact* or *exposure*.

Category V02 is used to identify a carrier or suspected carrier of an infectious disease. Fourth-digit codes are used to identify the type of infectious disease. The Official Guidelines state that category V02 is considered a **status code,** a code that indicates that a patient is either a carrier of a disease or has the sequelae or residual of a past disease or condition. The Official Guidelines state the following in relation to category code V02:

Official ICD-9-CM Coding Guideline:

V02   Carrier or suspected carrier of infectious diseases

Carrier status indicates that a person harbors the specific organisms of a disease without manifest symptoms and is capable of transmitting the infection. (See Appendix A, Section I, C18, d, 3.)

V codes from category V02 are located in the Alphabetic Index by referencing *carrier*.

Category codes V03–V06 are used when a patient receives a vaccination and/or inoculation against a disease. When locating these codes in the Alphabetic Index, the coder should reference the following main terms: *admission for vaccination* or *vaccination*. The Official Guidelines give direction when using V03–V06 codes.

Official ICD-9-CM Coding Guideline:

Inoculations and vaccinations

Categories V03–V06 are for encounters for inoculations and vaccinations. They indicate that a patient is being seen to receive a prophylactic inoculation against a disease. The injection itself must be represented by the appropriate procedure code. A code from V03–V06 may be used as a secondary code if the inoculation is given as a routine part of preventive health care, such as a well-baby visit. (See Appendix A, Section I, C18, d, 2.)

Persons with Need for Isolation and Other Prophylactic Measures (Category Code V07)

Category code V07 is used to classify encounters for **isolation,** when a patient is admitted for placement in a private area for protection against exposure to infectious diseases in their surroundings and for other prophlylactic measures, such as hormone replacement therapy, V07.4, or RhoGAM administration, V07.2. Category codes V07 are located in the Alphabetic Index by referencing *prophylactic, isolation,* and *desensitization*.

Exercise 23–1 Coding Category Codes V01–V07

Instructions: For each encounter select the appropriate V code.

Encounter	Code
1. Encounter for measles inoculation	_____
2. Exposure to rabies	_____
3. Hepatitis B carrier	_____
4. Vaccination for DTP + TAB	_____
5. Administration of tetanus antitoxin	_____

Asymptomatic Human Immunodeficiency Virus (HIV) Infection Status (Category Code V08)

Asymptomatic human immunodeficiency virus (HIV) infection status is coded to category V08. This is a serious health concern, and there are many regulations on the reporting of HIV. There are two types of HIV: type one or HIV-1 is the type commonly found in the United States; HIV-2 is found primarily in Africa and rarely seen in the United States. V08 is the correct code to assign when a patient has never had any HIV-related illnesses but is HIV positive. Code 042 is used for patients who are HIV positive and symptomatic.

ICD-9-CM Official Coding Guidelines clarify this.

Official ICD-9-CM Coding Guideline:

V08-Asymptomatic HIV infection status

This code indicates that a patient has tested positive for HIV but has manifested no signs or symptoms of the disease. (See Appendix A, Section I, C18, d, 3.)

Infection with Drug-Resistant Microorganism (Category Code V09)

Category V09, Infection with drug-resistant microorganisms, is used in very limited circumstances.

Official ICD-9-CM Coding Guideline:

V09-Infection with drug-resistant microorganisms

This category indicates that a patient has an infection that is resistant to drug treatment.

Sequence the infection code first. (See Appendix A, Section I, C18, d, 3.)

What this guideline means is that the V09 is never used as a primary diagnosis. The infectious condition is coded as the primary condition, with the V09 as the secondary condition. The drug resistance referred to here could be a result of the patient's not following prescribed treatments due to underuse, overuse, or just stopping midtreatment.

Persons with Potential Health Hazards Related to Personal and Family History (Category Codes V10–V19)

Category codes V10–V19 are used to report past personal or family histories of diseases. **Personal history codes** explain a patient's past medical condition that no longer exists. When these V codes are used, the patient is not receiving any treatment for the past illness but there is the potential for recurrence; therefore, the patient is being seen to monitor recurrence. **Family history codes** are used to indicate that a patient has one or more family member who have had a particular disease, therefore placing the patient at a higher risk of contracting it.

> **EXAMPLE:** A patient has a history of a malignant neoplasm of the breast and is being seen for a follow-up visit after a mastectomy. The coder should report V10.3, Personal history of malignant neoplasm of the breast, and V67.09, Follow-up examination following surgery. Because the reason for the encounter is the follow-up examination, V67.09 should be listed first, followed by V10.3.

It is common for providers to report codes for a past history of a malignant neoplasm incorrectly. A common error is to report that the patient still has the malignant neoplasm. Coders must review the medical documentation to determine whether the patient currently has the malignant neoplastic condition or was previously treated and the condition no longer exists. To locate the history codes, the coder should reference the following in the Alphabetic Index:

| "History (personal) of" | To locate personal history of an illness |
| "History (personal) of family" | To locate family history of an illness |

Indentations are key and need to be watched closely. For this reason, verifying the code chosen in the Tabular List is critical.

The Official Guidelines for coding gives the following advice for coding personal and family history codes:

> **Official ICD-9-CM Coding Guideline:**
>
> *Personal history codes may be used in conjunction with follow-up codes, and family history codes may be used in conjunction with screening codes to explain the need for a test or procedure. History codes are also acceptable on any medical record regardless of the reason for the visit. A history of an illness, even if no longer present, is important information that may alter the type of treatment ordered. (See Appendix A, Section I, C18, d, 4.)*

Persons Encountering Health Services in Circumstances Related to Reproduction and Development (Category Codes V20–V29)

This range of codes is used to report care given in relation to a child's development, in antepartum and postpartum care and examination, as well as in contraceptive and procreative management. The main terms to be referenced in Alphabetic Index for codes V20–V29 are:

- Admission for
- Contraception
- Checking (of)
- Checkup
- Encounter for
- Examination
- Fitting of

- Pregnancy, supervision of
- Supervision (of) contraceptive method
- Sterilization, admission for

The following is a summary of the category codes found in this section of the chapter:

Category Code	Description
V20	Health Supervision of Infant or Child—This category codes encounters in which a healthy infant or newborn is receiving care in cases of maternal illness, socioeconomic factors, or routine health checks.
V21	Constitutional States in Development—Codes from this category identify low birth weight status (2,500 grams or less), periods of rapid growth, puberty, and other states in development.
V22	Normal Pregnancy—This category code is used to record supervision of normal pregnancies. Fourth digits are used as follows: 0, normal first pregnancy; 1, other normal pregnancy; and 2, pregnant state incidental.
V23	Supervision of High-Risk Pregnancy—These codes are used to identify factors that place a pregnancy at risk. Fourth digits are used to identify the specific factor that is presenting a risk to the pregnancy. These codes are most commonly used for prenatal outpatient encounters.
V24	Postpartum Care and Examination—After delivery and birth, obstetrical patients are seen in the outpatient setting for follow-up care. Category V24 is used to report care and observation for uncomplicated cases. Code V24.0 is used to report cases when the mother delivers before admission to the hospital and then is admitted for routine care. This code is used only if no complications exist. Code V24.2 reports routine postpartum care. (Because this is a follow-up code category, Guideline Section 1, C18, d, 8 in Appendix A.)
V25	Encounter for Contraceptive Management—This category is used to report services in relation to contraceptive management. Code V25.2 is used to report sterilizations. This code can be reported either as a solo code or as a secondary code. This code is reported as a solo code when sterilization is the only reason for the patient encounter. This code is reported as a secondary code when a patient is receiving other care and sterilization is also performed. For example, a patient is receiving obstetrical care after a normal delivery, and during this admission the patient also has a sterilization procedure performed. The coder selects a code for the normal delivery, 650, and a code for the sterilization, V25.2, as well as a code from the V27 category to indicate the outcome of delivery.
V26	Procreative Management—This category code identifies encounters for the purpose of reproduction management, including fertility testing, artificial insemination, and sterilization reversal.
V27	Outcome of Delivery—A V27 code is included on every maternal medical record when a delivery occurs. These codes identify the number of infants that are liveborn or stillborn. Coders must review the record to identify the number of infants and whether the infant(s) were liveborn or stillborn. The V27 code is always a secondary code. Category code V27 is indexed in the Alphabetic Index by referencing "Outcome of delivery."
V28	Antenatal Screening—This category is used to report encounters for antenatal screening, including screenings for chromosomal anomalies and other abnormalities that present in amniotic fluids, as well as other fetal screenings.
V29	Observation and Evaluation of Newborns and Infants for Suspected Condition Not Found—This category is used for newborns, within the first 28 days of life, who are suspected of having an abnormal condition but do not present with any signs or symptoms. This category is used only if after examination and observation the newborn is found not to have the suspected condition. If the suspected condition is found, the case is reported by selecting a code for the suspected condition or signs and symptoms identified. Category codes are found in the Alphabetic Index by referencing "Observation (for), suspected, condition, newborn."

Exercise 23–2   Coding Category Codes V20–V29

Instructions: For each statement, select the appropriate ICD-9-CM codes.

Statement	Code
1. Patient is seen by her primary care provider for acute sinusitis and is also known to be 6 months pregnant.	_____
2. Male patient admitted for sterilization.	_____
3. Patient seen to determine postvasectomy sperm count.	_____
4. Male patient seen for sperm count for fertility testing.	_____
5. A single stillborn infant is delivered.	_____

Liveborn Infants According to Type of Birth (Category Codes V30–V39)

These categories of codes are used to report the birth of a liveborn infant and are reported on the child's record. When assigning codes from this range, coders should pay attention to the necessity of adding fourth and fifth digits to this category. A notation for the fourth and fifth digits appears in the code book as follows:

```
The following fourth-digit subdivisions are for use with categories V30-V39:
.0   Born in hospital (requires fifth digit)
.1   Born before admission to hospital
.2   Born outside of hospital and not hospitalized
The following two fifth digits are for use with the fourth-digit 0, Born in
hospital:
0    Delivered without mention of cesarean delivery
1    Delivered by cesarean delivery
```

The fifth digits are only assigned when the fourth digit of 0 is used to indicate that the infant was born in the hospital. The fourth digit of 1 is assigned when the infant is born outside the hospital and then admitted. It is not used if the infant was transferred from another hospital. The fourth digit of 2 is assigned when the infant is born outside the hospital and is not subsequently admitted. This fifth digit is, therefore, not assigned in the acute care record.

Persons with a Condition Influencing Their Health Status (Category Codes V40–V49)

Category codes V40–V49 are used to report the following conditions when the physician records them as a diagnosis or problem:

- Mental and behavioral problems
- Problems with special senses and functions
- Organ or tissue replacements
- Status conditions
- Postsurgical states
- Dependence on machines
- Other problems with body organs and parts

This is a summary of the category codes and descriptions found in this section:

Category Code	Description
V40	Mental and Behavioral Problems—These codes are used to indicate that a patient has a problem with learning or communication or other mental or behavioral problem that influences health status.
V41	Problems with Special Senses and Other Special Functions—These codes are used to indicate problems with sight, hearing, voice production, smell and taste, swallowing and mastication, and sexual function.
V42	Organ or Tissue Replaced by Transplant—These codes include homologous and heterologus organ transplant status. Currently, there are no complications.
V43	Organ or Tissue Replaced by Other Means—This category is used to indicate a patient's status after of an organ or tissue replacement. The replacement of the organ occurred with an artificial device, a mechanical device, or prosthesis.
V44	Artificial Opening Status—The presence of an artificial opening is reported by use of this category code. Fourth digits are used to identify the type of opening such as tracheostomy, V44.0; gastrostomy, V44.1; ileostomy, V44.2; colostomy, V44.3; and cystostomy, V44.5X. An Exclude: note at the start of the category code alerts the coder not to use these codes if the artificial opening requires attention or management; codes V55.0–V55.9 should be used in these cases.
V45	Other Postsurgical States—This category includes various postsurgical states. Common postsurgical states that are classified to this category include cardiac pacemaker, V45.01; renal dialysis status, V45.1; intrauterine contraceptive device, V45.51; cataract extraction status, V45.61; acquired absence of organ, V45.7X; breast implant status, V45.83; and insulin pump status, V45.85. Numerous notations and Exclude: notes appear in this category; therefore, it is imperative that coders read the notations and Exclude: notes that are contained in this code category.
V46	Other Dependence on Machines—This category is used to identify patients who depend on machines such as aspirators, respirators, supplemental oxygen, and other enabling machines. To locate these codes in the Alphabetic Index, the coder should reference "Dependence, on."
V47	Other Problems with Internal Organs—This category is used to code problems with internal organs such as deficiencies, mechanical, and motor problems.
V48	Problems with Head, Neck, and Trunk—This category is used to code problems that include mechanical and motor problems, as well as sensory and disfiguration problems.
V49	Other Conditions Influencing Health Status—The V49 category is used to identify deficiencies, disfigurations, sensory, motor, and mechanical problems that influence a patient's health status. Conditions that are classified to this category code include amputation status, asymptomatic postmenopausal status, dental sealant status, and other conditions that affect the limbs.

To locate codes in this range, coders should reference to following main terms in the Alphabetic Index:

- Dependence, on (type of machine)
- Postsurgery status
- Problem (with)
- Replacement by artificial or mechanical device
- Status

Some of these codes are considered status codes, in that they indicate a sequelae or residual of a past disease or condition and are commonly assigned as additional diagnoses. These codes indicate the presence of a condition that may influence the treatment given to a patient, such as a patient who has a pacemaker.

This range of codes also consists of codes for status and postsurgical states. These codes should be reported if they require or affect the treatment or case management of the patient. Postoperative status conditions should be reported if they require consideration in the management of patient care.

EXAMPLE: A patient is seen who complains of abdominal pain and tenderness. The patient previously had an intestinal bypass. No diagnosis is recorded at this time by the physician. The coder should code abdominal pain and tenderness, 789.0X, and the postsurgical intestinal bypass V45.3.

However, if the patient is being seen for an upper respiratory infection, there is no need to record the postsurgical intestinal bypass because it would not affect the management of patient care.

The ICD-9-CM Official Guidelines for Coding and Reporting give the following guidance:

Official ICD-9-CM Coding Guideline:

Categories V42–V46 and subcategories V49.6– V49.7 are for use only if there are no complications or malfunctions of the organ or tissue replaced, the amputation site, or the equipment on which the patient is dependent. (See Appendix A, Section I, C18, d, 3.)

Persons Encountering Health Services for Specific Procedures and Aftercare (Category Codes V50–V59)

This range of codes is used to report reasons for encounters involving aftercare, fitting and adjusting of devices, attention to artificial openings, rehabilitation procedures, radiotherapy and chemotherapy sessions, and organ or tissue donors. This care is being received to consolidate treatment, to care for residual states, or to prevent recurrences.

The main terms to reference in the Alphabetic Index are:

- Admission for adjustment
- Aftercare
- Attention to
- Chemotherapy
- Dialysis
- Donor
- Fitting
- Radiotherapy
- Rehabilitation
- Therapy

These codes are used for planned encounters, not for encounters due to complications or problems that have arisen from a previous condition or the presence of an artificial device or opening.

EXAMPLE: A patient is seen for cleansing of a tracheostomy. The coder selects code V55.0.

However, if a patient is seen for a tracheal stenosis due to a tracheostomy, the coder reports code 519.02, Mechanical complication of tracheostomy.

The ICD-9-CM Official Guidelines for Coding and Reporting provide the guidelines for reporting these codes:

> **Official ICD-9-CM Coding Guideline:**
>
> *Aftercare visit codes cover situations when the initial treatment of a disease or injury has been performed and the patient requires continued care during the healing or recovery phase or for the long-term consequences of the disease. The aftercare V code should not be used if treatment is directed at a current, acute disease or injury. The diagnosis code is to be used in these cases. (See Appendix A, Section I, C18, d, 7.)*

There are exceptions to these guidelines, including the codes V58.0, Radiotherapy, and V58.1, Chemotherapy. When a patient's encounter is solely to receive radiation or chemotherapy for treatment of a neoplasm, codes V58.0 or V58.1 are listed first, followed by the diagnosis code for the neoplasm. When a patient receives both chemotherapy and radiation therapy, both codes are reported with either one sequenced first.

New coders need to reference Appendix A, Section I, C18, d, 7 to read all the official guidelines that pertain to this section of codes.

Persons Encountering Health Services in Other Circumstances (Category Codes V60–V69)

Codes from this code range are used to report circumstances that affect patient management or the patient directly. This range is also used to report encounters with healthcare professionals when the patient is not currently ill but is convalescencing or receiving follow-up care. Main terms to reference in the Alphabetic Index are:

- Admission (encounter)
- Convalescence (following)

    for

    follow-up examination

- Follow-up
- Problem (with)

    family

    marital

    personal

    poverty

The V67 category, Follow-up examination, is used to report follow-up care and examinations. If follow-up is occurring after treatment has eliminated the condition, the previous condition should be reported by using a "history of" code from the V10–V15 range. If follow-up occurs and a condition is found, the V67 code should be reported as well as the code for the condition found.

EXAMPLE: A patient, with a previous diagnosis of malignant neoplasm of the bladder, had surgery 6 weeks ago. He is being seen for follow-up, and there is no evidence of secondary malignancy or recurrence. The coder selects code V67.0, Follow-up examination following surgery, and code V10.51, Personal history of malignant neoplasm of bladder.

If the same patient is seen but a secondary malignancy is found, then the coder codes the follow-up examination and the secondary malignancy.

The ICD-9-CM Official Guidelines for Coding and Reporting explain the V67 code as follows:

Official ICD-9-CM Coding Guideline:

The follow-up codes help to explain the continuing surveillance following completed treatment of a disease, condition, or injury. They imply that the condition has been fully treated and no longer exists. . . . Follow-up codes may be used in conjunction with history codes to provide the full picture of the healed condition and its treatment. The follow-up code is sequenced first, followed by the history code.

A follow-up code may be used to explain repeated visits. Should a condition be found to have recurred on the follow-up visit, then the diagnosis code should be used in place of the follow-up code. (See Appendix A, Section I, C18, d, 8.)

This guideline also pertains to category code V24, Postpartum care and evaluation, because it is also a follow-up code category.

Persons Without Reported Diagnosis Encountered During Examination and Investigation of Individuals and Populations (Category Codes V70–V82)

Category codes V70–V83 are used to report encounters for general medical examinations, observation, and evaluation for suspected conditions, and special investigations and examinations. The main terms to be located in the Alphabetic Index are:

- Evaluation
- Examination
- Observation (for)
- Screening
- Test

Category code V71 is used to report encounters that occur to determine whether a condition is present, and after such examination it is determined there is no need for further treatment or medical care.

When a patient is admitted to a hospital to receive evaluation, coding differences can occur between the physician's office reporting and the hospital reporting. The following situation is an example of coding requirement differences between physicians' offices and hospitals.

EXAMPLE: A patient is hospitalized to complete tests for suspected malignant neoplasm of bone. The physician's office reports code V71.1, Observation for suspected malignant neoplasm and any signs and symptoms that are present. The hospital coder reports the malignant neoplasm of bone. Hospital coders report any conditions to be ruled out as conditions that are present. It is imperative that physician's office coders recode hospital admissions, because the coding guidelines for physicians' offices and hospitals are different.

Codes from V71–V83 can be used to report encounters in which examinations, screenings, and tests are completed only for diagnostic purposes and no other service is provided. When these codes are used to report diagnostic services as the only reason for the encounter, the V code should be sequenced first, and the diagnosis or problem for which the services are being performed is sequenced second. See the chapter on coding guidelines and requirements for further explanations and examples.

When reporting V codes, the coder should be aware that some carriers will not pay for routine examinations and testing. When possible, in addition to the V code, list all symptoms, diagnosis, and conditions that are present. The primary role of V codes is as a supplemental classification. Therefore, a code from the main classification should accompany V codes to justify the claim. When a test or examination is performed and a condition is found to be present, the coder should code the condition found to be present in addition to the test or examination.

The guidelines in the chapter on coding guidelines and requirements provide additional information on selecting additional codes to be reported on claims.

Genetics (Category Codes V83–V84)

Category codes V83–V84 are used to report genetic carrier status and genetic susceptibility to disease. V83 codes indicate that a person carries a gene associated with a particular disease that may be passed to offspring who may develop that disease. Fourth and fifth digits are used to identify specific diseases. V84 codes include confirmed abnormal genes. Coders are also instructed to use an additional code to identify any associated family history of the disease. This is reported by using codes V16–V19.

Body Mass Index (Category Code V85)

These codes are used to report the body mass index (BMI). Codes V85.0, V85.1, V85.2X, V85.3X, and V85.4 are used to report the BMI for adults. V85.5X codes are used to report the BMI for pediatric patients.

Estrogen Receptor Status (Category Code V86)

Category code V86 is used to report estrogen receptor positive status (V86.0) and estrogen negative receptor status (V86.1). The code book instructs the coder to code first malignant neoplasm of the breast (codes 174.0–174.9 and 175.0–175.9).

Category Codes V87 to V89

Category V87 reports other specified personal exposures and history presenting hazards to health. The fourth and fifth digits denote the type of exposures. Category V88 reports acquired absence of organs and tissues such as the cervix and uterus. Category V89 reports suspected conditions not found elsewhere in ICD-9-CM and includes maternal and fetal conditions.

Extensive Coding Guidelines for V Codes

It should be noted that in the ICD-9-CM Official Guidelines for Coding and Reporting there are extensive coding guidelines for V codes. The guidelines also contain a table entitled V Code Table. This table is used to identify first-listed, first or additional, additional only, and nonspecific V codes. *(See Appendix A, Section I, C18 for the complete V code guidelines and table.)*

Summary

- "V Codes—Supplementary Classification of Factors Influencing Health Status and Contact with Health Services" classifies encounters for which circumstances other than a disease or injury prompts the encounter.

- V codes can be used as either a primary or a secondary diagnosis, depending on the situation of the encounter.

- There are four primary circumstances for the use of V codes: to report encounters for specific purposes even though the patient is not currently ill, to report the history of an illness whether it is personal or family, to report an encounter for chemotherapy or dialysis, and to indicate the outcome of a delivery.

- Coders need to pay careful attention to detail and to be familiar with the V code section of ICD-9-CM in order to assign the correct code.

Chapter Review

True/False: Indicate whether each statement is true (T) or false (F).

1. _____ V codes are always listed as the primary diagnosis.

2. _____ V codes must be used with an additional code from the main chapters of ICD-9-CM.

3. _____ An encounter for a routine physical examination is coded using a V code.

4. _____ Different V code categories exist for family and personal histories of diseases.

5. _____ A code from category V30 always appears on a maternal health record.

Fill-in-the-Blank: Enter the appropriate term(s) to complete each statement.

6. A normal pregnancy is classified to V code _____.

7. An outcome of delivery code, V27, is recorded on the _____ health record.

8. V codes are considered one of two _____ classifications of ICD-9-CM.

9. V codes are not used when a current, acute diagnosis is being treated. In these cases _____ codes should be used.

10. Category V24, Postpartum care and examination, is more commonly used in the _____ setting for uncomplicated follow-up care during the postpartum period.

Code Assignments

Instructions: Using an ICD-9-CM coding book, select the appropriate code for each statement.

Statement	Code
1. Repositioning of a tracheostomy tube	_____
2. Encounter to remove internal fixation device in the right arm	_____
3. Patient presents to ER with order for blood transfusion, no other diagnosis given	_____
4. Contact lens fitting and adjustment	_____
5. Counseling on use of oral contraceptive	_____
6. Exposure to rubella	_____
7. Suspected carrier of streptococcus	_____
8. Status post total hip replacement	_____
9. Cardiac pacemaker in situ	_____
10. Family history of diabetes mellitus	_____
11. DTP + TAB vaccine	_____
12. Hormone replacement therapy (postmenopausal)	_____
13. Personal history of malignant neoplasm of the esophagus	_____
14. Heart valve replaced by transplant	_____

15. Fitting and adjustment of artificial leg, partial   _____

16. Routine physical, adult   _____

17. Screening for viral diseases   _____

18. Genetic susceptibility to malignant neoplasm of the breast   _____

19. Personal history of allergy to eggs   _____

20. Routine examination, child   _____

21. Family history of polycystic kidney   _____

22. Personal history of malaria   _____

23. Exposure to rabies   _____

24. Personal history of malignant neoplasm of the ovary   _____

25. Genetic counseling   _____

Case Studies

Instructions: Review each case study, and select the correct ICD-9-CM V code.

CASE 1

Physician's Office Note of 2/6/XX

CHIEF COMPLIANT: This patient presents for a physical exam and to rule out any disease process.

General status reveals an alert, 80-year-old woman who is pleasant and cooperative. Vital signs: BP—128/67, P—72, R—24, wt—113 lbs. Routine labwork done on 2/3/XX, all within acceptable range. Family and social history noncontributory.

PHYSICAL EXAM:

HEENT:

HEAD: Normocephalic.

EYES: Cornea clear, conjunctivae pale pink, sclerae nonicteric, pupils react to light.

EARS: TMs are clear.

NECK: Supple, no JVD or bruit. Trachea midline. No lymphadenopathy or thyromegaly.

HEART: Regular rhythm, no murmurs. No peripheral cyanosis, pallor, or edema. She has very good distal pulses.

BREASTS: No masses palpated.

LUNGS: Good air entry, no adventitious sounds.

ABDOMEN: Soft, nondistended. Bowel sounds active.

EXTERNAL GENITALIA: Normal female.

RECTAL: Stool guaiac negative. Stool in the rectal vault.

MUSCULOSKELETAL: Functional range of motion of her joints.

NEUROLOGICAL: Cranial nerves 2–12 grossly intact bilaterally.

IMPRESSION: No findings.

PLAN: Patient to follow up in 1 year or sooner if any problems develop.

ICD-9-CM Code Assignment: _____

CASE 2

Physician's Office Note

This 39-year-old male presents following a fracture of the left ankle, which was casted when he was on vacation. Patient is doing excellently. X-rays taken 4 days ago show the fracture to be healed. He says there is no tenderness in the ankle.

Cast removed.

Ankle appeared to be healed.

Patient was referred for PT evaluation.

ICD-9-CM Code Assignment: _____

CASE 3

Physician's Office Note

This 16-year-old male patient presents for suture removal. The sutures were placed 1 week ago due to a laceration over the eye, which occurred while he was at wrestling practice.

Sutures were removed, and the area was examined and found to be healed with no signs of infection.

Patient instructed to return if any signs of infection occur.

ICD-9-CM Code Assignment: _____

CASE 4

Mrs. Kragan is a 78-year-old female with a history of recurrent pneumonia and was recently released from the hospital after a 10-day stay due to pneumonia. Her oxygen level has been running between 86% and 88%. She is here today for a follow-up to this hospital stay and also to get her set up on a long-term oxygen therapy. We filled out all paperwork for the insurance and got her set up with the agency who will be delivering the tanks to her.

ICD-9-CM Code Assignment: _____

CASE 5

Lacy presents today for a 1-year status postovarian cancer. She has been living a healthy lifestyle and taken all meds as directed. She finished her chemo and radiation therapy exactly 1 year ago, and all labs have come back within normal limits. A CT scan of the abdomen and pelvis is showing no signs of tumor activity. We will see Lacy back in 6 months or sooner if necessary.

ICD-9-CM Code Assignment: _____

E Codes—Supplementary Classification of External Causes of Injury and Poisoning

Chapter Outline

Objectives

At the conclusion of this chapter, the student will be able to:

1. Understand the purpose of E codes and how they are used.
2. Describe the instances in which E codes are used appropriately.
3. Discuss the specific coding guidelines that relate to E codes.
4. Select and code E codes from case studies.

Key Terms

Asphyxia

E Codes

Motor Vehicle Accident (MVA)

> **Reminder**
>
> *As you work through this chapter, you will need to have a copy of the ICD-9-CM coding book to reference.*

Introduction

Codes found in the "Supplementary Classification of External Causes of Injury and Poisoning" section of ICD-9-CM are referred to as E codes. These codes are located not only in the Table of Drugs and Chemicals but also in the Index to External Causes. The use of the Index to External Causes and the Table of Drugs and Chemicals was previously discussed in Chapter 3. Just like the main text of terms for ICD-9-CM coding, E codes have their own Alphabetic Index located immediately after the Table of Drugs and Chemicals. The E codes themselves are located immediately after V codes in the Tabular List.

Coding Guidelines for E Codes

E codes are codes that classify external causes, environmental events, or other conditions that cause an injury or other adverse effects. E codes are *never* used as a primary diagnosis but are used as a supplement to the main ICD-9-CM codes chosen. E codes are generally used for research and statistical purposes. Outpatient settings such as doctor's offices do not typically use E codes unless reporting for a motor vehicle accident (MVA), worker's compensation, or other instances in which they are required by the insurance companies. If a physician's office is involved in research, they may be required to report using E codes.

General coding guidelines for the use of E codes are found in Appendix A, Section 1, C19, a in this book. Outlined here are some of the basic guidelines for coding from this section.

Official ICD-9-CM Coding Guideline:

1. *An E code may be used with any code in the range of 001–V89, which indicates an injury, poisoning, or adverse effect due to an external cause.*

2. *Assign the appropriate E code for the initial encounter of an injury, poisoning, or adverse effect of drugs, not for subsequent treatment. External cause of injury codes (E codes) may be assigned while the acute fracture codes are still applicable.*

3. *Use the full range of E codes to completely describe the cause, the intent, and the place of occurrence, if applicable, for all injuries, poisonings, and adverse effects of drugs.*

4. *Assign as many E codes as necessary to fully explain each cause. If only one E code can be recorded, assign the E code most closely related to the principal diagnosis.*

5. *The selection of the appropriate E code is guided by the Index to External Causes, which is located after the alphabetic index to diseases and by Inclusion and Exclusion notes in the Tabular List.*

6. *An E code can never be a principal (first-listed) diagnosis.*

7. *An external cause code is not appropriate with a codes from subcategory 995.9, unless the patient also has an injury, poisoning, or adverse effect of drugs. (See Appendix A, Section II, C19, a 1–7)*

As in any coding done before this chapter, it is extremely important that the coder *not* code from the Alphabetic Index alone but refer to the Tabular Index to determine that the proper code was selected. Because of the varying scenarios that a coder may encounter with assigning E codes, as well as the volume of notes in the E code chapter, careful attention needs to be made to the Include: and Exclude: notes in each section of the E code chapter. The coder may also need to reference the official guidelines located in Appendix A of this book.

Coding E Codes

It is imperative that the coder read the medical documentation before reviewing the Index to External Causes to locate an E code. If the documentation is not specific, the coder should query the provider for clarification.

Transportation Accidents (Category Codes E800–E849)

Transport accidents are the first accidents classified to this chapter. Listed in these categories are aircraft, spacecraft, watercraft, motor vehicle, railway, and other road vehicle accidents. If more than one type of vehicle is involved, the E codes should be listed in the order given here, beginning with aircraft and ending with other road vehicles. If an accident occurs on land involving watercraft or aircraft, these vehicles are considered motor vehicles if on a highway or roadway and as off-road motor vehicles when parked off the road. Construction and farming vehicles that are on the road moving under their own power are considered transport; otherwise these vehicles are regarded as machinery. This includes bulldozers, cranes, and tractors. Fourth-digit classifications are used to identify the injured person. Codes from category E849 may also be assigned to indicate where the accident occurred. Category codes E800–E848 are summarized as follows:

E800–E807	Railway Accident—This category is used when the accident involves a train or other vehicle that travels on rails. It does not matter whether the vehicle is moving or stationary.
E810–E819	Motor Vehicle Traffic Accident—A **motor vehicle accident (MVA)** is an accident that occurs on the highway or roadway. An accident that involves an all-terrain vehicle (ATV) or a snowmobile is considered a nontraffic accident unless the vehicle is traveling on the road or highway.
E820–E825	Motor Vehicle Nontraffic Accident—Accidents that occur in places other than on public roadways are classified to these categories. Snowmobiles, ATVs, and other off-road vehicles are included in this section of codes. A person who has an accident while boarding or leaving a vehicle is classified to these categories of codes as well.
E826–E829	Other Road Vehicle Accidents—These codes are used for accidents that involve any vehicle other than motor vehicles. This might be a bicycle, an animal-drawn carriage, or a streetcar. Accidents involving an animal-drawn carriage include those due to breakage of any part of the vehicle.
E830–E838	Water Transport Accidents—Accidents involving recreational boating, vehicles used for transporting people or products, and any other vehicles that travel in the water are classified to these category codes.
E840–E845	Air and Space Transport Accidents—Any accident that is airline-related, whether commercial or noncommercial, as well as accidents involving spacecraft are reported with these categories of codes.
E846–E848	Vehicle Accidents Not Elsewhere Classifiable—The codes in this category are used when no other code describes the accident that involves a vehicle.

   Category E849 is used to indicate the place of occurrence for injuries and poisonings. Coders should follow these guidelines:

> **Official ICD-9-CM Coding Guideline:**
>
> *Place of Occurrence Guideline*
>
>   *Use an additional code from category E849 to indicate the place of occurrence for injuries and poisonings. The place of occurrence describes the place where the event occurred and not the patient's activity at the time of the event.*
>
>   *Do not use E849.9 if the place of occurrence is not stated. (See Appendix A, Section I, C19, b.)*

Accidental Poisoning by Drugs, Medicinal Substances, and Biologicals, and Other Solid and Liquid Substances, Gases and Vapors (Category Codes E850–E869)

The next section of the chapter categorizes accidental poisonings. These codes are located by using the Table of Drugs and Chemicals. These E codes are used to identify the following situations:

- Accidental overdose of a drug

- Wrong drug given or taken in error

- Drug taken inadvertently

- Accidents in the use of drugs and biologicals in medical and surgical procedures

The coder should read the Include: and Exclude: notations that appear at the start of the E850–E858 range of codes. The notations provide examples of accidents that are included and excluded from these codes.

The E codes found in this section are summarized as follows:

E850-E858	Accidental Poisoning by Drug, Medicinal Substances, and Biologicals—Codes included here classify different types of drugs that could cause an accidental poisoning by overdose, drug taken in error, and accidents in the use of biologicals in medical and surgical procedures.
E860-E869	Accidental Poisoning by Other Solid and Liquid Substances, Gases, and Vapors—Included in this group of codes are accidental poisoning by alcohol, cleansing agents, fertilizers, and vapors. Also included are codes for accidental poisoning by corrosives and caustics, which include types of acid.

Misadventures to Patients During and After Surgical and Medical Care (Category Codes E870–E879)

Sometimes patients have unusual or abnormal reactions after surgical or medical procedures. In these situations the following E codes are used to identify the misadventure.

E870-E876	Misadventures to Patients During Surgical and Medical Care—When medical errors occur, such as prescribing the wrong medication, operating a mechanical device incorrectly, completing a surgical procedure incorrectly, or administering an anesthetic improperly, E codes from this category of codes are used.
E878-E879	Surgical and Medical Procedures as the Cause of Abnormal Reaction of Patient or Later Complication, Without Mention of Misadventure at the Time of Procedure—After a surgical or medical procedure, the patient may have an abnormal reaction, which is coded from this category of codes. Sometimes the patient does not have a complication until after the procedure, such as a malfunction of a prosthetic device. Such codes are also found in this section.

Accidental Falls (Category Codes E880–E888); Accidents Caused by Fire and Flames (Category Codes E890–E899)

Falls are very common reasons for many injuries. Many elderly people fall each year, requiring medical attention to the injuries from their falls. Construction accidents are also another cause of falls. Accidental falls and accidents caused by fire are coded from the following categories of E codes:

E880-E888	Accidental Falls—The accidental fall codes are used most frequently when coding medical records of elderly patients. The accidental falls are broken down by specific types such as from stairs or off a ladder. A fall may be a result of a person striking an object. These codes are found in these category codes as well.
E890-E899	Accidents Caused by Fire and Flames—Accidents caused by fire include the injury that may be caused by flames. Also found here are codes for asphyxia or poisoning due to fire. Asphyxia is suffocation due to lack of oxygen when there is a fire. Most causes of death in a fire are not from the fire itself but from asphyxia.

Accidents Due to Natural and Environmental Conditions (Category Codes E900–E909); Accidents Caused by Submersion, Suffocation, and Foreign Bodies (E910–E915)

E900–E909 is used to classify situations that have occurred due to natural and environmental conditions such as exposure to excessive heat and cold, high and low air pressure, abandonment or neglect of infants and helpless persons, lightning, and other environmental and natural conditions. Codes E910–E915 are used to classify accidental drowning and submersion, inhalation and ingestion of food causing obstruction of the respiratory factor, and accidents caused by foreign bodies. This section of E codes is organized into the following categories:

E900–E909	Accidents Due to Natural and Environmental Factors—Accidents caused by excessive weather conditions, such as excessive heat or excessive cold, are classified here. Also found here is an injury caused by a lightning strike. Environmental factors might include snakebites or poisoning from plants.
E910–E915	Accidents Caused by Submersion, Suffocation, and Foreign Bodies—Drowning accidents are found in this section, as are suffocations. Foreign bodies accidentally entering an orifice are found here.
E916–E928	Other Accidents—This category lists codes that cannot be found in other categories or accidents that tend not to fall in any other more specific category. As stated in the guidelines, when the intent of an injury or poisoning is known but the cause is not, use code E928.9.

Late Effects of External Causes

Late effects of external causes are found in several categories in the E code chapter. Coding guidelines specify how the late effects should be used.

> ## Official ICD-9-CM Coding Guideline:
>
> 1. Late effect E codes exist for injuries and poisonings but not for adverse effects of drugs, misadventures, and surgical complications.
> 2. A late effect E code (E929, E959, E969, E977, E989, or E999.1) should be used with any report of a late effect or sequela resulting from a previous injury or poisoning (905–909).
> 3. A late effect E code should never be used with a related current nature of injury.
> 4. Use of a late effect E code for subsequent visits when a late effect of the initial injury or poisoning is being treated. There is no late effect E code for adverse effects of drugs. Do not use a late effect E code for subsequent visits for follow-up care (e.g., to assess healing, to receive rehabilitative therapy) of the injury or poisoning when no late effect of the injury has been documented. (See Appendix A, Section I, C19, H.)

The guidelines state specifically which codes fall into the late effect category. The tables in this book do not separate them out unless further clarification is necessary.

Drugs, Medicinal, and Biological Substances Causing Adverse Effects in Therapeutic Use (Category Codes E930–E949)

Patients can have an adverse effect to medicinal and biological substances that are prescribed for therapeutic use or that are taken as an over-the-counter treatment. When a patient has an adverse effect, this is usually described in the medical record as one of the following:

Allergy to

Allergic reaction

Hypersensitivity to a drug

Adverse reaction to a drug

Toxicity of a drug

When this situation occurs, the E code is located by referencing the Table of Drugs and Chemicals and selecting a code from the Therapeutic Use column. The coder should also remember the following when selecting E codes from category E930–E949:

| E930–E949 | Drugs, Medicinal, and Biological Substances Causing Adverse Effects in Therapeutic Use—Therapeutic use refers to doses of medication given correctly and taken as prescribed. This category does not contain codes for overdoses. Some patients may suffer from hypersensitivity or have an allergic reaction. |

Accidents Caused by Suicide and Homicide and Injuries Purposely Inflicted by Other Persons

When selecting codes, it is important to identify the action that occurred as part of the suicide or homicide, such as jumping or pushing a person before a moving object, rape, assault by poisoning, and so on. Injuries that occur as a result of suicide or homicide or that are purposely inflicted by other persons are classified as follows:

E950–E959	Suicide and Self-Inflicted Injury—These codes are used only if the condition is truly deemed a suicide or self-inflicted injury. Use of these codes on an insurance claim can have a devastating impact on how the claim is handled and can have far-reaching effects for a person who tries to obtain insurance in the future.
E960–E969	Homicide and Injury Purposely Inflicted by Other Persons—Assaults of any kind, whether they are with a firearm, poisoning, or corrosive substance, are included in this section. Fights and rape are also coded from this category, as are perpetrators of child or adult abuse.
E970–E978	Legal Intervention—Falling into this category of codes are injuries that may be a result of intervention by police officers or law enforcement during an arrest, maintaining order during a protest march or other large group gathering, or attending any other type of legal action.
E979	Terrorism—This category is used to identify the cause of injuries resulting from the unlawful use of force or violence against persons or property to intimidate or coerce a government, the civilian population, or any segment thereof, in the furtherance of a political or social objective.
E980–E989	Injury Undetermined Whether Accidentally or Purposely Inflicted—Any action that might be undetermined as to the specific cause or reason should be coded to this section.
E990–E999	Injury Resulting from Operations of War—These categories of codes are used in coding for military personnel during times of war. Training of military personnel does not fall under this category.

Remember that any number of E codes can be used to accurately describe an encounter. Coding guidelines explain the sequencing of E codes and the situations that warrant use of more than one E code. (See Appendix A, C19, d.) It is important for coders to identify how E codes will be used in the organization in which they work. It should also be noted that there are E code guidelines for child and adult abuse, late effects of external causes, and terrorism guidelines. These guidelines are found in Appendix A, Section I, C19.

Summary

- E codes are located by referencing the Index to External Causes and the Table of Drugs and Chemicals.

- E codes are never used as a principal or first-listed diagnosis.

- E codes classify external causes, environmental events, and other conditions that cause an injury or adverse effect.

- E codes are assigned for all initial treatments of an injury, poisoning, or adverse effect of drugs.

- Multiple E codes can be assigned to fully explain the cause of an injury or adverse effect.

- Numerous notations appear throughout the E code chapter of ICD-9-CM.

Chapter Review

True/False: Indicate whether each statement is true (T) or false (F).

1. _____ The E codes Tabular List is located immediately after the Table of Drugs and Chemicals.

2. _____ E codes are *never* used as a primary diagnosis.

3. _____ E codes should not be used with V codes.

4. _____ Late effect E codes exist for injuries and poisonings but not for adverse effects of drugs.

5. _____ When several vehicles are involved in an accident, the order of vehicles is aircraft, space-craft, and watercraft.

Fill-in-the-Blank: Enter the appropriate term(s) to complete each statement.

6. E codes can be used as a _____.

7. E code E849 is assigned to indicate _____.

8. A lightning strike accident is coded from category _____.

9. A person injured while falling from a ladder is classified to E code _____.

10. A suicide attempt by a cutting or piercing instrument is classified to E code _____.

Coding Assignments

Instructions: Using an ICD-9-CM coding book, select the appropriate codes and E codes for each statement.

Statement	Codes
1. Lacerations on arm due to being thrown from a snow vehicle	_____
2. Fracture of the left arm due to being tackled in a football game	_____
3. Laceration of face due to being hit by tree	_____
4. Obstruction of air passages due to vomiting of food	_____
5. Bruise of thigh caused by assault	_____
6. Skin rash for allergic reaction to antibiotic	_____
7. High fever due to reaction to administration of BCG vaccine correctly administrated	_____
8. Fracture of femur due to suicide attempt by jumping before a bicycle	_____
9. Burn on left shoulder due to a cigarette	_____
10. Laceration of chin due to jumping into a swimming pool	_____
11. Hip fracture due to fall from chair	_____
12. Abdominal pain due to object left in abdomen after surgery	_____
13. Coma due to wrong fluid in infusion	_____
14. Crushing injury of hand due to hand's being caught in hay rake	_____
15. Burn of right hand due to scalding by boiling water	_____
16. Surgical operation with implant of artificial internal device—heart valve prosthesis	_____
17. Accident caused by a fire in a fireplace in a private home	_____

18. Accident caused by a transmission cable _____

19. Accident caused by bad wiring in the toaster oven _____

20. Accidental poisoning by gas in a pipeline accident _____

21. Train accident involving a collision with a rock on the track _____

22. Suicide attempt with barbiturates _____

23. Injury due to building collapse _____

24. Crushed by avalanche _____

25. Cut due to electric knife _____

Case Studies

Instructions: Review each case study, and select the correct ICD-9-CM diagnostic and E codes.

CASE 1

Skilled Nursing Facility Note

Mrs. Jones is a 83-year-old female who has been a resident for 2 years. The nurse called me to the unit to examine Mrs. Jones because she fell from her wheelchair within the last 15 minutes and now is complaining of pain in her right arm.

PHYSICAL EXAM:

EXTREMITIES: All extremities are negative for bruising, but when I touch the right arm the patient complains of increased pain and discomfort.

PLAN: An ambulance was called to take Mrs. Jones to the ER for an X-ray to rule out a fracture.

ICD-9-CM Code Assignment: _____

CASE 2

Emergency Department Note

This 3-year-old patient was playing outside and was cut by a piece of broken glass.

EXAM:

There is a 1-cm laceration of the skin on the right hand.

PROCEDURE: The area was cleaned and sutured. See procedure note dictated.

PLAN: Patient is to follow up with his primary care provider in 1 week for suture removal.

ICD-9-CM Code Assignment: _____

CASE 3

Hospital Progress Note

This 35-year-old patient was given a dose of penicillin and has experienced a severe allergic reaction. The nurse called me to immediately come and examine the patient.

PHYSICAL EXAM: The patient is not responsive. Vitals as per nursing note.

HEART: Bradycardia present.

PLAN: Full neurological work up. Neurologist called for immediate consult. Orders are written.

ICD-9-CM Code Assignment: _____

CASE 4

Physician's Office Visit

This 42-year-old male was hiking in the Grand Canyon this afternoon and suffered a rattlesnake bite. The patient came upon the snake unexpectedly, startling both of them. The snake reacted by attacking and thus biting the patient. At the time of the bite, the patient stopped immediately and treated the wound as best as he could until he could get help. It has now been 45 minutes since the bite occurred. The wound looks good, and no further treatment is needed, but we will keep the patient overnight for observation and to redo some lab work to be sure the venom is out of his system.

ICD-9-CM Code Assignment: _____

CASE 5

Physician's Office Visit

This is a 22-year-old young man who received a shoulder injury as a result of a paintball game. He was with friends at the local paintball club and in the midst of their game, the patient was struck at close range in the right shoulder by a paintball. An X-ray of the area shows that there is no major injury to the shoulder. There is bruising and pain with movement, consistent with what the patient told us happened. At this time, the patient is advised to take Advil as needed and to alternate heat and ice.

ICD-9-CM Code Assignment: _____

ICD-9-CM Procedural Coding

Introduction to ICD-9-CM Procedure Coding

Chapter Outline

Introduction

Procedure Code Structure and Volume Format

Prefixes and Suffixes Relating to Procedures

Surgical and Procedural Terminology

Coding Conventions

Coding Canceled and Incomplete Procedures

Coding Endoscopic Procedures

Internet Links

Summary

Chapter Review

Objectives

At the conclusion of this chapter, the student will be able to:

1. Discuss the organization of volume 3 of ICD-9-CM.

2. Identify procedure phrases in operative reports.

3. Identify coding conventions used in volume 3 of ICD-9-CM.

4. Describe procedures.

5. Discuss the coding of endoscopic versus open procedures.

6. Explain the coding of cancelled procedures.

Key Terms

Ablation	Biopsy	Cysto-	Dilation
Amputation	Bypass	*Current Procedural Terminology, Fourth Edition (CPT)*	Drainage
Anastomosis	-cele		-ectomy
Ante-	-centesis	Debridement	Em-
-asis	Closure/correction	Dia-	Endoscopic

Reminder

As you work through this chapter, you will need to have a copy of the ICD-9-CM coding book to reference.

Evacuation	Infusion	Operation	Revision
Excision	Insertion	-ostomy	-rrhage
Exploration	Intra-	-plasty	-rrhagia
Fusion	Ligation	Procedure	-rrhaphy
Graft	Lysis	Puncture	-rrhea
-gram	Macro-	Radiography	-rrhexis
-graph	Manipulation	Reconstruction	-scopy
Healthcare Common Procedure Coding System (HCPCS)	Micro-	Reduction	Shunt
	Myelo-	Removal	Significant Procedure
Implant	-oma	Repair	Suture
Incision	Omit Code	Replacement	Volume 3 of ICD-9-CM
	Open Procedure	Resection	

Introduction

The ICD-9-CM, *International Classification of Diseases, Ninth Revision, Clinical Modification,* is organized into three volumes. Volumes 1 and 2 of ICD-9-CM were discussed earlier in this book. Volume 3 of the ICD-9-CM classifies procedures and contains both an Alphabetic Index and a Tabular List. The use of volume 3 will be discussed in the remaining chapters of this textbook. Volume 3 of ICD-9-CM contains procedure codes used by hospitals to report inpatient procedures and would not be used by physicians' offices or outpatient settings. The Uniform Hospital Discharge Data Set (UHDDS) requires that all significant procedures are coded and reported for hospital inpatients. A significant procedure is any procedure that carries an anesthetic or procedural risk, is surgical in nature, or requires the provider to have specialized training to complete the procedure. To bill and report physician and outpatient services, coders are required to use *Current Procedural Terminology, Fourth Edition (CPT),* and the Healthcare Common Procedure Coding System (HCPCS). Because facility policies vary for internal reporting requirements, some facilities also code outpatient procedures using ICD-9-CM procedure codes to capture information for internal data gathering.

Procedure Code Structure and Volume Format

ICD-9-CM procedure codes comprise up to four digits, with the first two digits followed by a decimal point. Three-digit codes are not used if a four-digit code is presented in ICD-9-CM. The two digits preceding the decimal point indicate the body system in which the procedure occurred or the site of the procedure. The one or two digits following the decimal point indicate a more specific code with relation to site, purpose, technique, or diagnosis.

Volume 3 of ICD-9-CM is organized in the same format as volumes 1 and 2; however, both the Alphabetic Index and Tabular List are contained together in this volume. The process of locating codes in the Alphabetic Index of Procedures and then verifying them in the Tabular List of Procedures is exactly the same as explained at the start of this book.

When trying to locate a procedure code in volume 3, the coder needs to identify the main term to reference in the Alphabetic Index to Procedures. The coder also needs to identify the procedure to be coded from a procedural phrase or statement.

EXAMPLE: Dr. Knife performed a mammoplasty of the breast with split-thickness graft. The main procedure completed is the mammoplasty; so the coder begins by locating this main term in the Alphabetic Index to Procedures. The entry appears in the Alphabetic Index to Procedures as:

```
Mammoplasty 85.89
 With
  full-thickness graft 85.83
  muscle flap 85.85
  pedicle graft 85.84
  split-thickness graft 85.82
```

After reviewing the list of codes found, the coder selects 85.82 to properly report the procedure completed. Verification in the Tabular List confirms the code choice.

The coder should always be guided by the Alphabetic Index for Procedures when coding procedures, because the Alphabetic Index for Procedures is far more comprehensive than the Tabular List for procedures. At times, procedures are listed in the Alphabetic Index that are not listed in the Tabular List.

Sometimes the procedure statement to be coded is identified by an eponym or acronym. In the case of an acronym, the procedure is usually found under the acronym itself, such as LASIK or laser-assisted in situ keratomileusis. In the case of an eponym, the procedure might be found by referencing the eponym itself, by referencing the type of procedure, or by looking up the procedure under the main term "operation." An example of this would be the Leadbetter-Politano operation. This procedure can be found under the main term "operation," the eponym "Leadbetter-Politano," or the type of procedure, a ureteroneocystostomy.

As in the Alphabetic Index in volume 2, the coder needs to pay close attention to the indentations that are present in the index. Remember to pull out that ruler to correctly identify the indentations! Remember that the main term is located first; then the coding becomes more specific the further the indention goes. The Alphabetic Index of Procedures does offer cross-references to other terms, but volume 3 cross-references are not as extensive as those in volume 2, which is why a knowledge of terminology is very important when coding procedures.

Prefixes and Suffixes Relating to Procedures

Medical terminology is broken down into word parts. Some common word parts that are helpful to understand when trying to code procedures are as follows:

Prefix	Meaning	Suffix	Meaning
ante-	Before, forward	-asis	State of or condition
cysto-	Bladder, sac	-cele	Hernia or swelling
dia-	Through, apart, across	-centesis	Remove fluid by surgical puncture
em-	In	-ectomy	Cut out by surgical means
intra-	Within	-gram	A drawing
macro-	Large	-graph	An instrument that records
micro-	Small	-lysis	Break up or dissolve
myelo-	Marrow, spinal cord	-oma	Tumor
para-	Beside, near	-ostomy	An artificial opening is formed
		-plasty	Type of surgical repair
		-scopy	Visual examination of the interior

One group of suffixes can be particularly confusing due to their similarity in appearance. They do, however, mean entirely different things. Please pay close attention to the differences between the following suffixes:

Suffix	Meaning
-rrhage, -rrhagia	Abnormal or excessive bleeding
-rrhea	Abnormal discharge of body fluids
-rrhexis	To rupture
-rrhaphy	Surgical repair by sutures or stitches

Exercise 25–1   Identifying Similar Suffixes

Instructions: Identify the correct suffix for the definition given.

Definition   **Suffix**

1. Abnormal discharge of body fluids   _____

2. An instrument that records   _____

3. An artificial opening   _____

4. Type of surgical repair   _____

5. To rupture   _____

6. Remove fluid by surgical puncture   _____

7. Surgical repair by sutures or stitches   _____

8. Hollow   _____

9. Break up or dissolve   _____

10. Abnormal or excessive bleeding   _____

Surgical and Procedural Terminology

Understanding the terminology is important when trying to locate a type of procedure. The type of procedure done—whether it is a repair, a removal, a puncture, or a scope—is easier to locate and code when the terminology is understood.

Some of the main terms that are used to locate procedures follow, each with a brief definition of what the term means. The coder needs to understand what exactly was being done in order to code it, so basic understanding of these terms is needed to code in volume 3.

Main Term	Definition
Ablation	Destruction with regard to function of a body part—Various techniques can be used to accomplish this, such as radiation, extreme cold, or electrocautery.
Amputation	Complete removal of a body part—Amputation can occur in circumstances in which an extremity or organ becomes so diseased that the body part does not function or causes gross infection and poses a threat to the life of the patient.

Anastomosis	Surgical joining of two tubular structures—This is usually found in surgeries in the gastrointestinal tract.
Aspiration (Surgical)	This is the drawing of fluids from the body, as in a joint aspiration.
Biopsy	A sampling of living tissue taken for diagnostic purposes—The physician is trying to determine if a growth is benign or malignant and if further treatment is needed.
Bypass	To go around or "bypass" a structure—In vascular procedures, the surgeon may need to bypass an artery to regain proper blood flow to an area.
Closure/Correction	In the context of procedures, these terms usually refer to a repair of some type.
Debridement	To clean out a wound to prevent infection or to cleanse a site
Destruction	To eliminate completely—This term may be seen with regard to any number of procedures and is used frequently with the term "removal."
Dilation	The expansion of, usually an opening—Frequently heard with regard to curettage, as in a D&C.
Drainage	To remove fluid, usually with a tube
Endoscopic	Visual inspection of inside the body—Coding for this needs to be handled carefully when the scope passes through more than one cavity.
Evacuation	The coder will be referred to "drainage," which means to remove from.
Excision	To surgically remove, as in a lesion or organ
Exploration	Usually a procedure that is diagnostic in nature—These procedures are used to establish a diagnosis. Once the procedure goes from a diagnostic exploratory procedure to a definite focused one, the exploration is not coded.
Fusion	Coming together—This term is used frequently in orthopedic or spinal surgeries.
Graft	To transplant any tissue—This is a common procedure with burn victims. The term may also be used in relation to vascular procedures.
Implant	To insert an object or material—This term may be used in relation to a graft but is commonly used with regard to a device such as a pacemaker.
Incision	To cut into—As a surgical approach, this is not coded separately.
Infusion	Movement of fluid into a vein—The therapeutic introduction of a medication or fluid into the body is usually through a vein.
Insertion	To put into—This is a broad term used for any number of procedures.
Ligation	To tie or bind off blood vessels or ducts using catgut, cotton, silk, or wire
Lysis	Destruction, loosening, or releasing—This is seen very frequently in abdominal procedures in which the surgeon is freeing up and removing adhesions. Sometimes this is an integral part of a more extensive surgery.
Manipulation	Movement in a skillful manner, as in physical therapy or joint movement to put back into place
Operation	Check under this term if you are unable to find the surgery or procedure performed anywhere else.
Procedure	Use this term when you are trying to find the code for a procedure that may not be located anywhere else.
Puncture	To pierce or penetrate with a sharp instrument
Radiography	Noninvasive way to look at the internal structures of the body through gamma rays or X-rays—A picture is produced and becomes part of the record.
Reconstruction	To rebuild—These procedures are done when rebuilding a part of the body such as breast reconstruction after mastectomy.

Main Term	Definition
Reduction	To correct or move back into place, as in a hernia, dislocation, or fracture
Removal	To take out completely—The removal or excision of something is a very common procedure, and the term is encountered frequently.
Repair	To fix—This is another term used frequently because most surgeries are necessary to fix something that is wrong.
Replacement	To insert tissue or organ needed for proper function—This is also used in reference to maintenance on devices, such as stents or tubes.
Resection	Removal of all or part of an organ or tissue
Revision	To surgically correct or fix
Shunt	A shunt is used to divert or bypass.
Suture	The procedure used to close an open wound or incision

Surgical coding requires knowledge of the intent of the procedure. First, distinction needs to be made between a diagnostic procedure, such as an exploratory procedure, and a procedure that is being done for treatment. The procedures being done for treatment take precedence over diagnostic procedures or surgeries.

EXAMPLE: Mike Spike was admitted with severe right lower-quadrant abdominal pain. He is not running a fever, and the lab work has come back inconclusive for appendicitis. It was decided to take the patient into the operating room for an exploratory procedure to determine what is causing his pain.

Patient was prepped for a laparoscopic approach to visualize any problems. Placement of the scope allowed for a clear view of the abdominal cavity, which revealed that the appendix was close to rupturing. The appendix was removed.

In this case, because the appendectomy was performed, the following is coded: Appendectomy, laparoscopic (47.01).

However, if the laparoscopy revealed no findings and no further procedure was performed, the following is coded: Laparoscopy (54.21).

Because the exploratory procedure turned into an actual treatment procedure, 47.01 is the procedure code used. Until such time as it turns into a treatment procedure, the 54.21 is correct. The use of both codes is incorrect and would result in a denial by the insurance company should the claim be submitted this way.

The approach for the procedures can sometimes guide the coder as to which term to reference in the Alphabetic Index. If the code cannot be located any other way, then reference can be made to the main term of "operation."

Coding Conventions

Coding conventions are used in volume 3 of ICD-9-CM just as they are in volumes 1 and 2. The conventions are virtually the same as those used in the coding of diseases. Attention needs to be paid to any Include: or Exclude: notes that are designated in both the Alphabetic Index and the Tabular List. These conventions are used to alert the coder of the need to include or exclude the use of additional codes. Here a brief discussion will describe some of the unique features of procedural conventions.

Code Also

The phrase *code also* is used in volume 3 to instruct coders to code an additional code if the referenced procedure was performed during this operative session. This convention is used in volume 3 to alert the coder to code each component of a operation or procedure that has more than one component commonly performed together or to code the use of special equipment or special adjunctive procedures.

> **EXAMPLE:** Dr. Light performs an extracapsular extraction of the lens by a temporal inferior route with the insertion of pseuodphakos. To code this, the coder references *extraction* in the Alphabetic Index and then the subterm *cataract,* followed by *extracapsular approach,* followed by *temporal inferior route.* When code 13.51 in the Tabular List is referenced, the instructional notation of "code also any synchronous insertion of pseudophakos (13.71)" appears. This instructs the coder to use the additional code of 13.71 to complete the coding assignment.

Omit Code

The **omit code** convention is used only in volume 3 of ICD-9-CM. This notation appears in both the Alphabetic Index and the Tabular List to indicate that no code is assigned. This convention commonly appears in the Alphabetic Index following the subterm "as operative approach," and it appears in the Tabular List following an Exclude: note. Examples for both appear as:

```
Example: Alphabetic Index
Thoracotomy (with drainage) 34.09
  as operative approach—omit code
  exploratory 34.02


Example: Tabular List
34.0 Incision of Chest Wall and Pleura
  Excludes: that as operative approach—omit code
```

This convention tells the coder that if the incision is part of a surgery and it is the approach to the procedure, it is not billed separately. The approach is considered an integral part of the surgery and is not normally coded separately.

Coding Canceled and Incomplete Procedures

In rare instances, a surgery is started and then, for any number of reasons, completion is not possible. If a procedure is started but not completed, the following guidelines should be used:

```
1. If an incision is made and the procedure is not completed, code to the
   incision site.
2. If a cavity space is entered and explored but the procedure is not completed,
   assign a code to describe the exploratory procedure.
3. If an endoscopic approach is started and the scope cannot reach the intended
   site to perform the definitive procedure, code the endoscopy only.
```

In some cases a patient is admitted and a scheduled procedure is canceled before it begins. This can occur because of a number of reasons, including the fact that a patient may have a medical condition that is a counterindication to surgery, the surgeon is unavailable, or the facility poses a problem such as staff scheduling or equipment failure. When this occurs, no procedure code is assigned; however, a code from category V64, Persons encountering health services for specific procedures not carried out, is assigned.

Coding Endoscopic Procedures

When a scope is used to perform a procedure, the coder should select the code for the completion of the endoscopic procedure. Endoscopic procedures are located in the Alphabetic Index by referencing the main term *endoscopy* or the term for the specific scope used. When a scope is passed through more than one body area, the code for the endoscopy should identify the farthest placement of the scope. Various types of endoscopic procedures include:

Arthroscopy

Bronchoscopy

Colonoscopy

Cystoscopy

Esophagoscopy

Esophagogastroduodenoscopy (EGD)

Laparoscopy

Laryngoscopy

Mediastinoscopy

Thoracoscopy

ICD-9-CM provides codes for most endoscopic procedures; however, when a separate code does not exist, the open procedure code is assigned.

Various types of endoscopes are used to perform procedures that were previously completed via an incision, also referred to as an open procedure. When an endoscopic procedure is started but has to be converted to an open procedure, the code for the open procedure is assigned. If a laparoscopic approach is converted to an open approach, then this case is also identified by the V code V64.41, Laparoscopic surgical procedure converted to open procedure.

Internet Links

To learn more about ICD-9-CM procedure codes and the process for requesting new and revised procedures codes and for a list of new and revised and deleted procedure codes, visit *www.cms.hhs.gov/ ICD9ProviderDiagnosticCodes/06_codes.asp.*

Summary

- Volume 3 of ICD-9-CM classifies procedures and surgeries.

- ICD-9-CM procedure codes are used to report inpatient procedures.

- ICD-9-CM procedure codes have up to four digits.

- Procedures are located in the Alphabetic Index of volume 3 by referencing the name of the procedure completed.

- The conventions used in volume 3 of ICD-9-CM are similar to the conventions used in volumes 1 and 2.

- Coders must differentiate between procedures completed for diagnostic purposes and procedures completed for therapeutic purposes.

- Procedures can be completed by using an endoscopic or open approach.

- To locate an endoscopic procedure in the Alphabetic Index, the coder should reference the main term "endoscopy" or the specific name of the scope used.

Chapter Review

True/False: Indicate whether the statement is true (T) or false (F).

1. _____ In volume 3, the Alphabetic Index and the Tabular List are contained together.

2. _____ Attention to the indentations found in the Alphabetic Index is not as important in volume 3 as it is in volumes 1 and 2.

3. _____ The suffix that means "to rupture" is -rrhea.

4. _____ Understanding terminology is essential in coding procedures.

5. _____ When an exploratory procedure turns into a treatment procedure, you would code both the exploratory procedure and the treatment.

6. _____ A procedure can be identified by an eponym or acronym.

7. _____ When a scope is used to perform a procedure, the approach is coded.

8. _____ Volume 3 codes are used to code inpatient procedures only.

9. _____ The prefix em- means "in."

10. _____ If an incision is made in a body cavity and the procedure is canceled, the coder selects the code for the indented procedure.

Short Answer: For each definition, give the correct procedure term.

Definition	Term
11. Surgical joining of two tubular structures	_____
12. The expansion of an opening	_____
13. Procedure used to establish a diagnosis	_____
14. To take out completely	_____
15. To pierce or penetrate with a sharp instrument	_____
16. Movement in a skillful manner to put back into place	_____
17. To insert an object or material	_____
18. To clean out a wound to prevent infection	_____
19. Destruction with regard to function of a body part	_____
20. The coming together	_____
21. Destruction, loosening, or releasing	_____
22. To transplant any tissue	_____
23. To rebuild	_____
24. To fix	_____

25. To close an open wound or incision   _____

26. To remove from   _____

27. To draw fluids from the body   _____

28. To remove fluid from the body, usually with a tube   _____

29. To cut into   _____

30. To surgically correct or fix   _____

Operations on the Nervous System

Chapter Outline

Introduction

Introduction to Body System Operations
and Procedures

Internet Links

Summary

Chapter Review

Coding Assignments

Case Studies

Objectives

At the conclusion of this chapter, the student will be able to:

1. Describe operations on the nervous system.
2. Explain the divisions of the nervous system.
3. Select and code operations on the nervous system.

Key Terms

Analgesia Injection

Biopsy of Spinal Cord or
Spinal Meninges

Closed Biopsy

Craniectomy

Craniotomy

Curettage of the Brain

Decompression of
Nerves

Debridement of the
Brain

Hemispherectomy

Inclusive

Lobectomy

Nerve Release

Neurolytic Agent

Open Biopsy

Release of Carpal
Tunnel

Release of Tarsal Tunnel

Spinal Tap

Reminder

As you work through this chapter, you should have a copy of volume 3 of ICD-9-CM to reference.

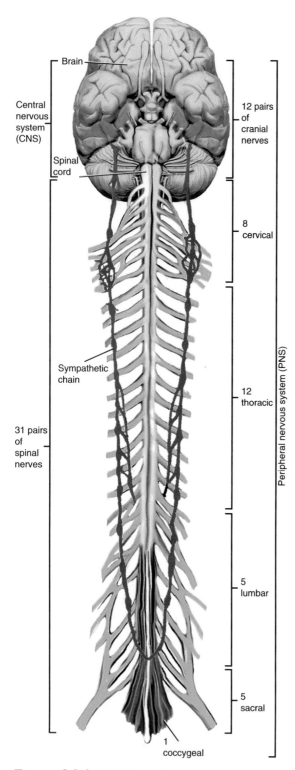

Figure 26-1 Divisions of the nervous system (From Caruthers B, Price P, Junge TL, et al. *Surgical Technology for the Surgical Technologist: A Positive Care Approach.* Clifton Park, NY: Delmar, Cengage Learning, 2001, p. 825.)

(Labels in figure: Brain; Central nervous system (CNS); Spinal cord; Sympathetic chain; 31 pairs of spinal nerves; 12 pairs of cranial nerves; 8 cervical; 12 thoracic; 5 lumbar; 5 sacral; 1 coccygeal; Peripheral nervous system (PNS))

Introduction

Chapter 1 of volume 3 of ICD-9-CM, "Operations on the Nervous System," is organized into categories 01–05:

01   Incision and Excision of Skull, Brain, and Cerebral Meninges

02   Other Operations on Skull, Brain, and Cerebral Meninges

03   Operations on Spinal Cord and Spinal Canal Structures

04   Operations on Cranial and Peripheral Nerves

05   Operations on Sympathetic Nerves or Ganglia

Introduction to Body System Operations and Procedures

Surgeries that are completed on the nervous system involve the brain, spinal cord, peripheral nerves, and the protective structures that surround these structures. The nervous system is divided into the central nervous system (CNS) and the peripheral nervous system (PNS). Figure 26-1 illustrates the divisions of the nervous system. Coders need to be familiar with the anatomy of the nervous system to identify the site of the procedures completed.

Incision and Excision of Skull, Brain, and Cerebral Meninges (Category Code 01)

Incisions and excisions are performed on the skull, brain, and cerebral meninges for a number of reasons. When an incision is made to perform surgery, the incision is not coded because it is considered to be part of the more complex procedure, or inclusive. At times, a craniotomy, the cutting open of a section of the skull bones, or a craniectomy, the removal of a section of the skull bones, is performed to remove excessive pressure within the skull or to explore the anatomical site. Figure 26-2 illustrates a craniotomy. Excisions are performed to remove a lesion, foreign body, or bone fragments.

Category code 01, Incision and excisions of skull, brain, and cerebral meninges, is divided into three-digit codes. (Note that fourth digits are also used throughout this category.)

Figure 26-2 Craniotomy with burr holes (From
Caruthers B, Price P, Junge TL, et al. *Surgical
Technology for the Surgical Technologist: A Positive Care
Approach.* Clifton Park, NY: Delmar, Cengage Learning,
2001, p. 852.)

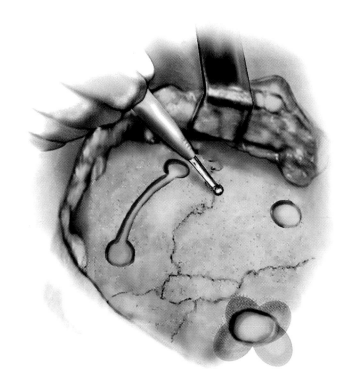

Three-Digit Codes	Description of Codes
01.0X	Cranial Puncture—These codes are used to code the penetration of the structures in the skull by a surgical instrument. These procedures are sometimes necessary to relieve pressure on the brain or to obtain cerebrospinal fluid through aspiration.
01.1X	Diagnostic Procedures on Skull, Brain, and Cerebral Meninges—This range of codes includes closed and open biopsies of the cerebral meninges and other diagnostic procedures on the brain. A biopsy is the removal of a piece of living tissue for examination. A closed biopsy is completed without making an incision to obtain the tissue, and it is completed percutaneously or endoscopically or by use of a needle. An open biopsy is completed by making an incision to obtain the tissue sample.
01.2X	Craniotomy and Craniectomy—A craniotomy is an incision into the skull, and a craniectomy is the removal of a section of the skull bones. A craniotomy is not coded when it is the operative approach. Coders should be familiar with the notations that appear in this code category because they guide code selection.
01.3X	Incision of Brain and Cerebral Meninges—These codes are used to code incisions of the brain and cerebral meninges. Drainage of an intracerebral hematoma is classified to code 01.39.
01.4X	Operations on Thalamus and Globus Pallidus—Operations classified to these codes include incisions and excisions, as well as therapeutic chemical destruction of the anatomical site.
01.5X	Other Excision or Destruction of Brain and Meninges—Procedures that are classified to 01.5X include hemispherectomy, the excision of a cerebral hemisphere; lobectomy, the excision of a lobe of the cerebrum; debridement of the brain, the removal of damaged brain tissue; and curettage of the brain, the removal of lesions from the brain surface.
01.6	Excision of Lesion of Skull—This code is for the removal of granulation tissue of the cranium. The coder should note that a biopsy of the skull and a sequestrectomy are excluded from this code.

Figure 26-3 illustrates a cross-section of the brain to help the coder understand the location of various brain structures.

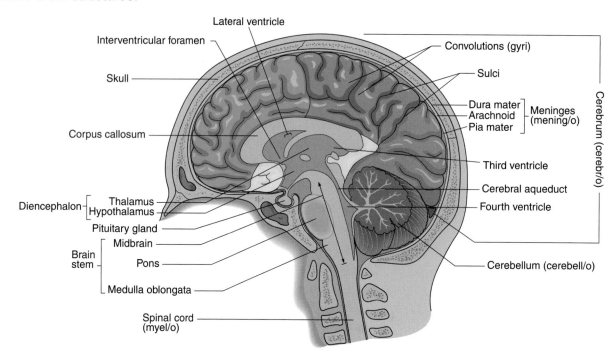

Figure 26-3 Cross-section of the brain (From Caruthers B, Price P, Junge TL, et al. *Surgical Technology for the Surgical Technologist: A Positive Care Approach.* Clifton Park, NY: Delmar, Cengage Learning, 2001, p. 830.)

Other Operations on Skull, Brain, and Cerebral Meninges (Category Code 02)

Category code 02 is also divided into third-digit codes:

02.0X	Cranioplasty—This is the surgical repair of the skull.
02.1X	Repair of the Cerebral Meninges—These codes include the simple suturing, ligation, and surgical creation of openings of the cerebral meninges.
02.2	Ventriculostomy—The creation of a surgical opening of the third ventricle. The insertion of a Holter valve is classified to this code and is completed to regulate the flow of cerebrospinal fluid.
02.3X	Extracranial Ventricular Shunt—Shunts are placed in the cerebral ventricle to redirect cerebrospinal fluid from a cerebral ventricle to a location outside the cranial vault via a tube. To select the proper code, coders must identify the anatomical site to which the tube is connected. For example, code 02.31 classifies a ventricular shunt that has been connected to a structure in the head and neck. Figure 26-4 illustrates a ventriculoatrial shunt.
02.4X	Revision, Removal, and Irrigation of Ventricular Shunt—Procedures that are completed to attend to ventricular shunts are classified to 02.4X. The coder must identify the procedure that was completed on the shunt, such as irrigation and exploration, replacement, or removal.
02.9X	Other Operations on Skull, Brain, and Cerebral Meninges—These codes include the implantation or replacement of intracranial neurostimulators and the insertion, replacement, and removal of skull tongs or halo traction devices.

Operations on Spinal Cord and Spinal Canal Structures (Category Code 03)

Procedures that are classified to category code 03, Operations on the spinal cord and spinal canal structures, include both therapeutic and diagnostic procedures. A notation at the start of the category instructs coders to code any application or administration of an adhesion barrier substance, code 99.77, in addition to codes selected from category code 03.

Codes 03.31–03.39 classify diagnostic procedures on the spinal cord and spinal canal structures. These procedures include the following:

Spinal Tap—The penetration of the spinal subarachniod space to remove cerebrospinal fluid to detect abnormal substances and variations in the fluid for examination, pressure recording, or injection.

Biopsy of Spinal Cord or Spinal Meninges—The removal of tissue of the spinal cord or spinal meninges for microscopic examination

Coders should note the Exclude: notation that appears as part of code 03.39, which excludes from this code the microscopic examination of a specimen from the nervous system or of spinal fluid.

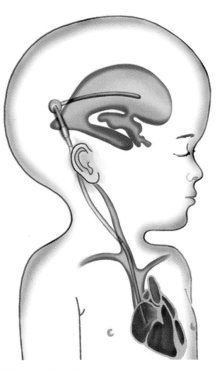

Figure 26-4 Ventriculoatrial shunt (From Caruthers B, Price P, Junge TL, et al. *Surgical Technology for the Surgical Technologist: A Positive Care Approach.* Clifton Park, NY: Delmar, Cengage Learning, 2001, p. 862.)

Operations on Cranial and Peripheral Nerves (Category Code 04)

Category 04, Operations on cranial and peripheral nerves, classifies therapeutic and diagnostic procedures that are completed on the cranial and peripheral nerves. Physicians often refer to cranial nerves by Roman numerals.

Many peripheral nerves are named after the body regions in which they are located. Figure 26-5 illustrates the peripheral nerves.

Please note that Chapter 11 of this textbook provides additional illustrations of the cranial and peripheral nerves.

The surgical removal of pressure on nerves, known as **decompression of nerves,** is completed to relieve the compression of nerves and is often referred to as a **nerve release.** Relief of compression of the median nerve at the wrist, known as **release of carpal tunnel,** is classified to code 04.43. Relief of compression of the tibial nerve at the ankle is classified to code 04.44 and is known as a **release of tarsal tunnel.**

Roman Numeral Reference	Nerve
I	Olfactory
II	Optic
III	Oculomotor
IV	Trochlear
V	Trigeminal
VI	Abducens
VII	Facial
VIII	Acoustic
IX	Glossopharyngeal
X	Vagus
XI	Accessory
XII	Hypoglossal

When selecting codes for some categories, such as category 04.7, coders must be able to identify the specific nerves for which the procedure was completed. Documentation must be read to identify the nerves before code selection.

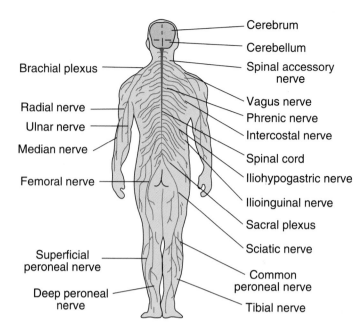

Figure 26-5 Peripheral nerves (From Sormunen C. *Terminology for Allied Health Professions,* 5th ed. Clifton Park, NY: Delmar, Cengage Learning, 2003, p. 529.)

Exercise 26–1   Procedures on Specific Nerves

Instructions: For each code listed, identify the specific nerve(s) for which the procedure was completed and provide the Roman numeral reference for each nerve.

Procedure Code	Nerve and Roman Reference
1. Code 04.02	_____
2. Code 04.73	_____
3. Code 04.71	_____
4. Code 04.72	_____

Operations on Sympathetic Nerves or Ganglia (Category Code 05)

Category code 05 classifies operations on the sympathetic nerves and ganglia. Codes 05.21–05.29 classify resections of a sympathetic nerve or ganglion, also known as sympathectomy or ganglionectomy. Fourth digits are used to identify the location of the resection.

Injections into Nerves

There are different types of nerve injections. Neurolytic agents are injected to cause the destruction of adhesions around a nerve. Neurolytic epidural injections are given to reduce pain around the spinal column. Another type of injection is called an analgesia injection. These types of injections are given to relieve pain. Codes used to report injections made into a sympathetic nerve or ganglion include codes 05.31, 05.32, and 05.39.

Internet Links

The official journal of the Congress of Neurological Surgeons can be found at *www.neurosurgery-online .com*. This Web site contains many articles and illustrations on neurosurgical procedures.

The official journal of the American Association of Neurological Surgeons can be found at *www.thejns-net.org/*.

The American Association of Neurological Surgeons and the Congress of Neurological Surgeons have a combined Web site at *www.neurosurgery.org*.

Two additional Web sites the contain information on neurosurgery are *www.neurosurgeryToday.org* and *www.neurosurgeon.org*.

Summary

- Chapter 1 of volume 3 of ICD-9-CM classifies operations on the nervous system.
- To accurately code, coders must be able to identify the specific nerves for which the procedure is completed.
- The cranial nerves are often referred to by using Roman numerals.
- A craniotomy is not coded when it is the operative approach.
- Cranioplasty is the surgical repair of the skull.
- Shunts are placed in the cerebral ventricle to redirect cerebrospinal fluid.
- Decompression of nerves is completed to relieve the compression of nerves.

Chapter Review

True/False: Indicate whether each statement is true (T) or false (F).

1. _____ The peripheral nerves are often referred to by Roman numeral references.

2. _____ A craniotomy is coded when it is an operative approach.

3. _____ A lobectomy is the excision of a lobe of the cerebrum.

4. _____ Code 04.71 is assigned to code an accessory-facial nerve anastomosis.

5. _____ The insertion of a Holter valve is completed to regulate the flow of cerebrospinal fluid.

Fill-in-the-Blank: Enter the appropriate term(s) to complete each statement.

6. A carpal tunnel release is completed to provide relief of a _____ of the median nerve at the wrist.

7. The removal of tissue of the spinal meninges for microscopic examination is known as a _____ of the spinal meninges.

8. The removal of damaged brain tissue is known as _____ of the brain.

Short Answer: For each cranial nerve listed, record the Roman numeral reference.

9. Facial _____

10. Vagus _____

11. Hypoglossal _____

12. Optic _____

13. Trochlear _____

14. Abducens _____

15. Glossopharyneal _____

Coding Assignments

Instructions: Using the ICD-9-CM coding book, select the code for each procedural statement.

Statement	Code
1. Drainage of intracerebral hematoma	_____
2. Replacement of skull plate	_____
3. Transection of spinal cord tracts	_____
4. Release of carpal tunnel	_____
5. Ventriculopleural anastomosis	_____
6. Replacement of ventricular shunt	_____
7. Presacral sympathectomy	_____
8. Peripheral nerve injection	_____
9. Reopening of laminectomy site	_____
10. Insertion of sphenoidal electrodes	_____
11. Biopsy of skull	_____
12. Aspiration of subdural space	_____
13. Hemispherectomy	_____
14. Repair of spinal meningocele	_____
15. Chordotomy	_____
16. Pallidotomy	_____
17. Reinsertion of Holter valve	_____
18. Opening of cranial suture	_____
19. Cauterization of choroid plexus	_____
20. Spinal subarachnoid-peritoneal shunt	_____
21. Excision of acoustic neuroma	_____

22. Insertion of halo traction device   _____

23. Removal of bone chip from spinal canal   _____

24. Sphenopalatine ganglionectomy   _____

25. Neurectasis   _____

Case Studies

Instructions: Review each case study, and select the correct ICD-9-CM diagnostic and procedural codes.

CASE 1

HISTORY OF PRESENT ILLNESS:

This is a 7-year-old male who was exhibiting no signs of ill health until just before mom called 911 after she went into the child's room to see if he was ready for school. She found him on the floor with his neck bent in a forward position and his eyes rolling back in his head. Mom noticed tremors in the right hand as his whole body was shaking. She said that patient did not respond when she spoke to him, and she believes he did not even recognize her. Mom realized what was happening and tried to keep her son from biting his tongue, which she did by inserting a spoon at the corner of his mouth. Upon arrival of the emergency squad, patient vomited once and, at that time, lost control of his bladder. The EMT noted slight tremor on right side, but that was the only movement noted on the trip to this hospital in the ambulance. Patient is now very lethargic and quiet. Entire episode lasted for approximately 15 to 20 minutes. ABGs on 4 LMP were 7.17/68/145/22. Repeat ABGs were 7.3/45/230/20, with saturation of 98%. Electrolytes were sodium 144, potassium 3.4, chloride 111, CO2 25, BUN 15, creatinine 0.4, and glucose 124. EKG and chest X-ray were normal. Patient given ceftriaxone 1 gram, 1 dose, and transferred to the Pediatric Intensive Care Unit. Vital signs were stable and noted at the top of this page. Upon arrival at this unit, patient had desaturated to 75%, but he came back up by himself.

ALLERGIES: NKA, Medications: None. Past Medical History: Noncontributory. No other illnesses in the house. Not exposed to anything that mom knows of. No family history that would indicate a problem here. Immunizations are up to date. Pediatrician does not go to hospital, so the hospitalist will follow him while here.

PHYSICAL EXAM: HEENT: Normal, no abnormalities noted. HEART: RRR, no JVD. LUNGS: Clear to auscultation. Remainder of exam unremarkable. Full examination is documented in the medical record for this date.

LABORATORY DATA: Electroencephalogram was done and showed sharp waves in the left temporal area. This is consistent with temporal lobe epilepsy. CT scan of brain was normal.

ASSESSMENT AND PLAN: Electroencephalogram confirmed diagnosis of new onset seizure disorder. The blood work and urinalysis were all within normal limits, which has ruled out sepsis and viral encephalitis. A lumbar puncture was done, and the cerebrospinal fluid was clear with glucose of 63, protein of less than 10. CIE and Gram stain were negative. Child was started on 50 mg of phenobarbital in the morning and 45 mg in the evening. No other medications or treatments are going to be implemented at this time. He will follow up with Dr. Sarah at Neurological Associates.

DIAGNOSIS: Seizure disorder, epileptic seizure, new onset

PROCEDURE: Lumbar puncture

ICD-9-CM Code Assignment: _____

CASE 2

HISTORY OF PRESENT ILLNESS: Patient came to my office several months ago with numbness, tingling, and pain in the left wrist. She had been symptomatic for approximately 6 months before she came to see me. She is a mother of two small boys and works part-time cleaning houses. She notes that at night the pain becomes worse, and sometimes she can't get to sleep. When she does finally sleep, the pain eventually wakes her up after several hours. Mornings are difficult until she gets moving around. She says by the end of the day she is in a good deal of pain and has difficulty moving her left wrist and hand.

It was determined after results of the nerve conduction studies, ibuprofen treatment, and application of splints both night and day, that surgery was necessary to correct the carpal tunnel syndrome as a last resort. The risks and benefits of this surgery were explained to the patient, and she has consented to the surgery because she is in extreme pain that is not getting better.

PROCEDURE: Patient was brought to the operating room; IV sedation was successfully administered. The left hand and forearm were draped and prepped. Marcaine plain was instilled, and an angled incision was made in the volar aspect of the wrist. The incision was taken down through subcutaneous tissue to the transverse carpal ligament, which was exposed and incised. It was incised proximally and distally. Bleeding was controlled with cauterization. By use of a metal groove director, contents of the carpal canal were protected. The median nerve was seen to be round with good vascular supply. Copious amounts of antibiotic irrigation were used in the wound. The wound was closed with nylon sutures. A volar splint and sterile dressing were applied. The patient was taken to the recovery room in good condition.

PREOP DIAGNOSIS: Carpal tunnel syndrome

POSTOP DIAGNOSIS: Same

PROCEDURE: Left carpal tunnel release

ICD-9-CM Code Assignment: _____

CASE 3

HISTORY OF PRESENT ILLNESS: Two days ago, patient was struck by a car and brought in by ambulance. Complained of headache and blurred vision. Right now, pupils are reactive and equal. CT scan was done and is showing some edema.

PHYSICAL: Deferred back to H&P done at time of admission. Current vital signs are noted at the top of this page. No other changes noted from admission H&P found in this medical record.

ASSESSMENT & PLAN: Traumatic diffuse brain swelling. Surgical intervention needed at this time to relieve swelling.

PROCEDURE: After informed consent, the patient was brought to the operating room. A curvilinear posterolateral concave incision was made in the right frontal scalp A right twist drill burr hole was placed in the right frontal skull. Using a #11 knife, the dura was opened and a ventricular catheter was placed 5.5 cm with good flow of blood-tinged cerebrospinal fluid out under pressure. There was intermittent interruption of fluid flow. This was due to diffuse brain edema, which caused collapse of the ventricular cath system. Once the catheter was tunneled out through a separate location in the posterior right frontal scalp, it was secured with 3-0 silk sutures. Scalp was closed in layers, and a sterile dressing was applied.

PREOP DIAGNOSIS: Diffuse brain swelling

POSTOP DIAGNOSIS: Same

PROCEDURE: Placement of ventriculostomy

ICD-9-CM Code Assignment: _____

CASE 4

Indications for Surgery: This 57-year-old male presents for decompression laminectomy of the lower lumbar region of the spine. Patient has had compression of the lower lumbar region due to nontraumatic displacement of the intervertebral disk in the lumbar region. Disk material has impinged this region and caused the patient a great deal of pain over the past 2 years. All forms of conservative therapy have been pursued prior to surgery.

Operation: Patient was placed in prone position, then prepped and draped in the usual sterile fashion. Using a paramedian incision with a #10 blade, the lumbar area identified by MRI scans was approached. The paraspinous muscles were separated from the area using osteotome and peristeal elevator, and the area was packed to help with hemostatis. Using Kerrison rongeur, the offending lamina and fragments of disk material were removed. Care was taken that no damage occurred to the nerve roots or epidural veins.

No fusion was necessary.

Wound was irrigated copiously with saline. All sponge and instrument counts were good. The incision was closed with heavy, interrupted sutures. Patient was returned to the recovery room in good, stable condition.

ICD-9-CM Code Assignment: _____

CASE 5

Jessica is a 3-month-old female who presents today for a craniectomy of a portion of the right posterior fossa. She was born with an additional malformed piece of this portion of the skull. It was explained to the parents that surgery at this time will allow for normal skull development as the child grows. All risks and benefits have been discussed, and the parents are in agreement that this is the best course of action at this time.

The patient was placed in the semi-Fowler position with her right posterior side exposed. The patient was prepped and draped in the usual sterile fashion. A vertical incision was made medial to the mastoid process with the suboccipital muscles and fascia incised and moved away from the bone. A Stille-Leur rongeur was used to burr addition bone away. The wound was closed using 3-0 catgut. The procedure went very well. The patient tolerated the procedure well and was returned to the recovery room in stable condition.

ICD-9-CM Code Assignment: _____

CHAPTER

27

Operations on the Endocrine System

Chapter Outline

Introduction

Introduction to Operations and Procedures on the Endocrine System

Internet Links

Summary

Chapter Review

Coding Assignments

Case Studies

Objectives

At the conclusion of this chapter, the student will be able to:

1. Understand pathologies associated with the endocrine system.
2. Describe procedures completed on the endocrine system.
3. Accurately code procedures completed on the endocrine system.
4. Select and code diagnoses and procedures from case studies.

Key Terms

Adrenalectomy

Pinealectomy

Pineal Gland

Reimplantation

Submental Incision

Transoral Incision

Reminder

As you work through this chapter, you should have a copy of the ICD-9-CM to reference.

Introduction

The procedure codes for chapter 2 of volume 3 of ICD-9-CM, "Operations on the Endocrine System," include category codes 06–07 and are used to classify procedures that are completed on the glands of the endocrine system.

Introduction to Operations and Procedures on the Endocrine System

The chapter begins with procedures on the thyroid and parathyroid glands. Figure 27-1 illustrates the location of the thyroid gland in relation to the throat.

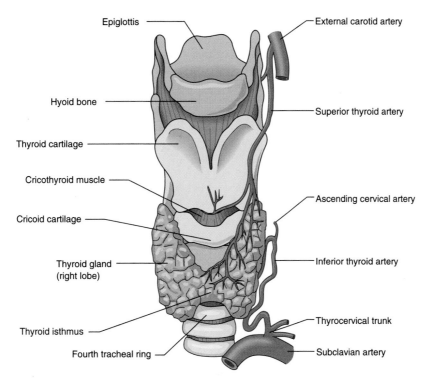

Figure 27-1 Anatomical position of the thyroid gland (From Price P, Frey KB, Junge TL. *Surgical Technology for the Surgical Technologist: A Positive Care Approach,* 2nd ed. Clifton Park, NY: Delmar, Cengage Learning, 2004, p. 1027.)

Operations on the Thyroid and Parathyroid (Category 06)

The first category of codes—06, Operations on the thyroid and parathyroid glands—classifies operations on the thyroid and parathyroid glands. The coder should note that after the category title, an inclusion note appears that reads:

```
Includes: Incidental resection of the hyoid bone
```

This note alerts the coder that if a resection of the hyoid bone occurs in association with another procedure from category 06, the resection of the hyoid bone is not coded with a separate code. The hyoid bone is unique in that it is a suspended bone that lies between the mandible and the larynopharynx. Figure 27-2 illustrates the anatomical position of the hyoid bone. It should be noted that fourth-digit classifications are necessary within this category of codes. A summary of some of the codes found in this category includes codes 06.0X to 06.9X.

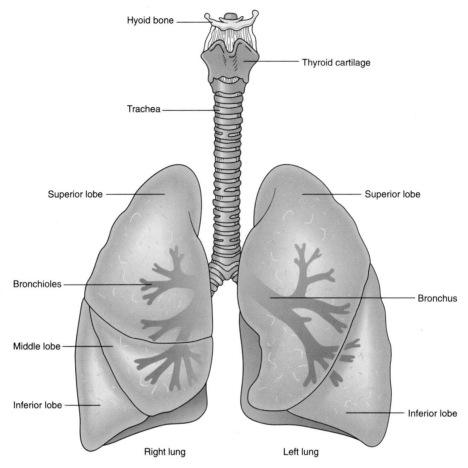

Figure 27-2 Position of the hyoid bone (From Ehrlich A, Schroeder CL. *Medical Terminology for Health Professions*, 4th ed. Clifton Park, NY: Delmar, Cengage Learning, 2001, p. 147.)

Procedure	Description
06.0X	Incision of Thyroid Field—These codes are used to code incisions made into the thyroid field for aspiration of fluid, reopening of a wound, and other reasons. Should a patient have hemorrhaging after thyroid surgery, codes from this section are used for reopening the wound. Foreign body removal and drainage of hematoma are also classified here.
06.1X	Diagnostic Procedures on Thyroid and Parathyroid Glands—This subcategory is used for diagnostic procedures performed on the thyroid and parathyroid glands. Open, closed, or needle biopsies of these glands are classified here. Coders should note that an Exclude: note appears for code 06.19 stating that radioisotope scans are excluded from this code.
06.3X, 06.4	Other Partial Thyroidectomy and Complete Thyroidectomy—When coding a thyroidectomy, coders must determine whether a partial or complete thyroidectomy is performed. A total or complete thyroidectomy is classified to code 06.4. For coding a partial thyroidectomy, refer to codes in the 06.3X section.
06.5X	Substernal Thyroidectomy—If the thyroid or tissue connected to the thyroid falls below the breastbone, codes from this subcategory are used for identification of such procedures.
06.6	Excision of Lingual Thyroid—This code is used to report the removal of diseased thyroid tissue. The tissue is removed from the base of the tongue and can include excision of the thryoid by submental or transoral route. A submental incision is made below the chin, and a transoral incision is made within the oral cavity.
06.7	Excision of the Thyroglossal Duct or Tract—An incision is made to remove the thyroglossal duct or tract.

06.8X	Parathyroidectomy—Should surgery necessitate removal of the parathyroid, codes from this subcategory are needed to accurately code the procedure. The coder identifies a complete versus a partial parathyroidectomy by selection of a fourth digit.
06.9X	Other Operations on Thyroid (region) and Parathyroid—The isthmus is the narrowest part of the thyroid, which at times needs to be narrowed or divided. Codes for this procedure are found here. In some instances, the tissue of the thyroid needs to be moved to another part of the thyroid to aid in functioning. This is called reimplantation. Codes for reimplantation of the thyroid and parathyroid are found here.

Operations on Other Endocrine Glands (Category Code 07)

Category 07, Operations on other endocrine glands, classifies procedures performed on other parts of the endocrine system such as the adrenal glands, pituitary gland, thymus, and pineal gland. To refresh your memory of the location of these glands, review Figure 8-1. Procedures completed on these glands are classified to codes 07.0X to 07.9X. Examples follow:

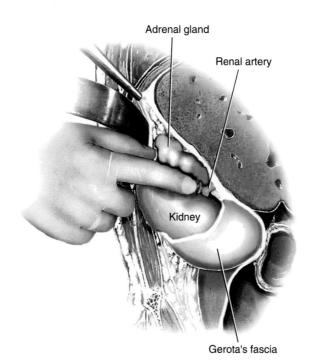

Figure 27-3 Open adrenalectomy (From Price P, Frey KB, Junge TL. *Surgical Technology for the Surgical Technologist: A Positive Care Approach,* 2nd ed. Clifton Park, NY: Delmar, Cengage Learning, 2004, p. 757.)

Procedure	Description
07.0X	Exploration of Adrenal Field—Codes 07.00 to 07.02 are used to report the surgical exploration of the adrenal and periadrenal field. The fourth digits differentiate among unspecified, unilateral, and bilateral explorations.
07.1X	Diagnostic Procedures on Adrenal, Pituitary, Pineal, and Thymus Glands—Diagnostic procedures are found in this subcategory. Biopsies of the adrenal, pituitary, pineal, and thymus glands are found here. Coders must identify whether the biopsy is an open or closed procedure.
07.2X, 07.3	Partial Adrenalectomy and Bilateral Adrenalectomy—This subcategory contains codes for partial adrenalectomy, as well as a complete procedure. An adrenalectomy is the surgical removal of either one adrenal gland or both. This surgery is generally done because of a tumor. The adrenal glands sit on top of each kidney, so an adrenalectomy might be bilateral or unilateral. The bilateral procedure is coded from subcategory 07.3. Figure 27-3 illustrates the location of the adrenal gland in relation to the kidney.

Procedure	Description
07.5X	Operations on Pineal Gland—This section starts the procedures on the pineal gland. The pineal gland is located in the brain near the corpus collosum and is associated with the onset of puberty. A pinealectomy is the removal of the pineal gland.
07.6X	Hypophysectomy—This subcategory is related to procedures having to do with the pituitary gland. The procedures include excision and destruction.
07.7X	Other Operations on Hypophysis—Codes 07.71 to 07.79 are used to report other operations on the hypophysis that include exploration of the pituitary fossa, incision of the pituitary gland, and insertion of pack into the sella turcica. It should be noted that code 07.72 reports exploration with incision of pituitary gland. Code 07.71 reports only an exploration.
07.8X	Thymectomy—Excisions of the thymus gland are classified to these codes. Fourth digits are used to identify partial versus total excisions.
07.9X	Other Operations on thymus—Codes 07.91 to 07.99 reports operation on the thymus that include open incisions of the thymus, repair and transplantation of thymus and thorascopic incision of thymus.

Internet Links

To view articles, illustrations, and videos on surgery performed on the endocrine system, visit *www .websurg.com*. Locate the heading Endocrine Surgery and select this area. Procedures completed on the adrenal, parathyroid, thymus, and thyroid glands are described here.

Summary

- Chapter 2 of volume 3 of ICD-9-CM classifies procedures completed on the various glands of the endocrine system.

- Procedures of the thyroid, parathyroid, adrenal, pituitary, pineal, and thymus glands are included.

- Procedures include biopsies, which are identified as both open and closed procedures.

- Partial and complete removal of glands are identified throughout chapter 2 by the use of fourth digits.

Chapter Review

True/False: Indicate whether the statement is true (T) or false (F).

1. _____ The thyroid gland is located in the abdominal cavity.

2. _____ An open biopsy of the thyroid gland is a diagnostic procedure.

3. _____ A coder must be able to identify whether a total or partial thyroidectomy has occurred to select the appropriate code, as ICD-9-CM provides separate codes.

4. _____ An open biopsy of the adrenal gland is coded to 07.12.

5. _____ A bilateral adrenalectomy is coded to 07.22.

Fill-in-the-Blank: Enter the appropriate term(s) to complete each statement.

6. The gland located in the brain near the corpus collosum that is associated with the onset of puberty is the _____ gland.

7. A thymectomy is a(n) _____ of the thymus gland.

8. Category code 07.3 classifies a(n) _____ adrenalectomy.

9. Category code 06, Operations on the thyroid and parathyroid glands, includes an incidental resection of the _____ bone.

10. An unilateral thyroid lobectomy is classified to code _____.

Coding Assignments

Instructions: Using an ICD-9-CM coding book, select the appropriate procedure code.

Procedure	Code
1. Ligation of thyroid vessels	_____
2. Biopsy thymus	_____
3. Total excision of pituitary gland, transsphenoidal approach	_____
4. Exploration of pituitary fossa with incision of pituitary gland	_____
5. Pinealectomy	_____
6. Repair of adrenal gland	_____
7. Aspiration of craniopharyngioma	_____
8. Percutaneous drainage of thyroid field	_____
9. Excision of lingual thyroid	_____
10. Open biopsy of adrenal gland	_____
11. Thymopexy	_____
12. Biopsy of pineal gland	_____
13. Exploration of thyroid field/gland	_____
14. Thyroidotomy	_____
15. Isthmectomy	_____
16. Closed percutaneous biopsy of adrenal gland	_____
17. Excision of lesion on pituitary, transfrontal approach	_____
18. Total excision of pineal gland	_____
19. Cryohypophysectomy, complete, transfrontal approach	_____
20. Rathke's pouch, aspiration	_____
21. Needle biopsy of the thyroid gland	_____
22. Exploration of the right adrenal gland	_____
23. Partial excision of pineal gland	_____
24. Repair of the thymus	_____
25. Partial substernal thyroidectomy	_____

Case Studies

Instructions: Review each case study, and select the correct ICD-9-CM diagnostic and procedural code.

CASE 1

PRE- AND POSTOPERATIVE DIAGNOSIS: Grave's disease

PROCEDURE: Thyroidectomy

This 46-year-old female patient was taken to the OR and placed in the supine position with neck extension. She was placed under general anesthesia, and a symmetrical transverse incision was made following the Langer lines over the thyroid using a #15 blade. The incision was then extended to the subcutaneous tissue, and the platysma muscle was divided. Retractors were placed to mobilize the superior and inferior flaps.

After the strap muscles were separated, the thyroid was exposed and the middle thyroid vein was visualized, divided, and then ligated with 3-0 plain catgut. The superior poles were retracted caudally, and the superior vessels and laryngeal nerves were visualized to divide and ligate the vessels. After the parathyroid glands, the inferior thyroid artery, and the laryneal nerve were identified, the parathyroid gland was mobilized. The branches of the inferior thyroid artery were divided and ligated. The superior connective tissue was divided, and hemostasis was achieved by use of an electrosurgical unit. The entire thyroid was then dissected from the trachea and a $1/4$-inch Penrose drain was placed. The wound site was irrigated with normal saline, and hemostasis was obtained. The muscle, fascial layer, and subcutaneous layer were closed with 3-0 plain chromic sutures. The skin was closed with 4-0 Dexon. The patient tolerated the procedure well and was sent to the recovery room in stable condition.

ICD-9-CM Code Assignment: _____

CASE 2

PREOPERATIVE DIAGNOSIS: Tumor of adrenal gland

POSTOPERATIVE DIAGNOSIS: Malignant adrenal gland cortical tumor

PROCEDURE: Adrenalectomy

This 56-year-old female patient was prepped and draped in the usual fashion with insertion of a Foley catheter. General anesthesia was given. A 2-cm flank incision was made on the right side using a #10 blade. The retroperitoneal space was exposed, and Gerota's fascia was opened. The superior perinephric fat was dissected, and blood vessels were ligated. Downward retraction of the kidney was achieved, and transection of the fibrous attachments to the adrenal surfaces was completed. The adrenal gland was then rotated, and the adrenal artery was clamped, transected, and ligated. The right adrenal gland was then removed. The wound was irrigated with saline, and hemostasis was achieved. A Penrose drain was placed, and the wound was closed in the usual fashion. The patient tolerated the procedure well and was transported to the recovery room.

ICD-9-CM Code Assignment: _____

CASE 3

A 10-year-old female presents today for removal of an adrenal tumor. The patient presented initially with complaints of excessive amount of facial hair. She was noted to have development of pubic hair by age 7 and had early appearance of acne, mainly on her forehead and back. Blood tests were done, which showed an abnormal DHEA-S blood level. The patient was monitored over the next year and began to have a change in her voice and then significant weight loss. More labs were done, which showed hormone levels that were at abnormal levels for a 10-year-old. DHEA-S was at 3,000 ng/ml; testosterone level was at 200 ng/dl. At this point we proceeded with an MRI, which confirmed a diagnosis of tumors of the adrenal gland on the left side. It was decided that she would have surgery to remove these tumors with the hopes of her hormone levels returning to normal for her age.

Patient was placed in supine position. The abdomen was prepped and draped in the usual sterile fashion. An incision was made that went through the walls of the abdomen. A small tumor was identified on the left adrenal and removed and sent for pathology. The postoperative diagnosis is benign tumor of the adrenal gland. The incision was closed and the patient was returned to the recovery room in stable condition.

ICD-9-CM Code Assignment: _____

CASE 4

INDICATIONS FOR SURGERY: This is a 38-year-old female who has had problems for the last 3 years with hypertrichosis, blurred vision, and a change in her skin, which has become very oily. Her voice has become deeper, and her nose now appears thickened. Lab tests indicated a problem with hormone levels, so additional X-rays and CT scans of the head and neck were performed. A lesion is present on the pituitary gland, which appears to be the problem for this patient.

PREOPERATIVE DX: Acromegaly

POSTOPERATIVE DX: Acromegaly, benign tumor of pituitary gland

OPERATION: The patient was prepped for a transphenoidal hypophysectomy. The nasal septum is exposed, and the mucosa is separated from the septal cartilage. The cartilage is resected, and the floor of the sphenoid sinus is removed so that the sella turcica can be viewed. A Kerrison rongeur and osteotome are used to put an opening in the sella turcica, allowing for exposure of the tumor. The tumor is removed along with part of the pituitary gland. The sellar cavity is packed with fat and fascia from the thigh area. The incision is closed, and the patient is returned to the recovery room in good condition.

ICD-9-CM Code Assignment: _____

CASE 5

INDICATIONS FOR SURGERY: This is a 58-year-old female who has noted weight gain, increased appetite, fatigue, thinning of her hair, and brittle nails. A TSH was done to determine whether the thyroid is involved in her problems. There was a noticeable problem because her levels were much lower than normal. A thyroid scan shows 63% uptake and 53% uptake after treatment with iodine-123. The patient is now having a fine needle biopsy of the lesion that is showing on the scan.

A fine needle biopsy was performed today on the thyroid nodule. Pathology reveals a benign lesion of the thyroid.

ICD-9-CM Code Assignment: _____

Operations on the Eye

Chapter Outline

Objectives

At the conclusion of this chapter, the student will be able to:

1. Identify pathologies that affect the eye.
2. Describe some of the procedures used to correct the pathologies.
3. Discuss procedures that are completed on the eye.
4. Select and code diagnoses and procedures from case studies.

Key Terms

Blepharoptosis	Epikeratophakia	Keratoplasty	Phacoemulsification
Cataracts	Evisceration	Lacrimal Structures	Pterygium
Chalazion	Fistulization	Laser	Rhytidectomy
Coreoplasty	Full-Thickness Excision	Lensectomy	Scleral Buckling
Cornea	Glaucoma	Meibomian Cyst	Tarsal Cyst
Correction of a Lid Retraction	Goniopuncture	Ophthalmoscopy	Thermocauterization
Dacryoadenectomy	Internal Hordeolum	Partial Thickness Excision	Visual Acuity
	Iridotomy		Vitreous Humor

Reminder

As you work through this chapter, you will need to have a copy of the ICD-9-CM coding book to reference.

Introduction

The codes found in chapter 3 of volume 3 of ICD-9-CM, "Operations on the Eye," classify procedures completed on the eyelid, conjunctiva, cornea, lens, retina, iris, and ciliary body of the eye. Any of the areas of the eye that can be corrected or operated on are found in this chapter.

Coding Operations on the Eye

The techniques for eye surgery vary, but laser surgery is one of the techniques that can be used. Laser is actually an acronym meaning light amplification by the stimulated emission of radiation. The use of light amplification to emit focused radiation as a surgical technique is used not only in eye surgery but in many specialties. Should the coder encounter laser surgery as a technique used, the following can be found in the Alphabetic Index of Procedures:

```
Laser—see also Coagulation, Destruction, and Photocoagulation by site
```

Normal vision is recognized as 20/20. The first number is the distance in feet from the Snellen chart, which is used to measure visual acuity. Visual acuity is the ability to see and distinguish objects at a distance. The second number is the deviation from normal. To review the different structures of the eye, reference Figure 11-4 of this textbook.

Operations on the eye are organized into the following categories in ICD-9-CM:

```
08    Operations on the Eyelid
09    Operations on Lacrimal System
10    Operations on Conjunctiva
11    Operations on Cornea
12    Operations on Iris, Ciliary Body, Sclera, and Anterior Chamber
13    Operation on Lens
14    Operations on Retina, Choroid, Vitreous, and Posterior Chamber
15    Operations on Extraocular Muscles
16    Operations on Orbit and Eyeball
```

A coder must be able to identify the various anatomical sites of the eye to select the proper code assignment.

Operations on Eyelids (Category Code 08)

The procedures found in chapter 3 of volume 3 begin with operations on the eyelids, including biopsy, lesion removal or destruction, and repair. It should be noted that category code 08 includes operations on the eyebrow as identified by the Include: note that appears after the category heading in ICD-9-CM.

Procedure Code	Description
08.1X	Diagnostic Procedures on Eyelid—This subcategory includes diagnostic procedures such as biopsy of the eyelid and microscopic examination of the tissue of the eyelid.
08.2X	Excision or Destruction of Lesion or Tissue of Eyelid—This subcategory of codes includes the excision and destruction of lesions found on the eyelid. Some codes in this category distinguish the thickness of the cutting that is done. A partial-thickness excision involves one-fourth or more of the lid margin and is not through all of the eyelid layers. A full-thickness excision involves one-fourth or more of the lid margin and is through all of the eyelid layers. Excision of a chalazion, a localized swelling of the eyelid resulting from an obstruction of a sebaceous gland of the eyelid, is classified to code 08.21. The coder may find that a chalazion is sometimes referred to as meibomian cyst, tarsal cyst, or internal hordeolum.
08.3X	Repair of Blepharoptosis and Lid Retraction—Blepharoptosis refers to a drooping eyelid, which is repaired by restoration of the eyelid by elevating or lengthening the frontalis or levator muscles of the eye. Fourth digits are used to identify the specific repair that is completed. Code 08.38 included in this subcategory codes a correction of a lid retraction, which is a procedure that moves the eyelid back to its normal position.

Procedure Code	Description
08.6X	Reconstruction of Eyelid with Flaps or Grafts—These procedures are completed for patients who have been victims of fire or accidents. These restore the eyelid with the use of flaps or grafts.
08.8X	Other Repair of Eyelid—This subcategory is referred to when coding a laceration repair of the eyelid or eyebrow. Wrinkle removal is also coded from this subcategory and is referred to as **rhytidectomy.**

Operations on Lacrimal System (Category Code 09)

The corner of the eye closest to the nose is the opening for the lacrimal sac. The **lacrimal structures** produce tears. The lacrimal gland is located over the outer corner of the eye. When this gland produces tears, they move across the surface of the eye and to the lacrimal sac, which opens into the nasolacrimal duct. Figure 28-1 illustrates the lacrimal system and its proximity to the eye and nose. This is why crying can also make your nose run. The tears produced also lubricate the eye and wash away foreign material. Operations of the lacrimal system are coded to the 09 category of codes.

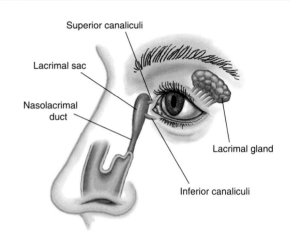

Figure 28-1 Lacrimal system (From Caruthers B, Price P, Junge TL, et al. *Surgical Technology for the Surgical Technologist: A Positive Care Approach.* Clifton Park, NY: Delmar, Cengage Learning, 2001, p. 449.)

Procedure Code	Description
09.1X	Diagnostic Procedures on Lacrimal System—Diagnostic procedures, such as biopsy of the lacrimal sac and biopsy of the lacrimal gland, are found in this subcategory.
09.2X	Excision of Lesion or Tissue of Lacrimal Gland—This subcategory deals with the lacrimal gland only. The coder will see the term *dacryoadenectomy* in this subcategory. **Dacryoadenectomy** is also known as excision of the lacrimal gland.
09.8X	Fistulization of Lacrimal Tract to Nasal Cavity—Because of the proximatiy to the nasal cavity, sometimes surgical intervention is needed to create a passage between the lacrimal sac and the nasal cavity or between the conjunctival sac and the nasal cavity. These codes are found in this section of the chapter.

Operations on Conjunctiva (Category Code 10)

Category 10, Operations on conjunctiva, contain codes related to diagnostic procedures as well as excision, destruction, and repair of the conjunctiva. As with the other subcategories in this chapter, this subcategory starts with incision and diagnostic procedures and then moves to other procedures.

Procedure Codes	Description
10.3X	Excision or Destruction of Lesion or Tissue of Conjunctiva—The codes for the excision or destruction of lesions fall into this subcategory. Remember that excision is the cutting removal of tissue, and destruction is the forcible death of tissue.
10.4X	Conjunctivoplasty—Conjunctivoplasty is commonly completed by plastic surgeons when restoring the conjunctiva. This subcategory of codes includes free grafts in conjunctiva repair.

Operations on Cornea (Category Code 11)

Category 11, Operations on cornea, is referred to frequently because numerous procedures are commonly completed on this anatomical site. The **cornea** is the layer of the eye located directly below the conjunctiva.

Procedure Code	Description
11.2X	Diagnostic Procedures on Cornea—Like other subcategories in this chapter, this category starts out with diagnostic procedures. Code 11.21 is used to identify the scraping of the cornea to obtain a sample of tissue for laboratory examination.
11.3X	Excision of Pterygium—A **pterygium** is a wing-shaped growth of conjunctiva. In some cases this growth can extend into the cornea, feeling like a foreign body. Sometimes treatment with a steroid is sufficient, but other times surgical intervention is required to remove the pterygium.
11.4X	Excision or Destruction of Tissue or Other Lesion of Cornea—This subcategory includes the mechanical removal of the outer layer of the cornea. Code 11.42 is used for the destruction of a corneal lesion by **thermocauterization.** This procedure uses a hot-tipped instrument to directly heat a lesion to destroy it.
11.5X	Repair of Cornea—Repair of the cornea, including suturing, is included in this subcategory. It should be noted that code 11.52 is used to identify a repair of a postoperative wound dehiscence of the cornea.
11.6X	Corneal Transplant—The coder may see the term *keratoplasty,* which is a term for corneal grafting. Different types of grafting are included in this category. Figure 28-2 illustrates a corneal transplant.
11.7X	Other Reconstructive and Refractive Surgery on Cornea—**Epikeratophakia** is coded to this subcategory even though it is a type of graft. This procedure requires the placement of stitches to connect a corneal graft to the central part of the cornea for the correction of a missing lens from the eye.

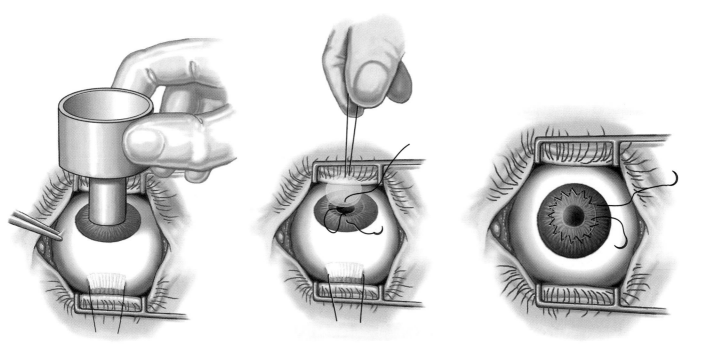

Figure 28-2 Corneal transplant (From Caruthers B, Price P, Junge TL, et al. *Surgical Technology for the Surgical Technologist: A Positive Care Approach.* Clifton Park, NY: Delmar, Cengage Learning, 2001, p. 466.)

Operations on the Iris, Ciliary Body, Sclera, and Anterior Chamber (Category Code 12)

Category 12, Operations on iris, ciliary body, sclera, and anterior chamber, encompasses codes for parts of the eye that are illustrated in Figure 11-5 of this textbook.

The sclera is the white part of the eye, and the iris is the colored part of the eye. The ciliary body is a group of muscles and ligaments that adjust the lens of the eye to focus light rays on the retina.

Procedure Codes	Description
12.0X	Removal of Intraocular Foreign Body from Anterior Segment of Eye—This subcategory includes the removal of an intraocular foreign body from the anterior section of the eye. Fourth digits are used to specify how the removal was performed. Magnets are sometimes used to move a foreign body from this portion of the eye, a procedure coded by using code 12.01.
12.1X	Iridotomy and Simple Iridectomy—Iridotomy is coded to this subcategory. **Iridotomy** is a surgical cutting or incision into the iris. This subcategory is *not* used when coding an iridotomy associated with cataract extraction, scleral fistulization, or removal of a lesion. An Exclude: note in the Tabular List after the start of category 12.1 identifies operations that are excluded from this subcategory.
12.2X	Diagnostic Procedures on Iris, Ciliary Body, Sclera, and Anterior Chamber—This subcategory contains the diagnostic procedures including biopsy of the iris. Code 12.21 is assigned when an aspiration of fluid from the anterior chamber occurs for diagnostic purposes.
12.3X	Iridoplasty and Coreoplasty—Lysis or destruction of lesions and adhesions are coded to this subcategory. The coder must be able to identify the site of the lysis, because fourth digits are used to specific the site. It should be noted that **coreoplasty**, which is a repair of a defect of the iris and is sometimes referred to as needling of the papillary membrane, is coded to this subcategory.
12.4X	Excision or Destruction of Lesion of Iris and Ciliary Body—The removal of lesions and dead tissue is coded to this section. The destruction of lesions of the iris can be done with cutting as well as cauterization (heat), cryotherapy (freezing), or photocoagulation (to solidify tissue after disruption by using light rays).
12.5X	Facilitation of Intraocular Circulation—The procedure **goniopuncture** is classified to this subcategory. This procedure is sometimes used in the treatment of glaucoma. A knife blade is used to make a slit through the cornea for filtering.
12.6X	Scleral Fistulization—**Fistulization** is the creation of a passage, usually for drainage. Because of how the sclera encompasses the eye, a fistula through the sclera is sometimes needed to relieve pressure. **Glaucoma** is caused by intraocular pressure, which can damage the optic nerve and lead to blindness.
12.7X	Other Procedures for Relief of Elevated Intraocular Pressure—Ciliary body tissue is destroyed by heat, freezing, or light-ray destruction in the treatment of glaucoma.
12.8X	Operations on Sclera—This subcategory includes codes for the excision, repair, and revision of the sclera.

Operations on the Lens (Category Code 13)

The lens of the eye works like the lens of a camera to focus images on the retina. It is found behind the iris and pupil. Category code 13 is used to classify operations on the lens.

Procedure Codes	Description
13.0X	Removal of Foreign Body from Lens—This subcategory contains codes needed to code procedures involving foreign body removal from the lens.
13.1X	Intracapsular Extraction of Lens—This is the section of codes that begins the cataract surgery codes. **Cataracts** are caused by a clouding of the lens of the eye. Cataract surgery is sometimes referred to as a **lensectomy**, because the cataract-clouded lens is removed and replaced. Intracapsular extraction involves a larger incision in which the entire capsule is removed (Figure 28-3).
13.2–13.5X	Extracapsular Extraction of Lens—These procedures use a smaller incision for removal of the lens but leave the capsule intact. Code 13.41 is a technique called **phacoemulsification**, which is the use of ultrasound to break up the lens; then the material is flushed and aspirated at the same time.
13.7X	Insertion of Prosthetic Lens (Pseudophakos)—When the natural lens is removed, an artificial lens is inserted to replace it. This subsection covers this insertion.

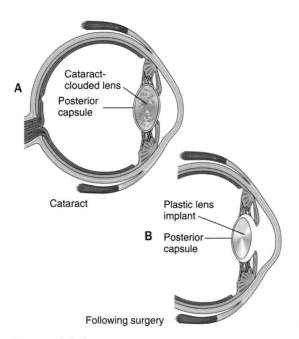

Figure 28-3 Lens implant surgery for cataracts. (A) Cataract. (B) After surgery. (From Hegner BR, Acello B, Caldwell E. *Nursing Assistant: A Nursing Process Approach,* 9th ed. Clifton Park, NY: Delmar, Cengage Learning, 2004, p. 699.)

Cataract extractions are often followed by an implantation of an artificial lens. When this occurs, codes are assigned for both the cataract extraction and lens implantation.

Operation on Retina, Choroid, Vitreous, and Posterior Chamber (Category Code 14)

Category 14, Operations on retina, choroid, vitreous, and posterior chamber, is organized in a similar fashion to the previous categories. These structures are located so closely in the eye that sometimes a procedure on one structure affects the others. Careful attention to detail in the notes is critical.

Procedure Codes	Description
14.2X	Destruction of Lesion of Retina and Choroid—These codes are used for the destruction of lesions by various methods, including laser, radiation, and cryotherapy.
14.3X	Repair of Retinal Tear—If there is a tear or defect of some kind in the retinal layer, codes from this subcategory are used for the repair. The repair can be done by various techniques such as laser, cryotherapy, or diathermy.
14.4X	Repair of Retinal Detachment with Scleral Buckling and Implant—Scleral buckling is a procedure used in the correction of retinal detachment. Figure 28-4 illustrates this procedure. The idea is to support any retinal breaks with a piece of silicone or silicone sponge. The silicone is stitched to the sclera to create a buckle, which pushes the retinal break together and closes it. Other repairs of retinal detachment are coded to subcategory 14.5X.
14.7X	Operations on Vitreous—This subcategory includes the removal of vitreous as well as the injection and other operations on this structure. The vitreous humor, or vitreous gel, is a gel-like substance that helps the eye keep its shape.

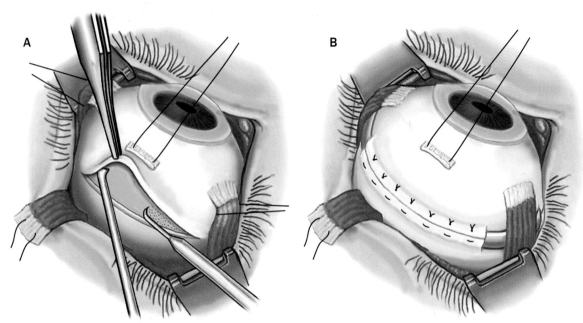

Figure 28-4 Scleral buckling. **(A)** Preparation of sclera buckling. **(B)** Scleral buckle sutured in place. (From Caruthers B, Price P, Junge TL, et al. *Surgical Technology for the Surgical Technologist: A Positive Care Approach.* Clifton Park, NY: Delmar, Cengage Learning, 2001, p. 458.)

Operations on Extraocular Muscles (Category Code 15)

The muscles of category 15, Operations on extraocular muscles, are illustrated in Figure 28-5. The six muscles needed to move the eye extend from the bones of the orbit and are collectively called the extraocular muscles.

Procedures completed on the extraocular muscles are classified to codes 15.0X–15.9.

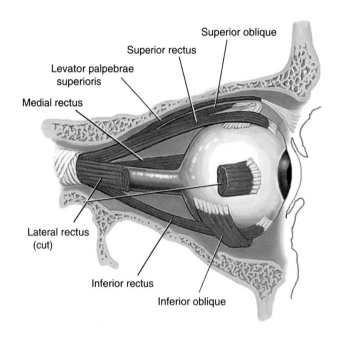

Figure 28-5 Extrinsic muscles of the eye (From Caruthers B, Price P, Junge TL, et al. *Surgical Technology for the Surgical Technologist: A Positive Care Approach.* Clifton Park, NY: Delmar, Cengage Learning, 2001, p. 448.)

Procedure Codes	Description
15.0X	Diagnostic Procedures on Extraocular Muscles or Tendons—Biopsies of the muscles or tendons and other diagnostic procedures are included in this subcategory.
15.1X	Operations on One Extraocular Muscle Involving Temporary Detachment from Globe—One muscle of the eye might need recession, advancement, or resection. For procedures involving more than one muscle, subcategories 15.3–15.4 are referenced.
15.7	Repair of Injury of Extraocular Muscle—Code 15.7 is used to classify a repair of a laceration, lysis of adhesions, or freeing of an entrapped muscle.

Operations on Orbit and Eyeball (Category Code 16)

Category 16, Operations on orbit and eyeball, finishes the chapter. The orbit of the eye is formed by seven bones in the face. The orbit is described like a house with a roof, floor, and inner and outer wall, as well as four angles, a base, and an apex. The orbit, along with the muscles, holds the eye in place.

Procedure Codes	Description
16.0X	Orbitotomy—This subcategory starts with orbitotomy, a procedure involving an incision of the orbit. One approach is through openings in the skull.
16.2X	Diagnostic Procedures on Orbit and Eyeball—Code 16.21 classifies an examination of the eye through a scope, known as an ophthalmoscopy. Code 16.23 includes the code for a biopsy of the orbit or eyeball.
16.3X	Evisceration of Eyeball—Evisceration is exposure through an open wound. It indicates an emergency situation and requires immediate surgical attention.
16.4X	Enucleation of Eyeball—Sometimes, because of an injury, disease, or defect, the eyeball needs to be removed and replaced. This subcategory contains these codes.
16.6X	Secondary Procedures after Removal of Eyeball—Notes are important to watch in this section because these codes are used in addition to a primary procedure. These codes are revision codes or secondary graft codes after the removal of the eyeball.

When a patient has an ocular condition that has impacted both eyes, surgery will be performed on one eye and then repeated on the second eye during a later episode of care.

Internet Links

To learn more about surgeries completed on the eye, visit the following Web sites: American Society of Cataract and Refractive Surgery, *www.ascrs.org*; American Academy of Ophthalmology, *www.aao.org*; American Society of Ophthalmic Plastic and Reconstructive Surgery, *www.asoprs.org*.

Summary

- Chapter 3 of volume 3 of ICD-9-CM classifies procedures that include the eyelid, conjunctiva, cornea, lens, retina, iris, and ciliary body of the eye.

- Laser surgery, diagnostic, biopsy, repair, removal, and destruction procedure codes are included in this chapter.

- Laser means light amplification by the stimulated emission of radiation.

- Procedures of the lacrimal structures are found in this chapter.

- Reconstruction and graft procedures of the eye are found in this chapter.

- The orbit holds the eyeball in place.

- Thermocauterization is performed by using a hot-tipped instrument.

- Iridotomy is a surgical cutting or incision into the iris.
- Cataracts are caused by a clouding of the lens and are corrected by removal of the lens.
- Keratoplasty refers to corneal grafting.

Chapter Review

True/False: Indicate whether the statement is true (T) or false (F).

1. _____ Laser is an acronym that stands for light amplification by the standard emission of radiation.

2. _____ Repair of lacerations of the eyelid is coded to the 08.8X subcategory of codes.

3. _____ Lysis of adhesions to the iris is coded to the 12.3X subcategory.

4. _____ The rhytidectomy produces tears to wash away foreign material from the eye.

5. _____ A procedure that directs heat to destroy a corneal lesion is called thermocauterization.

Fill-in-the-Blank: Enter the appropriate term(s) to complete each statement.

6. _____ is the ability to see and distinguish objects at a distance.

7. A drooping eyelid is known as _____.

8. The surgical correction of an absent lens in the eye is called _____.

9. Normal vision is recognized as _____.

10. The _____ structures produce tears.

Coding Assignments

Instructions: Using an ICD-9-CM coding book, select the code for each procedural statement.

Procedure	Code
1. Destruction of lesion of eyelid	_____
2. Biopsy of lacrimal sac	_____
3. Reconstruction of conjunctival cul-de-sac	_____
4. Repair of retinal detachment with laser photocoagulation	_____
5. Biopsy of eyeball	_____
6. Revision of extraocular muscle surgery	_____
7. Repair of blepharoptosis by tarsal technique	_____
8. Removal of ocular implant	_____
9. Perforating keratoplasty with autograph	_____
10. Lysis of adhesions of iris	_____

11. Radical orbitomaxillectomy   _____

12. Excision of verucca   _____

13. Cryotherapy of corneal lesion   _____

14. Repair of retinal detachment with diathermy   _____

15. Blepharorrhaphy   _____

16. Canthotomy   _____

17. Cataract extraction   _____

18. Repair of cornea   _____

19. Goniotomy with goniopuncture   _____

20. Incision and drainage of lacrimal cyst   _____

21. Removal of trachoma follicles   _____

22. Repair of canaliculus   _____

23. Biopsy of extraocular tendon   _____

24. Removal of foreign body from posterior segment of the eye using a magnet   _____

25. Excision of lesion of orbit   _____

Case Studies

Instructions: Review each case study, and select the correct ICD-9-CM diagnostic and procedural codes.

CASE 1

This is a 75-year-old female who presents with a diagnosis of nuclear sclerosis cataract in the left eye. The patient now presents for correction of cataract with lens implant. Prior to surgery, patient was experiencing blurring and halos in the left eye. Preop examination confirmed the diagnosis of advanced nuclear sclerosis cataract of left eye.

PROCEDURE: Patient was brought to the operating room and placed in supine position. The left eye was prepped and draped in usual sterile fashion, and a subciliary and then periretrobulbar injection was given. Open wire lid speculum and operating microscope were placed.

A superior conjunctival peritectomy, 4 mm, was fashioned with the Westcott scissors. The wet-field cautery was used for hemostasis. A general-shelf incision was then made with a crescent knife. A 2.5-mm sharp blade was used superiorly to enter the anterior chamber. The pupil was dilated to 5 mm. An inferior sphineterotomy was performed at 6 o'clock with bandage scissors. Healon was introduced into the anterior chamber, and a continuous-tear capsulotomy was performed with Utrata forceps. Remnants were removed from the eye. The nucleus was hydrodissected with balanced salt solution. The Storz premier handpiece was used, using a total time of 2 minutes 14 seconds at an average power of 24% with a nuclear cracking technique. The posterior capsular bag was then deepened with Healon, and a Staar foldable AA203V, +24.4 diopter, posterior chamber intraocular lens was then unfolded into the inferior and then superior capsular bag. Centration was verified.

Healon was removed from the eye and replaced with balanced salt solution. Miochol was used to constrict the pupil. Speculum was removed. Gentamicin drops were given. Pred Forte drops were also given. A patch and shield was placed. Patient was sent to recovery room in stable condition.

ICD-9-CM Code Assignment: _____

CASE 2

This is a 72-year-old male who is presenting for YAG laser surgery. He presents with a diagnosis of capsular fibrosis in the right eye. Preop physical is attached and shows no counterindications for surgery. Patient has noted vision loss over the last year and is unable to see a distance without a great deal of difficulty. Right eye is the only eye affected at this time. Good vision noted in the left.

Eye exam prior to surgery noted vision in the right eye to be 20/50; in the left eye, vision is noted to be 20/20. Tension: 18 bilaterally. Slit Exam: cornea—0; A/C—0, posterior capsule showing moderate opacity; view—20/80; retina—no tears.

The laser was used at 1.0 millijoules; patient had 34 spots treated to eradicate the fibrosis. Patient tolerated the procedure well and will return to office for postop visit.

ICD-9-CM Code Assignment: _____

CASE 3

This is a 30-year-old female who presented with symptoms of a blocked tear duct on the left side. Preop physical confirmed this diagnosis due to stenosis of the lacrimal sac. The left eye is somewhat inflamed and swollen. Patient has no counterindications for surgery.

PROCEDURE: Patient was placed in a supine position on the operating table. Patient was prepped and draped in the usual sterile fashion on the left side of the face. Patient was given general anesthesia and then a local injection of tetracain 1% with adrenaline 1:5,000, two drops in the conjunctival sac. A curved incision was made, conforming to the anterior lacrimal crest cut down to expose the lacrimal crest. Each side of the incision was retracted to allow for room to use blunt dissection in separating the lacrimal sac from the lacrimal fossa. This was retracted, and the periosteum was dissected away from the lacrimal fossa. The anterior lacrimal crest to the nasolacrimal duct was then removed using rongeur. An ostium was created using a burr. Debris was suctioned away to make visualization better. A window of bone was removed with bone forceps. The nasal mucosa was stripped using a mucoperiosteal elevator. A sphenoidal punch was used to trim the edges of the opening. After a vertical cut was made in the anterior wall of the lacrimal sac, a probe was passed into the lumen. There was a horizontal slit cut into the wall of the sac. The nasal mucosa was also slit horizontally. By using 9-0 monofilament nylon sutures, the flaps of the nasal mucosa and lacrimal sac were joined. Bleeding was well controlled, and we went on to close the incision. Patient tolerated the procedure well and was sent to the recovery room in good condition.

ICD-9-CM Code Assignment: _____

CASE 4

PREOPERATIVE DIAGNOSIS: Orbital mass, OS-left eye

POSTOPERATIVE DIAGNOSIS: Orbital mass, OS-left eye, herniated fat pad in the orbital area

PROCEDURE: Patient was prepped with proparacaine instilled in the left eye and 2% Lidocaine with 1:200,000 epinephrine injected in the superior aspect of the left orbit.

The upper lid was everted, and a herniated mass was located and measured at 0.50 cm in diameter. The herniated mass was clamped and excised. Cauterization was then used to stop the bleeding. The mass was sent to pathology, but the report came back as a fatty mass. The superior fornix was repaired, and antibiotic ointment was applied to the eye. An eye pad was placed over the eye. The patient tolerated the procedure well and was in good condition when sent to the recovery area.

ICD-9-CM Code Assignment: _____

CASE 5

Emergency Department Note

This is a 6-year-old male who presents to the emergency department with a laceration on the right upper lid of the eye due to a playground accident that occurred just prior to coming to the emergency department. Past medical history is noncontributory. No medical conditions.

Examination reveals a very deep laceration medial to the upper puctum. Upon further exam of the wound, canalicular involvement is found, so the patient was moved to the operating room for repair.

Surgical repair of the canaliculus was performed under conscious sedation using pigtail probes.

ICD-9-CM Code Assignment: _____

29 Operations on the Ear

Chapter Outline

Objectives

At the conclusion of this chapter, the student will be able to:

1. Identify pathologies and injuries of the ear.
2. Describe some of the procedures used to correct the pathologies and injuries.
3. Accurately code procedures completed on the ear.
4. Select and code diagnoses and procedures from case studies.

Key Terms

Auditory Ossicles	Incus	Myringoplasty	Perilymphatic Tap
Canaloplasty	Labyrinths	Myringotomy	Pinna
Cerumen	Malleus	Otitis Media	Stapedectomy
Eustachian Tubes	Mastoidectomy	Otoplasty	Stapes
Fenestration	Meatus	Otoscope	Tympanic Membrane

Reminder

As you work through this chapter, you will need to have a copy of the ICD-9-CM coding book to reference.

Introduction

Chapter 4 of ICD-9-CM volume 3 classifies operations and procedures completed on the inner, middle, and external or outer ear. It is important for the coder to identify in the medical documentation the component of the ear in which the surgery is completed.

Introduction to the Anatomy of the Ear

The outer ear consists of the pinna, sometimes called the auricle, and the meatus, or the external auditory canal. Some of the problems that can occur in the outer ear usually involve obstructions. Cerumen, or earwax, can cause problems with hearing. Another type of obstruction can be a foreign body. Children tend to put foreign bodies into their ears and, depending on the size of the foreign body, can push it in far enough where intervention by a healthcare professional is necessary.

The tympanic membrane is also called the eardrum. This is where the middle ear begins. The eardrum is normally shiny, translucent, and pearly gray in color. The middle ear is also where the auditory ossicles are located. The auditory ossicles are three bones named by their shapes. The hammer-shaped bone is called the malleus, the anvil-shaped bone is called the incus, and the stirrup-shaped bone is called the stapes. The stapes is the ossicle that is located next to the oval window, where the inner ear begins. Damage to any of these bones or the eardrum itself can result in loss of hearing. Sometimes fluid gets trapped in the middle ear and can cause otitis media, an acute inflammation known more commonly as an ear infection. Another problem that can be encountered in the middle ear occurs when there is unequal pressure between the middle ear and outside environment. This can make hearing difficult because the eardrum becomes distorted. This can happen when a person flies or climbs to a higher altitiude. The eustachian tubes are located in the middle ear and lead to the nasopharynx. The eustachian tubes are the channels that keep the air pressure within the ear in balance.

The inner ear is a series of canals and chambers, called labyrinths, that begin at the oval window. Located in the inner ear are the vestibule, cochlea, and semicircular canals. The vestibule and the canals are involved in equilibrium. The cochlea is the part of the labyrinth involved in hearing. Patients with inner ear problems may experience vertigo, tinnitus, or hearing loss. To review the anatomy of the ear, refer to Figure 11-7.

Coding Operations on the Ear

The chapter is divided into procedures of the external, middle, and inner ear. The arrangement of this chapter of ICD-9-CM works its way from the external ear inward.

Operations on the External Ear (Category Code 18)

This category classifies procedures completed on the external ear. An Include: note appears at the start of the category to identify the included operations.

```
Includes: Operations on:
 External auditory canal
 Skin and cartilage of:
  Auricle
  Meatus
```

Some procedures that are classified to this category include:

Procedure Codes	Description
18.0X	Incision of External Ear—Ear piercing is included in this series of codes. Although this procedure is done in the malls around the country, sometimes a provider performs this procedure, which is a billable service in the outpatient setting.
18.1X	Diagnostic Procedure on External Ear—Biopsy of the external ear and otoscopy are coded to this section. An **otoscope** is an instrument used to view the external ear canal and the middle ear.
18.2X	Excision or Destruction of Lesion of External Ear—Excisions and destructions of lesions of the external ear code to this subcategory. The types of destruction can be cauterization, cryosurgery, curettage, electrocoagulation, coagulation, or enucleation.
18.3X	Other Excision of External Ear—Other excisions of the external ear are the amputations of parts or all of external ear.

Subcategory 18.4 is coded when a laceration repair of the external ear is performed. Subcategory 18.5 is for the correction or reformation of outer ear, such as an ear pinning or setback. Reconstruction of the external ear or external auditory canal, also referred to as **canaloplasty** of the external auditory canal, is coded to 18.6.

Procedure Code	Description
18.7X	Other Plastic Repair of External Ear—A procedure known as an otoplasty is coded to this subcategory. An **otoplasty** is a repair of the outer ear. Prosthetic application in cases in which the external ear is missing is coded to this subcategory. In a case in which the external ear is being reattached after amputation, this subcategory is referenced.

The removal of a foreign body from the ear might be necessary but is coded to this chapter only if an incision is necessary.

Reconstructive Operations on the Middle Ear (Category Code 19)

Category 19 classifies reconstructive procedures of the middle ear; specific codes follow. All reconstructive procedures are completed to surgically reform a structure.

Procedure Codes	Description
19.1X	Stapedectomy—**Stapedectomy** is the surgical removal of part or all of the stapes. Reconstruction may also be done by the insertion of a prosthesis or by a homograft.
19.2X	Revision of Stapedectomy—When a surgical correction of a stapedectomy occurs at another operative session, it is coded to this subcategory.
19.3	Other Operations on Ossicular Chain—This is the subcategory used when the repair of the bones of the middle ear occurs at a second operative session. The unspecified removal of bones of the middle ear is also coded to this subcategory.
19.4	Myringoplasty—A **myringoplasty** refers to a repair of the tympanic membrane that may have ruptured due to internal pressure or some type of external trauma. This repair includes graft or cauterization. This is considered a type I repair.
19.5X	Other Tympanoplasty—This subcategory encompasses the type II through type V repairs. The extent of damage to the eardrum determines which type is assigned. The types are assigned as follows:
	Type II—Tympanic membrane and malleus
	Type III—Tympanic membrane, malleus, and incus
	Type IV—Tympanic membrane, malleus, incus, and stapes
	Type V—The same as type IV except that the footplate of the stapes is fixed

19.6	Revision of Tympanoplasty—This subcategory is a revision or correction of the middle ear done at a previous operative session. Medical documentation must be reviewed to ensure that the tympanoplasty is being completed to surgically correct a previous tympanoplasty.
19.9	Other Repair of Middle Ear—This subcategory includes any procedures that are not specified anywhere else. Included in this subcategory are the restoration of the mastoid muscle, the repair of mastoid fistula, and the removal of functional parts of the middle ear.

Other Operations on the Middle and Inner Ear (Category Code 20)

Some procedures of the middle ear are located in category 20, Other operations on middle and inner ear. Because the anatomy overlaps somewhat, the coding does as well. The category 20 codes also contain procedures involving the mastoid sinus. Figure 29-1 illustrates the mastoid sinus and structures that are involved in its makeup.

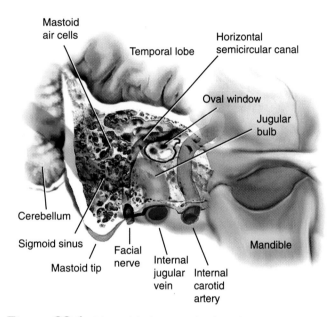

Figure 29-1 Mastoid sinus and related structures (From Price P, Frey KB, Junge TL. *Surgical Technology for the Surgical Technologist: A Positive Care Approach,* 2nd ed. Clifton Park, NY: Delmar, Cengage Learning, 2004, p. 588.)

Procedure Codes	Description
20.0X	Myringotomy—When tube placement is required, an incision is made in the eardrum for placement. The incision made into the eardrum is known as a **myringotomy**.
20.1	Removal of Tympanostomy Tube—This code is used to code the removal of a tympanic membrane tube.
20.2X	Incision of Mastoid and Middle Ear—The mastoid process of the temporal bones contains the air cells of the mastiod sinus. The tympanic antrum is an opening that leads into the mastoid sinus through the middle ear.
20.4X	Mastoidectomy—A **mastoidectomy** is the removal of mastoid process or bony portion of the mastoid air cells behind the ear. This subcategory contains codes for a simple mastoidectomy, which is the removal of the air cells only.
20.6X	Fenestration of Inner Ear—**Fenestration** is a procedure that is done in the labyrinth of the ear; a surgical opening is formed to restore hearing. Type V tympanoplasty is not included in this procedure.
20.7X	Incision, Excision, and Destruction of Inner Ear—Placement of a shunt to drain fluid from the inner ear is coded from this subcategory under 20.71, Endolymphatic shunt. Relief of pressure of the inner ear is also called either decompression or decompression of the labyrinth. If a fluid sac forms in the inner ear cavity, it may need to be punctured. This is called a **perilymphatic tap** and is coded to this subcategory.

Procedure Codes	Description
20.8	Operations on Eustachian Tube—This subcategory includes such procedures as catherization, inflation, injection, intubation, and politzerization.
20.9X	Other Operations on Inner and Middle Ear—This subcategory contains codes for procedures not specified elsewhere in the chapter. Cochlear implant surgery, which is relatively new, is coded to this section. Also coded to this subcategory is electromagnetic hearing device implantation.

Please note that new techniques for performing procedures on the ear occur each year. Coders must continuously research and learn about the new procedures.

Internet Links

To learn more about the latest treatments for disorders of the ear, visit the American Academy of Otolaryngology at *www.entnet.org*.

The National Library of Medicine provides information on operations and procedures at *www.nlm.nih.gov*. To locate specific information, type the name of the procedure you want to research in the search area; you will be amazed at the amount of information you will find. For information related to this chapter, search this site for tympanoplasty.

Summary

- The anatomy of the ear is divided into the outer ear, middle ear, and inner ear.
- The ICD-9-CM chapter follows the anatomy from the external or outer ear inward to the inner ear.
- Tympanoplasty is also referred to as a myringoplasty.
- The external ear is made up of the pinna and the external auditory canal.
- The middle ear contains the three auditory ossicles.
- The inner ear contains the labyrinths and the cochlea.
- Tympanoplasty is coded by types I–V, depending on the damage to the eardrum.

Chapter Review

True/False: Indicate whether the statement is true (T) or false (F).

1. _____ The eardrum is located in the inner ear.

2. _____ Reconstruction of the external ear is coded to 18.32.

3. _____ Tympanoplasty, type III, indicates damage to the tympanic membrane, malleus, incus, and stapes.

4. _____ The ear is made up of three parts: external, middle, and inner ears.

5. _____ Shunt placement for the drainage of fluid from the inner ear is coded from the 20.7X subcategory.

Fill-in-the-Blank: Enter the appropriate term(s) to complete each statement.

6. The three bones of the middle ear are called _____, _____, and the _____.

7. The instrument used to view the external ear canal is called an _____.

8. The _____ is the part of the inner ear involved in hearing.

9. The procedure done in the labyrinth of the ear in which a surgical opening is formed to restore hearing is called _____.

10. A _____ is when tube placement is required and a surgical incision is made in the eardrum for placement.

Coding Assignments

Instructions: Using an ICD-9-CM coding book, select the code for each procedural statement.

Procedure	Code
1. Excision of exostosis of external auditory canal	_____
2. Incudectomy	_____
3. Stapedectomy with incus replacement	_____
4. Revision of tympanoplasty	_____
5. Excision of preaucular sinus	_____
6. Removal of tympanostomy tube	_____
7. Suture of laceration of external ear	_____
8. Tympanoplasty, type III	_____
9. Biopsy of external ear	_____
10. Revision of fenestration of inner ear	_____
11. Ear pinning	_____
12. Catherization of eustachian tube	_____
13. Incision of mastoid	_____
14. Piercing of pinna	_____
15. Type II tympanoplasty	_____
16. Single-channel replacement of cochlear prosthetic device	_____
17. Otoplasty	_____
18. Implantation of multiple-channel cochlear prosthetic device	_____
19. Insufflation of eustachian tube	_____
20. Type I tympanoplasty	_____
21. Radical excision of lesion of external ear	_____

22. Reconstruction of auricle _____

23. Radical mastoidectomy _____

24. Electrocochleography _____

25. Injection of tympanum _____

Case Studies

Instructions: Review each case study, and select the correct ICD-9-CM diagnostic and procedural codes.

CASE 1

PRE- AND POSTOPERATIVE DIAGNOSIS: Persistent chronic adhesive otitis of the middle ear, right ear

PROCEDURE PERFORMED: Myringotomy and insertion of tympanotomy tube

ANESTHESIA: General

This 6-year-old male patient was prepared in the usual manner and was given general anesthesia. A speculum was placed in the right external auditory canal. The right ear was viewed via an operating microscope, and the canal was cleansed of wax. An incision was made in the inferior posterior portion of the right tympanic membrane. A PE tube was placed into the membrane without any difficulty. Final positioning was achieved, and the speculum was removed. Cortisporin was placed in the canal. The patient was sent to the recovery room in stable condition.

ICD-9-CM Code Assignment: _____

CASE 2

PREOPERATIVE DIAGNOSIS: Pain in left ear

POSTOPERATIVE DIAGNOSIS: Perforation of tympanic membrane, left ear due to trauma

PROCEDURE: Tympanoplasty

ANESTHESIA: General

This 30-year-old patient was placed in the supine position, and the patient's left ear was examined using an operating microscope. The tympanic membrane was assessed, and it was noted to be perforated. All debris was removed from the area, and the tympanic membrane was cauterized. The perforation was completely closed. Antibiotic solution was placed in the ear canal. The patient was awoken and transferred to the recovery room in excellent condition.

ICD-9-CM Code Assignment: _____

CASE 3

PREOPERATIVE DIAGNOSIS: Foreign body in ear canal

POSTOPERATIVE DIAGNOSIS: Same

ANESTHESIA: General

This 3-year-old child was placed in the supine position, and his right ear was examined using a scope. A paper clip-like structure was visualized. An incision was made in the external canal to remove the structure because the clip was embedded in canal tissue. The structure was removed, and there was no damage to the external canal. Vasodin was instilled in the canal, and the canal was packed with cotton. The patient tolerated the procedure well and was sent to the recovery room with minimal blood loss.

ICD-9-CM Code Assignment: _____

CASE 4

Physician's Office Note

Mrs. Kirk presents today with her 3-month-old baby girl, Kelly. Mom would like Kelly's ears pierced but does not want to go to "one of those mall places." She asked whether we would be able to perform this procedure. We explained the risks and benefits, and Mrs. Kirk wants to proceed with the procedure. We prepped Kelly for the procedure and prepared the piercing gun. Kelly's ears were pierced through the pinna, and she appeared to handle the procedure well. We will see her back in a week or sooner if there are any problems or complications.

ICD-9-CM Code Assignment: _____

CASE 5

Ambulatory Surgery Note

This is a 17-year-old male who presents today for a stapedectomy due to otosclerosis. The patient was accompanied by his parents. All risks and benefits were explained to the patient and his parents. All parties agreed this was the best option to correct the problem.

The external ear canal was injected with local anesthesia, and an operating microscope was used to visualize the middle ear. An ear speculum was inserted for proper visualization of the middle ear. Fluid was removed with suction. The tympanic membrane was elevated, and at this point we were able to visual the ossicular chain. A fine Rosen needle and forceps were utilized to fracture the stapes. A laser was used to create a hole in the footplate. The prosthesis is introduced into the middle ear and properly positioned. The patient's hearing was tested. Then moistened gelatin squares were placed around the prosthesis, and the site was dressed. Patient tolerated the procedure well.

ICD-9-CM Code Assignment: _____

Operations on the Nose, Mouth, and Pharynx

Chapter Outline

Objectives

At the conclusion of this chapter, the student will be able to:

1. Understand the pathologies associated with the nose, mouth, pharynx, and their associated structures.
2. Describe the procedures used to correct the pathologies.
3. Accurately code these procedures.
4. Select and code diagnoses and procedures from case studies.

Key Terms

Adenoids	Deciduous	Hard Palate	Neck
Alveolectomy	Epistaxis	Impacted Tooth	Orthodontics
Alveoli	Ethmoid Sinuses	Inlay	Packing
Alveoloplasty	Frenulum	Lavage	Palate
Antrotomy	Frontal Sinuses	Lingual Tonsils	Palatine Tonsils
Apicoectomy	Gingiva	Marsupialization	Paranasal Sinuses
Caldwell-Luc Procedure	Gingivoplasty	Maxillary Sinuses	Parotid Glands
Cilia	Glosso-	Nasal Septum	Pharynx
Crown	Gums	Nasopharyngeal Tonsils	Polyp

> **Reminder**
>
> *As you work through this chapter, you will need to have a copy of the ICD-9-CM coding book to reference.*

Polypectomy

Resection

Rhino-

Rhinoscopies

Root

Root Canal

Saliva

Salivary Glands

Septoplasty

Sialoadenectomy

Sinusotomy

Sinuses

Soft Palate

Sphenoid Sinuses

Sublingual Glands

Submandibular Glands

Tonsils

Uvula

Introduction

Coding for chapter 5 of volume 3 of ICD-9-CM involves procedures related to the nose, mouth, and pharynx. These structures fall under one chapter in procedural coding in ICD-9-CM due to their close proximity to each other.

Air enters the body through the nose and mouth. The pharynx, also called the throat, receives air from both structures. The pharynx has a unique function in that it acts as a common passage for air, as part of the respiratory tract, and for food and liquid, as part of the digestive tract. Figure 30-1 illustrates the location and relationship of the pharynx and related structures.

Coding Operations on the Nose, Mouth, and Pharynx

Coding for this chapter of ICD-9-CM begins with procedures that take place on the nose. The function of the nose is to receive and filter air coming into the body. Air enters the nasal cavity, where it is filtered and warmed before moving to the pharynx. The nose is lined with mucous membrane and cilia. Cilia are the fine hairs found right inside the nose that filter air coming into the body. The mucous membrane in the upper portion of the nasal cavity contains the receptors for our sense of smell. The coder should be aware of the prefix *rhino-*, which means "nose." Terminology for diagnoses and procedures of the nose often begin with this prefix.

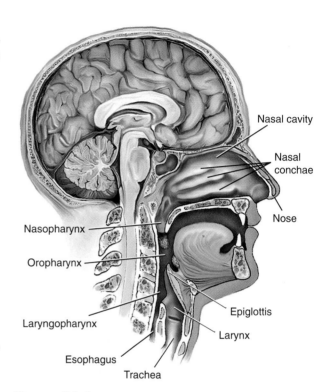

Figure 30-1 Three sections of the pharynx and related structures (From Price P, Frey KB, Junge TL. *Surgical Technology for the Surgical Technologist: A Positive Care Approach,* 2nd ed. Clifton Park, NY: Delmar, Cengage Learning, 2004, p. 619.)

Operations on the Nose (Category Code 21)

Category codes 21.0X–21.9X classifies operations and procedures completed on the nose.

Procedure Codes	Description
21.0X	Control of Epistaxis—Epistaxis is another name for bloody nose or nosebleed. Generally, nosebleeds that require treatment are posterior nosebleeds, in which the bleeding is difficult to stop and much more profuse. Surgical procedures include packing, cauterization, and ligation. Packing is a technique in which gauze is placed in the nose to provide pressure to stop the bleeding.
21.2X	Diagnostic Procedures on Nose—Diagnostic procedures are sometimes done with a scope. These scope procedures are called rhinoscopies.
21.3X	Local Excision or Destruction of Lesion of Nose—This subcategory contains codes for the local excision or destruction of lesions, including polypectomy. A polyp is a growth on the mucous membrane. Generally, a polyp is benign but can be precancerous. Polypectomy is the removal of these growths with a snare or forceps.

Procedure Codes	Description
21.4	Resection of Nose—**Resection** is the complete or partial removal of a structure. In this case, the nose is either amputated or partially removed.
21.6X	Turbinectomy—The turbinate or concha bone is either partially or totally removed. Also included in this subcategory is the destruction of the turbinate bone using cryosurgery (freezing) or diathermy (heating). In some cases, it is necessary to surgically break this bone, which is also coded to this subcategory.
21.7X	Reduction of Nasal Fracture—Fractures can be reduced with either an open procedure or a closed procedure. Both the open and closed procedures are coded to this subcategory.
21.8X	Repair and Plastic Operations on the Nose—Some of the repairs and plastic surgery that are done on the nose and mouth are a result of injury, but they may also be a result of a birth defect such as a fistula. There may be a hole or even a crack between the nose and lip, the nose and mouth, or even the nose and pharynx. Nasal reconstruction, revision, or augmentation are all coded to this subcategory. These are all referred to as types of rhinoplasty. Specifics of the procedure done are necessary in order to properly code the procedure. Also coded in this subcategory is septoplasty. The **nasal septum** divides the nasal cavity into two parts, posterior and anterior. The anterior portion is cartilage, and the posterior portion is bone. **Septoplasty,** or repair of the septum, can be performed on either of these two parts.
21.9X	Other Operations on Nose—This subcategory is used for coding procedures of the nose that are not coded more specifically elsewhere. This subcategory includes lysis of adhesions of the nose, anterior and posterior.

Operations on Nasal Sinuses (Category Code 22)

Category 22, Operations on nasal sinuses, is the next category in this chapter. Sinuses are air spaces located in bones around the nasal cavity. The sinuses, as a group, are sometimes referred to as paranasal sinuses. The specific sinuses are named after the bones they are located in. There are four sinus cavities, which are illustrated in Figure 30-2. They are the frontal, ethmoid, sphenoid, and maxillary sinuses.

Interestingly, with regard to the paranasal sinuses, only the maxillary sinuses are present at birth. The other sinuses develop as a person grows and develops. The frontal and sphenoid sinuses are

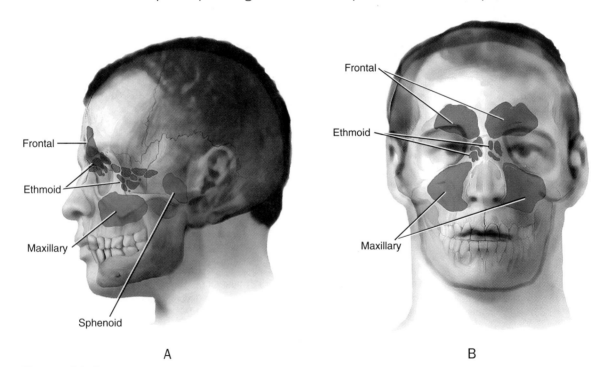

A B

Figure 30-2 Paranasal sinuses: **(A)** Lateral view, **(B)** Anterior view (From Price P, Frey KB, Junge TL. *Surgical Technology for the Surgical Technologist: A Positive Care Approach,* 2nd ed. Clifton Park, NY: Delmar, Cengage Learning, 2004, p. 603.)

developed by age 6 or 7, but the ethmoid sinuses do not complete development until a person is in the late teens to early twenties.

Procedure Codes	Description
22.0X	Aspiration and Lavage of Nasal Sinus—Some people have a problem with fluid building up in the sinus cavities. They require aspiration of this fluid; then the area is washed out or flushed. This washing is called lavage.
22.2	Intranasal Antrotomy—The antrotomy is done to surgically open up the sinus for drainage.
22.3X	External Maxillary Antrotomy—A physician may refer to the procedure of antrotomy in the maxillary sinus cavity as a Caldwell-Luc procedure. This is the approach used in reaching the maxillary cavity. An incision is made just above the canine and is used to clean out the sinus and establish drainage through the nose. If disease is noticed on portions of the antral wall, it is also removed.
22.4X	Frontal Sinusotomy and Sinusectomy—Drainage of the frontal sinus requires an external incision, usually along the eyebrow. The ethmoid sinus is entered first and then the frontal sinus. For drainage, a fistula is created.
22.5X	Other Nasal Sinusotomy—A sinusotomy, or incision into the sinus cavity, for the ethmoid and sphenoid sinuses is coded to this subcategory.
22.6X	Other Nasal Sinusectomy—Codes in this subcategory contain the excision of lesions in the sinuses as well as any bone removal that might be necessary.
22.7X	Repair of Nasal Sinus—These codes are for the repair of the sinus or closure of a fistula.

The age of the patient when coding certain procedures may be a factor due to development of the sinus area.

Removal and Restoration of Teeth (Category Code 23)

Category 23, Removal and restoration of teeth, is included in this chapter because the teeth are part of the mouth. Teeth aid in the breakdown of food and also assist with speech. The teeth of the upper jaw are imbedded in the maxillary process. The teeth of the lower jaw are embedded in the mandibular process. Figure 30-3 illustrates the location of the teeth in relation to the maxillary and mandibular bones.

Figure 30-4 illustrates the teeth and other structures that are in close proximaty.

Procedures are done on various parts of a tooth, so understanding the anatomy and the terminology is important. The part of the tooth that is above the gumline is called the crown. This is the part we brush and use to chew food. Below the gumline is the root of the tooth. The root of the tooth is connected to ligaments that are connected to the jaw and hold the tooth in place. The part of the tooth where the crown and the root meet is called the neck. Figure 30-5 illustrates the location of each of these parts.

Procedure Codes	Description
23.0X	Forceps Extraction of Tooth—Subcategory 23.01, Extraction of deciduous tooth, is the extraction of the primary or baby teeth. At about age 6 or 7, the permanent teeth begin to push the primary teeth out. This procedure does not usually require general anesthesia.
23.1X	Surgical Removal of Tooth—This subcategory is used for surgically removing an impacted tooth. An impacted tooth is one that is lodged below the gumline and is usually causing problems to the surrounding teeth.
23.2	Restoration of Tooth by Filling—A filling is a general procedure performed by the dentist repairing a hole in the enamel of a tooth.
23.3	Restoration of Tooth by Inlay—Inlay is a type of restoration in which a molded filling is cemented in.
23.4X	Other Dental Restoration—This includes the application of a crown, or a covering, on what might be a damaged tooth. This subcategory also includes insertion of a bridge or dentures, which can be fixed or removable.
23.7X	Apicoectomy and Root Canal Therapy—Apicoectomy is the removal of a tooth root. Root canals are mainly done to treat damaged tissue or roots of teeth to try and save the tooth before extraction.

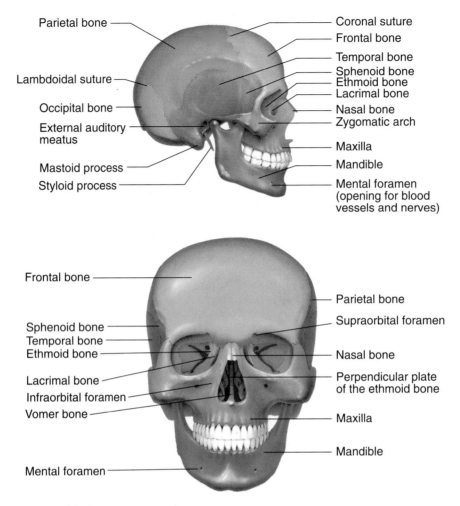

Figure 30-3 Head and facial bones (From Price P, Frey KB, Junge TL. *Surgical Technology for the Surgical Technologist: A Positive Care Approach*, 2nd ed. Clifton Park, NY: Delmar, Cengage Learning, 2004, p. 1028.)

Other Operations on Teeth, Gums, and Alveoli (Category Code 24)

Category 24, Other operations on teeth, gums, and alveoli, contains procedures that are related to orthodotics for the correction of teeth that are out of alignment. If teeth are out of alignment and correction is not made, problems can develop not only with other teeth but also with the jaw.

Also included in this subcategory are procedures that are done on the gums and alveoli. The gums are also referred to as gingiva. This is a mucous membrane that covers the lower part of the tooth and roots, as well as the bone of the jaw. This mucous membrane moves up to the inside of the cheek as well. The alveoli are also called the sockets. These are what help to hold the teeth in place. As with previous subcategories in the procedure section of this book, category 24 begins with procedure codes for incisions and then moves into diagnostic procedures.

Procedure Codes	Description
24.2	Gingivoplasty—Gingivoplasty is a type of repair performed on gum tissue.
24.3X	Other Operation on Gum—This subcategory contains codes for suturing and for performing lesion excision.
24.5	Alveoloplasty—The suffix -plasty, as previously explained, means repair. The alveoloplasty is a repair done on the tooth socket. Also included in this subcategory is the alveolectomy, which is a correction of the tooth socket. This may be simple, radical, or grafted.

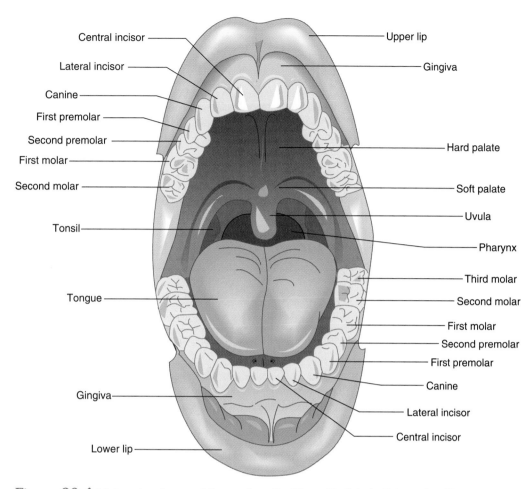

Figure 30-4 Major structures of the oral cavity (From Ehrlich A, Schroeder CL. *Medical Terminology for Health Professions,* 4th ed. Clifton Park, NY: Delmar, Cengage Learning, 2001, p. 167.)

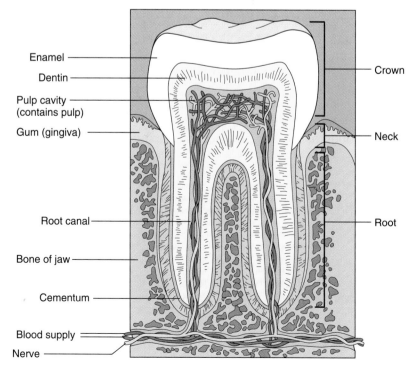

Figure 30-5 Structures and tissues of the tooth (From Ehrlich A, Schroeder CL. *Medical Terminology for Health Professions,* 4th ed. Clifton Park, NY: Delmar, Cengage Learning, 2001, p. 168.)

Procedure Codes	Description
24.7	Application of Orthodontic Appliance—This subcategory begins the orthodontic procedure codes. Included in this subcategory are the application, insertion, and fitting of wiring, peiodontal splint, arch bars, and orthodontic obtruators.
24.8	Other Orthodontic Operations—This subcategory includes procedures such as the closure of alveolar, the removal of arch bars, occlusal adjustment, and the repair of dental arch. The removal of nonorthodontic wiring is not coded to this subcategory. See the Excludes: note.

Operations on the Tongue (Category Code 25)

Operations on the tongue is the next category of this chapter. The tongue aids swallowing and, as do the teeth, speech and chewing. The top part of the tongue contains taste buds. The under part of the tongue is vascular. Because of the vascular nature, medications given under the tongue have a rapid absorpsion rate and tend to work quickly. An example of this is a cardiac patient who needs to take nitroglycerin for an angina attack. The nitro tablet is placed under the tongue and enters the bloodstream quickly.

Procedure Codes	Description
25.1	Excision or Destruction of Lesion or Tissue of Tongue—The procedures coded here deal with lesions that are directly on the tongue.
25.2–25.4	Glossectomy—These subcategories code procedures that consist of the partial, complete, or radical removal of the tongue. *Glosso-* is a prefix meaning "tongue." In the case of a complete or radical glossectomy, a tracheostomy or neck disection may be necessary. There is a note to code other procedures in additon to the glossectomy.
25.5X	Repair of Tongue and Glossoplasty—Any type of repair to the tongue, including sutures of laceration, is coded to this subsection. Fusion and graft procedures are also included here.
25.9X	Other Operations on Tongue—Frenotomy and frenectomy are both coded to this subsection. A **frenulum** is a small section of mucous membrane that limits the movement of an organ. In the mouth, there is a frenulum between the lower lip and gum and also connecting the upper lip and gum.

Operations on Salivary Glands and Ducts (Category Code 26)

Category 26, Operations on salivary glands and ducts, is the next section in this chapter. The **salivary glands** secrete **saliva.** When the enzyme in saliva mixes with chewed food, the digestion process begins. There are three pairs of salivary glands, and the coder should be familiar with the types as well as their locations to be sure the proper codes are being assigned. The first pair, called the **parotid glands,** are located in front of each ear. The next pair, the **sublingual glands,** are located under the tongue. The **submandibular glands** are found on the floor of the mouth. As with other subcategories in the procedure section, incisions and diagnostic procedures are found at the beginning of the subcategory.

Procedure Codes	Description
26.2X	Excision of Lesion of Salivary Gland—This subcategory is where the drainage of a cyst in the salivary gland is accomplished by creating a pouch of the cyst to promote healing. This procedure is called **marsupialization** (creation of the pouch).
26.3X	Sialoadenectomy—The term **sialoadenectomy** refers to the removal of a salivary gland. This subcategory includes partial, complete, and radical removal.
26.4X	Repair of Salivary Gland or Duct—Repair in this subcategory includes suture of the laceration and closure of a fistula. Transplantation of the duct opening is also included in this subcategory.

Other Operations on the Mouth and Face (Category Code 27)

Other procedures on the mouth and face are coded to category 27. This category should be referenced before a less specific code is assigned from another category. Included in this category are codes for operations on lips, palate, and soft tissue of the mouth and face, with the exclusion of the tongue and gingiva because they were covered earlier in this chapter.

Procedure Codes	Description
27.0	Drainage of Face and Floor of Mouth—This includes drainage of an abscess or cyst in the facial region.
27.1	Incision of Palate—The palate forms the roof of the mouth and is made up of two parts: the hard palate and the soft palate. The hard palate is bony and is found in the anterior portion of the roof of the mouth. The soft palate is found in the posterior portion and closes off the nasal passage when swallowing occurs. The soft palate is more flexible than the hard palate.
27.2X	Diagnostic Procedures on Oral Cavity—Biopsy procedures are coded to this subcategory of codes. The biopsy codes for palate, lip, and mouth are all found here. Also found here is the biopsy code for the uvula. The uvula primarily helps with sound production and speech.
27.3X	Excision of Lesion or Tissue of Bony Palate—Destruction is also included in this subcategory. The method of excision or destruction can be chemotherapy, cryotherapy, or cautery.
27.4X	Excision of Other Parts of the Mouth—This subcategory is the excision and destruction of the soft tissue of the mouth.
27.5X	Plastic Repair of Mouth—There is a specific suture repair code for the laceration of the lip, code 27.51, but the laceration repair for the rest of the mouth is coded to 27.52. Code 27.54 is used for the repair of a cleft lip. A cleft lip is a condition in which there is a gap between two sides of the lip, usually the upper lip, or the palate has not fused together. In some cases both the lip and the palate are affected.
27.6X	Palatoplasty—This series of codes involves the repair or correction of the palate.
27.7X	Operations on Uvula—This subcategory includes the incision, excision, and repair of the uvula.

Operations on Tonsils and Adenoids (Category Code 28)

The next category in this chapter is 28, Operations on tonsils and adenoids. The tonsils are located in the posterior wall of the nasopharynx. They are made up of lymphatic tissue and are considered the first line of defense for the respiratory system. The nasopharyngeal tonsils are also called the adenoids. The base of the tongue on the posterior surface contains the lingual tonsils. The palatine tonsils are what people commonly refer to as the tonsils. This pair of tonsils is visible through the mouth and comes off the soft palate to the base of the tongue. Figure 30-6 Illustrates the locations of the three types of tonsils.

Procedure Codes	Description
28.0	Incision and Drainage of Tonsil and Peritonsillar Structures—This procedure is not just the incision, as in previous categories. This procedure includes the incision and drainage of cysts or abscesses.
28.1X	Diagnostic Procedures on Tonsils and Adenoids—This subcategory includes biopsies or other diagnostic procedures done on the the tonsils and adenoids.
28.2-28.3	Tonsillectomy—The excision of the tonsils with or without the removal of adenoids is the distinction that needs to be made with these two codes.
28.6	Adenoidectomy Without Tonsillectomy—An adenoidectomy may be done without the removal of the other tonsils. This code is used in such a case.
28.7	Control of Hemorrhage after Tonsillectomy and Adenoidectomy—If the patient starts to hemorrhage once the procedure is completed and additional measures are needed to control the bleeding, this code is assigned in addition to the code for the removal of the tonsils and adenoids.
28.9	Other Operations on Tonsils and Adenoids—This subcategory includes the removal of a foreign body and excision of a lesion if the tonsil, adenoid, or both were not completely removed.

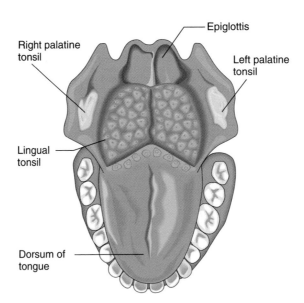

Figure 30-6 Tonsils and surrounding structures (From Ehrlich A, Schroeder CL. *Medical Terminology for Health Professions,* 4th ed. Clifton Park, NY: Delmar, Cengage Learning, 2001, p. 125.)

Operations on Pharynx (Category Code 29)

To end the chapter, category 29, Operations on pharynx, classifies procedures related directly to the pharynx. Coders should review the Includes: note at the start of the category.

Procedure Codes	Description
29.0	Pharyngotomy—This procedure code is used when an incision is made into the pharynx or when drainage of the pharyngeal bursa occurs.
29.1X	Diagnostic Procedures on Pharynx—Diagnostic procedures done with a scope; biopsies of the pharynx and any other diagnostic procedures are coded from this subcategory.
29.2	Excision of Brachial Cleft Cyst or Vestige—This procedure code is used when a brachial cleft cyst or remnants of a brachial cleft need to be removed.
29.3X	Excision or Destruction of Lesion or Tissue of Pharynx—These procedure codes are referenced if damaged tissue of the pharynx needs to be removed or excised.
29.5X	Other Repair of Pharynx—This includes the suture of a laceration, closure of a fistula, and lysis of adhesions of the pharynx.
29.9X	Other Operations on Pharynx—Any other procedure of the pharynx that is not specifically defined anywhere else in this chapter is coded to this subcategory.

With the advancement in the use of scopes, many procedures that were previously performed via incisions are now performed by use of scopes.

Internet Links

To learn more about operations on the nose, mouth, and pharynx, visit the American Academy of Otolaryngology at *www.entnet.org*.

Summary

- Chapter 5 of volume 3 of ICD-9-CM classifies operations completed on the nose, mouth, and pharynx.
- Nosebleeds, also known as epistaxis, that require treatment are packed with gauze.
- Polypectomy is the removal of growths with a snare or forceps.
- Nasal fractures are reduced by open and closed procedures.
- There are four sinus cavities: frontal, ethmoid, sphenoid, and maxillary.
- A sinusotomy is an incision into a sinus cavity.
- An impacted tooth is lodged below the gumline.
- Removal of a salivary gland is known as a sialoadenectomy.
- The nasopharyngeal tonsils are called the adenoids.

Chapter Review

True/False: Indicate whether the statement is true (T) or false (F).

1. _____ The maxillary sinuses are present at birth.

2. _____ The Caldwell-Luc procedure cleans out the frontal sinuses.

3. _____ Cilia filter and warm air coming into the body.

4. _____ The pharynx has a unique dual function as part of the respiratory and digestive tracts.

5. _____ Subcategory 24.3X is used to report gingivoplasty.

Fill-in-the-Blank: Enter the appropriate term(s) to complete each statement.

6. Our sense of smell comes from _____ found in the mucous membrane of the nose.

7. An incision into the sinus cavity is called _____.

8. The technique in which gauze is placed in the nose to stop bleeding is called _____.

9. The prefix meaning tongue is _____.

10. The condition in which there is a separation in the two parts of the lip is called a _____.

Coding Assignments

Instructions: Using an ICD-9-CM coding book, select the appropriate procedure code.

Procedure	Code
1. Suture laceration of the nose	_____
2. Excision of the odontogenic lesion	_____
3. Biopsy of nose	_____
4. Posterior packing of nose to control bleeding	_____
5. Lingual frenectomy	_____

6. Chondrotomy _____

7. Surgical fracture of turbinates _____

8. Closure of a salivary fistula _____

9. Plastic repair of nasolabial flaps _____

10. Correction of cleft palate _____

11. Control of epistaxis by ligation of ethmoidal arteries _____

12. Pharyngotomy _____

13. Tip rhinoplasty _____

14. Exploration of maxillary antrum with Caldwell-Luc procedure _____

15. Repair of nasal septum _____

16. Tonsillectomy with adenoidectomy _____

17. Biopsy of gum _____

18. Probing of salivary duct _____

19. Pharyngeal diverticulectomy _____

20. Graft of buccal sulcus _____

21. Aspiration and lavage of nasal sinus _____

22. Crown application _____

23. Dilation of pharynx _____

24. Partial sialoadenectomy _____

25. Drainage of facial abscess _____

Case Studies

Instructions: Review each case study, and select the correct ICD-9-CM diagnostic and procedural codes.

CASE 1

PREOPERATIVE DIAGNOSIS: Adenotonsillar hyperplasia

INDICATIONS: This is a 24-year-old female who has had an extensive history of tonsilitis and strep throat. This surgery was a last resort to end this cycle. She has been made aware of the risks and benefits of this surgery and has given written consent.

PROCEDURE: Patient presented to the operating room and was placed on the operating table in the supine position. She was induced with general anesthesia and then prepped and draped in the usual sterile fashion. Attention was directed to the right tonsil. The tonsil was clutched near the superior pole, retracted medially and inferiorly. The anterior pillar was dissected from the superior to inferior and then anterior to posterior. The tonsil was freed and removed. The left tonsil was removed in the same way. Attention was then directed to the adenoids through the nares. The soft palate was retracted superiorly, and the adenoid tissue was identified. An adenoid curette was used to remove the adenoids. Gauze packing was used, and then all points were cauterized. The procedure was completed, and the patient was sent to the recovery room in stable condition.

ICD-9-CM Code Assignment: _____

CASE 2

PREOPERATIVE/POSTOPERATIVE DIAGNOSIS: Nasal polyps

PROCEDURE: This is a 67-year-old male who was brought to the operating room for removal of nasal polyps. Preop workup shows 2 polyps located in the nasal cavity. Patient was placed under general anesthesia and placed in supine position with head tilted slightly back. The first polyp, located in the posterior right nare, was visualized and grasped with forceps, encircled with a polyp snare, and removed. Cautery was used to achieve hemostasis. Then attention was directed to the second polyp, which was quite far up in the posterior left nare. After several attemps, the polyp was grasped with forceps, and I was able to encircle this with the polyp snare and remove it. Again, cautery was used to achieve hemostasis. The nose was packed, and the patient was sent to the recovery room in stable condition.

ICD-9-CM Code Assignment: _____

CASE 3

INDICATIONS FOR SURGERY: This is a healthy 18-year-old male who presents today for removal of an impacted molar, tooth 32. The panoramic radiograph shows tooth 32 to be in good position now, but due to the pain it is causing this patient and the slight movement of the existing teeth, surgical intervention is needed to get the tooth out before any further movement can occur.

PROCEDURE: Patient was given conscious sedation using Versed. The site was also injected with 2% Lidocaine. The gingiva was removed from the surface with an elevator, and then a #15 blade was used to incise the gum line. The soft tissue was dissected to expose the impacted tooth (tooth 32) and was able to be removed in whole. The area was then rinsed and all debris removed before two sutures were placed with 4-0 silk. The patient was in good condition when returned to the recovery suite.

ICD-9-CM Code Assignment: _____

CASE 4

This patient presents today for application of Arch Bars to immobilize his jaw. This is a 22-year-old male who was in a fight outside a local bar last night. He was brought into the emergency department by friends immediately following this fight. He was examined and found to have taken several blows to the head area, resulting in a black eye on the left and a broken mandible. X-rays of the head reveal a closed fracture of the right mandible.

PROCEDURE: Patient was prepped and draped in the usual sterile fashion under general anesthesia. The arch bars are measured and shaped for proper fit. They are then attached to the maxilla using wires. A wire twister is used to apply and secure the 10-cm wires around each tooth. The second arch bar is anchored to the mandible with wire. The upper and lower jaws are stabilized to each other, and elastic loops are placed over the hooks of the arch bars, which are then tightened. A final rinse is applied. The patient tolerated the procedure well and was returned to the recovery suite in good condition.

ICD-9-CM Code Assignment: _____

CASE 5

This is a 30-year-old female who presents today for a Caldwell-Luc procedure to open up the maxillary sinus cavity because more conservative treatment has not worked. She has been suffering from chronic maxillary sinusitis for the past 5 years.

The patient was placed in supine position with her head tilted back and turned to the right side. Using a #15 blade, an incision was made in the gingiva above the canine tooth and second molar. The inferior wall of the maxilla was elevated, and the infraorbital nerve was retracted. The bone was perforated with a small drill, and the maxillary sinus was enlarged with a small rongeur. All purulent material was removed. Hemostasis was achieved and the nose was packed. The gingiva was sutured with absorbable suture material. The patient was returned to the recovery suite in stable condition.

ICD-9-CM Code Assignment: _____

31 Operations on the Respiratory System

Chapter Outline

Objectives

At the conclusion of this chapter, the student will be able to:

1. Understand the pathologies associated with the organs and associated structures of the respiratory system.
2. Describe some of the procedures used to correct the pathologies.
3. Accurately code these procedures.
4. Select and code diagnoses and procedures from case studies.

Key Terms

Alveoli

Artificial Pneumothorax

Arytenoidopexy

Bronchial Dilation

Bronchial Tree

Bronchioles

Bronchocutaneous

Bronchoesophageal

Bronchoscopy

Bronchovisceral

Decortication of the
  Lung

Diaphragm

En Bloc

Endoscopic Procedure

Epiglottidectomy

Epiglottis

False Vocal Cords

Hemilaryngectomy

Larynx

Lobe

Lobectomy

Lung Transplant

Lung Volume Reduction

Marsupialization

Mediastinum

Pleura

Pleurectomy

Plication

Pneumonectomy

Pneumoperitoneum

Rib Resection

Reminder

As you work through this chapter, you will need to reference an ICD-9-CM coding book.

Introduction

Chapter 6 of volume 3 of ICD-9-CM is entitled "Operations on the Respiratory System." Coding for this chapter begins with the procedures of the larynx and moves through the trachea, bronchus, lungs, and pleura. The respiratory system brings oxygen into the blood cells and then expels carbon dioxide and water. This air flow also plays a role in the ability to speak.

Coding Operations on the Respiratory System

Category codes 30–34 are used to code the following operations:

Category 30	Excision of Larynx
Category 31	Other Operations on the Larynx and Trachea
Category 32	Excision of Lung and Bronchus
Category 33	Other Operations on Lung and Bronchus
Category 34	Operations on Chest Wall, Pleura, Mediastinum, and Diaphragm

Excision of Larynx (Category Code 30)

Category 30 procedure codes deal with the larynx, or the voicebox. The larynx connects the pharynx and the trachea. It is made up of cartilage, which is attached by ligaments to the hyoid bone. There are actually two sets of vocal cords. The uppermost vocal cords, made of cartilage, are called the false vocal cords. Their function is to help keep food and liquid out of the lungs. The true vocal cords, or the lower pair, vibrate when air passes through them and produce sound. Figure 31-1 illustrates the larynx and vocal cords.

Procedure Codes	Description
30.0X	Excision or Destruction of Lesion or Tissue of Larynx—This subcategory is for excision or destruction of cysts or lesions of the larynx. Included in this subcategory is the marsupialization of a cyst. This procedure involves an incision of the cyst with the edges sutured to make a pouch.
30.1	Hemilaryngectomy—During this procedure only one half of the larynx is removed.
30.2X	Other Partial Laryngectomy—One of the cartilages that make up the larynx is called the epiglottis. The epiglottis is the structure at the base of the tongue, which keeps food from entering the larynx and the trachea. The epiglottis is assisted by the false vocal cords in this function. Removal of the epiglottis is called an epiglottidectomy and is coded to this subcategory. Removal of the vocal cords is also coded to this subcategory.
30.3	Complete Laryngectomy—This procedure may be done at the same time as a thyroidectomy or tracheostomy (defined later in this chapter).
30.4	Radical Laryngectomy—This code is used if the larynx is totally removed; incision is through the neck. The thyroid may be removed at the same time, and a tracheostomy may also be necessary during the same operative session.

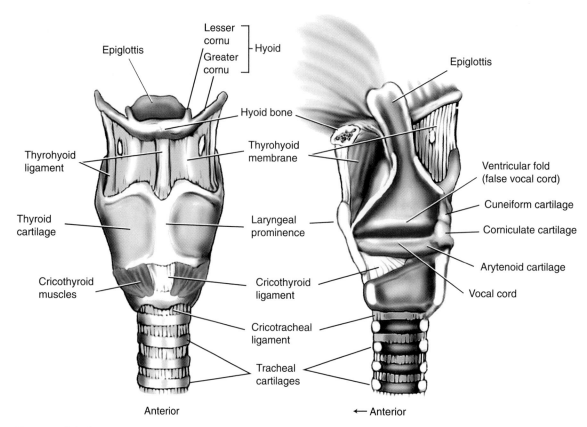

Figure 31-1 Larynx and related structures (From Price P, Frey KB, Junge TL. *Surgical Technology for the Surgical Technologist: A Positive Care Approach,* 2nd ed. Clifton Park, NY: Delmar, Cengage Learning, 2004, p. 620.)

Other Operations on Larynx and Trachea (Category Code 31)

Category 31, Other operations on larynx and trachea, classifies operations completed on the larynx and the trachea. The trachea is also known as the windpipe. It goes from the larynx to where it branches off to the bronchi. Figure 31-2 illustrates the location of the trachea in relation to the lungs.

Procedure Codes	Description
31.0	Injection of Larynx—Sometimes there is a need for an injection of inert material into the larynx or the vocal cords. This subcategory is the code for such an injection.
31.1	Temporary Tracheostomy—A tracheostomy is the surgical creation of a stoma in the trachea. A tracheotomy is the surgical opening made in the trachea for placement of a tube to assist in breathing, usually an emergency procedure. Because of the fine distinction between the two terms, they are sometimes used interchangeably. Tracheostomy and tracheotomy are procedures done to help with breathing or to gain access to an internal structure.
31.2X	Permanent Tracheostomy—The mediastinum is the space between the lungs in the thoracic cavity. This procedure involves placement of a breathing tube through the mediastinal area to the trachea for artificial breathing, usually for long-term use.
31.4X	Diagnostic Procedures on Larynx and Trachea—The procedures in this subcategory are usually done with a scope. The procedures are called endoscopic procedures and are performed by inserting a scope into the body or a structure for visual examination. There are different types of endoscopic procedures, and they are performed for various reasons, such as biopsies, the removal of foreign objects, repairs, or other surgical procedures. Open or closed biopsies are coded to this subcategory.
31.6X	Repair of Larynx—Repairs include suture and grafting. Revision of the larynx is also included in this subcategory. The revision procedure may be done if the larynx needs surgical correction. Arytenoidopexy is the surgical correction of cartilage of the larynx. If a surgical correction or repositioning of the vocal cords is needed, this subcategory is also used.

31.7X	Repair and Plastic Operations on Trachea—If a temporary tracheostomy has to be repaired or closed, codes from this subcategory are used. If there is a congenital anomoly in which there is an abnormal passage between the trachea and the esophagus, a procedure called a **tracheoesophageal fistulectomy** is needed. Should a tracheostomy function improperly, surgical revision might be necessary. This procedure is coded to this subcategory.
31.9X	Other Operations on Larynx and Trachea—Nerve division, lysis of adhesions, injection of therapeutic substance, dilation of larynx, and removal of a stent are all coded to this subcategory when the procedure is related to the larynx.

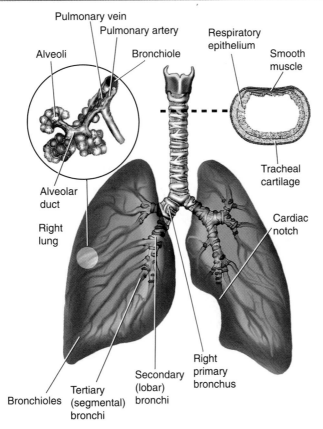

Figure 31-2 Trachea and lungs (From Price P, Frey KB, Junge TL. *Surgical Technology for the Surgical Technologist: A Positive Care Approach,* 2nd ed. Clifton Park, NY: Delmar, Cengage Learning, 2004, p. 621.)

Excision of Lung and Bronchus (Category Code 32)

The next category of this chapter classifies procedures completed on the lung and bronchi. Figure 31-3 illustrates the lungs and bronchus in relation to the trachea.

The trachea leads into the bronchi and branches off to form the **bronchial tree.** The bronchi continually divide to form smaller and smaller bronchi, which are called **bronchioles.** At the end of each bronchiole are clusters of grapelike structures called **alveoli.** Air exchange occurs through the walls of the alveoli. All these structures are encased in a sac or **lobe.** The lobe is covered by a thin serous membrane called the **pleura.** Figure 31-4 illustrates all the parts of the lung and their relationship to each other.

As illustrated in Figure 31-3, the lobes of the lung are further subdivided. The left lung has a superior and inferior lobe, which are separated by an oblique fissure. The right lung also has a superior and inferior part of the lobe, but it has a middle lobe as well due to the separations created by oblique and horizontal fissures.

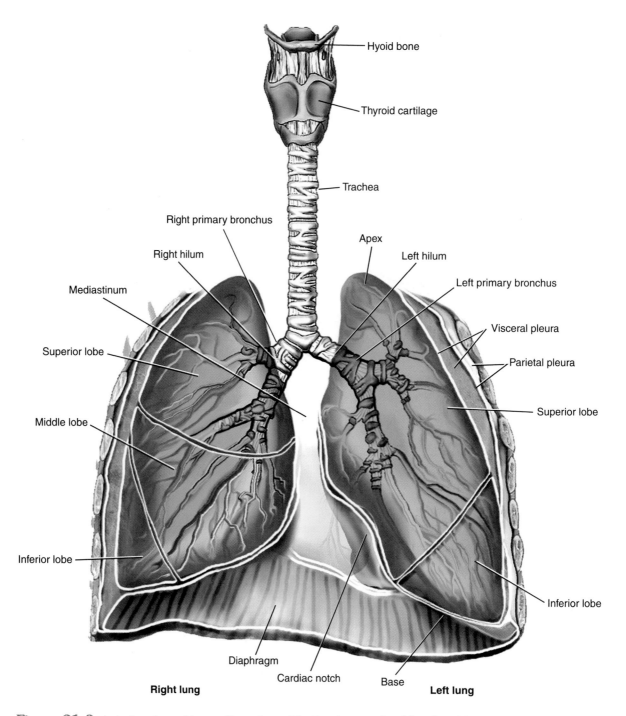

Figure 31-3 Anterior view of lungs (From Lazo DL. *Fundamentals of Sectional Anatomy: An Imaging Approach.* Clifton Park, NY: Delmar, Cengage Learning, 2005, p. 125.)

The lungs sit in the thoracic cavity. The thoracic cavity contains bone structures that protect the heart and lungs. Anteriorly are the sternum and costal cartilages, laterally are the ribs with the diaphragm inferiorly, and the thoracic vertebrae are found posteriorly. Some procedures discussed in the remaining categories and subcategories of this chapter contain descriptions to include these structures. Coders should review all medical documentation to ensure that the exact procedure performed is actually what is coded. Figure 31-5 illustrates the bone structures of the thoracic cavity.

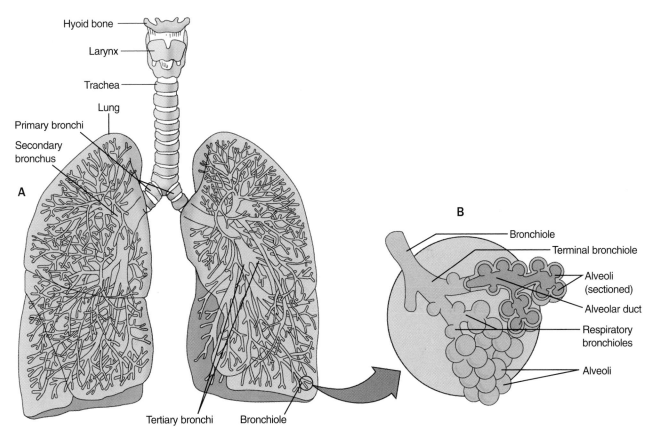

Figure 31-4 Bronchial tree: (**A**) Bronchial divisions, (**B**) bronchiole (From Price P, Frey KB, Junge TL. *Surgical Technology for the Surgical Technologist: A Positive Care Approach,* 2nd ed. Clifton Park, NY: Delmar, Cengage Learning, 2004, p. 867.)

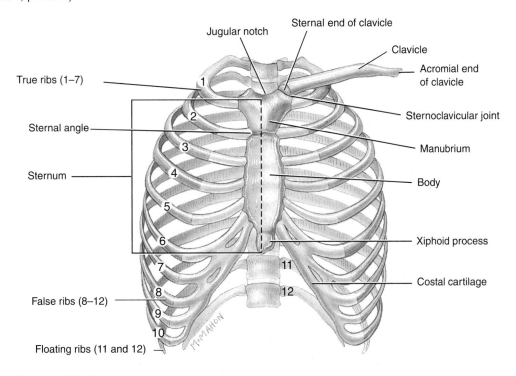

Figure 31-5 Anterior view of thoracic skeletal structures (From Lazo DL. *Fundamentals of Sectional Anatomy: An Imaging Approach.* Clifton Park, NY: Delmar, Cengage Learning, 2005, p. 124.)

Category 32, Excision of lung and bronchus, begins the section of procedure codes involving the lungs and bronchus. This category includes certain operative approaches such as rib resection, which means that the removal of a rib may be necessary for the surgeon to access organs of the thoracic cavity. Sternotomy, or the splitting of the sternum, is done by cutting into the sternum. Also, thoracotomy is an operative approach in which the incision is made through the chest wall. These are all considered part of the surgical procedure and are not coded separately but included in the codes in this section.

Procedure Codes	Description
32.0X	Local Excision or Destruction of Lesion or Tissue of Bronchus—Endoscopic excision or destruction of tissue or lesions of the bronchus is coded to this subcategory.
32.2X	Local Excision or Destruction of Lesion or Tissue of Lung—This subcategory contains a procedure called plication. Plication is the tucking or folding of a structure or tissue, in this case, emphysematous vesicles. Lung volume reduction is also coded to this subcategory and is the procedure in which there is partial excision of multiple lobes in one or both of the lobes to help the lung form a renewed expansion. Endoscopic procedures of the lung tissue are also coded here.
32.3X	Segmental Resection of Lung—This subcategory includes procedures in which the bronchovascular segments are excised or partial excision of the lobe is done.
32.4X	Lobectomy of Lung—A lobectomy is a procedure in which the whole lobe of the lung needs to be removed.
32.5X	Complete Pneumonectomy—Pneumonectomy is the complete removal of a lung and lung tissue.
32.6X	Radical Dissection of Thoracic Structures—Be sure to read the Include: notes with regard to this subcategory. Included in this procedure is the removal of any structures of the thoracic cavity that are associated with the lung. The coder may see the term *en bloc*, which means "to remove as a whole."

Other Operations of Lung and Bronchus (Category Code 33)

Category 33, Other operations of lung and bronchus, has the same Include: notes as does category 32. The operative approach is included in the procedure. Category 33 begins with procedure codes for incision of the bronchus and incision of the lung and then moves into diagnostic procedures.

Procedure Codes	Description
33.2X	Diagnostic Procedures on Lung and Bronchus—Bronchoscopies are coded to this subcategory. A bronchoscopy is a type of endoscopic procedure in which a rigid or flexible scope is inserted through a natural opening (the mouth) or an artificial one (a stoma) to view from the trachea into the bronchi. Figure 31-6 illustrates the rigid bronchoscopy. Figure 31-7 illustrates a flexible bronchoscopy. The coder may encounter the term *fiber-optic bronchoscopy*, which refers to a type of flexible bronchoscope. Open and closed biopsies of the lung and bronchus are coded to this section.
33.3X	Surgical Collapse of the Lung—Some patients require surgical collapse of the lung. This is an intentional procedure done to deflate or cave in the lung. Some of the codes listed in this subcategory are assigned by how the lung is collapsed. Artificial pneumothorax is a procedure in which gas or air is forced into the pleural space. Pneumoperitoneum is a procedure in which the gas or air is forced into the peritoneum. Thoracoplasty involves the collapse of a lung by removing ribs.
33.4X	Repair and Plastic Operation on Lung and Bronchus—The repair is usually accomplished by some type of suturing. Closure of a surgical wound created by a bronchostomy is coded to this subcategory. Repair of a fistula—whether it is between the bronchus and the skin, bronchocutaneous, or the bronchus and the esophagus, a bronchoesophageal—is coded to this subcategory. In some congenital situations, a bronchovisceral fistulectomy is necessary. This procedure is indicated when there is a fistula between the bronchus and a large internal organ.
33.5X	Lung Transplant—A lung transplant is a procedure in which a donor lung is transferred and implanted into the recipient.
	A Code also: note is associated with this subcategory of codes. The note tells the coder to code 39.61, Extracorporeal circulation auxiliary to open heart surgery. This code is used when the patient is placed on a machine that pumps blood throughout the body until surgery is completed. This subcategory breaks down the procedure codes to indicate whether one lung or both lungs were transplanted.

| 33.6 | Combined Heart-Lung Transplantation—This code is used when the patient receives both a heart and lung in the same operative session. |
| 33.9X | Other Operations on Lung and Bronchus—**Bronchial dilation** is where the bronchus is enlarged by stretching. Ligation of the bronchus and puncture of the lung are both coded to this subcategory. |

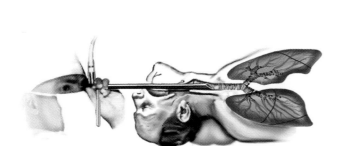

Figure 31-6 Rigid bronchoscopy (From Price P, Frey KB, Junge TL. *Surgical Technology for the Surgical Technologist: A Positive Care Approach,* 2nd ed. Clifton Park, NY: Delmar, Cengage Learning, 2004, p. 887.)

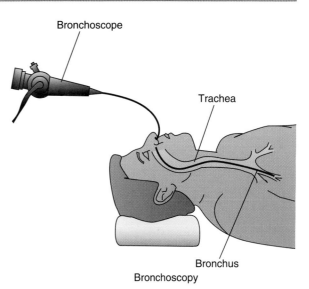

Figure 31-7 Bronchoscopy (From Ehrlich A, Schroeder CL. *Medical Terminology for Health Professions,* 4th ed. Clifton Park, NY: Delmar, Cengage Learning, 2001, p. 155.)

Operations on Chest Wall, Pleura, Mediastinum, and Diaphragm (Category Code 34)

Category 34, Operations on chest wall, pleura, mediastinum, and diaphragm, is the last set of procedure codes in this chapter. The **diaphragm** is the structure that separates the thoracic cavity from the abdominal cavity. This structure is essential in forcing air into and out of the lungs during respiration. Figure 31-8 illustrates the location and relationship of the diaphragm with other structures within the thoracic cavity.

Procedure Codes	Description
34.0X	Incision of Chest Wall and Pleura—The codes in this subcategory begin with the code for incision into the chest wall and pleura, but then the codes move into procedures for direct examination of the thoracic cavity, known as a **thoracotomy.** If the thoracotomy site needs to be reopened, this is coded to this subcategory. Should the chest cavity start to hold fluid, a tube may need to be inserted for drainage purposes. This is coded to this subcategory.
34.2X	Diagnostic Procedures on Chest Wall, Pleura, Mediastinum, and Diaphragm—This subcategory contains codes for biopsies of the chest wall, the pleura, the mediastinum, and the diaphragm. The procedures can be open or done with a scope as a closed procedure.
34.3	Excision or Destruction of Lesion or Tissue of Mediastinum—The excision of damaged tissue of the mediastinum is coded from this subcategory.
34.4	Excision or Destruction of Lesion of Chest Wall—If excision of the ribs is necessary to get to the site of the lesion, it is not coded separately.
34.5X	**Pleurectomy**—This is a procedure in which the pleura is removed. The pleura is a thin serous membrane, but if it thickens and needs to be thinned, **decortication of the lung** may be necessary. This procedure is coded to this subcategory.
34.6	Scarification of Pleura—**Scarification** does not relate to scarring. Scarification is the production of many tiny scratches or superficial punctures. In the pleura, this relates to the cells of the pleura that secrete fluid and need to be destroyed.

Procedure Codes	Description
34.7X	Repair of Chest Wall—This subcategory refers to repair procedures such as suturing of a laceration, the closure of a fistula, or the closure of a thoracostomy. Sternum repair is also coded to this subcategory.
34.8X	Operations on Diaphragm—This subcategory includes excisions, suture of lacerations, and repairs of the diaphragm.
34.9X	Other Operations on Thorax—Thoracentesis is a procedure coded to this subcategory in which a needle is inserted into the pleural cavity to draw fluid for diagnostic purposes, to drain fluid, or to re-expand a collapsed lung. The coder may also see the term *pleurocentesis,* which is the same as thoracentesis.

As noted in other chapters, coders must read the operative or procedural note carefully to determine whether the respiratory procedure was performed as an open or closed procedure, because this has an impact on code assignment.

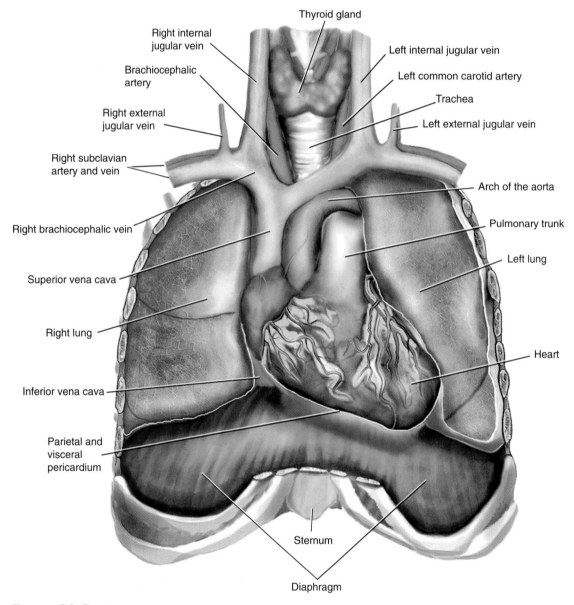

Figure 31-8 Structures with the thorax (From Price P, Frey KB, Junge TL. *Surgical Technology for the Surgical Technologist: A Positive Care Approach,* 2nd ed. Clifton Park, NY: Delmar, Cengage Learning, 2004, p. 870.)

Internet Links

To learn more about lung transplants, visit *www.lung-transplant.com*.

Comprehensive information about pulmonary procedures can be found at *www.medscape.com*.

Summary

- Chapter 6 of volume 3 of ICD-9-CM classifies procedures that correct problems of the respiratory system.
- The respiratory system brings air into the lungs and expels carbon dioxide and water.
- Procedures in this chapter begin at the larynx and move through the trachea, bronchi, lungs, and the thoracic cavity.
- A tracheotomy is a surgical opening made in the trachea.
- A thoracotomy is an incision made into the chest wall and is not coded if it is an operative approach.
- A lobectomy is the complete removal of a lung.
- A surgical collapse of the lung is performed to deflate the lung.
- Biopsies of respiratory sites are completed by both open and closed procedures.
- The terms *pleurocentesis* and *thoracentesis* are used interchangeably.

Chapter Review

True/False: Indicate whether the statement is true (T) or false (F).

1. _____ The trachea branches off to form the bronchi of the lungs.

2. _____ The true vocal cords assist the epiglottis in keeping food out of the lungs.

3. _____ All the structures of the lung are enclosed in a sac called the lobe.

4. _____ Biopsy of the trachea is coded to subcategory 31.6X.

5. _____ The 33.3X subcategory of codes is where you find the bronchoscopies.

Fill-in-the-Blank: Enter the appropriate term(s) to complete each statement.

6. The procedure in which half the larynx is removed is called _____.

7. The trachea is also known as the _____.

8. Biopsy of the larynx performed by inserting a scope into the larynx is called an _____ procedure.

9. The _____ contains bone structures that protect the heart and lungs.

10. The term _____ means to remove as whole.

Coding Assignments

Instructions: Using an ICD-9-CM coding book, select the code for each procedural statement.

Procedure	Code
1. Endoscopic biopsy of trachea	
2. Pneumoperitoneum for collapse of lung	
3. Closure of fistula of the thorax	
4. Laryngotracheal fistulectomy	
5. Transbronchial lung biopsy	
6. Puncture of lung	
7. Transposition of vocal cords	
8. Open biopsy of larynx	
9. Needle biopsy of lung	
10. Excision of laryngeal cartilage	
11. Closure of tracheotomy	
12. Revision of laryngostomy	
13. Lung transplant, right lobe only	
14. Stripping of vocal cords	
15. Thoracicoabdominal fistulectomy	
16. Epiglottidectomy	
17. Thoracoplasty	
18. Decortication of lung	
19. Open chest drainage	
20. Bronchial dilation	
21. Radical laryngectomy	
22. Suture of laceration of trachea	
23. Excision of lesion of mediastinum	
24. Repair of the pleura	
25. Radical dissection of thoracic structure	

Case Studies

Instructions: Review each case study, and select the correct ICD-9-CM diagnostic and procedural codes.

CASE 1

Operative Note

DIAGNOSIS: Airway obstruction at the level of the larynx due to disease process

PROCEDURE: Tracheotomy

This 86-year-old patient was brought to the OR for placement of a temporary tracheal tube because of airway obstruction that is causing difficult breathing. The patient was placed in the supine position with his neck extended under general anesthesia. A transverse symmetrical incision was made two fingerbreadths above the clavicular head and extended through the subcutaneous tissue and the platysma muscle. The platysma and strap muscles were separated, and the trachea and thyroid isthmus were visualized. A tracheal hook was placed on the tracheal ring, and an incision was made into the second tracheal ring using a #15 blade.

A tracheal spreader was placed with the obturator in place, and then the tracheotomy tube was placed in the incision. The obturator was withdrawn, and the inner cannula was placed and secretions were suctioned. The endotracheal balloon was inflated, and the tracheotomy tube was secured. The wound was closed with 4-0 Dexon. The patient tolerated the procedure well and was transported to PACU. Will review the need to remove tube in 5 to 6 days to evaluate whether it needs to be permanently placed.

ICD-9-CM Code Assignment: _____

CASE 2

PREOPERATIVE DIAGNOSIS: Laryngeal lesion

POSTOPERATIVE DIAGNOSIS: Deferred until pathology returns

PROCEDURE: Excision of lesion via bronchoscope

This 69-year-old patient was placed in the supine position. After induction of general anesthesia, she was intubated with a #6 endotracheal tube, and a flexible bronchoscopy was performed. A 1.4-cm lesion was visualized on the left side of the larynx, and this was removed via the scope. The lesion was sent to pathology. Hemostasis was noted, and blood loss was minimal. The scope was removed. The patient was awakened and sent to the recovery room in stable condition.

ICD-9-CM Code Assignment: _____

CASE 3

PREOPERATIVE DIAGNOSIS: Lung tissue damage due to cystic fibrosis with bronchiectasis

POSTOPERATIVE DIAGNOSIS: Same

OPERATIVE PROCEDURE: Lobectomy

This 24-year-old patient was prepped and draped in the usual fashion. A bronchoscopy was performed to view the right lung. A incision was made over the tip of the scapula and was carried through the chest wall muscles. Over the sixth rib, an incision was made and a rib spreader was placed. The right upper lobe of the right lung showed damage. Dissection of the right upper lobe of the right lung was completed. The bronchus was stapled and divided, and hemostasis was secured. A chest tube was placed, and the pleura was closed via suturing. The muscles of the chest wall were closed, and the subcutaneous tissue was closed. The skin was closed with 3-0 Dexon. The patient tolerated the procedure and was sent to the recovery room with insignificant blood loss.

ICD-9-CM Code Assignment: _____

CASE 4

This is a 30-year-old male who has a history of cocaine abuse. Recently he developed a paroxysmal, nonproductive cough. He smokes 1 pack of cigarettes per day. Two weeks ago he was given a prescription for an antibiotic, but he is unsure of the name of this medication. He said it hasn't helped.

Examination reveals a thin, ill-appearing male. Vital signs: BP: 112/80; T: 98.7; R: 24; P: 96. Neck: no lymphadenopathy. Lung: positive for bibasilar rales. Heart: RRR. Musculoskeletal and neurologic exam were within normal limits.

Lab tests were run, as were a liver function test and urinalysis. Results are in the medical record. Based on the test results and chest X-rays, it was determined that a fiber optic bronchoscopy be performed, for which the patient is here today. With the patient in the appropriate position, the bronchoscope was placed. The images were sent to radiology. Once we receive the results of this bronchoscopy, we will develop a plan of care.

Dx: Bibasilar pneumonia

ICD-9-CM Code Assignment: _____

CASE 5

Patient presents today for a mediastinoscopy. Patient has been having pain in this area and some coughing spells, but nothing is showing up on CT scans or X-rays. After risks and benefits were explained, the patient opted for this procedure in the hopes of getting a final diagnosis.

PREOPERATIVE DIAGNOSIS: Chest pain, cough

POSTOPERATIVE DIAGNOSIS: Enlarged lymph nodes, pathology pending

PROCEDURE: The patient was placed in the lateral position with right side exposed. The area was prepped and draped in the usual sterile fashion. A 1.5-cm incision was made and carried down through between the fifth and sixth intercostal space. A 10-mm trocar was positioned in the pleural space after the lung was deflated. The scope was moved through the trocar into the pleural cavity for examination of the mediastinum. The thoracic cavity was visualized for lesions or other abnormalities. At the area of the mediastinal lymph nodes, it was noted that several lymph nodes were enlarged; so a biopsy of the lymph nodes was taken. After all areas were visualized, the instruments were removed and a drainage tube was inserted. Incisions were sutured with 4-0 Vicryl. Patient tolerated the procedure well and was returned to the recovery room in good condition.

ICD-9-CM Code Assignment: _____

Operations on the Cardiovascular System

Chapter Outline

Objectives

At the conclusion of this chapter, the student will be able to:

1. Understand the pathologies associated with the organs and associated structures of the cardiovascular system.
2. Describe the procedures used to correct the pathologies.
3. Accurately code cardiovascular procedures.
4. Select and code diagnoses and procedures from case studies.

Key Terms

Aneurysm	Autograft	Clipping	Extracorporeal Circulation
Angioplasty	Bicuspid Valve	Congenital Anomaly	Heart
Angioscopy	Bypass	Drug-Eluting Stents	Hemodialysis
Annuloplasty	Cardiac Catheter	Electrode Catheter	Heterograft
Aorta	Cardiac Pacemaker	Electrodes	Homograft
Aortic Valve	Cardiovascular System	Embolus	Inferior Vena Cava
Arteries	Catheter	Endocardium	Infundibulectomy
Atria	Chordae Tendineae	Epicardium	

Reminder

As you work through this chapter, you will need to reference an ICD-9-CM coding book.

Mitral Valve

Myocardium

Open Heart Massage

Papillary Muscle

Percutaneous Transluminal Coronary Angioplasty (PTCA)

Pericardiocentesis

Pericardium

Pulmonary Valve

Pulse Generator

Revascularization

Septum

Shunt

Stent

Superior Vena Cava

Thrombus

Trabeculae Carneae Cordis

Transmyocardial Revascularization (TMR)

Tricuspid Valve

Valves

Varicose Veins

Veins

Ventricles

Introduction

Chapter 7 of volume 3 of ICD-9-CM classifies procedures completed on the cardiovascular system. The cardiovascular system encompasses the heart, arteries, veins, and blood. The category code range utilized is 35–39.

Introduction to the Cardiovascular System

The cardiovascular system is the system that pumps blood through the body, carrying oxygen and nutrients. Waste products are picked up by this system for disposal from the body.

The major organ of the cardiovascular system is the heart. The heart is a large muscle that acts like a pump and is located between the lungs in the thoracic cavity. The sac that encloses the heart is double-walled and called the pericardium. Figure 32-1 is an external view of the heart.

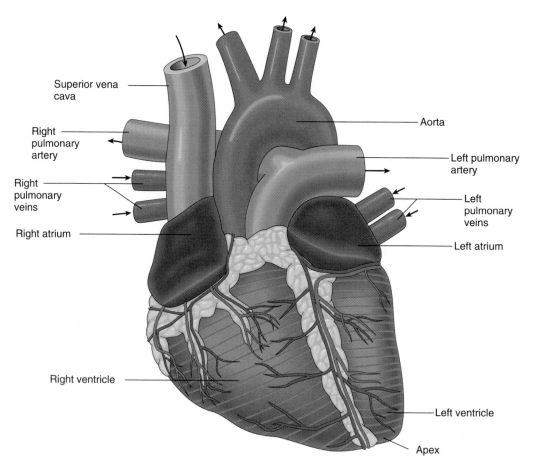

Figure 32-1 External view of the heart (From Ehrlich A, Schroeder CL. *Medical Terminology for Health Professions,* 4th ed. Clifton Park, NY: Delmar, Cengage Learning, 2001, p. 96.)

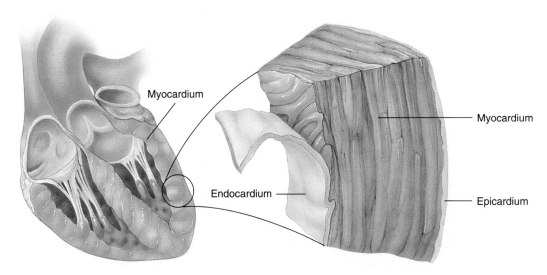

Figure 32-2 Layers of the heart's walls (From Ehrlich A, Schroeder CL. *Medical Terminology for Health Professions,* 4th ed. Clifton Park, NY: Delmar, Cengage Learning, 2001, p. 97.)

The walls of the heart are comprised of layers. The epicardium is the outermost layer. The middle layer is called the myocardium and is the thickest layer. The endocardium is the innermost layer and is sometimes referred to as the lining of the heart. Figure 32-2 illustrates the three layers of the heart.

The heart is divided into four chambers. The upper chambers receive blood from the veins and are called the atria. The lower chambers are called ventricles and send blood to the arteries. Blood enters the right atrium through the superior vena cava from the upper part of the body and through the inferior vena cava from the lower part of the body. Blood leaves the heart through the aorta and the pulmonary artery.

Coding Operations on the Cardiovascular System

Coding for the cardiovascular system begins with operations on the valves and septa of the heart, category code 35. The valves of the heart work like any other valves. They open and close, usually in one direction, to regulate the blood flow through the heart. The main valves of the heart are the aortic valve, the mitral valve, the pulmonary valve, and the tricuspid valve. The aortic valve sits between the aorta and the left ventricle. Blood pushes against the valve, which opens it, allowing flow from the ventricle, but closes before the blood pushes back up into the ventricle. The pulmonary valve sits between the pulmonary artery and the right ventricle and performs the same function as does the aortic valve in allowing blood to flow to through the ventricle. The tricuspid valve is the valve between the right atrium and right ventricle. The mitral valve, also called the bicuspid valve, is the valve between the left atrium and left ventricle.

The septa of the heart relate to the septum, or dividing wall. There are several septa in the heart, which divide the atria and the ventricles.

Procedure Codes	Description
35.0X	Closed Heart Valvotomy— A closed treatment, in this case, means treatment without an incision into the heart. The treatment of the valve is done with manipulation or with an incision into the valve itself, not the heart.
35.1X	Open Heart Valvuloplasty Without Replacement—Open repair of the valve involves an incision into the heart to repair a valve. In this subcategory of codes, valve replacement is not a part of the procedure. Cardiopulmonary bypass is also coded in addition if it is performed at the same operative session. Bypass is a procedure in which a graft is done with a healthy vessel to go around a diseased vessel.

Procedure Codes	Description
35.2X	Replacement of Heart Valve—This subcategory of codes includes the removal and replacement of a defective heart valve. As in the preceding subcategory, if a bypass is performed, it is coded in addition to the procedure from this subcategory. The valve replacements in this subcategory may be tissue grafts from the patient's own body, an autograft. The graft tissue may be from an animal; this is called a heterograft. Or the tissue used may be from another human, a homograft. Prosthetic or artificial material is also used in valve replacement procedures. Figure 32-3 illustrates the aortic valve replacement. Figure 32-4 illustrates mitral valve replacement.
35.3X	Operations on Structures Adjacent to Heart Valves—This subcategory of codes includes the division, reattachment, and repair of the papillary muscle, chordae tendineae, and the trabeculae carneae cordis. Papillary muscles are the smaller endocardial muscles that open the heart valves. The papillary muscles are connected to the valves by cordlike tendons called chordae tendineae. The trabeculae carneae cordis are the endocardial muscular ridges. Also found in this subcategory is an annuloplasty and infundibulectomy. An annuloplasty is a surgical repair of one or more of the circular orifices in the heart. These are the rings around the major heart valves. An infundibulectomy is the excision of the funnel-shaped structure around the outflow tract of the valves.
35.4X	Production of Septal Defect in Heart—The codes in this subcategory are referenced when there is a need to improve the function by enlarging or creating a septal defect between the atria.
35.5X	Repair of Atrial and Ventricular Septa with Prosthesis—This subcategory of codes includes repairs performed with a patch or synthetic implant. The repairs may be done as either open or closed procedures. If a bypass procedure is performed, it should be coded separately.
35.6X	Repair of Atrial and Ventricular Septa with Tissue Graft—This subcateory of codes is used when the repair of the atrial or ventricular septal defect is corrected by using tissue implants. If a bypass procedure is performed, it should be coded separately. Any repairs of the atrial or ventricular septal defects not found in these subcategories code to the 35.7X subcategory.
35.8X	Total Repair of Certain Congenital Cardiac Anomalies—A congenital anomaly is an abnormality that is present at birth. Some of these anomalies may not appear right away but may be discovered later in life. The codes in this subcategory are used if the repair done at one operative session totally corrected the anomaly. If the procedure had to be done in stages, this subcategory is not coded. If there was a partial repair or a staged repair, code the specific procedure.
35.9X	Other Operations on Valves and Septa of Heart—The codes in this subcategory should be researched well before assignment. Procedure notes should clearly state what was done, and then the coder should read the codes carefully. This subcategory of codes contains procedures that include shunt placement between different parts of the heart, such as between the right ventricle and pulmonary artery or between the left ventricle and the aorta. A shunt can be used to connect two structures, or it can be used to divert or bypass an area. Should a valve or the septum need revision of a correction that has already been done, code 35.95 is referenced for consideration.

Operations on Vessels of Heart (Category Code 36)

Category 36, Operations on vessels of heart, classifies procedures completed on the arteries and veins. Arteries are vessels that carry blood away from the heart to other parts of the body. Veins are vessels that carry blood back to the heart from other parts of the body. Even though many arteries and veins enter and leave the heart, several significant vessels act as the main tributaries for the other arteries and veins. The superior vena cava is the main vein through which blood flows from the upper portion of the body above the heart back to the heart. Blood flow from the lower portion of the body to the heart goes through the inferior vena cava. The pulmunary arteries carry blood from the heart to the lungs, where oxygen and carbon dioxide are exchanged. The aorta is the largest vessel in the body. This artery is where the oxygenated blood is sent out to the entire body. Figure 32-5 illustrates the blood flow to and from the heart and identifies the vessels in relation to the heart.

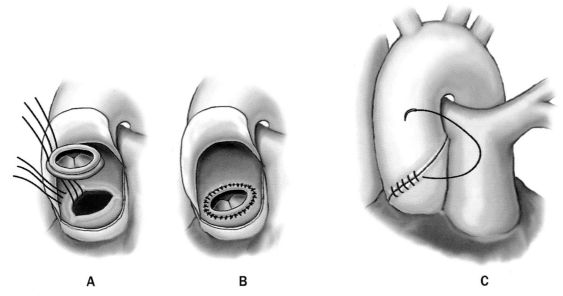

A   B   C

Figure 32-3 Prosthetic valve placement: (A) Sutures are placed through the annulus and the skirt of the valve prosthesis. (B) The valve is positioned and the sutures are tied. (C) The aortic incision is closed. (From Price P, Frey KB, Junge TL. *Surgical Technology for the Surgical Technologist: A Positive Care Approach,* 2nd ed. Clifton Park, NY: Delmar, Cengage Learning, 2004, p. 915.)

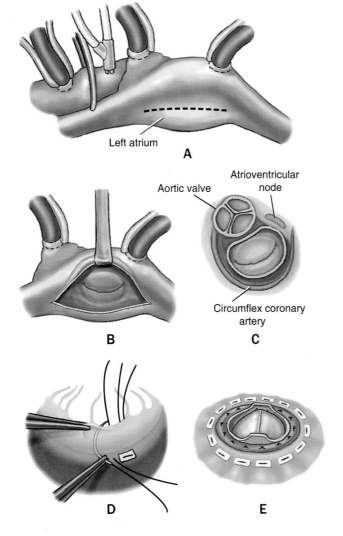

Left atrium

A

Aortic valve

Atrioventricular node

Circumflex coronary artery

B   C

D   E

Figure 32-4 Mitral valve replacement: (A) Atrial incision site, (B) mitral valve exposed, (C) cross-section showing related anatomical structures, (D) sutures placed in the annulus, (E) prosthesis in place (From Price P, Frey KB, Junge TL. *Surgical Technology for the Surgical Technologist: A Positive Care Approach,* 2nd ed. Clifton Park, NY: Delmar, Cengage Learning, 2004, p. 917.)

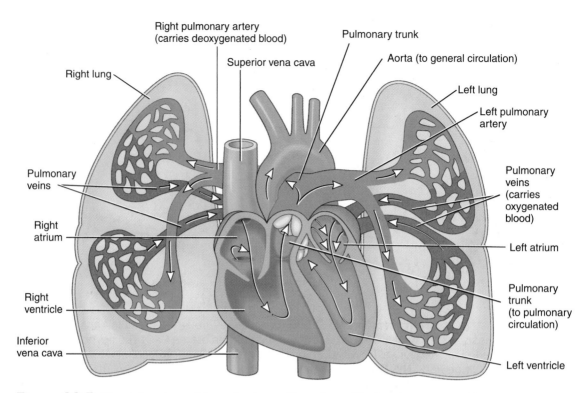

Figure 32-5 Blood flow to and from the heart (From Lazo DL. *Fundamentals of Sectional Anatomy: An Imaging Approach.* Clifton Park, NY: Delmar, Cengage Learning, 2005, p. 48.)

Procedure Codes	Description
36.0X	Removal of Coronary Artery Obstruction and Insertion of Stent(s)—A **stent** in relation to coronary procedures refers to a small device used to support a vessel but still allow the fluid, or blood, to pass through. Some stents are coated with a time-released drug that assists in restoring blood flow. These are called **drug-eluting stents. Angioplasty** is a procedure in which the vessel that is narrowed or occluded is opened up or dilated. **Percutaneous transluminal coronary angioplasty (PTCA)** is a procedure in which the obstructed artery is opened up by inserting a balloon-tipped catheter to the affected part of the artery through the skin, maneuvering it into position, and inflating it, allowing the blood flow to increase. The codes in this subcategory are for procedures done on a single vessel or multiple vessels, with or without thrombolytic agent. If there is any stent placement, this procedure is coded separately.
36.1X	Bypass Anastomosis for Heart Revascularization—**Revascularization** procedure codes are used when the blood flow to the heart can be restored by doing a bypass procedure around the defective area. The revascularization can be accomplished by using a catheter stent, prosthesis, or vein graft. The complexity of these types of procedures requires care in reading operation notes in order to assign the proper code.
36.2	Heart Revascularization by Arterial Implant—This code is used when the artery itself is connected to the heart directly.
36.3X	Other Heart Revascularization—Included in this subcategory is the **transmyocardial revascularization (TMR)**, which is a laser procedure that creates channels through the myocardium and allows for more blood flow to the myocardial tissue.
36.9X	Other Operations on Vessels of Heart—When a coronary vessel develops an aneurysm, the repair is coded to this subcategory. An **aneurysm** forms when the wall of an artery or vein weakens. When the wall weakens, it dilates, forming a sac. This sac is the aneurysm.

Other Operations on Heart and Pericardium (Category Code 37)

Category 37, Other operations on heart and pericardium, contains codes for procedures completed on the heart as well as on the thin lining surrounding the heart, known as the pericardium.

Procedure Codes	Description
37.0	Pericardiocentesis—**Pericardiocentesis** is a procedure in which a needle is surgically inserted into the pericardium and fluid is removed.
37.1X	Cardiotomy and Pericardiotomy—These series of codes are used for incision into the pericardium and heart.
37.2X	Diagnostic Procedures on Heart and Pericardium—The diagnostic procedures in this subcategory include cardiac catheterizations along with biopsies. A **catheter** is a fine tube that is inserted into the body to allow injections, fluid or air removal, obstruction removal, or monitoring. In this series of codes, the **cardiac catheter** is used to determine whether any cardiac abnormalities exist. An **electrode catheter** is sometimes used on patients to induce or stop cardiac arrhythmias.
37.3X	Pericardiectomy and Excision of Lesion of Heart—This subcategory includes codes for excisions of lesions located on any part of the heart. It also includes repair by excision of any aneurysms of the heart.
37.4	Repair of Heart and Pericardium—This code is used for the repair or restoration of the pericardium and heart if a more specific procedure was not completed.
37.5X	Heart Replacement Procedures—These codes are used for heart transplant procedures. These codes include donor and nondonor hearts and mechanisms.
37.6X	Implantation of Heart and Circulatory Assist System—This subcategory of codes contains codes for procedures that assist in the circulation of blood: heart pumps, balloon catheters that pump blood into the arteries of the heart, and other mechanical circulatory devices. If the assist device is no longer needed, the removal code is also found here.
37.7X	Insertion, Revision, Replacement, and Removal of Pacemaker Leads; Insertion of Temporary Pacemaker System; or Revison of Cardiac Device Pocket—A **cardiac pacemaker** is used to correct and manage heart dysrhythmias. The pacemaker is made up of a **pulse generator** that contains a lithium battery as its source of power. In most cases it lasts 6 to 10 years before it needs to be surgically replaced. The generator controls the heart rate, the energy output, and the pacing modes. The other part of the pacemaker consists of the **electrodes**. An electrode is inserted through the subclavian vein and advanced to the right ventricular apex. If a second lead, or electrode, is needed, it is fixed in the right atrial appendage. The electrodes are then attached to the pulse generator. The pulse generator is usually located in the upper right portion of the chest. This subcategory of codes includes the initial insertion, any revisions and replacement of leads.
37.8X	Insertion, Replacement, Removal, and Revision of Pacemaker Device—This subcategory of codes involves the actual pacemaker device itself. The insertion, replacement, or removal is all coded here. Insertion and maintenance on the leads are coded in addition to these codes.
37.9X	Other Operations on Heart and Pericardium—This subcategory of codes includes **open heart massage**, in which the thoracic cavity is opened and the surgeon actually massages the heart using rhythmic compressions.

Incision, Excision, and Occlusion of Vessels (Category Code 38)

Category 38, Incision, excision, and occlusion of vessels, contains a listing of fourth-digit subclassifications by vessel. It is important when coding to this category to pay attention to which vessel the procedure is being done on to properly assign this fourth digit.

Procedure Codes	Description
38.0X	Incision of Vessel—This subcategory includes the removal of a thrombus or an embolus. A **thrombus** is a blood clot. The blood clot adheres to the wall of the vessel, causing a problem. An **embolus** is an occlusion in the vessel, which can be a clot but could be a foreign object such as a piece of tissue or even air or gas, that obstructs the blood flow through the vessel.
38.2X	Diagnostic Procedures on Blood Vessels—This subcategory contains the codes for a biopsy of a vessel and angioscopy. **Angioscopy** is a procedure in which a puncture is made through a body wall and a scope is inserted to visualize blood vessels.

Procedure Codes	Description
38.3X	Resection of Vessel with Anastomosis—When part of a vessel needs to be removed and then is reconnected, the coder references this code.
38.4X	Resection of Vessel with Replacement—In this subcategory, part of the vessel is removed and then replaced. Fourth-digit assignment is needed to identify the exact site of the procedure.
38.5X	Ligation and Stripping of Varicose Veins—**Varicose veins** are veins that become out of shape. They become elongated, protrude when they become dilated, and can be extremely painful. Varicose veins are treated with a ligation and stripping procedure in which the saphenous vein and its tributaries are ligated and then removed using an intraluminal vein stripper. Another procedure used in the treatment of varicose veins involves injections into the varicosities that causes a fibrotic reaction, which destroys the lumen of the varicosity.
38.7	Interruption of Vena Cava—This surgical interruption of the blood flow to the vena cava may be necessary to stop an embolus from reaching the right ventricle.
38.8X	Other Surgical Occlusion of Vessels—Surgical occlusions that are coded to this subcategory are clamping, division, and ligation. These procedures are purposely done to interrupt blood flow.
38.9X	Puncture of Vessel—Puncture of a vessel is necessary to insert a catheter. The various vessel catherizations are coded to this subcategory, as are any other nonspecific punctures of arteries or veins.

Other Operations on Vessels (Category Code 39)

Because of the complexity of vascular coding, category 39, Other operations on vessels, should be reviewed by the coder. This category contains bypass surgeries along with shunt placement, endovascular repairs, stent placement, and repair codes.

Procedure Codes	Description
39.0	Systemic to Pulmonary Artery Shunt—This procedure includes anastomosis of the aorta, the subclavian artery, and arterial blood vessels to the pulmonary artery.
39.1	Intra-Abdominal Venous Shunt—In this subcategory, the anastomosis is between two veins in the abdomen, such as the superior mesenteric vein to the inferior vena cava. The key here is the vein-to-vein connection within the abdomen.
39.2X	Other Shunt or Vascular Bypass—The bypass in these code selections can include the aorta to subclavian and carotid arteries. Codes for bypass involving the aorta and renal arteries are included in this subcategory. This subcategory also contains a code for the creation of an arteriovenous fistula type return for renal dialysis access. Care in referencing the documentation is critical in proper code assignment.
39.3X	Suture of Vessel—This subcategory is referred to if a suture repair of a vessel is needed.
39.4X	Revision of Vascular Procedure—This subcategory of codes is referenced when a previous vascular surgery is completed but a revision or correction is necessary.
39.5X	Other Repair of Vessels—Angioplasty of noncoronary vessels is coded from this subcategory. **Clipping** of the aneurysm is a procedure in which the aneurysm is not allowed to move due to surgical placement of a device, which prevents the movement.
39.6X	Extracorporeal Circulation and Procedures Auxiliary to Heart Surgery—**Extracorporeal circulation** is a procedure that pumps the heart and oxygenates blood throughout the body while heart surgery is being performed.
39.7X	Endovascular Repair of Vessel—These procedures are performed within the vessel. The endovascular repair includes grafting and liquid tissue adhesive.
39.8	Operations on Carotid Body and Other Vascular Bodies—The body of a structure is the largest part of the structure.
39.9X	Other Operations on Vessels—This subcategory contains codes for nondrug-eluting stent placement for noncoronary arteries. Injections of agents to harden the walls of veins are found here, as are cannula replacements. **Hemodialysis,** a procedure that filters waste from the blood, is also coded from this subcategory.

Patients who have undergone procedures completed on the cardiovascular system continue to have a better survival rate as surgical techniques have improved over the past two decades.

Internet Links

To learn more about procedures completed on the cardiovascular system, visit *http://heartdisease.miningco.com* and *http://www.americanheart.org*.

Summary

- The procedures in chapter 7 of volume 3 of ICD-9-CM classify operations completed on the valves of the heart, pericardium, heart, veins, and arteries.
- Closed and open procedures of the heart are coded from this chapter.
- Operations on structures that are adjacent to the heart are also coded to this chapter.
- An autograft is from the patient's own body.
- A heterograft uses tissue from an animal.
- A homograft uses tissue from another human.
- A shunt is used to connect two structures, or it can be used to divert or bypass an area.
- Angioplasty is a procedure in which the vessel is opened up or dilated.
- Transmyocardial revascularization is a laser procedure that allows more blood flow to the myocardial tissue.
- Pericardiocentesis is the insertion of a needle into the pericardium to allow for fluid removal.
- A cardiac pacemaker is used to correct and manage heart dysrhythmias.

Chapter Review

True/False: Indicate whether the statement is true (T) or false (F).

1. _____ There are three layers in the wall of the heart.

2. _____ Prosthetic replacement of a heart valve is coded to the 35.2X subcategory.

3. _____ Coding for the insertion of a pacemaker includes the insertion of electrodes.

4. _____ Congenital repairs coded to the 35.8X subcategory are total repairs done in one operative session, not a staged procedure.

5. _____ The largest vessel in the body is the pulmonary artery.

Fill-in-the-Blank: Enter the appropriate term(s) to complete the statement.

6. The thickest layer of the heart is called the _____.

7. The small endocardial muscles that open the heart valves are called _____.

8. The main vein through which blood flows from the upper portion of the body back to the heart is called the _____.

9. The sac that forms when the wall of an artery or vein weakens and dialates is called an

   _____.

10. A _____ is used to correct and manage heart dysthythimias.

Coding Assignments

Instructions: Using an ICD-9-CM coding book, select the correct procedure code.

Procedure	**Code**
1. Open heart valvuloplasty of tricuspid valve without replacement	_____
2. Closed heart valvotomy, aortic valve	_____
3. Correction of arterial septal defect with tissue graft	_____
4. Infundibulectomy	_____
5. Autograft repair of pulmonary valve	_____
6. Thromboendarterectomy with patch graft	_____
7. Prosthetic mitral valve needs to be resutured	_____
8. Cardio-omentopexy	_____
9. Annuloplasty	_____
10. Ostiumprimum defect with prosthesis	_____
11. Percutaneous valvuloplasty	_____
12. Endovascular repair of carotid artery	_____
13. Insertion of drug-coated stent into the coronary artery	_____
14. Thrombectomy	_____
15. Blalock-Hanlon operation	_____
16. Anastomosis of thoracic artery to the coronary artery (single)	_____
17. Repositioning of electrode	_____
18. Denervation of aortic body	_____
19. Injection of therapeutic substance into pericardium	_____
20. Percutaneous cardiopulmonary bypass	_____
21. Endovascular grafts	_____
22. Pericardiectomy	_____
23. Double internal mammary-coronary artery bypass	_____
24. Insertion of heart assist system	_____
25. Insertion of left atrial filter	_____

Case Studies

Instructions: Review each case study, and select the appropriate ICD-9-CM diagnostic and procedure codes.

CASE 1

PREOPERATIVE DIAGNOSIS: Precordial chest pain

POSTOPERATIVE DIAGNOSIS: Coronary artery stenosis

INDICATIONS: This is a 62-year-old male who presented to the hospital with precordial chest pain. He has a history of chest pain, but previous stress tests have been negative. Today an EKG was done when the patient presented and showed T-wave inversion inferiorly and laterally. A new stress test was ordered, at which time the patient experienced more pain and slight abnormalities, which are included in this record. It was determined that a catherization was indicated. This was discussed with the patient, explanation of risks and benefits was given, and patient decided to proceed with catherization.

PROCEDURE: The patient was brought to the Cath Lab and was given 25 mg Benadryl, and 2 mg Valium through IV. The right groin area was prepped and draped in the usual sterile fashion. Using a thin-walled needle, the right femoral artery was punctured, and a #6 catheter introducer was placed using Selding technique. Catheter was moved into place, and angiography was performed. Left ventriculogram was performed in 30-degree ROA projection using 32 cc Optiray at 10 cc/sec. A 60% left main artery stenosis was found. On the right side, all coronary arteries appeared normal.

ICD-9-CM Code Assignment: _____

CASE 2

PREOPERATIVE/POSTOPERATIVE DIAGNOSIS: Heart block

INDICATIONS: This is a 77-year-old male who presented several days ago with chest pain. He has an extensive history of cardiac problems that are documented in this medical record. It was determined that he needs to have a pacemaker inserted. The risks as well as the benefits of the procedure were explained to the patient, and he agreed this was the correct course of action.

PROCEDURE: Patient was brought to the operating room and placed in supine position on the table. It was decided to go with a local anesthesia because he is at high risk for general anesthesia. After Xylocain was infiltrated and sensitivity had been checked, a small subfascial incision was made about 2 cm below the clavicle. The generator pocket was created. The subclavian vein was then cannulated, and the pacemaker atrial lead was threaded through to the left atrium and then through to the atrial septum. The second subclavian stick allowed the ventricular lead to be inserted in the right ventricular apex. Leads were connected to the pacemaker, tested, and then programmed. The wound was closed and dressed. The patient was taken to the recovery room in good condition.

ICD-9-CM Code Assignment: _____

CASE 3

This is a 58-year-old African American male with a long history of hypertension, COPD, and coronary artery disease. He presented today with complaints of chest pain. The patient's medical history revealed that he had a stress test done 1 month ago that was negative for ischemia. The lab tests did not support an MI. An arterial catheterization was scheduled.

PROCEDURE: Arterial catheterization

PROCEDURE: The patient was placed in supine position, and the brachial artery was accessed percutaneously. A dye solution was shot, no occlusions were noted. The catheter was removed, and pressure was applied until bleeding stopped. The patient tolerated the procedure well.

ICD-9-CM Code Assignment: _____

CASE 4

This is a 28-year-old Caucasian female who presents today for sclerotherapy injection treatment of her varicosities. There are two varicosities that are on the medial side of the left leg that measure 2 mm and 2.5 mm. Sodium chloride 23.4% and 3% sodium tetradecyl sulfate were injected. Patient tolerated the procedure well.

ICD-9-CM Code Assignment: _____

CASE 5

PREOPERATIVE DIAGNOSIS: Chronic pericarditis

POSTOPERATIVE DIAGNOSIS: Chronic pericarditis

PROCEDURE: Pericardiectomy

This is a 62-year-old female with a long-standing history of heart disease. Recent studies have now shown pericarditis. which is prompting this procedure. The diastolic filling of the ventricle is feared given her poor cardiac history.

The patient is supine on the operating table. Using median sternotomy as the approach, the phrenic nerves are identified and protected. Incision of the pericardium is then performed, and decortication begins at the left ventricle and proceeds until the ventricles, atria, and both the superior and inferior cavae are freed. Drainage tubes are placed, and the sternum is closed with stainless steel wire. The wound is then closed. The patient tolerated the procedure well and was returned to the recovery room in good condition.

ICD-9-CM Code Assignment: _____

Operations on the Hemic and Lymphatic System

Chapter Outline

Introduction
Introduction to the Hemic and
   Lymphatic System
Coding Operations on the Hemic and
   Lymphatic System

Internet Links
Summary
Chapter Review
Coding Assignments
Case Studies

Objectives

At the conclusion of this chapter, the student will be able to:

1. Understand the pathologies and traumas associated with the hemic and lymphatic system.
2. Describe procedures completed on the hemic and lymphatic system.
3. Accurately code procedures completed on the hemic and lymphatic system.
4. Select and code diagnoses and procedures from case studies.

Key Terms

Allogeneic Bone Marrow
   Transplant
Autologous Bone
   Marrow Transplant
Bone Marrow
Hematopoietic

Ligation of Peripheral
   Lymphatics
Lymphangiogram
Lymph Nodes
Marsupialization of
   Splenic Cyst

Obliteration of
   Peripheral Lymphatics
Partial Splenectomy
Purging
Radical Excision

Reconstruction of
   Peripheral Lymphatics
Regional Excision
Spleen
Transplantation of
   Peripheral Lymphatics

> **Reminder**
>
> *As you work through this chapter, you should have a copy of volume 3 of ICD-9-CM to reference.*

Introduction

The procedure codes for chapter 8 of volume 3 of ICD-9-CM, "Operations on the Hemic and Lymphatic System," include category codes 40–41 and are used to classify procedures that are completed on the lymph nodes, bone marrow, and spleen.

Introduction to the Hemic and Lymphatic System

To ensure proper coding, the coder must know the location of the various lymph nodes in the body. Lymph nodes are found in groups of two to more than 100 and are connected via lymph vessels. The primary purposes of **lymph nodes** is to provide a site for lymphocyte production, to produce antibodies, and to filter impurities, such as viruses and bacteria, from the body. Lymph nodes are named according to their anatomical location. Figure 33-1 illustrates lymph node sites and lymphatic circulation.

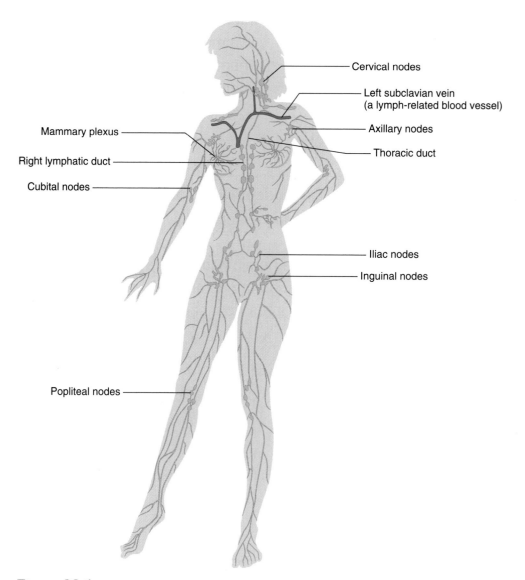

Figure 33-1 Lymph node locations and lymphatic circulation (From Ehrlich A, Schroeder CL. *Medical Terminology for Health Professions,* 4th ed. Clifton Park, NY: Delmar, Cengage Learning, 2001, p. 124.)

Procedures that involve bone marrow and hematopoietic cells are classified to chapter 8 of volume 3 of ICD-9-CM. Bone marrow is the site where blood cells are formed. The term hematopoietic, meaning pertaining to the formation of blood cells, is used to describe the function of bone marrow.

Diagnostic and therapeutic procedures that are completed on the spleen are also classified to this chapter of ICD-9-CM. The spleen is located in the left upper quadrant of the abdomen (Figure 33-2) and performs the following functions:

- Filters microorganisms and other material from the blood

- Forms lymphocytes and monocytes

- Removes and destroys worn-out red blood cells

- Stores erythrocytes

- Balances the amount of red blood cells and plasma in circulation

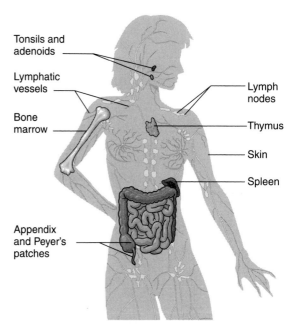

Figure 33-2 Anatomical site of the spleen (From Ehrlich A, Schroeder CL. *Medical Terminology for Health Professions,* 4th ed. Clifton Park, NY: Delmar, Cengage Learning, 2001, p. 126.)

Coding Operations on the Hemic and Lymphatic System

Only two category codes are found in this chapter of ICD-9-CM. Category code 40 classifies operations on the lymphatic system, and category code 41 classifies operations performed on bone marrow and the spleen.

Operations on the Lymphatic System (Category Code 40)

Category 40, Operations on the lymphatic system, classifies diagnostic and surgical procedures completed on lymphatic structures such as lymph nodes.

Procedure Codes	Description
40.0	Incision of Lymphatic Structures—This code is used for the cutting into lymphatic structures.
40.1X	Diagnostic Procedures on Lymphatic Structures—This subclassification is used to code biopsies of lymphatic structures and other diagnostic procedures. It is important for the coder to note the Exclude: notation that appears for code 40.19. A lymphangiogram, which is a radiographic study of the lymphatic vessels and nodes, is excluded from this code.
40.2X	Simple Excision of Lymphatic Structure—These excisions involve the removal of lymphatic structures that are limited to the lymph node. Fourth digits are used to identify the specific lymph node removed.
40.3	Regional Lymph Node Excision—Regional excisions classified to this code include the removal of groups of lymph nodes and other lymphatic structures that are grouped together in a region of the body. The Include: notation that appears for this code states that regional lymph node excisions with excisions of the lymphatic drainage area, including the skin, subcutaneous tissue, and fat, are classified to this code.
40.4X	Radical Excision of Cervical Lymph Nodes—A radical excision is the resection or removal of lymph nodes down to muscle and deep fascia. These codes classify the radical excision of the lymph nodes located in the neck. Fourth digits are used to identify the unilateral or bilateral removal of the nodes.
40.5X	Radical Excision of Other Lymph Nodes—These codes are used to code the radical excision of lymph nodes of the auxiliary, periaortic, iliac, groin, and other regions. Coders need to reference the procedural reports to identify the lymph nodes removed and to select proper fourth digits.

Procedure Codes	Description
40.6X	Operations on Thoracic Duct—These operations are completed on the thoracic duct, which is located in the thoracic cavity.
40.9	Other Operations on Lymphatic Structures—This code includes the following procedures: • Ligation of peripheral lymphatics—The tying off of a peripheral duct • Obliteration of peripheral lymphatics—The surgical elimination of the peripheral duct • Reconstruction of peripheral lymphatics—The surgical reforming of a peripheral duct • Transplantation of peripheral lymphatics—The grafting of a peripheral duct to reposition the duct Reference code 40.9 for additional procedures that are included.

Operations on Bone Marrow and Spleen (Category Code 41)

Category 41 classifies procedures completed on the bone marrow and the spleen.

Procedure Codes	Description
41.0X	Bone Marrow or Hematopoietic Stem Cell Transplant—These codes include the following types of transplants: • Autologous bone marrow transplant—The grafting of a patient's own bone marrow tissue • Allogeneic bone marrow transplant—The grafting of a human donor bone marrow tissue The coder must also identify whether the transplant was performed with or without purging. Purging is a process of isolating and purifying the transplanted bone marrow. Fourth digits are used to identify whether purging occurred.
41.1	Puncture of Spleen—This is the code for the surgical penetration of the spleen.
41.2	Splenotomy—This is the code for the incision of the spleen.
41.3X	Diagnostic Procedures on Bone Marrow and Spleen—These codes include biopsies of the spleen and bone marrow. Coders should note that the microscopic examination of specimens from bone marrow and spleen is excluded from this category. Exclusion notations appear to direct the coder.
41.4X	Excision or Destruction of Lesion or Tissue of Spleen—These codes are used to classify the following: • Marsupialization of splenic cyst—In this procedure an incision is made in a splenic cyst, and the cyst is sutured to create an open pouch. • Partial splenectomy—This procedure is the removal of a part of the spleen.
41.5	Total Splenectomy—This code is used for the complete removal of the spleen. Splenectomies are completed for the following reasons: • Injury to spleen due to trauma (the most common reason) • Intraoperative injury • Splenomegaly • Abscess of spleen • Thrombocytopenia • Presence of cysts • Rupture due to a disease process Figure 33-3 illustrates a splenectomy.
41.9X	Other Operations on the Spleen and Bone Marrow—These codes are used to classify other procedures that are not elsewhere classified in this chapter. It should be noted that code 41.91 is used to report the aspiration of bone marrow from a donor for transport. It occurs when healthy tissue is removed from a donor.

The coder should note that both diagnostic and therapeutic procedures are coded within this section of ICD-9-CM.

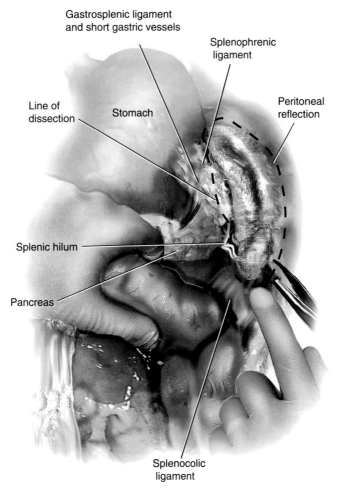

Figure 33-3 Splenectomy (From Price P, Frey KB, Junge TL. *Surgical Technology for the Surgical Technologist: A Positive Care Approach,* 2nd ed. Clifton Park, NY: Delmar, Cengage Learning, 2004, p. 355.)

Internet Links

To learn more about splenectomies, visit *http://www.sages.org/*.

To learn more about bone marrow transplants, visit: *www.ucsfhealth.org*.

To research any surgery, visit *http://archsurg.ama-assn.org* and search for the name of the surgery. For information related to this chapter, search "resection of lymph nodes." You will be amazed at the amount of information at this site.

Summary

- Chapter 8 of volume 3 of ICD-9-CM is entitled "Operations on the Hemic and Lymphatic System."

- Lymph nodes provide a site for lymphocyte production, produce antibodies, and filter impurities.

- Trauma is the most common reason for a splenectomy.

- Category code 40 classifies operations on the lymphatic system.

- Category code 41 classifies operations performed on bone marrow and the spleen.

- Excisions of lymph nodes are classified as simple, radical, and regional in ICD-9-CM.
- Separate codes are used to identify bone marrow or hematopoietic stem cell transplant with or without purging.
- Partial and total splenectomies are separately identified within ICD-9-CM.

Chapter Review

True/False: Indicate whether the statement is true (T) or false (F).

1. _____The cervical lymph nodes are located in the arm.

2. _____ An open biopsy of the spleen is a therapeutic procedure.

3. _____ A coder must be able to identify whether a total or partial splenectomy has occurred to select the appropriate code, because ICD-9-CM provides separate codes.

4. _____ A splenotomy is coded to code 41.2.

5. _____ A bilateral radical excision of the cervical lymph nodes is coded 40.40.

Fill-in-the-Blanks: Enter the appropriate term(s) to complete the statement.

6. The lymph nodes located in the area of the armpit are known as _____ lymph nodes.

7. The groin area of the lower abdomen is the location of the _____ lymph nodes.

8. Category code 40.41 classifies a _____ radical excision of the cervical lymph nodes.

9. Category code 40.19, Other diagnostic procedures on lymphatic structures, excludes an abdominal and cervical _____.

10. A simple lymphadenectomy is the surgical removal of a _____.

Coding Assignments

Instructions: Using an ICD-9-CM coding book, select the appropriate procedure code.

Procedure	Code
1. Ligation of thoracic duct	_____
2. Axillary lymph node excision	_____
3. Excision of lesion of spleen with application of adhesive barrier substance	_____
4. Purging of bone marrow with bone marrow transplant, using patient's own bone marrow	_____
5. Bone marrow biopsy	_____
6. Excision of inguinal lymph node	_____
7. Lymphangioma excision	_____

8. Repair of peripheral lymphatic duct _____

9. Fistulization of thoracic duct _____

10. Splenoplasty _____

11. Partial splenectomy _____

12. Splenorrhaphy _____

13. Radical excision of external mammary lymph node _____

14. Excision of lymphocele _____

15. Transplant of umbilical cord stem cells into a donor _____

16. Percutaneous biopsy of spleen _____

17. Aspiration of bone marrow from donor _____

18. Open biopsy of spleen _____

19. Hematopoietic stem cell transplant with purging from donor tissue _____

20. Radical dissection of lymph nodes of the groin _____

21. Excision of deep cervical lymph node _____

22. Allogeneic bone marrow transplant without purging _____

23. Marsupialization of splenic cyst _____

24. Extended regional lymph node excision _____

25. Cannulation of thoracic duct _____

Case Studies

Instructions: Review each case study, and select the correct ICD-9-CM diagnostic and procedural codes.

CASE 1

PRE- AND POSTOPERATIVE DIAGNOSIS: Splenic abscess

ANESTHESIA: General

This 64-year-old female patient was taken to the OR and placed in the supine position. An upper midline incision was made, and retractors were placed. The LUQ was explored, and splenic ligaments and the gastric veins were identified and divided. Dissection at the splenic hilum occurred, and the splenic vessels were identified. The splenic artery and vein were double ligated, suture ligated, and divided. The entire spleen was removed, and hemostasis was achieved. Blood loss was minimal. A drain was placed, and the wound was closed in layers with #3-0 Vicryl for the deep layers and #4-0 Vicryl for the skin.

The patient tolerated the procedure well and was taken to the postop recovery room in satisfactory condition.

Procedure: Splenectomy, no complications

ICD-9-CM Code Assignment: _____

CASE 2

PREOPERATIVE DIAGNOSIS: Lymph node enlargement

POSTOPERATIVE DIAGNOSIS: Right cervical lymphadenopathy

PROCEDURE: Cervical lymph node excision

This 29-year-old patient was prepped, and general anesthesia was administered. The right side of the patient's neck was prepped with Betadine. A transverse incision was made into the right cervical node region, and a 2.0-cm lymph node was removed with excision of scalene fat pad. Hemostasis was achieved, and the wound was closed in layers with Vicryl sutures. Steri-Strips and a sterile dressing were applied. The patient was sent to the recovery room, and the lymph node was sent to pathology for examination.

ICD-9-CM Code Assignment: _____

CASE 3

This is a 44-year-old Caucasian female presenting today for axillary lymph node biopsy. A very small (3.2-cm) lump was removed from the left breast 1 week ago. At that time the mass was sent for pathology, which came back with cells in situ in the lump. Margins were clear, but it was decided that a lymph node biopsy would be appropriate to be sure there was nothing suspicious in the lymph system.

ICD-9-CM Code Assignment: _____

CASE 4

This patient is an 8-year-old male who has previous complaints of pain in the lower extremities, fatigue, and now some unexplained weight loss. We suspect Leukemia but need the bone marrow biopsy for confirmation. The child presents today for a bone marrow biopsy. He is placed in supine position and injected with a local anesthetic agent. A needle was then inserted into the pelvic bone and rotated first right, then left, then withdrawn. This process was done one more time, when a viable sample was retrieved. The patient tolerated the procedure well.

ICD-9-CM Code Assignment: _____

Operations on the Digestive System

Chapter Outline

Objectives

At the conclusion of this chapter, the student will be able to:

1. Identify pathologies that affect the digestive system.
2. Describe some of the procedures used to correct the pathologies.
3. Discuss procedures completed on the structures of the digestive system.
4. Select and code diagnoses and procedures from case studies.

Key Terms

Anal Fistulectomy	Cholecystostomy	Esophagomyotomy	Hepatopexy
Anal Fistulotomy	Cholecystotomy	Esophagoscopy	Hepatotomy
Anal Sphincter	Cholecysto-	Esophagus	Hernia
Anoscopy	Chole/o-	Exteriorization	Hiatal Hernia
Antesternal	Colostomy	Femoral Hernia	High Gastric Bypass
Anastomosis	Direct Inguinal Hernia	Gastroduodenostomy	Ileostomy
Anus	Esophageal Web	Gastrotomy	Indirect Inguinal Hernia
Appendectomy	Esophagectomy	Hemorrhoids	Inguinal Hernia
Appendix	Esophagogastrostomy	Hepato-	Intestine

Reminder

As you work through this chapter, you will need to have a copy of the ICD-9-CM coding book to reference.

Large Intestine

Ligation of Esophageal Varices

Liver

Lobectomy

Myotomy of the Colon

Oddi

Pancreas

PEG Tube

Peptic Ulcer

Percutaneous Endoscopic Gastrostomy

Percutaneous Jejunostomy Done Endoscopically (PEJ)

Perfusion

Perianal Tissue

Perirectal Area

Proctostomy

Pyloromyotomy

Pyloroplasty

Pylorus

Rectum

Sigmoid Colon

Small Intestine

Stoma

Strangulated Hernia

Trocar

Umbilical Hernia

Vagus Nerve

Ventral Hernia

Introduction

This chapter codes operations and procedures of the digestive system, sometimes called the alimentary canal. Codes from the 42–54 categories are used. In a previous chapter, we covered codes for the mouth, pharynx, and trachea. This chapter starts with codes for procedures on the esophagus and moves through the digestive tract, including some accessory organs, such as the liver.

Coding Operations on the Digestive System

Coding operations on the digestive system are enhanced when the coder has a comprehensive understanding of the various procedures that are performed on this body system. Surgery completed on the digestive system is commonly completed by use of various endoscopes.

Operations on the Esophagus (Category Code 42)

Category 42 begins with procedures completed on the esophagus. The esophagus is found directly behind the trachea. It is the tube that moves food from the throat to the stomach. The position of the esophagus in relation to other structures of the digestive tract is illustrated in Figure 34-1.

Procedure Codes	Description
42.0X	Esophagotomy—An incision into the esophagus is coded to this subcategory, as is the cutting of the esophageal web. The esophageal web is a congenital condition in which tissue extends across the esophagus, causing problems with swallowing. It has a weblike appearance, which is how it got its name.
42.1X	Esophagostomy—This procedure creates a surgical opening in the esophagus. Exteriorization of the esophageal pouch involves moving part of the esophageal pouch to the exterior of the body.
42.2X	Diagnostic Procedures on Esophagus—Esophagoscopy by incision or through a stoma is coded to this subcategory. Esophagoscopy is a scope procedure, which is done to remove a foreign body or to biopsy a lesion by swabbing or brushing.
42.3X	Local Excision or Destruction of Lesion or Tissue of Esophagus—The destruction of the tissue or lesion happens through a cutting or endoscopic procedure.
42.4X	Excision of Esophagus—Esophagectomy is the excision of the esophagus. The procedure codes in this subcategory are for a partial removal or total removal of the esophagus. If a gastrostomy, interposition, or anastomosis, other than end-to-end, is performed at the same time, the procedure should be coded in addition to the excision.
42.5X	Intrathoracic Anastomosis of Esophagus—Esophagogastrostomy is a procedure in which the diseased part of the esophagus is removed; then there is a surgical connection to another structure such as the small bowel. If a gastrostomy or esophagectomy is performed at the same time, the procedure should be coded in addition to the anastomosis.

42.6X	Antesternal Anastomosis of Esophagus—**Antesternal anastomosis** is a procedure in which a surgical tunnel is created through substernal tissue to the esophagus. If a gastrostomy or esophagectomy is performed at the same time, the procedure should be coded in addition to the anastomosis.
42.7	**Esophagomyotomy**—This is an incision of the muscle tissue of the esophagus.
42.8X	Other Repair of Esophagus—Repairs in this subcategory include suturing of esophageal laceration, repair of esophageal fistula, grafting of the esophagus not elsewhere classified, and repair of esophageal stricture.
42.9X	Other Operations on Esophagus—This subcategory contains the code for **ligation of esophageal varices.** This is a procedure that involves the surgical tying off of esophageal veins that are dilated or painful.

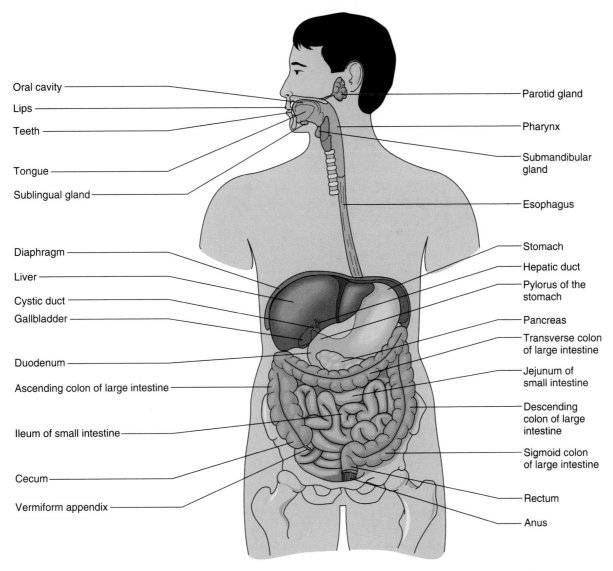

Figure 34-1 Digestive system (From Price P, Frey KB, Junge TL. *Surgical Technology for the Surgical Technologist: A Positive Care Approach,* 2nd ed. Clifton Park, NY: Delmar, Cengage Learning, 2004, p. 1026.)

Incision and Excision of the Stomach (Category Code 43)

Category 43, Incision and excision of stomach, begins the section on procedures of the stomach. The function of the stomach is to break down food. The esophagus connects to the stomach just below the upper portion, or the **fundus.** Figure 14-4 of this book illustrates the structures of the stomach.

Procedure Codes	Description
43.0	**Gastrotomy**—This is an incision into the stomach.
43.1X	**Gastrostomy**—This is a surgical opening into the stomach. The placement of a **percutaneous endoscopic gastrostomy** is a procedure that involves the surgical placement of a tube into the stomach through the abdominal wall. It is also called a **PEG tube** placement.
43.3	**Pyloromyotomy**—This is an incision into the muscles of the pylorus. The **pylorus** is the narrow passageway between the stomach and the duodenum at the start of the small intestine.
43.4X	Local Excision or Destruction of Lesion or Tissue of Stomach—These procedures can be done by incision or endoscopic technique. Removal of polyps and varices are coded to this subcategory.
43.5	Partial Gastrectomy with Anastomosis to Esophagus—This code is used when part of the stomach is excised and then the resection is sutured directly to the esophagus.
43.6	Partial Gastrectomy with Anastomosis to Duodenum—This procedure is sometimes referred to as **gastroduodenostomy**. An anastomosis connects the stomach directly with the duodenum. There is a partial excision of the stomach; in this case, the pylorus is usually taken. Figure 34-2 illustrates this procedure.
43.7	Partial Gastrectomy with Anastomosis to Jejunum—In this procedure, after partial excision of the stomach, the remaining portion of the stomach is connected to the jejunum.
43.8X	Other Partial Gastrectomy—When a partial gastrectomy procedure is done and a more specific code cannot be found, the procedure is coded to this subcategory.
43.9X	Total Gastrectomy—This is complete excision of the stomach. These procedures also include total excision of the stomach with anatomosis of the esophagus and the small intestine.

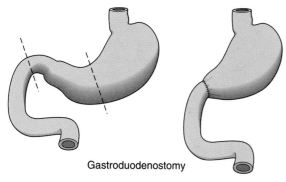

Gastroduodenostomy

Figure 34-2 Formation of an anastomosis in a gastroduodenostomy (From Ehrlich A, Schroeder CL. *Medical Terminology for Health Professions,* 4th ed. Clifton Park, NY: Delmar, Cengage Learning, 2001, p. 177.)

Other Operations on the Stomach (Category Code 44)

Category 44, Other operations on stomach, encompasses more procedure codes involving the stomach and surrounding structures. The category begins with procedures on the vagus nerve. The **vagus nerve** transmits sensory information, specifically sensory information for the regulation of the thoracic and abdominal organs. It is also involved with the inferior pharynx and the larynx. Figure 34-3 illlustrates the nerves and arteries of the stomach.

Procedure Codes	Description
44.0X	Vagotomy—This subcategory contains procedure codes for the interruption of impulses of the vagus nerve due to surgical intervention, as well as the excision of a segment or specific segments of the vagus nerve.
44.1X	Diagnostic Procedures on Stomach—Diagnostic procedures can be done through a gastroscope inserted through the abdominal wall or a stoma. Open or closed biopsies are also coded to this subcategory.
44.2X	**Pyloroplasty**—This is a surgical correction of the pylorus to relieve an obstruction. Dilation of the pylorus by endoscopic procedure or incision is also coded to this subcategory.
44.3X	Gastroenterostomy without Gastrectomy—A procedure known as a high gastric bypass is coded to this subcategory. The **high gastric bypass** is a procedure in which the jejunum and the upper portion of the stomach are connected by anastomosis and completely bypass the duodenum. Endoscopic and open procedures, such as a jejunostomy and conversion of a gastrostomy to a gastrojejunostomy, are coded to this subcategory.

44.4X	Control of Hemorrhage and Suture of Ulcer of Stomach or Duodenum—A peptic ulcer is an open sore of the mucous membrane at the lower end of the esophagus entering the stomach and is usually painful due to inflammation.
44.5	Revision of Gastric Anastomosis—This is a surgical correction of an anastomosis done at a prior operative session.
44.6X	Other Repair of Stomach—This subcategory contains a variety of surgical repair codes for the stomach and esophagus that are not coded more specifically anywhere else.
44.9X	Other Operations on the Stomach—This subcategory includes ligation of gastric varices and intraoperative manipulation of the stomach, which is done by hand during an operative session.

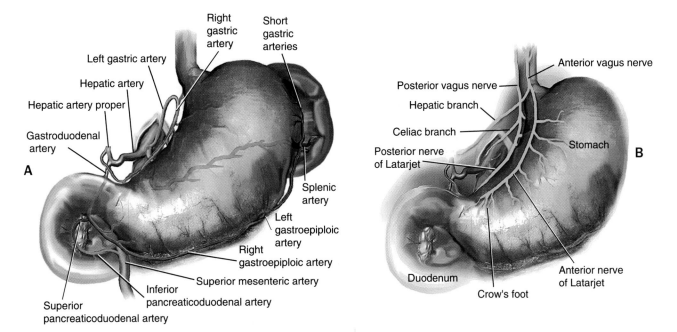

Figure 34-3 Stomach: **(A)** Arterial supply, **(B)** neural supply (From Price P, Frey KB, Junge TL. *Surgical Technology for the Surgical Technologist: A Positive Care Approach,* 2nd ed. Clifton Park, NY: Delmar, Cengage Learning, 2004, p. 390.)

Incision, Excision, and Anastomosis of the Intestines (Category Code 45)

Category 45 is called Incision, excision, and anastomosis of intestine. The intestine is made up of the small and large intestines. The small intestine begins at the pyloric sphincter and moves through the duodenum, jejunum, ileum, and the ileocecal sphincter. Most of the digestive process, including nutrient absorption, occurs in the small intestine. Some liquid is absorbed here; the rest is absorbed by the large intestine as waste passes through.

The large intestine begins with the cecum, the colon, the rectum, and the anus. The large intestine further breaks down food and holds it until it can be evacuated from the body.

Procedure Codes	Description
45.0X	Enterotomy—This is the surgical cutting into the intestine. Codes in this subcategory are specific to certain parts of the intestine.
45.1X	Diagnostic Procedures on Small Intestine—This subcategory includes diagnostic procedures done endoscopically, open and closed biopsies, and other diagnostic procedures on the small intestine. An intraoperative endoscopy is included in this procedure and not billed separately. A laparotomy is billed separately.
45.2X	Diagnostic Procedures on Large Intestine—This subcategory includes diagnostic procedures done endoscopically, open and closed biopsies, and other diagnostic procedures on the large intestine. An intraoperative endoscopy is included in this procedure and not billed separately. A laparotomy is billed separately.

Procedure Codes	Description
45.3X	Local Excision or Destruction of Lesion or Tissue of Small Intestine—This subcategory of codes includes endoscopic or other excision or destruction of lesions or tissue.
45.4X	Local Excision or Destruction of Lesion or Tissue of Large Intestine—This subcategory of codes includes endoscopic or other excision or destruction of lesions or tissue. The removal of polyps found in the large intestine is coded from this subcategory.
45.5X	Isolation of Intestinal Segment—The procedures in this subcategory involve surgically separating parts of the intestine. If an anastomosis, other than end-to-end, or an enterostomy is done in the same operative session, it is coded separately.
45.6X	Other Excision of Small Intestine—Codes in this subcategory include procedure codes for surgeries when multiple segments of small intestine are removed. Also the total removal of the small intestine is coded to this subcategory. If an anastomosis, other than end-to-end, a colostomy, or an enterostomy is done in the same operative session, it is coded separately.
45.7X	Partial Excision of Large Intestine—These procedures include the partial excision of one or more segments of the large intestine. If an anastomosis, other than end-to-end, or an enterostomy is done in the same operative session, it is coded separately.
45.8	Total Intra-Abdominal Colectomy—This code is used when the entire colon is removed from the ileum to the rectum. Figure 34-4 illustrates the various types of colectomies that can be done.
45.9X	Intestinal Anastomosis—These procedures are coded when part of the intestine is removed and the remaining ends are surgically connected to restore functional continuity.

Other Operations on Intestine (Category Code 46)

Category 46, Other operations on intestine, contains colostomy and ileostomy procedure codes and introduces procedure codes for dilation and manipulation of the intestine.

Procedure Codes	Description
46.0X	Exteriorization of Intestine—This procedure involves the transposition of part of the intestine to the exterior of the body. The small and large intestines are included in this subcategory.
46.1X	Colostomy—A **colostomy** is a surgical opening between part of the colon and the outside surface of the body. This opening is called a **stoma**. The colostomy is named for the part of the colon that meets with the stoma. An example of this is an **ileostomy;** the ileum meets with the opening in the abdominal wall. A colostomy can be permanent or temporary. Any resection done in the same operative session can be coded separately. If a colostomy needs to be reopened, it is coded to this subcategory.
46.2X	Ileostomy—As explained, an ileostomy is a type of colostomy in which the ileum is connected to an abdominal opening to outside of the body. An ileostomy can be permanent or temporary, and any resection done in the same operative session can be coded separately.
46.3X	Other Enterostomy—A **percutaneous jejunostomy done endoscopically (PEJ)** is a procedure in which a tube is guided endoscopically into the jejunum.
46.4X	Revision of Intestinal Stoma—This subcategory includes codes for procedures done in the large and small intestines. Also found here are procedure codes for hernia repair at the site of the colostomy.
46.5X	Closure of Intestinal Stoma—Procedure codes include stoma closure in the small or large intestine.
46.6X	Fixation of Intestine—The operation note needs to be reviewed to determine whether the fixation was to the abdominal wall or to a structure in the abdominal cavity.

46.7X	Other Repair of Intestine—Suture or repair of the small or large intestine, as well as the closure of a fistula, is also included in this subcategory.
46.8X	Dilation and Manipulation of Intestine—Coded to this subcategory is dilation of the intestine by balloon through an endoscopic procedure through the rectum or colostomy. Maniipulation using hands in the treatment of knots or twisted intestine is also coded to this subcategory.
46.9X	Other Operations on Intestines—This subcategory contains codes for the revision of the large and small intestines, myotomy of the colon, which is a surgical incision into the muscular layer of the colon and local perfusion of the large and small intestine. Perfusion is a process in which fluid is run through the structure.

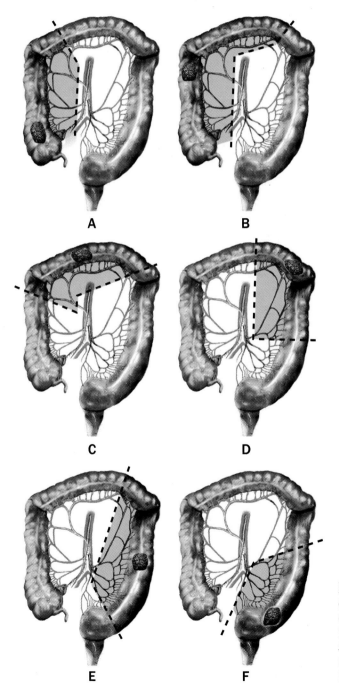

Figure 34-4 Colon resection: (**A**) Right colectomy, (**B**) right hemicolectomy, (**C**) transverse colectomy, (**D**) left colectomy, (**E**) left hemicolectomy, (**F**) abdominoperineal resection (From Price P, Frey KB, Junge TL. *Surgical Technology for the Surgical Technologist: A Positive Care Approach,* 2nd ed. Clifton Park, NY: Delmar, Cengage Learning, 2004, p. 426.)

Operation on the Appendix (Category Code 47)

Category 47, Operations on appendix, is the next category in this chapter. The appendix, sometimes referred to as the vermiform appendix, is found at the base of the cecum. An appendectomy is an excision of the appendix and is illustrated in Figure 34-5.

Procedure Codes	Description
47.0X	Appendectomy—As shown in Figure 34-5, an appendectomy can be done as an open procedure or done laparoscopically. Both procedures are coded from this subcategory.
47.1X	Incidental Appendectomy—In some cases, the surgeon takes the appendix just because he or she is in that portion of the abdomen during surgery. If the appendectomy is done as an incidental portion of a more extensive procedure, it may or may not be paid for by the carrier.
47.2	Drainage of Appendiceal Abscess—If the appendix is infected, this procedure is coded if the abscess is drained and the appendix is not removed.
47.9X	Other Operations on Appendix—If drainage of the appendix is necessary, there may be the need for an incision into the abdominal wall to the appendix. This procedure is called an appendicostomy and is coded from this subcategory.

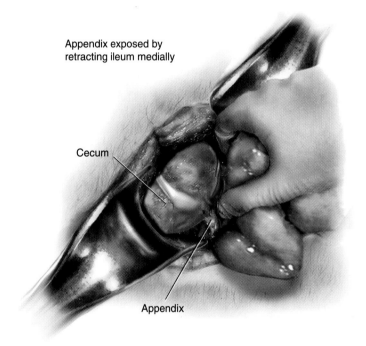

Appendix exposed by
retracting ileum medially

Cecum

Appendix

Figure 34-5 Appendectomy (From Price P, Frey KB, Junge TL. *Surgical Technology for the Surgical Technologist: A Positive Care Approach,* 2nd ed. Clifton Park, NY: Delmar, Cengage Learning, 2004, p. 423.)

Operations on the Rectum, Rectosigmoid, and Perirectal Tissue (Category Code 48)

Category 48, Operations on rectum, rectosigmoid, and perirectal tissue, contains procedure codes pertaining to the sigmoid colon, which is the S-part of the colon connecting to the rectum. The rectum is at the distal end of the large intestine, right before the anus. These structures move waste from the body.

Procedure Codes	Description
48.0	Proctotomy—Surgical incision of the rectum.
48.1	Proctostomy—When an opening needs to be created between the rectum and the body's surface, a proctostomy is done.
48.2X	Diagnostic Procedures on Rectum, Rectosigmoid, and Perirectal Tissue—The procedures in this subcategory include open and closed biopsies along with diagnostic scope procedures.
48.3X	Local Excision or Destruction of Lesion or Tissue of Rectum—The excision or destruction can be done by electrocoagulation, which is the use of an electrical current, or by the use of laser or cryosurgery. Endoscopic polypectomy of the rectum is coded to this subcategory.
48.4X	Pull-Through Resection of Rectum—This subcategory contains the procedure codes for the pull-through resection. If an anastomosis, other than end-to-end, is done in the same operative session, it can be coded separately.
48.5X	Abdominoperineal Resection of Rectum—This subcategory is coded if there is a removal of the rectum through an abdominal and perineal operative approach. If an anastomosis, other than end-to-end, is done in the same operative session, it can be coded separately. This procedure includes a colostomy.
48.6X	Other Resection of the Rectum—This subcategory contains codes that describe resection procedures not found in other subcategories of this chapter.
48.7X	Repair of Rectum—These procedure codes are for the repair of the rectum, closure of rectal fistula, fixation of the rectum and sigmoid colon within the abdomen to other structures, and repair of rectal prolapse.
48.8X	Incision or Excision of Perirectal Tissue or Lesion—The perirectal area is the area surrounding the rectum. The procedures in this subcategory include the incision and excision of perirectal tissue.
48.9X	Other Operations on Rectum and Perirectal Tissue—The release of a rectal stricture is coded to this subcategory, as is the repair of a perirectal fistula. The excision of muscle tissue of the rectum, known as an anorectal myectomy, is also coded to this subcategory.

Operations on the Anus (Category Code 49)

The anus is the very end of the digestive tract. It is the opening from the body through which solid waste is eliminated. Category 49, Operations on anus, contains procedure codes for this portion of the body.

Procedure Codes	Description
49.0X	Incision or Excision of Perianal Tissue—Perianal tissue is the tissue around the anus. The procedures in this area include the removal of perianal skin tags or other incisions and excisions of the perianal tissue.
49.1X	Incision or Excision of Anal Fistula—Anal fistulotomy is the cutting of an anal fistula. Anal fistulectomy is the removal of an anal fistula. Both procedures are coded to this subcategory.
49.2X	Diagnostic Procedures on Anus and Perianal Tissue—Biopsies of the perianal tissue and the anus itself are coded to this subcategory. The anoscopy is also coded to this subcategory. An anoscopy is an examination of the anus by way of a scope.
49.4X	Procedures on Hemorrhoids—Veins that supply circulation to the anal canal can sometimes become enlarged and painful. These enlarged veins are called hemorrhoids. Some of the procedures included in this subcategory are the cauterization and ligation of hemorrhoids. Cryotherapy and injections to hemorrhoids are also found here.
49.5X	Division of Anal Sphincter—The elimination of the waste from the body is controlled by the muscles of the anus, also known as anal sphincter. The code selection is based on how the incision is made: laterally, posteriorly, or other approach.
49.6	Excision of Anus—Removal of the anus.
49.7X	Repair of Anus—Repair codes are based on the type of repair. Suture repair and closure of anal fistula are included in this subcategory of codes.
49.9X	Other Operations on Anus—Procedure codes not more specifically described may be found in this subcategory. Electrical stimulator, incision of anal septum, and reduction of anal prolapse are coded to this subcategory.

Operations on the Liver (Category Code 50)

Category 50, Operations on liver, is the next category in this chapter. The liver is the largest organ in the human body. The function of the liver is to produce bile and enzymes, which aid in food digestion. The liver is located in the upper right quadrant of the abdomen. Figure 34-6 illustrates the location of the liver in relation to the intestines.

Some of the terms used in this category begin with the prefix *hepato-*. This prefix means "liver."

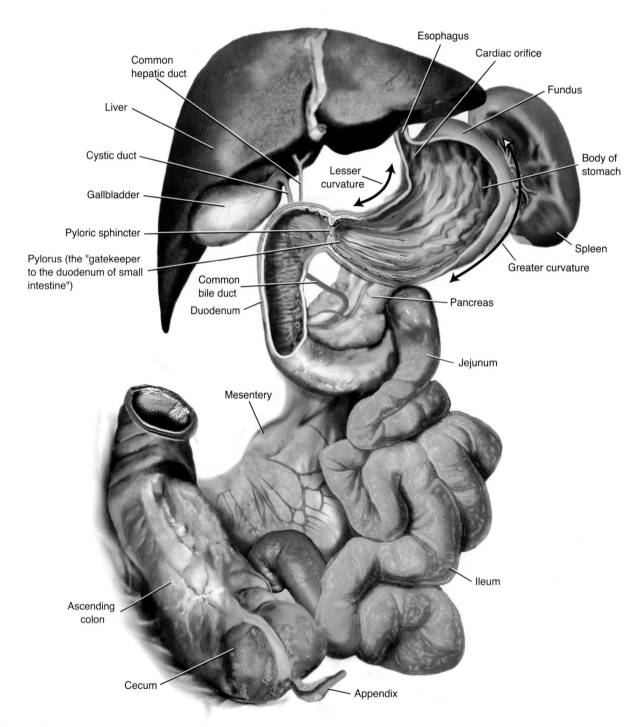

Figure 34-6 Anatomical location of liver in relation to the intestine (From Lazo DL. *Fundamentals of Sectional Anatomy: An Imaging Approach.* Clifton Park, NY: Delmar, Cengage Learning, 2005, p. 173.)

Procedure Codes	Description
50.0	Hepatotomy—This is a surgical cut into the liver.
50.1X	Diagnostic Procedures on Liver—This subcategory contains procedure codes for obtaining biopsies of the liver. The procedures may be done open or closed, usually with a needle to extract the tissue.
50.2X	Local Excision or Destruction of Liver Tissue or Lesion—Procedure codes in this subcategory include the removal of hepatic lesions or excision of part of the liver.
50.3	Lobectomy of Liver—A lobectomy is the complete removal of one of the four lobes of the liver. This code is also used if all of one lobe is removed with the partial removal of another lobe.
50.4	Total Hepatectomy—This is complete surgical removal of the liver.
50.5X	Liver Transplant—This is receipt of a donor liver.
50.6X	Repair of the Liver—The coder may see the term *hepatopexy* in an operative note. This term refers to the surgical repair of the liver.
50.9X	Other Operations on Liver—Should mechanical assistance be required for the liver to function properly, some of the procedure codes are found in this subcategory. Therapeutic injections and perfusions are also found in this subcategory.

Operations on the Gallbladder and Biliary Trac (Category Code 51)

Category 51, Operations on gallbladder and biliary tract, is the next set of procedures in this chapter. Figure 34-6 diagrams the location of the gallbladder and the various ducts in relation to the intestine and the liver. The gallbladder stores bile for later use in digestion. The prefix *chole/o-* refers to bile or gall. *Cholecysto-* is a prefix that refers to the gallbladder.

Procedure Codes	Description
51.0X	Cholecystotomy and Cholecystostomy—The cholecystostomy is a surgical opening being created into the gallbladder. This procedure is sometimes performed with an instrument called a trocar. A trocar is a cannula with a sharp point at the end. A cholecystostomy is the surgical cutting into the gallbladder.
51.1X	Diagnostic Procedures on Biliary Tract—The diagnostic procedures included in this subcategory include biopsy procedures and scope procedures. Some of the scope procedures include the injection of radiopaque contrast for radiologic examination of a structure.
51.2X	Cholecystectomy—The surgical removal of all or part of the gallbladder. This procedure may be done as an open procedure or laparoscopically.
51.3X	Anastomosis of Gallbladder or Bile Duct—The procedures found in this subcategory include a surgical connection between the gallbladder and the pancreas, stomach, or other structures.
51.4X	Incision of Bile Duct for Relief of Obstruction—If the bile ducts become obstructed and needs to be incised to clear the obstruction, procedure codes are found in this subcategory.
51.5X	Other Incision of Bile Duct—Should the bile duct need to be incised for exploration or other purposes, codes from this subcategory are used.
51.6X	Local Excision or Destruction of Lesion or Tissue of Biliary Ducts and Sphincter of Oddi—Oddi refers to Oddi's sphincter, which is located at the opening into the duodenum from the common bile duct.
51.7X	Repair of Bile Ducts—These procedure codes are used for suturing repair as well as the repair of the ducts.
51.8X	Other Operations on Biliary Ducts and Sphincter of Oddi—These codes include open repairs and endoscopic procedures. Stent insertion is coded to this subcategory, along with the removal of stones.
51.9X	Other Operations on Biliary Tract—Fistula repair, the removal of a prosthetic device, and the closure of an opening in the gallbladder are procedures coded to this subcategory.

Operations on the Pancreas (Category Code 52)

Category 52, Operation on pancreas, contains codes related to procedures on the pancreas. The pancreas has functions in both the digestive and endocrine systems. In the digestive system, the enzymes secreted by the pancreas through the pancreatic duct help neutralize stomach acids.

Procedure Codes	Description
52.0X	Pancreatotomy—This is the surgical cutting into the pancreas. Also found in this subcategory of procedure codes is the code for drainage of the pancreas by catheter placement.
52.1X	Diagnostic Procedures on Pancreas—This subcategory includes codes for open and closed biopsies, as well as endoscopic biopsies and some of the scope procedures that include the injection of radiopaque contrast for radiologic examination of a structure.
52.2X	Local Excision or Destruction of Pancreas and Pancreatic Duct—The endoscopic excision of a lesion or tissue is coded to this subcategory.
52.3	Marsupialization of Pancreatic Cyst—This procedure involves surgically cutting into the cyst in the pancreas and then suturing the open cyst.
52.4	Internal Drainage of Pancreatic Cyst—This procedure code includes the anastomosis of the pancreatic cyst to parts of the stomach and intestine.
52.5X	Partial Pancreatectomy—A part of the pancreas is surgically removed.
52.6	Total Pancreatectomy—The entire pancreas is removed.
52.7	Radical Pancreaticoduodenectomy—This is a complex procedure involving multiple anastomosis between the various parts of the intestine and the pancreas.
52.8X	Transplant of Pancreas—This subcategory of procedure codes involves the various forms of grafting pancreatic tissue. This subcategory also involves the implantation of cells of islets of Langerhans.
52.9X	Other Operations on Pancreas—These procedure codes include closure of a fistula of the pancreas, stent insertion, simple suturing, and anastomoses procedures not coded more specifically anywhere else in this chapter.

Repair of Hernias (Category Code 53)

Hernias are coded to category 53, Repair of hernias. A hernia is a bulging or protrusion through tissue of a structure or part of a structure that is normally contained in that tissue. Certain terminology is associated with different types of hernias. A hiatal hernia is a type of hernia that pushes the stomach upward into the mediastinal cavity through the diaphragm. An inguinal hernia is a bulging at the inguinal opening. In an indirect inguinal hernia, the hernia sac extends through the inguinal ring and into the inguinal canal, sometimes descending into the scrotum. A direct inguinal hernia is a type of inguinal hernia that protrudes into the abdominal wall by the Hesselbach triangle. A strangulated hernia is a hernia that develops gangrene because the sac is so tightly constricted. A ventral hernia is a hernia that protrudes through an abdominal scar where the abdominal wall is protected only by scar tissue.

Procedure Codes	Description
53.0X	Unilateral Repair of Inguinal Hernia—These procedure codes consist of repair codes for inguinal hernias that occur on only one side of the abdomen. The repair includes repair with graft or prosthesis. The Excludes: note should be reviewed as it states that laparoscopic unilateral repair of inguinal hernia is coded to 17.11 to 17.13.
53.1X	Bilateral Repair of Inguinal Hernia—These procedure codes are also for the repair of inguinal hernias, but this subcategory is for bilateral repair. It should be noted that an Excludes: note appears that states that laparoscopic bilateral repair of inguinal hernia code to 17.21 to 17.24.
53.2X	Unilateral Repair of Femoral Hernia—A femoral hernia occurs at the femoral ring of the intestine. The repair codes in this subcategory are for femoral hernias appearing on only one side of the body.
53.3X	Bilateral Repair of Femoral Hernia—These procedure codes are referenced when there is a bilateral repair of femoral hernias.

53.4X	Repair of Umbilical Hernia—An **umbilical hernia** is a hernia found in the part of the intestine that falls around the umbilicus.
53.5X	Repair of Other Hernia of Anterior Abdominal Wall (without Graft or Prosthesis)—These hernia repairs do not use tissue implantation or artificial material repair.
53.6X	Repair of Other Hernia of Anterior Abdominal Wall with Graft or Prosthesis—This subcategory of repair codes includes the tissue implantation or artificial material repair. Excludes: notes should be reviewed for this subcateogry.
53.7	Repair of Diaphragmatic Hernia, Abdominal Approach—This procedure code is used when the repair involves the protrusion of an abdominal organ through the wall of the diaphragm. The approach is through an abdominal cavity incision.
53.8X	Repair of Diaphragmatic Hernia, Thoracic Approach—This series of codes involve an incision into the thoracic cavity in order to perform the repair.
53.9	Other Hernia Repair—If there is not a more specific hernia repair code found in this chapter, this code is used.

Other Operations on the Abdominal Region (Category Code 54)

The last category of this chapter contains procedure codes for other operations on the abdominal region. The codes include procedures done in the epigastric, flank, groin, hypochondrium, inguinal, loin, male pelvic cavity, mesentery, omentum, peritoneum, and retroperitoneal regions.

Procedure Codes	Description
54.0	Incision of Abdominal Wall—The surgical cutting of the abdominal wall to drain an abscess is coded from this subcategory.
54.1X	Laparotomy—The codes in this subcategory are used when the surgeon is making a direct surgical examination. If this procedure is done in conjunction with an intra-abdominal surgery, it is not coded separately.
54.2X	Diagnostic Procedures of Abdominal Region—This subcategory is referenced for biopsies of the abdominal region that are not specified by another code in this chapter. Laparoscopic procedures are also found here.
54.3	Excision or Destruction of Lesion or Tissue of Abdominal Wall or Umbilicus—The surgical removal or destruction of tissue of the abdominal wall or umbilical region is coded to this subcategory.
54.4	Excision or Destruction of Peritoneal Tissue—The surgical removal or destruction of peritoneal tissue such as appendices epiploicae, lesions of mesenteric tissue, omental tissue, and peritoneal tissue.
54.5X	Lysis of Peritoneal Adhesions—The destruction of fibrous adherent tissue found in the peritoneal cavity is coded from this subcategory. The destruction can be done as an open procedure or laparoscopically.
54.6X	Suture of Abdominal Wall and Peritoneum—The surgical repair of wounds of the abdominal wall or peritoneum is coded to this subcategory.
54.7X	Other Repair of Abdominal Wall and Peritoneum—This includes procedure codes for the repair of the abdominal wall, peritoneum, omentum, and mesentery.
54.9X	Other Operations of Abdominal Region—This is a removal of a foreign body from the peritoneal cavity. The surgical creation of a fistula, incision, and injections of air into the peritoneal cavity are procedures coded to this subcategory.

Approaches to gastrointestinal surgery becomes less invasive each year; therefore, it is imperative that coders stay abreast of new gastrointestinal procedures.

Internet Links

To learn more about gastrointestinal surgery, visit *www.uphs.upenn.edu/surgery* and the Harvard Medical School Family health guide at *http://www.health.harvard.edu/* and check on "digestive system." Please note that this site contains information on numerous body systems.

Summary

- This chapter contains procedure codes for the digestive system, also known as the alimentary canal.
- The code range for this chapter is categories 42–54.
- This chapter begins with procedure codes for the esophogus and follows the digestive tract to the anus. It also contains codes for accessory organs such as the gallbladder and liver.
- Codes for hernia repairs are included in this chapter and to code range 17.1X to 17.24.

Chapter Review

True/False: Indicate whether the statement is true (T) or false (F).

1. _____ The esophagus is located directly in front of the trachea.

2. _____ The vagus nerve transmits sensory information.

3. _____ A PEG tube is placed through the abdominal wall into the stomach.

4. _____ Most digestion occurs in the large intestine.

5. _____ The prefix *hepato-* refers to the gallbladder.

Fill-in-the-Blank: Enter the appropriate term(s) to complete the statement.

6. The narrow passage between the stomach and small intestine is called the _____.

7. The _____ is a congenital condition in which tissue extends across the esophagus, causing problems.

8. A truncal vagotomy is coded to _____.

9. A _____ hernia is so constricted that it develops gangrene.

10. A surgical opening between part of the colon and the outside surface of the body is called a
_____.

Coding Assignments

Instructions: Using an ICD-9-CM coding book, select the appropriate procedure code.

Procedure	Code
1. Revision of the pylorus	_____
2. Placement of PEG tube	_____
3. Temporary colostomy	_____

4. Ligation of esophageal varices   _____

5. Open biopsy of bile duct   _____

6. Pyloromyotomy   _____

7. Endoscopic ablation of tumor of large intestine   _____

8. Esophagomyotomy   _____

9. Enucleation of liver   _____

10. Ligation of gastric varices   _____

11. Intrathoracic esophageal anastomosis with interposition of small bowel   _____

12. Laparoscopic cholecystectomy   _____

13. Esophagogastroplasty   _____

14. Bilateral repair of direct inguinal hernia with graft   _____

15. Closed endoscopic biopsy of esophagus   _____

16. Laparoscopic lysis of peritoneal adhesions   _____

17. Excision of redundant mucosa of ileostomy   _____

18. Dilation of duodenum   _____

19. Endoscopic insertion of stent tube into pancreatic duct   _____

20. Marsupialization of pancreatic cyst   _____

21. Gastric polypectomy by endoscopic approach   _____

22. Antesternal esophagogastrostomy   _____

23. Reopening of recent laparotomy site   _____

24. Creation of a cutaneoperitoneal fistula   _____

25. Pancreatic sphincteroplasty   _____

Case Studies

Instructions: Review each case study, and select the correct ICD-9-CM diagnostic and procedural codes.

CASE 1

PREOPERATIVE DIAGNOSIS: Chronic calculus cholecystitis

POSTOPERATIVE DIAGNOSIS: Common bile duct obstruction with hydrops

INDICATIONS: This 30-year-old male presented to the ER with severe right upper quadrant abdominal pain. Ultrasound showed dilated bile ducts. Laboratory workup showed elevated liver functions and elevated lipase.

PROCEDURE: Patient was prepped and draped in normal sterile fashion. He was placed in supine position and under general anesthesia with endotracheal intubation. A midline infraumbilical incision was carried through the intra-abdominal wall with #10 blade scalpel, where I entered the peritoneal cavity bluntly with my finger. I inserted the 10-mm port and insufflated the peritoneal cavity with carbon dioxide to 15 mm Hg pressure and inserted the laparoscope. Below the xiphoid process, I placed another 10-mm port; in the upper right quadrant, two 5-mm ports. I was able to triangulate the gallbladder, which was very distended, so I had to aspirate it. Upon examination of the syringe, we found there was white bile, diagnostic for hydrops of the gallbladder. Once the bile was removed, I used a harmonic scalpel to dissect into the hepatoduodenal ligament and triangle of Calot until the cystic duct and cystic artery were found. Because of the elevated liver functions, we did a cholangiogram, where we found stones impacted in the cystic duct. By using a Maryland dissector, I was able to milk them out of the duct until we were able to see bile come back. A repeat cholangiogram with good results occurred. I placed four clips proximally in cystic duct and transected it, then found the cystic artery, and placed two clips proximally on the artery and transected that distally. I continued to dissect the gallbladder out of the gallbladder fat. The gallbladder was placed into an Endo catch bag and removed through the umbilical wound. The area was irrigated with saline antibiotics. There was no bleeding, no bile leaking. The laparoscope was removed along with the ports. All wounds were sutured. The patient returned to the recovery room in stable condition.

ICD-9-CM Code Assignment: _____

CASE 2

This was a 23-year-old female who presented to the hospital with right lower quadrant pain. CAT scan and laboratory workup, including elevated white blood cell count, suggest appendicitis. Palpation of this area demonstrates tenderness and pain.

PREOPERATIVE DIAGNOSIS: Appendicitis

POSTOPERATIVE DIAGNOSIS: Nonruptured appendicitis

PROCEDURE: Patient was taken to operating room and placed in supine position. She underwent induction of general anesthesia with endotracheal intubation. A Foley catheter was inserted. The abdomen was prepped and draped in the usual sterile fashion. Using a 15-blade scalpel, I made a supraumbilical midline incision, which I carried down to the layers of the anterior abdominal wall with cautery. I entered the peritoneal cavity with my finger and inserted a 10-mm port. With carbon dioxide gas, the peritoneal cavity was insufflated, and the laparoscope was inserted. Another 10-mm port was placed below the pubis, and in the left lower quadrant I placed a 5-mm port.

I was then able to find the cecum, which I followed to the convergence of the teniae. I located the appendix, which was inflamed and had the beginnings of suppuration. I used a harmonic scalpel to take down the mesoappendix to ensure that the mesoappendix remnant was hemostatic, which it was. I used an EnodGIA 45 vascular load stapler across the base of the appendix, transecting the appendix. The appendix was then placed in the Endocatch bag and removed through the supraumbilical wound. I went back and copiously irrigated the area with saline antibiotics. The ports were removed, then the laparoscope. Incisions were sutured and dressed. The Foley catheter was removed. Patient went to recovery room in stable condition.

ICD-9-CM Code Assignment: _____

CASE 3

PROCEDURE: The patient was placed in supine position on the operating table. He underwent induction of general anesthesia. The groin area was prepped and draped in the usual sterile fashion on the left. A 4-cm incision was made with a #10 blade scalpel above the inguinal ligament. Upon dissection down to the subcutaneous tissue, I found a large hernia that attenuated the external oblique aponeurosis. I was able to dissect all adhesions away from the hernia sac and disconnect this from the spermatic cord, being sure not to injure the vas deferens or the blood supply to the testicle. Once the sac was dissected all the way back, I scored the transversalis fascia, which allowed me to move the sac back into the peritoneal cavity. I was then able to place two large PerFix mesh plugs. I sewed the plug to surrounding tissue with interrupted #2-0 Prolene suture. I irrigated the wound with saline and antibiotics and then placed a standard mesh onlay on top of the repair and sewed it to the pubic tubercle medially and the conjoined tendon superiorly. I brought the two limbs of the mesh and sewed them to each other around the top of the spermatic cord laterally, and then I sewed the inferior aspect of the mesh to the shelving portion of the inguinal ligament. The wound was again irrigated with saline and antibiotics. All counts were correct, and incision was sutured. Patient was returned to the recovery room in stable condition.

ICD-9-CM Code Assignment: _____

CASE 4

Hospital Procedural Note

This is a 45-year-old male who was placed in observation today with abdominal pain, chills, and weakness since 3 pm today. Last night the patient experienced some vomiting but no diarrhea. Patient has not had a bowel movement since 7:30 am, which the patient describes as "small and painful." No other medical history is pertinent as patient has been in good health and has had no surgeries to date.

Examination reveals a 45-year-old white male in mild abdominal discomfort. Vital signs are all within normal limits with a BP of 127/78, and temperature of 99, a pulse rate of 90, and respirations of 19. The abdomen is mildly distended, tympanic is tender. A CT scan of the abdomen and pelvis showed a solid mass in the duodenum.

Procedure: Patient was prepped and draped in the usual manner. An incision was made to complete a duodenotomy to release the impaction. No other problems were noted in the duodenum. The impacted material was removed. The incision was closed. The patient tolerated the procedure.

ICD-9-CM Code Assignment: _____

CASE 5

PREOPERATIVE DIAGNOSIS: Esophagitis, duodenitis, possible peptic ulcer

POSTOPERATIVE DIAGNOSIS: Peptic ulcer disease

PROCEDURE: The patient was prepped using adequate amounts of topical anesthetic, Xylocaine. When I was sure the patient was comfortable, the Olympus upper GI endoscope was introduced per the oral cavity and advanced down the esophagus. Proximal esophagus appeared normal, while the distal esophagus showed two small ulcerative lesions, one at 10 o'clock, which was red and irritated but not oozing, and one at 6 o'clock which also appeared red and irritated but was oozing. The scope was then advanced into the stomach and then the duodenum, which revealed no further lesions. The endoscope was removed. The patient tolerated the procedure well.

ICD-9-CM Code Assignment: _____

Chapter Outline

Objectives

At the conclusion of this chapter, the student will be able to:

1. Identify pathologies and injuries of the urinary system.
2. Describe the procedures used to correct the pathologies of the urinary system.
3. Accurately code procedures completed on the urinary system.
4. Select and code diagnoses and procedures from case studies.

Key Terms

Anastomosis

Aspiration of Kidney

Bilateral Nephrectomy

Calculus

Capsulectomy of Kidney

Cystostomy

Cystotomy

Fragmentation of
  Stones

Kelly-Kennedy Operation
  on the Urethra

Kelly-Stoeckell Urethral
  Plication

Nephropexy

Nephroscopy

Nephrostomy

Nephrotomy

Partial Nephrectomy

Pyeloscopy

Pyelostomy

Pyelotomy

Transurethral Clearance
  of the Bladder

Transurethral
  Cystoscopy

Unilateral Nephrectomy

Ureterectomy

Ureterotomy

Urethral Meatotomy

Urethrotomy

Vesicostomy

Reminder

As you work through this chapter, you will need to have a copy of the ICD-9-CM coding book to reference.

Introduction

Chapter 10 of ICD-9-CM volume 3 classifies operations and procedures completed on the urinary system. For purposes of this chapter, the procedures are completed on the kidneys, ureter, urinary bladder, urethra, and other structures of the urinary tract.

Coding Operations on the Urinary System

Categories found in chapter 10, "Operations on the Urinary System," include:

55	Operations on the kidney
56	Operations on the ureter
57	Operations on urinary bladder
58	Operations on urethra
59	Other operations on the urinary tract

The anatomical position of the structures of the urinary system can be reviewed by referencing Figure 15-1 of this book.

Operations on the Kidney (Category Code 55)

The function of the kidney is to filter the blood to remove waste products and to excrete the waste products as urine. The kidneys can become damaged because of injury or because of a disease process.

The coder should note the inclusion note at the start of the category stating that operations on the renal pelvis are included in this category. The inclusion note also instructs the coder to assign code 99.77 as an additional code when an adhesion barrier substance is applied or administered. Procedures that are completed on the kidney are discussed in this chapter.

Procedure Codes	Description
55.0X	Nephrotomy and Nephrostomy—A nephrotomy is an incision of the kidney. It can be completed to remove a renal cyst, to explore the kidney, or to remove a calculus. When the calculus, commonly referred to as a kidney stone, is removed by an incision, this code is assigned. The coder must pay close attention to the medical documentation to determine whether the calculus was removed by incision or via a scope or tube because separate codes exist. The coder should be guided by use of the Alphabetic Index of procedures. A nephrostomy is the surgical insertion of a tube into the kidney to create an opening to the exterior of the body. Coders must identify by what approach the nephrostomy was completed. Codes 55.03 and 55.04 classify percutaneous nephrostomies. The fourth digits further identify whether the fragmentation of stones occurred, which is the breaking apart of the stones.
55.1X	Pyelotomy and Pyelostomy—An incision into the renal pelvis is referred to as a pyelotomy, and an insertion of a tube into the renal pelvis is referred to as a pyelostomy. These procedures are completed to explore the renal pelvis or to insert a drainage tube.
55.2X	Diagnostic Procedures on Kidney—This subcategory includes diagnostic procedures that are completed on the kidney. The use of optical instruments to examine the kidney, known as nephroscopy, and the renal pelvis, known as pyeloscopy, is classified to codes 55.21 and 55.22. Closed and open biopsies of the kidneys are also classified in this subcategory. It is important for the coder to read the exclusion note that appears for code 55.29, because it instructs the coder to code to other procedural chapters for some diagnostic procedures completed on the kidney.
55.3X	Local Excision or Destruction of Lesion or Tissue of Kidney—This subcategory classifies the excision or destruction of renal tissue or lesions located in renal tissue.
55.4	Partial Nephrectomy—The removal of a portion of the kidney is known as a partial nephrectomy. This is completed to obtain a tissue sample for pathological review, to remove cancers, to treat tissue that has been damaged due to injury, and to remove calculi that have damaged tissue. This procedure is completed at either the lower or upper pole of the kidney. Figure 35-1 illustrates a partial nephrectomy.

Procedure Codes	Description
55.5X	Complete Nephrectomy—This subcategory is used to classify excisions of one or more kidneys. Code 55.51 classifies a unilateral nephrectomy, a removal of one kidney (Figure 35-2). A bilateral nephrectomy, which is the complete removal of both kidneys, is classified to code 55.54.
55.6X	Transplant of Kidney—This subcategory is used to report the implantation of a donor kidney. This code is used on the record of the patient who is receiving the kidney. To report the source of the kidney, additional codes are reported using codes 00.91–00.93. Organs used for transplant are obtained from living relatives, nonrelated persons, and cadavers. Figure 35-3 illustrates the placement of the new kidney after a transplant.
55.7	Nephropexy—This procedure is the surgical fixation of a floating kidney.
55.8X	Other Repair of Kidney—This subcategory includes the suturing, closure, and reduction of renal structures.
55.9X	Other Operations on Kidney—Procedures classified to this subcategory include: • Capsulectomy of kidney—The surgical removal of the capsule of the kidney • Aspiration of kidney—The withdrawal of fluid • Replacement of nephrostomy and pyelostomy tubes • Implantation and removal of mechanical kidney

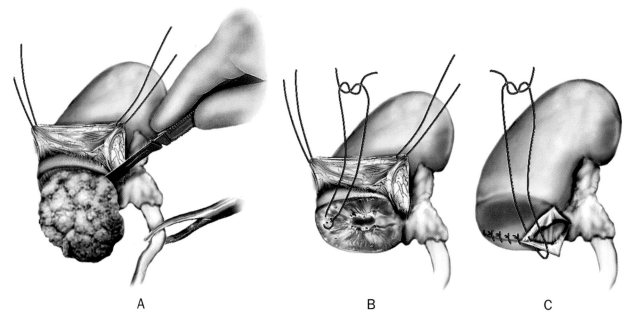

A   B   C

Figure 35-1 Partial nephrectomy: (**A**) Removal of diseased portion of kidney, (**B**) intrarenal vessels ligated, (**C**) defect closed with redundant renal capsule (From Price P, Frey KB, Junge TL. *Surgical Technology for the Surgical Technologist: A Positive Care Approach,* 2nd ed. Clifton Park, NY: Delmar, Cengage Learning, 2004, p. 758.)

Operations on the Ureter (Category Code 56)

The function of the two ureters is to carry urine from the kidneys to the urinary bladder. At times, the ureters become diseased or obstructed for a number of reasons, which can also impact the functioning of the kidneys. Therefore, procedures are completed to remove the obstruction or diseased tissue.

Procedure Codes	Description
56.0	Transurethral Removal of Obstruction from Ureter and Renal Pelvis—This code is used to classify the removal of a blood clot, calculi, or foreign body from the ureter or renal pelvis by inserting a tube through the urethra to the ureter. The coder should note that an incision is not completed.
56.1	Ureteral Meatotomy—This code is used to code an incision made into the ureteral meatus.

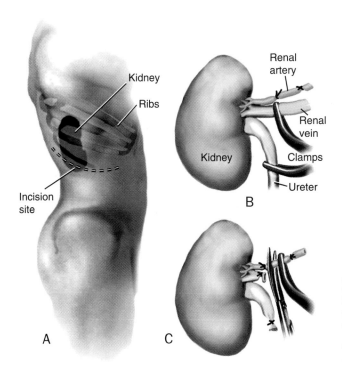

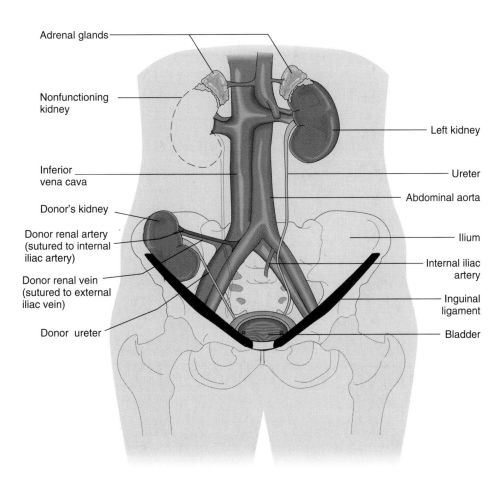

Figure 35-2 Simple nephrectomy: **(A)** Subcostal incision, **(B)** renal artery ligated first, **(C)** renal artery transected (From Price P, Frey KB, Junge TL. *Surgical Technology for the Surgical Technologist: A Positive Care Approach,* 2nd ed. Clifton Park, NY: Delmar, Cengage Learning, 2004, p. 758.)

Figure 35-3 In a renal transplant the new kidney is placed lower in the abdomen. (From Ehrlich A, Schroeder CL. *Medical Terminology for Health Professions,* 4th ed. Clifton Park, NY: Delmar, Cengage Learning, 2001, p. 195.)

Procedure Codes	Description
56.2	Ureterotomy—An incision of the ureter, known as a ureterotomy, is completed to remove calculi, to explore the ureter, or to allow for drainage of the ureter.
56.3X	Diagnostic Procedures on Ureter—Procedures included in this subcategory include both open and closed procedures that are completed for diagnostic purposes. Many diagnostic procedures are completed by use of scopes. Procedures include: • Cystourethroscopy • Uretral endoscopy • Ureteroscopy
56.4X	Ureterectomy—An excision of the ureter is known as an ureterectomy and is classified to this subcategory. Fourth digits are used to identify the extent of the ureterectomy as partial, total, or not otherwise specified. A notation appears for this subcategory that instructs the coder to code also the anastomosis other than end-to-end. An anastomosis is the surgical creation of a connection between two structures. At times, the ureter(s) are excised and connected to another structure of the body. The notation alerts the coder to use an additional code to code the anastomosis.
56.5X	Cutaneous Uretero-ileostomy—A cutaneous uretero-ileostomy is the surgical transplantation of the ureter(s) to the ileum with external diversion through the abdominal wall.
56.6X	Other External Urinary Diversion—This subcategory is used to classify the formation of a ureter diversion outside the body other than a cutaneous ureteroileostomy.
56.7X	Other Anastomosis or Bypass of Ureter—This code is used to classify all other anastomosis or bypass procedures completed on the ureter(s). Fourth digits are used to identify the type of diversion that was completed. Coders must read the operative report to determine the site to which the ureter(s) was diverted. For example, if an anastomosis of the ureter to the intestine occurred, code 56.71 is used, with an additional code assigned to code any colostomy. Coders should be guided by the index and inclusion notes when coding.
56.8X	Repair of the Ureter—Any repair or restoration of an ureteral defect is classified to this subcategory.
56.9X	Other Operations on Ureter—This subcategory includes the following procedures: dilation of the ureteral meatus, ligation of the ureter and implantation, and replacement and removal of electronic ureteral stimulators.

Operations on Urinary Bladder (Category Code 57)

The urinary bladder is responsible for storing urine before it is excreted from the body. If urinary bladder tissue is diseased or injured, the following procedures may be performed for diagnostic and therapeutic purposes. It should be noted that an additional code, 99.71, should be assigned if the application or administration of an adhesion barrier substance is used during a procedure that codes to category 57.

Procedure Codes	Description
57.0	Transurethral Clearance of Bladder—Drainage of the bladder can occur by the placement of an instrument through the urethra into the bladder. It is described as transurethral clearance of the bladder. This is completed to remove blood clots, calculi, and other foreign bodies from the bladder without an incision occurring.
57.1X	Cystotomy and Cystostomy—A cystotomy is an incision made into the bladder. A cystostomy is the surgical creation of an opening into the bladder, which is commonly completed for the insertion of a tube to remove urine. Figure 35-4 illustrates an open cystostomy with insertion of a cystostomy tube.
57.2X	Vesicostomy—Creation of an opening from the bladder to the skin is known as a vesicostomy.
57.3X	Diagnostic Procedures on the Bladder—A unique feature of this subcategory is that code 57.31 classifies the use of a scope for examination of the bladder that is performed through an artificial opening or stoma of the urinary tract. Therefore, when coding a cystoscopy, the coder must identify whether the scope was placed through an artificial stoma or through the urethra. When the scope is placed through the urethra, a transurethral cystoscopy occurs (Figure 35-5). Remember that when a scope is used as the approach, no code is assigned for the cystoscopic approach, because the transurethral approach is indicated in the title of the procedure and is therefore included in the code for the procedure.

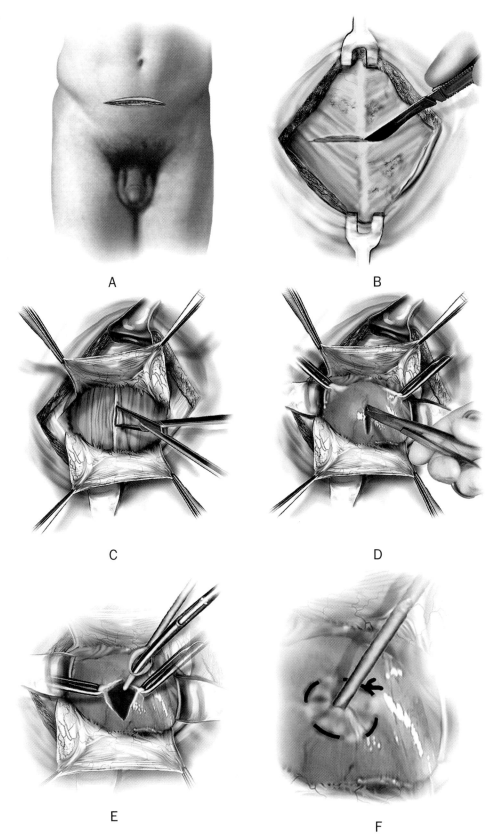

A

B

C

D

E

F

Figure 35-4 Open cystostomy: (**A**) Incision site, (**B**) fascia incised, (**C**) muscle split, (**D**) bladder incised, (**E**) cystostomy tube inserted, (**F**) cystostomy tube secured with pursestring suture (From Price P, Frey KB, Junge TL. *Surgical Technology for the Surgical Technologist: A Positive Care Approach,* 2nd ed. Clifton Park, NY: Delmar, Cengage Learning, 2004, p. 766.)

Procedure Codes	Description
57.4X	Transurethral Excision or Destruction of Bladder Tissue—This subcategory is used when an instrument is placed into the urethra to destroy or remove bladder tissue. No incision is made.
57.5X	Other Excision or Destruction of Bladder Tissue—In contrast to subcategory code 57.4X, subcategory code 57.5X is used for all excisions and destructions of bladder tissue that are completed other than by a transurethral approach.
57.6	Partial Cystectomy—A partial cystectomy is the removal of a portion of the urinary bladder.
57.7X	Total Cystectomy—A total cystectomy is the complete removal of the bladder. A coder must determine whether additional structures are removed. If additional structures are removed, this is referred to as a radical cystectomy. In a male the prostate, seminal vesicles, and fat may be additionally removed. In a female the urethra and fat may be additionally removed. It should be noted that an additional code should be assigned for lymph node dissection and urinary diversion when it occurs.
57.8X	Other Repair of the Urinary Bladder—This subcategory is used to classify other repairs of the urinary bladder, including suturing of the bladder, closure of a cystostomy, repairs of fistula of bladder, and other reconstruction procedures.
57.9X	Other Operations on Bladder—This subcategory includes sphincterotomy of the bladder, dilation of the bladder neck, and insertion, replacement, and implantation of electronic bladder stimulators.

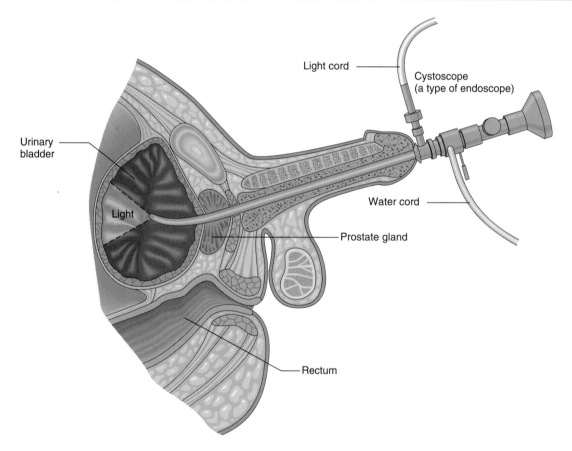

Figure 35-5 Use of a cystoscope to examine the interior of the bladder in a male (From Ehrlich A, Schroeder CL. *Medical Terminology for Health Professions,* 4th ed. Clifton Park, NY: Delmar, Cengage Learning 2001, p. 193.)

Operations on Urethra (Category Code 58)

The urethra is the tube from the bladder to the outside of the bladder. Operations on the urethra are classified to category code 58. At the start of the category, two notations appear. One notation informs the coder that operations on the bulbourethral gland, also known as Cowper's gland, and periurethral tissue are included in this category. The second notation instructs the coder to additionally code any application or administration of an adhesion barrier substance by using code 99.77. The operations that are classified to category code 58 include the procedures described here.

Procedure Codes	Description
58.0X	Urethrotomy—An incision made into the urethra is known as a urethrotomy. This is completed to remove an abnormal urethral membrane, to form an urethrovaginal or perineal fistula, or to remove calculi from the urethra by incision.
58.1	Urethral Meatotomy—An urethral meatotomy occurs when an incision of the external urethral opening is completed.
58.2X	Diagnostic Procedures on Urethra—Many diagnostic procedures use a urethroscope to view the urethra.
58.3X	Excision and Destruction of Lesion or Tissue of Urethra—This subcategory is used to classify the excision or destruction of urethral tissue.
58.4X	Repair of Urethra—This subcategory includes all repairs that are completed on the urethra to correct a urethral defect.
58.5	Release of Urethral Stricture —At times the urethra narrows due to injury or adhesions or a disease process. The urethral sphincter or the internal urinary meatus is incised to relieve the urethral narrowing.
58.6	Dilation of Urethra—This code is used when the urethra is stretched or dilated to increase the size of the urethra. No incision is made.
58.9X	Other Operations on Urethra and Periurethral Tissue—This subcategory includes incisions and excisions of the periurethral tissue and the implantation and removal of an artificial urinary sphincter.

Other Operations on the Urinary Tract (Category Code 59)

The last category code in this chapter of ICD-9-CM classifies other operations that are completed on the urinary tract.

Procedure Codes	Description
59.0X	Dissection of Retroperitoneal Tissue—Coders need to read the medical documentation to determine whether the dissection of the retroperitoneal tissue occurred with or without the use of the laparoscope, because fourth digits are used to distinguish the approach.
59.1X	Incision of Perivesical Tissue—This subcategory is used to classify incisions into the tissue adjacent to the bladder to destroy adhesive tissue or to explore the tissue.
59.2X	Diagnostic Procedures on Perirenal and Perivesical Tissue—This subcategory includes diagnostic procedures completed on the perirenal and perivesical areas and the retroperitoneum.
59.3	Plication of Urethrovesical Junction—The connective tissue between the vagina and the bladder can be sutured together to support the bladder and urethra. This code is used for this type of procedure and is often referred to by the following: Kelly-Kennedy operation on the urethra or Kelly-Stoeckell urethral plication.
59.4	Suprapubic Sling Operation—This code classifies restorative procedures that are competed to restore the bladder neck and urethral support by suturing to the suprapubic periosteum.
59.5	Retropubic Urethral Suspension—Procedures that are classified to this code also restore the bladder neck and urethral support, but the sutures are attached to the retropubic periosteum.
59.6	Paraurethral Suspension—This code also classifies a restoration procedure of the bladder neck and urethral support by using the musculofasical vaginal tissue ligature and attaching it to the pubis.
59.7X	Other Repair of Urinary Stress Incontinence—Fourth digits are used in the subcategory to describe the approach used to correct urinary stress incontinence. Treatment for incontinence depends on the cause of the incontinence.
59.8	Ureteral Catheterization—At times urine does not flow from the ureter(s), and a tube is inserted into the ureter to allow for the withdrawal of urine. This is known as ureteral catheterization. The coder should note that if an ureterotomy also occurs at the same time as the placement of the ureteral catheter, code 56.2 should also be assigned.
59.9X	Other Operations on Urinary System—This subcategory is used to classify excisions of perivesical tissue,and the replacement of ureterostomy and cystostomy tubes. Code 59.95 is used when urinary calculi are broken apart by ultrasonic sound waves; an additional code of 57.0 is also assigned when this procedure is completed.

Internet Links

To learn more about urinary problems and procedures completed to correct the urinary problem, visit *www.faqs.org/health/topics/32/Urinary-system.html*.

To learn how urinary procedures are completed, visit *http://www.emedicine.com*. Search on the name of procedure you want to research.

Pictures of various urinary scopes can be found at *http://www.medfix28.com*.

Summary

- Chapter 10 of volume 3 of ICD-9-CM classifies operations completed on the kidneys, ureters, urinary bladder, urethra, and other structures of the urinary tract.

- Coders should reference the start of categories to determine whether an inclusion note instructs the coder to assign code 99.77 as an additional code when an adhesion barrier substance is applied or administered.

- The medical suffix *-ostomy* is commonly included in this chapter, which means the surgical creation of an opening.

- The use of optical instruments to examine the organs of the urinary tract is common.

- ICD-9-CM provides separate codes for unilateral and bilateral nephrectomies.

- Two codes are used to report a kidney transplant: code 55.6X to indicate the transplant procedure and a code from 00.91–00.93 to report the source of the kidney.

- An anastomosis is the surgical creation of a connection between two structures.

- Partial and total cystectomies are given separate codes in ICD-9-CM volume 3.

Chapter Review

True/False: Indicate whether the statement is true (T) or false (F).

1. _____ A nephropexy is the surgical fixation of a floating kidney.

2. _____ Transurethral clearance of the bladder is completed only to remove blood clots.

3. _____ When a scope is placed through the ureter, the procedure is known as a transurethral cystoscopy.

4. _____ A partial cystectomy is the removal of a portion of the urinary bladder.

5. _____ An operative report states that the procedure completed is a urethral meatotomy. This is coded to code 58.1.

Fill-in-the-Blank: Enter the appropriate term(s) to complete the statement.

6. The creation of an opening from the bladder to the skin is known as a(n) _____.

7. The surgical creation of an opening into the bladder, also known as a(n) _____, is commonly completed for insertion of a tube to remove urine.

8. An optical instrument used to view the urethra is a(n) _____.

9. A(n) _____ occurs when a tube is inserted into the ureter to allow for the withdrawal of urine.

10. An incision made into the urethra is known as a(n) _____.

Coding Assignments

Instructions: Using an ICD-9-CM code book, select the code for each procedural statement.

Procedure	Code
1. Total unilateral nephrectomy with excision of bladder segment	_____
2. Percutaneous aspiration of bladder	_____
3. Transurethral biopsy of ureter	_____
4. Renipuncture for fluid removal	_____
5. Endoscopic destruction of urethral lesion	_____
6. V-Y plasty of bladder neck	_____
7. Implantation of inflatable bladder sphincter	_____
8. Ureteral meatotomy	_____
9. Biopsy of kidney, open procedure	_____
10. Nephrolithotomy	_____
11. Fluoroscopic guidance for percutaneous nephrostomy with fragmentation	_____
12. Wedge resection of kidney	_____
13. Ureterocalyceal anastomosis	_____
14. Placement of electronic ureteral stimulator	_____
15. Bladder incision for lysis of intraluminal adhesions	_____
16. Excision of bladder dome	_____
17. Closure of vesicostomy	_____
18. Repair of laceration of bladder due to old obstetric laceration	_____
19. Incision into urethra for removal of calculi	_____
20. Suprapubic cystostomy, percutaneous	_____
21. Nephrostomy	_____
22. Percutaneous ablation of renal lesion	_____
23. Retropubic urethral suspension	_____
24. Excision of periurethral tissue	_____
25. Closure of ureterostomy	_____

Case Studies

Instructions: Review each case study, and select the correct ICD-9-CM diagnostic and procedural codes.

CASE 1

PREOPERATIVE DIAGNOSIS: Chronic kidney obstruction

POSTOPERATIVE DIAGNOSIS: Chronic kidney obstruction

PROCEDURE: Nephrectomy

ANESTHESIA: General

This 73-year-old male patient was prepped and draped in the usual fashion. A Foley catheter was inserted; the patient was placed in the lateral position with his right side up. A #10 blade was used to make a subcostal flank incision 2 cm below the 12th rib. The soft tissue was retracted using Parker retractors. The latissimus dorsi, external oblique, and internal oblique muscles were transected using electrocautery. The subcostal neurovascular bundle was located and retracted. The lumbodorsal and Gerota's fascia were opened. By blunt dissection the renal pedicle was exposed both anteriorly and posteriorly, and the perinephritic fat and the adrenal gland were dissected. By using Mayo clamps, the ureter was doubly clamped, transected, and ligated. The right kidney was then superiorly retracted, and the renal artery and vein were located. The renal artery was clamped, and then the vein was clamped. The vessels were secured with sutures and transected, and the kidney was removed. After hemostasis was achieved, a drain was placed and the Gerota's fascia was closed. The skin was closed in layers with interrupted figure-eight stitches. The skin was stapled. The patient tolerated the procedure well and was sent to the recovery room.

ICD-9-CM Code Assignment: _____

CASE 2

PREOPERATIVE DIAGNOSIS: Stricture of left ureter

POSTOPERATIVE DIAGNOSIS: Same

PROCEDURE: Removal and insertion of nephrostomy tube

This 75-year-old female patient had a nephrostomy tube placed 2 months ago. Today she is having the tube replaced. She was prepped and draped in the usual fashion and given general anesthesia. Once the patient was adequately positioned, the tube was removed and a new tube was placed at the same site. The area was noted to be free of infection or any foreign bodies. The patient tolerated the procedure well and was sent to the recovery room.

ICD-9-CM Code Assignment: _____

CASE 3

This is a 62-year-old male who presents today for right hydronephrosis. He has been having trouble for the past few months, with other conservative measures being explored without success.

The patient was prepped and draped, and anesthesia was administered. The administration of 50 cc of Isovue-300 renal opacification was introduced into the right side under fluoroscopic guidance. Using an 8 French catheter with an 8 French nephrostomy tube, the tract was dilated. The left nephrostomy tube catheter was then advanced into the renal pelvis along the inferior margin of the lower pole calix. The contrast was injected. and excellent opacification of the right pyelocaliceal system could be visualized. No extravasation noted. Patient tolerated the procedure well.

ICD-9-CM Code Assignment: _____

CASE 4

This is a 72-year-old female who presents today for anterior urethropexy due to urinary incontinence. This has been a problem for this patient for several years. The risks and benefits of the surgery were explained and the patient agreed to the procedure.

This patient was brought to the operating room and prepped and draped in the usual sterile fashion. A midline incision was made from the symphysis pubis to the umbilicus. The incision was carried down through the rectus fascia where these muscles were split midline, and a Turner-Warwick retractor was used to hold the muscles in place while the clitoral vein complex was isolated. At this point the endopelvic fascia overlying the urethra was exposed. Sutures were placed through this layer to anchor the periosteum of the symphysis pubis. The sutures extended for the length of the urethra slightly beyond the bladder neck to the anterior bladder wall. A Foley catheter was placed and tested.

ICD-9-CM Code Assignment: _____

CASE 5

This is a 10-month-old male who has had problems voiding since birth. It was thought at first that this child had a congenital defect with the bladder. Further testing found that there was a congenital defect with the left ureter. The bladder is fine and functioning normally, as is the right ureter. The child is now going to undergo a ureteroureterostomy. The risks and benefits of this procedure were explained to the parents, and they agree that this is the best course of action.

The patient is prepped and draped in the usual sterile fashion. A curved incision is made on the left side of the abdomen through the skin and fascia directly above the ureter. The defect is found to be in the upper third of the ureter, which is dissected away. The anastomosis of the remaining segments is performed. A drainage tube is inserted to help with healing, but it should be able to be removed within a few days. A layered closure is performed. The patient tolerated the procedure well and was returned to the recovery room in good, stable condition.

ICD-9-CM Code Assignment: _____

36 Operations on the Male Genital Organs

Chapter Outline

Objectives

At the conclusion of this chapter, the student will be able to:

1. Identify pathologies and injuries of the male genital organs.
2. Describe the procedures used to correct the pathologies of the male genital organs.
3. Accurately code procedures completed on the male genital organs.
4. Select and code diagnoses and procedures from case studies.

Key Terms

Bilateral Orchiectomy

Circumcision

Epididymectomy

Epididymis

Foreskin

Glans Penis

Hydrocele

Orchectomy

Orchiectomy

Orchiopexy

Penis

Percutaneous Aspiration
of Seminal Vesicles

Perineal Prostratectomy

Prepuce

Radical Orchiectomy

Radical Prostatectomy

Retropubic
Prostatectomy

Scrotal Sac

Scrotum

Spermatocele

Spermatocelectomy

Suprapubic
Prostatectomy

Testectomy

Testes

Testicles

Transurethral Microwave
Thermotherapy of
Prostate

Transurethral Needle
Ablation of Prostate
(TUNA)

Transurethral
Prostatectomy

Transurethral Resection
of the Prostate (TURP)

Unilateral Orchiectomy

Reminder

As you work through this chapter, you will need to have a copy of the ICD-9-CM coding book to reference.

Introduction

Operations on the male genital organs, codes 60–64, are classified in chapter 11 of volume 3 of ICD-9-CM. The male genital organs include the prostate and seminal vesicles, scrotum, testes, spermatic cord, epididymis and vas deferens, and penis.

Coding Operations on the Male Genital Organs

Categories found in chapter 11, "Operations on the Male Genital Organs," include:

60	Operations on prostate and seminal vesicles
61	Operations on scrotum and tunica vaginalis
62	Operations on testes
63	Operations on spermatic cord, epididymis, and vas deferens
64	Operations on penis

The anatomical position of the structures of the male genital organs can be reviewed by referencing Figure 15-2 of this book.

Operations on the Prostate and Seminal Vesicles (Category Code 60)

The function of the prostate is to secrete a fluid that is part of the semen and that aids in the motility of sperm. The prostate is located under the bladder and surrounds the upper end of the urethra.

The coder should read the inclusion note at the start of the category stating that operations on the periprostatic tissue are included in category 66. The inclusion note also instructs the coder to assign code 99.77 as an additional code when an adhesion barrier substance is applied or administered. Procedures that are completed on the prostate and seminal vesicles are summarized in this chapter.

Procedure Codes	Description
60.0	Incision of Prostate—This procedure includes cutting into the prostate to drain an abscess or to remove a prostatic calculus.
60.1X	Diagnostic Procedures on Prostate and Seminal Vesicles—Open and closed biopsies and other diagnostic procedures are classified to this subcategory. Fourth digits are used to identify the site of the diagnostic procedures. For example, fourth digits 1 and 2 identify the prostate gland, and fourth digits 3 and 4 identify the seminal vesicles. Exclusion notations appear for fourth digits 8 and 9. These notations instruct the coder that X-rays and microscopic examinations of specimens from the prostate and seminal vesicles are classified to other categories in ICD-9-CM.
60.2X	Transurethral Prostatectomy—A transurethral prostatectomy is completed by inserting a scope into the urethra to resect prostatic tissue. This is also known as a transurethral resection of the prostate (TURP). Figure 36-1 illustrates this procedure.
60.3	Suprapubic prostatectomy—This type of prostatectomy is completed to remove tissue or adenomas that are too large to be removed via a scope. An abdominal suprapubic incision is made to remove the prostate. Figure 36-2 illustrates the procedure.
60.4	Retropubic Prostatectomy—A retropubic prostatectomy is completed by making an abdominal direct incision into the prostatic capsule. This approach is used to provide better visualization of the prostatic fossa.
60.5	Radical Prostatectomy—A radical prostatectomy is the surgical removal of the seminal vesicles, the entire prostate gland, and surrounding tissue.

Procedure Codes	Description
60.6X	Other Prostatectomy—This subcategory includes other prostatectomies and includes a perineal prostratectomy, which is completed by making an perineal incision. This approach is rarely used because it can present a serious risk of injury to the rectum.
60.7X	Operations on Seminal Vesicles—Operations classified to this category include: • Percutaneous aspiration of seminal vesicles—The removal of fluid by insertion of an instrument through the body wall • Incision of seminal vesicles • Excision of seminal vesicles—The removal of a seminal vesicle
60.8X	Incision or Excision of Periprostatic Tissue—The periprostatic tissue is the tissue that lies around the prostate gland. At times this area is drained to remove abscess material or excised to remove damaged tissue.
60.9X	Other Operations on the Prostate—This subcategory includes: • Percutaneous aspiration of the prostate • Control of (Postoperative) hemorrhage of prostate—This procedure is completed to control bleeding from the prostate. It is completed by coagulation of the prostatic bed or by use of cystoscope. • Transurethral microwave thermotherapy of prostate—This procedure is completed to destroy prostatic tissue by the use of microwave energy to heat the tissue. • Transurethral needle ablation of prostate (TUNA)—This procedure is completed to destroy prostatic tissue by using radiofrequency energy to heat the tissue.

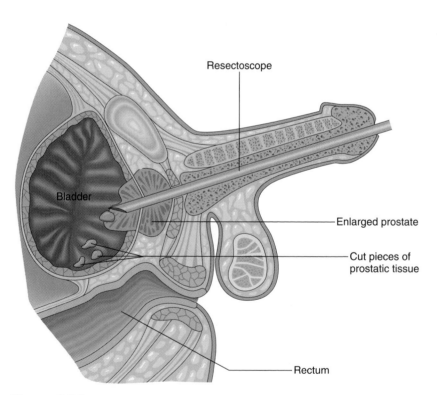

Figure 36-1 Transurethral resection of the prostate (From Ehrlich A, Schroeder CL. *Medical Terminology for Health Professions*, 4th ed. Clifton Park, NY: Delmar, Cengage Learning, 2001, p. 299.)

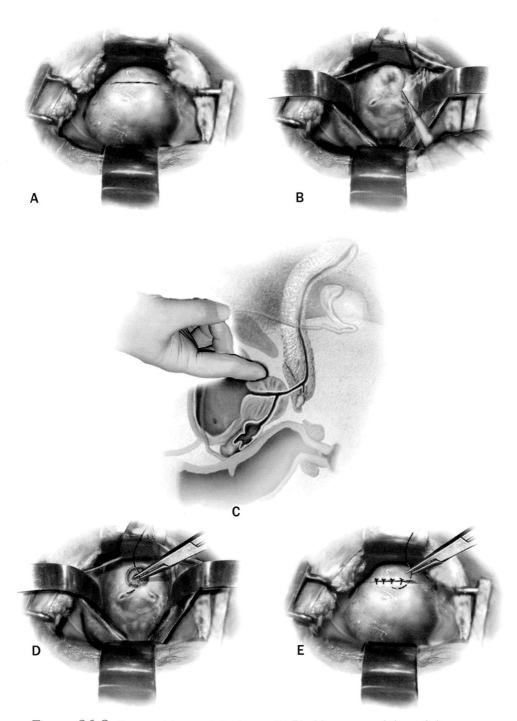

Figure 36-2 Suprapubic prostatectomy: **(A)** Bladder exposed through low transverse incision, **(B)** bladder entered, **(C)** blunt dissection of prostate, **(D)** prostate fossa sutured to bladder mucosa, **(E)** bladder closure (From Caruthers B, Price P, Junge TL, et al. *Surgical Technology for the Surgical Technologist: A Positive Care Approach*. Clifton Park, NY: Delmar, Cengage Learning, 2001, p. 466.)

Operations on Scrotum and Tunica Vaginalis (Category Code 61)

The **scrotum** encloses, protects, and supports the testicles. This area is also known as the **scrotal sac**. Figure 36-3 illustrates the structures within the scrotal sac. Category 61 includes these procedures.

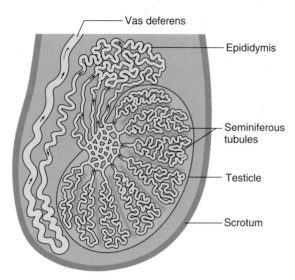

Figure 36-3 Cross-section of scrotum (From Ehrlich A, Schroeder CL. *Medical Terminology for Health Professions,* 4th ed. Clifton Park, NY: Delmar, Cengage Learning, 2001, p. 296.)

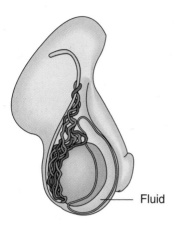

Figure 36-4 Hydrocele (From Sormunen C. *Terminology for Allied Health Professions,* 5th ed. Clifton Park, NY: Delmar, Cengage Learning, 2003, p. 529.)

Procedure Codes	Description
61.0	Incision and Drainage of Scrotum and Tunica Vaginalsis—This procedure is done to remove fluid from the scrotum and is completed by making an incision. Coders must identify that an incision has been made, because removal of fluid from this area can also occur without making an incision by using a percutaneous approach.
61.1X	Diagnostic Procedures on Scrotum and Tunica Vaginalis—This subcategory includes biopsies and other diagnostic procedures.
61.2	Excision of Hydrocele—A **hydrocele** is an accumulation of fluid in the scrotum surrounding the testes. This procedure is completed to remove the hydrocele. Figure 36-4 illustrates a hydrocele.
61.3	Excision or Destruction of Lesion or Tissue of Scrotum—This subcategory is used to classify procedures that are completed to remove or destroy scrotal tissue. Procedures that are classified to this code include: • Fulguration of lesion • Partial scrotectomy • Reduction of elephantiasis
61.4X	Repair of Scrotum and Tunica Vaginalis—Suturing of the scrotum, a repair of a scrotal fistula, and reconstruction of a scrotal or tunica vaginalis defect are classified to this code.
61.9X	Other Operations on Scrotum and Tunica Vaginalis—As discussed earlier, fluid can be removed by incision into the scrotal sac or by a nonincisional approach. Code 61.91 is used to code a percutaneous aspiration of fluid.

Operations on Testes (Category Code 62)

The **testes,** also known as the **testicles,** are located in the scrotal sac and are two glands that produce the sperm. Procedures in this category include the procedures discussed in this section.

Procedure Codes	Description
62.0	Incision of Testis—The surgical cutting into the testis.
62.1X	Diagnostic Procedures on Testes—Open and closed biopsies are classified to this subcategory.
62.2	Excision or Destruction of Testicular Lesion—This category includes both the surgical removal of testicular tissue and the forced death of testicular tissue.

62.3	Unilateral Orchiectomy—A unilateral orchiectomy is the surgical removal of one of the testes. An orchiectomy is also known as an orchidectomy, orchectomy, or testectomy. At times this procedure is completed with an epididymectomy, which is the surgical removal of the epididymis. The epididymis is a tubular structure that is found at the upper end of each testicle. Code 62.3 includes both a unilateral orichiectomy and an epididymectomy when completed at the same operative session. If an epididymectomy is performed without an orchiectomy, code 63.4 is assigned. Figure 36-5 illustrates a unilateral orchiectomy.
62.4X	Bilateral Orchiectomy—A bilateral orchiectomy is the surgical removal of both of the testicles. A radical orchiectomy is the surgical removal of both testicles and two epididymides. Fourth digits exist for this subcategory that identify the following: 62.41—Removal of both testes at the same operative episode. 62.42—Removal of remaining testis—This code is used when a patient has already had one testis removed and is currently having the second testis removed. If lymph node dissection also occurs during the same operative episode, code 40.3 or 40.5 is also assigned.
62.5	Orchiopexy—An orchiopexy is the surgical fixation of the testis in the scrotal sac. This procedure is completed when a testicle fails to descend or is retracted or to treat testicular torsion. Figure 36-6 illustrates an orchiopexy.
62.6X	Repair of Testes—This subcategory classifies the suturing of a laceration of the testis and other repairs of the testis. However, this code does not classify a reduction of a torsion of testes. An exclusion note appears that instructs the coder to assign code 63.52 for a reduction of a testicular torsion.
62.7	Insertion of Testicular Prosthesis—This code classifies the implantation of an artificial testicle.
62.9X	Other Operations on the Testes—This subcategory is used to classify: • The withdrawal of fluid from the testes, known as aspiration of testis • The injection of therapeutic substances into the testis

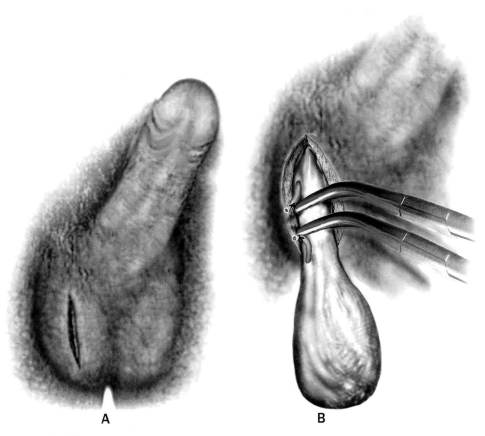

A   **B**

Figure 36-5 Unilateral orchiectomy: **(A)** Scrotal incision, **(B)** removal of testicle (From Caruthers B, Price P, Junge TL, et al. *Surgical Technology for the Surgical Technologist: A Positive Care Approach*. Clifton Park, NY: Delmar, Cengage Learning, 2001, p. 658.)

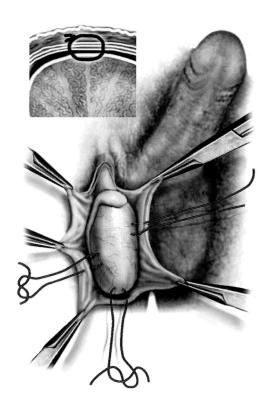

Figure 36-6 Orchiopexy (From Caruthers B, Price P, Junge TL, et al. *Surgical Technology for the Surgical Technologist: A Positive Care Approach.* Clifton Park, NY: Delmar, Cengage Learning, 2001, p. 658.)

Operations on Spermatic Cord, Epididymis, and Vas Deferens (Category Code 63)

Category code 63 classifies operations on the spermatic cord, epididymis, and the vas deferens. All of these structures are responsible for the transportation of sperm.

Procedure Codes	Description
63.0X	Diagnostic Procedures on Spermatic Cord, Epididymis, and Vas Deferens—This subcategory includes biopsies and other diagnostic procedures.
63.1	Excision of Varicocele and Hydrocele of Spermatic Cord—A spermatic cord varicocele is an enlarged dilated vein, and a spermatic cord hydrocele is the accumulation of fluid in the spermatic cord. An excision is completed to correct the defect. Figure 36-7 illustrates a varicocele.
63.2	Excision of Cyst of Epididymis —This category classifies both the surgical removal of a cyst of the epididymis and a spermatocelectomy. A spermatocele is a cyst of the epididymis that contains sperm.
63.4	Epididymectomy—This code is used when an epididymectomy is the only procedure performed. An exclusion note appears to guide the coder.
63.5X	Repair of Spermatic Cord and Epididymis—This subcategory classifies procedures that correct a spermatic cord or epididymal defect. It should be noted that code 63.52, Reduction of torsion of testis or spermatic cord, is used when this procedure is the only procedure performed. If the reduction occurs with an orchiopexy, code 62.5 is assigned. The coder should be guided by the notations in the code book.
63.6	Vasotomy—This procedure is performed to create an opening of a vas deferens or to simply make an incision into the vas deferens.
63.7X	Vasectomy and Ligation of Vas Deferens—This category is used to classify procedures that tie off the spermatic cord, or vas deferens. An excision of the vas deferens, known as a vasectomy, is also classified to this subcategory. Figure 36-8 illustrates a vasectomy.

63.8X	Repair of Vas Deferens and Epididymis—This subcategory classifies procedures that are completed to restore defects of the vas deferens or epididymis. These defects can be due to injury or can have been from procedures completed for sterilization.
63.9X	Other Operations on Spermatic Cord, Epididymis, and Vas Deferens—This subcategory includes the aspiration of a spermatocele, incisions of the spermatic cord, lysis of adhesions of the spermatatic cord, and insertion of a valve in the vas deferens.

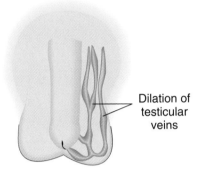

Figure 36-7 Varicocele (From Sormunen C. *Terminology for Allied Health Professions,* 5th ed. Clifton Park, NY: Delmar, Cengage Learning, 2003, p. 459.)

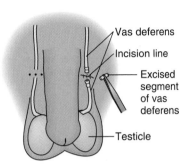

Figure 36-8 Vasectomy (From Ehrlich A, Schroeder CL. *Medical Terminology for Health Professions,* 4th ed. Clifton Park, NY: Delmar, Cengage Learning, 2001, p. 299.)

Operations on Penis (Category Code 64)

The last category code in this chapter of ICD-9-CM classifies operations on the penis. The penis is the male sex organ that is made up of the glans penis, the soft tip of the penis, and the prepuce or foreskin, which covers and protects the glans penis.

Procedure Codes	Description
64.0	Circumcision—At birth, the end of the penis is covered with a fold of skin known as the foreskin. An elective procedure known as circumcision is completed to remove the foreskin. Figure 36-9 illustrates a circumcision.
64.1X	Diagnostic Procedures on the Penis—Biopsies and other diagnostic procedures completed on the penis are classified to this subcategory.
64.2	Local Excision of Destruction of Lesion of Penis—This subcategory classifies excisions and destruction of lesions on the penis.
64.4X	Repair and Plastic Operation on Penis—The correction of defects of the penis are classified to this subcategory. The coder needs to read the operative note to ensure the correct assignment of codes, because codes in this subcategory identify the use of transplanted tissue and the cause of the defect.
64.5	Operations for Sex Transformation, Not Elsewhere Classified—This code is used to code operations for a sex change.
64.9X	Other Operations on Male Genital Organs—This subcategory includes: • Incision of penis • Fitting of external prosthesis of penis • Insertion and removal of penile prosthesis When using these codes, the coder must identify the type of prosthesis used and whether the procedure includes only the insertion or the removal of a previous prosthesis and the insertion of a new prosthesis.

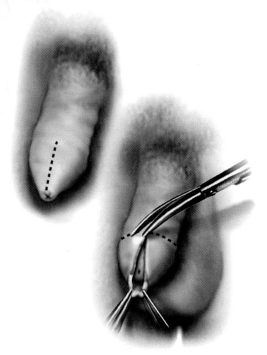

Figure 36-9 Circumcision (From Ehrlich A, Schroeder CL. *Medical Terminology for Health Professions,* 4th ed. Clifton Park, NY: Delmar, Cengage Learning, 2001, p. 655.)

Internet Links

Using the search field on the following Web sites, search by the name of the procedure you wish to research: *www.aafp.org, www.healthsquare.com,* and *www.uhseast.com.*

Summary

- Operations on the male genital organs are classified in chapter 11 of volume 3 of ICD-9-CM.
- A transurethral procedure is completed by inserting a scope into the urethra.
- A transurethral resection of the prostate is commonly abbreviated as TURP.
- ICD-9-CM assigns different codes for the various approaches used to complete a prostatectomy.
- A percutaneous aspiration of fluid is completed by insertion of an instrument through the body wall.
- A transurethral needle ablation of prostate is commonly abbreviated as TUNA.
- Unilateral and bilateral orchiectomies are classified to different codes in ICD-9-CM.
- A circumcision is completed to remove the foreskin and is an elective procedure.

Chapter Review

True/False: Indicate whether the statement is true (T) or false (F).

1. _____ An enlarged dilated spermatic vein is known as a hydrocele.

2. _____ A prostatectomy is the surgical removal of the seminal vesicles, the entire prostate gland, and surrounding tissue.

3. _____ A bilateral orchiectomy is the surgical removal of both testicles.

4. _____ A spermatocelectomy is classified to code 63.2.

5. _____ At birth, the end of the penis is covered with a fold of skin known as the foreskin.

Fill-in-the-Blank: Enter the appropriate term(s) to complete the statement.

6. An _____ is the surgical fixation of the testis in the scrotal sac.

7. The injection of therapeutic substances into the testis is classified to code _____.

8. The _____ is the tissue that lies around the prostate gland.

9. An orchiectomy is also known as a _____, orchectomy, or _____.

10. A _____ is the surgical removal of both testicles and two epididymides.

Coding Assignments

Instructions: Using an ICD-9-CM code book, select the code for each procedural statement.

Procedure	Code
1. Division of vas deferens	_____
2. Aspiration of fluid from testis	_____
3. Excision of hematocele of tunica vaginalis	_____
4. Destruction of prostate tissue by transurethral microwave thermotherapy	_____
5. Transurethral electrovaporization of prostate	_____
6. Cryosurgery of prostate	_____
7. Periprostatic tissue biopsy	_____
8. Needle biopsy of prostate	_____
9. Excision of Mullerian duct cyst	_____
10. Orchiopexy with reduction of testicular torsion	_____
11. Fulguration of lesion of scrotum	_____
12. Spermatocelectomy	_____
13. Destruction of lesion on penis	_____
14. Placement of valve in vas deferens	_____
15. Replacement of semirigid rod prosthesis into penis shaft	_____
16. External penis prosthesis	_____
17. Cystoscopy to control prostatic hemorrhage	_____
18. Scrotal fistula repair	_____
19. Suprapubic prostatectomy	_____
20. Incisional biopsy of seminal vesicles	_____
21. Percutaneous aspiration of prostate	_____

22. Radical prostatectomy _____

23. Reconstruction of penis _____

24. Hydrocelectomy of canal of Nuck _____

25. Removal of internal prosthesis of penis _____

Case Studies

Instructions: Review each case study, and select the correct ICD-9-CM diagnostic and procedural codes.

CASE 1

Operative Report

PREOPERATIVE DIAGNOSIS: Hydrocele

POSTOPERATIVE DIAGNOSIS: Hydrocele

ANESTHESIA: General

Under general anesthesia this 36-year-old male was prepped and draped in the usual fashion. After placing the patient in the lithotomy position, a 3.5-cm incision was made in the left scrotum, and a hydrocele was visualized. Hemostasis was achieved. The hydrocele was located in the tunica vaginalis and was dissected and brought through the incision site. The hydrocele was surgically excised, and a drain was placed. The wound was closed in layers by using 3-0 chromic sutures. The patient was sent to the recovery room in stable condition and tolerated the procedure well.

ICD-9-CM Code Assignment: _____

CASE 2

PREOPERATIVE DIAGNOSIS: Routine circumcision

POSTOPERATIVE DIAGNOSIS: Circumcision, uncomplicated

This 24-hour-old male infant was placed in the supine position and prepped and draped in the usual fashion. To provide hemostasis, a hemostat was applied to the posterior midline of the prepuce. A dorsal slit was created by using a #15 knife blade. Scissors were used to make a freehand cut around the shaft, and the skin was dissected away from the subcutaneous tissue. Hemostasis was obtained by electrocoagulation. The raw edges of the foreskin were pulled together and sutured. The glans and frenulum were exposed. A dressing was applied to the distal penis, and the patient was diapered. The patient tolerated the procedure well and was sent to the recovery area.

ICD-9-CM Code Assignment: _____

CASE 3

PREOPERATIVE DIAGNOSIS: Testicular torsion

POSTOPERATIVE DIAGNOSIS: Testicular torsion

ANESTHESIA: General

The patient was placed in the supine position under general anesthesia and prepped and draped. The external genitalia and surrounding area were prepped. Tension was applied to the scotum, and a #15 blade was used to make an incision. An incision was made through the skin and dartos muscle, and hemostasis was achieved by electrocautery pencil. The tunica vaginalis was opened, and the contents of the hemiscrotum were visualized. The left testicle was then properly positioned in the scrotal sac. The tunica albuginea was sutured to the dartos muscle, and the wound was closed in layers with interrupted sutures. The procedure was then completed on the right side. The patient's estimated blood loss was negligible, and he tolerated the procedure well. He was sent to the recovery room in stable condition.

ICD-9-CM Code Assignment: _____

CASE 4

This is a 35-year-old male who presents today for a vasectomy. He is a good candidate for surgery because he is in good health and has a full understanding of the risks and benefits of the procedure. His wife is here with him to accompany him home after the procedure and she is very supportive.

The patient was brought to the procedure room, at which time he was given Versed and local anesthetic was applied. A segment of the spermatic cord was pulled taught, which allowed the cord to be cut. This procedure was performed bilaterally. The patient tolerated the procedure well and was able to leave the procedure room in good condition.

ICD-9-CM Code Assignment: _____

CASE 5

This is a 47-year-old male who presents today for removal of penial lesion. This gentleman presented last week with complaint of a painful lesion, measuring approximately 0.75 cm located on the lateral portion of the shaft of the penis. He said this lesion appears to be changing in size and color, and he would like it removed. At this time, we do not know if it is benign or malignant. After excision, we will send for pathology.

The patient was prepped and draped in the usual sterile fashion. The lateral side of the penis was exposed, showing a 0.75-cm lesion. The lesion was removed in its entirety by excising with a #10 blade. The wound was repaired, and the patient left the operating suite in good condition. Lesion was sent for pathology.

ICD-9-CM Code Assignment: _____

Operations on the Female Genital Organs

Chapter Outline

Objectives

At the conclusion of this chapter, the student will be able to:

1. Identify pathologies that affect the female genital organs.
2. Describe some of the procedures used to correct the pathologies.
3. Discuss procedures that are completed on the structures of the female genital organs.
4. Select and code diagnoses and procedures from case studies.

Key Terms

Artificial Insemination	D&C	Oophorotomy	Rubin's Test
Bartholin's Glands	Dilation and Curettage	Ovaries	Salpingo-
Cervical Os	Fallopian Tubes	Ovario-	Salpingo-Oophorotomy
Cervix	Hysterectomy	Paracervical Uterine	Unilateral Oophorectomy
Clitoris	Hystero-	Denervation	Utero-
Colpo-	Insufflation	Pelvic Evisceration	Uterus
Conization	Metrio-	Perineum	Vagina
Curette	Metro-	Plication of Uterine	Vagino-
Cystocele	Oophoro-	Ligaments	Vulva
		Rectocele	

> **Reminder**
>
> *As you work through this chapter, you will need to have a copy of the ICD-9-CM coding book to reference.*

Introduction

Chapter 12 of the ICD-9-CM coding book encompasses procedures, open and laparoscopic, performed on the female genital organs. The female genital organs are made up of reproductive organs such as the ovaries, uterus, and fallopian tubes. Other structures of the female genitalia are the labia, clitoris, Bartholin's glands, and perineum.

Coding Operations on the Female Genital Organs

Category 65, Operations on ovary, begins the procedure codes for this chapter. Common prefixes that relate to the ovary are oophoro- and ovario-. The ovaries produce female hormones and eggs (ova). The eggs travel down the fallopian tubes to be fertilized or expelled in the uterus. The prefix that denotes the fallopian tubes is salpingo-. This category not only codes operations on the ovaries but also includes procedures that combine the ovaries and fallopian tubes.

Many of the procedures in this chapter can be done as either an open procedure or a laparoscopic procedure. Figure 37-1 illustrates a basic laparoscopic procedure.

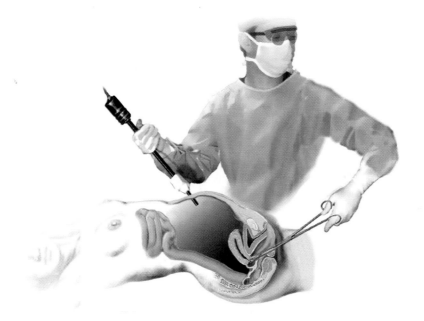

Figure 37-1 Laparoscopy with use of uterine manipulator and camera (From Caruthers B, Price P, Junge TL, et al. *Surgical Technology for the Surgical Technologist: A Positive Care Approach.* Clifton Park, NY: Delmar, Cengage Learning, 2001, p. 517.)

Procedure Codes	Description
65.0X	Oophorotomy—An oophorotomy is a surgical cut into the ovary. This subcategory includes the surgical cutting into the ovary and fallopian tubes, which is also referred to as a salpingo-oophorotomy. A laparoscopic approach is also coded from this subcategory.
65.1X	Diagnostic Procedures on Ovaries—This subcategory contains procedure codes for open and laparoscopic biopsies.
65.2X	Local Excision or Destruction of Ovarian Lesion or Tissue—This subcategory of codes contains procedures that are done as open procedures or with a laparoscope. There is a code for the wedge resection of the ovary, but this code is used only if an open procedure is done. This code should not be used if the procedure is performed laparoscopically.

Procedure Codes	Description
65.3X	**Unilateral Oophorectomy**—This procedure is the surgical removal of one of the ovaries. There are codes in this subcategory for open and laparoscopic procedures.
65.4X	Unilateral Salpingo-Oophorectomy—This procedure is the surgical removal of one of the ovaries and its fallopian tube. There are codes in this subcategory for open and laparoscopic procedures.
65.5X	Bilateral Oophorectomy—This procedure is the surgical removal of both of the ovaries. There are codes in this subcategory for open and laparoscopic procedures.
65.6X	Bilateral Salpingo-Oophorectomy—This procedure is the surgical removal of both of the ovaries and both fallopian tubes. There are codes in this subcategory for open and laparoscopic procedures.
65.7X	Repair of Ovary—These procedure codes involve the repair of the ovaries.
65.8X	Lysis of Adhesions of Ovary and Fallopian Tube—Adhesions on the ovaries or fallopian tubes that are surgically removed or destroyed are coded with this subcategory.
65.9X	Other Operations on Ovary—This subcategory includes aspiration of fluid on the ovary, transplantation of an ovary, and manual rupture of an ovarian cyst by the surgeon.

Operations on Fallopian Tubes (Category Code 66)

Category 66, Operations on fallopian tubes, contains procedure codes for operations done on the fallopian tubes only.

Procedure Codes	Description
66.0X	Salpingotomy and Salpingostomy—This is the surgical cutting into the fallopian tube.
66.1X	Diagnostic Procedures on Fallopian Tubes—Biopsies are coded to this subcategory.
66.2X	Bilateral Endoscopic Destruction or Occlusion of Fallopian Tubes—The bilateral procedure is performed on both fallopian tubes. Since the procedure states "bilateral," it is billed only once. The operations coded to this subcategory include destruction of obstruction, crushing and ligation of the tubes, and ligation and division of the tubes. The inclusion note in this subcategory gives the endoscopic approaches that are included in this subcategory.
66.3X	Other Bilateral Destruction or Occlusion of Fallopian Tubes—They are the same procedures as described in subcategory 66.2X, but these codes are used when the procedure is not done endoscopically.
66.4	Total Unilateral Salpingectomy—This is the surgical removal of one fallopian tube.
66.5X	Total Bilateral Salpingectomy—This subcategory contains codes for procedures in which both fallopian tubes are removed. If a fallopian tube was removed in a previous operative session and the second tube is now being removed in a separate session, the second surgery is coded from this subcategory.
66.6X	Other Salpingectomy—These procedures include cauterization of the fallopian tube, coagulation of tissue of the fallopian tube, electrocoagulation, and excision. This category also contains the procedure code for the removal of part of the fallopian tube to remove a tubal pregnancy.
66.7X	Repair of Fallopian Tubes—These procedures include grafting, reopening a divided tube, and repair of a defect of a fallopian tube. The repair procedure may also include an anastomosis of segments of the fallopian tube to other structures or even to another part of the same fallopian tube.
66.8	Insufflation of Fallopian Tube—To test the viability of the fallopian tube, gas or a liquid (such as saline) may be introduced under pressure. This test is called **insufflation** of the fallopian tube. The tube may be insufflated with air, gas, saline, or a dye. There is also an insufflation procedure called the **Rubin's test,** which introduces carbon dioxide into the fallopian tube and the uterus.
66.9X	Other Operations on Fallopian Tubes—These operations include the aspiration of the fallopian tube; the implantation, removal, or replacement of prosthesis; and the dilation of the fallopian tube.

Operations on the Cervix (Category Code 67)

Category 67, Operations on the cervix, is the next category in this chapter. The **cervix** is located at the lowest part of the uterus and extends to the vagina.

Procedure Codes	Description
67.0	Dilation of Cervical Canal—This procedure involves stretching the cervical canal.
67.1X	Diagnostic Procedures on Cervix—These procedure codes include biopsies of the cervix and the endocervical area.
67.2	Conization of Cervix—Conization is a procedure performed on the cervix in which a cold knife is used to surgically cut a cone-shaped portion of tissue for examination. A cold knife is used to better preserve the specimen. This procedure is illustrated in Figure 37-2.
67.3X	Other Excision or Destruction of Lesion or Tissue of Cervix—The codes in this subcategory are determined by the way the excision or destruction is performed. The procedure codes include cauterization and cryosurgery.
67.4	Amputation of Cervix—This procedure involves the surgical removal of the lowest part of the cervix. Should a cervicectomy be performed in the same operative session as a colporrhaphy, it is included in the amputation procedure, not coded separately.
67.5X	Repair of Internal Cervical Os—The cervical os is a bony part of the cervix. The codes are assigned by determining the approach, which can be vaginal or abdominal.
67.6X	Other Repair of Cervix—These repair codes include simple suture repair as well as the repair of a fistula. Should another type of repair be performed that is not coded more specifically, it is assigned a code from this subcategory.

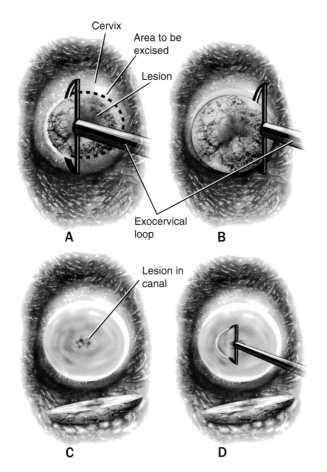

Figure 37-2 Cervical conization-LEEP technique: (**A**) Path of electrosurgical loop through distal cervix; (**B**) loop near completion of excision; (**C**) lesion identified in cervix; (**D**) loop excision of lesion (From Caruthers B, Price P, Junge TL, et al. *Surgical Technology for the Surgical Technologist: A Positive Care Approach.* Clifton Park, NY: Delmar, Cengage Learning, 2001, p. 534.)

Other Incision and Excision of Uterus (Category Code 68)

Category 68, Other incision and excision of uterus, contains procedure codes for operations performed on the uterus and vagina. The **uterus** is a muscular organ that carries a fetus. Some of the prefixes that indicate the term *uterus* are **hystero-, metro-, metrio-,** and **utero-.** The **vagina** is a muscular tube that connects on one end to the cervix and on the other end to outside the body. The prefixes that denote the vagina are colpo- and vagino-.

Procedure Codes	Description
68.0	Hysterotomy—The surgical cutting into the uterus.
68.1X	Diagnostic Procedures on Uterus and Supporting Structures—This includes open and closed biopsies. Hysteroscopic examination for diagnostic purposes is also included in this subcategory.
68.2X	Excision or Destruction of Lesion or Tissue of Uterus—This subcategory contains the lysis of uterine adhesions, the surgical removal of the congenital septum of the uterus, and endometrial ablation by use of coagulation or cauterization.
68.3X	Subtotal Abdominal Hysterectomy—A hysterectomy is the removal of the uterus, which may or may not include the cervix, the ovaries, and the fallopian tubes. This subcategory is for the removal of *only* the uterus.
68.4	Total Abdominal Hysterectomy—This code references the approach of the procedure. A surgical incision is made through the abdomen, and the uterus is then removed through the incision. Should the fallopian tubes and the ovaries be removed as well, additional codes for their removal should be assigned from the 65 category.
68.5X	Vaginal Hysterectomy—This code references the approach of the procedure. The uterus is removed through the vagina. Should the surgeon also use a laparoscope to assist with this approach, it is included in this subcategory. The removal of the fallopian tubes, the ovaries, and any other repairs are coded in addition to the code from this subcategory.
68.6	Radical Abdominal Hysterectomy—This is a very extensive procedure in which the uterus is removed through an abdominal approach, and perimetrial and vaginal tissue is also excised. A modified radical hysterectomy and Wertheim's operation are also coded to this subcategory.
68.7	Radical Vaginal Hysterectomy—This is a very extensive procedure in which the uterus is removed through a vaginal approach and perimetrial and vaginal tissue is also excised.
68.8	Pelvic Evisceration—Pelvic evisceration is an extensive surgery in which the uterus, vagina, ovaries, tubes, bladder, and urethra are removed. In some extreme cases, the sigmoid colon and the rectum are also removed. This is usually an emergent situation. Colostomy and urinary diversion are coded separately.
68.9	Other and Unspecified Hysterectomy—A hysterectomy that is not coded more specifically should be coded to this subcategory.

Other Operations on Uterus and Supporting Structures (Category Code 69)

Category 69, Other operations on uterus and supporting structures, includes excision, repair, and aspiration procedures.

Procedure Codes	Description
69.0X	Dilation and Curettage of Uterus—Figure 37-3 illustrates the dilation and curettage of the uterus. The cervix is opened up, or dilated, and then the uterus is scraped clean with an instrument called a curette. Suction might also be used. The procedure is sometimes referred to as a D&C.
69.1X	Excision or Destruction of Lesion or Tissue of Uterus and Supporting Structures—This is the surgical removal of lesions or damaged tissue of the uterus and supporting structures.
69.2X	Repair of Uterine Supporting Structures—This includes repositioning the bladder in relation to the uterus. A procedure called plication of uterine ligaments, in which the ligaments of the uterus are tucked, is coded to this subcategory.
69.3	Paracervical Uterine Denervation—This is a procedure in which nerve impulse pathways of the uterus are surgically destroyed.
69.4X	Uterine Repair—This subcategory contains procedure codes for the repair of lacerations or defects in the uterus.

69.5X	Aspiration Curettage of Uterus—This is the subcategory of procedure codes used when the suction curette is used to clean out the contents of the uterus.
69.6	Menstrual Extraction or Regulation—This procedure involves suction to stimulate menstruation.
69.7	Insertion of Intrauterine Contraceptive Device—To prevent pregnancy, the implantation of an intrauterine contraceptive device may be done.
69.9X	Other Operations on Uterus, Cervix, and Supporting Structures—The removal of a foreign body in the cervix is coded to this subcategory, as is artificial insemination. Artificial insemination is a way to achieve pregnancy for couples who have had fertility problems.

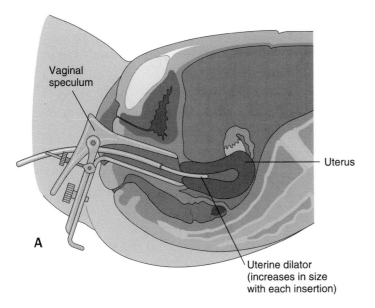

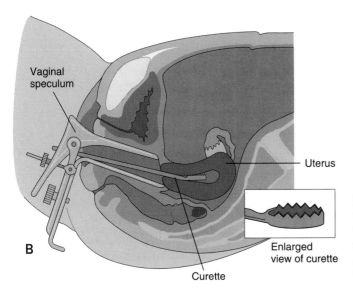

Figure 37-3 Dilation and curettage. (A) Dilation, the expansion of the cervical opening; (B) curettage, the removal of material from the surface of the uterus (From Ehrlich A, Schroeder CL. *Medical Terminology for Health Professions,* 4th ed. Clifton Park, NY: Delmar, Cengage Learning, 2001, p. 307.)

Operations on Vagina and Cul-de-Sac (Category Code 70)

Category 70, Operations on vagina and cul-de-sac, contains diagnostic, repair, reconstruction, and excision procedures.

Procedure Codes	Description
70.0	Culdocentesis—The surgical aspiration of fluid from the cul-de-sac.
70.1X	Incision of Vagina and Cul-de-Sac—The procedures in this subcategory include incision, lysis of adhesions of the vagina, and other vaginotomy procedures.
70.2X	Diagnostic Procedures on Vagina and Cul-de-Sac—This subcategory contains codes for procedures done for diagnostic purposes, such as biopsies and scope procedures.
70.3X	Local Excision or Destruction of Vagina and Cul-de-Sac—Lesions and damaged tissue of the vagina or cul-de-sac are coded from this subcategory.
70.4	Obliteration and Total Excison of Vagina—The surgical removal of the vagina.
70.5X	Repair of Cystocele and Rectocele—The cystocele is the anterior vaginal wall; the rectocele is the posterior vaginal wall. The walls of the vagina may protrude anteriorly from the bladder or posteriorly from the rectum. Procedures to correct these conditions are coded to this subcategory.
70.6X	Vaginal Construction and Reconstruction—This is the plastic surgical construction or restoration of a vagina.
70.7X	Other Repair of Vagina—The repair of fistulas that may be present between the vagina and other structures is coded to this subcategory.
70.8	Obliteration of Vaginal Vault—This is the surgical removal of the vaginal vault.
70.9X	Other Operations on the Vagina and Cul-de-Sac—Other procedures done on the vagina or cul-de-sac that are not more specifically coded elsewhere in this chapter are coded to this subcategory.

Operations on Vulva and Perineum (Category Code 71)

Category 71, Operations on vulva and perineum, is coded to the last category of the chapter. The vulva is a term used for the external female genital organs, including the labia and the vestibule of the vagina. The perineum is the area between the vaginal opening and the anus.

Procedure Codes	Description
71.0X	Incision of Vulva and Perineum—The surgical cutting of tissue of the vulva or perineum.
71.1X	Diagnostic Procedures on Vulva—This includes biopsies and other diagnostic procedures.
71.2X	Operations on Bartholin's Gland—Bartholin's glands are small glands located on either side of the vagina that secrete a mucus substance to lubricate the vagina. The procedures in this subcategory include marsupialization, incision, excision, and cyst aspiration.
71.3	Other Local Excision or Destruction of Vulva and Perineum—The surgical removal or destruction of lesions or damaged tissue of the vulva or perineum.
71.4	Operations on Clitoris—The clitoris is a small erectile structure in front of the vaginal opening. Procedures coded to this subcategory include incision and amputation.
71.5	Radical Vulvectomy—The surgical removal of the vulva and surrounding tissue.
71.6X	Other Vulvectomy—This subcategory distinguishes between a bilateral and a unilateral procedure.
71.7X	Repair of Vulva and Perineum—This is the surgical repair or stitching of a laceration of the vulva or perineum. The repair of the perineum as a result of childbirth is not coded to this subcategory but is found in the 75 category of obstetrical procedures.
71.8	Other Operations on Vulva—Should a procedure be performed on the vulva that is not coded more specifically in this chapter, this code is used.
71.9	Other Operations on Female Genital Organs—Should a procedure be performed on female genital organs that is not coded more specifically in this chapter, this code is used.

When coding for operations on the female genital organs, the coder must review the medical documentation to determine whether the procedure was completed via a scope or as an open procedure.

Internet Links

To research information on procedures completed on the female genital system visit *http://www .reproline.jhu.edu* and *http://www.abog.org*.

Summary

- Chapter 12 of volume 3 ICD-9-CM is entitled "Operations on the Female Genital Organs."
- The female genital organs include the ovaries, the uterus, and the fallopian tubes. Also coded by chapter 12 are procedure codes for the labia, clitoris, Bartholin's glands, and perineum.
- Open and laparoscopic procedures are both included in the procedure codes found in this chapter.
- Pelvic evisceration, artificial insemination, and dilation and curettage are procedures coded in this chapter.

Chapter Review

True/False: Indicate whether the statement is true (T) or false (F).

1. _____ If a fallopian tube is being removed at a second operative session, it is coded to the 66.4X subcategory.

2. _____ The codes found in subcategory 67.3X are determined by the method of destruction.

3. _____ Rubin's test introduces carbon dioxide into the fallopian tubes and the cervix to check the viability of the tube.

4. _____ A subtotal abdominal hysterectomy involves the surgical removal of the uterus while the cervix is left in place.

5. _____ Removal of a foreign body in the cervix is coded to subcategory 70.2X.

Fill-in-the-Blank: Enter the appropriate term(s) to complete the statement.

6. Introduction of saline into the fallopian tube to test its viability is a procedure called _____.

7. The surgical removal of the uterus is called a(n) _____.

8. _____ of uterine ligments is a procedure in which the ligaments are tucked.

9. The anterior vaginal wall is also called the _____.

10. The area between the vaginal opening and the anus is called the _____.

Coding Assignments

Instructions: Using an ICD-9-CM coding book, select the appropriate procedure code.

Diagnosis	Code
1. Endometrial ablation	_____
2. Hysterocopy	_____
3. Lysis of vulvar adhesions	_____

4. Biopsy of uterus

5. Repair of old obstetric laceration of perineum

6. Repair of old obstetric laceration of the cervix

7. Salpingo-uterostomy

8. Repair of cystocele

9. Repair of rectovaginal fistula

10. Removal of prosthesis of fallopian tube

11. Vaginal repair of chronic inversion of uterus

12. Laparoscopic marsupialization of ovarian cyst

13. Aspiration biopsy of ovary

14. Cauterization of ovary

15. Burying of fimbriae in uterine wall

16. Diagnostic D&C

17. Cryosurgical destruction of cervical lesion

18. Vulvectomy, bilateral

19. Laparoscopic unilateral oophorectomy

20. Culdoscopy

21. Marsupialization of ovarian cyst

22. Laparoscopic removal of remaining ovary

23. Total unilateral salpingectomy

24. Hysteroscopy

25. Hymenectomy

Case Studies

Instructions: Review each case study, and select the correct ICD-9-CM diagnostic and procedural codes.

CASE 1

PREOPERATIVE/POSTOPERATIVE DIAGNOSIS: Bartholin's gland cyst

PROCEDURE: This is a 40-year-old female who presents today for removal of Bartholin's gland cyst on the right side of the vagina.

She was brought to the operating room and, under general anesthesia, was prepped and draped in the usual sterile fashion. I began by pulling back the labia minor on the right and with 2-0 nylon stitched it back to expose the area of incision. I then made an elliptical incision in vaginal mucosa around the area of the duct and as close to the gland as possible without damage to any other structure. Blunt dissection was used to completely expose the gland, and Mayo scissors were then used to dissect the gland from its bed. The cyst was identified to be approximately 2 cm. Direct incision was made into the cyst. The cyst was drained, and then the incision made to the cyst was closed with three interrupted absorbable sutures. The cyst wall lining was then everted, and several sutures were placed to adhere it to the vaginal mucosa. The sutures that had been placed to hold back the labia minor were removed. All counts were good, dressing was applied, and patient was taken to the recovery room in good condition.

ICD-9-CM Code Assignment: _____

CASE 2

INDICATIONS: This is a 45-year-old female who has had excessive bleeding during menstruation and irregular bleeding between periods. Other measures of control have been tried and are documented in the patient's H&P found in this medical record. It was decided that we would try the D&C before medication was started because the patient really doesn't want to take any drugs. It was explained to the patient that if this procedure doesn't alleviate the problem, she will need to try medication to control the bleeding.

PREOPERATIVE/POSTOPERATIVE DIAGNOSIS: Menometrorrhagia

PROCEDURE: The patient presented to the operating room and was identified by me. She understood the procedure we were to perform as well as the risks and benefits. She underwent general anesthesia and was then prepped and draped in the usual sterile fashion.

The results of her pelvic exam, performed yesterday as part of her preop, are documented in her medical record. I did not, at that time, detect any masses, but the uterine wall was extremely thick. An Auvard weight speculum was placed in the posterior of the vagina and tucked under the os of the cervix. With the use of a single-toothed tenaculum, the cervix was grasped at the 12 o'clock position. A uterine sound was placed into the external os of the cervix. The uterine depth was determined, and the sound was removed. The curette was then introduced to the external os of the cervical mucosa and used to scrape. A specimen was taken and sent for pathology. The cervix was then progressively dilated. Randall forceps were placed, and the uterus was examined for fibroids or polyps. None were noted. This procedure was done twice more to be sure the uterus was clear. A curette was then introduced and advanced into the uterus. The endometrium was scraped, and samples were sent for pathology. Once this was completed, instruments were removed and the count was good. Patient was sent to the recovery room in stable condition.

ICD-9-CM Code Assignment: _____

CASE 3

Macy is a 27-year-old female in her second trimester who presents today for cerclage of her cervix. This is her second pregnancy. The first pregnancy required this procedure, which allowed her to carry her baby to term. We are confident of the same results this time as well.

With the patient in the dorsal lithotomy position, she was prepped and draped in the normal sterile fashion. Using a transvaginal approach, the cervix was found to be approximately 3 cm in length with the external os measuring 1 cm and showing to be closed. Retractors were placed, and, using ring forceps, the anterior and posterior lips of the cervix were grasped. A mersilene band was placed in a counterclockwise fashion approximately 3 cm superior to the external os and then tied off. The cervix looked to be closed, and the patient tolerated the procedure well.

ICD-9-CM Code Assignment: _____

CASE 4

This is a 42-year-old female who presents today for endometrial ablation because she has been suffering with menorrhagia for the last 2 years since her last pregnancy.

Patient was given Versed due to the high anxiety she is suffering prior to procedure. She was placed in the dorsal lithotomy position and prepped and draped in the usual sterile fashion. Once the patient was dilated successfully to #31 French, the ACMI GYN resectoscope was inserted and inspection was performed. Seeing no reason not to proceed, a systemic endometrial ablation was carried out starting at the tip of the fundus and, using a roller spindle, continued a 360-degree circle, at which time a continuous endometrial systemic ablation was done. Fulguration current was used; when necessary, some cutting was done. All viable tissue was coagulated as were the fallopian tube conus areas. After hemostasis was obtained, the patient was returned to the recovery room in stable condition.

ICD-9-CM Code Assignment: _____

CASE 5

This is a 54-year-old female who has had four children, all by vaginal delivery. At this time, she is experiencing problems indicative of early vaginal prolapse. A colpopexy has been scheduled for today.

With the patient in the dorsal position, an incision is made in the lower abdominal area. The vaginal vault does appear to need some repair. Mesh was sutured to the front of the internal sacral wall inside the pelvic cavity. The apex of the vagina was firmly secured with sutures to the bridge. The patient tolerated the procedure well and was returned to the recovery room in stable condition.

ICD-9-CM Code Assignment: _____

Obstetrical Procedures

Chapter Outline

Introduction
Coding Obstetrical Procedures
Internet Links
Summary

Chapter Review
Coding Assignments
Case Studies

Objectives

At the conclusion of this chapter, the student will be able to:

1. Identify procedures completed during the labor and delivery process.
2. Describe some of the procedures used to assist in delivery.
3. Discuss procedures that are completed on the fetus and the mother during labor and delivery.
4. Select and code diagnoses and procedures from case studies.

Key Terms

Amniocentesis
Amnioscopy
Breech Delivery
Cesarean Section

Episiotomy
Extraperitoneal
    Cesarean Section
Fetoscopy

Forceps Delivery
Induction of Labor
Laparoamnioscopy
Obstetrical Tamponade

Obstetrics
Placenta
Vacuum Extraction

Reminder

As you work through this chapter, you will need to have a copy of the ICD-9-CM coding book to reference.

Introduction

This chapter contains procedure codes related to obstetrics. Obstetrics is the specialty that deals with women during pregnancy, childbirth, and the period immediately after childbirth.

Most of the procedures in this chapter are performed during labor and delivery. Also included in this chapter are procedure codes that cover repairs that need to be made after the delivery.

Coding Obstetrical Procedures

Category 72, Forceps, vacuum, and breech delivery, classifies assisted deliveries. A forceps delivery involves the use of an instrument that has two blades and a handle and is inserted to help assist the fetus through the birth canal. Vacuum extraction is a delivery using a device that is applied to the head of the fetus to assist in delivery. Breech delivery is a type of delivery in which the fetus presents either feet, buttocks, or knees first.

A procedure known as an episiotomy is included in some of the procedures for this category. An episiotomy is an incision made at the vaginal opening to prevent tearing during delivery. Figure 38-1 illustrates an episiotomy and the types of repairs.

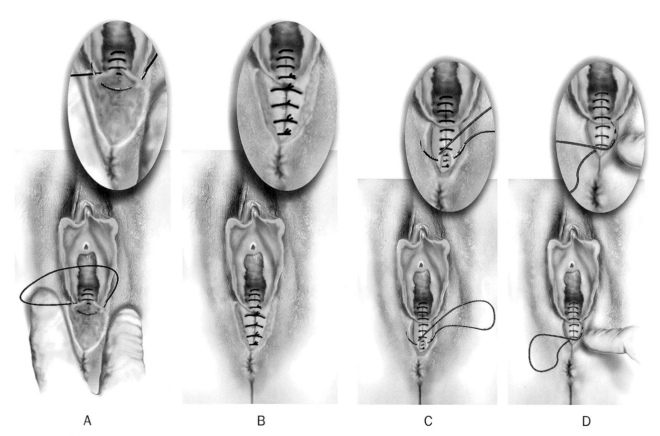

A   B   C   D

Figure 38-1 Episiotomy repair: (**A**) Closure of vaginal epithelium from apex to hymeneal ring, (**B**) interrupted sutures to close perineal fascia and levator ani muscles, (**C**) continuous closure of superficial fascia to the anal edge, (**D**) continuous closure of subcutaneous layer (From Price P, Frey KB, Junge TL. *Surgical Technology for the Surgical Technologist: A Positive Care Approach,* 2nd ed. Clifton Park, NY: Delmar, Cengage Learning, 2004, p. 758.)

Procedure Codes	Description
72.0	Low Forceps Operation—This is a type of delivery in which the forceps are used on the fetal head once the fetus is visible at the pelvic floor.
72.1	Low Forceps Operation with Episiotomy—This is a type of delivery in which the forceps are used on the fetal head once the fetus is visible at the pelvic floor. The vulva requires an incision, or episiotomy, to prevent tissue tear.
72.2X	Mid Forceps Operation—Mid forceps delivery is a type of assisted delivery in which the fetal head has begun entry to the pelvic floor. This subcategory contains a code for mid forceps operation with episiotomy
72.3X	High Forceps Operation—High forceps delivery is a type of assisted delivery in which the fetal head has not begun entry to the pelvic floor. This subcategory contains verbiage for the procedure with episiotomy.
72.4	Forceps Rotation of Fetal Head—The forceps are used to rotate the head of the fetus to help work its way down the birth canal.
72.5X	Breech Extraction—This subcategory of codes for breech delivery includes forceps assistance.
72.6	Forceps Application to Aftercoming Head—In this type of delivery procedure, the fetus is not positioned correctly, and partial delivery has already been made when the forceps are needed to help deliver the head.
72.7X	Vacuum Extraction—These procedures are for fetal delivery using a vacuum extraction device. This subcategory includes a procedure code for vacuum extraction with episiotomy.
72.8	Other Specified Instrumental Delivery—This code is used should a delivery be assisted with specified instruments other than forceps or vacuum.
72.9	Unspecified Instrumental Delivery—This code is used should a delivery be assisted with unspecified instruments other than forceps or vacuum.

Other Procedures Inducing or Assisting Delivery (Category Code 73)

Category 73, Other procedures inducing or assisting delivery, contains procedure codes that involve the induction of labor and manual assisted delivery.

Procedure Codes	Description
73.0X	Artificial Rupture of Membranes—This procedure involves the induction of labor. Induction of labor usually requires administering medication to force the fetus to begin movement through the birth canal. In this subcategory, the artificial rupture of the amniotic sack begins the labor process.
73.1	Other Surgical Induction of Labor—This induction can be done manually or by a procedure other than artificial rupture of membranes.
73.2X	Internal and Combined Version and Extraction—This type of delivery requires the practitioner to manually assist in rotating the fetus at the same time as some external manipulation is being performed. This procedure can be done with or without delivery.
73.3	Failed Forceps—This is coded if forceps are used but a delivery does not occur.
73.4	Medical Induction of Labor—This is coded if a chemical substance is given to the mother to induce labor.
73.5X	Manually Assisted Delivery—The fetus is assisted through the birth canal by the physician's reaching into the dilated cervix and assisting the fetus manually.
73.6	Episiotomy—This procedure is the surgical cutting of the vulvar orifice.
73.8	Operations on Fetus to Facilitate Delivery—In some cases, problems with the fetus inhibit delivery. Procedures that are done on the fetus to assist in the delivery are coded from this subcategory.
73.9X	Other Operations Assisting Delivery—This subcategory contains procedure codes that are not otherwise coded in this chapter involving procedures that might be necessary for delivery. These procedures include the replacement of a prolapsed umbilical cord and pubiotomy.

Cesarean Section and Removal of Fetus (Category code 74)

Category 74, Cesarean section and removal of fetus, contains codes for the surgical procedure of extracting the fetus from the uterus through the abdominal wall.

506 Section III ICD-9-CM Procedural Coding

Procedure Codes	Description
74.0	Classical Cesarean Section—This procedure is the removal of the fetus through an incision into the abdominal wall. In this procedure, the incision is made at the upper portion of the uterus.
74.1	Low Cervical Cesarean Section—This procedure involves an incision made lower into the uterus. The approach is usually through the pelvic cavity or abdominal peritoneal.
74.2	Extraperitoneal Cesarean Section—Not normally performed any more due to antibiotics, this procedure code is for the removal of a fetus from an infected uterus. The incision is usually made in the lower portion of the uterus, but entry is not made into the peritoneal cavity.
74.3	Removal of Extratubal Ectopic Pregnancy—An ectopic pregnancy is one in which an egg is fertilized outside the uterus. This code also includes removal of a fetus from the peritoneal or extraperitoneal cavity if rupture occurs.
74.4	Cesarean Section of Other Specified Types—This code is used for a specified type of cesarean section that is not coded more specifically in this chapter.
74.9X	Cesarean Section of Unspecified Type—Included in this subcategory is the hysterotomy, an incision into the uterus, to terminate a pregnancy.

Other Obstetric Operations (Category Code 75)

Category 75, Other obstetric operations, is the last category in this chapter. This category contains codes for various other conditions that might be encountered during a pregnancy or delivery.

Procedure Codes	Description
75.0	Intra-Amniotic Injection for Abortion—A substance is injected into the amniotic or uterine cavities to force an abortion. Prostaglandin and saline are two of the substances that may be injected to promote an abortion.
75.1	Diagnostic Amniocentesis—In amniocentesis, a needle is inserted into the amniotic sac to withdraw fluid for examination.
75.2	Intrauterine Transfusion—Should a problem with fetal blood be detected before delivery, a transfusion might be necessary. This procedure can involve blood exchange in the uterus, the insertion of a catheter into the abdomen of the fetus, or a transfusion into the fetal peritoneal cavity. Should the approach for this procedure be a hysterotomy, it should be coded in addition to the transfusion.
75.3X	Other Intrauterine Operations on Fetus and Amnion—A scope procedure to view the fetus in the amniotic sac is called an amnioscopy. This procedure may also be referred to as a fetoscopy or laparoamnioscopy. The scope procedures are found in this subcategory. Also found in this subcategory are codes for fetal monitoring and fetal electrocardiograph.
75.4	Manual Removal of Retained Placenta—The placenta is the organ present during pregnancy that is the site of metabolic exchange between the mother and fetus. As part of the delivery, the placenta is expelled after the fetus is born. If the placenta does not deliver on its own, it may be necessary for the provider to manually remove it. This procedure is coded to this subcategory.
75.5X	Repair of Current Obstetric Laceration of Uterus—Should a laceration of the cervix or uterus occur and need repair, but is not an old obstetrical laceration, it is coded to this subcategory. Note that this repair is for a current obstetric laceration.
75.6X	Repair of Current Obstetric Laceration—This subcategory is referred to for repair procedures that are performed on organs or tissue outside the uterus such as the pelvic floor, the bladder, and the vulva.
75.7	Manual Exploration of Uterine Cavity Postpartum—The physician may need to examine the uterine cavity internally by hand. This procedure is coded to this subcategory.
75.8	Obstetrical Tamponade of Uterus or Vagina—The surgical use of a tampon to compress the uterus or vagina is obstetrical tamponade.
75.9X	Other Obstetric Operations—The removal of hematoma and the surgical correction of an inverted uterus are included in this subcategory.

It is important for the coder to read the medical documentation to ensure that the procedure performed was necessary because of an obstetrical complication or injury.

Internet Links

Because of the close link between gynecology and obstetrics, the following links overlap with the links given in the previous chapter: *http://www.abog.org*, *www.greenjournal.org*, and *www.mayoclinic.org/obstetrics*.

Summary

- A forceps delivery involves the use of an instrument to assist the fetus through the birth canal, and a vacuum extraction is a delivery using a device that is applied to the head of the fetus.

- An incision made at the vaginal opening to prevent tearing during delivery is known as an episiotomy.

- Induction of labor usually requires administering medication to force the fetus to begin movement through the birth canal.

- A cesarean section is a surgical procedure of extracting the fetus from the uterus through the abdominal wall.

- In amniocentesis, a needle is inserted into the amniotic sac to withdraw fluid for examination.

- A scope procedure to view the fetus in the amniotic sac is known as an amnioscopy, fetoscopy, or laparoamnioscopy.

Chapter Review

True/False: Indicate whether the statement is true (T) or false (F).

1. _____ An episiotomy is an incision to prevent tissue tear during delivery.

2. _____ In a high forceps delivery, the head of the fetus has not reached the pelvic floor.

3. _____ A prior obstetrical laceration of the uterus needs repair. The proper subcategory for this repair is 75.5X.

4. _____ Intrauterine blood transfusions are done by placing a catheter into the arm of the fetus.

5. _____ Replacement of a prolapsed umbilical cord is coded to 73.9X.

Fill-in-the-Blank: Enter the appropriate term(s) to complete the statement.

6. A type of delivery in which the fetus presents knees first is called a(n) _____ delivery.

7. Administering medication to force the fetus through the birth canal is known as _____ of labor.

8. A needle inserted into the amniotic sac to withdraw fluid is called _____.

9. The type of pregnancy in which the egg is fertilized outside the uterus is called a(n) _____.

10. The _____ is the site of metabolic exchanges between mother and baby.

Coding Assignments

Instructions: Using an ICD-9-CM coding book, select the appropriate procedure code.

Procedure	Code
1. Classic cesarean section	_____
2. Replacement of prolapsed umbilical cord	_____
3. Vaginal cesarean section	_____
4. Delee maneuver	_____
5. Artificial rupture of membranes	_____
6. Removal of ectopic abdominal pregnancy	_____
7. Amnioinfusion	_____
8. Obstetrical abdominouterotomy	_____
9. Manual rotation of fetal head	_____
10. Obstetrical tamponade of vagina	_____
11. Fetal monitoring	_____
12. Surgical correction of inverted uterus	_____
13. Low forceps operation with episiotomy	_____
14. Vacuum extraction	_____
15. Fetal blood sampling	_____
16. Clavicotomy on fetus	_____
17. Postpartum manual exploration of uterine cavity	_____
18. Piper forceps operation	_____
19. Repair of current obstetric laceration of corpus uteri	_____
20. Exchange transfusion in utero	_____
21. Low forceps operation	_____
22. Failed forceps	_____
23. Repair of current obstetric laceration of bladder and urethra	_____
24. Hysterotomy to terminate pregnancy	_____
25. Correction of fetal defect	_____

Case Studies

Instructions: Review each case study, and select the correct ICD-9-CM diagnostic and procedural codes.

CASE 1

INDICATIONS FOR PROCEDURE: This is a 29-year-old gravida 1, para 0, who is 37 weeks' gestational age by dates and ultrasound. She has presented with elevated blood pressure of 151/103. Lab values showed platelet count of 54,000, normal liver function test, a hematocrit of 35.0, and normal PT and PTT. It was felt that the patient was suffering from pre-eclampsia when examination revealed intrauterine growth retardation and hematemesis. Contractions were occurring but not regular. Patient was dilated 3 cm, but due to the problems presented, we felt delivery could not wait. Patient was advised that an emergency cesarean was needed, and she agreed.

PROCEDURE: This 29-year-old female was brought to the OR, after which epidural anesthesia was administered. Once patient showed no response to sensitivity, we proceeded. Patient was supine and right hip was slightly elevated to keep pressure off the vena cava. A low transverse incision with a #10 blade was carried to the level of the fascia. Mayo scissors were used to open the incision laterally. The posterior fascia was dissected bluntly from the rectus abdominus muscle. The aponeurosis was cut superiorly near the umbilicus and inferiorly to the symphysis pubis. Clamps were placed, and Metzenbaum scissors were then used to make a longitudinal peritoneal incision and extend the facial opening. At this point, we were able to palpate the uterus, and fetal position was good. The bladder was freed from the uterus and retracted, a small transverse incision was made in the lower uterine segment, and the amniotic sac was exposed and incised. I then manipulated the fetus from the uterus. The infant female was drawn out, and the mouth and nose were immediately suctioned. The umbilical cord was clamped and cut, and cord samples were sent for pathology. The placenta was then recovered, and then a laparotomy sponge was used to clean the interior before a layered closure was performed: 2-0 absorbable sutures were used when closing the uterus. 3-0 Vicryl was used to close the bladder. The skin was closed with staples. Patient tolerated procedure well; mother and baby were fine.

ICD-9-CM Code Assignment: _____

CASE 2

INDICATIONS FOR SURGERY: A 34-year-old female presents with severe abdominal pain. After examination was completed and ultrasound results were reviewed, it was determined that patient had an ectopic pregnancy and surgical intervention was needed.

PROCEDURE: Patient was taken to the operating room, and after general anesthesia was induced, she was prepped and draped in the usual sterile fashion. Examination was performed after anesthesia, which showed a normal-sized, nontender uterus, a left adnexal mass, and a fullness in the vagina, all consistent with hyperperitoneum. A 10-mm trocar was inserted directly into the abdomen through a small incision in the umbilicus. Using 3.5 liters of carbon dioxide, a pneumoperitoneum was created. The hemoperitoneum was noticed, and another 10-mm trocar was placed in a small suprapubic incision. Two 5-mm ports were also placed under direct visualization in both the right and left lower quadrants. With an irrigator and aspirator, the hemoperitoneum was reduced. The left fallopian tube was noted to be almost to the point of rupture due to a mass in the tube. The fallopian tube was distended beyond repair, so this needed to be removed. The tube was tied off and removed with its contents through an Endo Catch bag through the 10-mm port. Inspection of the abdomen noted no other problems; adequate hemostasis was noted, and ports were removed. Defects were closed with 0 Vicryl, and the skin was closed with 4-0 Dexon. She was sent to the recovery room in stable condition.

ICD-9-CM Code Assignment: _____

CASE 3

This patient is a 23-year-old female who presents in active labor. Dr. Smith is her OB; however, due to the breech presentation of this fetus, I was called in to turn the fetus. Due to the patient being in active labor, an IV was started in which tocolytic drug therapy was started to stop contractions during the manipulation. The abdomen was palpated to determine the exact position of the fetus. At this point, the fetus was slowly turned without incident so that the head was moved into a downward position. The IV was stopped and contractions continued. The fetal monitor showed the baby to be doing nicely. The baby was born at 1:23 pm.

ICD-9-CM Code Assignment: _____

CASE 4

This is a 27-year-old female, G1 P0, who presents today in active labor with regular uterine contractions, every 2–3 minutes lasting 40–50 seconds. The antepartum course was unremarkable to date. Sonogram and amniocentesis performed during this pregnancy were normal. Exam shows all vital signs normal, with patient at 10 cm dilated. Normal spontaneous delivery, no forceps or vacuum, but a midline episiotomy was performed. Baby weighed 6 lb 2 oz and had Apgar scores of 8 at 1 minute and 9 at 5 minutes. Mother and baby are fine.

ICD-9-CM Code Assignment: _____

CASE 5

DISCHARGE DIAGNOSIS: False labor without delivery, antepartum complication

This patient is a 20-year-old female who presents today dilated 7 cm with contractions occurring every 3–4 minutes lasting 30–40 seconds. This mother is also an admitted cocaine addict who is worried about how her baby will be when born. At this time we are going to try to obtain a blood sample of the fetus to determine whether we need to have any special services on standby in the NICU.

The fetal monitor is showing a stable heart rate at this time. The amniotic sac is broken, and the amnioscope is inserted through the vagina. A 0.05-mm incision is made in the scalp and a blood sample is aspirated into a tube for a STAT to the lab. Contractions stopped, and the baby was not delivered at this time.

ICD-9-CM Code Assignment: _____

Operations on the Musculoskeletal System

Chapter Outline

Objectives

At the conclusion of this chapter, the student will be able to:

1. Identify pathologies that affect the musculoskeletal system.
2. Describe procedures used to correct the pathologies.
3. Discuss procedures that are completed on the structures of the musculoskeletal system.
4. Select and code diagnoses and procedures from case studies.

Key Terms

Amputation	Bursectomy	Hemimaxillectomy	Osse-
Appendicular Skeleton	Cranium	Internal Fixation	Osteo-
Arthro-	Debridement	Intervertebral Disc	Osteoarthrotomy
Arthrocentesis	Disarticulation	Joint Replacement	Osto-
Arthrodesis	Dislocation	Luxation	Rotator Cuff Repair
Arthroplasty	Epiphysis	Macroadactyly	Sequestrectomy
Arthroscopy	External Fixation Device	Muscles	Spinal Fusion
Arthrotomy	Fascia	Opponensplasty	Subluxation
Axial Skeleton	Hallux Valgus	Orthognathic	Synovial Membrane
Bunionectomy	Hammer Toe	Ossi-	Tendons

Reminder

As you work through this chapter, you will need to have a copy of the ICD-9-CM coding book to reference.

Introduction

Operations on the musculoskeletal system, category codes 76–84, include procedures completed on the bones, bone marrow, cartilage, ligaments, joints, bursa, and some of the linings and fluid of the joints. The musculoskeletal system is the framework of the body and also protects internal organs. The human skeleton consists of 206 bones. The skull, vertebral column, ribs, and sternum make up what is called the axial skeleton. The bones in the arms, legs, shoulders, and pelvis make up the appendicular skeleton.

This chapter classifies procedures as simple as setting a fracture to procedures as complex as spinal surgery. Medical terms that begin with the prefixes osse-, ossi-, osteo-, and osto- refer to bone. Medical terms that begin with the prefix arthro- refer to joints.

Coding Operations on the Musculoskeletal System

The chapter begins with category 76, Operations on facial bones and joints. The face is comprised of 14 bones. The cranium, the bone that encloses the brain, is made up of eight bones. Figure 39-1 illustrates the bones of the head and face.

Procedure Codes	Description
76.0X	Incision of Facial Bone Without Division—These procedures involve cutting into the bone without separating it altogether. A sequestrectomy procedure is a procedure in which a piece of bone becomes necrosed, or dead, and needs to be removed.
76.1X	Diagnostic Procedures on Facial Bones and Joints—Biopsies of the facial bones and joints are coded to this subcategory.
76.2	Local Excision or Destruction of Lesion of Facial Bone—If bone tissue becomes diseased or damaged and needs to be removed, this code is used.
76.3X	Partial Ostectomy of Facial Bone—The surgical removal of part of a facial bone. Also coded to this subcategory is a hemimaxillectomy with bone graft or prosthesis. In this procedure, half of the maxilla is surgically removed and reconstructed by using prosthetics or bone grafting.
76.4X	Excision and Reconstruction of Facial Bones—The bone is cut and removed, and reconstruction is done during the same operative session.
76.5	Temporomandibular Arthroplasty—Arthroplasty is the repair of a joint. In this case, the temporomandibular joint is repaired by using plastic surgery.
76.6X	Other Facial Bone Repair and Orthognathic Surgery— The term orthognathic refers to the branch of oral medicine relating to the treatment of bones of the jaw. If bone grafting or synthetic implants are performed during the same operative session, they are coded in addition to the other procedure.
76.7X	Reduction of Facial Fracture—The correction of facial fractures by manipulation. If an internal fixation device is applied, this application is included in the procedure code. If bone grafting or synthetic implants are performed during the same operative session, they are coded in addition to the other procedure.
76.9X	Other Operations on Facial Bones and Joints—The removal of an internal fixation device is coded to this subcategory. Open and closed reduction of the temporomandibular bone is also coded to this subcategory. If inert foreign body material is implanted in the facial bone, that is also coded to this subcategory.

Incision, Excision, and Division of Other Bones (Category Code 77)

Category 77, Incision, excision, and division of other bones, is the next category in this chapter. Some of the codes in this category require a fourth digit to identify the location of the procedure. Attention to notes and symbols is essential for proper coding in this category.

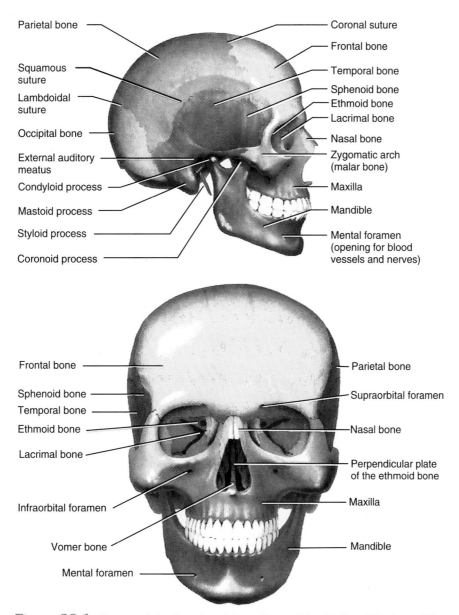

Figure 39-1 Bones of the head and face (From Price P, Frey KB, Junge TL. *Surgical Technology for the Surgical Technologist: A Positive Care Approach,* 2nd ed. Clifton Park, NY: Delmar, Cengage Learning, 2004, p. 968.)

Procedure Codes	Description
77.0X	Sequestrectomy—This procedure is the surgical removal of a piece of dead bone.
77.1X	Other Incision of Bone Without Division—This is a surgical cut into a bone without complete separation from the site.
77.2X	Wedge Osteotomy—This procedure involves surgically removing a piece of bone that has a wedge shape.
77.3X	Other Division of Bone—This procedure involves the surgical separation of part of a bone. Osteoarthrotomy is a procedure in which the articular end of a bone is surgically removed. This procedure is included in this subcategory.
77.4X	Biopsy of Bone—Part of the living tissue of the bone is surgically removed and microscopically examined.

Procedure Codes	Description
77.5X	Excision and Repair of Bunion and Other Toe Deformities—Bunionectomy is a procedure in which a bony exostosis is removed from the great toe. A bunion can also be referred to as hallux valgus. Also coded to this subcategory is the repair of hammer toe. A hammer toe is a condition in which the first phalanx shows dorsal flexion and there is plantar flexion of the second and third phalanges.
77.6X	Local Excision of Lesion or Tissue of Bone—If a lesion or other diseased or damaged tissue needs to be removed, the procedure is coded to this subcategory.
77.7X	Excision of Bone for Graft—Should bone tissue be needed for grafting to another site, the procedure code from this subcategory is used.
77.8X	Other Partial Ostectomy—This is the surgical removal of part of a bone.
77.9X	Total Ostectomy—This is the surgical removal of the bone.

Other Operations on Bones, Except Facial Bones (Category Code 78)

Category 78, Other operations on bones, except facial bones, contains procedures related to grafting, the shortening and lengthening of bones, and repair. This category requires fourth-digit assignment to denote the site of the procedure.

Procedure Codes	Description
78.0X	Bone Graft—This procedure code includes the graft of tissue from a donor bone bank. If bone is surgically removed for grafting, it is coded in addition to the graft.
78.1X	Application of External Fixator Device—The application of an external fixation device is a procedure used to stabilize a fractured bone in which wires, pins, or screws are placed through the soft tissue into the bone and then are held in place with an external device. This is done without any surgical correction of the bone. This device is illustrated in Figure 39-2.
78.2X	Limb Shortening Procedures—This procedure deals with the epiphysis of the bone. The epiphysis is located in the joint and is the point of active growth for bones. Figure 39-3 illustrates the structure of the bone, along with the location of the epiphysis. This procedure surgically adjusts the length of the bone.
78.3X	Limb-Lengthening Procedures—These procedures surgically adjust the length of the bone, including bone grafting and bone division. If an external fixation device is also used, this procedure is coded in addition to the lengthening procedure.
78.4X	Other Repair or Plastic Operations on Bone—This subcategory is coded if no more specific code is found in this chapter for repairs or plastic operations on bone.
78.5X	Internal Fixation of Bone Without Fracture Reduction—Internal fixation is an open procedure using wire, pins, plates, and screws to correct a fracture. This procedure can sometimes be referred to as open reduction internal fixation (ORIF). Figure 39-4 illustrates the use of an internal fixation device. This subcategory is also used to code the procedure in which a fixation device becomes loose or displaced and has to be adjusted.
78.6X	Removal of Implanted Devices from Bone—Should the external or internal fixation device need to be removed invasively, this subcategory is used to code the procedure.
78.7X	Osteoclasis—Should a bone need to be surgically fractured or refractured, this subcategory is used to code the procedure.
78.8X	Diagnostic Procedures on Bone, Not Elsewhere Classified—A diagnostic procedure that is not coded more specifically in this chapter is coded to this subcategory.
78.9X	Insertion of Bone Growth Stimulator—This subcategory includes the insertion of an electrical device used to stimulate bone growth and also bone healing. A noninvasive device is not coded from this subcategory.

Reduction of Fracture and Dislocation (Category Code 79)

As explained earlier in this book, a fracture is a break in the bone. A reduction is one way to correct the fracture. The codes for this procedure are found in category 79, Reduction of fracture and dislocation. If the procedure for the reduction involves the insertion of a traction device, this is included, not coded separately.

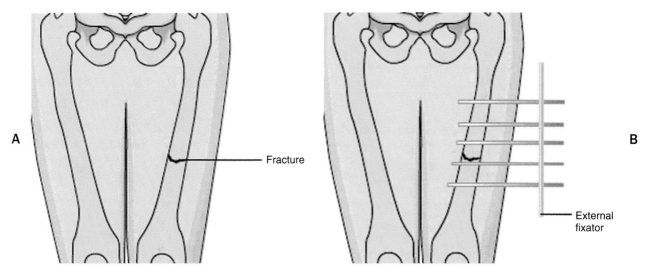

Figure 39-2 External fixation: **(A)** Fracture of the epiphysis of a femur, **(B)** external fixation to stabilize the bone (removed after the bone has healed) (From Ehrlich A, Schroeder CL. *Medical Terminology for Health Professions,* 4th ed. Clifton Park, NY: Delmar, Cengage Learning, 2001, p. 63.)

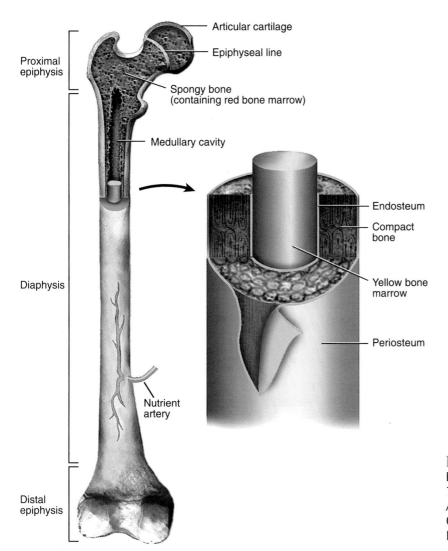

Figure 39-3 Structure of bone (From Price P, Frey KB, Junge TL. *Surgical Technology for the Surgical Technologist: A Positive Care Approach,* 2nd ed. Clifton Park, NY: Delmar, Cengage Learning, 2004, p. 795.)

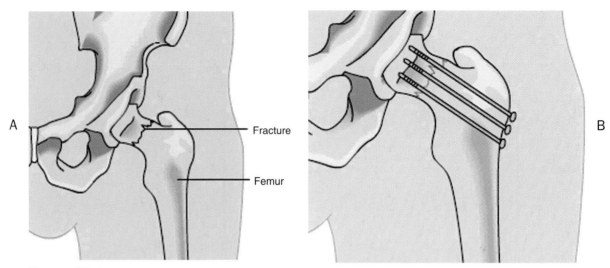

Figure 39-4 Internal fixation: (**A**) Fracture of the femoral neck, (**B**) internal fixation pins placed to stabilize the (not removed) (From Ehrlich A, Schroeder CL. *Medical Terminology for Health Professions,* 4th ed. Clifton Park, NY: Delmar, Cengage Learning, 2001, p. 64.)

External fixation devices are coded separately. The procedures in this category include the application of a cast or splint. Fourth-digit code assignment is needed in most subcategories to indicate the site.

Procedure Codes	Description
79.0X	Closed Reduction of Fracture Without Internal Fixation—This procedure requires the physician to manipulate the bone back into place without making an incision.
79.1X	Closed Reduction of Fracture with Internal Fixation—This procedure involves the manipulation of the bone to correct the fracture with the application of an internal fixation device.
79.2X	Open Reduction of Fracture Without Internal Fixation—Through an incision at the fracture site, the manipulation of the fracture is done to correct the injury.
79.3X	Open Reduction of Fracture with Internal Fixation—Through an incision at the fracture site, the manipulation of the fracture is done to correct the injury with the application of an internal fixation device.
79.4X	Closed Reduction of Separated Epiphysis—An epiphysis that has separated from its proper position is moved back into position without an incision at the injury site.
79.5X	Open Reduction of Separated Epiphysis—An epiphysis that has separated from its proper position is moved back into position with an incision at the injury site.
79.6X	Debridement of Open Fracture Site—**Debridement,** as already explained, is the cleaning out of a wound. In this case, the fracture site is cleaned out of dirt, foreign objects, or damaged tissue.
79.7X	Closed Reduction of Dislocation—**Dislocation** is when a bone is out of place. Another name for dislocation is luxation. **Subluxation** is when the bone is partially displaced. This subcategory is coded when the reduction procedure is done without incision.
79.8X	Open Reduction of Dislocation—An incision is made at the site of the dislocation so that corrective manipulation can be performed.
79.9X	Unspecified Operation on Bone Injury—Any procedure not coded in any other section of the chapter.

Incision and Excision of Joint Structures (Category Code 80)

Category 80, Incision and excision of joint structures, includes operations on ligaments, meniscus, synovial membrane, cartilage, and joint capsules. This category requires a fourth digit to identify the site of the operation.

Procedure Codes	Description
80.0X	Arthrotomy for Removal of Prosthesis—**Arthrotomy** is a surgical cut into the joint. This procedure involves a surgical cut into the joint to remove a prosthesis.
80.1X	Other Arthrotomy—This procedure code is used for any incision in the joint for anything other than removal of a prosthesis.
80.2X	Arthroscopy—An **arthroscopy** is a visual examination of the joint with a scope.
80.3X	Biopsy of Joint Structure—This procedure code is used for any biopsy done on a structure of the joint. This also includes an aspiration biopsy.
80.4X	Division of Joint Capsule, Ligament, or Cartilage—The procedures coded to this subcategory include the division of tissue that constricts joint movement. Also coded to this subcategory is the separation of joint and ligament tissue.
80.5X	Excision or destruction and other repair of intervertebral disc—An **intervertebral disc** is found in the spinal column. These discs are made up of cartilage and cushion the vertebrae. The procedures include the cervical, thoracic, and lumbar disks. Additional codes are assigned for concomitant decompression of spinal nerve root and any concurrent spinal fusion.
80.6	Excision of Semilunar Cartilage of Knee—The knee joint contains a crescent-shaped disc. The surgical removal of this disk is coded to this subcategory. Surgical removal of the meniscus is also coded to this subcategory.
80.7X	Synovectomy—The **synovial membrane** of a joint is the source of fluid the joint needs to move. The removal of the synovial membrane can be partial or complete.
80.8X	Other Local Excision or Destruction of Lesion of Joint—If the removal or destruction of joint tissue is not more specifically coded in this chapter, it is coded to this subcategory.

Repair and Plastic Operations on Joint Structures (Category Code 81)

Category 81, Repair and plastic operations on joint structures, includes procedures that repair the joint. Various types of procedures and techniques are used to repair joints. Close attention should be paid to inclusion notes in this category.

Procedure Codes	Description
81.0X	**Spinal Fusion**—This is a procedure that joins two or more vertebrae to immobilize part of the spine. **Arthrodesis** is another name for fusion and is also included in this subcategory. The various fusion codes found in this subcategory are coded by the location and technique used. Bone graft and internal fixation are included in this subcategory.
81.1X	Arthrodesis and arthroereisis of Foot and Ankle—These procedure codes are used when the immobilization of the parts of the foot or ankle joints is performed. Bone graft and application of an external fixation device are included.
81.2X	Arthrodesis of Other Joint—This subcategory of procedure codes is reported when a surgical fixation of a joint, other than the foot or ankle, occurs. The code choice depends on the location of the procedure. Bone graft and external fixation device application are included.
81.3X	Refusion of Spine—This code is used if correction of a prior surgical fusion is needed. Code selection is based on location and technique.
81.4X	Other Repair of Joint of Lower Extremity—The repair of the knee, hip, and ankle is included in this subcategory. Arthroplasty includes bone graft, external traction or fixation application, and internal fixation application.
81.5X	Joint Replacement of Lower Extremity—**Joint replacement** is a procedure in which a prosthetic implant is surgically placed in the joint area. This subcategory of codes includes joint replacement procedures of the lower extremities. Also included in this subcategory is the revision of replacement procedures.
81.6X	Other Procedures on Spine—Included in this subcategory of procedure codes are fusion codes for more than one vertebra.
81.7X	Arthroplasty and Repair of Hand, Fingers, and Wrist—These procedures are focused on the joints of the hand, wrist, and fingers. Wrist replacement and plastic surgery of the hand, fingers, and wrist are also coded to this subcategory.

Procedure Codes	Description
81.8X	Arthroplasty and Repair of Shoulder and Elbow—Total shoulder and elbow replacements are coded in this subcategory.
81.9X	Other Operations on Joint structures—This subcategory includes a procedure in which joint fluid is withdrawn by needle, also called an **arthrocentesis.** The revision of upper extremity joint replacement is also coded to this subcategory.

Operations on Muscle, Tendon, and Fascia of Hand (Category Code 82)

Category 82, Operations on muscle, tendon, and fascia of hand, includes repairs, suturing, grafting, and excision procedures. **Muscles** make body and organ movement possible. **Tendons** are the tissues that connect muscle to bone. **Fascia** is the tissue that covers and separates muscles. Inclusion notes should be read carefully in this category.

Procedure Codes	Description
82.0	Incision of Muscle, Tendon, Fascia, and Bursa of Hand—This is the surgical cutting of the muscle, fascia, and bursa of the hand. The bursa acts as a cushion and contains synovial fluid to ease movement.
82.1X	Division of Muscle, Tendon, and Fascia of Hand—This procedure consists of surgically cutting and separating the muscle, tendon, or fascia of the hand.
83.2X	Excision of Lesion of Muscle, Tendon, and Fascia of Hand—The procedures coded from this subcategory include excision of lesions or damaged tissue.
82.3X	Other Excision of Soft Tissue of the Hand—This subcategory includes procedure codes for the excision and removal of tendons and muscles of the hand that are not more specifically coded in this chapter.
82.4X	Suture of Muscle, Tendon, and Fascia of Hand—This is the repair of muscle, tendon, or fascia by stitching.
82.5X	Transplantation of Muscle and Tendon of Hand—These procedures involve surgeries that detach and reattach muscles and tendons of the hand.
82.6X	Reconstruction of Thumb—Should the thumb need to be constructed due to an accident or birth defect, this subcategory of codes is referenced for the procedure. This subcategory includes bone and skin grafts, as well as the transfer of the digit if necessary. The amputation of this digit is coded separately.
82.7X	Plastic Operation on Hand with Graft or Implant—This subcategory includes tendon graft to the hand. Restoring opposing tendons, known as **opponensplasty,** is coded to this subcategory.
82.8X	Other Plastic Operations on Hand—The procedures in this subcategory include the repair of cleft hand, mallet finger, and macrodactyly. **Macroadactyly** is a condition in which fingers are abnormally large.
82.9X	Other Operations on Muscle, Tendon, and Fascia of Hand—The lysis of adhesions, aspirations, and injections are coded this subcategory. Any procedure on the muscles, tendons, and fascia of the hand that is not coded more specifically in this chapter is coded from this subcategory.

Operations on Muscle, Tendon, Fascia, and Bursa, Except Hand (Category Code 83)

Category 83, Operations on muscle, tendon, fascia, and bursa, except hand, encompasses the procedures on these structures that are located outside the area of the hand. This category includes procedures for tendon expansion, revisions, lysis of adhesions, and excisions. The synovial membrane of the bursa, as well as tendon sheaths, is included in this category of codes.

Procedure Codes	Description
83.0X	Incision of Muscle, Tendon Fascia, and Bursa—This subcategory includes procedures in which the muscle, tendon, fascia, or bursa is incised.
83.1X	Division of Muscle, Tendon, and Fascia—This is the surgical separation of muscle, tendons, or fascia for locations other than the hand.

83.2X	Diagnostic Procedures on Muscle, Tendon, Fascia, and Bursa, Including That of Hand—This subcategory includes biopsies and other diagnostic procedures.
83.3X	Excision of Lesion of Muscle, Tendon, Fascia, and Bursa—Should any of these structures be damaged or develop lesions, the surgical removal of the lesion or damaged tissue is coded to this subcategory.
83.4X	Other Excision of Muscle, Tendon, and Fascia—The excision of muscle, tendons, or fascia to be used for grafting at another site is coded to this subcategory.
83.5	Bursectomy—This is the surgical removal of the bursa. This procedure code should not be used for bursectomy of the hand.
83.6X	Suture of Muscle, Tendon, and Fascia—Rotator cuff repair is the correction of the musculomembrane that surrounds the capsule of the shoulder joint. This repair is coded to this subcategory.
83.7X	Reconstruction of Muscle and Tendon—These procedures involve surgeries that detach and reattach muscles and tendons at locations other than the hand. Arthroplasty is not included in this subcategory.
83.8X	Other Plastic Operations on Muscle, Tendon, and Fascia—Tendon and muscle graft, release of clubfoot, and hamstring lengthening are all included in this subcategory.
83.9X	Other Operations on Muscle, Tendon, Fascia, and Bursa—This subcategory includes lysis of adhesions, injections, and aspiration procedures. The insertion or replacement of skeletal muscle stimulator, including the electrodes, is coded to this subcategory.

Other Procedures on Musculoskeletal System (Category Code 84)

Category 84, Other procedures on musculoskeletal system, codes amputation and disarticulation procedures. Also coded to this category is the fitting of a prosthesis after amputation. Amputation is the removal of a limb or organ. In reference to procedure codes in this category, the amputations are done surgically. Disarticulation is a form of amputation, but done at the joint. There are different types of amputation procedures. The coder should reference the inclusion notes to be sure of proper code assignment.

Procedure Codes	Description
84.0X	Amputation of Upper Limb—Amputation and disarticulation of the upper limbs of the body, including hand and finger amputation.
84.1X	Amputation of Lower Limb—Amputation and disarticulation of the lower limbs of the body, including foot and toe amputation.
84.2X	Reattachment of Extremity—If an extremity is amputated owing to an accidental cause, an attempt may be made to surgically reattach this extremity. This subcategory contains the code for this procedure.
84.3	Revision of Amputation Stump—This is the procedure code used should a previous amputation site need surgical correction.
84.4X	Implantation or Fitting of Prosthetic Limb Device—The fitting and placement of an artificial limb device are coded to this subcategory. Documentation for this procedure requires note of measurements for placement.
84.5X	Implantation of Other Musculoskeletal Devices and Substances—This subcategory includes the placement of cages or spacers into the spine. Also included here is the placement of morphoenetic protein material to stimulate new bone formation.
84.9X	Other Operations on Musculoskeletal System—Procedures that are not coded more specifically in this chapter are referenced to this subcategory.

Each year, new approaches are used to surgically treat injuries and illnesses that affect the musculoskeletal system. It is essential for coders to increase their knowledge of these procedures.

Internet Links

To learn more about operations and procedures completed on the musculoskeletal system visit *http://omni.ac.uk*, *http://www.fpnotebook.com*, and *http://www.righthealth.com/topic/orthopedic?*.

Summary

- Chapter 14 of volume 3 of ICD-9-CM is entitled "Operations on the Musculoskeletal System."
- The musculoskeletal system is the framework of the body and protects internal organs.
- *Osse-, ossi-, osteo-,* and *osto-* are prefixes that refer to bone. *Arthro-* is a prefix that refers to the joint.
- The procedures in this chapter refer to operations performed on bones, bone marrow, cartilage, ligaments, joints, bursa, snyovial membranes, muscles, tendons, and fascia.
- Amputations and disarticulations are coded to this chapter.

Chapter Review

True/False: Indicate whether the statement is true (T) or false (F).

1. _____ A bunion is also referred to as a "hammer toe."

2. _____ ORIF is an abbreviation for open reduction internal fixation.

3. _____ The revision of an upper extremity joint replacement is coded to subcategory 80.9X.

4. _____ Code 83.5 can be used for bursectomy of hand.

5. _____ Intervertebral disk destruction is found in subcategory 80.5X.

Fill-in-the-Blank: Enter the appropriate term(s) to complete the statement.

6. Should an internal fixation device become loose or displaced, correction of this is coded to subcategory _____.

7. The procedure in which bony exostosis is removed from the great toe is called _____.

8. _____ is a condition in which the bone is not fractured but is out of place.

9. Amputation at the joint is called _____.

10. Synovial fluid is secreted by the _____ to ease in movement of the joint.

Coding Assignments

Instructions: Using an ICD-9-CM coding book, select the appropriate procedure code.

Procedure	Code
1. Debridement of open fracture of femur	_____
2. Quadricepsplasty	_____
3. Disarticulation of shoulder	_____

4. Open reduction of dislocation of knee   _____

5. Arthrodesis of shoulder   _____

6. Intervertebral chemonucleolysis   _____

7. Bunionectomy with soft tissue correction   _____

8. Removal of implanted fixation device of the femur   _____

9. Refusion of lumbar spine, anterior technique   _____

10. Augmentation genioplasty   _____

11. Insertion of osteogenic electrodes for bone growth, humerus   _____

12. Open reduction of wrist dislocation   _____

13. Arthoscopy of knee   _____

14. Sequestrectomy of facial bone   _____

15. Total hip replacement   _____

16. Heel cord shortening   _____

17. Total ostectomy of three phalanges on left foot   _____

18. Fitting of a prosthetic arm   _____

19. Open reduction of the radius with internal fixation   _____

20. Reattachment of Achilles tendon   _____

21. Hemimaxillectomy with bone graft   _____

22. Local excision of lesion of the left tarsal bone   _____

23. Aspiration biopsy of elbow   _____

24. Arthrodesis of C1 using anterolateral technique   _____

25. Repair of macrodactyly   _____

Case Studies

Instructions: Review each case study, and select the correct ICD-9-CM diagnostic and procedural codes.

CASE 1

PREOPERATIVE/POSTOPERATIVE DIAGNOSIS: Ischemic right leg with nonreconstructible rest pain

PROCEDURE: This is a 69-year-old male who had previous angioplasty and stenting procedures that have ultimately been unsuccessful. It was determined that the right leg would be amputated above the knee. The patient was taken to the operating room, placed in the supine position, and given general anesthesia with endotracheal intubation. The right leg was prepped and draped in the usual sterile fashion. A standard fish-mouth incision was made above the knee with a 10 blade scalpel. Cautery was used to dissect down through subcutaneous tissue and muscle. Hemostasis was maintained; any time bleeding was encountered it was cauterized, and small and medium hemoclips were used for control. I came across the main arteries with clamps and then cut and suture ligated them with #2-0 Vicryl suture ties. The fibular nerve was found, clamped, cut, suture ligated with #2-0 Vicryl suture ties, and allowed to retract into the muscle proximally. I was then able to transect the femur 4 cm above the level of the skin incision with the oscillating saw. The lower leg was handed off to the scrub nurse. We went back and made sure the wound was hemostatic with cautery and more clips and sutures.

The wound was irrigated with saline and antibiotics. A little bone wax was applied to prevent any bleeding from the marrow space, and then I reapproximated the anterior and posterior fascia with interrupted #2-0 Vicryl suture. The skin was then reapproximated with #3-0 Ethilon vertical mattress sutures. A ½-inch Penrose drain was placed from medial to lateral in the wound. All counts were correct. Wound was dressed, and patient was taken to recovery room in stable condition.

ICD-9-CM Code Assignment: _____

CASE 2

PREOPERATIVE/POSTOPERATIVE DIAGNOSIS: Maisonneuve fracture, right ankle

This is a 39-year-old woman who presented for syndesmotic screw placement following a right ankle injury.

PROCEDURE: Patient presented to operating room for placement of syndesmotic screw in the right ankle to obtain proper alignment and prevent displacement of ankle fracture. Patient was prepped and draped in the usual sterile fashion. Induction of general anesthesia was done intravenously.

Using image intensification, a guidewire was applied to the external surface of the ankle, which allowed us to obtain proper placement of the screw. The right ankle was incised with a 15-blade scalpel. The guidewire was placed through the fibula into the tibia using imaging guidance. This went through three cortices, and a 50-mm 4.0 cannulated screw was placed over the guidewire. The guidewire was then removed. The placement was verified under imaging guidance, and then the incision was closed with 3-0 Vicryl suture. Cast was applied in plantigrade position to the right ankle, and the patient was sent to the recovery room in stable condition.

ICD-9-CM Code Assignment: _____

CASE 3

PREOPERATIVE/POSTOPERATIVE DIAGNOSIS: Status postsyndesmotic disruption of right ankle to correct Maisonneuve fracture

Patient is a 39-year-old female who returns to have hardware removed from ankle that was placed a little over 3 months ago.

PROCEDURE: The patient was taken to the operating room, where IV sedation was given. The right ankle was prepped and draped in the usual sterile fashion. At the old incision site, a #15 blade scalpel was used to open the old incision. Dissection was carried down to the screw, which was easily removed with a screwdriver. The wound was irrigated and closed with #3-0 nylon interrupted sutures. A sterile dressing was applied. The patient was taken to the recovery room in stable condition.

ICD-9-CM Code Assignment: _____

CASE 4

Patient is an 8-year-old male who presents today with right wrist pain. Patient was riding his skateboard when he hit a crack in the sidewalk and fell forward. His arms were outstretched when he hit the concrete. He denies loss of consciousness, which was confirmed by witnesses. He has not had any vomiting, abdominal pain, or dizziness.

X-ray of the right arm and wrist reveals a dislocation of the right wrist. Using the X-ray as a guide, a closed reduction of the distal radioulnar joint was performed. Follow-up X-ray revealed that the bones are now in place. The child is fitted for a splint and shoulder immobilizer, which are to be worn for the next 10 days, after which we will reassess the injury site. If all is well, he will be able to resume normal activity.

ICD-9-CM Code Assignment: _____

CASE 5

This is a 33-year-old male who presents with a fibrous cyst of the left proximal tibia. Biopsies have already been performed, and no malignancy is present. The patient now needs curettage of the tibial cyst to gain more comfort and ambulation.

The patient's left leg was prepped and draped in the usual sterile fashion after general anesthesia was administered. The proximal tibia was incised at the same site as the previous biopsy. The cyst contained some chalky material, which was sent to pathology, but there was no evidence of infection or malignancy, as previously stated. The cyst was totally removed and the site was irrigated. The site was closed in layered fashion. The patient tolerated the procedure well and was returned to the recovery room in good condition.

ICD-9-CM Code Assignment: _____

Operations on the Integumentary System

Chapter Outline

Objectives

At the conclusion of this chapter, the student will be able to:

1. Identify pathologies that affect the integumentary system.
2. Describe the procedures used to correct the pathologies.
3. Discuss procedures that are completed on the structures of the integumentary system.
4. Select and code diagnoses and procedures from case studies.

Key Terms

Augmentation Mammoplasty	Escharotomy	Integumentary System	Pedicle Graft
Chemical Peel	Free Skin Graft	Mammo-	Resection of a Quadrant of a Breast
Debridement	Fulguration	Mammotomy	Subcutaneous Mammectomy
Dermabrasion	Heterografting	Mastectomy	
Dermal Regenerative Graft	Homograft	Masto-	Transposition of a Nipple
Electrolysis	Incision and Drainage (I&D)	Mastopexy	
		Mastotomy	

Reminder

As you work through this chapter, you will need to have a copy of the ICD-9-CM coding book to reference.

Introduction

The integumentary system is another name for the skin. The skin has several functions in that it protects the internal body from possible infection, prevents fluid loss, and is the receptor for our sense of touch.

The procedure codes in this chapter include procedures on the breast, the removal of skin lesions and foreign bodies, and skin grafting.

Coding Operations on the Integumentary System

Category 85, Operations on the breast, includes the skin and subcutaneous tissue of the breast. The codes in this category are not gender specific and may be used for procedure coding on males and females. Some common prefixes used to reference the breast are mammo- and masto-.

Procedure Codes	Description
85.0	Mastotomy—This is a surgical incision into the breast. The term *mammotomy* is also used for this procedure.
85.1X	Diagnostic Procedures on Breast—Diagnostic procedures in this subcategory include open biopsy of the breast as well as a percutaneous needle biopsy.
85.2X	Excision or Destruction of Breast Tissue—This subcategory of codes includes the excision or destruction of breast tissue, as well as a resection of a quadrant of a breast, in which one of the quadrants of the breast is removed.
85.3X	Reduction Mammoplasty and Subcutaneous Mammectomy—This subcategory contains procedure codes for breast reduction procedures. Subcutaneous mammectomy is also coded to this subcategory. This is a procedure in which the subcutaneous tissue of the breast is removed but the skin and nipple are left intact.
85.4X	Mastectomy—A mastectomy is the surgical removal of a breast. This subcategory contains procedure codes for different types of mastectomies. Figure 40-1 shows the different types of breast surgery options. This subcategory also distinguishes between a bilateral and a unilateral procedure.
85.5X	Augmentation Mammoplasty—This is a type of plastic surgery in which the breast is reconstructed to a larger size. Breast injections and breast implants are also coded to this subcategory. This subcategory also distinguishes between a bilateral and a unilateral procedure.
85.6	Mastopexy—A mastopexy is a form of mammaplasty in which the breast is surgically reconstructed.
85.7X	Total Reconstruction of Breast—This is a procedure used to totally form a new breast. If this procedure is performed after a radical mastectomy, it is usually done in a separate operative session.
85.8X	Other Repair and Plastic Operations on Breast—This subcategory contains procedure codes for graft procedures done to the skin and muscle tissue of the breast. The transposition of the nipple is also coded to this subcategory. Transposition of a nipple is a procedure in which the nipple is surgically relocated.
85.9X	Other Operations on the Breast—This subcategory includes the aspiration of breast fluid, revision and removal of breast implants, and insertion of breast tissue expanders.

Operations on the Skin and Subcutaneous Tissue (Category Code 86)

Category 86, Operations on skin and subcutaneous tissue, includes injection, incision, excision, debridement, and grafting procedures. This category contains many inclusion and exclusion notes that the coder should be aware of.

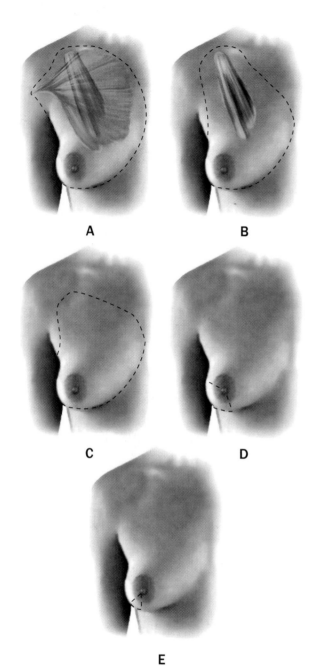

Figure 40-1 Breast surgery options: **(A)** Radical mastectomy, **(B)** modified radical mastectomy, **(C)** simple mastectomy, **(D)** segmental resection, **(E)** lumpectomy (From Price P, Frey KB, Junge TL. *Surgical Technology for the Surgical Technologist: A Positive Care Approach,* 2nd ed. Clifton Park, NY: Delmar, Cengage Learning, 2004, p. 458.)

Procedure Codes	Description
86.0X	Incision of Skin and Subcutaneous Tissue—Aspirations of an abscess, hematoma, or seroma are all included in this subcategory. Incision and drainage procedures are coded to this subcategory. An incision and drainage procedure (I&D) involves surgically cutting and then withdrawing fluid from the skin. Another procedure coded to this subcategory is called an escharotomy. This procedure is the surgical cutting into the edges of a scab formed by a burn.
86.1X	Diagnostic Procedures on Skin and Subcutaneous Tissue—This subcategory contains the procedure code for the biopsy of the skin and subcutaneous tissue.
86.2X	Excision or Destruction of Lesion or Tissue of Skin and Subcutaneous Tissue—This subcategory contains codes for procedures such as wound debridement, debridement of the nail and surrounding area, chemical peel, and dermabrasion. Debridement of the skin and nails involves the surgical removal of damaged tissue. Chemical peel is a procedure in which chemicals are use to destroy and remove skin. Dermabrasion is a procedure in which the skin is surgically removed by planing with chemicals, fine sandpaper, wire brush, or laser.

86.3	Other Local Excision or Destruction of Lesion or Tissue of Skin and Subcutaneous Tissue—The destruction of skin by laser, cauterization, cryosurgery, and fulguration is included in this subcategory. Fulguration is a procedure in which a high-frequency electric current is used to destroy the skin.
86.4	Radical Excision of Skin Lesion—This procedure is a wide-margined excison of a skin lesion. The excision is deep and may involve adjacent structures.
86.5X	Suture or Other Closure of Skin and Subcutaneous Tissue—This is the closure of skin by means of sutures, staples, or adhesives such as Dermabond.
86.6X	Free Skin Graft—In a free skin graft, the donor tissue is completely removed from its site before it is applied to the recipient site. This subcategory also includes a graft of nonhuman material, such as pigskin, to the donor, a procedure called heterografting. Should the donor skin belong to another human, the procedure is called homograft. Should the patient's own skin be cultured or regenerated by using a substance to promote growth for the grafting procedure, the code for dermal regenerative graft is used.
86.7X	Pedicle Grafts or Flaps—A pedicle graft is a type of graft that remains attached to its blood supply.
86.8X	Other Repair and Reconstruction of Skin and Subcutaneous Tissue—This subcategory includes procedures for the repair of facial weakness, surgical repair of excess facial skin, liposuction, and repair of the nail or nailbed.
86.9X	Other Operations on Skin and Subcutaneous Tissue—This subcategory includes the surgical removal of skin for use in grafting, the insertion of tissue expander, and electrolysis. Electrolysis is the removal of hair by use of electric current.

When coding in this chapter of ICD-9-CM, it is important for the coder to read the medical documentation to determine the layer of skin in which the procedures are performed. The coder must identify whether the procedure was performed on the epidermis, dermis, or subcutaneous tissue. The coder should also note whether muscle tissue was involved.

Internet Links

To research procedures on performed on the integumentary system, visit *http://www.lib.uiowa.edu*, *http://dermatlas.med.jhmi.edu*, and *http://tray.dermatology.uiowa.edu*.

Summary

- Chapter 15 of volume 3 of ICD-9-CM is entitled "Operations on the Integumentary System."
- The integumentary system protects the internal body from infection and fluid loss.
- Breast procedures, such as mastectomy and mammoplasty, are coded to this chapter.
- These breast procedures are not gender specific.
- Other procedures found in this chapter include repair of skin, excision of lesions, and grafting.

Chapter Review

True/False: Indicate whether the statement is true (T) or false (F).

1. _____ Liposuction is coded to subcategory 86.83.

2. _____ Breast augmentation is a procedure in which the breast is reduced in size.

3. _____ Breast procedures in category 85 are not gender specific.

4. _____ Grafting using donor skin, pigskin, or regenerative skin is coded to the 86.7X subcategory.

5. _____ Breast reconstruction after a radical mastectomy is coded to 85.7.

Fill-in-the-Blank: Enter the appropriate term(s) to complete the phrase:

6. The procedure in which the nipple is surgically moved is called _____.

7. The surgical removal of a breast is called a _____.

8. Surgical removal of damaged tissue is called _____.

9. Removal of hair by electric current is called _____.

10. A _____ is a type of graft that remains attached to its blood supply.

Coding Assignments

Instructions: Using an ICD-9-CM coding book, select the appropriate procedure code.

Procedure	Code
1. Bilateral breast implant	_____
2. Full-thickness skin graft to hand	_____
3. Bilateral subcutaneous mammectomy with synchronous implant	_____
4. Bilateral extended simple mastectomy	_____
5. Escharotomy	_____
6. Onychoplasty	_____
7. Laceration repair of hand, three sutures	_____
8. Removal of breast implant	_____
9. Relaxation of web contracture	_____
10. Lumpectomy	_____
11. Cryosurgery on skin lesion	_____
12. Unilateral simple mastectomy	_____
13. Facial rhytidectomy	_____
14. Muscle flap graft to breast	_____
15. Dermabrasion	_____
16. Subtotal mastectomy	_____
17. Chemosurgery of skin	_____
18. Bilateral radical mastectomy	_____
19. Punch biopsy of skin of arm	_____
20. Excision of nipple	_____

21. Insertion of tissue expander of the scalp   _____

22. Repair for facial weakness   _____

23. Bilateral injection into breast for augmentation   _____

24. Bilateral simple mastectomy   _____

25. Split-thickness graft to breast   _____

Case Studies

Instructions: Review each case study, and select the correct ICD-9-CM diagnostic and procedural codes.

CASE 1

PREOPERATIVE DIAGNOSIS: Left breast lump at 3 o'clock
Microcalcification, suspicious, left breast at 12 o'clock

POSTOPERATIVE DIAGNOSIS: Pending path report

INDICATIONS: This is a 45-year-old female who, upon self-breast exam, found a suspicious lump in her left breast at the 3 o'clock position. A mammogram was performed, and a second suspicious cluster of microcalcification was noted in the 12 o'clock position. We discussed options with the patient, and it was agreed that a needle biopsy of these lesions would be the best course of action.

PROCEDURE: Prior to being brought to the operating room, the patient had guide wire placement. She was placed in the supine position, and general anesthesia was induced. The left breast was prepped and draped in the normal sterile fashion. A 3-cm-long incision was made between the two wire sites in the upper portion of the breast. Cautery dissection was used to elevate the skin flaps. Hemostasis was obtained, and the dissection was carried down to remove the tissue surrounding the mare lateral wire. A biopsy was obtained by removing a segment of tissue measuring 3 cm × 5 cm. Then the next specimen was addressed and dissected. Tissue measuring 3 cm × 3 cm was removed. No other suspicious areas were noted, and the wounds were carefully closed and dressed. Both specimens were sent immediately to pathology.

ICD-9-CM Code Assignment: _____

CASE 2

The patient is a 32-year-old male who was accidentally shot in the right forearm when the gun his father was cleaning discharged. There are bullet fragments in the skin, but the bullet missed the radius and ulnar arteries.

PROCEDURE: The patient was prepped and draped in the usual sterile fashion. While in supine position, general anesthesia was administered. The right arm was examined and the wound was explored. There were found to be multiple linear wounds measuring 6 cm, 4 cm, and 10 cm in the right forearm. There is exposed tendon and muscle, which appear intact. All subcutaneous tissue, as well as the tissue surrounding the wound, was extensively debrided. Antibiotic solution was used to irrigate the wound, and all palpable and visible bullet fragments were removed. Cautery was used to achieve hemostasis, and a Penrose drain was placed into the muscle compartment using 2-0 Vicryl. The skin was closed with staples. The patient tolerated the procedure well and was returned to the recovery room in stable condition.

ICD-9-CM Code Assignment: _____

CASE 3

This is a 71-year-old male who presents today for follow-up to surgery to remove a lesion on the left flank. The procedure was performed 1 week ago while he was out of town. The patient spent 3 months in Florida before returning home for the summer months. A postoperative seroma is present at the site of the excision.

The left flank was prepped and draped in the usual sterile fashion. An anesthetic mixture of 5 cc Lidocaine with epinephrine was injected in the area. A 16-gauge needle was then used to puncture and aspirate 20 cc of fluid. A pressure dressing was applied. The patient tolerated the procedure well and will return in 3–4 days for a wound check.

ICD-9-CM Code Assignment: _____

CASE 4

Patient is a 54-year-old female who presents today for removal of right breast lumps. The right breast shows a 2-cm lump in the 9:00 position and a 3-cm lump in the 6:00 position. The patient has had the breast marked with a marking pen preoperatively.

Addressing the lump in the 6:00 position, first an incision was made with the Bovie. Using Lahey tenaculum, the breast mass was grasped and dissected using sharp dissection. No other lumps, cysts, or abnormalities were noted by inspection or palpation. This 3-cm lump was sent for pathology in its entirety. Moving to the 9:00 position, dissection was carried from the medial aspect of the incision to the subcutaneous tissue where the mass was identified. Using the Lahey tenaculum and sharp dissection, this mass was also removed in its entirety, approximately 2.5 cm. This lump was also sent to pathology. Hemostasis was obtained with the Bovie. The wound was irrigated with saline, and each wound was closed using 4-0 Monocryl for the skin and 2-0 Vicryl for the subcutaneous tissue. Patient was returned to the recovery room in good condition.

ICD-9-CM Code Assignment: _____

CASE 5

This is a 40-year-old woman who presents today for a dermabrasion treatment. We have discussed the risks and benefits, and she is willing to proceed. Her face was prepped, and using the rotary instrument, we began with the forehead and worked in a clockwise motion around the face until all surface area was treated. Once the procedure was completed, the patient was given water; then hypoallergenic cream was applied to lessen the redness. She will return in 6 months.

ICD-9-CM Code Assignment: _____

Miscellaneous Procedures and Interventions

Chapter Outline

Objectives

At the conclusion of this chapter, the student will be able to:

1. Identify procedures that fall under the miscellaneous category because they are not coded more specifically in the procedure section of ICD-9-CM.
2. Describe some of the procedures that are coded to the Miscellaneous Procedures and Interventions chapter of ICD-9-CM.
3. Discuss some of the more unusual procedures that might be encountered by a coder.
4. Select and code diagnoses and procedures from case studies.

Key Terms

Angiocardiography
Arteriography
Autopsy
Computerized Axial
  Tomography
Contrast
Diagnostic Radiology

Echogram
Electrocardiogram
  (EKG, ECG)
Extracorporeal Shock
  Wave Lithotripsy
Infusion
Inhaled
Injection

Magnetic Resonance
  Imaging (MRI)
Nuclear Medicine
Pharmaceuticals
Phlebography
Physical Therapy
Respiratory Therapy

Retrograde
Sonogram
Therapeutic Ultrasound
Thermography
Tomography
Tonometry
Ultrasound

Reminder

As you work through this chapter, you will need to have a copy of the ICD-9-CM coding book to reference.

Introduction

This chapter discusses procedures that are coded to the 00 category, Procedures and interventions, not elsewhere classified. Also, categories 87–99, miscellaneous diagnostic and therapeutic procedures that are found in ICD-9-CM volume 3, are included in this chapter because of the similarities in the procedure codes found in both categories.

Procedures found in these categories include therapeutic procedures, the injection of pharmaceuticals, cardiovascular procedures, radiologic procedures, stress testing, and physical, speech, and occupational therapy procedures.

Coding Procedures and Interventions (Category Code 00)

Category 00, Procedures and interventions not elsewhere classified, is the only category in this chapter of the ICD-9-CM code book. The category further breaks down into subcategories for the procedures listed.

Some of the subcategories in this chapter include therapeutic ultrasound, pharmaceuticals, and other cardiovascular procedures. Ultrasound is a form of imaging in which high-frequency sound waves reflect from body tissue and the pulses are recorded and viewed as images. Pharmaceuticals are medications or a combination of medications used to treat a condition.

Procedure Codes	Description
00.0X	Therapeutic ultrasound—This is the use of ultrasound to treat diseased or damaged tissue. Therapeutic ultrasound is used in peripheral vascular vessels, vessels of the head and neck, and the heart and its vessels.
00.1X	Pharmaceuticals—These can be injected, infused, or inhaled. Injection is the delivery of medication by inserting a needle into the skin; the needle is then removed. The process is very short in time duration. Infusion is a form of injection, but the needle is placed intravenously and medication is passed through for a length of time that can span from minutes to days. Inhaled occurs when medication is passed through a device that allows the patient to breathe in the medication through the nose and mouth. Figure 41-1 illustrates types of intravenous delivery methods.
00.5X	Other Cardiovascular Procedures—Pacemaker procedures are coded to chapter 7, "Operations on Cardiovascular System," of ICD-9-CM, volume 3. This subcatergory codes procedures for the implantation of resynchronization systems. These are implanted to improve cardiac output by assisting the pacemaker in simultaneous ventricular contractions.

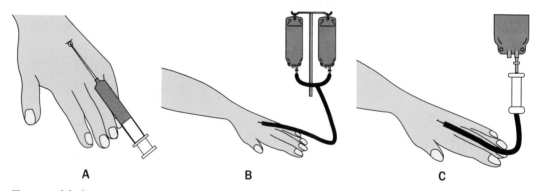

   A   B   C

Figure 41-1 Intravenous delivery of medication: (**A**) Intravenous push, (**B**) intravenous piggyback (intermittent), (**C**) infusion (continuous) (From Sormunen C. *Terminology for Allied Health Professions,* 5th ed. Clifton Park, NY: Delmar, Cengage Learning, 2003, p. 68.)

Miscellaneous Diagnostic and Therapeutic Procedures (Category Codes 87–99)

Chapter 16, "Miscellaneous Diagnostic and Therapeutic Procedures," is the final chapter of the procedure codes of ICD-9-CM. The procedure codes in this chapter report radiology procedures, therapies, and other procedures that are not coded to a more specific category.

Diagnostic Radiology (Category Code 87)

Category 87, Diagnostic radiology, is the first category in this chapter. Diagnostic radiology is the use of X-ray to photograph specific areas to determine whether pathology is present.

Procedure Codes	Description
87.0X	Soft-Tissue X-Ray of Face, Head, and Neck—The X-ray procedures represented in this subcategory involve the soft tissue of the face, head, and neck. These procedures also include X-ray with contrast. Contrast is used to X-ray parts of the body that normally cannot be X-rayed. The contrast material is usually barium or iodine based. Also found throughout this category of codes is a procedure called tomography. Tomography is a technique in imaging that involves taking an image of one layer of the body while blocking layers above and below it. In computerized axial tomography, the computer is used to produce a cross-section image of a structure. The view is three-dimensional.
87.1X	Other X-Ray of Face, Head, and Neck—This subcategory contains codes for procedures performed on areas of the face, head, and neck that are not coded in subcategory 87.0X.
87.2X	X-Ray of Spine—This subcategory contains codes for X-ray imaging of the cervical, thoracic, and lumbar spinal areas.
87.3X	Soft Tissue X-Ray of Thorax—X-ray imaging coded to this subcategory includes the breast, the chest wall, and the bronchus. Images of the thoracic area taken after administering contrast material are also coded to this subcategory.
87.4X	Other X-Ray of Thorax—This subcategory contains codes for procedures performed on areas of the thorax that are not coded in subcategory 87.3X
87.5X	Biliary Tract X-Ray—This subcategory contains codes for X-ray imaging of the biliary tract and includes the bile duct and the gallbladder.
87.6X	Other X-Ray of Digestive System—This subcategory contains the imaging codes for the upper and lower gastrointestinal tract. This subcategory also contains imaging with contrast.
87.7X	X-Ray of Urinary System—This subcategory contains imaging codes for the urinary system. The coder might notice the term *retrograde* in this subcategory. Retrograde, when used in the imaging process, means going against the normal direction of blood flow. Contrast medium is injected against the normal direction of blood flow of the area.
87.8X	X-Ray of Female Genital Organs—This is the imaging of the female genital organs.
87.9X	X-Ray of Male Genital Organs—The imaging of male genital organs is coded to this subcategory.

Other Diagnostic Radiology and Related Techniques (Category Code 88)

Category 88, Other diagnostic radiology and related techniques, is the next category in this chapter. These procedures are not coded in the 87 category.

Procedure Codes	Description
88.0X	Soft-Tissue X-Ray of Abdomen—This subcategory contains soft-tissue X-rays, including tomography, of the abdomen.
88.1X	Other X-Ray of Abdomen—Imaging procedure codes of the abdomen that do not include the soft tissue.
88.2X	Skeletal X-Ray of Extremities and Pelvis—These procedure codes are for X-rays done on the bones of the pelvis, arms, legs, hands, and feet.
88.3X	Other X-Ray—This subcategory includes procedure codes on the soft tissue of the extremities, contrast injections, and X-rays of multiple parts of the skeleton.
88.4X	Arteriography Using Contrast Material—Arteriography is the imaging of an artery or an arterial family after the injection of material into the bloodstream. The inclusion notes for this subcategory are important because they guide the coder on what is included in the code being used. The fourth-digit subclassification notes the site viewed, not the site of the injection of contrast material.
88.5X	Angiocardiography Using Contrast Material—Similar to the arteriography, the angiocardiography takes images of the arteries with the use of contrast material, but it is specifically used for images of the heart and the great vessels.
88.6X	Phlebography—This uses contrast material to take images of the veins. Similar to the angiography, the inclusion notes are important in assigning the correct code and understanding what is included in the code being assigned from this subcategory.

Procedure Codes	Description
88.7X	Diagnostic Ultrasound—An ultrasound uses sound waves to bounce off a structure and produce an image of the structure. The record that is generated by an ultrasound is called a sonogram or an echogram. Diagnostic ultrasounds are performed on pregnant women to check the progress of a pregnancy.
88.8X	Thermography—This is a type of imaging that uses infrared photography of body temperature of a structure to project an image.
88.9X	Other Diagnostic Imaging—This subcategory is where we find the procedure codes for magnetic resonance imaging (MRI). The fourth-digit classification identifies the location where the procedure is being performed.

Interview, Evaluation, Consultation, and Examination (Category Code 89)

Category 89, Interview, evaluation, consultation, and examination, contains procedure codes that identify types of consultations and interviews. The examinations in this subcategory are of specific areas of different body systems. Cardiac procedures that are not found in chapter 7, "Operations on the Cardiovascular System," are found in this category.

Procedure Codes	Description
89.0X	Diagnostic Interview, Consultation, and Evaluation—The procedure code selected in this subcategory depends on the documentation the provider has written or dictated in the patient's medical record. The codes range from brief to comprehensive.
89.1X	Anatomic and Physiologic Measurements and Manual Examinations, Nervous System and Sense Organs—This subcategory contains procedure codes for the measurement of intraocular pressure, called a tonometry, and nasal function studies. Sleep studies and neurologic examinations are also found in this subcategory.
89.2X	Anatomic and Physiologic Measurements and Manual Examinations, Genitourinary System—This subcategory contains various procedure codes that measure urethral pressure and urine flow, as well as pelvic examination.
89.3X	Other Anatomic and Physiologic Measurements and Manual Examinations—This subcategory includes codes for dental examination, manual breast examination, and digital rectal examination.
89.4X	Cardiac Stress Tests, Pacemaker and Defibrillator Checks—Various types of procedure codes are available for a cardiac stress test, depending on whether a simple treadmill test is done or exercise on a bicycle. Regardless of the type of exercise required, an electrocardiogram is generated. The pacemaker checks are done routinely on the various parts of the pacemaker to be sure they are working properly.
89.5X	Other Nonoperative Cardiac and Vascular Diagnostic Procedures—This subcategory includes an electrocardiogram (EKG), which is an electrical record of the activity of the heart. This may also be referred to as an ECG.
89.6X	Circulatory Monitoring—These procedure codes include monitoring of central venous pressure as well as arterial pressure. Measurement of blood gases is also coded to this subcategory.
89.7	General Physical Examination—This is the procedure code for a regular physical examination.
89.8	Autopsy—An autopsy is the postmortem internal and external examination of a body.

Category Codes 90–99

Category 90, Microscopic examination-I, and category 91, Microscopic examination-II, involve the procedure codes for the examination of tissue under a microscope. A fourth-digit subclassification is used in both of these categories for identifying the type of examination performed, such as bacterial smear, culture and sensitivity, and toxicology.

Category 92, Nuclear medicine, encompasses procedures that use radioactive or atomic energy to treat disease or diagnosis conditions. This category is where the various scanning procedures are located. A code selection is made depending on the site of the scan.

Also included in category 92 are the radiation procedures used to treat some forms of cancer. The implantation or insertion of radioactive substances is also found in this category.

Category 93, Physical therapy, respiratory therapy, rehabilitation, and related procedures, contains various exercises and treatments used by these different providers. Physical therapy is a type of treatment offered by a trained professional who uses exercise, massage, and other forms of physical movement to treat disease or disorders.

Respiratory therapy is a form of treatment administered by a trained professional who uses various techniques to assist and enhance a patient's respiratory function. Procedures such as oxygen therapy and mist therapy with a nebulizer are just two of the procedures found in this section of category 93.

Category 94, Procedures related to psyche, contains procedure codes related to mental health conditions. The procedures in this category deal with psychological testing, drug therapy, crisis intervention, and counseling. Also included in this category are procedure codes related to alcohol and drug rehabilitation.

Category 95, Ophthalmologic and otologic diagnosis and treatment, contains procedure codes that fall outside surgical intervention for the eye and ear. Eye examinations, hearing tests, X-ray studies, and fitting of hearing aids are the more frequently referenced codes in this subcategory.

Category 96, Nonoperative intubation and irrigation, contains procedure codes for gastrointestinal and respiratory intubation. Also coded to this category are packing procedures and nonoperative manipulations. This category contains codes for all areas of the body that are not specifically defined within the chapter of operation codes for the particular body system.

Category 97, Replacement and removal of therapeutic appliances, encompasses procedure codes for all body areas. This subcategory of codes is referenced when a packing or appliance application procedure is completed, some time passes, and now removal or replacement of the appliance or packing is necessary. The third-digit classification notes the body system and the fourth-digit classification identifies the type of appliance or packing.

Category 98, Nonoperative removal of foreign body or calculus, contains procedure codes for the removal of a foreign body without an incision. An example of this is extracorporeal shock wave lithotripsy, a procedure in which kidney stones are broken up by a machine that is positioned outside the body and that generates high-voltage waves that break up the stones inside the body so that they can be passed through the kidneys.

Category 99, Other nonoperative procedures, is the last category of the ICD-9-CM procedure codes. Any procedures that are not coded more specifically elsewhere in volume 3 might be referenced to this section of the book. Blood transfusions, allergy injections, vaccinations, therapeutic injections, acupuncture, and ultraviolet light therapy are all found in this category.

Internet Links

Information about radiological procedures can be found at *www.radiologyinfo.org*.

Cardiac procedures can be researched at *www.medicinenet.com*.

Physical therapy procedures can be reviewed at *www.apta.org*.

Occupational therapy procedures can be reviewed at *www.aota.org*.

Summary

- Category 00 of volume 3 of ICD-9-CM classifies procedures and interventions not found elsewhere in volume 3.

- Chapter 16 of volume 3 classifies diagnostic and therapeutic procedures not classified elsewhere in volume 3.

- Therapeutic procedures, injections of pharmaceuticals as well as vaccinations, and radiological procedures are all found in these chapters.
- Ultrasound procedures, thermography, angiography, electrocardiography, and magnetic resonance imaging procedures are coded to these chapters.
- Examinations, consultations, interviews, and counseling are coded to these chapters.
- Microscopic and nuclear medicine are also coded to these chapters.

Chapter Review

True/False: Indicate whether the statement is true (T) or false (F).

1. _____ MRI stands for magnetic resonance imaging.

2. _____ Subcategory 88.4X requires a fourth-digit code assignment that indicates the site injected with contrast material.

3. _____ Subcategory 87.5X contains procedure codes for X-ray imaging of the gallbladder and pancreas.

4. _____ The term *retrograde* in this chapter means going against the normal direction of blood flow.

5. _____ Contrast material is usually iodine or barium based.

Fill-in-the-Blanks: Enter the appropriate term(s) to complete the statement.

6. _____ is an imaging technique that involves a three-dimensional picture of one layer of the body.

7. The procedure used to take images of a vein using contrast material is called _____.

8. The record generated by an ultrasound is called a _____ or an _____.

9. A type of treatment performed by trained professionals in which they use exercise and massage is called _____.

10. _____ is a form of injection in which medication is passed through for a length of time.

Coding Assignments

Instructions: Using an ICD-9-CM coding book, select the correct code for each procedure.

Procedure	Code
1. Intravascular imaging of renal vessels	_____
2. Vaccination against cholera	_____
3. Drug detoxification	_____
4. Audiometry	_____
5. Urinary manometry	_____
6. Retrograde pyelogram	_____

7. Percutaneous insertion of intracranial vascular stent _____

8. Iontophoresis _____

9. Percutaneous hysterogram _____

10. Decompression chamber _____

11. Infusion of nesiritide _____

12. Psychoanalysis _____

13. Application of Shanz dressing _____

14. Irrigation of ear _____

15. Routine chest X-ray _____

16. Barium swallow _____

17. MRI of chest and myocardium _____

18. Coronary arteriography using a single catheter _____

19. Dysphasia training _____

20. Removal of dental packing _____

21. Antirestenotic ultrasound _____

22. Intravascular imaging of extracranial cerebral vessels _____

23. Contrast radiogram of nasopharynx _____

24. Cardiac tomogram _____

25. Insertion of three vascular stents _____

Case Studies

Instructions: Review each case study, and select the correct ICD-9-CM diagnostic and procedure codes.

CASE 1

PREOPERATIVE DIAGNOSIS: Left back and flank pain

POSTOPERATIVE DIAGNOSIS: Renal stone, left ureter

PROCEDURE: Extracorporeal shockwave lithotripsy

PROCEDURE: The patient was placed in the supine position, and general anesthesia was administered. Fluoroscopy was used to position the patient. The stone was visualized in the left ureter. Shockwaves were used to break up the stone. A total of 4,200 shocks were used with a power of 2.8. The patient tolerated the procedure, was awoken, and sent to the recovery room. Discharge instructions were written.

ICD-9-CM Code Assignment: _____

CASE 2

This 88-year-old woman was referred for 24-hour Holter monitoring. The Holter monitor basically revealed the patient was in normal sinus rhythm. The average heart rate was 83, maximum was 153, minimum about 60. Total number of the aberrant beats were about 200. Ventricular ectopic beats were 77, 71 were isolettes and 3 were couplets.

The patient's QRS is normal. At the time, 3:20, there were 12 beats SVT. The patient has PVCs, which are monomorphic but very infrequent. The patient had another bout of SVT at about 3:20.

CONCLUSION:

1. Normal sinus rhythm with normal QRS, normal PR, and normal QT intervals

2. Brief periods of tachycardia

RECOMMENDATIONS:

This mild tachycardia probably should not be treated.

ICD-9-CM Code Assignment: _____

CASE 3

Department of Radiology

STUDY REQUESTED: Left foot and ankle X-ray

CONDITION OF PATIENT: Wheelchair

REPORT OF EXAM:

LEFT ANKLE:

Examination of the left ankle revealed no definite evidence of fracture, dislocation, or bone destruction. The bony articular structures appear intact.

IMPRESSION: Osseous pathology noted

LEFT FOOT:

Examination of the left foot revealed no definite evidence of fracture, dislocation, or bone destruction. The bony articular structures appear intact. A small osteophytic spur is noted off the plantar aspect of the calcaneus.

IMPRESSION: No acute osseous pathology.

ICD-9-CM Code Assignment: _____

CASE 4

The patient is a 3-year-old little girl who was brought into this office by her mother. The mother states this child has seen a dentist only once prior to this visit due to finances. She has not been eating very much lately, and mother is concerned that there might be some dental pain. Child still takes a bottle at night, which mom is trying to wean her from.

A full-mouth X-ray was taken following the dental examination. Intraorally the teeth are in good shape.

Postprocedure diagnosis: Encounter for dental examination

ICD-9-CM Code Assignment: _____

CASE 5

INDICATIONS: Previous brain tumor, status postradiation therapy

PROCEDURE: MRI brain

A large irregular abnormality of the right frontal and temporal region seen on previous studies has a marked decrease in size. There is no signal of abnormality noted throughout the periventricular white matter. All other signals are normal. Mass noted previously has decreased in size, and no metastasis is present.

ICD-9-CM Code Assignment: _____

Appendix A: ICD-9-CM Official Guidelines for Coding and Reporting

Effective October 1, 2008
Narrative changes appear in bold text
Items underlined have been moved within the guidelines since October 1, 2007
The guidelines include the updated V Code Table

The Centers for Medicare and Medicaid Services (CMS) and the National Center for Health Statistics (NCHS), two departments within the U.S. Federal Government's Department of Health and Human Services (DHHS) provide the following guidelines for coding and reporting using the International Classification of Diseases, 9th Revision, Clinical Modification (ICD-9-CM). These guidelines should be used as a companion document to the official version of the ICD-9-CM as published on CD-ROM by the U.S. Government Printing Office (GPO).

These guidelines have been approved by the four organizations that make up the Cooperating Parties for the ICD-9-CM: the American Hospital Association (AHA), the American Health Information Management Association (AHIMA), CMS, and NCHS. These guidelines are included on the official government version of the ICD-9-CM, and also appear in "*Coding Clinic for ICD-9-CM*" published by the AHA.

These guidelines are a set of rules that have been developed to accompany and complement the official conventions and instructions provided within the ICD-9-CM itself. These guidelines are based on the coding and sequencing instructions in Volumes I, II and III of ICD-9-CM, but provide additional instruction. Adherence to these guidelines when assigning ICD-9-CM diagnosis and procedure codes is required under the Health Insurance Portability and Accountability Act (HIPAA). The diagnosis codes (Volumes 1-2) have been adopted under HIPAA for all healthcare settings. Volume 3 procedure codes have been adopted for inpatient procedures reported by hospitals. A joint effort between the healthcare provider and the coder is essential to achieve complete and accurate documentation, code assignment, and reporting of diagnoses and procedures. These guidelines have been developed to assist both the healthcare provider and the coder in identifying those diagnoses and procedures that are to be reported. The importance of consistent, complete documentation in the medical record cannot be overemphasized. Without such documentation accurate coding cannot be achieved. The entire record should be reviewed to determine the specific reason for the encounter and the conditions treated.

The term encounter is used for all settings, including hospital admissions. In the context of these guidelines, the term provider is used throughout the guidelines to mean physician or any qualified health care practitioner who is legally accountable for establishing the patient's diagnosis. Only this set of guidelines, approved by the Cooperating Parties, is official.

The guidelines are organized into sections. Section I includes the structure and conventions of the classification and general guidelines that apply to the entire classification, and chapter-specific guidelines that correspond to the chapters as they are arranged in the classification. Section II includes guidelines for selection of principal diagnosis for non-outpatient settings. Section III includes guidelines for reporting additional diagnoses in non-outpatient settings. Section IV is for outpatient coding and reporting.

Section I. Conventions, general coding guidelines and chapter specific guidelines

The conventions, general guidelines and chapter-specific guidelines are applicable to all health care settings unless otherwise indicated.

A. Conventions for the ICD-9-CM

The conventions for the ICD-9-CM are the general rules for use of the classification independent of the guidelines. These conventions are incorporated within the index and tabular of the ICD-9-CM as instructional notes. The conventions are as follows:

1. Format:

The ICD-9-CM uses an indented format for ease in reference

2. Abbreviations

a. Index abbreviations

NEC   "Not elsewhere classifiable"
This abbreviation in the index represents "other specified" when a specific code is not available for a condition the index directs the coder to the "other specified" code in the tabular.

b. Tabular abbreviations

NEC   "Not elsewhere classifiable"
This abbreviation in the tabular represents "other specified". When a specific code is not available for a condition the tabular includes an NEC entry under a code to identify the code as the "other specified" code.
(See Section I.A.5.a. "Other" codes").

NOS   "Not otherwise specified"
This abbreviation is the equivalent of unspecified.
(See Section I.A.5.b., "Unspecified" codes)

3. Punctuation

[ ]   Brackets are used in the tabular list to enclose synonyms, alternative wording or explanatory phrases. Brackets are used in the index to identify manifestation codes.
(See Section I.A.6. "Etiology/manifestations")

( )   Parentheses are used in both the index and tabular to enclose supplementary words that may be present or absent in the statement of a disease or procedure without affecting the code number to which it is assigned. The terms within the parentheses are referred to as nonessential modifiers.

: Colons are used in the Tabular list after an incomplete term which needs one or more of the modifiers following the colon to make it assignable to a given category.

4.   Includes and Excludes Notes and Inclusion terms

Includes: This note appears immediately under a three-digit code title to further define, or give examples of, the content of the category.

Excludes: An excludes note under a code indicates that the terms excluded from the code are to be coded elsewhere. In some cases the codes for the excluded terms should not be used in conjunction with the code from which it is excluded. An example of this is a congenital condition excluded from an acquired form of the same condition. The congenital and acquired codes should not be used together. In other cases, the excluded terms may be used together with an excluded code. An example of this is when fractures of different bones are coded to different codes. Both codes may be used together if both types of fractures are present.

Inclusion terms: List of terms is included under certain four and five digit codes. These terms are the conditions for which that code number is to be used. The terms may be synonyms of the code title, or, in the case of "other specified" codes, the terms are a list of the various conditions assigned to that code. The inclusion terms are not necessarily exhaustive. Additional terms found only in the index may also be assigned to a code.

5.   Other and Unspecified codes

a.   "Other" codes

Codes titled "other" or "other specified" (usually a code with a 4th digit 8 or fifth-digit 9 for diagnosis codes) are for use when the information in the medical record provides detail for which a specific code does not exist. Index entries with NEC in the line designate "other" codes in the tabular. These index entries represent specific disease entities for which no specific code exists so the term is included within an "other" code.

b.   "Unspecified" codes

Codes (usually a code with a 4th digit 9 or 5th digit 0 for diagnosis codes) titled "unspecified" are for use when the information in the medical record is insufficient to assign a more specific code.

6. Etiology/manifestation convention ("code first", "use additional code" and "in diseases classified elsewhere" notes)

Certain conditions have both an underlying etiology and multiple body system manifestations due to the underlying etiology. For such conditions, the ICD-9-CM has a coding convention that requires the underlying condition be sequenced first followed by the manifestation. Wherever such a combination exists, there is a "use additional code" note at the etiology code, and a "code first" note at the manifestation code. These instructional notes indicate the proper sequencing order of the codes, etiology followed by manifestation.

In most cases the manifestation codes will have in the code title, "in diseases classified elsewhere." Codes with this title are a component of the etiology/manifestation convention. The code title indicates that it is a manifestation code. "In diseases classified elsewhere" codes are never permitted to be used as first listed or principal diagnosis codes. They must be used in conjunction with an underlying condition code and they must be listed following the underlying condition.

There are manifestation codes that do not have "in diseases classified elsewhere" in the title. For such codes a "use additional code" note will still be present and the rules for sequencing apply.

In addition to the notes in the tabular, these conditions also have a specific index entry structure. In the index both conditions are listed together with the etiology code first followed by the manifestation codes in brackets. The code in brackets is always to be sequenced second.

The most commonly used etiology/manifestation combinations are the codes for Diabetes mellitus, category 250. For each code under category 250 there is a use additional code note for the manifestation that is specific for that particular diabetic manifestation. Should a patient have more than one manifestation of diabetes, more than one code from category 250 may be used with as many manifestation codes as are needed to fully describe the patient's complete diabetic condition. The category 250 diabetes codes should be sequenced first, followed by the manifestation codes.

"Code first" and "Use additional code" notes are also used as sequencing rules in the classification for certain codes that are not part of an etiology/manifestation combination.
See - Section I.B.9. "Multiple coding for a single condition".

7. "And"

The word "and" should be interpreted to mean either "and" or "or" when it appears in a title.

8.   "With"

The word "with" in the alphabetic index is sequenced immediately following the main term, not in alphabetical order.

9.   "See" and "See Also"

The "see" instruction following a main term in the index indicates that another term should be referenced. It is necessary to go to the main term referenced with the "see" note to locate the correct code.

A "see also" instruction following a main term in the index instructs that there is another main term that may also be referenced that may provide additional index entries that may be useful. It is not necessary to follow the "see also" note when the original main term provides the necessary code.

B. General Coding Guidelines

1.   Use of Both Alphabetic Index and Tabular List

Use both the Alphabetic Index and the Tabular List when locating and assigning a code. Reliance on only the Alphabetic Index or the Tabular List leads to errors in code assignments and less specificity in code selection.

2.   Locate each term in the Alphabetic Index

Locate each term in the Alphabetic Index and verify the code selected in the Tabular List. Read and be guided by instructional notations that appear in both the Alphabetic Index and the Tabular List.

3.   Level of Detail in Coding

Diagnosis and procedure codes are to be used at their highest number of digits available.

ICD-9-CM diagnosis codes are composed of codes with 3, 4, or 5 digits. Codes with three digits are included in ICD-9-CM as the heading of a category of codes that may be further subdivided by the use of fourth and/or fifth digits, which provide greater detail.

A three-digit code is to be used only if it is not further subdivided. Where fourth-digit subcategories and/or fifth-digit subclassifications are provided, they must be assigned. A code is invalid if it has not been coded to the full number of digits required for that code. For example, Acute myocardial infarction, code 410, has fourth digits that describe the location of the infarction (e.g., 410.2, Of inferolateral wall), and fifth digits that identify the episode of care. It would be incorrect to report a code in category 410 without a fourth and fifth digit.

ICD-9-CM Volume 3 procedure codes are composed of codes with either 3 or 4 digits. Codes with two digits are included in ICD-9-CM as the heading of a category of codes that may be further subdivided by the use of third and/or fourth digits, which provide greater detail.

4. Code or codes from 001.0 through V89.09

The appropriate code or codes from 001.0 through **V89.09** must be used to identify diagnoses, symptoms, conditions, problems, complaints or other reason(s) for the encounter/visit.

5. Selection of codes 001.0 through 999.9

The selection of codes 001.0 through 999.9 will frequently be used to describe the reason for the admission/encounter. These codes are from the section of ICD-9-CM for the classification of diseases and injuries (e.g., infectious and parasitic diseases; neoplasms; symptoms, signs, and ill-defined conditions, etc.).

6. Signs and symptoms

Codes that describe symptoms and signs, as opposed to diagnoses, are acceptable for reporting purposes when a related definitive diagnosis has not been established (confirmed) by the provider. Chapter 16 of ICD-9-CM, Symptoms, Signs, and Ill-defined conditions (codes 780.0 - 799.9) contain many, but not all codes for symptoms.

7. Conditions that are an integral part of a disease process

Signs and symptoms that are associated routinely with a disease process should not be assigned as additional codes, unless otherwise instructed by the classification.

8. Conditions that are not an integral part of a disease process

Additional signs and symptoms that may not be associated routinely with a disease process should be coded when present.

9. Multiple coding for a single condition

In addition to the etiology/manifestation convention that requires two codes to fully describe a single condition that affects multiple body systems, there are other single conditions that also require more than one code. "Use additional code" notes are found in the tabular at codes that are not part of an etiology/manifestation pair where a secondary code is useful to fully describe a condition. The sequencing rule is the same as the etiology/manifestation pair - , "use additional code" indicates that a secondary code should be added.

For example, for infections that are not included in chapter 1, a secondary code from category 041, Bacterial infection in conditions classified elsewhere and of unspecified site, may be required to identify the bacterial organism causing the infection. A "use additional code" note will normally be found at the infectious disease code, indicating a need for the organism code to be added as a secondary code.

"Code first" notes are also under certain codes that are not specifically manifestation codes but may be due to an underlying cause. When a "code first" note is present and an underlying condition is present the underlying condition should be sequenced first.

"Code, if applicable, any causal condition first", notes indicate that this code may be assigned as a principal diagnosis when the causal condition is unknown or not applicable. If a causal condition is known, then the code for that condition should be sequenced as the principal or first-listed diagnosis.

Multiple codes may be needed for late effects, complication codes and obstetric codes to more fully describe a condition. See the specific guidelines for these conditions for further instruction.

10.   Acute and Chronic Conditions

If the same condition is described as both acute (subacute) and chronic, and separate subentries exist in the Alphabetic Index at the same indentation level, code both and sequence the acute (subacute) code first.

11.   Combination Code

A combination code is a single code used to classify:
Two diagnoses, or
A diagnosis with an associated secondary process (manifestation)
A diagnosis with an associated complication

Combination codes are identified by referring to subterm entries in the Alphabetic Index and by reading the inclusion and exclusion notes in the Tabular List.

Assign only the combination code when that code fully identifies the diagnostic conditions involved or when the Alphabetic Index so directs. Multiple coding should not be used when the classification provides a combination code that clearly identifies all of the elements documented in the diagnosis. When the combination code lacks necessary specificity in describing the manifestation or complication, an additional code should be used as a secondary code.

12.   Late Effects

A late effect is the residual effect (condition produced) after the acute phase of an illness or injury has terminated. There is no time limit on when a late effect code can be used. The residual may be apparent early, such as in cerebrovascular accident cases, or it may occur months or years later, such as that due to a previous injury. Coding of late effects generally requires two codes sequenced in the following order: The condition or nature of the late effect is sequenced first.   The late effect code is sequenced second.

An exception to the above guidelines are those instances where the code for late effect is followed by a manifestation code identified in the Tabular List and title, or the late effect code has been expanded (at the fourth and fifth-digit levels) to include the manifestation(s). The code for the acute phase of an illness or injury that led to the late effect is never used with a code for the late effect.

13.   Impending or Threatened Condition

Code any condition described at the time of discharge as "impending" or "threatened" as follows:
> If it did occur, code as confirmed diagnosis.
> If it did not occur, reference the Alphabetic Index to determine if the condition has a subentry term for "impending" or "threatened" and also reference main term entries for "Impending" and for "Threatened."
> If the subterms are listed, assign the given code.
> If the subterms are not listed, code the existing underlying condition(s) and not the condition described as impending or threatened.

14.   Reporting Same Diagnosis Code More than Once

Each unique ICD-9-CM diagnosis code may be reported only once for an encounter. This applies to bilateral conditions or two different conditions classified to the same ICD-9-CM diagnosis code.

15.   Admissions/Encounters for Rehabilitation

When the purpose for the admission/encounter is rehabilitation, sequence the appropriate V code from category V57, Care involving use of rehabilitation procedures, as the principal/first-listed diagnosis. The code for the condition for which the service is being performed should be reported as an additional diagnosis.

Only one code from category V57 is required. Code V57.89, Other specified rehabilitation procedures, should be assigned if more than one type of rehabilitation is performed during a single encounter. A procedure code should be reported to identify each type of rehabilitation therapy actually performed.

16.   Documentation for BMI and Pressure Ulcer Stages

For the Body Mass Index (BMI) and pressure ulcer stage codes, code assignment may be based on medical record documentation from clinicians who are not the patient's provider (i.e., physician or other

qualified healthcare practitioner legally accountable for establishing the patient's diagnosis), since this information is typically documented by other clinicians involved in the care of the patient (e.g., a dietitian often documents the BMI and nurses often documents the pressure ulcer stages). However, the associated diagnosis (such as overweight, obesity, or pressure ulcer) must be documented by the patient's provider. If there is conflicting medical record documentation, either from the same clinician or different clinicians, the patient's attending provider should be queried for clarification.

The BMI and pressure ulcer stage codes should only be reported as secondary diagnoses. As with all other secondary diagnosis codes, the BMI and pressure ulcer stage codes should only be assigned when they meet the definition of a reportable additional diagnosis (see Section III, Reporting Additional Diagnoses).

C. Chapter-Specific Coding Guidelines

In addition to general coding guidelines, there are guidelines for specific diagnoses and/or conditions in the classification. Unless otherwise indicated, these guidelines apply to all health care settings. Please refer to Section II for guidelines on the selection of principal diagnosis.

1.   Chapter 1: Infectious and Parasitic Diseases (001-139)

a.   Human Immunodeficiency Virus (HIV) Infections

1)   Code only confirmed cases

Code only confirmed cases of HIV infection/illness. This is an exception to the hospital inpatient guideline Section II, H.

In this context, "confirmation" does not require documentation of positive serology or culture for HIV; the provider's diagnostic statement that the patient is HIV positive, or has an HIV-related illness is sufficient.

2)   Selection and sequencing of HIV codes

(a)   Patient admitted for HIV-related condition

If a patient is admitted for an HIV-related condition, the principal diagnosis should be 042, followed by additional diagnosis codes for all reported HIV-related conditions.

(b) **Patient with HIV disease admitted for unrelated condition**

If a patient with HIV disease is admitted for an unrelated condition (such as a traumatic injury), the code for the unrelated condition (e.g., the nature of injury code) should be the principal diagnosis. Other diagnoses would be 042 followed by additional diagnosis codes for all reported HIV-related conditions.

(c) **Whether the patient is newly diagnosed**

Whether the patient is newly diagnosed or has had previous admissions/encounters for HIV conditions is irrelevant to the sequencing decision.

(d) **Asymptomatic human immunodeficiency virus**

V08 Asymptomatic human immunodeficiency virus [HIV] infection, is to be applied when the patient without any documentation of symptoms is listed as being "HIV positive," "known HIV," "HIV test positive," or similar terminology. Do not use this code if the term "AIDS" is used or if the patient is treated for any HIV-related illness or is described as having any condition(s) resulting from his/her HIV positive status; use 042 in these cases.

(e) **Patients with inconclusive HIV serology**

Patients with inconclusive HIV serology, but no definitive diagnosis or manifestations of the illness, may be assigned code 795.71, Inconclusive serologic test for Human Immunodeficiency Virus [HIV].

(f) **Previously diagnosed HIV-related illness**

Patients with any known prior diagnosis of an HIV-related illness should be coded to 042. Once a patient has developed an HIV-related illness, the patient should always be assigned code 042 on every subsequent admission/encounter. Patients previously diagnosed with any HIV illness (042) should never be assigned to 795.71 or V08.

(g) **HIV Infection in Pregnancy, Childbirth and the Puerperium**

During pregnancy, childbirth or the puerperium, a patient admitted (or presenting for a health care encounter) because of an HIV-related illness should receive a principal diagnosis code of 647.6X, Other specified infectious and parasitic diseases in the mother classifiable elsewhere, but complicating the pregnancy, childbirth or the puerperium, followed by 042 and the code(s) for the HIV-related illness(es). Codes from Chapter 15 always take sequencing priority.

Patients with asymptomatic HIV infection status admitted (or presenting for a health care encounter) during pregnancy, childbirth, or the puerperium should receive codes of 647.6X and V08.

(h)   **Encounters for testing for HIV**

If a patient is being seen to determine his/her HIV status, use code V73.89, Screening for other specified viral disease. Use code V69.8, Other problems related to lifestyle, as a secondary code if an asymptomatic patient is in a known high risk group for HIV. Should a patient with signs or symptoms or illness, or a confirmed HIV related diagnosis be tested for HIV, code the signs and symptoms or the diagnosis. An additional counseling code V65.44 may be used if counseling is provided during the encounter for the test.

When a patient returns to be informed of his/her HIV test results use code V65.44, HIV counseling, if the results of the test are negative.

If the results are positive but the patient is asymptomatic use code V08, Asymptomatic HIV infection. If the results are positive and the patient is symptomatic use code 042, HIV infection, with codes for the HIV related symptoms or diagnosis. The HIV counseling code may also be used if counseling is provided for patients with positive test results.

b.   **Septicemia, Systemic Inflammatory Response Syndrome (SIRS), Sepsis, Severe Sepsis, and Septic Shock**

1)   **SIRS, Septicemia, and Sepsis**

(a)   The terms *septicemia* and *sepsis* are often used interchangeably by providers, however they are not considered synonymous terms. The following descriptions are provided for reference but do not preclude querying the provider for clarification about terms used in the documentation:

(i) Septicemia generally refers to a systemic disease associated with the presence of pathological microorganisms or toxins in the blood, which can include bacteria, viruses, fungi or other organisms.

(ii) Systemic inflammatory response syndrome (SIRS) generally refers to the systemic response to infection, trauma/burns, or other insult (such as cancer) with symptoms including fever, tachycardia, tachypnea, and leukocytosis.

(iii)Sepsis generally refers to SIRS due to infection.

(iv)Severe sepsis generally refers to sepsis with associated acute organ dysfunction.

(b) **The Coding of SIRS, sepsis and severe sepsis**

The coding of SIRS, sepsis and severe sepsis requires a minimum of 2 codes: a code for the underlying cause (such as infection or trauma) and a code from subcategory 995.9 Systemic inflammatory response syndrome (SIRS).

(i) The code for the underlying cause (such as infection or trauma) must be sequenced before the code from subcategory 995.9 Systemic inflammatory response syndrome (SIRS).

(ii) Sepsis and severe sepsis require a code for the systemic infection (038.xx, 112.5, etc.) and either code 995.91, Sepsis, or 995.92, Severe sepsis. If the causal organism is not documented, assign code 038.9, Unspecified septicemia.

(iii)Severe sepsis requires additional code(s) for the associated acute organ dysfunction(s).

(iv)If a patient has sepsis with multiple organ dysfunctions, follow the instructions for coding severe sepsis.

(v) Either the term sepsis or SIRS must be documented to assign a code from subcategory 995.9.

(vi) See Section I.C.17.g), Injury and poisoning, for information regarding systemic inflammatory response syndrome (SIRS) due to trauma/burns and other non-infectious processes.

(c) Due to the complex nature of sepsis and severe sepsis, some cases may require querying the provider prior to assignment of the codes.

2)   Sequencing sepsis and severe sepsis

(a)   Sepsis and severe sepsis as principal diagnosis

If sepsis or severe sepsis is present on admission, and meets the definition of principal diagnosis, the systemic infection code (e.g., 038.xx, 112.5, etc) should be assigned as the principal diagnosis, followed by code 995.91, Sepsis, or 995.92, Severe sepsis, as required by the sequencing rules in the Tabular List. Codes from subcategory 995.9 can never be assigned as a principal diagnosis. A code should also be assigned for any localized infection, if present.

If the sepsis or severe sepsis is due to a postprocedural infection, see Section I.C.1.b.10 for guidelines related to sepsis due to postprocedural infection.

(b)   Sepsis and severe sepsis as secondary diagnoses

When sepsis or severe sepsis develops during the encounter (it was not present on admission), the systemic infection code and code 995.91 or 995.92 should be assigned as secondary diagnoses.

(c)   Documentation unclear as to whether sepsis or severe sepsis is present on admission

Sepsis or severe sepsis may be present on admission but the diagnosis may not be confirmed until sometime after admission. If the documentation is not clear whether the sepsis or severe sepsis was present on admission, the provider should be queried.

3) Sepsis/SIRS with Localized Infection

If the reason for admission is both sepsis, severe sepsis, or SIRS and a localized infection, such as pneumonia or cellulitis, a code for the systemic infection (038.xx, 112.5, etc) should be assigned first, then code 995.91 or 995.92, followed by the code for the localized infection. If the patient is admitted with a localized infection, such as pneumonia, and sepsis/SIRS doesn't develop until after admission, see guideline I.C.1.b.2.b).

If the localized infection is postprocedural, *see Section I.C.1.b.10 for guidelines related to sepsis due to postprocedural infection.*

Note: The term urosepsis is a nonspecific term. If that is the only term documented then only code 599.0 should be assigned based on the default for the term in the ICD-9-CM index, in addition to the code for the causal organism if known.

4) Bacterial Sepsis and Septicemia

In most cases, it will be a code from category 038, Septicemia, that will be used in conjunction with a code from subcategory 995.9 such as the following:

(a) Streptococcal sepsis

If the documentation in the record states streptococcal sepsis, codes 038.0, Streptococcal septicemia, and code 995.91 should be used, in that sequence.

(b) Streptococcal septicemia

If the documentation states streptococcal septicemia, only code 038.0 should be assigned, however, the provider should be queried whether the patient has sepsis, an infection with SIRS.

5) Acute organ dysfunction that is not clearly associated with the sepsis

If a patient has sepsis and an acute organ dysfunction, but the medical record documentation indicates that the acute organ dysfunction is related to a medical condition other than the sepsis, do not assign code 995.92, Severe sepsis. An acute organ dysfunction must be associated with the sepsis in order to assign the severe sepsis code. If the documentation is not clear as to whether an acute organ dysfunction is related to the sepsis or another medical condition, query the provider.

6)   Septic shock

(a)   Sequencing of septic shock

Septic shock generally refers to circulatory failure associated with severe sepsis, and, therefore, it represents a type of acute organ dysfunction.

For all cases of septic shock, the code for the systemic infection should be sequenced first, followed by codes 995.92 and 785.52. Any additional codes for other acute organ dysfunctions should also be assigned. As noted in the sequencing instructions in the Tabular List, the code for septic shock cannot be assigned as a principal diagnosis.

(b)   Septic Shock without documentation of severe sepsis

Septic shock indicates the presence of severe sepsis.

Code 995.92, Severe sepsis, must be assigned with code 785.52, Septic shock, even if the term severe sepsis is not documented in the record. The "use additional code" note and the "code first" note in the tabular support this guideline.

7)   Sepsis and septic shock complicating abortion and pregnancy

Sepsis and septic shock complicating abortion, ectopic pregnancy, and molar pregnancy are classified to category codes in Chapter 11 (630-639).
See section I.C.11.

8)   Negative or inconclusive blood cultures

Negative or inconclusive blood cultures do not preclude a diagnosis of septicemia or sepsis in patients with clinical evidence of the condition, however, the provider should be queried.

9)   Newborn sepsis

See Section I.C.15.j for information on the coding of newborn sepsis.

10)   Sepsis due to a Postprocedural Infection

(a)   Documentation of causal relationship

As with all postprocedural complications, code assignment is based on the provider's documentation of the relationship between the infection and the procedure.

(b)   Sepsis due to postprocedural infection

In cases of postprocedural sepsis, the complication code, such as code 998.59, Other postoperative infection, or 674.3x, Other complications of obstetrical surgical wounds should be coded first followed by the appropriate sepsis codes (systemic infection code and either code 995.91or 995.92). An additional code(s) for any acute organ dysfunction should also be assigned for cases of severe sepsis.

11)   External cause of injury codes with SIRS

Refer to Section I.C.19.a.7 for instruction on the use of external cause of injury codes with codes for SIRS resulting from trauma.

12)   Sepsis and Severe Sepsis Associated with Non-infectious Process

In some cases, a non-infectious process, such as trauma, may lead to an infection which can result in sepsis or severe sepsis. If sepsis or severe sepsis is documented as associated with a non-infectious condition, such as a burn or serious injury, and this condition meets the definition for principal diagnosis, the code for the non-infectious condition should be sequenced first, followed by the code for the systemic infection and either code 995.91, Sepsis, or 995.92, Severe sepsis. Additional codes for any associated acute organ dysfunction(s) should also be assigned for cases of severe sepsis. If the sepsis or severe sepsis meets the definition of principal diagnosis, the systemic infection and sepsis codes should be sequenced before the non-infectious condition. When both the associated non-infectious condition and the sepsis or severe sepsis meet the definition of principal diagnosis, either may be assigned as principal diagnosis.

See Section I.C.1.b.2)(a) for guidelines pertaining to sepsis or severe sepsis as the principal diagnosis.

Only one code from subcategory 995.9 should be assigned. Therefore, when a non-infectious condition leads to an infection resulting in sepsis or severe sepsis, assign either code 995.91 or 995.92. Do not additionally assign code 995.93, Systemic inflammatory response syndrome due to non-infectious process without acute organ dysfunction, or 995.94, Systemic inflammatory response syndrome with acute organ dysfunction.

See Section I.C.17.g for information on the coding of SIRS due to trauma/burns or other non-infectious disease processes.

c. Methicillin Resistant *Staphylococcus aureus* (MRSA) Conditions

1) Selection and sequencing of MRSA codes

(a) Combination codes for MRSA infection

When a patient is diagnosed with an infection that is due to methicillin resistant *Staphylococcus aureus* (MRSA), and that infection has a combination code that includes the causal organism (e.g., septicemia, pneumonia) assign the appropriate code for the condition (e.g., code 038.12, Methicillin resistant Staphylococcus aureus septicemia or code 482.42, Methicillin resistant pneumonia due to Staphylococcus aureus). Do not assign code 041.12, Methicillin resistant Staphylococcus aureus, as an additional code because the code includes the type of infection and the MRSA organism. Do not assign a code from subcategory V09.0, Infection with microorganisms resistant to penicillins, as an additional diagnosis.

See Section C.1.b.1 for instructions on coding and sequencing of septicemia.

(b) Other codes for MRSA infection

When there is documentation of a current infection (e.g., wound infection, stitch abscess, urinary tract infection) due to MRSA, and that infection does not have a combination code that includes the causal organism, select the appropriate code to identify the condition along with code 041.12, Methicillin resistant Staphylococcus aureus, for the MRSA infection. Do not assign a code from subcategory V09.0, Infection with microorganisms resistant to penicillins.

(c)   **Methicillin susceptible Staphylococcus aureus (MSSA) and MRSA colonization**

The condition or state of being colonized or carrying MSSA or MRSA is called colonization or carriage, while an individual person is described as being colonized or being a carrier. Colonization means that MSSA or MSRA is present on or in the body without necessarily causing illness. A positive MRSA colonization test might be documented by the provider as "MRSA screen positive" or "MRSA nasal swab positive".

Assign code V02.54, Carrier or suspected carrier, Methicillin resistant Staphylococcus aureus, for patients documented as having MRSA colonization. Assign code V02.53, Carrier or suspected carrier, Methicillin susceptible Staphylococcus aureus, for patient documented as having MSSA colonization. Colonization is not necessarily indicative of a disease process or as the cause of a specific condition the patient may have unless documented as such by the provider.

Code V02.59, Other specified bacterial diseases, should be assigned for other types of staphylococcal colonization (e.g., S. *epidermidis, S. saprophyticus)*. Code V02.59 should not be assigned for colonization with any type of *Staphylococcus aureus* (MRSA, MSSA).

(d)   **MRSA colonization and infection**

If a patient is documented as having both MRSA colonization and infection during a hospital admission, code V02.54, Carrier or suspected carrier, Methicillin resistant *Staphylococcus aureus*, and a code for the MRSA infection may both be assigned.

2.   Chapter 2: Neoplasms (140-239)

<u>General guidelines</u>

Chapter 2 of the ICD-9-CM contains the codes for most benign and all malignant neoplasms. Certain benign neoplasms, such as prostatic adenomas, may be found in the specific body system chapters. To properly code a neoplasm it is necessary to determine from the record if the neoplasm is benign, in-situ, malignant, or of uncertain histologic behavior. If malignant, any secondary (metastatic) sites should also be determined.

The neoplasm table in the Alphabetic Index should be referenced first. However, if the histological term is documented, that term should be referenced first, rather than going immediately to the Neoplasm Table, in order to determine which column in the Neoplasm Table is appropriate. For example, if the documentation indicates "adenoma," refer to the term in the Alphabetic Index to review the entries under this term and the instructional note to "see also neoplasm, by site, benign." The table provides the proper code based on the type of neoplasm and the site. It is important to select the proper column in the table that corresponds to the type of neoplasm. The tabular should then be referenced to verify that the correct code has been selected from the table and that a more specific site code does not exist. *See Section I. C. 18.d.4. for information regarding V codes for genetic susceptibility to cancer.*

a.   Treatment directed at the malignancy

If the treatment is directed at the malignancy, designate the malignancy as the principal diagnosis.

The only exception to this guideline is if a patient admission/encounter is solely for the administration of chemotherapy, immunotherapy or radiation therapy, assign the appropriate V58.x code as the first-listed or principal diagnosis, and the diagnosis or problem for which the service is being performed as a secondary diagnosis.

b.   Treatment of secondary site

When a patient is admitted because of a primary neoplasm with metastasis and treatment is directed toward the secondary site only, the secondary neoplasm is designated as the principal diagnosis even though the primary malignancy is still present.

c.   Coding and sequencing of complications

Coding and sequencing of complications associated with the malignancies or with the therapy thereof are subject to the following guidelines:

1)   Anemia associated with malignancy

When admission/encounter is for management of an anemia associated with the malignancy, and the treatment is only for anemia, the appropriate anemia code (such as code 285.22, Anemia in neoplastic disease) is designated as the principal diagnosis and is followed by the appropriate code(s) for the malignancy.

Code 285.22 may also be used as a secondary code if the patient suffers from anemia and is being treated for the malignancy.

2)   Anemia associated with chemotherapy, immunotherapy and radiation therapy

When the admission/encounter is for management of an anemia associated with chemotherapy, immunotherapy or radiotherapy and the only treatment is for the anemia, the anemia is sequenced first followed by code E933.1. The appropriate neoplasm code should be assigned as an additional code.

3)   Management of dehydration due to the malignancy

When the admission/encounter is for management of dehydration due to the malignancy or the therapy, or a combination of both, and only the dehydration is being treated (intravenous rehydration), the dehydration is sequenced first, followed by the code(s) for the malignancy.

4)   Treatment of a complication resulting from a surgical procedure

When the admission/encounter is for treatment of a complication resulting from a surgical procedure, designate the complication as the principal or first-listed diagnosis if treatment is directed at resolving the complication.

d.   Primary malignancy previously excised

When a primary malignancy has been previously excised or eradicated from its site and there is no further treatment directed to that site and there is no evidence of any existing primary malignancy, a code from category V10, Personal history of malignant neoplasm, should be used to indicate the former site of the malignancy. Any mention of extension, invasion, or metastasis to another site is coded as a secondary malignant neoplasm to that site. The secondary site may be the principal or first-listed with the V10 code used as a secondary code.

e.   Admissions/Encounters involving chemotherapy, immunotherapy and radiation therapy

1)   Episode of care involves surgical removal of neoplasm

When an episode of care involves the surgical removal of a neoplasm, primary or secondary site, followed by adjunct chemotherapy or radiation treatment during the same episode of care, the neoplasm code should be assigned as principal or first-listed diagnosis, using codes in the 140-198 series or where appropriate in the 200-203 series.

2)   Patient admission/encounter solely for administration of chemotherapy, immunotherapy and radiation therapy

If a patient admission/encounter is solely for the administration of chemotherapy, immunotherapy or radiation therapy assign code V58.0, Encounter for radiation therapy, or V58.11, Encounter for antineoplastic chemotherapy, or V58.12, Encounter for antineoplastic immunotherapy as the first-listed or principal diagnosis. If a patient receives more than one of these therapies during the same admission more than one of these codes may be assigned, in any sequence.

The malignancy for which the therapy is being administered should be assigned as a secondary diagnosis.

3)   Patient admitted for radiotherapy/chemotherapy and immunotherapy and develops complications

When a patient is admitted for the purpose of radiotherapy, immunotherapy or chemotherapy and develops complications such as uncontrolled nausea and vomiting or dehydration, the principal or first-listed diagnosis is V58.0, Encounter for radiotherapy, or V58.11, Encounter for antineoplastic chemotherapy, or V58.12, Encounter for antineoplastic immunotherapy followed by any codes for the complications.

f.   Admission/encounter to determine extent of malignancy

When the reason for admission/encounter is to determine the extent of the malignancy, or for a procedure such as paracentesis or thoracentesis, the primary malignancy or appropriate metastatic site is designated as the principal or first-listed diagnosis, even though chemotherapy or radiotherapy is administered.

g. Symptoms, signs, and ill-defined conditions listed in Chapter 16 associated with neoplasms

Symptoms, signs, and ill-defined conditions listed in Chapter 16 characteristic of, or associated with, an existing primary or secondary site malignancy cannot be used to replace the malignancy as principal or first-listed diagnosis, regardless of the number of admissions or encounters for treatment and care of the neoplasm.
See section I.C.18.d.14, Encounter for prophylactic organ removal.

h. Admission/encounter for pain control/management

See Section I.C.6.a.5 for information on coding admission/encounter for pain control/management.

i. Malignant neoplasm associated with transplanted organ

A malignant neoplasm of a transplanted organ should be coded as a transplant complication. Assign first the appropriate code from subcategory 996.8, Complications of transplanted organ, followed by code 199.2, Malignant neoplasm associated with transplanted organ. Use an additional code for the specific malignancy.

3. Chapter 3: Endocrine, Nutritional, and Metabolic Diseases and Immunity Disorders (240-279)

a. Diabetes mellitus

Codes under category 250, Diabetes mellitus, identify complications/manifestations associated with diabetes mellitus. A fifth-digit is required for all category 250 codes to identify the type of diabetes mellitus and whether the diabetes is controlled or uncontrolled.

See I.C.3.a.7 for secondary diabetes

1) Fifth-digits for category 250:

The following are the fifth-digits for the codes under category 250:

0   type II or unspecified type, not stated as uncontrolled
1   type I, [juvenile type], not stated as uncontrolled
2   type II or unspecified type, uncontrolled
3   type I, [juvenile type], uncontrolled

The age of a patient is not the sole determining factor, though most type I diabetics develop the condition before reaching puberty. For this reason type I diabetes mellitus is also referred to as juvenile diabetes.

2)   Type of diabetes mellitus not documented

If the type of diabetes mellitus is not documented in the medical record the default is type II.

3)   Diabetes mellitus and the use of insulin

All type I diabetics must use insulin to replace what their bodies do not produce. However, the use of insulin does not mean that a patient is a type I diabetic. Some patients with type II diabetes mellitus are unable to control their blood sugar through diet and oral medication alone and do require insulin. If the documentation in a medical record does not indicate the type of diabetes but does indicate that the patient uses insulin, the appropriate fifth-digit for type II must be used. For type II patients who routinely use insulin, code V58.67, Long-term (current) use of insulin, should also be assigned to indicate that the patient uses insulin. Code V58.67 should not be assigned if insulin is given temporarily to bring a type II patient's blood sugar under control during an encounter.

4)   Assigning and sequencing diabetes codes and associated conditions

When assigning codes for diabetes and its associated conditions, the code(s) from category 250 must be sequenced before the codes for the associated conditions. The diabetes codes and the secondary codes that correspond to them are paired codes that follow the etiology/manifestation convention of the classification *(See Section I.A.6., Etiology/manifestation convention)*. Assign as many codes from category 250 as needed to identify all of the associated conditions that the patient has. The corresponding secondary codes are listed under each of the diabetes codes.

(a)   Diabetic retinopathy/diabetic macular edema

Diabetic macular edema, code 362.07, is only present with diabetic retinopathy. Another code from subcategory 362.0, Diabetic retinopathy, must be used with code 362.07. Codes under subcategory 362.0 are diabetes manifestation codes, so they must be used following the appropriate diabetes code.

5)   Diabetes mellitus in pregnancy and gestational diabetes

(a) For diabetes mellitus complicating pregnancy, see Section I.C.11.f., Diabetes mellitus in pregnancy.

(b) For gestational diabetes, see Section I.C.11, g., Gestational diabetes.

6) Insulin pump malfunction

(a) Underdose of insulin due insulin pump failure

An underdose of insulin due to an insulin pump failure should be assigned 996.57, Mechanical complication due to insulin pump, as the principal or first listed code, followed by the appropriate diabetes mellitus code based on documentation.

(b) Overdose of insulin due to insulin pump failure

The principal or first listed code for an encounter due to an insulin pump malfunction resulting in an overdose of insulin, should also be 996.57, Mechanical complication due to insulin pump, followed by code 962.3, Poisoning by insulins and antidiabetic agents, and the appropriate diabetes mellitus code based on documentation.

7) Secondary Diabetes Mellitus

Codes under category 249, Secondary diabetes mellitus, identify complications/manifestations associated with secondary diabetes mellitus. Secondary diabetes is always caused by another condition or event (e.g., cystic fibrosis, malignant neoplasm of pancreas, pancreatectomy, adverse effect of drug, or poisoning).

(a) Fifth-digits for category 249:

A fifth-digit is required for all category 249 codes to identify whether the diabetes is controlled or uncontrolled.

(b) Secondary diabetes mellitus and the use of insulin

For patients who routinely use insulin, code V58.67, Long-term (current) use of insulin, should also be assigned. Code V58.67 should not be assigned if insulin is given temporarily to bring a patient's blood sugar under control during an encounter.

(c)   **Assigning and sequencing secondary diabetes codes and associated conditions**

When assigning codes for secondary diabetes and its associated conditions (e.g. renal manifestations), the code(s) from category 249 must be sequenced before the codes for the associated conditions. The secondary diabetes codes and the diabetic manifestation codes that correspond to them are paired codes that follow the etiology/manifestation convention of the classification. Assign as many codes from category 249 as needed to identify all of the associated conditions that the patient has. The corresponding codes for the associated conditions are listed under each of the secondary diabetes codes. For example, secondary diabetes with diabetic nephrosis is assigned to code 249.40, followed by 581.81.

(d)   **Assigning and sequencing secondary diabetes codes and its causes**

The sequencing of the secondary diabetes codes in relationship to codes for the cause of the diabetes is based on the reason for the encounter, applicable ICD-9-CM sequencing conventions, and chapter-specific guidelines.

If a patient is seen for treatment of the secondary diabetes or one of its associated conditions, a code from category 249 is sequenced as the principal or first-listed diagnosis, with the cause of the secondary diabetes (e.g. cystic fibrosis) sequenced as an additional diagnosis.

If, however, the patient is seen for the treatment of the condition causing the secondary diabetes (e.g., malignant neoplasm of pancreas), the code for the cause of the secondary diabetes should be sequenced as the principal or first-listed diagnosis followed by a code from category 249.

(i) **Secondary diabetes mellitus due to pancreatectomy**

For postpancreatectomy diabetes mellitus (lack of insulin due to the surgical removal of all or part of the pancreas), assign code 251.3, Postsurgical hypoinsulinemia. A code from subcategory 249 should not be assigned for secondary diabetes mellitus due to pancreatectomy. Code also any diabetic manifestations (e.g. diabetic nephrosis 581.81).

(ii) Secondary diabetes due to drugs

Secondary diabetes may be caused by an adverse effect of correctly administered medications, poisoning or late effect of poisoning.
See section I.C.17.e for coding of adverse effects and poisoning, and section I.C.19 for E code reporting.

4.   Chapter 4: Diseases of Blood and Blood Forming Organs (280-289)

a.   Anemia of chronic disease

Subcategory 285.2, Anemia in chronic illness, has codes for anemia in chronic kidney disease, code 285.21; anemia in neoplastic disease, code 285.22; and anemia in other chronic illness, code 285.29. These codes can be used as the principal/first listed code if the reason for the encounter is to treat the anemia. They may also be used as secondary codes if treatment of the anemia is a component of an encounter, but not the primary reason for the encounter. When using a code from subcategory 285 it is also necessary to use the code for the chronic condition causing the anemia.

1)   Anemia in chronic kidney disease

When assigning code 285.21, Anemia in chronic kidney disease, it is also necessary to assign a code from category 585, Chronic kidney disease, to indicate the stage of chronic kidney disease.
See I.C.10.a. Chronic kidney disease (CKD).

2)   Anemia in neoplastic disease

When assigning code 285.22, Anemia in neoplastic disease, it is also necessary to assign the neoplasm code that is responsible for the anemia. Code 285.22 is for use for anemia that is due to the malignancy, not for anemia due to antineoplastic chemotherapy drugs, which is an adverse effect.
See I.C.2.c.1 Anemia associated with malignancy.
See I.C.2.c.2 Anemia associated with chemotherapy, immunotherapy and radiation therapy.

See I.C.17.e.1. Adverse effects.

5.   Chapter 5: Mental Disorders (290-319)

Reserved for future guideline expansion

6.   Chapter 6: Diseases of Nervous System and Sense Organs (320-389)

a. Pain - Category 338

1)   General coding information

Codes in category 338 may be used in conjunction with codes from other categories and chapters to provide more detail about acute or chronic pain and neoplasm-related pain, unless otherwise indicated below.

If the pain is not specified as acute or chronic, do not assign codes from category 338, except for post-thoracotomy pain, postoperative pain, neoplasm related pain, or central pain syndrome.

A code from subcategories 338.1 and 338.2 should not be assigned if the underlying (definitive) diagnosis is known, unless the reason for the encounter is pain control/ management and not management of the underlying condition.

(a)   Category 338 Codes as Principal or First-Listed Diagnosis

Category 338 codes are acceptable as principal diagnosis or the first-listed code:

*   When pain control or pain management is the reason for the admission/encounter (e.g., a patient with displaced intervertebral disc, nerve impingement and severe back pain presents for injection of steroid into the spinal canal). The underlying cause of the pain should be reported as an additional diagnosis, if known.

*   When an admission or encounter is for a procedure aimed at treating the underlying condition (e.g., spinal fusion, kyphoplasty), a code for the underlying condition (e.g., vertebral fracture, spinal stenosis) should be assigned as the principal

diagnosis. No code from category 338 should be assigned.

- When a patient is admitted for the insertion of a neurostimulator for pain control, assign the appropriate pain code as the principal or first listed diagnosis. When an admission or encounter is for a procedure aimed at treating the underlying condition and a neurostimulator is inserted for pain control during the same admission/encounter, a code for the underlying condition should be assigned as the principal diagnosis and the appropriate pain code should be assigned as a secondary diagnosis.

(b)   Use of Category 338 Codes in Conjunction with Site Specific Pain Codes

(i) Assigning Category 338 Codes and Site-Specific Pain Codes

Codes from category 338 may be used in conjunction with codes that identify the site of pain (including codes from chapter 16) if the category 338 code provides additional information. For example, if the code describes the site of the pain, but does not fully describe whether the pain is acute or chronic, then both codes should be assigned.

(ii) Sequencing of Category 338 Codes with Site-Specific Pain Codes

The sequencing of category 338 codes with site-specific pain codes (including chapter 16 codes), is dependent on the circumstances of the encounter/admission as follows:

- If the encounter is for pain control or pain management, assign the code from category 338 followed by the code identifying the specific site of pain (e.g., encounter for pain management for acute neck pain from trauma is assigned code 338.11, Acute pain due to trauma, followed by code 723.1, Cervicalgia, to identify the site of pain).

- If the encounter is for any other reason except pain control or pain management, and a related definitive diagnosis has not been established (confirmed) by the provider, assign the code for the specific site of pain first, followed by the appropriate code from category 338.

2)   Pain due to devices, implants and grafts

Pain associated with devices, implants or grafts left in a surgical site (for example painful hip prosthesis) is assigned to the appropriate code(s) found in Chapter 17, Injury and Poisoning. Use additional code(s) from category 338 to identify acute or chronic pain due to presence of the device, implant or graft (338.18-338.19 or 338.28-338.29).

3)   Postoperative Pain

Post-thoracotomy pain and other postoperative pain are classified to subcategories 338.1 and 338.2, depending on whether the pain is acute or chronic. The default for post-thoracotomy and other postoperative pain not specified as acute or chronic is the code for the acute form.

Routine or expected postoperative pain immediately after surgery should not be coded.

(a)   Postoperative pain not associated with specific postoperative complication

Postoperative pain not associated with a specific postoperative complication is assigned to the appropriate postoperative pain code in category 338.

(b)   Postoperative pain associated with specific postoperative complication

Postoperative pain associated with a specific postoperative complication (such as painful wire sutures) is assigned to the appropriate code(s) found in Chapter 17, Injury and Poisoning. If appropriate, use additional code(s) from category 338 to identify acute or chronic pain (338.18 or 338.28). If pain control/management is the reason for the encounter, a code from category 338 should be assigned as the principal or first-listed diagnosis in accordance with *Section I.C.6.a.1.a above*.

(c) **Postoperative pain as principal or first-listed diagnosis**

Postoperative pain may be reported as the principal or first-listed diagnosis when the stated reason for the admission/encounter is documented as postoperative pain control/management.

(d) **Postoperative pain as secondary diagnosis**

Postoperative pain may be reported as a secondary diagnosis code when a patient presents for outpatient surgery and develops an unusual or inordinate amount of postoperative pain.

The provider's documentation should be used to guide the coding of postoperative pain, as well as *Section III. Reporting Additional Diagnoses* and *Section IV. Diagnostic Coding and Reporting in the Outpatient Setting*.

See Section II.I.2 for information on sequencing of diagnoses for patients admitted to hospital inpatient care following post-operative observation.

See Section II.J for information on sequencing of diagnoses for patients admitted to hospital inpatient care from outpatient surgery.

See Section IV.A.2 for information on sequencing of diagnoses for patients admitted for observation.

4) **Chronic pain**

Chronic pain is classified to subcategory 338.2. There is no time frame defining when pain becomes chronic pain. The provider's documentation should be used to guide use of these codes.

5) **Neoplasm Related Pain**

Code 338.3 is assigned to pain documented as being related, associated or due to cancer, primary or secondary malignancy, or tumor. This code is assigned regardless of whether the pain is acute or chronic.

This code may be assigned as the principal or first-listed code when the stated reason for the admission/encounter is documented as pain control/pain management. The underlying neoplasm should be reported as an additional diagnosis.

When the reason for the admission/encounter is management of the neoplasm and the pain associated with the neoplasm is also documented, code 338.3 may be assigned as an additional diagnosis.

See Section I.C.2 for instructions on the sequencing of neoplasms for all other stated reasons for the admission/encounter (except for pain control/pain management).

6)   Chronic pain syndrome

This condition is different than the term "chronic pain," and therefore this code should only be used when the provider has specifically documented this condition.

7.   Chapter 7: Diseases of Circulatory System (390-459)

a.   Hypertension

Hypertension Table

The Hypertension Table, found under the main term, "Hypertension", in the Alphabetic Index, contains a complete listing of all conditions due to or associated with hypertension and classifies them according to malignant, benign, and unspecified.

1)   Hypertension, Essential, or NOS

Assign hypertension (arterial) (essential) (primary) (systemic) (NOS) to category code 401 with the appropriate fourth digit to indicate malignant (.0), benign (.1), or unspecified (.9). Do not use either .0 malignant or .1 benign unless medical record documentation supports such a designation.

2)   Hypertension with Heart Disease

Heart conditions (425.8, 429.0-429.3, 429.8, 429.9) are assigned to a code from category 402 when a causal relationship is stated (due to hypertension) or implied (hypertensive). Use an additional code from category 428 to identify the type of heart failure in those patients with heart failure. More than one code from category 428 may be assigned if the patient has systolic or diastolic failure and congestive heart failure.

The same heart conditions (425.8, 429.0-429.3, 429.8, 429.9) with hypertension, but without a stated causal relationship, are coded separately. Sequence according to the circumstances of the admission/encounter.

3) Hypertensive Chronic Kidney Disease

Assign codes from category 403, Hypertensive chronic kidney disease, when conditions classified to category 585 are present. Unlike hypertension with heart disease, ICD-9-CM presumes a cause-and-effect relationship and classifies chronic kidney disease (CKD) with hypertension as hypertensive chronic kidney disease.

Fifth digits for category 403 should be assigned as follows:

- 0 with CKD stage I through stage IV, or unspecified.
- 1 with CKD stage V or end stage renal disease.
The appropriate code from category 585, Chronic kidney disease, should be used as a secondary code with a code from category 403 to identify the stage of chronic kidney disease.
See Section I.C.10.a for information on the coding of chronic kidney disease.

4) Hypertensive Heart and Chronic Kidney Disease

Assign codes from combination category 404, Hypertensive heart and chronic kidney disease, when both hypertensive kidney disease and hypertensive heart disease are stated in the diagnosis. Assume a relationship between the hypertension and the chronic kidney disease, whether or not the condition is so designated. Assign an additional code from category 428, to identify the type of heart failure. More than one code from category 428 may be assigned if the patient has systolic or diastolic failure and congestive heart failure.

Fifth digits for category 404 should be assigned as follows:
- 0 without heart failure and with chronic kidney disease (CKD) stage I through stage IV, or unspecified
- 1 with heart failure and with CKD stage I through stage IV, or unspecified
- 2 without heart failure and with CKD stage V or end stage renal disease

- 3 with heart failure and with CKD stage V or end stage renal disease

The appropriate code from category 585, Chronic kidney disease, should be used as a secondary code with a code from category 404 to identify the stage of kidney disease.
See Section I.C.10.a for information on the coding of chronic kidney disease.

5) Hypertensive Cerebrovascular Disease

First assign codes from 430-438, Cerebrovascular disease, then the appropriate hypertension code from categories 401-405.

6) Hypertensive Retinopathy

Two codes are necessary to identify the condition. First assign the code from subcategory 362.11, Hypertensive retinopathy, then the appropriate code from categories 401-405 to indicate the type of hypertension.

7) Hypertension, Secondary

Two codes are required: one to identify the underlying etiology and one from category 405 to identify the hypertension. Sequencing of codes is determined by the reason for admission/encounter.

8) Hypertension, Transient

Assign code 796.2, Elevated blood pressure reading without diagnosis of hypertension, unless patient has an established diagnosis of hypertension. Assign code 642.3x for transient hypertension of pregnancy.

9) Hypertension, Controlled

Assign appropriate code from categories 401-405. This diagnostic statement usually refers to an existing state of hypertension under control by therapy.

10) Hypertension, Uncontrolled

Uncontrolled hypertension may refer to untreated hypertension or hypertension not responding to current therapeutic regimen. In either case, assign the appropriate code from categories 401-405 to designate the stage and type of hypertension. Code to the type of hypertension.

11) Elevated Blood Pressure

For a statement of elevated blood pressure without further specificity, assign code 796.2, Elevated blood pressure reading without diagnosis of hypertension, rather than a code from category 401.

b. Cerebral infarction/stroke/cerebrovascular accident (CVA)

The terms stroke and CVA are often used interchangeably to refer to a cerebral infarction. The terms stroke, CVA, and cerebral infarction NOS are all indexed to the default code 434.91, Cerebral artery occlusion, unspecified, with infarction. Code 436, Acute, but ill-defined, cerebrovascular disease, should not be used when the documentation states stroke or CVA.

See Section I.C.18.d.3 for information on coding status post administration of tPA in a different facility within the last 24 hours.

c. Postoperative cerebrovascular accident

A cerebrovascular hemorrhage or infarction that occurs as a result of medical intervention is coded to 997.02, Iatrogenic cerebrovascular infarction or hemorrhage. Medical record documentation should clearly specify the cause- and-effect relationship between the medical intervention and the cerebrovascular accident in order to assign this code. A secondary code from the code range 430-432 or from a code from subcategories 433 or 434 with a fifth digit of "1" should also be used to identify the type of hemorrhage or infarct.

This guideline conforms to the use additional code note instruction at category 997. Code 436, Acute, but ill-defined, cerebrovascular disease, should not be used as a secondary code with code 997.02.

d. Late Effects of Cerebrovascular Disease

1) Category 438, Late Effects of Cerebrovascular disease

Category 438 is used to indicate conditions classifiable to categories 430-437 as the causes of late effects (neurologic deficits), themselves classified elsewhere. These "late effects" include neurologic deficits that persist after initial onset of conditions classifiable to 430-437. The neurologic deficits caused by cerebrovascular disease may be present from the onset or may arise at any time after the onset of the condition classifiable to 430-437.

2)   Codes from category 438 with codes from 430-437

Codes from category 438 may be assigned on a health care record with codes from 430-437, if the patient has a current cerebrovascular accident (CVA) and deficits from an old CVA.

3)   Code V12.54

Assign code V12.54, Transient ischemic attack (TIA), and cerebral infarction without residual deficits (and not a code from category 438) as an additional code for history of cerebrovascular disease when no neurologic deficits are present.

e.   Acute myocardial infarction (AMI)

1)   ST elevation myocardial infarction (STEMI) and non ST elevation myocardial infarction (NSTEMI)

The ICD-9-CM codes for acute myocardial infarction (AMI) identify the site, such as anterolateral wall or true posterior wall. Subcategories 410.0-410.6 and 410.8 are used for ST elevation myocardial infarction (STEMI). Subcategory 410.7, Subendocardial infarction, is used for non ST elevation myocardial infarction (NSTEMI) and nontransmural MIs.

2)   Acute myocardial infarction, unspecified

Subcategory 410.9 is the default for the unspecified term acute myocardial infarction. If only STEMI or transmural MI without the site is documented, query the provider as to the site, or assign a code from subcategory 410.9.

3)   AMI documented as nontransmural or subendocardial but site provided

If an AMI is documented as nontransmural or subendocardial, but the site is provided, it is still coded as a subendocardial AMI. If NSTEMI evolves to STEMI, assign the STEMI code. If STEMI converts to NSTEMI due to thrombolytic therapy, it is still coded as STEMI.

See Section I.C.18.d.3 for information on coding status post administration of tPA in a different facility within the last 24 hours.

8. **Chapter 8: Diseases of Respiratory System (460-519)**

See I.C.17.f. for ventilator-associated pneumonia.

a. **Chronic Obstructive Pulmonary Disease [COPD] and Asthma**

1) **Conditions that comprise COPD and Asthma**

   The conditions that comprise COPD are obstructive chronic bronchitis, subcategory 491.2, and emphysema, category 492. All asthma codes are under category 493, Asthma. Code 496, Chronic airway obstruction, not elsewhere classified, is a nonspecific code that should only be used when the documentation in a medical record does not specify the type of COPD being treated.

2) **Acute exacerbation of chronic obstructive bronchitis and asthma**

   The codes for chronic obstructive bronchitis and asthma distinguish between uncomplicated cases and those in acute exacerbation. An acute exacerbation is a worsening or a decompensation of a chronic condition. An acute exacerbation is not equivalent to an infection superimposed on a chronic condition, though an exacerbation may be triggered by an infection.

3) **Overlapping nature of the conditions that comprise COPD and asthma**

   Due to the overlapping nature of the conditions that make up COPD and asthma, there are many variations in the way these conditions are documented. Code selection must be based on the terms as documented. When selecting the correct code for the documented type of COPD and asthma, it is essential to first review the index, and then verify the code in the tabular list. There are many instructional notes under the different COPD subcategories and codes. It is important that all such notes be reviewed to assure correct code assignment.

4) **Acute exacerbation of asthma and status asthmaticus**

   An acute exacerbation of asthma is an increased severity of the asthma symptoms, such as wheezing and shortness of breath. Status asthmaticus refers to a patient's failure to respond to therapy administered during an asthmatic episode and is a life threatening complication that requires emergency care. If status asthmaticus is documented by the provider with any type of COPD or with acute bronchitis, the status asthmaticus should be sequenced first. It supersedes any type of COPD including that with acute exacerbation or acute bronchitis. It is inappropriate to assign an asthma code with 5th digit 2, with acute exacerbation, together with an asthma code with 5th digit 1, with status asthmatics. Only the 5th digit 1 should be assigned.

b.   Chronic Obstructive Pulmonary Disease [COPD] and Bronchitis

1)   Acute bronchitis with COPD

Acute bronchitis, code 466.0, is due to an infectious organism. When acute bronchitis is documented with COPD, code 491.22, Obstructive chronic bronchitis with acute bronchitis, should be assigned. It is not necessary to also assign code 466.0. If a medical record documents acute bronchitis with COPD with acute exacerbation, only code 491.22 should be assigned. The acute bronchitis included in code 491.22 supersedes the acute exacerbation. If a medical record documents COPD with acute exacerbation without mention of acute bronchitis, only code 491.21 should be assigned.

c.   Acute Respiratory Failure

1)   Acute respiratory failure as principal diagnosis

Code 518.81, Acute respiratory failure, may be assigned as a principal diagnosis when it is the condition established after study to be chiefly responsible for occasioning the admission to the hospital, and the selection is supported by the Alphabetic Index and Tabular List. However, chapter-specific coding guidelines (such as obstetrics, poisoning, HIV, newborn) that provide sequencing direction take precedence.

2)   Acute respiratory failure as secondary diagnosis

Respiratory failure may be listed as a secondary diagnosis if it occurs after admission, or if it is present on admission, but does not meet the definition of principal diagnosis.

3)   Sequencing of acute respiratory failure and another acute condition

When a patient is admitted with respiratory failure and another acute condition, (e.g., myocardial infarction, cerebrovascular accident, **aspiration pneumonia**), the principal diagnosis will not be the same in every situation. **This applies whether the other acute condition is a respiratory or nonrespiratory condition.** Selection of the principal diagnosis will be dependent on the circumstances of admission. If both the respiratory failure and the other acute condition are equally responsible for occasioning the admission to the hospital, and there are no chapter-specific sequencing rules, the guideline regarding two or more diagnoses that equally meet the definition for principal diagnosis *(Section II, C.)* may be applied in these situations.

If the documentation is not clear as to whether acute respiratory failure and another condition are equally responsible for occasioning the admission, query the provider for clarification.

d. Influenza due to identified avian influenza virus (avian influenza)

Code only confirmed cases of avian influenza. This is an exception to the hospital inpatient guideline Section II, H. (Uncertain Diagnosis).

In this context, "confirmation" does not require documentation of positive laboratory testing specific for avian influenza. However, coding should be based on the provider's diagnostic statement that the patient has avian influenza.

If the provider records "suspected or possible or probable avian influenza," the appropriate influenza code from category 487 should be assigned. Code 488, Influenza due to identified avian influenza virus, should not be assigned.

9. Chapter 9: Diseases of Digestive System (520-579)

Reserved for future guideline expansion

10. Chapter 10: Diseases of Genitourinary System (580-629)

a. Chronic kidney disease

1) Stages of chronic kidney disease (CKD)

The ICD-9-CM classifies CKD based on severity. The severity of CKD is designated by stages I-V. Stage II, code 585.2, equates to mild CKD; stage III, code 585.3, equates to moderate CKD; and stage IV, code 585.4, equates to severe CKD. Code 585.6, End stage renal disease (ESRD), is assigned when the provider has documented end-stage-renal disease (ESRD).

If both a stage of CKD and ESRD are documented, assign code 585.6 only.

2)   Chronic kidney disease and kidney transplant status

Patients who have undergone kidney transplant may still have some form of CKD, because the kidney transplant may not fully restore kidney function. Therefore, the presence of CKD alone does not constitute a transplant complication. Assign the appropriate 585 code for the patient's stage of CKD and code V42.0. If a transplant complication such as failure or rejection is documented, see section I.C.17.f.**2**.b for information on coding complications of a kidney transplant. If the documentation is unclear as to whether the patient has a complication of the transplant, query the provider.

3)   Chronic kidney disease with other conditions

Patients with CKD may also suffer from other serious conditions, most commonly diabetes mellitus and hypertension. The sequencing of the CKD code in relationship to codes for other contributing conditions is based on the conventions in the tabular list.
See I.C.3.a.4 for sequencing instructions for diabetes.
See I.C.4.a.1 for anemia in CKD.
See I.C.7.a.3 for hypertensive chronic kidney disease.
See I.C.17.f.2.b, Kidney transplant complications, for instructions on coding of documented rejection or failure.

11.   Chapter 11: Complications of Pregnancy, Childbirth, and the Puerperium (630-679)

a.   General Rules for Obstetric Cases

1)   Codes from chapter 11 and sequencing priority

Obstetric cases require codes from chapter 11, codes in the range 630-679, Complications of Pregnancy, Childbirth, and the Puerperium. Chapter 11 codes have sequencing priority over codes from other chapters. Additional codes from other chapters may be used in conjunction with chapter 11 codes to further specify conditions. Should the provider document that the pregnancy is incidental to the encounter, then code V22.2 should be used in place of any chapter 11 codes. It is the provider's responsibility to state that the condition being treated is not affecting the pregnancy.

2) Chapter 11 codes used only on the maternal record

Chapter 11 codes are to be used only on the maternal record, never on the record of the newborn.

3) Chapter 11 fifth-digits

Categories 640-648, 651-676 have required fifth-digits, which indicate whether the encounter is antepartum, postpartum and whether a delivery has also occurred.

4) Fifth-digits, appropriate for each code

The fifth-digits, which are appropriate for each code number, are listed in brackets under each code. The fifth-digits on each code should all be consistent with each other. That is, should a delivery occur all of the fifth-digits should indicate the delivery.

b. Selection of OB Principal or First-listed Diagnosis

1) Routine outpatient prenatal visits

For routine outpatient prenatal visits when no complications are present codes V22.0, Supervision of normal first pregnancy, and V22.1, Supervision of other normal pregnancy, should be used as the first-listed diagnoses. These codes should not be used in conjunction with chapter 11 codes.

2) Prenatal outpatient visits for high-risk patients

For prenatal outpatient visits for patients with high-risk pregnancies, a code from category V23, Supervision of high-risk pregnancy, should be used as the first-listed diagnosis. Secondary chapter 11 codes may be used in conjunction with these codes if appropriate.

3) Episodes when no delivery occurs

In episodes when no delivery occurs, the principal diagnosis should correspond to the principal complication of the pregnancy, which necessitated the encounter. Should more than one complication exist, all of which are treated or monitored, any of the complications codes may be sequenced first.

4)   When a delivery occurs

When a delivery occurs, the principal diagnosis should correspond to the main circumstances or complication of the delivery. In cases of cesarean delivery, the selection of the principal diagnosis should correspond to the reason the cesarean delivery was performed unless the reason for admission/encounter was unrelated to the condition resulting in the cesarean delivery.

5)   Outcome of delivery

An outcome of delivery code, V27.0-V27.9, should be included on every maternal record when a delivery has occurred. These codes are not to be used on subsequent records or on the newborn record.

c.   Fetal Conditions Affecting the Management of the Mother

1)   Codes from category 655

Known or suspected fetal abnormality affecting management of the mother, and category 656, Other fetal and placental problems affecting the management of the mother, are assigned only when the fetal condition is actually responsible for modifying the management of the mother, i.e., by requiring diagnostic studies, additional observation, special care, or termination of pregnancy. The fact that the fetal condition exists does not justify assigning a code from this series to the mother's record.

See I.C.18.d. for suspected maternal and fetal conditions not found

2)   In utero surgery

In cases when surgery is performed on the fetus, a diagnosis code from category 655, Known or suspected fetal abnormalities affecting management of the mother, should be assigned identifying the fetal condition. Procedure code 75.36, Correction of fetal defect, should be assigned on the hospital inpatient record.

No code from Chapter 15, the perinatal codes, should be used on the mother's record to identify fetal conditions. Surgery performed in utero on a fetus is still to be coded as an obstetric encounter.

d. HIV Infection in Pregnancy, Childbirth and the Puerperium

During pregnancy, childbirth or the puerperium, a patient admitted because of an HIV-related illness should receive a principal diagnosis of 647.6X, Other specified infectious and parasitic diseases in the mother classifiable elsewhere, but complicating the pregnancy, childbirth or the puerperium, followed by 042 and the code(s) for the HIV-related illness(es).

Patients with asymptomatic HIV infection status admitted during pregnancy, childbirth, or the puerperium should receive codes of 647.6X and V08.

e. Current Conditions Complicating Pregnancy

Assign a code from subcategory 648.x for patients that have current conditions when the condition affects the management of the pregnancy, childbirth, or the puerperium. Use additional secondary codes from other chapters to identify the conditions, as appropriate.

f. Diabetes mellitus in pregnancy

Diabetes mellitus is a significant complicating factor in pregnancy. Pregnant women who are diabetic should be assigned code 648.0x, Diabetes mellitus complicating pregnancy, and a secondary code from category 250, Diabetes mellitus, **or category 249, Secondary diabetes** to identify the type of diabetes.

Code V58.67, Long-term (current) use of insulin, should also be assigned if the diabetes mellitus is being treated with insulin.

g. Gestational diabetes

Gestational diabetes can occur during the second and third trimester of pregnancy in women who were not diabetic prior to pregnancy. Gestational diabetes can cause complications in the pregnancy similar to those of pre-existing diabetes mellitus. It also puts the woman at greater risk of developing diabetes after the pregnancy. Gestational diabetes is coded to 648.8x, Abnormal glucose tolerance. Codes 648.0x and 648.8x should never be used together on the same record.

Code V58.67, Long-term (current) use of insulin, should also be assigned if the gestational diabetes is being treated with insulin.

h.   Normal Delivery, Code 650

1)   Normal delivery

Code 650 is for use in cases when a woman is admitted for a full-term normal delivery and delivers a single, healthy infant without any complications antepartum, during the delivery, or postpartum during the delivery episode. Code 650 is always a principal diagnosis. It is not to be used if any other code from chapter 11 is needed to describe a current complication of the antenatal, delivery, or perinatal period. Additional codes from other chapters may be used with code 650 if they are not related to or are in any way complicating the pregnancy.

2)   Normal delivery with resolved antepartum complication

Code 650 may be used if the patient had a complication at some point during her pregnancy, but the complication is not present at the time of the admission for delivery.

3)   V27.0, Single liveborn, outcome of delivery

V27.0, Single liveborn, is the only outcome of delivery code appropriate for use with 650.

i.   The Postpartum and Peripartum Periods

1)   Postpartum and peripartum periods

The postpartum period begins immediately after delivery and continues for six weeks following delivery. The peripartum period is defined as the last month of pregnancy to five months postpartum.

2)   Postpartum complication

A postpartum complication is any complication occurring within the six-week period.

3)   Pregnancy-related complications after 6 week period

Chapter 11 codes may also be used to describe pregnancy-related complications after the six-week period should the provider document that a condition is pregnancy related.

4) Postpartum complications occurring during the same admission as delivery

Postpartum complications that occur during the same admission as the delivery are identified with a fifth digit of "2." Subsequent admissions/encounters for postpartum complications should be identified with a fifth digit of "4."

5) Admission for routine postpartum care following delivery outside hospital

When the mother delivers outside the hospital prior to admission and is admitted for routine postpartum care and no complications are noted, code V24.0, Postpartum care and examination immediately after delivery, should be assigned as the principal diagnosis.

6) Admission following delivery outside hospital with postpartum conditions

A delivery diagnosis code should not be used for a woman who has delivered prior to admission to the hospital. Any postpartum conditions and/or postpartum procedures should be coded.

j. Code 677, Late effect of complication of pregnancy

1) Code 677

Code 677, Late effect of complication of pregnancy, childbirth, and the puerperium is for use in those cases when an initial complication of a pregnancy develops a sequelae requiring care or treatment at a future date.

2) After the initial postpartum period

This code may be used at any time after the initial postpartum period.

3) Sequencing of Code 677

This code, like all late effect codes, is to be sequenced following the code describing the sequelae of the complication.

k. Abortions

1) Fifth-digits required for abortion categories

Fifth-digits are required for abortion categories 634-637. Fifth-digit 1, incomplete, indicates that all of the products of conception have not been expelled from the uterus. Fifth-digit

2, complete, indicates that all products of conception have been expelled from the uterus.

2)   Code from categories 640-648 and 651-659

A code from categories 640-648 and 651-659 may be used as additional codes with an abortion code to indicate the complication leading to the abortion.

Fifth digit 3 is assigned with codes from these categories when used with an abortion code because the other fifth digits will not apply. Codes from the 660-669 series are not to be used for complications of abortion.

3)   Code 639 for complications

Code 639 is to be used for all complications following abortion. Code 639 cannot be assigned with codes from categories 634-638.

4)   Abortion with Liveborn Fetus

When an attempted termination of pregnancy results in a liveborn fetus assign code 644.21, Early onset of delivery, with an appropriate code from category V27, Outcome of Delivery. The procedure code for the attempted termination of pregnancy should also be assigned.

5)   Retained Products of Conception following an abortion

Subsequent admissions for retained products of conception following a spontaneous or legally induced abortion are assigned the appropriate code from category 634, Spontaneous abortion, or 635 Legally induced abortion, with a fifth digit of "1" (incomplete). This advice is appropriate even when the patient was discharged previously with a discharge diagnosis of complete abortion.

12. Chapter 12: Diseases Skin and Subcutaneous Tissue (680-709)

a. Pressure ulcer stage codes

1) Pressure ulcer stages

Two codes are needed to completely describe a pressure ulcer: A code from subcategory 707.0, Pressure ulcer, to identify the site of the pressure ulcer and a code from subcategory 707.2, Pressure ulcer stages.

The codes in subcategory 707.2, Pressure ulcer stages, are to be used as an additional diagnosis with a code(s) from subcategory 707.0, Pressure Ulcer. Codes from 707.2, Pressure ulcer stages, may not be assigned as a principal or first-listed diagnosis. The pressure ulcer stage codes should only be used with pressure ulcers and not with other types of ulcers (e.g., stasis ulcer).

The ICD-9-CM classifies pressure ulcer stages based on severity, which is designated by stages I-IV and unstageable.

2) Unstageable pressure ulcers

Assignment of code 707.25, Pressure ulcer, unstageable, should be based on the clinical documentation. Code 707.25 is used for pressure ulcers whose stage cannot be clinically determined (e.g., the ulcer is covered by eschar or has been treated with a skin or muscle graft) and pressure ulcers that are documented as deep tissue injury but not documented as due to trauma. This code should not be confused with code 707.20, Pressure ulcer, stage unspecified. Code 707.20 should be assigned when there is no documentation regarding the stage of the pressure ulcer.

3) Documented pressure ulcer stage

Assignment of the pressure ulcer stage code should be guided by clinical documentation of the stage or documentation of the terms found in the index. For clinical terms describing the stage that are not found in the index, and there is no documentation of the stage, the provider should be queried.

4) Bilateral pressure ulcers with same stage

When a patient has bilateral pressure ulcers (e.g., both buttocks) and both pressure ulcers are documented as being the same stage, only the code for the site and one code for the stage should be reported.

5) Bilateral pressure ulcers with different stages

When a patient has bilateral pressure ulcers at the same site (e.g., both buttocks) and each pressure ulcer is documented as being at a different stage, assign one code for the site and the appropriate codes for the pressure ulcer stage.

6) Multiple pressure ulcers of different sites and stages

When a patient has multiple pressure ulcers at different sites (e.g., buttock, heel, shoulder) and each pressure ulcer is documented as being at different stages (e.g., stage 3 and stage 4), assign the appropriate codes for each different site and a code for each different pressure ulcer stage.

7) Patients admitted with pressure ulcers documented as healed

No code is assigned if the documentation states that the pressure ulcer is completely healed.

8) Patients admitted with pressure ulcers documented as healing

Pressure ulcers described as healing should be assigned the appropriate pressure ulcer stage code based on the documentation in the medical record. If the documentation does not provide information about the stage of the healing pressure ulcer, assign code 707.20, Pressure ulcer stage, unspecified.

If the documentation is unclear as to whether the patient has a current (new) pressure ulcer or if the patient is being treated for a healing pressure ulcer, query the provider.

9) Patient admitted with pressure ulcer evolving into another stage during the admission

> **If a patient is admitted with a pressure ulcer at one stage and it progresses to a higher stage, assign the code for highest stage reported for that site.**

13.   Chapter 13: Diseases of Musculoskeletal and Connective Tissue (710-739)

a.   Coding of Pathologic Fractures

1)   Acute Fractures vs. Aftercare

Pathologic fractures are reported using subcategory 733.1, when the fracture is newly diagnosed. Subcategory 733.1 may be used while the patient is receiving active treatment for the fracture. Examples of active treatment are: surgical treatment, emergency department encounter, evaluation and treatment by a new physician.

Fractures are coded using the aftercare codes (subcategories V54.0, V54.2, V54.8 or V54.9) for encounters after the patient has completed active treatment of the fracture and is receiving routine care for the fracture during the healing or recovery phase. Examples of fracture aftercare are: cast change or removal, removal of external or internal fixation device, medication adjustment, and follow up visits following fracture treatment.

Care for complications of surgical treatment for fracture repairs during the healing or recovery phase should be coded with the appropriate complication codes.

Care of complications of fractures, such as malunion and nonunion, should be reported with the appropriate codes.

See Section I. C. 17.b for information on the coding of traumatic fractures.

14.   Chapter 14: Congenital Anomalies (740-759)

a.   Codes in categories 740-759, Congenital Anomalies

Assign an appropriate code(s) from categories 740-759, Congenital Anomalies, when an anomaly is documented. A congenital anomaly may be the principal/first listed diagnosis on a record or a secondary diagnosis.

When a congenital anomaly does not have a unique code assignment, assign additional code(s) for any manifestations that may be present.

When the code assignment specifically identifies the congenital anomaly, manifestations that are an inherent component of the anomaly should not be coded separately. Additional codes should be assigned for manifestations that are not an inherent component.

Codes from Chapter 14 may be used throughout the life of the patient. If a congenital anomaly has been corrected, a personal history code should be used to identify the history of the anomaly. Although present at birth, a congenital anomaly may not be identified until later in life. Whenever the condition is diagnosed by the physician, it is appropriate to assign a code from codes 740-759.

For the birth admission, the appropriate code from category V30, Liveborn infants, according to type of birth should be sequenced as the principal diagnosis, followed by any congenital anomaly codes, 740-759.

15.   Chapter 15: Newborn (Perinatal) Guidelines (760-779)

For coding and reporting purposes the perinatal period is defined as before birth through the 28th day following birth. The following guidelines are provided for reporting purposes. Hospitals may record other diagnoses as needed for internal data use.

a.   General Perinatal Rules

1)   Chapter 15 Codes

They are <u>never</u> for use on the maternal record. Codes from Chapter 11, the obstetric chapter, are never permitted on the newborn record. Chapter 15 code may be used throughout the life of the patient if the condition is still present.

2)   Sequencing of perinatal codes

Generally, codes from Chapter 15 should be sequenced as the principal/first-listed diagnosis on the newborn record, with the exception of the appropriate V30 code for the birth episode, followed by codes from any other chapter that provide additional detail. The "use additional code" note at the beginning of the chapter supports this guideline. If the index does not provide a specific code for a perinatal condition, assign code 779.89, Other specified conditions originating in the perinatal period, followed by the code from another chapter that specifies the condition. Codes for signs and symptoms may be assigned when a definitive diagnosis has not been established.

3) Birth process or community acquired conditions

If a newborn has a condition that may be either due to the birth process or community acquired and the documentation does not indicate which it is, the default is due to the birth process and the code from Chapter 15 should be used. If the condition is community-acquired, a code from Chapter 15 should not be assigned.

4) Code all clinically significant conditions

All clinically significant conditions noted on routine newborn examination should be coded. A condition is clinically significant if it requires:

- clinical evaluation; or
- therapeutic treatment; or
- diagnostic procedures; or
- extended length of hospital stay; or
- increased nursing care and/or monitoring; or
- has implications for future health care needs

Note: The perinatal guidelines listed above are the same as the general coding guidelines for "additional diagnoses", except for the final point regarding implications for future health care needs. Codes should be assigned for conditions that have been specified by the provider as having implications for future health care needs. Codes from the perinatal chapter should not be assigned unless the provider has established a definitive diagnosis.

b. Use of codes V30-V39

When coding the birth of an infant, assign a code from categories V30-V39, according to the type of birth. A code from this series is assigned as a principal diagnosis, and assigned only once to a newborn at the time of birth.

c. Newborn transfers

If the newborn is transferred to another institution, the V30 series is not used at the receiving hospital.

d.   Use of category V29

1)   Assigning a code from category V29

Assign a code from category V29, Observation and evaluation of newborns and infants for suspected conditions not found, to identify those instances when a healthy newborn is evaluated for a suspected condition that is determined after study not to be present. Do not use a code from category V29 when the patient has identified signs or symptoms of a suspected problem; in such cases, code the sign or symptom.

A code from category V29 may also be assigned as a principal code for readmissions or encounters when the V30 code no longer applies. Codes from category V29 are for use only for healthy newborns and infants for which no condition after study is found to be present.

2)   V29 code on a birth record

A V29 code is to be used as a secondary code after the V30, Outcome of delivery, code.

e.   Use of other V codes on perinatal records

V codes other than V30 and V29 may be assigned on a perinatal or newborn record code. The codes may be used as a principal or first-listed diagnosis for specific types of encounters or for readmissions or encounters when the V30 code no longer applies.
See Section I.C.18 for information regarding the assignment of V codes.

f.   Maternal Causes of Perinatal Morbidity

Codes from categories 760-763, Maternal causes of perinatal morbidity and mortality, are assigned only when the maternal condition has actually affected the fetus or newborn. The fact that the mother has an associated medical condition or experiences some complication of pregnancy, labor or delivery does not justify the routine assignment of codes from these categories to the newborn record.

g.   Congenital Anomalies in Newborns

For the birth admission, the appropriate code from category V30, Liveborn infants according to type of birth, should be used, followed by any congenital anomaly codes, categories 740-759.   Use additional secondary codes from other chapters to specify conditions associated with the anomaly, if applicable.

Also, see Section I.C.14 for information on the coding of congenital anomalies.

h. Coding Additional Perinatal Diagnoses

1) Assigning codes for conditions that require treatment

Assign codes for conditions that require treatment or further investigation, prolong the length of stay, or require resource utilization.

2) Codes for conditions specified as having implications for future health care needs

Assign codes for conditions that have been specified by the provider as having implications for future health care needs.

Note: This guideline should not be used for adult patients.

3) Codes for newborn conditions originating in the perinatal period

Assign a code for newborn conditions originating in the perinatal period (categories 760-779), as well as complications arising during the current episode of care classified in other chapters, only if the diagnoses have been documented by the responsible provider at the time of transfer or discharge as having affected the fetus or newborn.

i. Prematurity and Fetal Growth Retardation

Providers utilize different criteria in determining prematurity. A code for prematurity should not be assigned unless it is documented. The 5th digit assignment for codes from category 764 and subcategories 765.0 and 765.1 should be based on the recorded birth weight and estimated gestational age.

A code from subcategory 765.2, Weeks of gestation, should be assigned as an additional code with category 764 and codes from 765.0 and 765.1 to specify weeks of gestation as documented by the provider in the record.

j. Newborn sepsis

Code 771.81, Septicemia [sepsis] of newborn, should be assigned with a secondary code from category 041, Bacterial infections in conditions classified elsewhere and of unspecified site, to identify the organism.

A code from category 038, Septicemia, should not be used on a newborn record. **Do not assign code 995.91, Sepsis, as c**ode 771.81 describes the sepsis. **If applicable, use additional codes to identify severe sepsis (995.92) and any associated acute organ dysfunction.**

16.   Chapter 16: Signs, Symptoms and Ill-Defined Conditions (780-799)

Reserved for future guideline expansion

17.   Chapter 17: Injury and Poisoning (800-999)

a.   Coding of Injuries

When coding injuries, assign separate codes for each injury unless a combination code is provided, in which case the combination code is assigned. Multiple injury codes are provided in ICD-9-CM, but should not be assigned unless information for a more specific code is not available. These codes are not to be used for normal, healing surgical wounds or to identify complications of surgical wounds.

The code for the most serious injury, as determined by the provider and the focus of treatment, is sequenced first.

1)   Superficial injuries

Superficial injuries such as abrasions or contusions are not coded when associated with more severe injuries of the same site.

2)   Primary injury with damage to nerves/blood vessels

When a primary injury results in minor damage to peripheral nerves or blood vessels, the primary injury is sequenced first with additional code(s) from categories 950-957, Injury to nerves and spinal cord, and/or 900-904, Injury to blood vessels. When the primary injury is to the blood vessels or nerves, that injury should be sequenced first.

b.   Coding of Traumatic Fractures

The principles of multiple coding of injuries should be followed in coding fractures. Fractures of specified sites are coded individually by site in accordance with both the provisions within categories 800-829 and the level of detail furnished by medical record content. Combination categories for multiple fractures are provided for use when there is insufficient detail in the medical record (such as trauma cases transferred to another hospital), when the reporting form limits the number of codes that can be used in reporting pertinent clinical data, or when there is insufficient specificity at the fourth-digit or fifth-digit level. More specific guidelines are as follows:

1) **Acute Fractures vs. Aftercare**

Traumatic fractures are coded using the acute fracture codes (800-829) while the patient is receiving active treatment for the fracture. Examples of active treatment are: surgical treatment, emergency department encounter, and evaluation and treatment by a new physician.

Fractures are coded using the aftercare codes (subcategories V54.0, V54.1, V54.8, or V54.9) for encounters after the patient has completed active treatment of the fracture and is receiving routine care for the fracture during the healing or recovery phase. Examples of fracture aftercare are: cast change or removal, removal of external or internal fixation device, medication adjustment, and follow up visits following fracture treatment.

Care for complications of surgical treatment for fracture repairs during the healing or recovery phase should be coded with the appropriate complication codes.

Care of complications of fractures, such as malunion and nonunion, should be reported with the appropriate codes.

Pathologic fractures are not coded in the 800-829 range, but instead are assigned to subcategory 733.1. *See Section I.C.13.a for additional information.*

2) **Multiple fractures of same limb**

Multiple fractures of same limb classifiable to the same three-digit or four-digit category are coded to that category.

3) **Multiple unilateral or bilateral fractures of same bone**

Multiple unilateral or bilateral fractures of same bone(s) but classified to different fourth-digit subdivisions (bone part) within the same three-digit category are coded individually by site.

4) **Multiple fracture categories 819 and 828**

Multiple fracture categories 819 and 828 classify bilateral fractures of both upper limbs (819) and both lower limbs (828), but without any detail at the fourth-digit level other than open and closed type of fractures.

5)   Multiple fractures sequencing

Multiple fractures are sequenced in accordance with the severity of the fracture. The provider should be asked to list the fracture diagnoses in the order of severity.

c.   Coding of Burns

Current burns (940-948) are classified by depth, extent and by agent (E code). Burns are classified by depth as first degree (erythema), second degree (blistering), and third degree (full-thickness involvement).

1)   Sequencing of burn and related condition codes

Sequence first the code that reflects the highest degree of burn when more than one burn is present.

a.   When the reason for the admission or encounter is for treatment of external multiple burns, sequence first the code that reflects the burn of the highest degree.

b.   When a patient has both internal and external burns, the circumstances of admission govern the selection of the principal diagnosis or first-listed diagnosis.

c.   When a patient is admitted for burn injuries and other related conditions such as smoke inhalation and/or respiratory failure, the circumstances of admission govern the selection of the principal or first-listed diagnosis.

2)   Burns of the same local site

Classify burns of the same local site (three-digit category level, 940-947) but of different degrees to the subcategory identifying the highest degree recorded in the diagnosis.

3)   Non-healing burns

Non-healing burns are coded as acute burns.
Necrosis of burned skin should be coded as a non-healed burn.

4)   Code 958.3, Posttraumatic wound infection

Assign code 958.3, Posttraumatic wound infection, not elsewhere classified, as an additional code for any documented infected burn site.

5)   Assign separate codes for each burn site

When coding burns, assign separate codes for each burn site. Category 946 Burns of Multiple specified sites, should only be used if the location of the burns are not documented. Category 949, Burn, unspecified, is extremely vague and should rarely be used.

6)   Assign codes from category 948, Burns

Burns classified according to extent of body surface involved, when the site of the burn is not specified or when there is a need for additional data. It is advisable to use category 948 as additional coding when needed to provide data for evaluating burn mortality, such as that needed by burn units. It is also advisable to use category 948 as an additional code for reporting purposes when there is mention of a third-degree burn involving 20 percent or more of the body surface.

In assigning a code from category 948:

Fourth-digit codes are used to identify the percentage of total body surface involved in a burn (all degree).

Fifth-digits are assigned to identify the percentage of body surface involved in third-degree burn.

Fifth-digit zero (0) is assigned when less than 10 percent or when no body surface is involved in a third-degree burn.

Category 948 is based on the classic "rule of nines" in estimating body surface involved: head and neck are assigned nine percent, each arm nine percent, each leg 18 percent, the anterior trunk 18 percent, posterior trunk 18 percent, and genitalia one percent. Providers may change these percentage assignments where necessary to accommodate infants and children who have proportionately larger heads than adults and patients who have large buttocks, thighs, or abdomen that involve burns.

7)   Encounters for treatment of late effects of burns

Encounters for the treatment of the late effects of burns (i.e., scars or joint contractures) should be coded to the residual condition (sequelae) followed by the appropriate late effect code (906.5-906.9). A late effect E code may also be used, if desired.

8)   Sequelae with a late effect code and current burn

When appropriate, both a sequelae with a late effect code, and a current burn code may be assigned on the same record (when both a current burn and sequelae of an old burn exist).

d.   Coding of Debridement of Wound, Infection, or Burn

Excisional debridement involves surgical removal or cutting away, as opposed to a mechanical (brushing, scrubbing, washing) debridement.

For coding purposes, excisional debridement is assigned to code 86.22.

Nonexcisional debridement is assigned to code 86.28.

e.   Adverse Effects, Poisoning and Toxic Effects

The properties of certain drugs, medicinal and biological substances or combinations of such substances, may cause toxic reactions. The occurrence of drug toxicity is classified in ICD-9-CM as follows:

1)   Adverse Effect

When the drug was correctly prescribed and properly administered, code the reaction plus the appropriate code from the E930-E949 series. Codes from the E930-E949 series must be used to identify the causative substance for an adverse effect of drug, medicinal and biological substances, correctly prescribed and properly administered. The effect, such as tachycardia, delirium, gastrointestinal hemorrhaging, vomiting, hypokalemia, hepatitis, renal failure, or respiratory failure, is coded and followed by the appropriate code from the E930-E949 series.

Adverse effects of therapeutic substances correctly prescribed and properly administered (toxicity, synergistic reaction, side effect, and idiosyncratic reaction) may be due to (1) differences among patients, such as age, sex, disease, and genetic factors, and (2) drug-related factors, such as type of drug, route of administration, duration of therapy, dosage, and bioavailability.

2)   Poisoning

(a)   Error was made in drug prescription

Errors made in drug prescription or in the administration of the drug by provider, nurse, patient, or other person, use the appropriate poisoning code from the 960-979 series.

(b)   Overdose of a drug intentionally taken

If an overdose of a drug was intentionally taken or administered and resulted in drug toxicity, it would be coded as a poisoning (960-979 series).

(c)   Nonprescribed drug taken with correctly prescribed and properly administered drug

If a nonprescribed drug or medicinal agent was taken in combination with a correctly prescribed and properly administered drug, any drug toxicity or other reaction resulting from the interaction of the two drugs would be classified as a poisoning.

(d)   Interaction of drug(s) and alcohol

When a reaction results from the interaction of a drug(s) and alcohol, this would be classified as poisoning.

(e)   Sequencing of poisoning

When coding a poisoning or reaction to the improper use of a medication (e.g., wrong dose, wrong substance, wrong route of administration) the poisoning code is sequenced first, followed by a code for the manifestation. If there is also a diagnosis of drug abuse or dependence to the substance, the abuse or dependence is coded as an additional code. *See Section I.C.3.a.6.b. if poisoning is the result of insulin pump malfunctions and Section I.C.19 for general use of E-codes.*

3)   Toxic Effects

(a)   Toxic effect codes

When a harmful substance is ingested or comes in contact with a person, this is classified as a toxic effect. The toxic effect codes are in categories 980-989.

(b)   Sequencing toxic effect codes

A toxic effect code should be sequenced first, followed by the code(s) that identify the result of the toxic effect.

(c)   External cause codes for toxic effects

An external cause code from categories E860-E869 for accidental exposure, codes E950.6 or E950.7 for intentional self-harm, category E962 for assault, or categories E980-E982, for undetermined, should also be assigned to indicate intent.

f.   Complications of care

1)   Complications of care

(a)   Documentation of complications of care
As with all procedural or postprocedural complications, code assignment is based on the provider's documentation of the relationship between the condition and the procedure.

2)   Transplant complications

(a)   Transplant complications other than kidney
Codes under subcategory 996.8, Complications of transplanted organ, are for use for both complications and rejection of transplanted organs. A transplant complication code is only assigned if the complication affects the function of the transplanted organ. Two codes are required to fully describe a transplant complication, the appropriate code from subcategory 996.8 and a secondary code that identifies the complication.

Pre-existing conditions or conditions that develop after the transplant are not coded as complications unless they affect the function of the transplanted organs.

See I.C.18.d.3) for transplant organ removal status

See I.C.2.i for malignant neoplasm associated with transplanted organ.

(b)   Chronic kidney disease and kidney transplant complications
Patients who have undergone kidney transplant may still have some form of chronic kidney disease (CKD) because the kidney transplant may not fully restore kidney function. Code 996.81 should be assigned for documented complications of a kidney transplant, such as transplant failure or rejection **or other transplant complication.** Code 996.81 should

not be assigned for post kidney transplant patients who have chronic kidney (CKD) unless a transplant complication such as transplant failure or rejection is documented. If the documentation is unclear as to whether the patient has a complication of the transplant, query the provider.

For patients with CKD following a kidney transplant, but who do not have a complication such as failure or rejection, *see section I.C.10.a.2, Chronic kidney disease and kidney transplant status.*

3)   Ventilator associated pneumonia

(a)   Documentation of Ventilator associated Pneumonia

As with all procedural or postprocedural complications, code assignment is based on the provider's documentation of the relationship between the condition and the procedure.

Code 997.31, Ventilator associated pneumonia, should be assigned only when the provider has documented ventilator associated pneumonia (VAP). An additional code to identify the organism (e.g., Pseudomonas aeruginosa, code 041.7) should also be assigned. Do not assign an additional code from categories 480-484 to identify the type of pneumonia.

Code 997.31 should not be assigned for cases where the patient has pneumonia and is on a mechanical ventilator but the provider has not specifically stated that the pneumonia is ventilator-associated pneumonia.

If the documentation is unclear as to whether the patient has a pneumonia that is a complication attributable to the mechanical ventilator, query the provider.

(b)   Patient admitted with pneumonia and develops VAP

A patient may be admitted with one type of pneumonia (e.g., code 481, Pneumococcal pneumonia) and subsequently develop VAP. In this

instance, the principal diagnosis would be the appropriate code from categories 480-484 for the pneumonia diagnosed at the time of admission. Code 997.31, Ventilator associated pneumonia, would be assigned as an additional diagnosis when the provider has also documented the presence of ventilator associated pneumonia.

g.   SIRS due to Non-infectious Process

The systemic inflammatory response syndrome (SIRS) can develop as a result of certain non-infectious disease processes, such as trauma, malignant neoplasm, or pancreatitis. When SIRS is documented with a noninfectious condition, and no subsequent infection is documented, the code for the underlying condition, such as an injury, should be assigned, followed by code 995.93, Systemic inflammatory response syndrome due to noninfectious process without acute organ dysfunction, or 995.94, Systemic inflammatory response syndrome due to non-infectious process with acute organ dysfunction. If an acute organ dysfunction is documented, the appropriate code(s) for the associated acute organ dysfunction(s) should be assigned in addition to code 995.94. If acute organ dysfunction is documented, but it cannot be determined if the acute organ dysfunction is associated with SIRS or due to another condition (e.g., directly due to the trauma), the provider should be queried.

When the non-infectious condition has led to an infection that results in SIRS, *see Section I.C.1.b.12 for the guideline for sepsis and severe sepsis associated with a non-infectious process.*

18.   Classification of Factors Influencing Health Status and Contact with Health Service (Supplemental V01-V89)

Note: The chapter specific guidelines provide additional information about the use of V codes for specified encounters.

a.   Introduction

ICD-9-CM provides codes to deal with encounters for circumstances other than a disease or injury. The Supplementary Classification of Factors Influencing Health Status and Contact with Health Services (V01.0 - **V89.09**) is provided to deal with occasions when circumstances other than a disease or injury (codes 001-999) are recorded as a diagnosis or problem.

There are four primary circumstances for the use of V codes:

1) A person who is not currently sick encounters the health services for some specific reason, such as to act as an organ donor, to receive prophylactic care, such as inoculations or health screenings, or to receive counseling on health related issues.

2) A person with a resolving disease or injury, or a chronic, long-term condition requiring continuous care, encounters the health care system for specific aftercare of that disease or injury (e.g., dialysis for renal disease; chemotherapy for malignancy; cast change). A diagnosis/symptom code should be used whenever a current, acute, diagnosis is being treated or a sign or symptom is being studied.

3) Circumstances or problems influence a person's health status but are not in themselves a current illness or injury.

4) Newborns, to indicate birth status

b. V codes use in any healthcare setting

V codes are for use in any healthcare setting. V codes may be used as either a first listed (principal diagnosis code in the inpatient setting) or secondary code, depending on the circumstances of the encounter. Certain V codes may only be used as first listed, others only as secondary codes.
See Section I.C.18.e, V Code Table.

c. V Codes indicate a reason for an encounter

They are not procedure codes. A corresponding procedure code must accompany a V code to describe the procedure performed.

d. Categories of V Codes

1) Contact/Exposure

Category V01 indicates contact with or exposure to communicable diseases. These codes are for patients who do not show any sign or symptom of a disease but have been exposed to it by close personal contact with an infected individual or are in an area where a disease is epidemic. These codes may be used as a first listed code to explain an encounter for testing, or, more commonly, as a secondary code to identify a potential risk.

2) Inoculations and vaccinations

Categories V03-V06 are for encounters for inoculations and vaccinations. They indicate that a patient is being seen to receive a prophylactic inoculation against a disease. The injection itself must be represented by the appropriate procedure code. A code from V03-V06 may be used as a secondary code if the inoculation is given as a routine part of preventive health care, such as a well-baby visit.

3)   Status

Status codes indicate that a patient is either a carrier of a disease or has the sequelae or residual of a past disease or condition. This includes such things as the presence of prosthetic or mechanical devices resulting from past treatment. A status code is informative, because the status may affect the course of treatment and its outcome. A status code is distinct from a history code. The history code indicates that the patient no longer has the condition.

A status code should not be used with a diagnosis code from one of the body system chapters, if the diagnosis code includes the information provided by the status code. For example, code V42.1, Heart transplant status, should not be used with code 996.83, Complications of transplanted heart. The status code does not provide additional information. The complication code indicates that the patient is a heart transplant patient.

The status V codes/categories are:

V02   Carrier or suspected carrier of infectious diseases
        Carrier status indicates that a person harbors the specific organisms of a disease without manifest symptoms and is capable of transmitting the infection.

V07.5X   Prophylactic use of agents affecting estrogen receptors and estrogen level
This code indicates when a patient is receiving a drug that affects estrogen receptors and estrogen levels for prevention of cancer.

V08   Asymptomatic HIV infection status
        This code indicates that a patient has tested positive for HIV but has manifested no signs or symptoms of the disease.

V09   Infection with drug-resistant microorganisms
        This category indicates that a patient has an infection that is resistant to drug treatment. Sequence the infection code first.

V21	Constitutional states in development
V22.2	Pregnant state, incidental
	This code is a secondary code only for use when the pregnancy is in no way complicating the reason for visit. Otherwise, a code from the obstetric chapter is required.
V26.5x	Sterilization status
V42	Organ or tissue replaced by transplant
V43	Organ or tissue replaced by other means
V44	Artificial opening status
V45	Other postsurgical states

Assign code V45.87, Transplant organ removal status, to indicate that a transplanted organ has been previously removed. This code should not be assigned for the encounter in which the transplanted organ is removed. The complication necessitating removal of the transplant organ should be assigned for that encounter.

See section I.C17.f.2. for information on the coding of organ transplant complications.

Assign code V45.88, Status post administration of tPA (rtPA) in a different facility within the last 24 hours prior to admission to the current facility, as a secondary diagnosis when a patient is received by transfer into a facility and documentation indicates they were administered tissue plasminogen activator (tPA) within the last 24 hours prior to admission to the current facility.

This guideline applies even if the patient is still receiving the tPA at the time they are received into the current facility.

The appropriate code for the condition for which the tPA was administered (such as cerebrovascular disease or myocardial infarction) should be assigned first.

Code V45.88 is only applicable to the receiving facility record and not to the transferring facility record.

V46	Other dependence on machines

V49.6   Upper limb amputation status

V49.7   Lower limb amputation status

        Note: Categories V42-V46, and subcategories V49.6, V49.7 are for use only if there are no complications or malfunctions of the organ or tissue replaced, the amputation site or the equipment on which the patient is dependent.

V49.81   Postmenopausal status

V49.82   Dental sealant status

V49.83   Awaiting organ transplant status

V58.6x   Long-term (current) drug use

        Codes from this subcategory indicate a patient's continuous use of a prescribed drug (including such things as aspirin therapy) for the long-term treatment of a condition or for prophylactic use. It is not for use for patients who have addictions to drugs. **This subcategory is not for use of medications for detoxification or maintenance programs to prevent withdrawal symptoms in patients with drug dependence (e.g., methadone maintenance for opiate dependence). Assign the appropriate code for the drug dependence instead.**

        Assign a code from subcategory V58.6, Long-term (current) drug use, if the patient is receiving a medication for an extended period as a prophylactic measure (such as for the prevention of deep vein thrombosis) or as treatment of a chronic condition (such as arthritis) or a disease requiring a lengthy course of treatment (such as cancer). Do not assign a code from subcategory V58.6 for medication being administered for a brief period of time to treat an acute illness or injury (such as a course of antibiotics to treat acute bronchitis).

V83   Genetic carrier status

        Genetic carrier status indicates that a person carries a gene, associated with a particular disease, which may be passed to offspring who may develop that disease. The person does not have the disease and is not at risk of developing the disease.

V84   Genetic susceptibility status

        Genetic susceptibility indicates that a person has a gene that increases the risk of that person developing the disease.

Codes from category V84, Genetic susceptibility to disease, should not be used as principal or first-listed codes. If the patient has the condition to which he/she is susceptible, and that condition is the reason for the encounter, the code for the current condition should be sequenced first. If the patient is being seen for follow-up after completed treatment for this condition, and the condition no longer exists, a follow-up code should be sequenced first, followed by the appropriate personal history and genetic susceptibility codes. If the purpose of the encounter is genetic counseling associated with procreative management, a code from subcategory V26.3, Genetic counseling and testing, should be assigned as the first-listed code, followed by a code from category V84. Additional codes should be assigned for any applicable family or personal history.

See Section I.C. 18.d.14 for information on prophylactic organ removal due to a genetic susceptibility.

V86   Estrogen receptor status

V88   Acquired absence of other organs and tissue

4)   **History (of)**

There are two types of history V codes, personal and family. Personal history codes explain a patient's past medical condition that no longer exists and is not receiving any treatment, but that has the potential for recurrence, and therefore may require continued monitoring. The exceptions to this general rule are category V14, Personal history of allergy to medicinal agents, and subcategory V15.0, Allergy, other than to medicinal agents. A person who has had an allergic episode to a substance or food in the past should always be considered allergic to the substance.

Family history codes are for use when a patient has a family member(s) who has had a particular disease that causes the patient to be at higher risk of also contracting the disease.

Personal history codes may be used in conjunction with follow-up codes and family history codes may be used in conjunction with screening codes to explain the need for a test or procedure. History codes are also acceptable on any medical record regardless of the reason for visit. A history of an illness, even if no longer present, is important information that may alter the type of treatment ordered.

The history V code categories are:

V10	Personal history of malignant neoplasm
V12	Personal history of certain other diseases
V13	Personal history of other diseases
	Except: V13.4, Personal history of arthritis, and V13.6, Personal history of congenital malformations. These conditions are life-long so are not true history codes.
V14	Personal history of allergy to medicinal agents
V15	Other personal history presenting hazards to health
	Except: V15.7, Personal history of contraception.
V16	Family history of malignant neoplasm
V17	Family history of certain chronic disabling diseases
V18	Family history of certain other specific diseases
V19	Family history of other conditions
V87	**Other specified personal exposures and history presenting hazards to health**

5) **Screening**

Screening is the testing for disease or disease precursors in seemingly well individuals so that early detection and treatment can be provided for those who test positive for the disease. Screenings that are recommended for many subgroups in a population include: routine mammograms for women over 40, a fecal occult blood test for everyone over 50, an amniocentesis to rule out a fetal anomaly for pregnant women over 35, because the incidence of breast cancer and colon cancer in these subgroups is higher than in the general population, as is the incidence of Down's syndrome in older mothers.

The testing of a person to rule out or confirm a suspected diagnosis because the patient has some sign or symptom is a diagnostic examination, not a screening. In these cases, the sign or symptom is used to explain the reason for the test.

A screening code may be a first listed code if the reason for the visit is specifically the screening exam. It may also be used as an additional code if the screening is done during an office visit for other health problems. A screening code is not necessary if the screening is inherent to a routine examination, such as a pap smear done during a routine pelvic examination.

Should a condition be discovered during the screening then the code for the condition may be assigned as an additional diagnosis.

The V code indicates that a screening exam is planned. A procedure code is required to confirm that the screening was performed.

The screening V code categories:
V28   Antenatal screening
V73-V82   Special screening examinations

6)   **Observation**

There are **three** observation V code categories. They are for use in very limited circumstances when a person is being observed for a suspected condition that is ruled out. The observation codes are not for use if an injury or illness or any signs or symptoms related to the suspected condition are present. In such cases the diagnosis/symptom code is used with the corresponding E code to identify any external cause.

The observation codes are to be used as principal diagnosis only. The only exception to this is when the principal diagnosis is required to be a code from the V30, Live born infant, category. Then the V29 observation code is sequenced after the V30 code. Additional codes may be used in addition to the observation code but only if they are unrelated to the suspected condition being observed.

Codes from subcategory V89.0, Suspected maternal and fetal conditions not found, may either be used as a first listed or as an additional code assignment depending on the case. They are for use in very limited circumstances on a maternal record when an encounter is for a suspected maternal or fetal condition that is ruled out during that encounter (for example, a maternal or fetal condition may be suspected due to an abnormal test result). These codes should not be used when the condition is confirmed. In those cases, the confirmed condition should be coded. In addition, these codes are not for use if an illness or any signs or symptoms related to the suspected condition or problem are present. In such cases the diagnosis/symptom code is used.

Additional codes may be used in addition to the code from subcategory V89.0, but only if they are unrelated to the suspected condition being evaluated.

Codes from subcategory V89.0 may not be used for encounters for antenatal screening of mother. *See Section I.C.18.d., Screening).*

For encounters for suspected fetal condition that are inconclusive following testing and evaluation, assign the appropriate code from category 655, 656, 657 or 658.

The observation V code categories:

V29   Observation and evaluation of newborns for suspected condition not found
            For the birth encounter, a code from category V30 should be sequenced before the V29 code.

V71   Observation and evaluation for suspected condition not found

V89   **Suspected maternal and fetal conditions not found**

7)   **Aftercare**

Aftercare visit codes cover situations when the initial treatment of a disease or injury has been performed and the patient requires continued care during the healing or recovery phase, or for the long-term consequences of the disease. The aftercare V code should not be used if treatment is directed at a current, acute disease or injury. The diagnosis code is to be used in these cases. Exceptions to this rule are codes V58.0, Radiotherapy, and codes from subcategory V58.1, Encounter for chemotherapy and immunotherapy for neoplastic conditions. These codes are to be first listed, followed by the diagnosis code when a patient's encounter is solely to receive radiation therapy or chemotherapy for the treatment of a neoplasm. Should a patient receive both chemotherapy and radiation therapy during the same encounter code V58.0 and V58.1 may be used together on a record with either one being sequenced first.

The aftercare codes are generally first listed to explain the specific reason for the encounter. An aftercare code may be used as an additional code when some type of aftercare is provided in addition to the reason for admission and no diagnosis code is applicable. An example of this would be the closure of a colostomy during an encounter for treatment of another condition.

Aftercare codes should be used in conjunction with any other aftercare codes or other diagnosis codes to provide better detail on the specifics of an aftercare encounter visit, unless otherwise directed by the classification. The sequencing of multiple aftercare codes is discretionary.

Certain aftercare V code categories need a secondary diagnosis code to describe the resolving condition or sequelae, for others, the condition is inherent in the code title.

Additional V code aftercare category terms include fitting and adjustment, and attention to artificial openings.

Status V codes may be used with aftercare V codes to indicate the nature of the aftercare. For example code V45.81, Aortocoronary bypass status, may be used with code V58.73, Aftercare following surgery of the circulatory system, NEC, to indicate the surgery for which the aftercare is being performed. Also, a transplant status code may be used following code V58.44, Aftercare following organ transplant, to identify the organ transplanted. A status code should not be used when the aftercare code indicates the type of status, such as using V55.0, Attention to tracheostomy with V44.0, Tracheostomy status.

See Section I. B.16 Admissions/Encounter for Rehabilitation

The aftercare V category/codes:

V51.0	**Encounter for breast reconstruction following mastectomy**
V52	Fitting and adjustment of prosthetic device and implant
V53	Fitting and adjustment of other device
V54	Other orthopedic aftercare
V55	Attention to artificial openings
V56	Encounter for dialysis and dialysis catheter care
V57	Care involving the use of rehabilitation procedures
V58.0	Radiotherapy
V58.11	Encounter for antineoplastic chemotherapy
V58.12	Encounter for antineoplastic immunotherapy
V58.3x	Attention to dressings and sutures
V58.41	Encounter for planned post-operative wound closure
V58.42	Aftercare, surgery, neoplasm

V58.43	Aftercare, surgery, trauma
V58.44	Aftercare involving organ transplant
V58.49	Other specified aftercare following surgery
V58.7x	Aftercare following surgery
V58.81	Fitting and adjustment of vascular catheter
V58.82	Fitting and adjustment of non-vascular catheter
V58.83	Monitoring therapeutic drug
V58.89	Other specified aftercare

8)   Follow-up

The follow-up codes are used to explain continuing surveillance following completed treatment of a disease, condition, or injury. They imply that the condition has been fully treated and no longer exists. They should not be confused with aftercare codes that explain current treatment for a healing condition or its sequelae. Follow-up codes may be used in conjunction with history codes to provide the full picture of the healed condition and its treatment. The follow-up code is sequenced first, followed by the history code.

A follow-up code may be used to explain repeated visits. Should a condition be found to have recurred on the follow-up visit, then the diagnosis code should be used in place of the follow-up code.

The follow-up V code categories:

V24	Postpartum care and evaluation
V67	Follow-up examination

9)   Donor

Category V59 is the donor codes. They are used for living individuals who are donating blood or other body tissue. These codes are only for individuals donating for others, not for self donations. They are not for use to identify cadaveric donations.

10)   Counseling

Counseling V codes are used when a patient or family member receives assistance in the aftermath of an illness or injury, or when support is required in coping with family or social problems. They are not necessary for use in conjunction with a diagnosis code when the counseling component of care is considered integral to standard treatment.

The counseling V categories/codes:

V25.0	General counseling and advice for contraceptive management
V26.3	Genetic counseling
V26.4	General counseling and advice for procreative management
V61.**X**	Other family circumstances
V65.1	Person consulted on behalf of another person
V65.3	Dietary surveillance and counseling
V65.4	Other counseling, not elsewhere classified

11)   Obstetrics and related conditions

See Section I.C.11., the Obstetrics guidelines for further instruction on the use of these codes.

V codes for pregnancy are for use in those circumstances when none of the problems or complications included in the codes from the Obstetrics chapter exist (a routine prenatal visit or postpartum care). Codes V22.0, Supervision of normal first pregnancy, and V22.1, Supervision of other normal pregnancy, are always first listed and are not to be used with any other code from the OB chapter.

The outcome of delivery, category V27, should be included on all maternal delivery records. It is always a secondary code.

V codes for family planning (contraceptive) or procreative management and counseling should be included on an obstetric record either during the pregnancy or the postpartum stage, if applicable.

Obstetrics and related conditions V code categories:

V22	Normal pregnancy
V23	Supervision of high-risk pregnancy Except: V23.2, Pregnancy with history of abortion. Code 646.3, Habitual aborter, from the OB chapter is required to indicate a history of abortion during a pregnancy.
V24	Postpartum care and evaluation
V25	Encounter for contraceptive management Except V25.0x *(See Section I.C.18.d.11, Counseling)*
V26	Procreative management Except V26.5x, Sterilization status, V26.3 and V26.4 *(See Section I.C.18.d.11., Counseling)*
V27	Outcome of delivery

V28   Antenatal screening
(See Section I.C.18.d.6., Screening)

12)   Newborn, infant and child

See Section I.C.15, the Newborn guidelines for further instruction on the use of these codes.

Newborn V code categories:
V20   Health supervision of infant or child
V29   Observation and evaluation of newborns for suspected condition not found
       (See Section I.C.18.d.7, Observation)
V30-V39 Liveborn infant according to type of birth

13)   Routine and administrative examinations

The V codes allow for the description of encounters for routine examinations, such as, a general check-up, or, examinations for administrative purposes, such as, a pre-employment physical. The codes are not to be used if the examination is for diagnosis of a suspected condition or for treatment purposes. In such cases the diagnosis code is used. During a routine exam, should a diagnosis or condition be discovered, it should be coded as an additional code. Pre-existing and chronic conditions and history codes may also be included as additional codes as long as the examination is for administrative purposes and not focused on any particular condition.

Pre-operative examination V codes are for use only in those situations when a patient is being cleared for surgery and no treatment is given.

The V codes categories/code for routine and administrative examinations:

V20.2   Routine infant or child health check
         Any injections given should have a corresponding procedure code.
V70   General medical examination
V72   Special investigations and examinations
         Codes V72.5 and V72.6 may be used if the reason for the patient encounter is for routine laboratory/radiology testing in the absence of any signs, symptoms, or associated diagnosis. If routine testing is performed during the same encounter as a test to evaluate a sign, symptom, or diagnosis, it is

appropriate to assign both the V code and the code describing the reason for the non-routine test.

14)   Miscellaneous V codes

The miscellaneous V codes capture a number of other health care encounters that do not fall into one of the other categories. Certain of these codes identify the reason for the encounter, others are for use as additional codes that provide useful information on circumstances that may affect a patient's care and treatment.

Prophylactic Organ Removal

For encounters specifically for prophylactic removal of breasts, ovaries, or another organ due to a genetic susceptibility to cancer or a family history of cancer, the principal or first listed code should be a code from subcategory V50.4, Prophylactic organ removal, followed by the appropriate genetic susceptibility code and the appropriate family history code.

If the patient has a malignancy of one site and is having prophylactic removal at another site to prevent either a new primary malignancy or metastatic disease, a code for the malignancy should also be assigned in addition to a code from subcategory V50.4. A V50.4 code should not be assigned if the patient is having organ removal for treatment of a malignancy, such as the removal of the testes for the treatment of prostate cancer.

Miscellaneous V code categories/codes:

V07	Need for isolation and other prophylactic measures **Except V07.5, Prophylactic use of agents affecting estrogen receptors and estrogen levels**
V50	Elective surgery for purposes other than remedying health states
V58.5	Orthodontics
V60	Housing, household, and economic circumstances
V62	Other psychosocial circumstances
V63	Unavailability of other medical facilities for care
V64	Persons encountering health services for specific procedures, not carried out
V66	Convalescence and Palliative Care
V68	Encounters for administrative purposes
V69	Problems related to lifestyle
V85	Body Mass Index

15)   Nonspecific V codes

Certain V codes are so non-specific, or potentially redundant with other codes in the classification, that there can be little justification for their use in the inpatient setting. Their use in the outpatient setting should be limited to those instances when there is no further documentation to permit more precise coding. Otherwise, any sign or symptom or any other reason for visit that is captured in another code should be used.

Nonspecific V code categories/codes:

V11	Personal history of mental disorder
	A code from the mental disorders chapter, with an in remission fifth-digit, should be used.
V13.4	Personal history of arthritis
V13.6	Personal history of congenital malformations
V15.7	Personal history of contraception
V23.2	Pregnancy with history of abortion
V40	Mental and behavioral problems
V41	Problems with special senses and other special functions
V47	Other problems with internal organs
V48	Problems with head, neck, and trunk
V49	Problems with limbs and other problems

Exceptions:

V49.6	Upper limb amputation status
V49.7	Lower limb amputation status
V49.81	Postmenopausal status
V49.82	Dental sealant status
V49.83	Awaiting organ transplant status

V51.**8**	**Other a**ftercare involving the use of plastic surgery
V58.2	Blood transfusion, without reported diagnosis
V58.9	Unspecified aftercare
	See Section IV.K. and Section IV.L. of the Outpatient guidelines.

V CODE TABLE
October 1, 2008 (FY2009)
Items in bold indicate a new entry or change from the October 2007 table
Items underlined have been moved within the table since October 2007

The V code table below contains columns for 1st listed, 1st or additional, additional only, and non-specific. Each code or category is listed in the left hand column, and the allowable sequencing of the code or codes within the category is noted under the appropriate column.

As indicated by the footnote in the "1st Dx Only" column, the V codes designated as first-listed only are generally intended to be limited for use as a first-listed only diagnosis, but may be reported as an additional diagnosis in those situations when the patient has more than one encounter on a single day and the codes for the multiple encounters are combined, or when there is more than one V code that meets the definition of principal diagnosis (e.g., a patient is admitted to home healthcare for both aftercare and rehabilitation and they equally meet the definition of principal diagnosis). The V codes designated as first-listed only should not be reported if they do not meet the definition of principal or first-listed diagnosis.

See Section II and Section IV.A for information on selection of principal and first-listed diagnosis.

See Section II.C for information on two or more diagnoses that equally meet the definition for principal diagnosis.

Code(s)	Description	1st Dx Only[1]	1st or Add'l Dx[2]	Add'l Dx Only[3]	Non-Specific Diagnosis[4]
V01.X	Contact with or exposure to communicable diseases		X		
V02.X	Carrier or suspected carrier of infectious diseases		X		
V03.X	Need for prophylactic vaccination and inoculation against bacterial diseases		X		
V04.X	Need for prophylactic vaccination and inoculation against certain diseases		X		
V05.X	Need for prophylactic vaccination and inoculation against single diseases		X		

[1] Generally for use as first listed only but may be used as additional if patient has more than one encounter on one day or there is more than one reason for the encounter
[2] These codes may be used as first listed or additional codes
[3] These codes are only for use as additional codes
[4] These codes are primarily for use in the nonacute setting and should be limited to encounters for which no sign or symptom or reason for visit is documented in the record. Their use may be as either a first listed or additional code.

Code(s)	Description	1st Dx Only[1]	1st or Add'l Dx[2]	Add'l Dx Only[3]	Non-Specific Diagnosis[4]
V06.X	Need for prophylactic vaccination and inoculation against combinations of diseases		X		
V07.0	**Isolation**		**X**		
V07.1	**Desensitization to allergens**		**X**		
V07.2	**Prophylactic immunotherapy**		**X**		
V07.3X	**Other prophylactic chemotherapy**		**X**		
V07.4	**Hormone replacement therapy (postmenopausal)**			**X**	
V07.5X	**Prophylactic use of agents affecting estrogen receptors and estrogen levels**			**X**	
V07.8	**Other specified prophylactic measure**		**X**		
V07.9	**Unspecified prophylactic measure**				**X**
V08	Asymptomatic HIV infection status		X		
V09.X	Infection with drug resistant organisms			X	
V10.X	Personal history of malignant neoplasm		X		
V11.X	Personal history of mental disorder				X
V12.X	Personal history of certain other diseases		X		
V13.0X	Personal history of other disorders of urinary system		X		
V13.1	Personal history of trophoblastic disease		X		
V13.2X	Personal history of other genital system and obstetric disorders		X		
V13.3	Personal history of diseases of skin and subcutaneous tissue		X		
V13.4	Personal history of arthritis				X
V13.5**X**	Personal history of other musculoskeletal disorders		X		
V13.61	Personal history of hypospadias			X	
V13.69	Personal history of congenital malformations				X
V13.7	Personal history of perinatal problems		X		
V13.8	Personal history of other specified diseases		X		
V13.9	Personal history of unspecified disease				X
V14.X	Personal history of allergy to medicinal agents			X	
V15.0X	Personal history of allergy, other than to medicinal agents			X	

[1]Generally for use as first listed only but may be used as additional if patient has more than one encounter on one day or there is more than one reason for the encounter
[2]These codes may be used as first listed or additional codes
[3]These codes are only for use as additional codes
[4]These codes are primarily for use in the nonacute setting and should be limited to encounters for which no sign or symptom or reason for visit is documented in the record. Their use may be as either a first listed or additional code.

Code(s)	Description	1st Dx Only[1]	1st or Add'l Dx[2]	Add'l Dx Only[3]	Non-Specific Diagnosis[4]
V15.1	Personal history of surgery to heart and great vessels			X	
V15.2X	**Personal history of surgery to other organs**			X	
V15.3	Personal history of irradiation			X	
V15.4X	Personal history of psychological trauma			X	
V15.5X	Personal history of injury			X	
V15.6	Personal history of poisoning			X	
V15.7	Personal history of contraception				X
V15.81	Personal history of noncompliance with medical treatment			X	
V15.82	Personal history of tobacco use			X	
V15.84	Personal history of exposure to asbestos			X	
V15.85	Personal history of exposure to potentially hazardous body fluids			X	
V15.86	Personal history of exposure to lead			X	
V15.87	Personal history of extracorporeal membrane oxygenation [ECMO]			X	
V15.88	History of fall		X		
V15.89	Other specified personal history presenting hazards to health			X	
V16.X	Family history of malignant neoplasm		X		
V17.X	Family history of certain chronic disabling diseases		X		
V18.X	Family history of certain other specific conditions		X		
V19.X	Family history of other conditions		X		
V20.X	Health supervision of infant or child	X			
V21.X	Constitutional states in development			X	
V22.0	Supervision of normal first pregnancy	X			
V22.1	Supervision of other normal pregnancy	X			
V22.2	Pregnancy state, incidental			X	
V23.X	Supervision of high-risk pregnancy		X		
V24.X	Postpartum care and examination	X			
V25.X	Encounter for contraceptive management		X		

[1]Generally for use as first listed only but may be used as additional if patient has more than one encounter on one day or there is more than one reason for the encounter

[2]These codes may be used as first listed or additional codes

[3]These codes are only for use as additional codes

[4]These codes are primarily for use in the nonacute setting and should be limited to encounters for which no sign or symptom or reason for visit is documented in the record. Their use may be as either a first listed or additional code.

Code(s)	Description	1ˢᵗ Dx Only[1]	1ˢᵗ or Add'l Dx[2]	Add'l Dx Only[3]	Non-Specific Diagnosis[4]
V26.0	Tuboplasty or vasoplasty after previous sterilization		X		
V26.1	Artificial insemination		X		
V26.2X	Procreative management investigation and testing		X		
V26.3X	Procreative management, genetic counseling and testing		X		
V26.4X	Procreative management, genetic counseling and advice		X		
V26.5X	Procreative management, sterilization status			X	
V26.81	Encounter for assisted reproductive fertility procedure cycle	X			
V26.89	Other specified procreative management		X		
V26.9	Unspecified procreative management		X		
V27.X	Outcome of delivery			X	
V28.X	Encounter for antenatal screening of mother		X		
V29.X	Observation and evaluation of newborns for suspected condition not found		X		
V30.X	Single liveborn	X			
V31.X	Twin, mate liveborn	X			
V32.X	Twin, mate stillborn	X			
V33.X	Twin, unspecified	X			
V34.X	Other multiple, mates all liveborn	X			
V35.X	Other multiple, mates all stillborn	X			
V36.X	Other multiple, mates live- and stillborn	X			
V37.X	Other multiple, unspecified	X			
V39.X	Unspecified	X			
V40.X	Mental and behavioral problems				X
V41.X	Problems with special senses and other special functions				X
V42.X	Organ or tissue replaced by transplant			X	
V43.0	Organ or tissue replaced by other means, eye globe			X	
V43.1	Organ or tissue replaced by other means, lens			X	
V43.21	Organ or tissue replaced by other means, heart assist device			X	

[1]Generally for use as first listed only but may be used as additional if patient has more than one encounter on one day or there is more than one reason for the encounter

[2]These codes may be used as first listed or additional codes

[3]These codes are only for use as additional codes

[4]These codes are primarily for use in the nonacute setting and should be limited to encounters for which no sign or symptom or reason for visit is documented in the record. Their use may be as either a first listed or additional code.

Code(s)	Description	1ˢᵗ Dx Only[1]	1ˢᵗ or Add'l Dx[2]	Add'l Dx Only[3]	Non-Specific Diagnosis[4]
V43.22	Fully implantable artificial heart status		X		
V43.3	Organ or tissue replaced by other means, heart valve			X	
V43.4	Organ or tissue replaced by other means, blood vessel			X	
V43.5	Organ or tissue replaced by other means, bladder			X	
V43.6X	Organ or tissue replaced by other means, joint			X	
V43.7	Organ or tissue replaced by other means, limb			X	
V43.8X	Other organ or tissue replaced by other means			X	
V44.X	Artificial opening status			X	
V45.0X	Cardiac device in situ			X	
V45.1X	Renal dialysis status			X	
V45.2	Presence of cerebrospinal fluid drainage device			X	
V45.3	Intestinal bypass or anastomosis status			X	
V45.4	Arthrodesis status			X	
V45.5X	Presence of contraceptive device			X	
V45.6X	States following surgery of eye and adnexa			X	
V45.7X	Acquired absence of organ		X		
V45.8X	Other postprocedural status			X	
V46.0	Other dependence on machines, aspirator			X	
V46.11	Dependence on respiratory, status			X	
V46.12	Encounter for respirator dependence during power failure	X			
V46.13	Encounter for weaning from respirator [ventilator]	X			
V46.14	Mechanical complication of respirator [ventilator]		X		
V46.2	Other dependence on machines, supplemental oxygen			X	
V46.3	**Wheelchair dependence**			**X**	

[1]Generally for use as first listed only but may be used as additional if patient has more than one encounter on one day or there is more than one reason for the encounter
[2]These codes may be used as first listed or additional codes
[3]These codes are only for use as additional codes
[4]These codes are primarily for use in the nonacute setting and should be limited to encounters for which no sign or symptom or reason for visit is documented in the record. Their use may be as either a first listed or additional code.

Code(s)	Description	1st Dx Only[1]	1st or Add'l Dx[2]	Add'l Dx Only[3]	Non-Specific Diagnosis[4]
V46.8	Other dependence on other enabling machines			X	
V46.9	Unspecified machine dependence				X
V47.X	Other problems with internal organs				X
V48.X	Problems with head, neck and trunk				X
V49.0	Deficiencies of limbs				X
V49.1	Mechanical problems with limbs				X
V49.2	Motor problems with limbs				X
V49.3	Sensory problems with limbs				X
V49.4	Disfigurements of limbs				X
V49.5	Other problems with limbs				X
V49.6X	Upper limb amputation status		X		
V49.7X	Lower limb amputation status		X		
V49.81	Asymptomatic postmenopausal status (age-related) (natural)		X		
V49.82	Dental sealant status			X	
V49.83	Awaiting organ transplant status			X	
V49.84	Bed confinement status		X		
V49.85	Dual sensory impairment			X	
V49.89	Other specified conditions influencing health status		X		
V49.9	Unspecified condition influencing health status				X
V50.X	Elective surgery for purposes other than remedying health states		X		
V51.0	**Encounter for breast reconstruction following mastectomy**	X			
V51.8	**Other aftercare involving the use of plastic surgery**				X
V52.X	Fitting and adjustment of prosthetic device and implant		X		
V53.X	Fitting and adjustment of other device		X		
V54.X	Other orthopedic aftercare		X		
V55.X	Attention to artificial openings		X		
V56.0	Extracorporeal dialysis	X			

[1]Generally for use as first listed only but may be used as additional if patient has more than one encounter on one day or there is more than one reason for the encounter
[2]These codes may be used as first listed or additional codes
[3]These codes are only for use as additional codes
[4]These codes are primarily for use in the nonacute setting and should be limited to encounters for which no sign or symptom or reason for visit is documented in the record. Their use may be as either a first listed or additional code.

Code(s)	Description	1st Dx Only[1]	1st or Add'l Dx[2]	Add'l Dx Only[3]	Non-Specific Diagnosis[4]
V56.1	Encounter for fitting and adjustment of extracorporeal dialysis catheter		X		
V56.2	Encounter for fitting and adjustment of peritoneal dialysis catheter		X		
V56.3X	Encounter for adequacy testing for dialysis		X		
V56.8	Encounter for other dialysis and dialysis catheter care		X		
V57.X	Care involving use of rehabilitation procedures	X			
V58.0	Radiotherapy	X			
V58.11	Encounter for antineoplastic chemotherapy	X			
V58.12	Encounter for antineoplastic immunotherapy	X			
V58.2	Blood transfusion without reported diagnosis				X
V58.3X	Attention to dressings and sutures		X		
V58.4X	Other aftercare following surgery		X		
V58.5	Encounter for orthodontics				X
V58.6X	Long term (current) drug use			X	
V58.7X	Aftercare following surgery to specified body systems, not elsewhere classified		X		
V58.8X	Other specified procedures and aftercare		X		
V58.9	Unspecified aftercare				X
V59.X	Donors	X			
V60.X	Housing, household, and economic circumstances			X	
V61.X	Other family circumstances		X		
V62.X	Other psychosocial circumstances			X	
V63.X	Unavailability of other medical facilities for care		X		
V64.X	Persons encountering health services for specified procedure, not carried out			X	
V65.X	Other persons seeking consultation without complaint or sickness		X		
V66.0	Convalescence and palliative care following surgery	X			
V66.1	Convalescence and palliative care following radiotherapy	X			

[1]Generally for use as first listed only but may be used as additional if patient has more than one encounter on one day or there is more than one reason for the encounter

[2]These codes may be used as first listed or additional codes

[3]These codes are only for use as additional codes

[4]These codes are primarily for use in the nonacute setting and should be limited to encounters for which no sign or symptom or reason for visit is documented in the record. Their use may be as either a first listed or additional code.

Code(s)	Description	1st Dx Only[1]	1st or Add'l Dx[2]	Add'l Dx Only[3]	Non-Specific Diagnosis[4]
V66.2	Convalescence and palliative care following chemotherapy	X			
V66.3	Convalescence and palliative care following psychotherapy and other treatment for mental disorder	X			
V66.4	Convalescence and palliative care following treatment of fracture	X			
V66.5	Convalescence and palliative care following other treatment	X			
V66.6	Convalescence and palliative care following combined treatment	X			
V66.7	Encounter for palliative care			X	
V66.9	Unspecified convalescence	X			
V67.X	Follow-up examination		X		
V68.X	Encounters for administrative purposes	X			
V69.X	Problems related to lifestyle		X		
V70.0	Routine general medical examination at a health care facility	X			
V70.1	General psychiatric examination, requested by the authority	X			
V70.2	General psychiatric examination, other and unspecified	X			
V70.3	Other medical examination for administrative purposes	X			
V70.4	Examination for medicolegal reasons	X			
V70.5	Health examination of defined subpopulations	X			
V70.6	Health examination in population surveys	X			
V70.7	Examination of participant in clinical trial		X		
V70.8	Other specified general medical examinations	X			
V70.9	Unspecified general medical examination	X			
V71.X	Observation and evaluation for suspected conditions not found	X			
V72.0	Examination of eyes and vision		X		
V72.1X	Examination of ears and hearing		X		

[1]Generally for use as first listed only but may be used as additional if patient has more than one encounter on one day or there is more than one reason for the encounter
[2]These codes may be used as first listed or additional codes
[3]These codes are only for use as additional codes
[4]These codes are primarily for use in the nonacute setting and should be limited to encounters for which no sign or symptom or reason for visit is documented in the record. Their use may be as either a first listed or additional code.

Code(s)	Description	1st Dx Only[1]	1st or Add'l Dx[2]	Add'l Dx Only[3]	Non-Specific Diagnosis[4]
V72.2	Dental examination		X		
V72.3X	Gynecological examination		X		
V72.4X	Pregnancy examination or test		X		
V72.5	Radiological examination, NEC		X		
V72.6	Laboratory examination		X		
V72.7	Diagnostic skin and sensitization tests		X		
V72.81	Preoperative cardiovascular examination		X		
V72.82	Preoperative respiratory examination		X		
V72.83	Other specified preoperative examination		X		
V72.84	Preoperative examination, unspecified		X		
V72.85	Other specified examination		X		
V72.86	Encounter for blood typing		X		
V72.9	Unspecified examination				X
V73.X	Special screening examination for viral and chlamydial diseases		X		
V74.X	Special screening examination for bacterial and spirochetal diseases		X		
V75.X	Special screening examination for other infectious diseases		X		
V76.X	Special screening examination for malignant neoplasms		X		
V77.X	Special screening examination for endocrine, nutritional, metabolic and immunity disorders		X		
V78.X	Special screening examination for disorders of blood and blood-forming organs		X		
V79.X	Special screening examination for mental disorders and developmental handicaps		X		
V80.X	Special screening examination for neurological, eye, and ear diseases		X		
V81.X	Special screening examination for cardiovascular, respiratory, and genitourinary diseases		X		
V82.X	Special screening examination for other conditions		X		
V83.X	Genetic carrier status		X		

[1]Generally for use as first listed only but may be used as additional if patient has more than one encounter on one day or there is more than one reason for the encounter
[2]These codes may be used as first listed or additional codes
[3]These codes are only for use as additional codes
[4]These codes are primarily for use in the nonacute setting and should be limited to encounters for which no sign or symptom or reason for visit is documented in the record. Their use may be as either a first listed or additional code.

Code(s)	Description	1st Dx Only[1]	1st or Add'l Dx[2]	Add'l Dx Only[3]	Non-Specific Diagnosis[4]
V84.X	Genetic susceptibility to disease			X	
V85	Body mass index			X	
V86	Estrogen receptor status			X	
V87.0X	**Contact with and (suspected) exposure to hazardous metals**		**X**		
V87.1X	**Contact with and (suspected) exposure to hazardous aromatic compounds**		**X**		
V87.2	**Contact with and (suspected) exposure to other potentially hazardous chemicals**		**X**		
V87.3X	**Contact with and (suspected) exposure to other potentially hazardous substances**		**X**		
V87.4X	**Personal history of drug therapy**			**X**	
V88.0X	**Acquired absence of cervix and uterus**			**X**	
V89.0X	**Suspected maternal and fetal anomalies not found**		**X**		

[1]Generally for use as first listed only but may be used as additional if patient has more than one encounter on one day or there is more than one reason for the encounter

[2]These codes may be used as first listed or additional codes

[3]These codes are only for use as additional codes

[4]These codes are primarily for use in the nonacute setting and should be limited to encounters for which no sign or symptom or reason for visit is documented in the record. Their use may be as either a first listed or additional code.

19.   Supplemental Classification of External Causes of Injury and Poisoning (E-codes, E800-E999)

Introduction: These guidelines are provided for those who are currently collecting E codes in order that there will be standardization in the process. If your institution plans to begin collecting E codes, these guidelines are to be applied. The use of E codes is supplemental to the application of ICD-9-CM diagnosis codes. E codes are never to be recorded as principal diagnoses (first-listed in non-inpatient setting) and are not required for reporting to CMS.

External causes of injury and poisoning codes (E codes) are intended to provide data for injury research and evaluation of injury prevention strategies. E codes capture how the injury or poisoning happened (cause), the intent (unintentional or accidental; or intentional, such as suicide or assault), and the place where the event occurred.

Some major categories of E codes include:
>   transport accidents
>   poisoning and adverse effects of drugs, medicinal substances and biologicals
>   accidental falls
>   accidents caused by fire and flames
>   accidents due to natural and environmental factors
>   late effects of accidents, assaults or self injury
>   assaults or purposely inflicted injury
>   suicide or self inflicted injury

These guidelines apply for the coding and collection of E codes from records in hospitals, outpatient clinics, emergency departments, other ambulatory care settings and provider offices, and nonacute care settings, except when other specific guidelines apply.

a.   General E Code Coding Guidelines

1)   Used with any code in the range of 001-V89

An E code may be used with any code in the range of 001-**V89**, which indicates an injury, poisoning, or adverse effect due to an external cause.

2)   Assign the appropriate E code for all initial treatments

Assign the appropriate E code for the initial encounter of an injury, poisoning, or adverse effect of drugs, not for subsequent treatment.

External cause of injury codes (E-codes) may be assigned while the acute fracture codes are still applicable. *See Section I.C.17.b.1 for coding of acute fractures*.

3) Use the full range of E codes

Use the full range of E codes to completely describe the cause, the intent and the place of occurrence, if applicable, for all injuries, poisonings, and adverse effects of drugs.

4) Assign as many E codes as necessary

Assign as many E codes as necessary to fully explain each cause. If only one E code can be recorded, assign the E code most related to the principal diagnosis.

5) The selection of the appropriate E code

The selection of the appropriate E code is guided by the Index to External Causes, which is located after the alphabetical index to diseases and by Inclusion and Exclusion notes in the Tabular List.

6) E code can never be a principal diagnosis

An E code can never be a principal (first listed) diagnosis.

7) External cause code(s) with systemic inflammatory response syndrome (SIRS)

An external cause code is not appropriate with a code from subcategory 995.9, unless the patient also has an injury, poisoning, or adverse effect of drugs.

b. Place of Occurrence Guideline

Use an additional code from category E849 to indicate the Place of Occurrence for injuries and poisonings. The Place of Occurrence describes the place where the event occurred and not the patient's activity at the time of the event.

Do not use E849.9 if the place of occurrence is not stated.

c. Adverse Effects of Drugs, Medicinal and Biological Substances Guidelines

1) Do not code directly from the Table of Drugs

Do not code directly from the Table of Drugs and Chemicals. Always refer back to the Tabular List.

2)   Use as many codes as necessary to describe

Use as many codes as necessary to describe completely all drugs, medicinal or biological substances.

3)   If the same E code would describe the causative agent

If the same E code would describe the causative agent for more than one adverse reaction, assign the code only once.

4)   If two or more drugs, medicinal or biological substances

If two or more drugs, medicinal or biological substances are reported, code each individually unless the combination code is listed in the Table of Drugs and Chemicals. In that case, assign the E code for the combination.

5)   When a reaction results from the interaction of a drug(s)

When a reaction results from the interaction of a drug(s) and alcohol, use poisoning codes and E codes for both.

6)   If the reporting format limits the number of E codes

If the reporting format limits the number of E codes that can be used in reporting clinical data, code the one most related to the principal diagnosis. Include at least one from each category (cause, intent, place) if possible.

If there are different fourth digit codes in the same three digit category, use the code for "Other specified" of that category. If there is no "Other specified" code in that category, use the appropriate "Unspecified" code in that category.

If the codes are in different three digit categories, assign the appropriate E code for other multiple drugs and medicinal substances.

7)   Codes from the E930-E949 series

Codes from the E930-E949 series must be used to identify the causative substance for an adverse effect of drug, medicinal and biological substances, correctly prescribed and properly administered. The effect, such as tachycardia, delirium, gastrointestinal hemorrhaging, vomiting, hypokalemia, hepatitis, renal failure, or respiratory failure, is coded and followed by the appropriate code from the E930-E949 series.

d.   Multiple Cause E Code Coding Guidelines

If two or more events cause separate injuries, an E code should be assigned for each cause. The first listed E code will be selected in the following order:

E codes for child and adult abuse take priority over all other E codes.
See Section I.C.19.e., Child and Adult abuse guidelines.

E codes for terrorism events take priority over all other E codes except child and adult abuse

E codes for cataclysmic events take priority over all other E codes except child and adult abuse and terrorism.

E codes for transport accidents take priority over all other E codes except cataclysmic events and child and adult abuse and terrorism.

The first-listed E code should correspond to the cause of the most serious diagnosis due to an assault, accident, or self-harm, following the order of hierarchy listed above.

e.   Child and Adult Abuse Guideline

1)   Intentional injury

When the cause of an injury or neglect is intentional child or adult abuse, the first listed E code should be assigned from categories E960-E968, Homicide and injury purposely inflicted by other persons, (except category E967). An E code from category E967, Child and adult battering and other maltreatment, should be added as an additional code to identify the perpetrator, if known.

2)   Accidental intent

In cases of neglect when the intent is determined to be accidental E code E904.0, Abandonment or neglect of infant and helpless person, should be the first listed E code.

f.   Unknown or Suspected Intent Guideline

1)   If the intent (accident, self-harm, assault) of the cause of an injury or poisoning is unknown

If the intent (accident, self-harm, assault) of the cause of an injury or poisoning is unknown or unspecified, code the intent as undetermined E980-E989.

2) If the intent (accident, self-harm, assault) of the cause of an injury or poisoning is questionable

If the intent (accident, self-harm, assault) of the cause of an injury or poisoning is questionable, probable or suspected, code the intent as undetermined E980-E989.

g. Undetermined Cause

When the intent of an injury or poisoning is known, but the cause is unknown, use codes: E928.9, Unspecified accident, E958.9, Suicide and self-inflicted injury by unspecified means, and E968.9, Assault by unspecified means.

These E codes should rarely be used, as the documentation in the medical record, in both the inpatient outpatient and other settings, should normally provide sufficient detail to determine the cause of the injury.

h. Late Effects of External Cause Guidelines

1) Late effect E codes

Late effect E codes exist for injuries and poisonings but not for adverse effects of drugs, misadventures and surgical complications.

2) Late effect E codes (E929, E959, E969, E977, E989, or E999.1)

A late effect E code (E929, E959, E969, E977, E989, or E999.1) should be used with any report of a late effect or sequela resulting from a previous injury or poisoning (905-909).

3) Late effect E code with a related current injury

A late effect E code should never be used with a related current nature of injury code.

4) Use of late effect E codes for subsequent visits

Use a late effect E code for subsequent visits when a late effect of the initial injury or poisoning is being treated. There is no late effect E code for adverse effects of drugs.
Do not use a late effect E code for subsequent visits for follow-up care (e.g., to assess healing, to receive rehabilitative therapy) of the injury or poisoning when no late effect of the injury has been documented.

i.   Misadventures and Complications of Care Guidelines

1)   Code range E870-E876

Assign a code in the range of E870-E876 if misadventures are stated by the provider.

2)   Code range E878-E879

Assign a code in the range of E878-E879 if the provider attributes an abnormal reaction or later complication to a surgical or medical procedure, but does not mention misadventure at the time of the procedure as the cause of the reaction.

j.   Terrorism Guidelines

1)   Cause of injury identified by the Federal Government (FBI) as terrorism

When the cause of an injury is identified by the Federal Government (FBI) as terrorism, the first-listed E-code should be a code from category E979, Terrorism. The definition of terrorism employed by the FBI is found at the inclusion note at E979. The terrorism E-code is the only E-code that should be assigned. Additional E codes from the assault categories should not be assigned.

2)   Cause of an injury is suspected to be the result of terrorism

When the cause of an injury is suspected to be the result of terrorism a code from category E979 should not be assigned. Assign a code in the range of E codes based circumstances on the documentation of intent and mechanism.

3)   Code E979.9, Terrorism, secondary effects

Assign code E979.9, Terrorism, secondary effects, for conditions occurring subsequent to the terrorist event. This code should not be assigned for conditions that are due to the initial terrorist act.

4)   Statistical tabulation of terrorism codes

For statistical purposes these codes will be tabulated within the category for assault, expanding the current category from E960-E969 to include E979 and E999.1.

Section II. Selection of Principal Diagnosis

The circumstances of inpatient admission always govern the selection of principal diagnosis. The principal diagnosis is defined in the Uniform Hospital Discharge Data Set (UHDDS) as "that condition established after study to be chiefly responsible for occasioning the admission of the patient to the hospital for care."

The UHDDS definitions are used by hospitals to report inpatient data elements in a standardized manner. These data elements and their definitions can be found in the July 31, 1985, Federal Register (Vol. 50, No, 147), pp. 31038-40.

Since that time the application of the UHDDS definitions has been expanded to include all non-outpatient settings (acute care, short term, long term care and psychiatric hospitals; home health agencies; rehab facilities; nursing homes, etc).

In determining principal diagnosis the coding conventions in the ICD-9-CM, Volumes I and II take precedence over these official coding guidelines.
(See Section I.A., Conventions for the ICD-9-CM)

The importance of consistent, complete documentation in the medical record cannot be overemphasized. Without such documentation the application of all coding guidelines is a difficult, if not impossible, task.

A. Codes for symptoms, signs, and ill-defined conditions

Codes for symptoms, signs, and ill-defined conditions from Chapter 16 are not to be used as principal diagnosis when a related definitive diagnosis has been established.

B. Two or more interrelated conditions, each potentially meeting the definition for principal diagnosis.

When there are two or more interrelated conditions (such as diseases in the same ICD-9-CM chapter or manifestations characteristically associated with a certain disease) potentially meeting the definition of principal diagnosis, either condition may be sequenced first, unless the circumstances of the admission, the therapy provided, the Tabular List, or the Alphabetic Index indicate otherwise.

C. Two or more diagnoses that equally meet the definition for principal diagnosis

In the unusual instance when two or more diagnoses equally meet the criteria for principal diagnosis as determined by the circumstances of admission, diagnostic workup and/or therapy provided, and the Alphabetic Index, Tabular List, or another coding guidelines does not provide sequencing direction, any one of the diagnoses may be sequenced first.

D. Two or more comparative or contrasting conditions.

In those rare instances when two or more contrasting or comparative diagnoses are documented as "either/or" (or similar terminology), they are coded as if the diagnoses were confirmed and the diagnoses are sequenced according to the circumstances of the admission. If no further determination can be made as to which diagnosis should be principal, either diagnosis may be sequenced first.

E. A symptom(s) followed by contrasting/comparative diagnoses

When a symptom(s) is followed by contrasting/comparative diagnoses, the symptom code is sequenced first. All the contrasting/comparative diagnoses should be coded as additional diagnoses.

F. Original treatment plan not carried out

Sequence as the principal diagnosis the condition, which after study occasioned the admission to the hospital, even though treatment may not have been carried out due to unforeseen circumstances.

G. Complications of surgery and other medical care

When the admission is for treatment of a complication resulting from surgery or other medical care, the complication code is sequenced as the principal diagnosis. If the complication is classified to the 996-999 series and the code lacks the necessary specificity in describing the complication, an additional code for the specific complication should be assigned.

H. Uncertain Diagnosis

If the diagnosis documented at the time of discharge is qualified as "probable", "suspected", "likely", "questionable", "possible", or "still to be ruled out", or other similar terms indicating uncertainty, code the condition as if it existed or was established. The bases for these guidelines are the diagnostic workup, arrangements for further workup or observation, and initial therapeutic approach that correspond most closely with the established diagnosis.

Note: This guideline is applicable only to inpatient admissions to short-term, acute, long-term care and psychiatric hospitals.

I.   Admission from Observation Unit

1.   Admission Following Medical Observation

When a patient is admitted to an observation unit for a medical condition, which either worsens or does not improve, and is subsequently admitted as an inpatient of the same hospital for this same medical condition, the principal diagnosis would be the medical condition which led to the hospital admission.

2.   Admission Following Post-Operative Observation

When a patient is admitted to an observation unit to monitor a condition (or complication) that develops following outpatient surgery, and then is subsequently admitted as an inpatient of the same hospital, hospitals should apply the Uniform Hospital Discharge Data Set (UHDDS) definition of principal diagnosis as "that condition established after study to be chiefly responsible for occasioning the admission of the patient to the hospital for care."

J. Admission from Outpatient Surgery

When a patient receives surgery in the hospital's outpatient surgery department and is subsequently admitted for continuing inpatient care at the same hospital, the following guidelines should be followed in selecting the principal diagnosis for the inpatient admission:

- If the reason for the inpatient admission is a complication, assign the complication as the principal diagnosis.
- If no complication, or other condition, is documented as the reason for the inpatient admission, assign the reason for the outpatient surgery as the principal diagnosis.
- If the reason for the inpatient admission is another condition unrelated to the surgery, assign the unrelated condition as the principal diagnosis.

Section III. Reporting Additional Diagnoses

GENERAL RULES FOR OTHER (ADDITIONAL) DIAGNOSES

For reporting purposes the definition for "other diagnoses" is interpreted as additional conditions that affect patient care in terms of requiring:

clinical evaluation; or
therapeutic treatment; or
diagnostic procedures; or
extended length of hospital stay; or
increased nursing care and/or monitoring.

The UHDDS item #11-b defines Other Diagnoses as "all conditions that coexist at the time of admission, that develop subsequently, or that affect the treatment received and/or the length of stay. Diagnoses that relate to an earlier episode which have no bearing on the current hospital stay are to be excluded." UHDDS definitions apply to inpatients in acute care, short-term, long term care and psychiatric hospital setting. The UHDDS definitions are used by acute care short-term hospitals to report inpatient data elements in a standardized manner. These data elements and their definitions can be found in the July 31, 1985, Federal Register (Vol. 50, No, 147), pp. 31038-40.

Since that time the application of the UHDDS definitions has been expanded to include all non-outpatient settings (acute care, short term, long term care and psychiatric hospitals; home health agencies; rehab facilities; nursing homes, etc).

The following guidelines are to be applied in designating "other diagnoses" when neither the Alphabetic Index nor the Tabular List in ICD-9-CM provide direction. The listing of the diagnoses in the patient record is the responsibility of the attending provider.

A. Previous conditions

If the provider has included a diagnosis in the final diagnostic statement, such as the discharge summary or the face sheet, it should ordinarily be coded. Some providers include in the diagnostic statement resolved conditions or diagnoses and status-post procedures from previous admission that have no bearing on the current stay. Such conditions are not to be reported and are coded only if required by hospital policy.

However, history codes (V10-V19) may be used as secondary codes if the historical condition or family history has an impact on current care or influences treatment.

B. Abnormal findings

Abnormal findings (laboratory, x-ray, pathologic, and other diagnostic results) are not coded and reported unless the provider indicates their clinical significance. If the findings are outside the normal range and the attending provider has ordered other tests to evaluate the condition or prescribed treatment, it is appropriate to ask the provider whether the abnormal finding should be added.

Please note: This differs from the coding practices in the outpatient setting for coding encounters for diagnostic tests that have been interpreted by a provider.

C. Uncertain Diagnosis

If the diagnosis documented at the time of discharge is qualified as "probable", "suspected", "likely", "questionable", "possible", or "still to be ruled out" or other similar terms indicating uncertainty, code the condition as if it existed or was established. The bases for these guidelines are the diagnostic workup, arrangements for further workup or observation, and initial therapeutic approach that correspond most closely with the established diagnosis.

Note: This guideline is applicable only to inpatient admissions to short-term, acute, long-term care and psychiatric hospitals.

Section IV. Diagnostic Coding and Reporting Guidelines for Outpatient Services

These coding guidelines for outpatient diagnoses have been approved for use by hospitals/ providers in coding and reporting hospital-based outpatient services and provider-based office visits.

Information about the use of certain abbreviations, punctuation, symbols, and other conventions used in the ICD-9-CM Tabular List (code numbers and titles), can be found in Section IA of these guidelines, under "Conventions Used in the Tabular List." Information about the correct sequence to use in finding a code is also described in Section I.

The terms encounter and visit are often used interchangeably in describing outpatient service contacts and, therefore, appear together in these guidelines without distinguishing one from the other.

Though the conventions and general guidelines apply to all settings, coding guidelines for outpatient and provider reporting of diagnoses will vary in a number of instances from those for inpatient diagnoses, recognizing that:

> The Uniform Hospital Discharge Data Set (UHDDS) definition of principal diagnosis applies only to inpatients in acute, short-term, long-term care and psychiatric hospitals.

> Coding guidelines for inconclusive diagnoses (probable, suspected, rule out, etc.) were developed for inpatient reporting and do not apply to outpatients.

A. Selection of first-listed condition

> In the outpatient setting, the term first-listed diagnosis is used in lieu of principal diagnosis.

> In determining the first-listed diagnosis the coding conventions of ICD-9-CM, as well as the general and disease specific guidelines take precedence over the outpatient guidelines.

> Diagnoses often are not established at the time of the initial encounter/visit. It may take two or more visits before the diagnosis is confirmed.

> The most critical rule involves beginning the search for the correct code assignment through the Alphabetic Index. Never begin searching initially in the Tabular List as this will lead to coding errors.

1.   Outpatient Surgery

> When a patient presents for outpatient surgery, code the reason for the surgery as the first-listed diagnosis (reason for the encounter), even if the surgery is not performed due to a contraindication.

2.   Observation Stay

> When a patient is admitted for observation for a medical condition, assign a code for the medical condition as the first-listed diagnosis.

When a patient presents for outpatient surgery and develops complications requiring admission to observation, code the reason for the surgery as the first reported diagnosis (reason for the encounter), followed by codes for the complications as secondary diagnoses.

B. Codes from 001.0 through V89

The appropriate code or codes from 001.0 through **V89** must be used to identify diagnoses, symptoms, conditions, problems, complaints, or other reason(s) for the encounter/visit.

C. Accurate reporting of ICD-9-CM diagnosis codes

For accurate reporting of ICD-9-CM diagnosis codes, the documentation should describe the patient's condition, using terminology which includes specific diagnoses as well as symptoms, problems, or reasons for the encounter. There are ICD-9-CM codes to describe all of these.

D. Selection of codes 001.0 through 999.9

The selection of codes 001.0 through 999.9 will frequently be used to describe the reason for the encounter. These codes are from the section of ICD-9-CM for the classification of diseases and injuries (e.g. infectious and parasitic diseases; neoplasms; symptoms, signs, and ill-defined conditions, etc.).

E. Codes that describe symptoms and signs

Codes that describe symptoms and signs, as opposed to diagnoses, are acceptable for reporting purposes when a diagnosis has not been established (confirmed) by the provider. Chapter 16 of ICD-9-CM, Symptoms, Signs, and Ill-defined conditions (codes 780.0 - 799.9) contain many, but not all codes for symptoms.

F. Encounters for circumstances other than a disease or injury

ICD-9-CM provides codes to deal with encounters for circumstances other than a disease or injury. The Supplementary Classification of factors Influencing Health Status and Contact with Health Services (V01.0- **V89**) is provided to deal with occasions when circumstances other than a disease or injury are recorded as diagnosis or problems. *See Section I.C. 18 for information on V-codes.*

G. Level of Detail in Coding

1.   ICD-9-CM codes with 3, 4, or 5 digits

ICD-9-CM is composed of codes with either 3, 4, or 5 digits. Codes with three digits are included in ICD-9-CM as the heading of a category of codes that may be further subdivided by the use of fourth and/or fifth digits, which provide greater specificity.

2.   Use of full number of digits required for a code

A three-digit code is to be used only if it is not further subdivided. Where fourth-digit subcategories and/or fifth-digit subclassifications are provided, they must be assigned. A code is invalid if it has not been coded to the full number of digits required for that code.

See also discussion under Section I.b.3., General Coding Guidelines, Level of Detail in Coding.

H. ICD-9-CM code for the diagnosis, condition, problem, or other reason for encounter/visit

List first the ICD-9-CM code for the diagnosis, condition, problem, or other reason for encounter/visit shown in the medical record to be chiefly responsible for the services provided. List additional codes that describe any coexisting conditions. In some cases the first-listed diagnosis may be a symptom when a diagnosis has not been established (confirmed) by the physician.

I. Uncertain diagnosis

Do not code diagnoses documented as "probable", "suspected," "questionable," "rule out," or "working diagnosis" or other similar terms indicating uncertainty. Rather, code the condition(s) to the highest degree of certainty for that encounter/visit, such as symptoms, signs, abnormal test results, or other reason for the visit.

Please note: This differs from the coding practices used by short-term, acute care, long-term care and psychiatric hospitals.

J. Chronic diseases

Chronic diseases treated on an ongoing basis may be coded and reported as many times as the patient receives treatment and care for the condition(s)

K. Code all documented conditions that coexist

Code all documented conditions that coexist at the time of the encounter/visit, and require or affect patient care treatment or management. Do not code conditions that were previously treated and no longer exist. However, history codes (V10-V19) may be used as secondary codes if the historical condition or family history has an impact on current care or influences treatment.

L. Patients receiving diagnostic services only

For patients receiving diagnostic services only during an encounter/visit, sequence first the diagnosis, condition, problem, or other reason for encounter/visit shown in the medical record to be chiefly responsible for the outpatient services provided during the encounter/visit. Codes for other diagnoses (e.g., chronic conditions) may be sequenced as additional diagnoses.

For encounters for routine laboratory/radiology testing in the absence of any signs, symptoms, or associated diagnosis, assign V72.5 and V72.6. If routine testing is performed during the same encounter as a test to evaluate a sign, symptom, or diagnosis, it is appropriate to assign both the V code and the code describing the reason for the non-routine test.

For outpatient encounters for diagnostic tests that have been interpreted by a physician, and the final report is available at the time of coding, code any confirmed or definitive diagnosis(es) documented in the interpretation. Do not code related signs and symptoms as additional diagnoses.

Please note: This differs from the coding practice in the hospital inpatient setting regarding abnormal findings on test results.

M. Patients receiving therapeutic services only

For patients receiving therapeutic services only during an encounter/visit, sequence first the diagnosis, condition, problem, or other reason for encounter/visit shown in the medical record to be chiefly responsible for the outpatient services provided during the encounter/visit. Codes for other diagnoses (e.g., chronic conditions) may be sequenced as additional diagnoses.

The only exception to this rule is that when the primary reason for the admission/encounter is chemotherapy, radiation therapy, or rehabilitation, the appropriate V code for the service is listed first, and the diagnosis or problem for which the service is being performed listed second.

N. Patients receiving preoperative evaluations only

For patients receiving preoperative evaluations only, sequence first a code from category V72.8, Other specified examinations, to describe the pre-op consultations. Assign a code for the condition to describe the reason for the surgery as an additional diagnosis. Code also any findings related to the pre-op evaluation.

O. Ambulatory surgery

For ambulatory surgery, code the diagnosis for which the surgery was performed. If the postoperative diagnosis is known to be different from the preoperative diagnosis at the time the diagnosis is confirmed, select the postoperative diagnosis for coding, since it is the most definitive.

P. Routine outpatient prenatal visits

For routine outpatient prenatal visits when no complications are present, codes V22.0, Supervision of normal first pregnancy, or V22.1, Supervision of other normal pregnancy, should be used as the principal diagnosis. These codes should not be used in conjunction with chapter 11 codes.

Appendix I
Present on Admission Reporting Guidelines

Introduction

These guidelines are to be used as a supplement to the *ICD-9-CM Official Guidelines for Coding and Reporting* to facilitate the assignment of the Present on Admission (POA) indicator for each diagnosis and external cause of injury code reported on claim forms (UB-04 and 837 Institutional).

These guidelines are not intended to replace any guidelines in the main body of the *ICD-9-CM Official Guidelines for Coding and Reporting*. The POA guidelines are not intended to provide guidance on when a condition should be coded, but rather, how to apply the POA indicator to the final set of diagnosis codes that have been assigned in accordance with Sections I, II, and III of the official coding guidelines. Subsequent to the assignment of the ICD-9-CM codes, the POA indicator should then be assigned to those conditions that have been coded.

As stated in the Introduction to the ICD-9-CM Official Guidelines for Coding and Reporting, a joint effort between the healthcare provider and the coder is essential to achieve complete and accurate documentation, code assignment, and reporting of diagnoses and procedures. The importance of consistent, complete documentation in the medical record cannot be overemphasized. Medical record documentation from any provider involved in the care and treatment of the patient may be used to support the determination of whether a condition was present on admission or not. In the context of the official coding guidelines, the term "provider" means a physician or any qualified healthcare practitioner who is legally accountable for establishing the patient's diagnosis.

These guidelines are not a substitute for the provider's clinical judgment as to the determination of whether a condition was/was not present on admission. The provider should be queried regarding issues related to the linking of signs/symptoms, timing of test results, and the timing of findings.

General Reporting Requirements

All claims involving inpatient admissions to general acute care hospitals or other facilities that are subject to a law or regulation mandating collection of present on admission information.

Present on admission is defined as present at the time the order for inpatient admission occurs -- conditions that develop during an outpatient encounter, including emergency department, observation, or outpatient surgery, are considered as present on admission.

POA indicator is assigned to principal and secondary diagnoses (as defined in Section II of the Official Guidelines for Coding and Reporting) and the external cause of injury codes.

Issues related to inconsistent, missing, conflicting or unclear documentation must still be resolved by the provider.

If a condition would not be coded and reported based on UHDDS definitions and current official coding guidelines, then the POA indicator would not be reported.

Reporting Options

Y - Yes

N - No

U - Unknown

W – Clinically undetermined

Unreported/Not used **(or "1" for Medicare usage)** – (Exempt from POA reporting)

For more specific instructions on Medicare POA indicator reporting options, refer to http://www.cms.hhs.gov/HospitalAcqCond/02_Statute_Regulations_Program_Instructi ons.asp#TopOfPage

Reporting Definitions

Y = present at the time of inpatient admission

N = not present at the time of inpatient admission

U = documentation is insufficient to determine if condition is present on admission

W = provider is unable to clinically determine whether condition was present on admission or not

Timeframe for POA Identification and Documentation

There is no required timeframe as to when a provider (per the definition of "provider" used in these guidelines) must identify or document a condition to be present on admission. In some clinical situations, it may not be possible for a provider to make a definitive diagnosis (or a condition may not be recognized or reported by the patient) for a period of time after admission. In some cases it may be several days before the provider arrives at a definitive diagnosis. This does not mean that the condition was not present on admission. Determination of whether the condition was present on admission or not will be based on the applicable POA guideline as identified in this document, or on the provider's best clinical judgment.

If at the time of code assignment the documentation is unclear as to whether a condition was present on admission or not, it is appropriate to query the provider for clarification.

Assigning the POA Indicator

Condition is on the "Exempt from Reporting" list

Leave the "present on admission" field blank if the condition is on the list of ICD-9-CM codes for which this field is not applicable. This is the only circumstance in which the field may be left blank.

POA Explicitly Documented

Assign Y for any condition the provider explicitly documents as being present on admission.

Assign N for any condition the provider explicitly documents as not present at the time of admission.

Conditions diagnosed prior to inpatient admission

Assign "Y" for conditions that were diagnosed prior to admission (example: hypertension, diabetes mellitus, asthma)

Conditions diagnosed during the admission but clearly present before admission

Assign "Y" for conditions diagnosed during the admission that were clearly present but not diagnosed until after admission occurred.

Diagnoses subsequently confirmed after admission are considered present on admission if at the time of admission they are documented as suspected, possible, rule out, differential diagnosis, or constitute an underlying cause of a symptom that is present at the time of admission.

Condition develops during outpatient encounter prior to inpatient admission

Assign Y for any condition that develops during an outpatient encounter prior to a written order for inpatient admission.

Documentation does not indicate whether condition was present on admission

Assign "U" when the medical record documentation is unclear as to whether the condition was present on admission. "U" should not be routinely assigned and used only in very limited circumstances. Coders are encouraged to query the providers when the documentation is unclear.

Documentation states that it cannot be determined whether the condition was or was not present on admission

Assign "W" when the medical record documentation indicates that it cannot be clinically determined whether or not the condition was present on admission.

Chronic condition with acute exacerbation during the admission

If the code is a combination code that identifies both the chronic condition and the acute exacerbation, see POA guidelines pertaining to combination codes.

If the combination code only identifies the chronic condition and not the acute exacerbation (e.g., acute exacerbation of CHF), assign "Y."

Conditions documented as possible, probable, suspected, or rule out at the time of discharge

If the final diagnosis contains a possible, probable, suspected, or rule out diagnosis, and this diagnosis was suspected at the time of inpatient admission, assign "Y."

If the final diagnosis contains a possible, probable, suspected, or rule out diagnosis, and this diagnosis was based on symptoms or clinical findings that were not present on admission, assign "N".

Conditions documented as impending or threatened at the time of discharge

If the final diagnosis contains an impending or threatened diagnosis, and this diagnosis is based on symptoms or clinical findings that were present on admission, assign "Y".

If the final diagnosis contains an impending or threatened diagnosis, and this diagnosis is based on symptoms or clinical findings that were not present on admission, assign "N".

Acute and Chronic Conditions

Assign "Y" for acute conditions that are present at time of admission and N for acute conditions that are not present at time of admission.

Assign "Y" for chronic conditions, even though the condition may not be diagnosed until after admission.

If a single code identifies both an acute and chronic condition, see the POA guidelines for combination codes.

Combination Codes

Assign "N" if any part of the combination code was not present on admission (e.g., obstructive chronic bronchitis with acute exacerbation and the exacerbation was not present on admission; gastric ulcer that does not start bleeding until after admission; asthma patient develops status asthmaticus after admission)

Assign "Y" if all parts of the combination code were present on admission (e.g., patient with diabetic nephropathy is admitted with uncontrolled diabetes)

If the final diagnosis includes comparative or contrasting diagnoses, and both were present, or suspected, at the time of admission, assign "Y".

For infection codes that include the causal organism, assign "Y" if the infection (or signs of the infection) was present on admission, even though the culture results may not be known until after admission (e.g., patient is admitted with pneumonia and the provider documents pseudomonas as the causal organism a few days later).

Same Diagnosis Code for Two or More Conditions

When the same ICD-9-CM diagnosis code applies to two or more conditions during the same encounter (e.g. bilateral condition, or two separate conditions classified to the same ICD-9-CM diagnosis code):

Assign "Y" if all conditions represented by the single ICD-9-CM code were present on admission (e.g. bilateral fracture of the same bone, same site, and both fractures were present on admission)

Assign "N" if any of the conditions represented by the single ICD-9-CM code was not present on admission (e.g. dehydration with hyponatremia is assigned to code 276.1, but only one of these conditions was present on admission).

Obstetrical conditions

Whether or not the patient delivers during the current hospitalization does not affect assignment of the POA indicator. The determining factor for POA assignment is whether the pregnancy complication or obstetrical condition described by the code was present at the time of admission or not.

If the pregnancy complication or obstetrical condition was present on admission (e.g., patient admitted in preterm labor), assign "Y".

If the pregnancy complication or obstetrical condition was not present on admission (e.g., 2nd degree laceration during delivery, postpartum hemorrhage that occurred during current hospitalization, fetal distress develops after admission), assign "N".

If the obstetrical code includes more than one diagnosis and any of the diagnoses identified by the code were not present on admission assign "N".
> (e.g., Code 642.7, Pre-eclampsia or eclampsia superimposed on pre-existing hypertension).

If the obstetrical code includes information that is not a diagnosis, do not consider that information in the POA determination.
> (e.g. Code 652.1x, Breech or other malpresentation successfully converted to cephalic presentation should be reported as present on admission if the fetus was breech on admission but was converted to cephalic presentation after admission (since the conversion to cephalic presentation does not represent a diagnosis, the fact that the conversion occurred after admission has no bearing on the POA determination).

Perinatal conditions

Newborns are not considered to be admitted until after birth. Therefore, any condition present at birth or that developed in utero is considered present at admission and should be assigned "Y". This includes conditions that occur during delivery (e.g., injury during delivery, meconium aspiration, exposure to streptococcus B in the vaginal canal).

Congenital conditions and anomalies

Assign "Y" for congenital conditions and anomalies. Congenital conditions are always considered present on admission.

External cause of injury codes

Assign "Y" for any E code representing an external cause of injury or poisoning that occurred prior to inpatient admission (e.g., patient fell out of bed at home, patient fell out of bed in emergency room prior to admission)

Assign "N" for any E code representing an external cause of injury or poisoning that occurred during inpatient hospitalization (e.g., patient fell out of hospital bed during hospital stay, patient experienced an adverse reaction to a medication administered after inpatient admission)

Categories and Codes
Exempt from
Diagnosis Present on Admission Requirement
Effective Date: October 1, 2008

Note: "Diagnosis present on admission" for these code categories are exempt because they represent circumstances regarding the healthcare encounter or factors influencing health status that do not represent a current disease or injury or are always present on admission

137-139, Late effects of infectious and parasitic diseases

268.1, Rickets, late effect

326, Late effects of intracranial abscess or pyogenic infection

412, Old myocardial infarction

438, Late effects of cerebrovascular disease

650, Normal delivery

660.7, Failed forceps or vacuum extractor, unspecified

677, Late effect of complication of pregnancy, childbirth, and the puerperium

905-909, Late effects of injuries, poisonings, toxic effects, and other external causes

V02, Carrier or suspected carrier of infectious diseases

V03, Need for prophylactic vaccination and inoculation against bacterial diseases

V04, Need for prophylactic vaccination and inoculation against certain viral diseases

V05, Need for other prophylactic vaccination and inoculation against single diseases

V06, Need for prophylactic vaccination and inoculation against combinations of diseases

V07, Need for isolation and other prophylactic measures

V10, Personal history of malignant neoplasm

V11, Personal history of mental disorder

V12, Personal history of certain other diseases

V13, Personal history of other diseases

V14, Personal history of allergy to medicinal agents

V15.01-V15.09, Other personal history, Allergy, other than to medicinal agents

V15.1, Other personal history, Surgery to heart and great vessels

V15.2, Other personal history, Surgery to other major organs

V15.3, Other personal history, Irradiation

V15.4, Other personal history, Psychological trauma

V15.5, Other personal history, Injury

V15.6, Other personal history, Poisoning

V15.7, Other personal history, Contraception

V15.81, Other personal history, Noncompliance with medical treatment

V15.82, Other personal history, History of tobacco use

V15.88, Other personal history, History of fall

V15.89, Other personal history, Other

V15.9 Unspecified personal history presenting hazards to health

V16, Family history of malignant neoplasm

V17, Family history of certain chronic disabling diseases

V18, Family history of certain other specific conditions

V19, Family history of other conditions

V20, Health supervision of infant or child

V21, Constitutional states in development

V22, Normal pregnancy

V23, Supervision of high-risk pregnancy

V24, Postpartum care and examination

V25, Encounter for contraceptive management

V26, Procreative management

V27, Outcome of delivery

V28, Antenatal screening

V29, Observation and evaluation of newborns for suspected condition not found

V30-V39, Liveborn infants according to type of birth

V42, Organ or tissue replaced by transplant

V43, Organ or tissue replaced by other means

V44, Artificial opening status

V45, Other postprocedural states

V46, Other dependence on machines

V49.60-V49.77, Upper and lower limb amputation status

V49.81-V49.84, Other specified conditions influencing health status

V50, Elective surgery for purposes other than remedying health states

V51, Aftercare involving the use of plastic surgery

V52, Fitting and adjustment of prosthetic device and implant

V53, Fitting and adjustment of other device

V54, Other orthopedic aftercare

V55, Attention to artificial openings

V56, Encounter for dialysis and dialysis catheter care

V57, Care involving use of rehabilitation procedures

V58, Encounter for other and unspecified procedures and aftercare

V59, Donors

V60, Housing, household, and economic circumstances

V61, Other family circumstances

V62, Other psychosocial circumstances

V64, Persons encountering health services for specific procedures, not carried out

V65, Other persons seeking consultation

V66, Convalescence and palliative care

V67, Follow-up examination

V68, Encounters for administrative purposes

V69, Problems related to lifestyle

V70, General medical examination

V71, Observation and evaluation for suspected condition not found

V72, Special investigations and examinations

V73, Special screening examination for viral and chlamydial diseases

V74, Special screening examination for bacterial and spirochetal diseases

V75, Special screening examination for other infectious diseases

V76, Special screening for malignant neoplasms

V77, Special screening for endocrine, nutritional, metabolic, and immunity disorders

V78, Special screening for disorders of blood and blood-forming organs

V79, Special screening for mental disorders and developmental handicaps

V80, Special screening for neurological, eye, and ear diseases

V81, Special screening for cardiovascular, respiratory, and genitourinary diseases

V82, Special screening for other conditions

V83, Genetic carrier status

V84, Genetic susceptibility to disease

V85, Body Mass Index

V86 Estrogen receptor status

V87.4, Personal history of drug therapy

V88, Acquired absence of cervix and uterus

V89, Suspected maternal and fetal conditions not found

E800-E807, Railway accidents

E810-E819, Motor vehicle traffic accidents

E820-E825, Motor vehicle nontraffic accidents

E826-E829, Other road vehicle accidents

E830-E838, Water transport accidents

E840-E845, Air and space transport accidents

E846-E848, Vehicle accidents not elsewhere classifiable

E849.0-E849.6, Place of occurrence

E849.8-E849.9, Place of occurrence

E883.1, Accidental fall into well

E883.2, Accidental fall into storm drain or manhole

E884.0, Fall from playground equipment

E884.1, Fall from cliff

E885.0, Fall from (nonmotorized) scooter

E885.1, Fall from roller skates

E885.2, Fall from skateboard

E885.3, Fall from skis

E885.4, Fall from snowboard

E886.0, Fall on same level from collision, pushing, or shoving, by or with other person, In sports

E890.0-E890.9, Conflagration in private dwelling

E893.0, Accident caused by ignition of clothing, from controlled fire in private dwelling

E893.2, Accident caused by ignition of clothing, from controlled fire not in building or structure

E894, Ignition of highly inflammable material

E895, Accident caused by controlled fire in private dwelling

E897, Accident caused by controlled fire not in building or structure

E898.0-E898.1, Accident caused by other specified fire and flames

E917.0, Striking against or struck accidentally by objects or persons, in sports without subsequent fall

E917.1, Striking against or struck accidentally by objects or persons, caused by a crowd, by collective fear or panic without subsequent fall

E917.2, Striking against or struck accidentally by objects or persons, in running water without subsequent fall

E917.5, Striking against or struck accidentally by objects or persons, object in sports with subsequent fall

E917.6, Striking against or struck accidentally by objects or persons, caused by a crowd, by collective fear or panic with subsequent fall

E919.0-E919.1, Accidents caused by machinery

E919.3-E919.9, Accidents caused by machinery

E921.0-E921.9, Accident caused by explosion of pressure vessel

E922.0-E922.9, Accident caused by firearm and air gun missile

E924.1, Caustic and corrosive substances

E926.2, Visible and ultraviolet light sources

E928.0-E928.8, Other and unspecified environmental and accidental causes

E929.0-E929.9, Late effects of accidental injury

E959, Late effects of self-inflicted injury

E970-E978, Legal intervention

E979, Terrorism

E981.0-E981.8, Poisoning by gases in domestic use, undetermined whether accidentally or purposely inflicted

E982.0-E982.9, Poisoning by other gases, undetermined whether accidentally or purposely inflicted

E985.0-E985.7, Injury by firearms, air guns and explosives, undetermined whether accidentally or purposely inflicted

E987.0, Falling from high place, undetermined whether accidentally or purposely inflicted, residential premises

E987.2, Falling from high place, undetermined whether accidentally or purposely inflicted, natural sites

E989, Late effects of injury, undetermined whether accidentally or purposely inflicted

E990-E999, Injury resulting from operations of war

POA Examples

General Medical Surgical

1. Patient is admitted for diagnostic work-up for cachexia. The final diagnosis is malignant neoplasm of lung with metastasis.

    Assign "Y" on the POA field for the malignant neoplasm. The malignant neoplasm was clearly present on admission, although it was not diagnosed until after the admission occurred.

2. A patient undergoes outpatient surgery. During the recovery period, the patient develops atrial fibrillation and the patient is subsequently admitted to the hospital as an inpatient.

    Assign "Y" on the POA field for the atrial fibrillation since it developed prior to a written order for inpatient admission.

3. A patient is treated in observation and while in Observation, the patient falls out of bed and breaks a hip. The patient is subsequently admitted as an inpatient to treat the hip fracture.

    Assign "Y" on the POA field for the hip fracture since it developed prior to a written order for inpatient admission.

4. A patient with known congestive heart failure is admitted to the hospital after he develops decompensated congestive heart failure.

    Assign "Y" on the POA field for the congestive heart failure. The ICD-9-CM code identifies the chronic condition and does not specify the acute exacerbation.

5. A patient undergoes inpatient surgery. After surgery, the patient develops fever and is treated aggressively. The physician's final diagnosis documents "possible postoperative infection following surgery."

    Assign "N" on the POA field for the postoperative infection since final diagnoses that contain the terms "possible", "probable", "suspected" or "rule out" and that are based on symptoms or clinical findings that were not present on admission should be reported as "N".

6. A patient with severe cough and difficulty breathing was diagnosed during his hospitalization to have lung cancer.

    Assign "Y" on the POA field for the lung cancer. Even though the cancer was not diagnosed until after admission, it is a chronic condition that was clearly present before the patient's admission.

7. A patient is admitted to the hospital for a coronary artery bypass surgery. Postoperatively he developed a pulmonary embolism.

    Assign "N" on the POA field for the pulmonary embolism. This is an acute condition that was not present on admission.

8. A patient is admitted with a known history of coronary atherosclerosis, status post myocardial infarction five years ago is now admitted for treatment of impending myocardial infarction. The final diagnosis is documented as "impending myocardial infarction."

    Assign "Y" to the impending myocardial infarction because the condition is present on admission.

9. A patient with diabetes mellitus developed uncontrolled diabetes on day 3 of the hospitalization.

    Assign "N" to the diabetes code because the "uncontrolled" component of the code was not present on admission.

10. A patient is admitted with high fever and pneumonia. The patient rapidly deteriorates and becomes septic. The discharge diagnosis lists sepsis and pneumonia. The documentation is unclear as to whether the sepsis was present on admission or developed shortly after admission.

    Query the physician as to whether the sepsis was present on admission, developed shortly after admission, or it cannot be clinically determined as to whether it was present on admission or not.

11. A patient is admitted for repair of an abdominal aneurysm. However, the aneurysm ruptures after hospital admission.

    Assign "N" for the ruptured abdominal aneurysm. Although the aneurysm was present on admission, the "ruptured" component of the code description did not occur until after admission.

12. A patient with viral hepatitis B progresses to hepatic coma after admission.

    Assign "N" for the viral hepatitis B with hepatic coma because part of the code description did not develop until after admission.

13. A patient with a history of varicose veins and ulceration of the left lower extremity strikes the area against the side of his hospital bed during an inpatient hospitalization. It bleeds profusely. The final diagnosis lists varicose veins with ulcer and hemorrhage.

Assign "Y" for the varicose veins with ulcer. Although the hemorrhage occurred after admission, the code description for varicose veins with ulcer does not mention hemorrhage.

14. The nursing initial assessment upon admission documents the presence of a decubitus ulcer. There is no mention of the decubitus ulcer in the physician documentation until several days after admission.

    Query the physician as to whether the decubitus ulcer was present on admission, or developed after admission. Both diagnosis code assignment and determination of whether a condition was present on admission must be based on provider documentation in the medical record (per the definition of "provider" found at the beginning of these POA guidelines and in the introductory section of the ICD-9-CM Official Guidelines for Coding and Reporting). If it cannot be determined from the provider documentation whether or not a condition was present on admission, the provider should be queried.

15. **A urine culture is obtained on admission. The provider documents urinary tract infection when the culture results become available a few days later.**

    Assign "Y" to the urinary tract infection since the diagnosis is based on test results from a specimen obtained on admission. It may not be possible for a provider to make a definitive diagnosis for a period of time after admission. There is no required timeframe as to when a provider must identify or document a condition to be present on admission.

16. **A patient tested positive for Methicillin resistant Staphylococcus (MRSA) on routine nasal culture on admission to the hospital. During the hospitalization, he underwent insertion of a central venous catheter and later developed an infection and was diagnosed with MRSA sepsis due to central venous catheter infection.**

    Assign "Y" to the positive MRSA colonization. Assign "N" for the MRSA sepsis due to central venous catheter infection since the patient did not have a MRSA infection at the time of admission.

Obstetrics

1. A female patient was admitted to the hospital and underwent a normal delivery.

   Leave the "present on admission" (POA) field blank. Code 650, Normal delivery, is on the "exempt from reporting" list.

2. Patient admitted in late pregnancy due to excessive vomiting and dehydration. During admission patient goes into premature labor

   Assign "Y" for the excessive vomiting and the dehydration.
   Assign "N" for the premature labor

3. Patient admitted in active labor. During the stay, a breast abscess is noted when mother attempted to breast feed. Provider is unable to determine whether the abscess was present on admission

    Assign "W" for the breast abscess.

4. Patient admitted in active labor. After 12 hours of labor it is noted that the infant is in fetal distress and a Cesarean section is performed

    Assign "N" for the fetal distress.

5. **Pregnant female was admitted in labor and fetal nuchal cord entanglement was diagnosed. Physician is queried, but is unable to determine whether the cord entanglement was present on admission or not.**

    Assign "W" for the fetal nuchal cord entanglement.

Newborn

1. A single liveborn infant was delivered in the hospital via Cesarean section. The physician documented fetal bradycardia during labor in the final diagnosis in the newborn record.

    Assign " Y" because the bradycardia developed prior to the newborn admission (birth).

2. A newborn developed diarrhea which was believed to be due to the hospital baby formula.

    Assign " N" because the diarrhea developed after admission.

3. **A newborn born in the hospital, birth complicated by nuchal cord entanglement.**

    Assign "Y" for the nuchal cord entanglement on the baby's record. Any condition that is present at birth or that developed in utero is considered present at admission, including conditions that occur during delivery.

Appendix B: Anatomical Diagrams

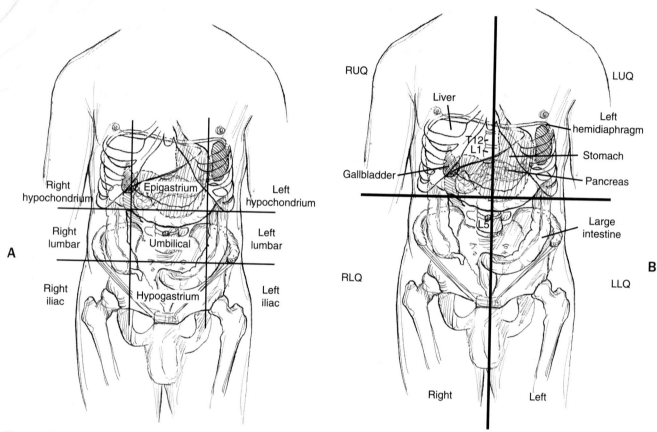

Figure 1 **(A)** Abdominopelvic region; **(B)** Abdominopelvic quadrants (From Caruthers B, Price P, Junge TL, et al. *Surgical Technology for the Surgical Technologist: A Positive Care Approach.* Albany, NY: Thomson Delmar Learning, 2001, p. 292.)

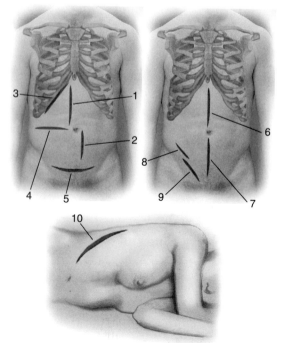

Figure 2 Abdominal incisions: right upper paramedian (1), left lower paramedian (2), right subcostal (3), right midline transverse (4), Pfannenstiel (5), upper longitudinal midline (6), lower longitudinal midline (7), McBurney's (8), right inguinal, oblique (9), and left thoracoabdominal (10) (From Caruthers B, Price P, Junge TL, et al. *Surgical Technology for the Surgical Technologist: A Positive Care Approach.* Albany, NY: Thomson Delmar Learning, 2001, p. 310.)

Glossary

A

ablation the destruction with regard to function of a body part.

ABO isoimmunization a condition in which the mother with type O blood carries a fetus with blood type A or B.

abruptio placentae the premature detachment of the placenta from the wall of the uterus.

abscess a collection of pus that is localized and indicates tissue destruction.

accessory organs secondary organs.

accident overdose of a drug, wrong substance given or taken in error, drug taken inadvertently, wrong dosage.

Accrediting Bureau of Health Education Schools (ABHES) accredits medical assisting programs that allow students to sit for the certification exam.

acne oversecretion of sebaceous glands, causing pores to clog.

acquired condition a condition that occurs during a person's life.

acquired deformity a malformation of an anatomical structure that is caused by infections, injury to soft tissue, or a late effect of fracture.

acute bronchitis inflammation of the bronchus that lasts for a short period of time and is typically caused by a spreading inflammation from the nasopharynx.

acute renal failure when renal function is interrupted suddenly.

adenoids nasopharyngeal tonsils.

Administration Simplification developed standards for the electronic exchange of healthcare data for administrative and financial transactions.

adnexa accessory or appendage of an organ.

adrenalectomy the surgical removal of either one or both adrenal glands, located above the kidneys.

adult onset diabetes a condition in which the body is unable to produce sufficient amounts of insulin and which develops later in life. Also known as type II diabetes mellitus.

adverse effect a reaction to the correct administration of a drug or a reaction between two or more drugs prescribed by a physician.

agranulocytes a type of leukocyte that does not have a granular appearance.

alcohol abuse drinking alcohol to excess but not having a physical dependence on it.

alcohol dependence occurs when a person has become dependent on alcohol and is unable to stop drinking. Also known as alcoholism.

alcoholism occurs when a person has become dependent on alcohol and is unable to stop drinking. Also known as alcohol dependence.

alimentary canal pertaining to nourishment. Also known as the digestive system.

allogeneic bone marrow transplant the grafting of human donor bone marrow tissue.

alopecia hair loss.

Alphabetic Index an alaphabetic listing of the codes found in volume 1.

Alphabetic Index to External Causes of Injury and Poisoning the index for E codes, which classify environmental events.

Alphabetic Index to Poisoning and External Causes of Adverse Effects of Drugs and Other Chemical Substances the index used to classify poisonings by a drug or chemical, as well as external causes of an adverse effect of a drug or chemical. Also known as Table of Drugs and Chemicals.

altered state of consciousness a state in which the patient does not lose consciousness completely but may stare or have an altered loss of awareness.

alveolectomy the correction of the tooth socket.

alveoli grapelike structures at the end of each bronchiole; the sockets that hold the teeth in place.

alveoloplasty a repair done on the tooth socket.

Alzheimer's disease a disease in which brain structure changes, leading to memory loss, personality changes, and ultimately impaired ability to function.

American Academy of Professional Coders (AAPC) founded in an effort to elevate the standards of medical coding and provide networking opportunities through local chapter memberships and conferences.

American Association of Medical Assistants (AAMA) represents individuals trained in performing both routine administrative and clinical jobs, including coding, that keep medical offices and clinics running efficiently and smoothly.

American Health Information Management Association (AHIMA) represents health information professionals who manage, organize, process, and manipulate patient data.

American Medical Technologists (AMT) professionals who perform the same tasks as a Certified Medical Assistant.

amniocentesis an ultrasonic-guided procedure in which a needle is inserted into the amniotic sac to withdraw fluid for examination.

amnioscopy a procedure in which a scope is used to view the fetus in the amniotic sac. Also known as fetoscopy or laparoamnioscopy.

amputation removal of a limb or body part by surgery.

anal fistulectomy removal of an anal fistula.

anal fistulotomy the surgical cutting of an anal fistula.

analgesia injection a type of injection given to relieve pain.

anal sphincter a circular muscle constricting the anus.

anastomosis the surgical creation of a connection between two tubular structures.

anatomical site the body system or location on the body.

anemia a condition marked by a decrease in red blood cells, hemoglobin, or hematocrit.

anencephalus   a birth defect in newborns in which the neural groove closes early in the first trimester. There may be no cranial vault.

aneurysm   when the wall of an artery or vein weakens.

angina pectoris   severe chest pains caused by an insufficient amount of blood reaching the heart.

angiocardiography   the imaging of the arteries of the heart and the great vessels by the use of a contrast material.

angiohemophilia   the most common of the inherited bleeding disorders, caused by a deficiency in clotting factor and platelet function and categorized as a hereditary autosomal dominant disorder. Also known as Von Willebrand's disease.

angioplasty   a procedure in which the vessel that is narrowed or occluded is opened up or dilated.

angioscopy   a scope is inserted to visualize blood vessels.

anisorcoria   unequal pupils.

ankylosis   a complete fusion of the vertebrae.

ankylosing spondylitis   a form of rheumatoid arthritis.

annuloplasty   the surgical repair of one or more of the circular orifices in the heart.

anomaly   a birth defect.

anoscopy   an endoscopic examination of the anus.

anoxia   the complete lack of oxygen.

ante-   a prefix meaning "before," "forward."

antepartum   the time before childbirth.

antepartum complication   any problem that occurs while the patient is pregnant until childbirth.

anterior   in front of or forward of.

antesternal anastomosis   a procedure in which a surgical tunnel is created through the substernal tissue to the esophagus.

anticoagulants   medications that prevent the formation of blood clots, such as heparin or Coumadin.

antrotomy   a surgically created opening in the sinus for drainage.

anus   the distal-most structure of the digestive tract.

aorta   the largest vessel in the body, through which oxygenated blood is sent out to the entire body.

aortic valve   one of the main valves of the heart that sits between the aorta and the left ventricle.

apicoectomy   the removal of a tooth root.

aplastic anemia   a type of anemia caused by the failure of bone marrow to produce blood components.

appendectomy   the removal of the appendix.

appendices   sections of a book containing reference information.

appendicitis   the appendix becomes inflamed or infected.

appendicular skeleton   the bones in the arms, legs, shoulders, and pelvis.

appendix   the wormlike structure that is found at the blind end of the cecum.

Appendix A   Morphology of Neoplasms   the volume 1 appendix that contains a nomenclature of the morphology of neoplasms adapted from the International Classification of Diseases (ICD) of Oncology; used with codes from chapter 2, depending on the setting of the encounter.

Appendix C   Classification of Drugs by American Hospital Formulary Service List Number and their ICD-9-CM Equivalents   the volume 1 appendix that lists the ICD-9-CM diagnosis code for the coding of poisonings by drugs and medicinal and biological substances in relation to the listing of drugs by the American Hospital Formulary Service.

Appendix D   Classification of Industrial Accidents According to Agency   the volume 1 appendix that lists industrial accidents as defined by the Tenth International Conference of Labor Statisticians.

Appendix E   List of Three-Digit Categories   the volume 1 appendix that lists all the three-digit categories found in ICD-9-CM.

Appendix I   Present on Admission Reporting Guidelines   the section of the ICD-9-CM Official Guidelines for Coding and Reporting outlines the guidelines for reporting present on admission indicators.

arteries   carry oxygen-rich blood from the heart to the body.

arteriography   the imaging of an artery or an arterial family after the injection of material into the bloodstream.

arteriosclerotic heart disease   the arteries narrow over a long period of time. Also known as chronic ischemic heart disease.

arthritis   inflammation of a joint.

arthro-   prefix for "pertaining to the joint."

arthrocentesis   a procedure in which the joint space is entered with a needle to remove an accumulation of fluid.

arthrodesis   the surgical immobilization of a joint.

arthropathy   a disorder of the joint.

arthroplasty   the surgical repair of a joint.

arthropods   parasitic organisms, including insects, ticks, spiders, and mites.

arthroscopy   a visual examination of the joint with a scope.

arthrotomy   the surgical incision of a joint.

artificial insemination   a mechanical procedure by which semen is placed into the vagina.

artificial pneumothorax   a procedure in which gas or air is forced into the pleural space.

arytenoidopexy   the surgical correction of the cartilage of the larynx.

asbestosis   a result of exposure to asbestos.

-asis   suffix meaning "state of" or "condition."

asphyxia   lack of oxygen in the air that is inhaled.

aspiration   the surgically draw of fluids from the body.

aspiration of kidney   the withdrawal of fluid from a kidney.

aspiration of testis   the withdrawal of fluid from the testes.

aspiration pneumonia   occurs when a solid or liquid is inhaled into the lung.

assault   injury or poisoning inflicted by another person with the intent to injure or kill.

asthma   a stricture of the airway, causing difficulty in breathing.

atria   the upper chambers of the heart that receive blood from the veins.

auditory ossicles   located in the middle ear, the three bones named by their shapes.

augmentation mammoplasty   a type of plastic surgery in which the breast is reconstructed to a larger size.

autograft   a tissue graft from patient's own body.

autologous bone marrow transplant   the grafting of a patient's own bone marrow tissue.

autonomic nervous system   regulates the activities of the cardiac muscle, smooth muscle, and glands and is part of the peripheral nervous system.

autopsy the internal and external examination of a body postmortem.

avulsion a ripping or tearing away.

axial skeleton the bones of the skull, vertebral column, ribs, and sternum.

B

bacilli the plural of bacillus.

bacillus a straight rod bacterium.

bacteria one-celled organisms named according to their shapes and arrangements.

Bartholin's glands small glands located on either side of the vagina that secrete a mucus substance to lubricate the vagina.

bedsores pressure ulcers.

Bell's palsy a disorder of the facial nerve caused by a lesion on a facial nerve, producing facial distortion and unilateral paralysis of the face.

benign hypertension mildly elevated blood pressure that remains relatively stable over many years.

benign neoplasm the usually non-life-threatening abnormal growth of cells. Also known as a nonmalignant tumor.

benign prostatic hypertophy (BPH) affects men, usually over 60 years of age, in which there is an abnormal enlargement of the prostate.

bicuspid valve the valve between the left atrium and left ventricle. Also called the mitral valve.

bilateral nephrectomy the removal of both kidneys.

bilateral orchiectomy the surgical removal of both of the testicles.

bile breaks down fat.

bilirubin a pigment in bile produced from the destruction of hemoglobin and released by the liver.

biopsy the removal of tissue for pathological examination to differentiate between malignant and benign tissue.

biopsy of spinal cord the removal of tissue of the spinal cord.

biopsy of spinal meninges the removal of tissue of the spinal meninges.

bipolar disorders occurrences of an elevated mood alternating with depressive episodes. Also known as manic-depressive episodes.

birth defect an anomaly.

birth trauma occurs when there is an injury to the fetus during the delivery process.

blepharoptosis drooping eyelid.

boil a staphylococcal infection around hair follicles. Also known as a furuncle.

bone marrow the site where blood cells are formed.

bones connective tissue that protects the internal organs and serves as the framework of the body.

braces used to connect a series of terms appearing on the left of the brace to a common term on the right of the brace.

breech delivery a type of delivery in which the fetus presents feet, buttocks, or knees first.

broncheoesophageal the bronchus and the esophagus.

bronchi found in the lobes of the lungs and are formed when the trachea branches off in the chest.

bronchial dilation the bronchus is enlarged by stretching.

bronchial tree the trachea leads into the bronchi and branches off.

bronchioles when the bronchus divides to form smaller and smaller bronchi.

bronchitis an inflammation of the bronchus that can be diagnosed as acute or chronic.

bronchocutaneous the area of the bronchus and the skin.

bronchoesophageal term referring to a repair between the bronchus and the esophagus.

bronchoscopy a type of endoscopic procedure in which a rigid or flexible scope is used.

bronchovisceral term referring to a repair between the bronchus and a large internal organ.

bronchvisceral fistulectomy the repair of a fistula between the bronchus and a large internal organ.

bunionectomy a procedure in which a bony exostosis is removed from the great toe.

burn an injury to body tissue as a result of heat, flame, sun, chemicals, radiation, or electricity.

bursa the synovial-filled sac that works as a cushion to assist in movement.

bursectomy the excision of the bursa.

bypass to go around a structure.

C

ca in situ (CIS) neoplastic cells that are undergoing malignant changes that are confined to the original epithelium site without invading surrounding tissues. Also known as carcinoma in situ.

calculus a kidney stone.

Caldwell-Luc procedure the approach used to reach the maxillary cavity.

canaloplasty the reconstruction of the external ear or external auditory canal.

cancer malignant cells that multiply excessively and invade or infiltrate other normal tissue, creating a life-threatening condition.

cancerous growth the life-threatening, malignant growth of abnormal cells. Also called a malignant neoplasm.

candidal onychia fungal infection of the skin and nails.

candidal vulvovaginitis fungal infection of the vulva and vagina. Also called monilial vulvovaginitis.

candidiasis a fungal infection caused by candida.

capsulectomy of kidney the surgical removal of the capsule of the kidney.

carbuncle furuncles cluster and form a pus-filled sac.

carcinoma in situ (CIS) neoplastic cells that are undergoing malignant changes that are confined to the original epithelium site without invading surrounding tissues. Also known as ca in situ.

cardiac catheter used to determine whether cardiac abnormalities exist.

cardiac dysrhythmias abnormal cardiac rhythm.

cardiac pacemaker used to correct and manage heart dysrhythmias.

cardiomyopathy diseases of the heart muscle.

cardiovascular system   the system that pumps blood through the body, carrying oxygen and nutrients.

cartilage   the smooth, nonvascular connective tissue that comprises the more flexible parts of the skeleton, such as the outer ear.

cataracts   opacity of the eye lens.

category   the level where three-digit codes are referenced.

catheter   a fine tube that is inserted into the body to allow for injections, fluid or air removal, obstruction removal, or monitoring.

cecum   beginning of the large intestine.

-cele   suffix meaning "hollow."

cellulitis   a type of skin infection resulting from an ulcer, laceration, or wound.

Centers for Medicare and Medicaid Services (CMS)   one of the agencies that are overseen by the U.S. Department of Health and Human Services and that is responsible for all the annual ICD-9-CM modifications in the United States.

-centesis   suffix meaning "remove fluid by surgical puncture."

central nervous system (CNS)   the part of the nervous system that contains the brain and spinal cord.

cerebral hemorrhage   bleeding within the brain or layers of brain lining.

cerebral infarction   the death of cerebral tissue due to inadequate blood supply.

cerebrovascular accident (CVA)   a disruption in the normal blood supply to the brain. Also called a stroke.

cerebrovascular disease   condition that affects the cerebral arteries.

Certified Coding Associate (CCA)   a level of certification and credentialing by the AHIMA.

Certified Coding Specialist (CCS)   a level of certification and credentialing by the AHIMA.

Certified Coding Specialist, Physician-Based (CCS-P)   a level of certification and credentialing by the AHIMA.

Certified Healthcare Privacy and Security (CHPS)   a level of certification and credentialing by the AHIMA.

Certified in Healthcare Privacy (CHP)   a level of certification and credentialing by the AHIMA.

Certified in Healthcare Security (CHS)   a level of certification and credentialing by the AHIMA.

Certified Medical Assistant (CMA)   the title for a credentialed medical assistant.

Certified Professional Coder (CPC)   the certification for professional coders in a physician's office or clinic setting.

Certified Professional Coder, Hospital-Based (CPC-H)   the certification for professional coders in a hospital setting.

cerumen   earwax.

cervical os   the bony structure of the cervix.

cervix   a female organ located at the lowest part of the uterus that extends to the vagina.

cesarean delivery   delivery of the fetus by way of an incision through the abdominal wall into the uterus.

cesarean section   a surgical procedure of extracting the fetus from the uterus through the abdominal wall.

chalazion   a localized swelling of the eyelid resulting from an obstruction of a sebaceous gland of the eyelid. Also called meibomian cyst, tarsal cyst, or internal hordeolum.

chemical peel   a procedure in which chemicals are use to destroy and remove skin.

childbirth   the delivery of one or more infants.

cholecystitis   a sudden and severe onset of inflammation of the gallbladder.

cholecysto-   a prefix that refers to the gallbladder.

cholecystostomy   a surgical opening created into the gallbladder.

cholecystotomy   a surgical cut into the gallbladder.

cholelithiasis   the formation or presence of gallstones.

chole/o-   a prefix that refers to bile or gall.

chondropathy   disorder of the cartilage.

chordae tendineae   the cordlike tendons that connect the papillary muscles to the valves of the heart.

chorea   involuntary movements of the face, tongue, and upper extremities.

chronic bronchitis   a prolonged inflammation of the bronchus, usually lasting for more than three months and occurring for two consecutive years.

chronic ischemic heart disease   the arteries narrow over time. Also called arteriosclerotic heart disease.

chronic obstructive pulmonary (lung) disease (COPD)   when the obstructive lung disease is long term and not likely to resolve.

chronic renal failure   a progressive disease in which renal function deteriorates, causing multisystem problems.

chronic sinusitis   a prolonged inflammation of one or more of the sinus cavities.

cilia   the fine hairs found right inside the nose that filter air coming into the body.

ciliary body   a group of muscles and ligaments that adjust the lens of the eye to focus light rays on the retina.

circumcision   an elective procedure completed to remove the foreskin.

Classification of Disease and Injuries   a section of the Tabular List of Diseases and Injuries that contains a numerical listing of diseases and injuries found in ICD-9-CM and that consists of 17 chapters.

cleft lip   a congenital defect that results in a deep groove or opening of the lip, running upward to the nose. Also called a harelip.

cleft palate   a congenital groove or opening of the palate that involves the hard palate or soft palate and upper lip.

clipping   a procedure in which the aneurysm is not allowed to move due to the surgical placement of a device that prevents movement.

clitoris   a small erectile structure in front of the vaginal opening.

closed biopsy   a removal of a piece of living tissue without making an incision to obtain the tissue.

closed fracture   a type of fracture in which the bone is broken but the skin has not been broken. Also known as a complete or simple fracture.

closure/correction   in the context of procedures, a repair.

clubfoot   a congenital turning of the foot. Also known as a talipes.

coagulation   the process of blood cells joining together to form a blood clot.

coagulation defects   occurs when there is a deficiency in one or more of the blood clotting factors, resulting in prolonged clotting time and possibly serious bleeding.

code first underlying disease, cause, or condition notation that must always be followed, because it instructs the coder to use an additional code to identify an underlying condition that is present.

cocci the plural of coccus.

coccus a spherical or round bacterium.

coding the assignment of numerical or alphanumerical digits and characters to specific diagnostic and procedural phrases.

colitis an inflammation of the colon.

Colles' fracture a wrist fracture that typically occurs when a person tries to break a fall by extending the arm.

colon the last part of the intestine, consisting of the ascending, transverse, descending, and sigmoid sections.

colostomy surgical opening between part of the colon and the outside surface of the body.

colpo- prefix meaning "pertaining to the vagina."

coma a condition in which the person is in a deep state of unconsciousness.

combination code assignment a single code used to classify two diagnoses.

Commission on Accreditation of Allied Health Education Programs (CAAHEP) one of the organizations involved in accrediting medical assistants.

complete fracture a type of fracture in which the bone is broken but the skin has not been broken. Also known as a closed or simple fracture.

complete placenta previa the abnormal implantation of the placenta near or at the opening of the uterine cervix.

complete prolapse when the entire uterus descends and protrudes beyond the introitus, and the vagina becomes inverted.

complicated fracture a fracture in which an internal organ has been injured as a direct result of the fracture.

compound fracture a fracture that has broken through the skin at the fracture site. Also known as an open fracture.

compression fracture of the spine occurs when the vertebrae in the spine become weak and collapse under low stress.

computerized axial tomography a type of tomography that uses a computer to produce a cross-section image of a body structure.

concussion a violent shaking or jarring of the brain.

conductive hearing loss a mild form of hearing loss, usually involving the external or middle ear.

congenital anomaly an abnormality that occurs before or during birth.

conization a procedure performed on the cervix in which a cold knife is used to surgically cut a cone-shaped portion of tissue for examination.

conjunctivitis an inflammation of the conjunctiva.

contiguous two adacent sites.

contrast material, usually barium or iodine based, that is used to X-ray parts of the body that normally cannot be X-rayed.

conventions a group of instructional notations, punctuation marks, abbreviations, and symbols.

Cooperating Parties for ICD-9-CM organizations that cooperatively developed and approved the ICD-9-CM Official Coding Guidelines.

coreoplasty a repair of a defect of the iris. Also known as needling of the papillary membrane.

cornea the layer of the eye located directly below the conjunctiva.

correction in the context of procedures, a repair.

correction of a lid retraction a procedure that moves the eyelid back to its normal position.

craniectomy the removal of a section of the skull bones.

craniotomy the cutting open of a section of the skull bones.

cranium the bone that encloses the brain and that is made up of eight parts.

Crohn's disease a form of inflammatory bowel disease that can cause thickening and scarring of the abdominal wall. Also known as regional enteritis.

crown the part of a tooth that is above the gumline.

culture and sensitivity test (C&S) a test used to accurately diagnose a specific bacterial infection that is affecting a patient.

curettage of the brain the removal of lesions from the brain surface.

curette an instrument used to perform a curettage of the uterus.

Current Procedural Terminology, Fourth Edition (CPT) the coding book published by the American Medical Association that lists procedure codes.

cystitis an inflammation of the bladder.

cysto- a prefix meaning "bladder" or "sac."

cystocele a bladder hernia that protrudes into the vagina.

cyst of breast an encapsulated fluid-filled sac of the breast.

cystostomy a surgical creation of an opening into the bladder.

cystotomy an incision made into the bladder.

D

dacryoadenectomy the excision of the lacrimal gland.

D&C a procedure in which the cervix is opened up or dilated; then the uterus is scraped clean with an instrument. Also known as dilation and curettage.

debridement the cleaning out of a wound to prevent infection or to cleanse a site.

debridement of the brain the removal of damaged brain tissue.

deciduous primary or baby teeth.

decompression of nerves the surgical removal of pressure on nerves. Also known as nerve release.

decortication of the lung a procedure to thin out the serous membrane of the pleura.

decubitus ulcer the result of continuous pressure in an area that eventually limits or stops circulation and oxygen flow to an area.

deformity a problem in the structure or form, which may or may not be disfiguring.

degenerative joint disease the degeneration of the articular cartilage. Also known as a type of osteoarthritis.

dehydration an excess loss of fluids.

delirium a confused, disoriented state with the inability to think clearly.

delusional disorders a disorder associated with the feeling of paranoia, in which the patient has a constant distrust and suspicion of others.

delusions   a false perception that is maintained by a person despite proof that it is contrary.

dementia   a slowly progressive decrease in mental abilities.

depressive features   the loss of interest or pleasure in activities or a depressed mood state.

dermabrasion   a procedure in which the skin is surgically removed by chemicals, fine sandpaper, wire brush, or laser.

dermal regenerative graft   the grafting of a patient's own skin to be cultured or regenerated using a substance to promote growth for the grafting procedure.

dermatitis   an inflammation of the upper layer of the skin.

dermis   the thick layer of tissue located directly below the epidermis.

destruction   complete elimination.

dia-   prefix meaning "through" or "apart."

diabetes mellitus   a complex metabolic disease characterized by hyperglycemia caused by defects in insulin secretion, insulin action, or both.

Diagnostic and Statistical Manual of Mental Disorders, Fourth Revision (DSM-IV)   a publication containing the nomenclature established by the American Psychiatric Association.

diagnostic radiology   the use of X-rays to photograph specific areas to determine whether pathology is present.

diaphragm   the structure that separates the thoracic cavity from the abdominal cavity.

diastolic blood pressure   the pressure on the arterial walls during relaxation of the heart muscle.

diff   identifies the percentage of each type of white cell relative to the total number of leukocytes. Also known as differential white blood count or differential leukocyte count.

differential leukocyte count   identifies the percentage of each type of white cell relative to the total number of leukocytes. Also known as differential white blood count or diff.

differential white blood cell count   identifies the percentage of each type of white cell relative to the total number of leukocytes. Also known as diff or differential leukocyte count.

dilation   the expansion of, usually of an opening.

dilation and curettage (D&C)   a procedure in which the cervix is opened up or dilated; then the uterus is scraped clean with an instrument.

diplo-   a medical prefix meaning "pairs," in reference to arrangements of bacteria.

direct inguinal hernia   a protrusion in the groin area.

disarticulation   amputation through a joint.

dislocation   the displacement of any part of a bone from its normal position in a joint.

diverticula   pouches or sacs in the lining of the intestine.

diverticulitis   when the sacs or pouches become inflamed.

diverticulosis   a condition of diverticula without inflammation.

dorsopathy   a disorder of the back.

drainage   the removal of fluid, usually with a tube.

drug abuse   taking drugs to excess but not having a dependence on them.

drug dependence   a chronic use of drugs that creates a compulsion to take them in order to experience their effects.

drug-eluting stent   a stent coated with a time-released drug that assists in restoring blood flow.

dual code assignment   occurs when two codes are needed to code a diagnostic statement.

duodenal ulcer   an ulcer that occurs in the upper part of the small intestine.

duodenum   where the small intestine begins.

dysplasia of cervix   the abnormal development or growth of cells of the cervix.

E

echogram   the record that is generated by an ultrasound.

E codes   codes that classify external causes.

E. coli   a common term for *Escherichia coli*.

-ectomy   suffix meaning "cut out by surgical means."

ectopic pregnancy   a pregnancy that occurs outside the uterus.

electrocardiogram (EKG, ECG)   an electrical record of the activity of the heart.

electrode   one end is attached to the apex of the heart and other is attached to the pulse generator.

electrode catheter   sometimes used on patients to induce or stop cardiac arrhythmias.

electrolysis   the removal of hair by the use of electric current.

em-   prefix meaning "in."

embolus   an occlusion in the vessel, which can be a clot, foreign object, air, or gas, that obstructs the blood flow through the vessel.

embryo   the developing child through the eighth week of pregnancy.

emphysema   a loss of lung function due to the progressive decrease in the number of alveoli in the bronchus of the lung.

empyema   an infection in the pleural cavity.

enamel   the hard tissue of the teeth.

en bloc   a term meaning "to remove as a whole."

encapsulated   enclosed or surrounded by a capsule.

encephalitis   an inflammation of the brain.

encephalomyelitis   an inflammation of both the brain and the spinal cord.

endocarditis   an inflammation of the inner layer of the heart.

endocardium   the innermost wall or lining of the heart.

endocrine system   glands and structures used to produce or secrete hormones.

endometriosis   an abnormal growth of the endometrium outside the uterus.

endoscopic   the visual inspection of inside the body.

endoscopic procedure   performed by inserting a scope into the body or structure for visual examination.

end-stage renal disease (ESRD)   when chronic renal failure progresses to late stages.

enteritis   an inflammation of the intestines.

epicardium   the outermost wall of the heart.

epidermis   the outermost layer of the skin.

epididymectomy   the surgical removal of the epididymis.

epididymis   a tubular structure found at the upper end of each testicle.

epiglottidectomy   the removal of the epiglottis.

epiglottis   the structure at the base of the tongue that keeps food from entering the larynx and the trachea.

epikeratophakia   a procedure that requires the placement of stitches to connect a corneal graft to the central part of the cornea for correction of a missing lens from the eye.

epilepsy   a transient disturbance of cerebral function that is recurrent and characterized by episodes of seizures.

epiphysis   located in the joint, the point of active growth for bones.

episiotomy   an incision made at the vaginal opening to prevent tearing during delivery.

epistaxis   nosebleed.

erythematosquamous dermatosis   a condition that presents as a scaly inflammation on the scalp and face.

erythrocyte count   identifies the number of red blood cells found in a cubic millimeter of blood. Also known as red blood cell count or RBC.

erythrocytes   disc-shaped red blood cells that contain hemoglobin. Also known as red blood cells.

erythrocyte sedimentation rate (ESR)   measures the rate at which red blood cells settle out of unclotted blood in an hour. Also known as ESR or sed rate.

escharotomy   the surgical cutting into the edges of a scab formed by a burn.

Escherichia coli (E. coli)   a rod-shaped bacillus found in the large intestine of humans.

esophageal web   a congenital condition in which tissue extends across the esophagus, causing problems with swallowing.

esophagectomy   the excision of the esophagus.

esophagitis   an inflammation of the esophagus due to reflux of acid and pepsin from the stomach.

esophagogastrostomy   a procedure that is completed to remove part of a diseased esophagus and to surgically connect the remaining portion to another structure, such as the small bowel.

esophagomyotomy   an incision of the muscle tissue of the esophagus.

esophagoscopy   an endoscopic procedure completed to remove a foreign body, to biopsy a lesion, or to view the esophagus.

esophagus   an organ of the digestive system located directly behind the trachea that connects the throat to the stomach.

ethmoid sinuses   found in the ethmoid bone.

etiology   the cause of a disease.

eustachian tubes   located in the middle ear and leading to the nasopharynx.

evacuation   removal from; the coder is referred to the term "drainage."

evisceration   exposure through an open wound.

excision   surgical removal.

Excludes: used to signify that the conditions listed are not assigned to the chapter, section, category, or fourth- or fifth-digit code listed. Also known as an exlusion note.

exclusion note   used to signify that the conditions listed are not assigned to the chapter, section, category, or fourth- or fifth-digit code listed. Also known as an Excludes:.

exploration   a procedure used to establish a diagnosis.

exteriorization   a surgical procedure that moves a structure of the body to the exterior of the body.

external fixation device   device such as a wire, pin, or screw placed through the soft tissue into the bone and then held in place with an external device, with the purpose of stabilizing a fractured bone.

extracorporeal circulation   a procedure in which a pump completes the work of the heart and oxygenates blood throughout the body while heart surgery is being performed.

extracorporeal shock wave lithotripsy   a procedure in which kidney stones are broken up by a machine that is positioned outside the body and that generates high-voltage waves to break up the stones inside the body.

extraperitoneal cesarean section   a procedure for the removal of a fetus from an infected uterus. An incision is usually made in the lower portion of the uterus, but entry is not made into the peritoneal cavity.

F

fallopian tubes   the organ that allows the eggs to travel from the ovaries to the uterus.

false vocal cords   an organ that function to keep food and liquid out of the lungs.

family history code   used to indicate that a patient has one or more family members who have had a particular disease.

fascia   connective tissue that not only covers but supports and separates muscles.

female genitalia   function in reproduction and as part of the urinary system; made up of the uterus, vagina, ovaries, fallopian tubes, cervix, perineum, clitoris, labia, and mammary glands.

femoral hernia   a protrusion of the intestine at the femoral ring.

fenestration   a procedure that is done in the labyrinth of the ear in which a surgical opening is formed to restore hearing.

fetal immaturity   a birth weight of less than 1,000 grams.

fetoscopy   a procedure in which a scope is used to view the fetus in the amniotic sac. Also known as a amnioscopy or laparo-amnioscopy.

fetus   the developing child from the ninth week until delivery.

fibrocystic disease of the breast   the presence of a single or multiple cysts of the breast.

filling   a general procedure in which a dentist repairs a hole in the enamel of a tooth

fistulization   the surgical production of an artificial channel.

forceps delivery   the use of an instrument that has two blades and a handle and that is inserted to assist the fetus through the birth canal.

foreskin   a structure that covers and protects the glans penis.

fracture (Fx)   a broken bone resulting from undue force or pathological changes.

fragmentation of stones   the breaking apart of stones.

free skin graft   a graft in which the donor tissue is completely removed from its site before it is applied to the recipient site.

frenulum   a small section of mucous membrane that limits the movement of an organ.

frontal sinuses   mucosa-lined air spaces within the frontal bones.

fulguration   a procedure in which a high-frequency electric current is used to destroy the skin.

full thickness excision   the excision of the full thickness of the skin and subcutaneous layers of the skin.

fungi   microscopic plant life that lack chlorophyll and must have a source of matter for nutrition because they cannot manufacture their own food.

furuncle   a staphylococcal infection around hair follicles. Also known as a boil.

fusion   the coming together.

G

gallbladder   stores bile until it is needed for digestion.

gastric ulcer   the erosion of the membrane of the stomach.

gastroduodenostomy   an anastomosis that connects the stomach directly to the duodenum.

gastroesophageal reflux disease (GERD)   the reflux of gastric contents into the esophagus.

gastrointestinal (GI) tract   pertaining to the stomach and intestines.

gastrojejunal ulcer   an ulcer that occurs in the stomach and jejunum.

gastrotomy   a surgical incision made into the stomach.

genital prolapse   the downward displacement of the genital organs.

geographic tongue   a condition in which irregularly shaped patches show on the tongue and resemble land forms on a map.

gestational diabetes   a condition that can occur during the second and third trimesters of pregnancy in women who were not diabetic prior to pregnancy.

gingiva   the mucous membrane that covers the lower part of the tooth and roots and also covers the bone of the jaw. Also called gums.

gingivoplasty   a type of repair performed on gum tissue.

glans penis   the soft tip of the penis.

glaucoma   caused by intraocular pressure, which can damage the optic nerve and lead to blindness.

glomerulonephritis   an inflammation of the glomeruli of the kidney.

glosso-   a prefix meaning "tongue."

glucose   used by the cells to properly function, supplying energy for the body's metabolic functions.

goiter   the enlargement of the thyroid gland.

goniopuncture   a procedure sometimes used in the treatment of glaucoma.

gout   a form of arthritis, commonly of the peripheral joints, that can become disabling when an acute attack occurs; caused by too much uric acid in the blood, which in some patients forms hard crystals in the joint area.

graft   a transplant of any tissue.

-gram   a suffix meaning "a drawing."

Gram-negative bacteria   the stain test for bacterial meningitis identification in which the dye turns from violet to colorless.

Gram-positive bacteria   the stain test for bacterial meningitis identification in which the dye retains the violet color.

grand mal   the most severe form of a seizure.

granulocytes   a type of leukocyte that has granular appearance.

-graph   a suffix meaning an "instrument that records."

gravida   pregnant woman.

gums   mucous membrane that covers the lower part of the tooth and roots and also covers the bone of the jaw. Also called gingiva.

H

hair   a form of protection used by the body to keep foreign material from entering through the skin.

hallux valgus   a bunion.

hammer toe   a condition in which the first phalanx shows dorsal flexion and there is plantar flexion of the second and third phalanges.

hard palate   bony part of the anterior portion of the roof of the mouth.

harelip   a congenital defect that results in a deep groove or opening of the lip, running upward to the nose. Also called a cleft lip.

healed myocardial infarction   when a patient has had an myocardial infarction in the past but currently is not experiencing any symptoms. Also called an old myocardial infarction.

Healthcare Common Procedure Coding System (HCPCS)   the coding book that contains alphanumeric codes for durable medical equipment and certain drugs.

Health Insurance Portability and Accountability Act of 1996 (HIPAA)   law passed by Congress to improve the portability and continuity of healthcare coverage.

heart   a muscular organ located between the lungs and to the left of the midline of the body, which pumps blood throughout the body.

heart attack   occurs when there is inadequate blood supply to a section or sections of the heart. Also known as a myocardial infarction.

heart failure   a decreased ability of the heart to pump a sufficient amount of blood to the body's tissue.

heavy-for-dates   birth weight of 4,500 grams or more regardless of gestation period.

helminths   parasitic organisms that include flatworms, roundworms, and flukes.

hematocrit (Hct)   determines the percentage of red blood cells in whole blood. Also known as packed cell volume.

hematopoietic   pertaining to the formation of blood cells.

hematuria   a condition in which blood appears in the urine.

hemilaryngectomy   a procedure in which half of the larynx is removed.

hemimaxillectomy   half of the maxilla is surgically removed and reconstructed using prosthetics or bone grafting.

hemiparesis   a condition in which one side of the body is paralyzed due to brain hemorrhage, cerebral thrombosis, embolus, or a tumor of the cerebrum. Also known as hemiplegia.

hemiplegia   a condition in which one side of the body is paralyzed due to brain hemorrhage, cerebral thrombosis, embolus, or a tumor of the cerebrum. Also known as hemiparesis.

hemispherectomy   the excision of a cerebral hemisphere.

hemodialysis   a procedure that filters waste from the blood.

hemoglobin (Hgb)   absorbs oxygen and transports the oxygen to the tissue of the body.

hemolysis   the destruction of red blood cells of the fetal blood can occur when the antibodies from the mother cross the placenta into the fetus.

hemolytic anemia a type of anemia that occurs when red blood cells are broken down at a faster rate than bone marrow can produce them; thus, there is an abnormal reduction of red blood cells.

hemorrhoids enlarged veins in or near the anus.

hepatic pertaining to the liver.

hepato- prefix that refers to the liver.

hepatopexy the surgical repair of the liver.

hepatotomy a surgical incision made into the liver.

hernia a bulging or protrusion through tissue of a structure or part of a structure.

herniated disc a rupture of the material in the center of the disc.

heterograft a tissue graft from an animal.

heterografting the grafting of nonhuman material, such as pigskin, to the donor.

hiatal hernia a type of hernia that pushes the stomach upward into the mediastinal cavity through the diaphragm.

high gastric bypass a procedure in which the jejunum and the upper portion of the stomach are connected by anastomosis and completely bypass the duodenum.

hirsutism excessive hair growth.

hives an allergic disorder marked by raised red patches of skin or mucous membrane.

homograft the grafting of human material.

hormones chemical substance produced by the body to keep organs and tissues functioning properly.

host the organism that a parasite lives off of or within.

hydrocele an accumulation of fluid in the scrotum surrounding the testes.

hydrocephalus an accumulation of fluid within the cranial meninges.

hypertension an increase in the systolic blood pressure, the diastolic blood pressure, or both.

hypertension table the table within the Alphabetic Index of ICD-9-CM that directs the coder to locate codes for various forms of hypertension.

hypertensive heart disease heart disease that is due to hypertension.

hypertensive chronic kidney disease renal diseases that are caused by hypertension.

hyperthyroidism the thyroid oversecretes hormones, causing excessive amounts of thyroid hormones in the blood.

hypotension low blood pressure.

hypothyroidism underactive thyroid, resulting in a deficiency of thyroid hormone secretions.

hypoxia below-normal levels of oxygen in the cells.

hysterectomy the removal of the uterus.

hystero- prefix meaning "pertaining to the uterus."

I

ICD-8 an abbreviation for *International Classification of Diseases, Eighth Revision.*

ICD-9-CM an abbreviation for *International Classification of Diseases, Ninth Revision, Clinical Modification.*

ICD-9-CM Official Guidelines for Coding and Reporting a way of assisting coders in consistently assigning correct ICD-9-CM codes.

IDDM insulin-dependent diabetes mellitus.

ileostomy a surgical passage created to exteriorize a segment of the ileum.

ileum the last part of the small intestine.

impacted tooth a tooth that is lodged below the gumline, usually causing problems to the surrounding teeth.

implant to insert an object or material.

incision a surgical cut into tissue.

incision and drainage (I&D) the surgically cutting and withdrawal of fluid from the skin.

Includes: used to define or give examples of the content of the chapter section, category, or subcategory code. Also known as an inclusion note.

inclusion note used to define or give examples of the content of the chapter section, category, or subcategory code. Also known as an Include:.

inclusive part of a more complete procedure.

incomplete abortion abortion in which all the products of conception have not been expelled from the uterus.

incomplete prolapse when the uterus descends into the introitus.

incus the anvil-shaped bone in the middle ear; one of the auditory ossicles.

Index to Diseases and Injuries the section of volume 2 that is the key to the coding system.

indirect inguinal hernia a hernia sac that extends through the inguinal ring and into the inguinal canal, sometimes descending into the scrotum.

induction of labor requires administering medication to force the fetus to begin movement through the birth canal.

infantile cerebral palsy a disorder that is present at birth, is chronic and nonprogressive, and impairs motor function of the brain.

infectious diseases diseases that occur when a pathogen invades the body.

inferior vena cava the main vein through which blood flows from the lower portion of the body to the heart.

infundibulectomy excision of the funnel-shaped structure around the outflow tract of the valves.

infusion a form of injection when the needle is placed intravenously and medication is passed for a length of time that can span from minutes to days.

inguinal canal tubular structure that passes through the lower layers of the abdominal wall.

inguinal hernia occurs when a part of the intestine passes through a weak point or tear in the wall that holds the abdominal organs.

inhaled medication is passed through a device that allows the patient to breathe in the medication through the nose and mouth.

injection a process in which a needle is inserted into the skin, medication is delivered, and the needle is removed.

inlay a type of restoration by which a molded filling is cemented in.

insertion to put into.

instructional notations phrases or notes that appear in all three volumes of the code book and provide information related to code selection.

insufflation   a procedure used to test the viability of the fallopian tube by introducing a gas or a liquid, such as saline, under pressure into the fallopian tube.

insulin   used within the body to process glucose.

insulin-dependent diabetes mellitus (IDDM)   a form of diabetes mellitus in which the patient uses insulin.

integumentary   pertaining to a covering or outer layer.

integumentary system   another name for the skin.

internal fixation   an open procedure using wire, pins, plates, and screws to correct a fracture.

internal hordeolum   a localized swelling of the eyelid resulting from an obstruction of a sebaceous gland of the eyelid. Also known as chalazion, meibomian cyst, or tarsal cyst.

International Classification of Diseases, Ninth Revision (ICD-9-CM)   developed by the World Health Organization to arrange and classify diagnosis codes, the ninth revision.

International Classification of Diseases, Ninth Revision, Clinical Modification   an arrangement of classes or groups of diagnoses and procedures by systematic division.

intervertebral disc   a structure located between the bones of the spinal column that are made up of cartilage and that cushion the vertebrae.

intestine   an organ that is made up of the small and large intestines.

intra-   a suffix meaning "within."

iridotomy   a surgical cutting or incision into the iris.

iris   the colored part of the eye.

iron deficiency anemia   a type of anemia that occurs when there is an insufficient supply of iron in the blood.

ischemic heart disease   occurs when there is an inadequate supply of blood to the heart that is caused by a blockage.

isoimmunization   the immunization or incompatability of the blood of an Rh-negative mother mixing with the Rh-positive blood of the fetus.

isolation   when a patient is admitted for placement in a private area to protect the patient from exposure to infectious diseases.

italicized brackets   used to enclose a second code that must be assigned when coding.

J

jaundice   excess bilirubin is released into the bloodstream. Also known as hyperbilirubinemia.

jejunum   the middle portion of the small intestine.

joint replacement   a procedure in which a prosthetic implant is surgically placed in the joint area.

joints   allow for bending and rotating movements.

juvenile diabetes   can occur between birth and adulthood, in which the pancreas is not functioning properly or at all in the production of insulin. Also known as type I diabetes mellitus.

K

Kelly-Kennedy operation on the urethra   a procedure in which the connective tissue between the vagina and the bladder is sutured together to support the bladder and the urethra.

Kelly-Stoeckell urethral plication   a procedure in which the connective tissue between the vagina and the bladder is sutured together to support the bladder and the urethra.

keratoplasty   corneal grafting.

kidney   filters blood constantly to remove waste.

L

labor   the process by which the fetus moves from the uterus to birth.

labor and delivery   the process of childbirth.

labyrinths   the series of canals and chambers that make up the inner ear.

lacrimal structures   produce tears.

laparoamnioscopy   a procedure in which a scope is used to view the fetus in the amniotic sac. Also known as an amnioscopy or fetoscopy.

large intestine   part of the intestines that includes the cecum, colon, rectum, and anus.

larynx   made up of cartilage and ligaments, which compose the vocal cords.

laser   acronym meaning light amplification by the stimulated emission of radiation. The use of light amplification to emit focused radiation as a surgical technique is used not only in eye surgery but in many specialties.

late effect   the condition produced after the acute phase of an illness or injury has terminated.

lateral   away from the midline toward the side.

lavage   when an area is washed out or flushed.

legally induced abortion   an abortion that is induced by medical personnel working within the law.

Legionnaire's disease   occurs when a contaminated water source becomes airborne.

lensectomy   removal of lens of the eye; cataract surgery.

leukemia   cancer of the blood-forming organs in which the bone marrow is replaced with malignant cancer cells.

leukocyte count   identifies the number of white blood cells found in a cubic millimeter of blood. Also known as white blood cell count or WBC.

leukocytes   pale-colored cells with an irregular ball-like shape that provide the body's natural defense against injury and disease. Also known as white blood cells (WBCs).

ligaments   bands of connective tissue that connect the joints where the tendons connect muscle to bone.

ligation   to tie or bind off blood vessels or ducts using catgut, cotton, silk, or wire.

ligation of esophageal varices   the surgical tying off of esophageal veins that are dilated or painful.

ligation of peripheral lymphatics   the tying off of a peripheral duct.

light-for-dates   underweight infants that are showing signs of fetal malnutrition.

lingual tonsils   located on the posterior surface of the tongue.

lipoma   a benign neoplasm of adipose tissue.

liver   filters red blood cells, produces glycogen, and secretes bile.

lobar pneumonia   pneumonia in a lobe of the lung.

lobe   encases the structures of the lung.

lobectomy   the complete removal of a lobe of an organ such as the lung, the cerebrum, and the liver.

lungs   the organs where oxygen and carbon dioxide are exchanged.

lung transplant   a procedure in which a donor lung is transferred and implanted in the recipient.

lung volume reduction   the partial excision of multiple lobes in one or both of the lungs to help the lungs form a renewed expansion.

luxation   dislocation of a bone.

lymphangiogram   a radiographic study of the lymphatic vessels and nodes.

lymph nodes   provide a site for lymphocyte production, produce antibodies, and filter impurities such as viruses and bacteria from the body.

lymphoma   cancer of the lymph nodes and immune system.

-lysis   a suffix meaning "break up" or "dissolve."

M

macro-   a prefix meaning "large."

macrodactyly   a condition in which the fingers are abnormally large.

magnetic resonance imaging (MRI)   an imaging technique that uses a combination of a strong magnetic field and radio waves to produce images.

main terms   identify the disease, sign, symptom, condition, or injury to be coded.

male genitalia   function in reproduction and as part of the urinary system; made up of the scrotum, testicles, and penis.

malignant hypertension   a severe form of hypertension with common blood pressure reading of 200/140.

malignant neoplasm   the life-threatening, uncontrolled abnormal growth of cells. Also called cancerous growth.

malignant primary   the column of the neoplasm table that is used for the originating site of the tumor.

malignant secondary   the column of the neoplasm table that is used for the site where the neoplasm has spread from the originating site of the tumor.

malleus   the hammer-shaped bone in the middle ear; one of the auditory ossicles.

malocclusion   a condition in which the bite alignment is abnormal.

malunion fracture   occurs when the fracture site is malaligned.

mammo-   prefix meaning "pertaining to the breast."

mammotomy   the surgical incision of the breast.

manic-depressive episodes   occurrences of an elevated mood alternating with depressive episodes. Also known as bipolar disorder.

manipulation   movement in a skillful manner.

marsupialization   the creation of a pouch.

marsupialization of splenic cyst   an incision is made in a splenic cyst, and the cyst is sutured to create an open pouch.

mastectomy   the surgical removal of the breast.

masto-   prefix meaning "pertaining to the breast."

mastoidectomy   the removal of the mastoid process, or bony portion of the mastoid air cells behind the ear.

mastopexy   the correction of the breast by surgical fixation and plastic surgery.

mastotomy   a surgical incision of the breast.

maxillary sinuses   found in the maxillary bone.

mean corpuscular hemoglobin (MCH)   identifies the average weight of hemoglobin in an average red blood cell.

mean corpuscular hemoglobin concentration (MCHC)   measures the average concentration or percentage of hemoglobin within each red blood cell.

mean corpuscular volume (MCV)   describes the average size of an individual red blood cell in cubic microns.

meatus   the external auditory canal.

meconium   a tarlike material that collects in the intestine of the fetus and is usually the first stools of the newborn.

medial   the closest or nearest to the midline of a structure.

mediastinum   the space between the lungs in the thoracic cavity.

meibomian cyst   a localized swelling of the eyelid resulting from an obstruction of a sebaceous gland of the eyelid. Also called chalazion, tarsal cyst, or internal hordeolum.

melanocytes   cells that produce dark pigment.

melanoma   a fast-growing cancer of the skin.

meningitis   an inflammation of the membranes or the meninges of the spinal cord or brain.

menopause   a time in a woman's life when her menstrual cycle ceases.

mental retardation   the mind of the patient never fully develops.

metabolism   the rate at which energy is used by the body and the rate at which body functions occur.

metastasize   the spread of cancer cells that originate in one area of the body to other body parts.

metrio-   a prefix meaning "pertaining to the uterus."

metro-   a prefix meaning "pertaining to the uterus."

micro-   a prefix meaning "small."

micturate   urination or voiding.

mild mental retardation   an IQ of 50 to 70.

missed abortion   a fetus that has died before completion of 22 weeks' gestation with retention of the dead fetus or products of conception up to 4 weeks after demise.

mitral valve   the valve between the left atrium and left ventricle. Also called the bicuspid valve.

moderate mental retardation   an IQ of 35 to 49.

molar pregnancy   when a blighted ovum in the uterus develops into a mole.

molds   fungal infections caused by long filament-shaped fungi.

monilial vulvovaginitis   a fungal infection of the vulva and vagina. Also called candial vulvovaginitis.

Moniliasis   a fungal infection found mainly in the skin, nails, mouth, vagina, bronchi, or lungs but may invade the bloodstream. Now called candidiasis.

morbidity   a diseased state.

morphology   the form and structure of a cell.

mortality   the rate or frequency of death.

motor vehicle accident (MVA)   an accident that occurs on a roadway in a car or truck.

multiple gestation   indicates twins, triplets, quadruplets, or other specified multiple fetuses.

multiple sclerosis   an inflammatory disease of the central nervous system in which T cells and macrophages break down the myelin fibers.

muscles   a type of tissue that allows for movement of the body.

myelitis   an inflammation of the spinal cord.

myelo-   a prefix meaning "marrow, spinal cord."

myelopathy   disorder of the spinal cord.

myocardial infarction (MI)   occurs when there is inadequate blood supply to a section or sections of the heart. Also known as a heart attack.

myocarditis   inflammation of the heart muscle.

myocardium   the middle wall of the heart.

myotomy of the colon   a surgical incision into the muscular layer of the colon and local perfusion of the large and small intestine.

myringoplasty   the repair of the tympanic membrane that may have ruptured due to internal pressure or trauma.

myringotomy   an incision is made in the eardrum for tube placement.

N

nails   hardened cells of the epidermis.

nasal septum   divides the nasal cavity into two parts, posterior and anterior.

nasopharyngeal tonsils   adenoids.

National Center for Health Statistics (NCHS)   coordinates the modifications of the disease classification.

neck   in reference to the oral cavity, the part of the tooth where the crown and the root meet.

neoplasm   an ucontrolled abnormal growth of cells characterized as malignant or benign. Also called a tumor.

neoplasm of uncertain behavior   the neoplasm exhibits the characteristics of both benign and malignant behavior after pathological investigation.

neoplasm of unspecified nature   a neoplasm in which the behavior or morphology is not specified in the patient's medical record.

nephritis   an inflammation of the kidneys.

nephrons   work within the kidney to filter, reabsorb, and secrete urine.

nephropathy   a disease or disorder of the kidney. Also known as nephrosis.

nephropexy   the surgical fixation of a floating kidney.

nephroscopy   the use of optical instruments to examine the kidneys.

nephrosis   a disease or disorder of the kidney. Also known as nephropathy.

nephrostomy   the surgical insertion of a tube into the kidney to create an opening to the exterior of the body.

nephrotomy   an incision of the kidney.

nerve release   the surgical removal of pressure on nerves. Also known as decompression of nerves.

nervous system   the system that controls all the bodily activities.

neurolytic agents   material injected to cause the destruction of adhesions around a nerve.

neurotic disorders   disturbances or symptoms that cause a person to feel distressed.

neutropenia   an abnormal decrease of granular leukocytes in the blood occurring in patients who receive chemotherapy.

NIDDM   non-insulin-dependent diabetes mellitus.

non-insulin-dependent diabetes mellitus (IDDM)   a form of diabetes mellitus in which the patient does not use insulin.

nonmalignant tumors   usually non-life-threatening abnormal growths of cells. Also known as a benign neoplasm.

nonunion fracture   occurs when the fracture fragments fail to unite.

not elsewhere classifiable (NEC)   used with poorly defined terms to warn the coder that specified forms of the diagnosis being coded are classified to different code numbers. Used only if more precise information is not available.

not otherwise specified (NOS)   codes that are not specific and should be used only after the coder has clarified with provider that a more specific diagnosis is not available.

noxious influence   a substance that is harmful to one's health.

nuclear medicine   procedures that use radioactive or atomic energy to treat disease or to diagnose conditions.

O

obliteration of peripheral lymphatics   the process of surgically eliminating the peripheral duct.

obstetrical care   medical care that occurs during pregnancy and delivery.

obstetrical period   the time from pregnancy until six weeks after delivery.

obstetrical tamponade   the surgical use of a tampon to compress the uterus or vagina.

obstetrics   the medical specialty that treats women during pregnancy, childbirth, and the period immediately after childbirth.

obstructive lung disease   a decrease in airflow within the lungs.

occlusion   a blockage or constriction of an arterial blood vessel.

occult prolapse   when the umbilical cord is trapped in front of a shoulder or is expelled before the presenting part.

oddi   refers to Oddi's sphincter, which is located at the opening into the duodenum from the common bile duct.

old myocardial infarction   when a patient has had a myocardial infarction in the past but currently is not experiencing any symptoms. Also called a healed myocardial infarction.

-oma   a suffix meaning "tumor."

omit code   indicates that no code is assigned.

oophoro-   a prefix meaning "pertaining to the ovary."

oophorotomy   an incision of the ovary.

open biopsy   a removal of a piece of living tissue by making an incision to obtain the tissue.

open fracture   a fracture that has broken through the skin at the fracture site. Also known as a compound fracture.

open heart massage   the thoracic cavity is opened, and the surgeon actually massages the heart using rhythmic compressions.

open procedure   a procedure completed via an incision.

operation   a surgical procedure.

ophthalmoscopy   use of a scope to examine the eye.

opponensplasty   the reforming or restoration of opposing tendons.

opportunistic infections   caused by opportunistic parasites when a patient has a weakened immune system.

opportunistic mycotic infection a fungal infection that occurs in a compromised host, typically a patient who has a chronic disease or a weakened immune system.

opportunistic parasites yeast and molds that infect human tissue.

orbitotomy an incision of the orbit.

orchectomy the surgical removal of a testicle.

orchiectomy the surgical removal of a testicle.

orchiopexy the suturing of an undescended testicle in the scrotal sac.

orthodontics for correction of teeth that are out of alignment.

orthognathic refers to the branch of oral medicine relating to the treatment of bones of the jaw.

ossi- a prefix meaning "pertaining to the bone."

ossie- a prefix meaning "pertaining to the bone."

osteo- a prefix meaning "pertaining to the bone."

osteoarthritis (OA) the degeneration of the articular cartilage.

osteoarthrotomy a procedure in which the articular end of a bone is surgically removed.

osteomyelitis an inflammation of bone tissue and marrow caused by a bacterial organism.

osteopathy a disorder of the bone.

osteoporosis a reduction in bone mass.

osto- a prefix meaning "pertaining to the bone."

-ostomy a suffix meaning "formation of artificial opening."

otitis media fluid gets trapped in the middle ear, causing an acute inflammation. Also called an ear infection.

otoplasty the repair of the outer ear.

otosclerosis the stapes becomes fixed and does not move any more.

otoscope an instrument used to view the external ear canal and the middle ear.

ovarian cyst the encapsulated sac of the ovary that is filled with a semisolid or liquid material.

ovaries produce female hormones and eggs (ova).

ovario- prefix meaning "pertaining to the ovary."

overt prolapse occurs with ruptured membranes when the cord is in front of the presenting part.

P

packed cell volume (PCV) determines the percentage of red blood cells in whole blood. Also known as hematocrit.

packing a technique in which gauze is placed in the nose to provide pressure to stop bleeding.

palate the roof of the mouth, made up of the hard and soft palates.

palatine tonsils the pair of tonsils that are visible through the mouth and come off the soft palate to the base of the tongue.

pancreas functions in both the digestive and endocrine systems, secreting the juices necessary for digestion and releasing the hormone insulin.

papillary muscles small endocardial muscles that open the heart valves.

para a woman has produced a viable infant weighing over 500 grams or reaching the age of over 20 weeks' gestation; a prefix meaning "beside" or "near."

paracentesis a surgical puncture of the abdominal cavity for the aspiration of fluid.

paracervical uterine denervation a procedure in which there is the surgical destruction of the nerve impulse pathways of the uterus.

paralysis the loss of sensation or voluntary motion, which may be permanent or temporary, depending on the type and site of the injury.

paranasal sinuses the sinuses as a group.

parasite lives on or in another organism to nourish itself.

parasitic diseases occur when an organism lives on or in another organism.

parasympathetic nervous system controls digestion, the constriction of the pupil of the eye, and smooth-muscle contraction.

parentheses used around terms providing additional information about the main diagnostic term.

Parkinson's disease a progressive disease characterized by a masklike facial expression, weakened muscles, trembling, and involuntary movement.

parotid glands a pair of salivary glands located at the side of the face just below and in front of the ears.

partial nephrectomy removal of part of a kidney.

partial placenta previa when the placenta covers part of the cervical os.

partial splenectomy removal of a part of the spleen.

partial-thickness excision describes the thickness of the cutting done to accomplish the excision.

pathogen a microorganism that can cause disease in humans.

pathologic fracture a break of diseased bone that occurs from a minor stress or injury and that would not normally occur in healthy bone.

pedicle graft a type of graft that remains attached to its blood supply.

PEG tube a procedure that involves the surgical placement of a tube into the stomach through the abdominal wall. Also known as percutaneous endoscopic gastrostomy.

pelvic evisceration an extensive surgery in which the uterus, vagina, ovaries, tubes, bladder, and urethra are removed.

penis male sex organ that is made up of the glans penis and the prepuce.

peptic ulcer an open sore of the mucous membrane at the lower end of the esophagus entering the stomach.

percutaneous aspiration of seminal vesicles the removal of fluid by the insertion of an instrument through the body wall.

percutaneous endoscopic gastrostomy the surgical placement of a tube into the stomach through the abdominal wall. Also known as a PEG tube placement.

percutaneous jejunostomy done endoscopically (PEJ) an endoscopic procedure in which a tube is guided into the jejunum.

percutaneous transluminal coronary angioplasty (PTCA) a procedure in which the obstructed artery is opened up by inserting a balloon-tipped catheter to the affected part of the artery.

perfusion a process by which fluid is run through the structure.

perianal tissue the tissue around the anus.

periapical abscess   an infection of the pulp and surrounding tissue.

pericardiocentesis   a procedure in which a needle is surgically inserted into the pericardium and fluid is removed.

pericarditis   an inflammation of the outer layers of the heart.

pericardium   the sac that encloses the heart.

perilymphatic tap   the puncture of a fluid sac that has formed in the inner ear cavity.

perimenopausal   when symptoms of menopause begin.

perinatal period   a period of time before birth, which can include time of delivery, and up to 28 days after birth.

perineal prostratectomy   the removal of the prostate by making a perineal incision.

perineum   the area between the vaginal opening and the anus.

peripheral nervous system (PNS)   is the part of the nervous system that directly branches off the central nervous system.

perirectal area   the area surrounding the rectum.

peritonitis   an inflammation of the lining of the abdominal cavity.

pernicious anemia   a severe anemia marked by a decrease in the number and increase in the size of the red blood cells.

personal history code   explains a patient's past medical condition that no longer exists.

personality disorders   defined as a pattern of maladaptive and inflexible traits that last throughout an individual's lifetime.

petit mal   a less severe form of a seizure.

phacoemulsification   the use of ultrasound to break up the lens; then the material is flushed and aspirated at the same time.

pharmaceuticals   the use of medication or a combination of medications to treat a condition.

pharyngitis   a sore throat.

pharynx   acts as a passage for air as part of the respiratory tract, as well as for food and liquid as part of the digestive tract. Also called the throat.

phlebitis   an inflammation of a vein.

phlebography   the use of contrast material to take images of the veins.

physical therapy   treatment offered by trained professional who uses exercise, massage, and other forms of physical movement to treat diseases or disorders.

pineal gland   located in the brain near the corpus callosum and associated with the onset of puberty.

pinealectomy   the removal of the pineal gland.

pinna   the outer part of the ear, sometimes called the auricle.

placenta   an organ that is present during pregnancy and that is the site of metabolic exchange between the mother and fetus.

placenta previa   the abnormal positioning of the placenta in the lower uterus that partially or completely covers the cervical os.

plasma   the liquid portion of the blood without its cellular elements.

-plasty   a suffix meaning a "type of surgical repair."

platelets   ovoid-shaped structures that function in the initiation of blood-clotting or coagulation. Also known as thrombocytes.

pleura   the thin serous membrane that covers the lobe.

pleurectomy   a procedure in which the pleura is removed.

pleurisy   an inflammation of the thoracic cavity.

plication   the tucking or folding of a structure or tissue.

plication of uterine ligaments   a procedure in which the ligaments of the uterus are tucked.

pneumonectomy   the complete removal of a lung and lung tissue.

pneumonia   a condition in which exudates and pus infiltrate the lung and cause an inflammation.

pneumoperitoneum   procedure in which the gas or air is forced into the peritoneum.

POA indicator   an indicator that reports diagnosis and external cause of injury codes that are present at the time a patient is admitted.

poisoning   when a drug, chemical, or biological substance has been taken by a patient when it was not given under the direction of a physician.

polycystic kidney disease   a slowly progressive disorder in which the normal tissue of the kidneys is replaced with multiple grapelike cysts.

polyp   a growth on mucous membrane.

polypectomy   the removal of growth or polyp with snare or forceps.

portal vein thrombosis   the formation of a blood clot in the main vein of the liver.

postconcussion syndrome   term that describes the symptoms after a concussion, such as headache, fatigue, depression, and anxiety.

posterior   the opposite of anterior, in back of or behind.

postmenopausal   when a woman has not had a period for at least one year until the time she celebrates her 100th birthday.

postpartum   period immediately after delivery and lasting for six weeks.

postpartum complication   any complication occurring within the six-week period after delivery.

premenopausal   the time period right before menopause.

prenatal period   the time surrounding the birth of a child up to 28 days after birth.

prepuce   covers and protects the glans penis.

pressure ulcers   a form of decubitus ulcer. Also known as bedsores.

preterm infant   birth that is before completion of 40 weeks with a birth weight of 1,000–2,499 grams.

primary osteoarthritis   a form of localized osteoarthritis, most often affecting the joints of the spine, knee, hip, and small joints of the hands and feet.

principal diagnosis   a condition esablished after the study to be chiefly responsible for occasioning the admission or encounter of the patient.

procedure   a type of surgery or operation.

proctostomy   the surgical creation of an opening between the rectum and the body's surface.

profound mental retardation   an IQ of under 20.

prostate gland   secretes a fluid that is part of the semen and also aids in the motility of the sperm.

prothrombin time   measures the time it takes for blood to clot. Also known as protime.

protime   an abbreviation for prothrombin time.

protozoa one-celled organisms that live on living matter and are classified by how they move.

psychosis a mental disorder that interferes with a person's ability to carry on the activities of daily living.

pterygium a wing-shaped growth of the conjunctiva.

Public Law 104-191 actual law number for the Health Insurance Portability and Accountability Act of 1996.

puerperium relates to the postpartum period.

pulmonary artery carries deoxygenated blood from the heart to the lungs, where oxygen and carbon dioxide are exchanged.

pulmonary valve one of the main valves of the heart that sits between the pulmonary artery and the right ventricle.

pulmonary vein carries oxygenated blood back to the heart.

pulp the center of a tooth.

pulpitis an abscess of the pulp.

pulse generator the part of the pacemaker containing lithium battery as its source of power.

puncture to pierce or penetrate with a sharp instrument.

purging a process of isolating and purifying the transplanted bone marrow.

purpura an accumulation of blood under the skin that forms multiple pinpoint hemorrhages.

pyeloscopy the use of optical instruments to examine the renal pelvis.

pyelostomy the insertion of a tube into the renal pelvis.

pyelotomy an incision into the renal pelvis.

pyloromyotomy an incision into the muscles of the pylorus.

pyloroplasty a surgical correction of the pylorus to relieve an obstruction.

pylorus a narrow passageway between the stomach and the duodenum at the start of the small intestine.

R

radical excision the resection or removal of lymph nodes down to muscle and deep fascia.

radical orchiectomy the surgical removal of both testicles and two epididymides.

radical prostatectomy the surgical removal of the seminal vesicles, the entire prostate, and the surrounding tissue.

radiography a noninvasive way to look at the internal structures of the body through gamma rays or X-rays.

reconstruction rebuilding.

reconstruction of peripheral lymphatics the surgical reforming of a peripheral duct.

rectocele the herniation of the posterior vaginal wall with the anterior wall of the rectum.

rectum the part of the colon at the distal end of the large intestine.

red blood cell count identifies the number of red blood cells found in a cubic millimeter of blood. Also known as RBC or erythrocyte count.

red blood cells (RBC) disc-shaped blood cells that contain hemoglobin.

reduction correcting or moving back into place.

regional enteritis a form of inflammatory bowel disease that can cause thickening and scarring of the abdominal wall. Also known as Crohn's disease.

regional excision the removal of pathologies grouped together in a region of the body.

Registered Health Information Administrator (RHIA) a level of certification and credentialing by the AHIMA.

Registered Health Information Technician (RHIT) a level of certification and credentialing by the AHIMA.

Registered Medical Assistant (RMA) a student who has completed a college level program approved by the U.S. Department of Education and who is able to sit for RMA credentialing.

reimplantation tissue of one organ area is moved to another part of that organ.

release of carpal tunnel the relief of compression of the median nerve at the wrist.

release of tarsal tunnel the relief of compression of the tibial nerve at the ankle.

removal taking out completely.

repair fixing.

replacement inserting tissue, organ, or maintenance devices needed for proper function.

resection the complete or partial removal of a structure.

resection of a quadrant of a breast the removal of one of the quadrants of the breast.

respiratory failure a severe condition that interrupts the flow of oxygen or carbon dioxide to the point at which the patient is in extreme danger.

respiratory system comprises the structures that exchange oxygen and carbon dioxide in the body.

respiratory therapy a form of treatment administered by a trained professional who uses various techniques to assist and enhance a patient's respiratory function.

retina the innermost layer of the eye, where the rods and cones are located, which distinguish color from black and white.

retrograde a term used to describe an imaging process by which a contrast medium is injected into the body against the normal direction of blood flow.

retropubic prostatectomy a procedure completed by making an abdominal direct incision into the prostatic capsule.

revascularization procedure used to restore blood flow to the heart.

revision surgically correcting or fixing.

rheumatism a disorder of the joints, muscles, tendons, and their attachments; an inflammation of the connective tissues.

rheumatoid arthritis (RA) a disease of the autoimmune system in which the synovial membranes are inflamed and thickened.

rhino- a prefix meaning "nose."

rhinoscopy a diagnostic procedure done with the scope to examine the nose.

rhytidectomy wrinkle removal.

rib resection the removal of a rib.

root the part of the tooth below the gumline.

root canal mainly done to treat damaged tissue or roots of a tooth to try and save the tooth before extraction.

rotator cuff repair the correction of the musculomembrane that surrounds the capsule of the shoulder joint.

-rrhage a suffix meaning "abnormal or excessive bleeding."

-rrhagia a suffix meaning "abnormal or excessive bleeding."

-rrhaphy a suffix meaning "surgical repair by sutures or stitches."

-rrhea   a suffix meaning "abnormal discharge of body fluids."

-rrhexis   a suffix meaning "rupture."

Rubin's test   a type of insufflation procedure in which carbon dioxide is introduced into the fallopian tube and the uterus.

S

saliva   an enzyme in saliva that mixes with chewed food, beginning digestion.

salivary glands   secrete saliva.

salpingo-   prefix meaning "pertaining to the fallopian tubes."

salpingo-oophorotomy   surgically cutting into the ovary and fallopian tubes.

sarcoma   cancer of supportive tissue, such as blood vessels, bones, cartilage, and muscles.

scarification   the production of many tiny scratches or punctures that are superficial.

schizophrenic disorder   a psychotic disorder characterized by disruptive behavior, hallucinations, delusions, and disorganized speech.

sclera   the white part of the eye.

scleral buckling   a procedure used in the correction of retinal detachment.

-scopy   a suffix meaning visual examination of the interior.

scrotal sac   encloses, protects, and supports the testicles. Also known as the scrotum.

scrotum   the structure that encloses, protects, and supports the testicles. Also known as the scrotal sac.

sebaceous cyst of the breast   an encapsulated cyst of a sebaceous gland of the breast that contains yellowish, fatty material.

sebaceous glands   located in the skin and produce an oily secretion that conditions the skin.

secondary diagnosis   conditions that coexist at the time of admission or encounter that affect the treatment received or length of stay.

secondary hypertension   high arterial blood pressure due to another disease such as central nervous system disorders, renal disorders, and endocrine and vascular diseases.

secondary osteoarthritis   a localized osteoarthritis that is most often due to illness or injury.

Section I—Conventions, General Coding Guidelines and Chapter-Specific Guidelines   the first section in the ICD-9-CM Official Guidelines for Coding and Reporting; outlines coding guidelines.

Section II—Selection of Principal Diagnosis   the second section in the ICD-9-CM Official Guidelines for Coding and Reporting; outlines the selection of principal diagnosis.

Section III—Reporting Additional Diagnoses   the third section in the ICD-9-CM Official Guidelines for Coding and Reporting; outlines the selection of additional diagnosis.

Section IV—Diagnostic Coding and Reporting Guidelines for Outpatient Services   the fourth section in the ICD-9-CM Official Guidelines for Coding and Reporting; outlines the selection of codes for outpatient services.

sections   contain a series of three-digit category codes that code conditions or related conditions.

Section I   Conventions, General Coding Guidelines, and Chapter-Specific Guidelines

Section II   Selection of Principal Diagnosis

Section III   Reporting Additional Diagnosis

Section IV   Diagnostic Coding and Reporting Guidelines for Outpatient Services

sed rate   measures the rate at which red blood cells settle out of unclotted blood in an hour.

See: instructs the coder to cross-reference the term or diagnosis that follows the notation.

See also: refers the coder to another location in the Alphabetical Index when the initial listing does not contain all the necessary information to accurately select a code.

see category   signals the coder to reference a specific category in the Tabular List.

sepsis   the systemic inflammatory response syndrome due to infection.

septicemia   a systemic infection with the presence of pathological organisms or their toxins in the blood.

septic shock   sepsis with hypotension, which is a failure of the cardiovascular system.

septoplasty   the repair of the septum.

septum   a dividing wall.

sequestrectomy   a procedure in which a piece of necrosed bone is removed.

severe mental retardation   an IQ of 20 to 34.

severe sepsis   sepsis with organ dysfunction.

shunt   used to connect two structures or to divert or bypass an area.

sialoadenectomy   the removal of a salivary gland.

sickle-cell anemia   occurs when a patient receives the genetic trait from both parents and therefore develops an abnormal type of hemoglobin in the red blood cells, causing decreased oxygenation in the tissues.

sickle-cell trait   an asymptomatic condition in which the patient received the genetic trait for sickle-cell anemia from only one parent.

sigmoid colon   the S-shaped part of the colon that connects to the rectum.

sign   can be measured or evaluated; part of the objective information.

significant procedure   any procedure that carries an anesthetic or procedural risk, is surgical in nature, or requires the provider to have specialized training in order to complete the procedure.

simple fracture   a type of fracture in which the bone is broken but the skin has not been broken. Also known as a closed or complete fracture.

single code assignment   occurs when only one code is needed to code a diagnostic statement.

sinuostomy   an incision into the sinus cavity.

sinuses   air spaces located in bones around the nasal cavity.

slanted brackets   enclose a second code that must be assigned when coding.

small intestine   part of the intestines that begins at the pyloric sphincter and includes the duodenum, jejunum, ileum, and the ileocecal sphincter.

soft palate   is found in the posterior portion of the roof of the mouth and closes off the nasal passage when swallowing.

sonogram   the record that is generated by an ultrasound.

spermatocele   a cyst of the epididymis that contains sperm.

spermatocelectomy a surgical removal of a cyst of the epididymis.

sphenoid sinuses found in the sphenoid bone.

spina bifida congenital condition in which there is failure of the spinal canal to close around the spinal cord.

spinal fusion a procedure that joins two or more vertebrae to immobilize part of the spine.

spinal tap the penetration of the spinal subarachnoid space to remove cerebrospinal fluid to detect abnormal substances and variations in the fluid from examination, pressure recording, or injection.

spirilla the plural of spirillum.

spirillum a spiral, corkscrew-shaped, or slightly curved bacterium.

spleen filters microorganisms and other material from the blood, forms lymphocytes and monocytes, removes and destroys worn-out red blood cells, stores erythrocytes, and balances the amount of red blood cells and plasma in circulation.

spondylosis an inflammation of the vertebrae.

spontaneous abortion the complete or incomplete expulsion of products of conception before a pregnancy goes beyond 22 weeks' gestation.

sprain an injury to a joint, specifically the ligament of the joint, which becomes stretched.

square brackets enclose synonyms, alternative wording, abbreviations, or explanatory phrases.

stapedectomy the surgical removal of part or all of the stapes.

stapes stirrup-shaped bone in the middle ear; one of the auditory ossicles.

staphylo- a medical prefix meaning "clustered," in reference to the arrangement of bacteria.

status asthmaticus a severe asthmatic attack that does not respond to treatment.

status code a code that indicates that a patient is either a carrier of a disease or has the residual of a past disease or condition.

stenosis the narrowing of the cerebral arteries that supply blood to the brain.

stent in relation to coronary procedures, a small device used to support a vessel but still allow fluid or blood to pass through.

sternotomy a splitting of the sternum.

stoma an artificially created opening between two passages.

stomach a pouchlike structure that connects to the esophagus on one end and to the duodenum on the other end.

strain an injury to the muscle or to the tendon attachment of a joint.

strangulated hernia a hernia that develops gangrene.

strepto- a medical prefix meaning "chains," in reference to the arrangement of bacteria.

stress fracture occurs when there is repetitive force applied to a bone over a period of time.

stroke a disruption in the normal blood supply to the brain. Also called a cerebrovascular accident.

subcategory the level at which four-digit codes are referenced.

subclassification the level of codes at which five-digit codes are referenced.

subcutaneous below the skin.

subcutaneous mammectomy the subcutaneous tissue of the breast is removed, but the skin and nipple are left intact.

sublingual glands a pair of salivary glands located under the tongue.

subluxation when the bone is partially displaced.

submandibular glands found on the floor of the mouth.

submental incision an incision made below the chin.

suicide attempt self-inflicted attempts, using drugs and chemicals, to end one's own life.

superior vena cava the main vein through which blood flows from the upper portion of the body above the heart back to the heart.

suprapubic prostatectomy a procedure completed to remove tissue or adenomas that are too large to be removed via a scope.

Supplementary Classification of External Causes of Injury and Poisoning (E codes) provide a classification for external causes of injuries and poisonings.

Supplementary Classification of Factors Influencing Health Status and Contact with Health Services (V codes) used to code conditions or circumstances that are recorded as the reason for the patient encounter when the patient is not currently ill, or when a factor is present that affects the patient's health status and/or medical management of the case.

Supplementary Classifications the second subdivision of volume 1, also known as V codes and E codes.

suture the procedure used to close an open wound or incision.

sympathetic nervous system controls the reaction to stress. Also known as the fight or flight reaction.

symptom a change in the body that brings a patient in to see the doctor; part of the subjective information.

syncope a brief loss of consciousness due to lack of oxygen to the brain. Also known as fainting.

synovia fluid that acts as a lubricant for the joints.

synovial membrane a membrane that secretes a clear lubricating fluid of the joints.

systemic inflammatory response syndrome (SIRS) the body's systemic response to infection or trauma.

systolic blood pressure the pressure on the arterial walls during the heart muscle contraction.

T

Table of Drugs and Chemicals the section of the Alphabetic Index used to classify poisonings by a drug or chemical, as well as to classify external causes of an adverse effect of a drug or chemical.

Tabular List and Alphabetic Index of Procedures the section of volume 3 that contains both the alphabetic and tabular list for procedures and surgeries.

Tabular List of Diseases and Injuries volume 1 of ICD-9-CM, containing a numerical listing of diseases and injuries. Each chapter of this volume is subdivided into sections, categories, and subcategories.

talipes also known as clubfoot.

tarsal cyst a localized swelling of the eyelid resulting from an obstruction of a sebaceous gland of the eyelid. Also called a chalazion, meibomian cyst, or internal hordeolum.

tendons tissues that connect muscle to bone.

teratogens   agents that cause defects in an embryo.

testectomy   the surgical removal of the testes.

testes   male genital glands that are located in the scrotal sac and produce sperm. Also known as testicles.

testicles   male genital glands that are located in the scrotal sac and produce sperm. Also known as testes.

therapeutic ultrasound   the use of ultrasound to treat diseased or damaged tissue.

therapeutic use   not used with poisoning code; used when there is an adverse effect.

thermocauterization   a procedure that uses a hot-tipped instrument to directly heat a lesion to destroy it.

thermography   a type of imaging using infrared photography of the body temperature of a structure to project an image.

thoracentesis   a procedure in which a needle is inserted into the pleural cavity to draw fluid for diagnostic purposes, to drain fluid, or to re expand a collapsed lung.

thoracic cavity   contains bone structures that protect the heart and lungs.

thoracoplasty   the collapse of a lung by removing ribs.

thoracotomy   an incision into the chest wall for direct examination of the thoracic cavity.

thrombocytes   ovoid-shaped structures that function in the initiation of blood-clotting or coagulation. Also known as platelets.

thrombocytopenia   an abnormal decrease in platelet count, causing purpural hemorrhages.

thrombolytic therapy   the intravenous administration of thrombolytic agents, often completed to open the coronary artery occlusion and to restore blood flow to the cardiac tissue.

thrombophlebitis   the inflammation of a vein with the formation of a thrombus.

thrombus   a blood clot.

thrush   a fungal infection of the mouth.

thyroid gland   secretes hormones that regulate growth and metabolism.

thyroiditis   an inflammation of the thyroid gland.

thyrotoxic crisis   the symptoms of hyperthyroidism are so severe that they put the patient in a life-threatening situation. Also called thyrotoxic storm.

thyrotoxic storm   the symptoms of hyperthyroidism are so severe that they put the patient in a life-threatening situation. Also called thyrotoxic crisis.

tomography   a technique in imaging that involves taking an image of one layer of the body while blocking layers above and below it.

tonometry   the measurement of intraocular pressure.

tonsils   located in the posterior wall of the nasopharynx and condsidered the first line of defense for the respiratory system.

toxic shock syndrome   an acute infection, caused by staphylococcus or streptococcus bacteria with an abrupt onset of symptoms.

trabeculae carneae cordis   endocardial muscular ridges.

trachea   tube of cartilage that extends from the larynx to the bronchi. Also known as the windpipe.

tracheoesophageal fistulectomy   the repair of a congenital anomoly in which there is an abnormal passage between the trachea and the esophagus.

tracheostomy   the surgical creation of a stoma in the trachea.

tracheotomy   a surgical opening made in the trachea for the placement of a tube to assist in breathing.

transient cerebral ischemia   the temporary restriction of blood flow to cerebral arteries.

transient hypertension   elevated blood pressure but the physician has not made a diagnosis of hypertension.

transmyocardial revascularization (TMR) a laser procedure that creates channels through the myocardium and allows for more blood flow to the myocardial tissue.

transoral incision   an incision made across the oral cavity.

transplantation of peripheral lymphatics   the grafting of a peripheral duct to reposition the duct.

transposition of a nipple   a procedure in which the nipple is surgically relocated.

transurethral clearance of the bladder   drainage of the bladder by the placement of an instrument through the urethra into the bladder.

transurethral cystoscopy   the placement of a scope through the urethra.

transurethral microwave thermotherapy of prostate   a procedure completed to destroy prostatic tissue by use of microwave energy to heat the tissue.

transurethral needle ablation of prostate (TUNA)   a procedure completed to destroy prostatic tissue by using radiofrequency energy to heat the tissue.

transurethral prostatectomy   a procedure completed using a scope that is inserted into the urethra to resect prostatic tissue. Also known as a transurethral resection of the prostate (TURP).

transurethral resection of the prostate (TURP)   a procedure completed using a scope that is inserted into the urethra to resect prostatic tissue. Also known as a transurethral prostatectomy.

tricuspid valve   the valve between the right atrium and right ventricle.

trocar   a cannula with a sharp point at the end.

true vocal cords   cords that vibrate when air passes through, producing sound.

truncated codes   codes that are not carried out to the most specific classification available for a category.

tumor   an uncontrolled abnormal growth of cells and characterized as malignant or benign. Also called a neoplasm.

tympanic membrane   eardrum.

type I diabetes mellitus   can occur between birth and adulthood in which the pancreas is not functioning properly or at all in the production of insulin. Also known as juvenile diabetes.

type II diabetes mellitus   results from the body's inability to produce sufficient amounts of insulin, which develops later in life. Also known as adult-onset diabetes.

U

ulcerative colitis   an inflammation of the colon, causing ulcers to develop in the lining.

ulcers   erosions of the skin in which the tissue becomes inflamed and then is lost.

ultrasound   a form of imaging in which high-frequency sound waves are reflected from body tissue and the pulses are recorded and viewed as images.

umbilical hernia   a hernia found in the part of the intestine that falls around the umbilicus.

undetermined code codes used when the intent of the poisoning cannot be determined.

unilateral nephrectomy the removal of one kidney.

unilateral oophorectomy the surgical removal of one of the ovaries.

unilateral orchiectomy the surgical removal of one of the testicles.

unspecified hypertension hypertension that is not specified as malignant or benign in the diagnostic statement.

unspecified mental retardation the medical documentation states that the patient is mentally retarded but the level of functioning is not recorded.

unstable angina an accelerating, or crescendo, pattern of chest pain that occurs at rest or mild exertion, typically lasting a long time and not responsive to medications.

ureterectomy the removal of the ureter.

ureterotomy an incision into the ureter, usually completed to remove calculi, explore the ureter, or allow for drainage of the ureter.

ureters very narrow tubes that move urine from the kidney to the bladder.

urethra a small tube extending from the bladder to outside the body.

urethral meatotomy an incision of the external urethral opening.

urethrotomy an incision made into the urethra.

urinary bladder holds urine until it moves to the urethra.

urinary system maintains a balance of the contents of the body fluids within the body.

urinary tract infection (UTI) an abnormal presence of microorganisms in the urine.

urine excess fluid that is expelled from the body by way of the bladder.

urticaria another term for hives.

use additional code signals the coder to add a second code to fully code the diagnosis.

utero- a prefix meaning "pertaining to the uterus."

uterus sits above the cervix and is the part of the female anatomy that houses the fetus until birth.

uvula primarily helps with sound production and speech.

V

vacuum extraction a delivery using a device that is applied to the head of the fetus to assist in delivery.

vagina a muscular tube that connects the cervix to the vulva.

vagino- a prefix meaning "pertaining to the vagina."

vagus nerve transmits sensory information.

valves open and close to regulate blood flow through the heart.

varicose veins veins that become elongated, may protrude when they become dilated, and can be extremely painful.

vasa previa dangerous condition in which the umbilical cord is the presenting part.

vault of the skulll the three bones of the skull: the two parietal bones and the frontal bone.

veins carry deoxygenated blood from the body back to the heart.

ventral hernia a hernia that protrudes through an abdominal scar.

ventricles lower chambers of the heart that send blood to the arteries.

vertebral column the structure that shields the spinal column, made up of the cervical, thoracic, and lumbar vertebra.

vesicostomy the creation of an opening from the bladder to the skin.

viruses the smallest infectious pathogens, which penetrate cells and release their DNA or RNA into the nucleus of a cell, causing damage to the human cell.

visual acuity the ability to see and distinguish objects at a distance.

vitreous humor a gel-like substance that helps the eye keep its shape.

vocal cords where sound or speech is produced.

voiding urination.

Volkmann's deformity a congenital dislocation of the tibiotarsal.

volume 3 of ICD-9-CM classifies procedures and contains both an Alphabetic Index and a Tabular List.

Von Willebrand's disease a genetic disorder characterized by mucosal bleeding due to abnormal blood vessels.

vulva portion of the female external genitalia.

W

white blood cells (WBC) pale-colored cells with an irregular ball-like shape that provide the body's natural defense against injury and disease.

white blood cell count identifies the number of white blood cells found in a cubic millimeter of blood. Also known as leukocyte count or WBC.

World Health Organization (WHO) prepares and publishes the revisions to International Classification of Diseases.

Y

yeast infection a fungal infection caused by a unicellular fungus.

Index